THE GOLFSMITH
PRACTICAL CLUBFITTING
PROGRAM

By
Tom W. Wishon

Edited By
Russell Caver

Photography By
Duane Osborn

Illustration & Artwork By
James Blunt
Tanya Davison

Published By
Golfsmith International, Inc.
11000 North IH-35
Austin, TX 78753
800-456-3344
(512) 837-4810

Golfsmith International, Inc.
11000 North IH-35
Austin, TX 78753
800-456-3344
(512) 837-4810

Manufactured in the United States of America

Distributed by Golfsmith International, Inc.

ISBN – 0-913563-05-6

TABLE OF CONTENTS

INTRODUCTION

HOW TO USE THIS BOOK TO IMPROVE YOUR CLUBFITTING PROCEDURES

PLEASE! Read this section first before reading any succeeding portion of this book!

DO NOT BE INTIMIDATED BY THE LENGTH OF THIS BOOK!! The Golfsmith Practical Fitting Program is indeed practical in its nature. This book has been written in a manner to allow you to obtain the information you need without having to read the book from cover to cover. To learn how best to use this book to improve your fitting and club selection, while at the same time making the experience of learning compatible with the level of your interest in clubmaking, please take the time to read this section of the book first.

This Golfsmith Practical Fitting Program has been written in an attempt to introduce a new way to approach the confusing task of how to select the best set of golf clubs for any golfer. Since the 1970s, much has been learned about the scientific workings of golf clubs which should help the golfer or the clubmaker make more accurate decisions as to what the specifications of the golf clubs need to be to maximize the potential of the golfer. However, all that has really happened from this accumulation of technical information is confusion over what the various changes in golf club specifications will truly do to the flight of the ball for any golfer. As a result, the process of fitting the golfer with the best set of golf clubs for their individual abilities has become little more than a trial and error session which takes entirely too much time to conduct.

As one of the fortunate few who has had the opportunity to research, publish and teach clubmakers the various aspects of clubfitting, I am just as guilty as anyone of contributing to making the fitting session a protracted, confusing venture which does not always end up helping the golfer get more out of his/her game. The problem has been that we have been approaching the fitting session from the wrong direction; the more we discovered and published about the various specifications of the golf club, the more we turned the fitting session into a process of trying to fit the specifications, individually, one by one, to the golfer. With as many as 20 different specifications making up a golf club, the fitting session gradually became too long and evolved to the point where the clubmaker is under the impression that numerous test clubs are required to pinpoint the right equipment.

When test clubs become a major part of the fitting decision, the fitting session has de-evolved into little more than a process of trial and error.

The approach to fitting golf clubs, which I am attempting to teach in this book, still consists of identifying the changes in the golf club specifications which will get the most out of the golfer's physical abilities. However, the approach which I call the Practical Fitting program does not focus on moving one by one through each of the 20 different golf club specifications. The Practical Fitting Program approaches the task by first determining what the golfer wants to change and improve in his/her game, and then identifies which of the 20 golf club specifications have the power to help make those desired changes come about. The result is an approach to fitting which is far more accurate, far more predictable, and one which takes far less time to obtain the desired results.

To learn the Practical Clubfitting Program to improve your fitting and club selection:

1. You must first understand which of the 20 golf club specifications have a **MAJOR**, a **MEDIUM** or a **MINOR** effect on changing the golfer's **Distance, Accuracy, Trajectory, Backspin** and **Feel** with the clubs.

2. You must be able to measure a few of the specifications on the golfer's current set of golf clubs to know if any of the shotmaking problems are being caused by poorly fit equipment, as well as to know if the changes you will prescribe will make an improvement.

3. You must learn how to conduct 4 simple measurements of the golfer which provide data necessary to make certain fitting decisions.

4. You must then be able to put all this information together to compile a list of specifications for the new set which will most effectively address the shotmaking needs of the player.

This book has been written in an attempt to be two books contained in one. Because it is a completely new approach to fitting, it has to contain every possible bit of information to explain every nuance of the fitting program. Because it takes a PRACTICAL approach to the fitting process, there are certain points which might be somewhat controversial because this information disagrees with some technical points which had been established in previous fitting publications.

For example, when I say that lie angle is a **MAJOR** factor of **Accuracy** in the short irons, but is a **MEDIUM** factor in the middle irons and only a **MINOR** factor in the long irons and woods, some clubmakers are going to be confused or even disagree, for the reason that previous publications teach that lie angle is important in all the clubs. It isn't. And the same thing can be said about many other golf club specifications and their real versus perceived effect on ball flight. Some specifications matter and many do not. That is one of the main points of the entire Practical Fitting Program. As such, I needed the space to fully explain why a specification is a **MAJOR**, a **MEDIUM** or only a **MINOR** factor.

But I also understand from my years in the clubmaking industry that not everyone wants to read on and on about why lie is only important in the short and middle irons, why shaft flex can only do so much, or why a comfortable grip size is more important than a properly fit grip size. Because of that, I incorporated two things in the book which you need to know – bold face print and a series of paragraphs also printed in bold face type which I have called FAST FACTS.

If all you do is read the bold face sentences and FAST FACT paragraphs within each section of the book, you can learn enough about the Practical Fitting Program to begin to fit golf clubs much more accurately and more confidently than ever before.

I do not expect every clubmaker or golfer to agree with the **MAJOR**, **MEDIUM** or **MINOR** ranking awarded to each of the specifications; hence the reason for the protracted explanations. While there is always a chance one of the specifications could be debated as having a **MEDIUM** instead of a **MINOR** effect on one of the five ball striking factors, the main point is that not all specifications have a **MAJOR** effect on helping the golfer to hit the ball better or more solidly. Focusing only on making the changes in those specifications which have a **MAJOR** effect on **Distance, Accuracy, Trajectory, Backspin** or **Feel**, then using the **MEDIUM** effect specifications when that specification is not so well fit to the golfer in his/her current set, and virtually ignoring all of the rest of the specifications which have a **MINOR** effect, will result in a better set of clubs for the golfer.

To get the most out of the Practical Fitting Program, I urge you to eventually find the time to read and study each page in the book. If you do not have the time nor the immediate inclination to study this program that extensively, I suggest you use this book in the following manner:

1. Read Chapter 1 entirely to fully understand the principles of the Practical Fitting Program – first, to learn that there are only 5 ways you can help a golfer through a change in his/her equipment specifications and second, which of the 20 different specifications contained in the clubs have a **MAJOR, MEDIUM,** or **MINOR** effect on changing the five game improvement factors. Keep the charts on pages 6 and 7 at close hand every time you perform a fitting session so you know which specifications to concentrate on to make the desired change for the golfer in improving **Distance, Accuracy, Trajectory, Backspin** or **Feel**.

2. Read the bold passages and FAST FACT paragraphs in Chapter 2 so you understand what each specification is, and why each is ranked as having either a **MAJOR, MEDIUM** or **MINOR** effect on **Distance, Accuracy, Trajectory, Backspin** or **Feel**.

3. Keep a copy of the Player Interview Form close at hand while you read the FAST FACT paragraphs which correspond to each section of the form. This will help you understand what the golfer wants to improve and how the information on the Player Interview Form can help you to make changes in only the **MAJOR** and **MEDIUM** effect specifications which pertain to the game improvement factor desired by the golfer.

4. Turn to the very end of Chapter 4 and study the section titled, "QUICK REFERENCE TO PERFORMING THE EQUIPMENT EVALUATION FOR THE GOLFSMITH PRACTICAL FITTING PROGRAM". This section will teach you which specifications are important to measure on the golfer's existing clubs to determine which specifications are helping the golfer and which are not. If you do not know how to measure the necessary specifications, turn to that section in Chapter 4 for the proper instruction.

5. Skip Chapter 5 unless you really want to add the knowledge of what the movements of the golf swing are which can help tip off the ability of the golfer to gain improvement from a change in the golf club specifications.

6. In chapter 6, study the example fitting for golfer Bob Johnson. Find the example Player Interview Form, the example Equipment Evaluation and

read the explanation for why the particular specifications were chosen for Mr. Johnson's future set. Learning the Practical Fitting Program by example is always the best way, so expect to spend a little time with this section of Chapter 6 so you have more confidence in knowing how to combine the information from the Player Interview and the information from the Equipment Evaluation. This section will also teach you how to reference that information to the **MAJOR**, **MEDIUM** and **MINOR** effect specifications for each desired game improvement factor, to make the Preliminary Fitting Recommendation.

7. Because the specifications for the Shaft, Lie Angle, Grip Size and Length do require you to obtain a few measurements from the golfer, try to spend enough time in Chapter 7, in the Procedures for Measurement sections of each of these four areas, to learn how to obtain this information. Of particular importance will be the procedures for fitting the shaft on its own, which are detailed with examples in Chapter 7. Do not skip the shaft fitting section of chapter 7 or you will not be able to properly fit the shaft to the golfer.

8. To build up the most confidence you can in your fitting skills, plan to read the FAST FACT paragraphs of Chapter 8. Here you will find out how to make that final decision for any of the specifications you might need to change to help the golfer achieve his/her game improvement goals.

9. If you totally ignore short game fitting in your current fitting session, or if you need to gain an edge on your competition, plan to spend time studying the **MAJOR** effect specifications outlined in the KEY SPECIFICATIONS FOR WEDGE AND PUTTER FITTING sections of Chapter 9. For your information, Chapter 9 on its own is the most complete explanation of short game fitting procedures ever written. So, if you feel the short game is important to playing better, you need to become more familiar at least with the **MAJOR** effect specifications for wedge and putter fitting.

10. Finally, by referencing the bold print passages in Chapter 10, you will have a much better background in being able to handle special fitting situations such as juniors, physically challenged or low handicap players.

Once you understand the principles of the Practical Fitting Program, you'll also see how important all of the rest of the sections of the book can be to making your education as a clubfitter as complete as possible. Remember, once you know the key principles of this system, most of the fitting session can be done in your mind, with a minimum of fitting aids. Most importantly though, and I truly believe this after spending more than 25 years in clubmaking and clubfitting, not every change in a golf club specification will be noticed by the golfer. This is because the modern business of golf has done its best to fool all of us into believing a new golf club can add to the golfer's skills.

When you approach a fitting session with any golfer, I urge you to keep this simple thought in mind:

The golf club can not add to what the golfer has in terms of physical ability. At the very best, it can only enhance that ability to the point of allowing the golfer to achieve the most potential he or she may bring to the golf course. However, at the worst, it can tear down and detract from the golfer's abilities to the point of severely limiting the potential the golfer brings to play. As a result, the benefits of accurate clubfitting are more often subtle in their effect. No set of clubs will eliminate bad shots. It can only maximize the potential of the golfer, whatever that potential may be.

Good Luck and Best wishes in Your Clubfitting,

Tom Wishon

Tom Wishon

Chapter One

THE GOLFSMITH PRACTICAL FITTING PROGRAM

FOCUSING ON THE GOLF CLUB SPECIFICATIONS THAT MAKE A DIFFERENCE AND FORGETTING THE ONES THAT DON'T

THE FIVE SHOTMAKING FACTORS OF GAME IMPROVEMENT

Real game improvement for any golfer can come in one of only two ways – by taking lessons from a competent teaching professional and practicing the changes that are advised, or by acquiring a custom-fit set of golf clubs that employ changes in design to overcome poor swing movements and accentuate the proper motions the golfer makes in the swing.

PGA Master Professional Gary Wiren, considered to be one of the finest teachers and theoreticians of the golf swing in the world, has been quoted as saying that a major change to correct a swing error requires no less than 10,000 repetitions of the new movement before it can be considered to be a permanent part of the golfer's swing.

Such thinking assumes that the golfer has the physical and athletic ability to make the swing change the teacher has recommended, and the golfer will be able to make the correct movement every time it is practiced. In golf, the statement, "practice makes perfect" is not true. As Mr. Wiren has also stated, "It is only perfect practice that makes perfect." Therefore, for each of the 10,000 required swings to work toward cementing the change, each one has to be absolutely correct, with no slipping back into the old incorrect movement.

In order to make a noticeable, permanent improvement in **Accuracy** or **Distance**, the golfer has to hit 10,000 shots! At the rate of hitting one large bucket of balls every day at the driving range, that means it will take nearly five months to make such a swing change. While 10,000 swings could result in an improvement in **Accuracy** for most players who get the right swing advice and who are physically mobile enough to make the change, when it comes to **Distance**, not every golfer has the physical or athletic ability to make the swing change that will result in an increase in yardage.

After all, **Distance** is a product of the force with which a certain mass can be delivered to the ball, a feat which is directly related to strength and leverage. In other words, if the golfer doesn't have the strength and coordination to increase the velocity of the club as it moves through impact, there is little chance those five months of hitting balls will ever increase the **Distance** off the tee.

In a choice between lessons and custom-fit golf clubs, the decision really has to come down to the question of how many golfers have the opportunity, much less the time and commitment, to hit balls every day for five months under proper supervision? Not many. That is precisely why custom fitting, and particularly, accurate custom fitting, is really one of the few effective ways that a golfer has at his or her disposal to improve shotmaking to the point of playing better golf.

It should be completely understood and accepted by clubmakers and golfers alike that there is nothing "wrong" with "buying a better game," as some of the critics of custom clubfitting have stated. In no way can pursuing game improvement through custom fitting be considered "cheating," because golf club design has not yet become so advanced that it can create a golf club that will allow a 70mph swinger to hit the ball 250 yards off the tee or to enable a player with a 15° outside-to-inside swing path to hit 14 fairways in a round. Even if it had; the United States Golf Association would step in and rule such equipment as non-conforming to protect the integrity of the game.

It will always require a good swing movement to hit the ball long and straight. Custom-made clubs are realistically intended to help golfers make the most out of their swing and avoid losing anything from what ability they have, rather than to completely erase a swing error. In fact, many of the most successful custom fitting sessions are those in which the old set was discovered to be so badly suited to the golfer's game that the set was detracting from the golfer's potential, instead of making the most of it.

The Golfsmith Practical Golf Clubfitting Program is based on the realization that the only way to improve shotmaking is to make a change in golf equipment which will truly alter the flight pattern of the ball and the performance of the club for the golfer. To this end, the Practical Fitting Program identifies that there are only five ways that a change in clubs can result in a change in ball flight or shotmaking performance. It is possible to make a change in the golf club to create a change in Distance, Accuracy, Trajectory, Backspin and the Feel of the club. That's it. No matter how you look at it , there are only five shotmaking factors that can be affected by a change in the specifications of the golf club – DISTANCE, ACCURACY, TRAJECTORY, BACK-SPIN and FEEL.

THE SPECIFICATIONS OF GOLF CLUBS AND THEIR EFFECT ON THE FIVE SHOTMAKING FACTORS OF THE GAME

All golf clubs can be described by a list of their specifications. Clubmakers and golfers who have studied clubfitting are familiar with many of the specifications of golf clubs such as loft, lie, face angle, length, shaft flex, shaft torque, shaft bend point, grip size, etc., just to name a few. While there are different opinions in the golf equipment industry of how many true specifications there are in any golf club, if a detailed analysis is made of the subject, as many as 16 or more can be measured and described.

The Golfsmith Practical Fitting Program identifies a total of 20 different golf club specifications 19 of which can have an effect on shotmaking and one more which pertains to the set as a whole. Eight of these 20 specifications are found only on the clubhead, five deal with the shaft by itself, two specifications center on the grip and four deal with how the components are assembled into the finished golf club. The one that pertains to the set as a whole – set makeup – is kept separate from the 20 golf club specifications because it has nothing to do with how the club is made. Set makeup describes the complement of the clubs that comprise the set and does not directly or indirectly affect any of the five factors of **Distance, Accuracy, Trajectory, Backspin** and **Feel**. However, it is identified as part of the Practical Fitting Program because it can have a powerful effect on the golfer's ability to score.

CLUBHEAD SPECIFICATIONS
- Loft
- Lie
- Face Angle
- Clubhead Design (Center of Gravity/Weight Distribution)
- Horizontal Bulge
- Vertical Roll
- Sole Angle/Sole Radius
- Hosel Offset/Face Progression

SHAFT SPECIFICATIONS
- Weight
- Flex
- Torque
- Bend Point
- Balance Point

GRIP SPECIFICATIONS
- Size/Type
- Weight

GOLF CLUB SPECIFICATIONS
- Length
- Swingweight
- Total Weight
- Golf Club Balance Point

Set of Clubs
- Set Make Up

THE MAJOR, MEDIUM AND MINOR EFFECTS OF THE GOLF CLUB SPECIFICATIONS ON THE FIVE SHOTMAKING PERFORMANCE FACTORS

Each of the golf club specifications listed do not have the same effect on the five factors of shotmaking – **Distance, Accuracy, Trajectory, Backspin** and **Feel**. In fact, some have no effect on the five shot performance factors. From observing the result of numerous actual fitting situations, the Golfsmith Practical Fitting Program recognizes that the golf club specifications which do have an effect on **Distance, Accuracy, Trajectory, Backspin** and **Feel** have either a **MAJOR** effect, a **MEDIUM** effect or only a **MINOR** effect.

Shotmaking Factor	Total Specs	Major Effect Specs	Medium Effect Specs	Minor Effect Specs	Total Affecting The Factor
DISTANCE	20	4	8	3	15
ACCURACY	20	3	8	8	19
TRAJECTORY	20	1	3	6	10
BACKSPIN	20	1	2	3	6
FEEL	20	7	5	3	15

The above chart shows the number of specifications that have an effect on the five shotmaking performance factors and breaks those down into how many have a **MAJOR**, **MEDIUM** or **MINOR** effect on each one of the shotmaking factors. This is one obvious way to show that not every specification has an effect on shotmaking. Even more important, the chart shows how few of the specifications have a **MAJOR**, **MEDIUM** or a **MINOR** effect on changing a player's game.

A **MAJOR** effect specification is defined as a design parameter that can create the most noticeable change in one of the five factors of shotmaking performance. In other words, when a **MAJOR** effect specification is changed, the golfer should notice an immediate change in that shotmaking performance factor. In prescribing a new set of specifications to help a golfer improve, the majority of the changes will need to be chosen from the **MAJOR** effect specifications.

A **MEDIUM** effect specification is defined as a design parameter which, when changed in the golf club, will have some effect on one of the shotmaking performance factors, but the amount of change is primarily determined by how well or how poorly that specification was fit to the golfer in the previous set or club(s). If a **MEDIUM** effect specification was pretty well fit to the needs of the golfer in the previous set, then the change in the new set or club will not be strongly evident. However, if that **MEDIUM** effect specification was poorly fit to the golfer in the existing set, the result from the change will be much more evident, in some cases close to being as noticeable as a change in a **MAJOR** effect specification.

Finally, a **MINOR** effect specification is defined as a design parameter which, when changed in the golf club, will have very little, if any, effect on the shotmaking performance factor. The only way that a **MINOR** effect specification will be noticed by the golfer is if this same specification was very poorly fit to the golfer in the previous set of clubs. However, even in these cases, the effect on shotmaking performance will still be very slight and will likely create very little long-term change for the golfer.

Therefore, the goal of the Golfsmith Practical Golf Clubfitting Program is to help golfers improve by identifying which of the five shotmaking factors of **Distance, Accuracy, Trajectory, Backspin** and **Feel** require a change or upgrade. Next, the total specifications for the new set are compiled, focusing first on the specifications that have a **MAJOR** effect on the desired shot performance factor, then on the specifications which have a **MEDIUM** effect on that shotmaking factor, and then virtually ignoring the specifications which have a **MINOR** effect on that shotmaking factor. In short, the Golfsmith Practical Fitting Program focuses on changing the specifications that will make a difference and ignoring the ones that won't.

For example, if a golfer wishes to improve the **Distance** he/she hits the ball, the clubmaker would look only at those specifications which have an effect on **Distance**. Of all the 20 specifications that make up a golf club, only 15 have any effect whatsoever on **Distance**. First and foremost, the clubmaker would focus on changing the four specifications which have a **MAJOR** effect on **Distance**. Next, the clubmaker would study the seven specifications which have a **MEDIUM** effect on **Distance** and determine if changing any of these specifications would make any real change on **Distance**. Finally, the clubmaker would note the four specifications which have a **MINOR** effect on Distance and determine if there is any reason to consider changing these specifications on the new clubs as a final effort to do everything possible to improve the player's desire for more yardage. NOTE: The reason why each specification is ranked as a **MAJOR, MEDIUM** or **MINOR** effect specification is explained fully in Chapter Two, The Golf Clubfitting Specifications.

On the following pages all of the golf club specifications are listed individually and ranked according to whether they have a MAJOR, a MEDIUM or a MINOR effect on the five shot performance factors of Distance, Accuracy, Trajectory, Backspin and Feel. Knowing and having access to a list of these relationships is the most important part of being able to use the Golfsmith Practical Fitting Program for more accurate and predictable fitting.

To make your understanding and use of these relationships as simple as possible, the specifications and their effect on the factors of shotmaking performance are cross referenced in two different ways.

*Chart #1 lists the specifications in order of their effect on the shotmaking factors, with the **MAJOR** effect specifications listed first, followed by the **MEDIUM** and then the **MINOR** effect specifications.*

*Chart #2 then cross references the specifications in order of the factors of shotmaking performance, starting first with all the specifications that have an effect on **Distance**, then the specifications which have an effect on **Accuracy**, then **Trajectory, Backspin** and finally which of all the specifications have an effect on the **Feel** of the golf club.*

In addition, a special reference card has been included with each copy of the book. Clubmakers are strongly advised to keep this **MAJOR, MEDIUM** and **MINOR** effect chart with them while performing any clubfitting session. (Again, see Chapter Two for a complete explanation of each specification and its effect on the five shotmaking performance factors.)

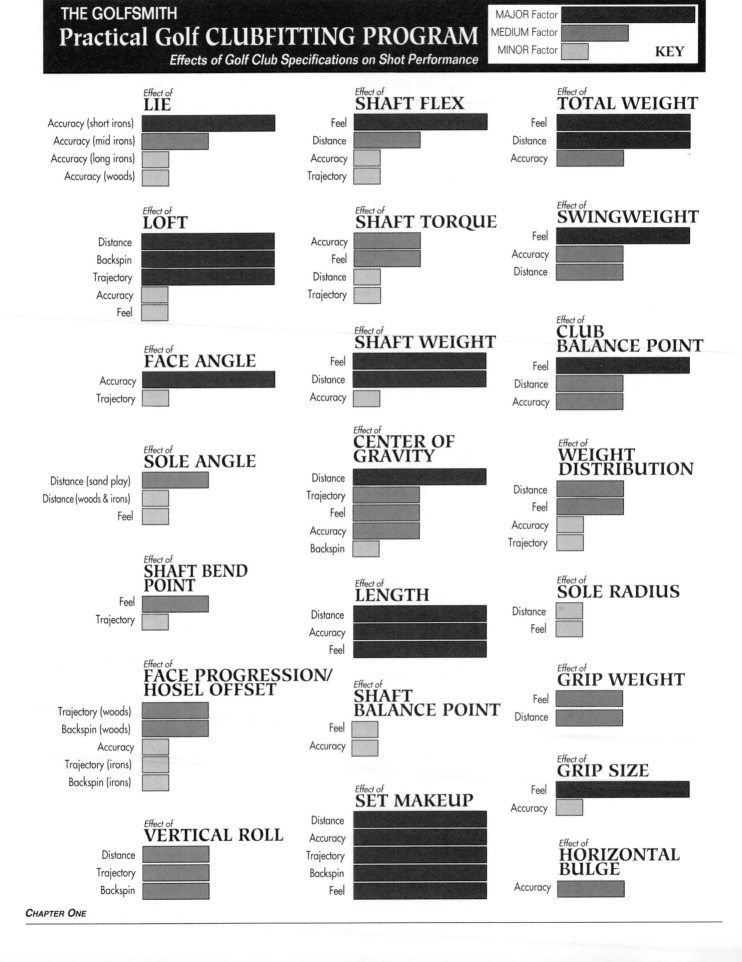

THE GOLFSMITH
Practical Golf CLUBFITTING PROGRAM
Effects of Golf Club Specifications on Shot Performance

KEY
MAJOR Factor
MEDIUM Factor
MINOR Factor

Effect of LIE
- Accuracy (short irons)
- Accuracy (mid irons)
- Accuracy (long irons)
- Accuracy (woods)

Effect of LOFT
- Distance
- Backspin
- Trajectory
- Accuracy
- Feel

Effect of FACE ANGLE
- Accuracy
- Trajectory

Effect of SOLE ANGLE
- Distance (sand play)
- Distance (woods & irons)
- Feel

Effect of SHAFT BEND POINT
- Feel
- Trajectory

Effect of FACE PROGRESSION/HOSEL OFFSET
- Trajectory (woods)
- Backspin (woods)
- Accuracy
- Trajectory (irons)
- Backspin (irons)

Effect of VERTICAL ROLL
- Distance
- Trajectory
- Backspin

Effect of SHAFT FLEX
- Feel
- Distance
- Accuracy
- Trajectory

Effect of SHAFT TORQUE
- Accuracy
- Feel
- Distance
- Trajectory

Effect of SHAFT WEIGHT
- Feel
- Distance
- Accuracy

Effect of CENTER OF GRAVITY
- Distance
- Trajectory
- Feel
- Accuracy
- Backspin

Effect of LENGTH
- Distance
- Accuracy
- Feel

Effect of SHAFT BALANCE POINT
- Feel
- Accuracy

Effect of SET MAKEUP
- Distance
- Accuracy
- Trajectory
- Backspin
- Feel

Effect of TOTAL WEIGHT
- Feel
- Distance
- Accuracy

Effect of SWINGWEIGHT
- Feel
- Accuracy
- Distance

Effect of CLUB BALANCE POINT
- Feel
- Distance
- Accuracy

Effect of WEIGHT DISTRIBUTION
- Distance
- Feel
- Accuracy
- Trajectory

Effect of SOLE RADIUS
- Distance
- Feel

Effect of GRIP WEIGHT
- Feel
- Distance

Effect of GRIP SIZE
- Feel
- Accuracy

Effect of HORIZONTAL BULGE
- Accuracy

THE GOLFSMITH
Practical Golf CLUBFITTING PROGRAM
Effects of Golf Club Specifications on Shot Performance

KEY
- MAJOR Factor
- MEDIUM Factor
- MINOR Factor

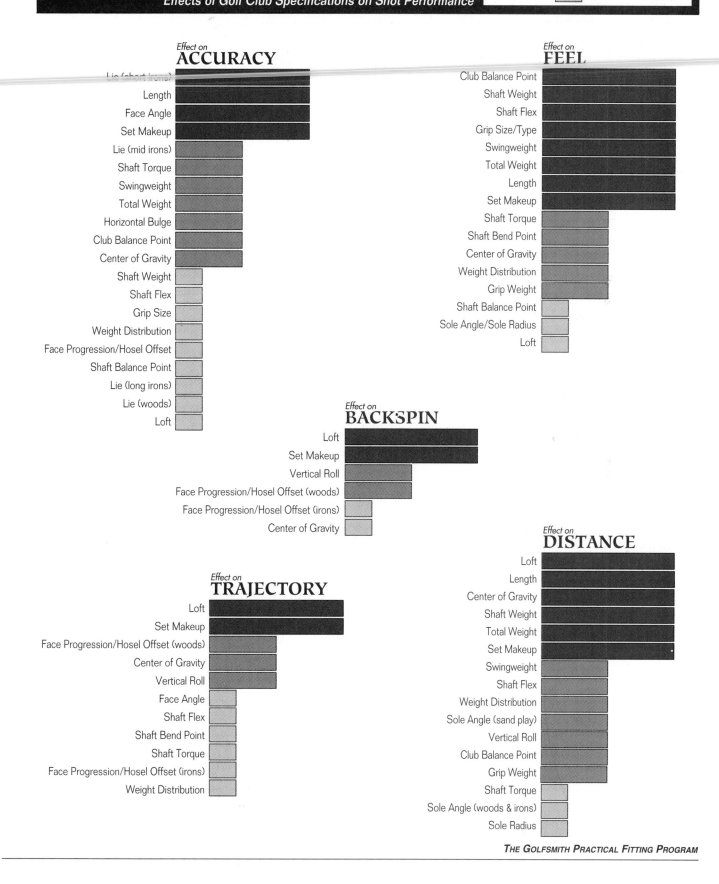

Effect on ACCURACY
- Lie (short irons)
- Length
- Face Angle
- Set Makeup
- Lie (mid irons)
- Shaft Torque
- Swingweight
- Total Weight
- Horizontal Bulge
- Club Balance Point
- Center of Gravity
- Shaft Weight
- Shaft Flex
- Grip Size
- Weight Distribution
- Face Progression/Hosel Offset
- Shaft Balance Point
- Lie (long irons)
- Lie (woods)
- Loft

Effect on FEEL
- Club Balance Point
- Shaft Weight
- Shaft Flex
- Grip Size/Type
- Swingweight
- Total Weight
- Length
- Set Makeup
- Shaft Torque
- Shaft Bend Point
- Center of Gravity
- Weight Distribution
- Grip Weight
- Shaft Balance Point
- Sole Angle/Sole Radius
- Loft

Effect on BACKSPIN
- Loft
- Set Makeup
- Vertical Roll
- Face Progression/Hosel Offset (woods)
- Face Progression/Hosel Offset (irons)
- Center of Gravity

Effect on TRAJECTORY
- Loft
- Set Makeup
- Face Progression/Hosel Offset (woods)
- Center of Gravity
- Vertical Roll
- Face Angle
- Shaft Flex
- Shaft Bend Point
- Shaft Torque
- Face Progression/Hosel Offset (irons)
- Weight Distribution

Effect on DISTANCE
- Loft
- Length
- Center of Gravity
- Shaft Weight
- Total Weight
- Set Makeup
- Swingweight
- Shaft Flex
- Weight Distribution
- Sole Angle (sand play)
- Vertical Roll
- Club Balance Point
- Grip Weight
- Shaft Torque
- Sole Angle (woods & irons)
- Sole Radius

How to use the Golfsmith Practical Fitting Program to accurately fit golf clubs

Once it has been accepted that only a few golf club specifications have any effect on shotmaking — and of those, which ones have a **MAJOR, MEDIUM** or **MINOR** effect on each of the five factors of shotmaking — it is possible to envision how simple and practical this system can be for fitting. First, most custom-fitting recommendations likely will come from the **MAJOR** and **MEDIUM** effect lists, since the **MINOR** effect specifications have so little real effect on the five shotmaking performance factors of **Distance, Accuracy, Trajectory, Backspin** and **Feel**. Thus, this program eliminates guesswork and needless testing and evaluation allowing both the clubmaker and golfer to realize maximum benefits in the minimum time.

The proper procedure for using the Practical Fitting Program, which will take all factors into account and result in the most accurate recommendations, is as follows:

1. **The Player Interview**. Identify from the golfer which of the five shot-making performance factors of **Distance, Accuracy, Trajectory, Backspin** and **Feel** they are having the most problems with and which they wish to address or improve the most in the new set.

2. **The Equipment Evaluation**. Measure or evaluate the golfer's current set or club(s) to see if any of the specifications of those clubs are the cause of some of the problems the player is experiencing with **Distance, Accuracy, Trajectory, Backspin** and **Feel.**

3. **The Preliminary Fitting Recommendation**. Use the information from the Player Interview and the Equipment Evaluation to guide a thorough search through the list of the **MAJOR, MEDIUM** and **MINOR** effect specifications to determine which specifications need to be changed in the new clubs to have a real effect on making a change in the desired shotmaking performance factor.

4. **The Final Fitting Procedures**. There are a few specifications, namely the lie angle, the shaft, the grip size and length, which require some form of measurement or test to determine. This segment of the Practical Fitting Program completes the determination of the new specifications because the tests will usually be simple tests which require no test clubs and only a minimum number of fitting aids.

5. **The Swing Evaluation** (OPTIONAL). If desired, the fitting session can end at this point because of the obtained knowledge on the **MAJOR, MEDIUM** and **MINOR** specifications that make the difference versus those that do not will make this fitting recommendation very accurate. However, if the clubmaker and the golfer wish to do so, the fitting session can continue with an evaluation of the golfer's swing to determine how the golfer's particular swing movements match up with the recommended fitting changes.

6. **The Verification/Modification of the Fitting Recommendation**. Finally, the clubmaker may choose to build a sample driver and a 7-iron, for example, to the new specifications and allow the golfer to hit them before finishing the set. This way the golfer will know that the fitting recommendations have been fine tuned and are correct.

To paraphrase, the simplest and fastest approach to practical clubfitting consists of asking the golfer what he/she wants to improve, finding out whether the existing set is helping or hurting the player in any of the five shotmaking areas, listing all the specs that could be changed to make improvements in the desired shotmaking factors, and then building the set. If the golfer and the clubmaker wish to spend more time, the clubmaker can evaluate the golfer's swing movements using the principles taught in Chapter Five and can test for the specifications by using test clubs or by building a sample club(s) for the golfer to try out.

Next, in Chapter Two, the Practical Fitting Program will list each of the 20 clubfitting specifications and explain exactly what these specifications are and why they are ranked as possessing a **MAJOR,** a **MEDIUM** or just a **MINOR** effect on the five shotmaking performance factors of **Distance, Accuracy, Trajectory, Backspin** and **Feel.**

Chapter Two

THE FITTING SPECIFICATIONS AND THEIR REAL EFFECT ON BALL FLIGHT

THE SPECIFICATIONS OF THE CLUBHEAD

> **NOTE FOR CHAPTER TWO:** While we urge clubmakers to read and study the information contained in Chapter Two about the 20 clubfitting specifications, we understand not every clubmaker will have the time or the commitment to study such information in the detail that it is provided. To assist in making the information easy to follow and understand, the chapter has been written to follow an outline form, using shorter paragraphs to express all of the information about each specification.
>
> For clubmakers who wish to pick up the important points for each clubfitting specification, we direct your attention to the bold face FAST FACT entries under each section. These FAST FACT paragraphs stand as a condensed version of the information that is detailed for each specification.

I. LOFT ANGLE
A. Wood Loft

Definition:

The angle in degrees between a plane that intersects the center of the striking face and a vertical plane which is perpendicular to the sole line.

Terminology of Loft:

A loft angle for any clubhead which is less than the accepted standard for that club is termed **strong**, and a loft angle for any clubhead which is greater than the accepted standard for that club is termed **weak**. While there have been **standard loft** angles for each wood head, variations in design from one company to another have prevented the creation of a standard for

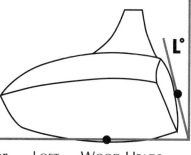

LOFT — WOOD HEADS

loft dimensions in the various wood heads.

■ **Effect of Loft on the shotmaking performance factors:**

In all cases, the effect of any specification on the shotmaking performance factors of **Distance, Accuracy, Trajectory, Backspin** and **Feel** can be modified depending on the way the golfer swings the club into impact. The explanations of how each specification affects the performance factors are based on normal impact conditions. For a full understanding of how the movements in the golf swing affect fitting, see Chapter Five -The Golf Swing as it Relates to Fitting.

• Loft is a **MAJOR** factor of **Distance** in the woods

In general, the greater the loft, the less the distance; the less amount of loft, the greater distance off the clubface. This is due to the glancing blow nature of the impact. More loft = a more glancing blow at impact and less

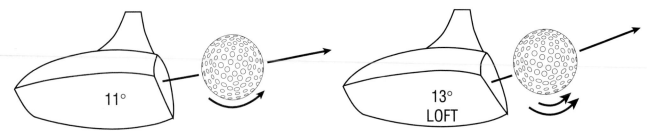

AT THE SAME CLUBHEAD SPEED, MORE LOFT = HIGHER TRAJECTORY AND GREATER BACKSPIN AND LESS DISTANCE

energy transferred into the ball while less loft = a less glancing blow at impact and more energy transferred into the ball.

Whether a stronger loft translates into more distance is determined by the golfer's ability to achieve the optimum launch angle which in turn creates maximum carry. Traditionally, golfers with slower swing speed need more loft in the driver to be able to generate the proper launch angle for maximum carry and with it, maximum distance.

In contrast, players with higher swing speeds can generate the proper launch angle with their ability to impart more backspin on the ball from the higher swing speed. This increase in driver backspin means a greater trajectory and for them, the proper carry achieving their maximum **Distance**.

Fast Fact:
For higher clubhead speed players (> 80 to 85mph with the driver) - the less the loft, the longer the shot in all clubs. For lower clubhead speed players (< 80mph), more loft in the driver and long irons can deliver more Distance while less loft in the fairway woods and middle to short irons will mean more Distance. The exception to this will be the player with a slow clubhead speed who, because of the swing or the ball position, already hits the driver inordinately high for his/her ability.

• Loft is a **MAJOR** factor of **Trajectory** in the woods

The greater the loft, the higher the shot; the lesser the loft, the lower the shot. This is again due to the nature of the impact. More loft = a more glancing blow on the face and the launch angle is increased. Less loft = a less glancing blow and the launch angle is decreased.

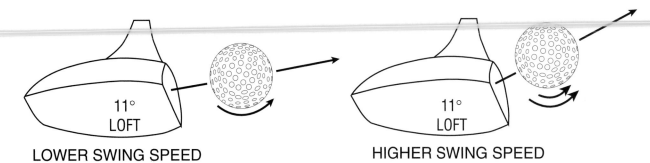

LOWER SWING SPEED   HIGHER SWING SPEED

However, swing speed again plays a role in the effect of loft on trajectory because the greater the clubhead speed, the greater the amount of backspin generated by any lofted plane. More **Backspin** = greater lift and with it, a higher trajectory. Therefore, between a fast swing speed player and a slower swinger who both hit a club with the same loft, the higher swing speed player will almost always generate more **Backspin**, which in turn will normally cause the ball to fly higher. (This can be modified by the position of the golfer's hands at the impact position, i.e. hands ahead of the ball = lower launch angle and lower **Trajectory**.)

Fast Fact:
   The greater the loft, the higher the shot. The less loft, the lower the shot. However, higher trajectory does not always mean a shorter shot. (See Loft as a MAJOR factor of Distance for the same explanation.)

• Loft is a **MAJOR** factor of **Backspin** in the woods

The more the loft, the greater the **Backspin**; the lesser the loft, the less amount of **Backspin**. This is also due to the nature of the impact. More loft = more **Backspin** because the ball slides and rolls more up the face. Less loft = less **Backspin** because the ball slides and rolls less up the face. Scorelines do not cause **Backspin**. The launch angle along with the amount the ball skids and rolls up the clubface are the **MAJOR** factors that dictate the amount of **Backspin** imparted on the ball.

Fast Fact:
   The desire for more backspin is normally isolated to the irons and not the woods. Be careful when increasing loft of the irons to increase backspin because a loss of distance can also occur with this increase.

• Loft is a **MINOR** factor of **Accuracy** in the woods

The greater the loft, the more **Backspin** will be imparted on the ball with a reduced amount of sidespin generated at impact. When the amount of **Backspin** is considerably greater than the sidespin, the ball will tend not to spin as far off-line. This is why short irons are not as likely to be hit off-line as are woods and long irons.

However, a golfer cannot play the game entirely with short irons in an effort to hit the ball straighter. Obviously, golfers will need woods for longer shots and an assortment of irons for hitting approach shots into the greens. Because different clubs are needed to hit the ball different distances, it is not possible to vary the loft enough within each individual club to affect a significant change in the **Accuracy**. For example, it is possible to change from a 9° to a 12° driver to hit the ball straighter, but the actual change of 3° will not have a **MAJOR** effect on **Accuracy** because 9° and 12° are so close in terms of their ability to generate misdirectional sidespin.

Fast Fact:
A 12°, 13° or higher lofted driver will hit the ball straighter than a 10° driver, but not by as much as you've been led to believe. If the golfer is just hitting the rough but is inside the treeline, a higher lofted driver can help find the short grass. If the golfer is in or outside the treeline, greater loft will not be enough to find the short grass. Look to face angle or a shorter length and then look at the other specifications that affect Accuracy.

• Loft is a **MINOR** factor of **Feel** in the woods

The greater the loft, the more glancing the blow at impact and the less solid the impact will **Feel** to the golfer. The less the loft, the less glancing the blow at impact and the more solid the impact will **Feel** to the golfer. However, because most golfers' sets of woods change in loft only from 11° to 25°, the variation in solidness of feel due to loft is not as dramatic as with the irons, where the loft can range from 17° in the 1-iron to 56° or more in the wedges.

Fast Fact:
Don't use loft as a way to change the feel of a golf club. The difference between the loft of one driver and another, or between any iron and a different lofted version of the same iron will not create enough of a change in feel to be worth the trade-off in how the loft change may affect Distance, Trajectory or Accuracy. Look to the MAJOR factors that affect Feel first.

B. IRON, WEDGE AND PUTTER LOFT

Definition:

The angle in degrees between the vertical plane of the face and the center line of the hosel.

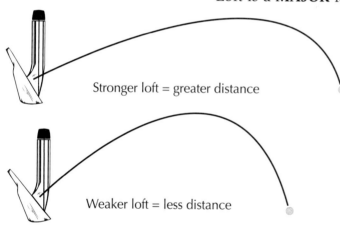

LOFT – IRONS AND PUTTERS

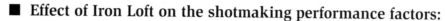

Terminology of Loft:

A loft angle for any clubhead that is less than the accepted standard for that club is termed **strong**, and a loft angle for any clubhead which is greater than the accepted standard for that club is termed **weak**.

While there have been standard loft angles for each iron head, variations in design from one company to another have prevented a standard for loft dimensions in the various iron heads.

■ Effect of Iron Loft on the shotmaking performance factors:

In all cases, the golfer's swing into impact can have a modifying effect on the performance factors of **Distance, Accuracy, Trajectory, Backspin, Feel** and consistency. The explanations of how each specification affects the performance factors are based on normal impact conditions. For a full understanding of how the movements in the golf swing affect fitting, see the Chapter, The Swing as it Relates to Fitting.

• Loft is a **MAJOR** factor of **Distance** in the irons

Stronger loft = greater distance

Weaker loft = less distance

The greater the loft, the shorter the **Distance**; the lesser the loft, the more the **Distance**. This is due to the glancing blow nature of the impact. More loft = a more glancing blow at impact and less energy transferred into a forward direction of force. Less loft = a less glancing blow at impact and more energy is transferred into a forward direction of force.

Unlike the woods, virtually all irons have enough loft so that a change in loft is seen in the same general manner by all golfers. In other words, with the driver, an increase in loft for slower swinging players can often result in a distance increase because the greater loft has allowed the golfer to achieve his/her optimum **Trajectory** for maximum carry **Distance**. However, when the loft is increased with the irons, the **Trajectory** will be slightly higher and the shot **Distance** will be decreased. When the loft is decreased, the **Trajectory** will be slightly lower and the shot **Distance** will be increased.

For average ability golfers, the effect of loft change on **Trajectory** and distance in the irons becomes greater as loft increases. In other words, for the average player, a 2° decrease in the loft of the 3-iron will not usually guarantee the same amount of **Trajectory** decrease and **Distance** increase as will a 2° decrease in the loft of the 7-iron. Again, this is because the greater the loft, the easier it is for the golfer to achieve the optimum **Trajectory** for maximum carry.

Fast Fact:

The stronger the loft, the longer the shot in all the irons for higher clubhead speed players (>65mph with the 5-iron). More loft in the long irons can deliver more Distance for lower clubhead speed players (<60mph). Less loft in the middle to short irons will mean more yards, regardless of how high the golfer already hits the ball.

- Loft is a **MAJOR** factor of **Trajectory** in the irons

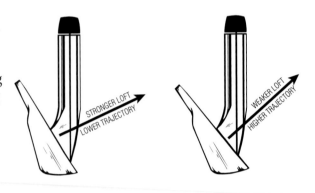

The greater the loft of the iron, the higher the shot; the less the loft of the iron, the lower the shot. This is primarily due to the glancing blow nature of the impact. More loft creates a more glancing blow at impact and the launch angle is increased, causing a higher **Trajectory**. Less loft creates a less glancing blow at impact and the launch angle is decreased, causing a lower **Trajectory** due to the friction at impact. However, at no time is the launch angle of the ball off the face ≥ the loft of the clubhead. (See explanation of Loft vs. **Distance** for more information on Loft vs. **Trajectory**.)

Fast Fact:

Greater (weaker) loft in the irons will increase Trajectory and help stop the ball better on the greens, but it will almost always decrease Distance as well. The golfer must be informed of this fact before making any adjustment to increase Trajectory in the irons.

- Loft is a **MAJOR** factor of **Backspin** in the irons

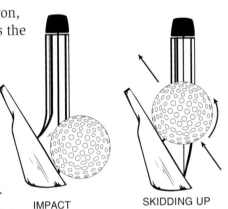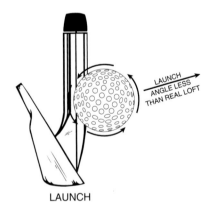

IMPACT   SKIDDING UP   LAUNCH

The greater the loft of the iron, the more the **Backspin**; the less the loft of the iron, the less the **Backspin**. This is due to the glancing blow nature of impact. More loft creates more backspin because the ball slides and rolls more up the face. Less loft creates less **Backspin** because the ball slides and rolls less up the face.

Scorelines do not cause **Backspin**, with the only exception being higher lofted irons that are swung at less than full swing speed. Identical iron heads, with and without scorelines, have been tested for **Backspin** and the ability to stop the ball on the green. In all cases with the golfers hitting full shots, there is virtually no difference in the rpm (revolutions per minute) of **Backspin** or in ability of the clubface to stop the ball on the green. Scorelines may be an additional factor to loft in creating **Backspin** at very slow clubhead velocities, such as hitting a wedge with far less than a full swing. In these cases, the ball moves so much slower up the face that the edges of the scorelines actually have a chance to "grab" the cover of the ball and impart more spin. Still, this is usually more of a factor when using wedges with square-shaped scorelines rather than the conventional V-shaped grooves.

Fast Fact:
Weaker loft in the irons will increase Backspin and help stop the ball better on the greens but will almost always decrease Distance as well. The golfer must be informed of this 'good news/bad news' fact before making any adjustment to increase Backspin in the irons. However, if the golfer can be convinced that a Backspin increase will be helpful to the overall game if only done in the wedges, it is possible to add a third or fourth wedge in place of a long iron and still provide the golfer with enough clubs to cover all the required distances while delivering more Backspin.

• Loft is a **MEDIUM** factor of **Feel** in the irons

The greater the loft, the more the impact will be a glancing blow and the less solid it will **Feel** to the golfer. The less the loft, the less glancing the blow will be at impact and the more solid the impact will **Feel** to the golfer. Because sets of irons change in loft from approximately 17° to 56° or more, the variation in solidness of **Feel** due to loft is much more dramatic in the irons than in the woods.

The reason Loft is rated as a **MEDIUM** factor in the **Feel** of the irons is because the difference in **Feel** between a long iron and a short iron is much more dramatic than the difference in **Feel** between a driver and a fairway wood. From a fitting standpoint, this means nothing because it is virtually an identical factor in all sets of irons. I.E. You never make sweeping changes in the loft of irons just to change the **Feel** of the set or else you disrupt the **Distance** the golfer can achieve with the set.

Fast Fact:
Never make 2-3° alterations in the loft of irons just to change the Feel of the set or you will disrupt the Distance the golfer can achieve with the set. The best way to change the Feel through the manipulation of loft is to get rid of as many long irons as possible for average players and replace them with higher lofted woods.

• Loft is a **MINOR** factor of **Accuracy** in the irons

The greater the loft, the more **Backspin** will be imparted on the ball and the less the amount of sidespin can be generated. When the amount of **Backspin** is considerably greater than the sidespin, the ball will tend not to spin as far off-line. This is why the short irons are not as likely to be hit off-line as are the middle and long irons.

However, a golfer cannot play the game entirely with short irons just in an effort to hit the ball straighter. Obviously golfers will need an assortment of irons for hitting different length approach shots to the greens. Because irons must change in loft from club to club by between 3° and 5°, it is not possible to vary the loft enough within each individual club to affect a significant change in the **Accuracy**. For example, it is possible to change from a 28° to a 30° loft 5-iron in order to hit the ball straighter, but the actual change of 2° will not usually have a dramatic effect on **Accuracy** because the 28° and 30° lofts are so close in terms of their ability to generate misdirectional sidespin. In addition, the difference in **Distance** between clubs and the overall **Distance** achieved would be adversely affected to the point that the overall ability to play the game would be hurt. Therefore, you cannot think of changing loft in the irons as a way to help improve **Accuracy**.

Fast Fact:
   Do not change the loft of the irons to try to improve Accuracy (by choosing more loft) or the tradeoff in terms of loss of Distance and/or Trajectory might not be worth the effort. The best way to manipulate loft to improve Accuracy is to work within the set makeup. If the player hits the fairway woods crooked and the longer irons straight, drop the woods and add on long irons. However, the opposite is more often the case, so always consider replacing long irons with high-lofted fairway woods, even to the point of eliminating the use of the 1, 2, 3 or 4-iron for an average to less skilled golfer.

II. LIE ANGLE

Definition:

The angle in degrees between the center line of the hosel and the sole of the clubhead, when the sole is touching the ground at the center of the face scoring area.

Terminology of Lie:

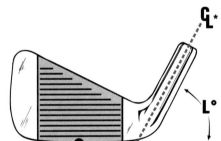

A clubhead with a lie angle that is lower in degrees than the accepted standard for that head is termed **flat**; a clubhead with a lie angle that is the same as the accepted standard for that head is termed **standard**; a clubhead with a lie angle that is greater than the accepted standard for that head is termed **upright**.

Despite changes from manufacturer to manufacturer in design philosophies, within the golf industry there are accepted general standard lie angles for each golf clubhead. (See Chapter 4 - Measuring the Golf Club Specifications - Lie Angle for the list of standard lie angle dimensions.)

■ **Effect on the shotmaking performance factors:**

   • Lie is a **MAJOR** factor of **Accuracy** in the short irons.
   • Lie is a **MEDIUM** factor of **Accuracy** in the middle irons.
   • Lie is a **MINOR** factor of **Accuracy** in the long irons and woods.

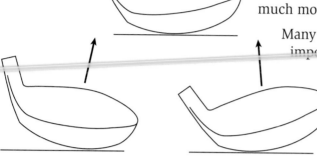

The greater the loft angle, the more dramatic the misdirection will be directly off the face. Additionally, a greater loft angle also means more **Backspin**, but if the blade is tilted upright or flat, some of that **Backspin** is translated into sidespin, which makes the shot fly further offline. This second factor is why lie in the short irons is much more important than in the woods.

Many clubmakers believe that lie in the woods is just as important as it is in the short irons because the extra distance gained in the woods multiplies the lesser misdirection angle into being the same amount of **Distance** off-line at the point of carry. Again, this is not true because when the face is tilted due to an incorrect lie, the greater **Backspin** in the short irons turns into sidespin, which exaggerates the off-line nature of the shot.

The misdirection factor of an improperly fit lie is less for the woods than the irons. In the irons, the misdirection factor becomes much greater as the loft increases.

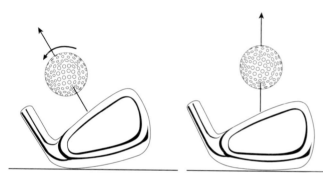
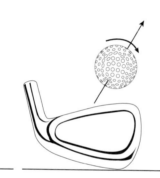

Fast Fact:
Lie is an important specification to fit to the golfer and set yourself apart as a quality source of golf equipment compared to shops that do not offer custom fitting. When fitting lie for the entire set, understand that the critical clubs to fit as closely as possible are the middle and short irons because they have more loft. The greater the loft of the clubhead, the more the face will point right or left when the toe or heel is up in the air due to an incorrect lie angle.

III. FACE ANGLE

Definition:

The angle in degrees between the face and the target line when the hosel bore is perpendicular to the target line. Face angle is a specification restricted to woods and does not exist in an iron or putter. This is because a wood is allowed to rest flat on its sole in the address position, thus revealing its face angle. With irons, the club is held by the golfer with the leading edge of the blade perpendicular to the target line. In this case, there is never a face angle on the iron. However, if the iron or putter is allowed to rest on its sole, and if it has a bounce sole angle, the face will turn hooked, or will turn open if the sole has a scoop sole angle. This is particularly important to know for the golfer who has a putter that "sits hooked" or "sits open," because of the bounce or scoop sole angle and is not being held with the leading edge perpendicular to the hole. (See Chapter 9 - Short Game Fitting, Putters).

Closed (2°) Face Angle   Square (0°) Face Angle   Open (2°) Face Angle

Terminology of Face Angle:

When allowed to sit flat on its sole in the address position, a face angle that points to the hook side of the target is termed **closed**; a face angle that points directly at the target is termed **square**; and a face angle that points to the slice side of the target is termed **open**. The face angle can be expressed in the number of degrees it is open or closed from the square position. If the face angle is square, it is always expressed as **0° square**. This is done to make sure there is no confusion between a 0° square measured face angle and a square appearing face angle. A square appearing face angle is usually measured at a 1-2° open face angle. This is due to an optical illusion created when both eyes are focused on the face when the club is addressed in the playing position.

■ Effect on the shotmaking performance factors:

• Face Angle is a **MAJOR** factor of **Accuracy**

Clubhead path and face angle are the two parts of the golf swing which control **Accuracy**. By changing the face angle of the club, the direction the clubface points at impact is altered. The effect of a face angle change of 2° or more can usually be noticed by golfers of all abilities. In fact, for changing shot direction, face angle is the single most effective specification to use.

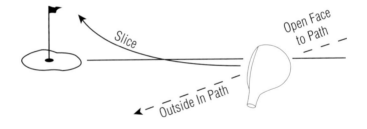

How a face angle change corrects the most common cause of a slice.

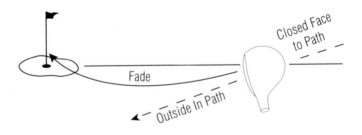

Fast Fact:
Face angle is the single most important specification for changing Accuracy. A clubmaker forgetting to use face angle to correct a slice or hook is as close to a clubmaking cardinal sin as exists.

- Face Angle is a **MINOR** factor of **Trajectory**

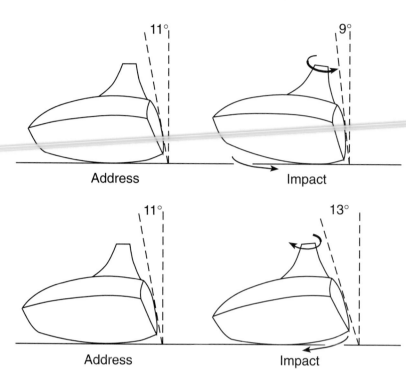

The principle of effective loft.

Due to the principle of effective loft, the more the face angle is closed (hooked), the greater the loft is at impact when the golfer rotates the hook faced club more square into the ball. The more the face angle is open (slice), the less the loft is at impact when the golfer rotates the open face club more square into the ball.

Effective loft can only operate under the premise that if a golfer slices or hooks the ball, then the player has a habit of making an incorrect movement with the hands during the downswing by either rotating the face open (slice) or closed (hook). Thus, a closed face wood in the hands of a person who slices the ball can be rotated more open at impact due to the swing error made by the slicer (and vice versa for ther person who hooks the ball).

Effective loft has never been proven to have a significant effect on shot **Trajectory**. If the player who hits the ball high, wants to reduce **Trajectory** but requires a closed face angle because he slices the ball, then reduce the real loft of the head to change the **Trajectory**.

Likewise, if the player hits the ball low, wants to increase the trajectory and requires an open face angle because he hooks the ball, then increase the real loft of the head as an additional and separate fitting recommendation for **Trajectory** control.

Fast Fact:
Face angle can interact with loft to create a MINOR factor called effective loft. With this, a hook face angle increases effective loft at impact while an open face angle decreases the effective loft at impact. However, the effect of this factor on Trajectory is <u>very slight</u> at best. If you give a hook face angle to a slicer who already hits the ball high and you are concerned it will make the player hit the ball too high, think of it this way... If the golfer thinks he hits the ball too high with the slice, you will make that correction through a change in real loft. Once that is done, the more closed face angle corrects the slice, the loft decrease corrects the high shot pattern and everything is OK without overanalyzing the situation by awarding more credence to effective loft than it deserves.

IV. CLUBHEAD DESIGN —
CENTER OF GRAVITY (CG) AND WEIGHT DISTRIBUTION

Definition of Center of Gravity:

The intersection of all balance points on the clubhead is the center of gravity.

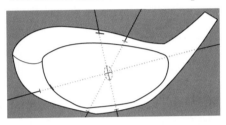 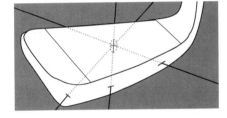

Definition of Weight Distribution:

The arrangement and positioning of the clubhead mass about its center of gravity.

Cavity Back - Perimeter Weighted   Muscle Back - Center Weighted

Terminology of Center of Gravity

The center of gravity is sometimes referred to as the **"sweet spot"** of the clubhead. While this can express the **Feel** of hitting the ball on the clubhead's center of gravity, in truth, the center of gravity is one small point inside the clubhead. The sweet spot then must be understood as the portion of the striking face on the clubhead where an off-center impact does not substantially twist the clubhead or vibrate the hands.

Other commonly used terms in clubmaking are **low center of gravity** and **high center of gravity**, which denote a general location of the point of balance on the head. There is no defined location for a low or a high CG.

For **Accuracy** and true comparison, the center of gravity of any clubhead can be described along the X, Y and Z axes within space.

Described in this context, it is then possible to locate the center of gravity in terms of the (X) vertical, (Y) horizontal and (Z) depth planes within the head. Points can be defined on each of the three axes, keeping in mind that there is only one point that is the actual CG in the head – the intersection of those three axes.

Using the measurements indicated in the drawing, it is possible to see that the CG is located 18.5mm up from the sole line on the X axis. This is the vertical location of the CG and is the coordinate that indicates how low the CG is, giving the clubmaker an idea of how easy the club will be to get the ball airborne. On the Y axis, the -0.5mm coordinate means that the CG is located 0.5mm toward the heel side of the center of the face, indicating the horizontal location of the CG. Finally, the tricky measurement to understand is the Z axis coordinate. In this example, the CG is located 11.3mm back from the intersection of the X, axes. To better understand the Z axis CG location — the greater the loft of an iron, the greater will be the Z axis measurement. (For more information, see the section in Chapter Three – Specification Measurement Procedures, which pertains to center of gravity measurement).

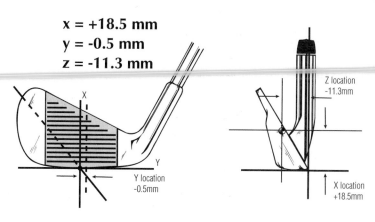

x = +18.5 mm
y = -0.5 mm
z = -11.3 mm

Z location -11.3mm

Y location -0.5mm

X location +18.5mm

Terminology of weight distribution:

Weight distribution can be expressed in different terms that describe the arrangement of the clubhead's mass on the head. For irons or metal woods, **perimeter-weighting** refers to a condition in which a significant portion of the clubhead's mass is positioned around and farther away from the center of gravity(i.e. around the perimeter of the clubhead.) **Muscleback** describes a type of weight distribution in irons where the mass is positioned more behind the center of gravity. Other terms describe particular types of weight distribution which have varying degrees of either perimeter weighting or a muscleback weight distribution, such as **hollow iron, flange back, flow weighting, heel weighting or toe weighting**.

Weight distribution is used to control the moment of inertia on the clubhead, which is a factor describing the head's ability to resist the force of rotation in response to any impact that occurs off-center.

■ Effect Center of Gravity on the shotmaking performance factors:

• Center of Gravity is a **MAJOR** factor of **Distance**.

A shot hit off the toe will cause the head to twist, losing the ability to transfer maximum energy to the shot.

The closer the center of gravity of the clubhead is in line with the ball's center of gravity, the greater the **Distance** of the shot. This is the only way the golfer's maximum energy can be transferred to the ball and achieve the maximum **Distance** generated by the golfer. (Of course if the loft angle is not properly matched to the golfer, a perfect alignment of the CG of the head and CG of the ball will not result in maximum **Distance**. However, this is a matter of loft and the launch angle it creates, not CG of the head on its own.)

Past research in impact dynamics has estimated that for every 1/2" the ball is struck horizontally off the center of gravity in a wood, seven percent of the golfer's potential **Distance** can be lost, and for every 1/2" the ball is struck horizontally off the CG in an iron, five percent can be lost. This is largely because the CG of the clubhead is not in line with the CG of the ball. The result is less energy transferred to the ball and a rotation of the head during impact, which results in a loss of **Distance**. While perimeter-weighting can slightly mask the feeling of the rotation (vibration) of the head, it cannot make up for all of the energy that has been lost.

In contrast, missing the CG on the vertical plane, or hitting the ball on its CG directly above or below the clubhead's CG will not result in the same type of vibration and loss of energy as hitting the ball on the toe or heel side of the clubhead's CG. This is because no horizontal twisting will occur in the clubhead when the CG of the ball is vertically in line with the CG of the head. If the ball is hit above the the CG of the head, there will be a very slight rotation of the clubhead around its own CG on a vertical plane. This vertical rotation around the clubhead's CG is much less than the horizontal rotation will be from a heel or toe hit because the shaft acts as a brace against such a motion, in addition to there being less area above or below the CG than there is to either side of the CG.

When the ball is hit high on the face, but still vertically in line with the CG, the ball will take off on a much higher launch angle and with less **Backspin**. This is due to two factors:

Balloon Shot

1) Vertical roll, or curvature of the face up and down, dictates that the loft angle is greater above the CG and,

2) The CG of the head is lower than the ball CG at impact causing the ball to take off at a higher **Trajectory**. The slight rotation of the head in response to the high face impact reduces the rolling of the ball up the face and decreases **Backspin**.

Skyed Shot

As a result, if the ball is hit well above the clubhead's CG and the top edge of the wood head face is below the CG of the ball, the shot takes off in what is commonly called a "skyed shot," resulting in a very high **Trajectory** and a severe loss of **Distance**.

If the ball is hit above the CG of the head but with the top of the face in line with, or slightly above the CG of the ball, the result is a "ballooned shot." The ball immediately jumps high into the air, but then reaches a point where it quits climbing and tends to float down the fairway. In some cases, a "ballooned" shot can fly farther than a shot hit in the center of the face because of a lack of **Backspin**, and because the golfer may have achieved a better **Trajectory** for carry **Distance** than a shot hit in the center of the face.

If the same type of impact occurs with an iron, the results are much less successful because there is less mass high on the top of an iron to support the impact. Therefore, a high hit with an iron results in a greater loss in **Distance** than a high hit with a wood.

The last condition of CG misalignment is when the CG of the clubhead is above the CG of the ball at impact. If the leading edge of the clubface is below the CG of the ball, but the CG of the head is still above the ball's CG, the shot will get airborne, but will fly in a much lower **Trajectory** than if impact occurs in the center of the face.

When the ball is hit low on the face and vertically in line with the CG, the ball will take off on a much lower launch angle. This lower launch angle is due to two factors:

Thin Shot

With High Swing Velocity

With Lower Swing Velocity

1) Vertical roll, or curvature of the face up and down, dictates the loft angle is less below the head's CG and,

2) With the CG of the head higher than the CG of the ball at impact, the ball will take off at a much lower **Trajectory**. **Backspin** is still imparted on the shot because there is still some loft low on the face and because the slight rotation of the head in response to the high face impact causes some rolling of the ball up the face.

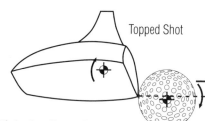

Topped Shot

If the ball is hit well below the clubhead's CG, so that the bottom edge of the face of the wood head is above the CG of the ball, the shot is topped and never gets airborne. If the CG of the ball makes contact with the face below the CG of the head but with the bottom edge of the face in line with or slightly above the CG of the ball, the result is a "thin shot." The ball takes off very low, does not carry very far and achieves most of its **Distance** from rolling on the fairway.

If the leading edge of the wood or iron is above the CG of the ball at impact, the ball will not get airborne.

In some cases, a "thin shot" can actually travel farther than a shot hit perfectly in the center of the face. This "747" type of shot (as some players refer to it) takes off low, flies low for a short period and then begins to climb, after which it peaks in its **Trajectory**, then comes down and rolls a significant **Distance**. This unique type of flight pattern occurs primarily with higher clubhead speed players because it requires a great deal of force to generate enough **Backspin** from a low face hit to be able to rise in **Trajectory** after taking off in a low flight pattern.

If the same type of low face impact occurs with an iron, the results are usually a little more successful than with a wood head hit because there is more loft on an iron. As long as the bottom edge of the iron contacts the ball below its CG, the shot will get airborne and will carry closer to the club's prescribed normal **Distance** than would a low face shot off a wood head. For an iron, it is only when the bottom edge of the face is level with the CG of the ball that the shot flies extraordinarily low.

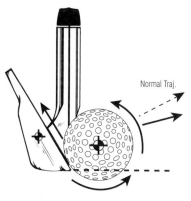

Normal Traj.

A thin shot still generates some backpsin as long as the CG of the ball is above the leading edge of the clubhead.

While there are ways to trick the CG at impact to result in a shot of adequate **Distance**, there is no way the player can consistently achieve maximum **Distance** unless the CG of the head and ball align with each other vertically. Missing the CG toward the toe or heel is an absolute sure way to rob a player of significant **Distance**. In order for the golfer to hit the ball to his or her maximum potential **Distance**, it should always be the goal of clubmaker to choose specifications for the player which will enhance his/her ability to hit the ball in line with the CG of the clubhead.

Fast Fact:
  Missing the center of gravity on the clubhead toward the toe or heel at impact is the most definite way to lose Distance. Making contact with the ball on the CG, or with the CG of the ball just above the CG of the clubhead is a sure way for the golfer to achieve his or her maximum potential Distance. The clubmaker must focus on doing whatever is necessary to allow the golfer to hit the ball on center in order to deliver the most Distance possible.

• Center of Gravity is a **MEDIUM** factor of **Accuracy**

  The closer the center of gravity of the clubhead is vertically with the CG of the ball, the less sidespin imparted on the ball and the straighter the shot. This is because sidespin results when the ball contacts the head on the toe or heel, making the head rotate and impart sidespin on the ball. If the ball hits above or below the CG of the clubhead, sidespin cannot be affected because the head will not rotate in a toe/heel or heel/toe direction.

  However, the reason CG is only a **MEDIUM** factor of **Accuracy** and not a **MAJOR** factor is because it is not controlled solely by the alignment of the clubhead's CG with the CG of the ball. **Accuracy** is controlled by the path the clubhead travels coming into impact and the face angle of the clubhead relative to that path. Only after path and face angle are factored into the accuracy of the shot can the amount of sidespin coming from an off-center hit add to the **Accuracy** results.

  There are three basic paths the clubhead is known to travel into impact as indicated in the above drawing – outside moving to inside, which is the most common cause of a slice; inside moving to the outside, which is the primary cause of a draw; and square, which the clubhead comes slightly from the inside, travels on the target line through impact and then travels back toward the inside again. Obviously, the very straightest hitters all have a square clubhead path.

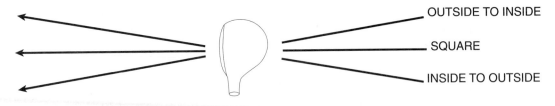

CLUBHEAD PATH

OUTSIDE TO INSIDE

SQUARE

INSIDE TO OUTSIDE

  In addition to the three basic clubhead paths, the clubface can also be open, square or closed to each of the three paths. For example, with the outside to inside clubhead path, (see drawing) the clubface can be open, square, or closed to that outside/in path. The clubhead path controls the initial direction that the ball will take off when it is struck, unless the face angle is so far open or closed that it alone overpowers the effect of the path.

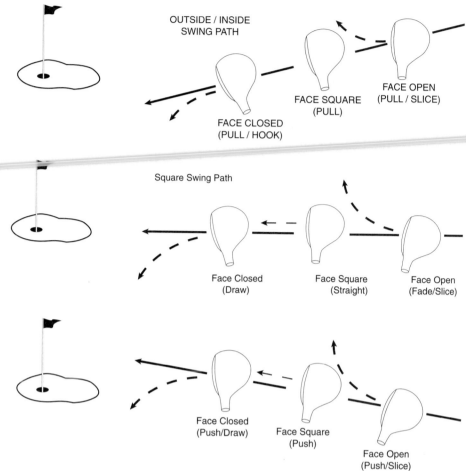

OUTSIDE / INSIDE
SWING PATH

FACE OPEN
(PULL / SLICE)

FACE SQUARE
(PULL)

FACE CLOSED
(PULL / HOOK)

Square Swing Path

Face Closed
(Draw)

Face Square
(Straight)

Face Open
(Fade/Slice)

Face Closed
(Push/Draw)

Face Square
(Push)

Face Open
(Push/Slice)

(NOTE: All descriptions to follow refer to a right handed player)

If the face is slightly open to the outside/inside path, the ball will start a little to the left of the target line and then slice to the right of the target line. However, if the clubface is severely open, the ball could start to the right of the target line and then slice farther to the right. Obviously, the interaction of the two factors, path and face angle, can both control and offset each other's effect on the shot direction, depending upon how severe each may be.

If the clubface is square to the outside/inside path, the ball will start to the left and travel with no curvature on the line of the path, constituting a pulled shot. Finally, if the clubface is closed to the outside/inside path, the ball will start to the left of the path and hook more to the left.

The same analysis can be made with each of the other path directions as follows:

Square path/open face = ball starts straight and slices to the right
Square path/square face = ball starts straight and goes straight (no sidespin)
Square path/closed face = ball starts straight and hooks to the left

Inside to outside path/open face = ball starts right and slices more right
Inside to outside path/square face = ball starts right and is a push (no sidespin)
Inside to outside path/closed face = ball starts slightly right and hooks back to center

Outside to inside path/open face = ball starts slightly left and slices to the right
Outside to inside path/square face = ball starts left and is a dead pull (no sidespin)
Outside to inside path/closed face = ball starts left and hooks farther to the left

Fast Fact:

Missing the CG of the clubhead toward the toe or heel at impact is the most definite way to lose Distance and create enough sidespin to affect Accuracy as well. Making contact with the ball on the CG, or just above the CG is a sure way for the golfer to achieve his or her maximum potential Accuracy. The clubmaker must focus on doing whatever is necessary to allow the golfer to hit the ball on center in order to deliver the most Accuracy possible.

• Center of gravity is a **MEDIUM** factor of **Trajectory**

The lower the CG of the clubhead in relation to the CG of the ball at impact, the higher the **Trajectory**. Likewise, the higher the center of gravity of the clubhead in relation to the CG of the ball at impact, the lower the **Trajectory**.

This effect on **Trajectory** occurs because of the combination of several factors. The lower the CG of the head compared to the CG of the ball, the more the ball will cause the head to pitch slightly back, thus increasing the loft and with it, the height of the shot as it leaves the face. In addition, the lower the CG of the head in relation to the CG of the ball, the more the ball can skid or slide up the face before it starts spinning. This action of more sliding up the face results in less friction with the face and accordingly, a higher launch angle.

Conversely, the higher the CG of the head compared to the CG of the ball, the more the ball will cause the head to pitch or rotate slightly forward, thus decreasing the loft and with it, lowering the height of the shot as it leaves the face. In addition, the higher the CG of the head in relation to the CG of the ball, the less the ball will slide up the face before it starts spinning. This action of less sliding up the face results in more friction with the face and accordingly, a lower launch angle.

The length of the grass from where a shot is struck is also a very significant factor in controlling the **Trajectory** of the shot in relation to the clubhead and ball's CG. The higher the ball sits up in the grass, the lower will be the CG of the club compared to the ball. In this case, you could have a high CG clubhead that reacts at impact like a low CG club, thus hitting the ball very high.

And, as the case is many times in clubhead dynamics, the opposite is true for hard ground and short, thin grass. The lower the ball sits down in the grass, the higher will be the CG of the club compared to the ball. In this case, you could have a low CG clubhead that reacts at impact like a high CG club, hitting the ball lower than normal.

Suffice it to say, hitting a ball slightly above or below the CG of the clubhead is far better from an accuracy standpoint than hitting the ball to the right or left of the CG.

The closer the CG to the face of the clubhead, the lower the **Trajectory** for any given loft. The farther back the CG is, the higher the **Trajectory** for any given loft. This means that wooden heads with backweights or jumbo oversized wood heads will result in a slightly higher **Trajectory** than similarly lofted heads without each of the mentioned features.

The reason a rear located CG will result in a higher **Trajectory** is because the CG causes the head to "turn under" very slightly coming into impact, adding dynamic loft to the head. This occurs because under the influence

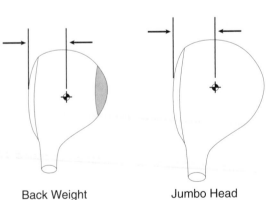

Back Weight   Jumbo Head

Two design factors which move the CG farther back from the face.

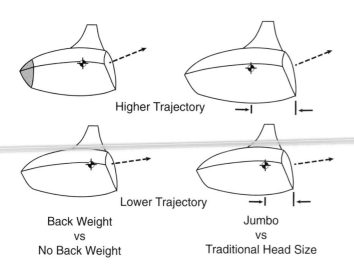

Higher Trajectory →| |←

Lower Trajectory →| |←

Back Weight
vs
No Back Weight

Jumbo
vs
Traditional Head Size

of the force of the downswing, the CG tries to align itself with the axis of the shaft. Depending on how far back in the head the CG may be shifted due to the backweight or jumbo head shape, the amount of **Trajectory** increase may or may not be noticeable to the golfer. Recent studies have shown that for every 1/8" the CG is moved back from the face, the **Trajectory** from any given loft will increase by about seven feet.

Fast Fact:
    The lower the CG, the higher the Trajectory for any given loft. This means among two clubs of the same loft, the one with the lower CG will hit the ball higher. This is why any golfer in search of a higher Trajectory needs to look for a low CG clubhead. According to research performed by Titleist Golf Company, and published in the book *Science and Golf II*, lowering the CG in an iron by 1/4" will increase the launch angle by 1°, which is not that significant. In a wood club, lowering the CG by 1/8" will increase the Trajectory by 30-35 feet, which is a more significant change. However, a portion of the wood head's increase in Trajectory is achieved because the CG is much farther back from the face, a point that does not occur on an iron due to the natural thickness difference in shape between the heads. Bigger, jumbo heads hit the ball higher because the CG is farther back from the face, while shallow woods hit the ball higher because the CG is much lower than it would be on a jumbo wood. This provides the clubmaker with two types of wood head choices to help the golfer hit the ball higher.

• Center of gravity is a **MINOR** factor of **Backspin**

    Testing performed by Titleist Golf Company, and published in the book *Science and Golf II*, has shown that decreasing the center of gravity by 1/4" on an iron will cause an increase of approximately 250 - 300 rpm of **Backspin**. While this may sound significant, increasing the **Backspin** of a 5-iron 250-300 rpm represents a 3.5 percent increase, which is not much in shotmaking terms and certainly not enough to make any real difference in stopping the ball on the green. In addition, it has to be understood that finding two different irons with a 1/4" vertical difference in the CG would require finding two iron designs that differ substantially in blade height. This is because it is almost impossible to have two clubs with the same blade height due to limitations in positioning the mass around the head.

Since the woods have much less loft than irons, even though a **Trajectory** increase in the woods is more dramatic when the CG is lower, the actual **Backspin** increase is not that significant. This will make a wood stop the ball faster. However, because the difference in **Trajectory** between a low and high CG iron is not that significant, the effect on the iron's ability to stop the ball is not that significant, except with players with high swing speeds.

Fast Fact:
The lower the CG, the greater the amount of Backspin generated by the club on the ball. However, the amount of increase is slight and is not enough to make a significant difference in stopping the ball on the green except for the stronger golfer. If the player needs to increase Backspin significantly, the change will have to first come in the form of a swing change, and second, in the form of increased loft.

• Center of Gravity is a **MEDIUM** factor in the **Feel** of a golf club

The closer the ball is hit to the CG of the clubhead, the more solid the shot will **Feel**. The farther from the CG of the head the ball is struck, the less solid the impact will **Feel**. The only reason the CG is considered to be a **MEDIUM** factor in the **Feel** of the club instead of a **MAJOR** factor is because the other factors such as shaft flex, shaft weight, shaft bend point, swingweight, total weight and grip size play a more important role.

However, it must be accepted that of all the factors which can affect the **Feel** of the club, CG is the most important. Plainly stated, CG has to be considered the most important of all the specifications of a golf club. Here is why –

Choose the right specifications of the total golf club so the golfer hits the ball on-center the greatest percentage of the time, more consistently and as far and straight as the golfer's physical abilities permit. Therefore, finding the combination of specifications which will enable the golfer to hit the CG more often has to be the single overall goal of any custom fitting program.

Fast Fact:
No club will Feel as solid when it is hit off center toward the toe or heel as it will Feel if hit on center, or just above the CG, regardless of perimeter weighting. Of course, there are many other factors which affect the Feel of the club, but for any clubhead to Feel solid, making contact with the center of gravity is the most important. Again, that is why it is so important to work with all the factors that affect Accuracy and Feel to find the right specifications that will help the golfer hit the ball on center the highest percentage of the time.

■ **Effect of Weight Distribution on shotmaking performance factors:**

• Weight Distribution is a **MEDIUM** factor of **Distance**

As a clubhead design specification, center of gravity was ranked as a **MAJOR** factor of **Distance** because of the dramatic loss of energy and **Distance** when a ball is hit off of the CG. To contrast, weight distribution does not have the same effect. If the clubhead makes contact with the ball in line with the CG on a perimeter-weighted and a muscleback iron head, which are identical in shape, size, loft and weight, the ball travels the same **Distance** on both heads.

However, when an off-center impact occurs on the identical muscle-back and perimeter-weighted heads, both will lose **Distance**, but the perimeter-weighted head will lose slightly less. While advertisements have led golfers to believe that perimeter-weighted clubheads will recover significant **Distance** on off-center impact as compared to a muscleback head, the real difference is not as great as the advertisements declare.

Still, because the perimeter-weighted head will vibrate and twist less from an off-center hit when compared to a muscleback style head, there will be slightly more **Distance** retained from the perimeter-weighted clubhead, which makes this specification a **MEDIUM** factor of **Distance**.

Fast Fact:
The more perimeter weighting on a clubhead, the less twisting of the head in response to an off-center hit and with it, the more Distance which can be recovered. Regardless of perimeter weighting, missing the CG will cause a definite loss of Distance. Using a perimeter-weighted club can make a difference in restoring some of the Distance that would have been lost on the off-center hit, but under no circumstances will a perimeter-weighted head restore all the lost Distance from hitting the ball off center.

• Weight distribution is a **MEDIUM** factor of **Feel**

Perhaps the most important contribution of weight distribution to fitting is its ability to enhance the **Feel** of impact. Due to the fact that perimeter weighting reduces the amount of rotation, twisting and vibration resulting from an off-center hit, the effect is the sensation of making more solid contact with the ball. While perimeter weighting will have a very slight effect on **Trajectory** or **Accuracy**, its effect on **Feel** is more perceptible to most players.

In other words, if you hit a perimeter-weighted club on the toe or heel, the impact will not be as solid as an on-center hit, but it will not transmit the feeling of vibration to the golfer's hands as badly as an off-center impact with a muscleback style of weight distribution. Still, an off-center shot hit with a perimeter-weighted clubhead will not **Feel** as solid as when the ball is hit on center. This is why weight distribution has to be ranked as having a **MEDIUM** effect on **Feel**.

Fast Fact:
The type of weight distribution that creates a perimeter-weighted design will have a noticeable effect on the Feel of the club at impact. Therefore, any golfer who hits the ball off-center a high percentage of the time will be better off from a Feel standpoint with a perimeter-weighted clubhead.

• Weight Distribution is a **MINOR** factor of **Accuracy**

If a golf club is designed with perimeter weighting (a high moment of inertia), contacting the ball off-center toward the heel or toe will prevent the club from twisting or vibrating as much as would a non-perimeter-weighted clubhead. If the head vibrates or twists less, there will be less sidespin created from the off-center hit and a more accurate shot will be the result.

However, **Accuracy** comes primarily from the clubhead path and the face angle movements during the golf swing, not from the weight distribution of the golf club. It is true that an off-center shot hit with a perimeter-weighted club will not have as much sidespin as an off-center hit with a muscleback club, but the reduction in sidespin is minimal. The reason a player often thinks he/she hits the ball straighter and better with the perimeter-weighted club is because off-center shots don't **Feel** as unsolid due to the reduction in rotation/twisting of the head.

Still, the choice for whether a player needs a perimeter-weighted head must be made chiefly on whether the player hits the ball off-center a high percentage of the time and not simply because the player hits it off-line. The perimeter-weighted head will help **Accuracy** a minimal amount, but not as much as some of the other factors in the Practical Fitting Program.

Fast Fact:
The more perimeter weighted the clubhead, the less sidespin imparted to the ball on off-center hits. However, the amount of Accuracy help will be minimal for a player who already hits the ball off line a high percentage of the time due to mistakes he/she makes in his/her clubhead path and/or face angle.

• Weight Distribution is a **MINOR** factor of **Trajectory**

If the weight distribution is low on a head, the center of gravity will also be low, which will increase the **Trajectory** of the shot. In addition, most cavity-back, perimeter-weighted irons heads also have more hosel offset, which in turn can increase the **Trajectory**. While this is not directly related to weight distribution, it is still worth mentioning in the whole context of weight distribution as a fitting factor.

On the other hand, if the weight distribution is designed to create a high moment of inertia, and the center of gravity is normal for a game improvement club (normal sole width instead of wide sole, for example), the **Trajectory** will not be affected by the weight distribution.

Fast Fact:
Weight distribution can only affect Trajectory if the weight distribution design includes enough mass positioned low on the clubhead to create a low center of gravity.

V. HORIZONTAL FACE BULGE

Definition:

The intentional heel-to-toe curvature designed on the face of a wood head that is required to counteract the sidespin imparted on the ball when impact is made off the center of gravity of the clubhead.

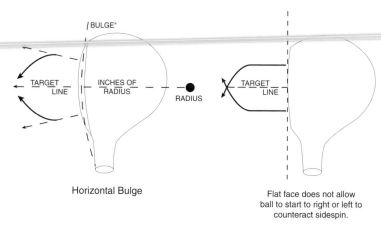

Horizontal Bulge

Flat face does not allow ball to start to right or left to counteract sidespin.

Terminology of Horizontal Bulge:

Horizontal bulge is normally referred to simply as bulge, with the assumption that **bulge** only refers to curvature in the horizontal plane, toe to heel on the wood head. Bulge is measured in inches or millimeters of the curvature and is different for each wood head, depending upon the breadth of the head. Therefore, an 8", 10", 12" or 14" bulge are the most common examples of how the specification is expressed.

■ Effect of Horizontal Bulge on the shotmaking performance factors:

• Horizontal Bulge is a **MEDIUM** factor of **Accuracy**

When the ball makes contact with the wood head on the toe, it normally picks up hooking sidespin. When it is hit off the heel, it picks up a slicing sidespin. This occurs because the off-center hit forces the clubhead to rotate about its own center of gravity. When the head begins to rotate, the ball will also begin to rotate in response, rolling and skidding toward the center of the face. As a result, a hooking sidespin is generated from toe shots and slicing sidespin from heel shots. This is what is referred to as the "gear effect."

To keep a hooking or fading shot under control, the curvature of the horizontal bulge allows the shot to start more to the right or left of the target so the hook or slice spin has the effect of moving the ball back toward the middle of the fairway. This result is based on the clubhead path and the face angle being relatively square.

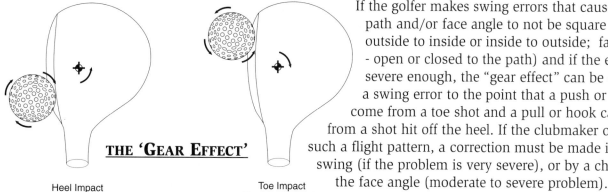

THE 'GEAR EFFECT'

Heel Impact
Fading Sidespin

Toe Impact
Hooking Sidespin

If the golfer makes swing errors that cause the path and/or face angle to not be square (path - outside to inside or inside to outside; face angle - open or closed to the path) and if the error is severe enough, the "gear effect" can be offset by a swing error to the point that a push or slice can come from a toe shot and a pull or hook can come from a shot hit off the heel. If the clubmaker observes such a flight pattern, a correction must be made in the swing (if the problem is very severe), or by a change in the face angle (moderate to severe problem).

Also, if the bulge is too great (too much curvature), the ball will not develop draw spin from a toe shot or fade spin from a heel impact. Likewise, if too little bulge is placed on the wood head, the ball will not start its flight direction far enough to the right or left to counter-act the hooking or slicing sidespin generated from the "gear effect."

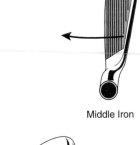

Too much bulge can offset the Gear Effect

Flat face does not allow ball to start to right or left to counteract side spin.

Irons are not designed with horizontal bulge for the single reason that the "gear effect" does not occur nearly as much from an off-center shot. This is because the center of gravity of most irons is much closer to the face of the iron than it is on a wood head. The "gear effect" is also reduced because the majority of the irons all have much more loft than do woods. The greater loft causes the ball to skid and roll more up the face rather than across, thus cre-ating much more **Backspin** than sidespin on the ball. The result is that long irons, with their lower loft, can generate some hooking spin from toe shots and fading spin from heel shots. Middle irons create less sidespin, while virtually no sidespin is created from a toe or heel impact on the short irons.

Long Iron

Middle Iron

Fast Fact:

Horizontal bulge is the intentional curvature from heel to toe on every wood head. It is not present on an iron because the center of gravity is much closer to the face of an iron than it is on a wood. The closer the CG is to the face and the more loft on the clubhead, the less hook or slice sidespin will occur from hitting the ball on the toe or heel.

Bulge must be present on a wood to help start the ball to the right or the left of the target to counteract the hooking or slicing sidespin generated by the off-center hit. Without it, every time the golfer hits the ball on the toe or heel, the ball would hook or fade much more off line while not traveling nearly as far.

The key point to remember about fitting for bulge is to inspect the wood heads you choose for the golfer to make sure they are not designed with too much bulge (too much curva-ture), or with too little bulge (too flat), both which could create even more Accuracy problems.

Short Iron

VI. VERTICAL FACE ROLL

Definition:

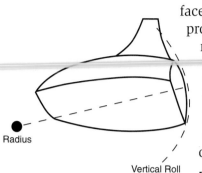

Radius

Vertical Roll

The intentional curvature designed from top to bottom, vertically, on the face of a wood head. While bulge has a definite purpose and is required for proper shotmaking, the same cannot be said for roll. There is no real explanation for why roll should be part of the design of a wood head. Wood heads have been produced with no roll and have proven to be very playable. In fact, wood heads with no roll are more playable for golfers who hit the ball high and/or low on the clubface. than the same wood head made with roll, yet roll is still used in virtually all wood head designs. (See the effects of roll on the shotmaking factors in this section of this chapter for a full understanding of this point.)

Terminology of Vertical Roll:

Vertical roll is normally referred to simply as **roll**, with the assumption that roll only refers to curvature in the vertical plane. Roll, like bulge, is also measured in inches or millimeters of the curvature and may be different for each wood head, depending upon the loft of the head. A 10", 12", 14" and 16" roll are the most common examples of how the specification is expressed. By tradition only, roll is generally designed to be 2" more in radius flatter than bulge on each wood head.

(**NOTE**: Virtually all Golfsmith wood heads are designed with at least 4" or more roll flatter than the bulge. This is because we feel excessive roll can be detrimental to most golfers who hit the ball low or high on the face. (Again, see the explanations that follow in the effect of vertical roll on the shotmaking performance factors.)

■ Effect of Vertical Roll on the shotmaking performance factors:

• Vertical Roll is a MEDIUM factor of Distance

Depending on the amount of vertical roll on the clubface and the point of impact, roll can create more loft on top of the face and less loft on the bottom of the face than the real loft which is measured in the middle of the face.

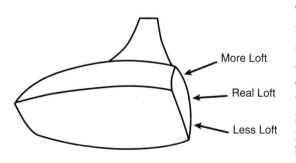

More Loft

Real Loft

Less Loft

Therefore, if the golfer hits the ball high on the face of the wood, the ball will fly higher. For most golfers, this results in the same or even more **Distance** because the **Trajectory** is higher and the ball is flying through the air with less friction due to decreased **Backspin**. In effect, the shot hit high off the face of the wood head is similar to a "flier" hit from tall grass with an iron. This type of shot does not have an accepted name, but is most commonly referred to as a "ballooned" shot because the ball takes off high and stays high in the air as it travels.

NOTE: This high face impact/greater **Distance** phenomenon only occurs if the impact is made with the top edge of the face in line with or above the center of gravity of the ball. If the top edge of the face is under the CG of the ball, a "skyed" shot will occur, which results in a very high **Trajectory** and a definite loss of **Distance**.

If impact occurs low on the face and below the CG of the clubhead, the ball will fly on a much lower **Trajectory** and will carry shorter than a shot hit higher on the face. This is what most golfers refer to as a thin shot and will usually result in less total **Distance**, unless the fairway is very parched and hard or the hole is downhill!

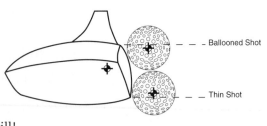

Balloned Shot

Thin Shot

Because loft is a **MAJOR** factor of **Distance**, the effect of vertical roll on **Distance** can create a visible change in the shot, depending upon the radius of the roll. However, because the effect of roll on **Distance** is only noticed when the golfer hits the ball high or low on the face, and especially if the roll is excessive, the overall effect of roll on **Distance** has to be ranked as **MEDIUM**.

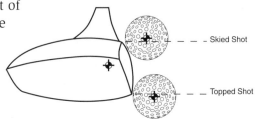

Skied Shot

Topped Shot

In effect, it is theoretically possible for roll to be individually customized for the golfer's impact habits. If the golfer hits the ball either low or high on the face a significant portion of the time, the roll should be less than normal (a flatter face, i.e. a higher number of inches of radius). This would create a face with approximately the same loft on the bottom, middle and top of the face, which in turn would mean a more consistent **Trajectory** and **Distance** when the golfer hits the ball high, low or in the middle of the clubface.

Fast Fact:
Vertical roll has no proven function for being a part of the design of a wood head. Despite this fact, roll does affect the Distance of a shot when the face is curved vertically and there is more loft on the top and less loft on the bottom of the face. This normally means that shots hit low on the face will fly lower and carry much shorter than a normal impact shot. A shot hit high on the face will fly higher because of the increased loft.
However, depending on the golfer's swing speed, swing ability and the exact location where the high face impact occurred with respect to the top edge of the clubface, the ball might fly farther or shorter than normal. Generally, players with a driver swing speed greater than 90mph who also hit the ball on a relatively high trajectory from an on-center shot will not usually gain Distance from a shot hit high on the face. It is the player who hits the ball with a lower than normal Trajectory and possesses a driver clubhead speed less than 90mph who is more likely to experience greater Distance from shots hit higher on the face. Remember, this does not refer to a "skyed" shot which flies very high and very short.

• Vertical Roll is a **MEDIUM** factor of **Trajectory**

Depending upon the amount of roll, a shot hit high on the face of the wood head will fly higher, and a shot hit low on the face will fly lower. While most golfers and clubmakers notice very significant changes in

Trajectory for this type of high or low face shot, the reason this is a **MEDIUM** and not a **MAJOR** factor is because the effect only occurs when the shot is not hit in the proper position on the face. In other words, the effect only occurs when the golfer incorrectly hits the shot. However, if the golfer suffers from high or low face shots a majority of the time, the roll should be reduced (choosing wood heads that are more flat from top to bottom to reduce loft on top of the face and increase loft on the bottom) to offset the high or low impact tendency.

The other significant reason a shot hit high or low on the face of the wood will result in a high or low **Trajectory** is because of the position of the ball's CG with respect to the CG of the clubhead in such impact conditions. Therefore, roll is not the only reason that a high or low impact will change **Trajectory**. In fact, even if the roll is made to be more flat, a high face shot still has to fly higher than a low face shot because of the position of impact relative to the CG of the head.

For roll itself to be a noticeable factor on **Trajectory**, it has to be engineered to be either much more (more curvature, lower number of inches of radius), or much less (less curvature, higher number of inches of radius) than what is normal for a wood head so there is either much more loft on top of the face or much less on the bottom than a normal roll or a flatter roll would create. In addition, it is possible, if the wood head has normal roll with a very deep face height (2 + ”), a high face shot would fly much higher and a low face shot much lower. This is because the taller the face, the more the effect of radius on creating more loft on the top and less loft on the bottom of the face.

Normal Face Height

Deep Face Height

Higher Trajectory

12"

12"

A shot hit high on the face of a deep face wood will fly higher due to CG and roll combined.

Just as the effect of roll is on **Distance** if the golfer hits the ball too high, the clubmaker can try to find a wood head with less roll (flatter face) so the loft will not be as great on the high face hits and as low on low face hits. Realistically, it is difficult to find wood heads made with so little roll to be able to correct high **Trajectory** problems by just addressing the roll. (If such woods were available, the much flatter roll would help lower the **Trajectory** of high face shots and raise the **Trajectory** of low face shots.) Therefore, the golfer's needs for a change in **Trajectory** should be addressed by its **MAJOR** effect factor of loft first, and the **MEDIUM** effect of center of gravity on the head second.

Fast Fact:
The greater the roll on the face of a wood or the taller the face height of a wood, the more the Trajectory will be affected by shots hit high or low on the face. With greater roll (more curvature, lower number of inches of radius), or a deep face height, a high face shot will fly higher and a low face shot will fly lower. This is primarily due to the fact that greater roll means more loft on the top of the face and less loft on the bottom of the face.

CG also plays a factor in the Trajectory as well. The farther the CG is below the ball's point of impact, the higher the shot. Conversely, the closer the CG is to the ball's point of impact on the face, the lower the shot. However, for golfers who have a problem hitting the ball too high, loft then followed by CG will be the chief specifications to address for the reason that vertically flat faced stainless steel and titanium metal woods basically do not exist (a wooden wood or an aluminum wood head could be filed or machined with no roll).

• Vertical Roll is a **MEDIUM** factor of **Backspin**

The greater the roll on the face, the more the **Backspin** can be affected by a shot hit high or low on the face. However, the effect of such shots hit high or low on the face on **Backspin** is a little different than what might be thought at first. Shots hit high on the face of the wood head fly with less **Backspin** and those hit low on the face with more **Backspin** because of "vertical gear effect."

When a wood head strikes the ball high or low on the face, the clubhead rotates slightly in the vertical plane about its own CG. A rotation that is similar to the horizontal movement of the head which occurs when the ball is struck on the toe or heel, the "vertical gear effect" is not nearly as significant as is the "horizontal gear effect" for two reasons. First, because wood heads are always designed to be longer from toe to heel than they are taller, it is possible to strike the ball farther from its CG toward the toe or heel than it is up or down. The farther the impact occurs from the CG, the more rotational force imparted to the head. Second, the vertical rotation is impeded more by the presence of the shaft than is the horizontal rotation. Because the stiffness axis of the shaft is roughly parallel to the vertical plane, any attempt the head makes to rotate vertically about its own CG is decreased slightly by the rigidity of the shaft.

Regardless of the difference, there is some vertical rotation of the head that does occur from a shot hit high or low on the face. This can have the effect of creating more **Backspin** on a low face shot and reducing the amount of **Backspin** that is imparted on a high face shot. The vertical gear effect cannot create topspin (overspin) on the high face shot because the face has loft and the CG of the head is below the CG of the ball, the two factors which create **Backspin**. Besides, if a ball ever takes off the face with true overspin it cannot get airborne because topspin cannot create lift on the ball. High face shots still have **Backspin**, but less than a ball hit in the middle of the face.

High face shots still have backspin, but not as much, due to slight rotation of the head.

The reason roll is a **MEDIUM** factor of **Trajectory** is because since the loft is greater on the top of the face, the vertical gear effect reduces the amount of **Backspin** applied to the ball when hit in this increased loft area of the face. For low face shots, the decrease in **Backspin** due to the loft being less on the bottom is offset by the vertical gear effect's ability to impart **Backspin** on the ball on low

Low face shots cause the head to slightly rotate.

face shots. This explains why sometimes a thin (not topped) shot stops a little faster on the green than what the golfer might have thought for such a low **Trajectory** shot.

Fast Fact:
Vertical roll creates more loft on the top of the wood face and less on the bottom of the face. Loft on its own is considered a MAJOR factor of Trajectory. The reason roll is only a MEDIUM factor is because the amount of actual loft increase or decrease due to roll on any wood head is minimal. Again, if a golfer is suffering from hitting the ball too high on the clubface, decreasing loft and raising the CG of the clubhead are the first two factors to correct in order to produce the most significant change. If it is possible to find woods with less roll, then this change should also be made for the golfer in search of a different Trajectory.

VII. SOLE ANGLE AND SOLE RADIUS

Definition:

Sole Angle

Typically seen on wedges but also occasionally seen on full sets of irons, the sole angle is the angle in degrees as measured between the sole line and the ground line when the clubhead is held in the playing position so the leading edge of the face is perpendicular to the target line.

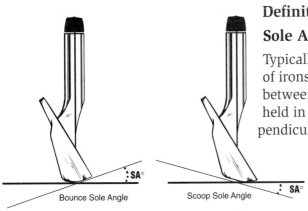

Bounce Sole Angle   Scoop Sole Angle

NOTE: Sole angle is not a specification on a wood head because a wood is intended addressed to be with the sole flat on the ground. When this is done, the wood head's face angle will come into play, causing the wood to aim left (hook face) or right (open face) or directly at the target (square face). To contrast, an iron is always intended to be played with the golfer holding the club so the leading edge is perpendicular to the target line.

When this is done, an iron with a bounce sole angle will rest on the turf on its trailing (back) edge while an iron with a scoop sole angle will rest with its leading edge on the turf.

Definition:

Sole Radius

The curvature on the sole of a wood head, iron head or putter head, expressed in inches or millimeters of radius, either from leading edge to trailing edge (front to back) or from toe to heel.

Terminology of Sole Angle:

There are three different conditions of sole angle. A bounce or positive sole angle describes the condition when the

Toe/Heel
Sole Radius

Front to Back
Sole Radius

leading edge is higher than the trailing edge, when the iron or wedge is placed in the playing position.

A **square** sole angle is when the leading edge is at the same level as the trailing edge, regardless of curvature of the sole, when the iron or wedge is placed in the playing position.

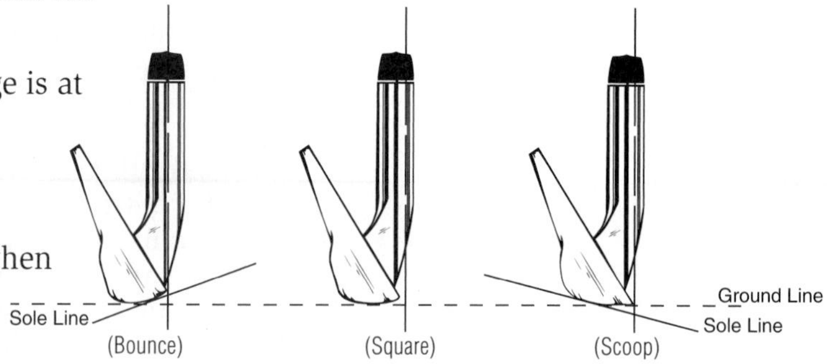

A **scoop, negative** or **digger** sole angle is when the leading edge is lower than the trailing edge when an iron or wedge is placed in the playing position. The scoop sole angle is bad for any iron or wedge and should be avoided for the reason it promotes the chance of hitting more "fat" shots. Sole angle is expressed in the number of degrees of bounce or scoop. A square sole angle is always expressed as a 0° sole angle.

(Bounce) (Square) (Scoop)

Ground Line
Sole Line
Sole Line

Terminology of Sole Radius:

Sole radius must first be expressed as **front-to-back radius** or as **toe-heel radius** to describe the direction of sole curvature being referenced.

The terms sole camber and tour grind can also be used to express the presence of a front to back sole radius. **Flat sole** is a term used to describe a design that has no radius from front to back. Because a wood or iron almost always has toe-heel radius, the term flat sole is accepted as referring only to a non-radiused sole from front to back.

The following effects of sole angle and sole radius on ball flight have less to do with the five basic factors of **Distance, Accuracy Trajectory Backspin** and **Feel**, than do the other primary specifications of a golf club. However, because sole angle and sole radius are a part of the golf club and they have an effect on how solid the shot may be hit, with solidness of a shot equating to **Distance** and **Feel**, it is important to qualify what they do in the Practical Fitting Program.

■ Effect of Sole Angle on the shotmaking performance factors:

• Sole Angle is a **MINOR** factor in the irons for **Distance** and **Feel**

Of the three sole angle conditions for the #1 – 9-irons, bounce, square and scoop, virtually any degree of scoop sole angle could contribute to hitting "fat" shots (hitting behind the ball). In addition, levels of bounce in excess of 5° on the #1 – 9-irons can cause "thin" or "skulled" shots. The bounce sole angle and its effect on hitting thin or fat shots also depends on the length of the grass and the condition of the ground. An iron with a greater bounce sole (more than 5°) is easier to play from tall grass, soft turf or on creeping type fairway grasses but is much more diffi-cult to play from hard ground such as dirt or hardpan or thin grass.

In very warm climates, most golf courses use a creeping type of turf for the fairways and rough such as bermuda or kikuyu grass. A slight bounce sole angle (5° or less) can be beneficial for use on this type of turf because it will help resist the tendency of the creeping grasses to "grab" the leading edge through impact and thus can reduce the chance of a "fat" shot.

The reason a scoop sole can dig into the ground behind the ball and promote a "fat" shot is because the first part of the iron to contact the ground is often the leading edge. Without a broad surface (the sole) to help the sole glide through the turf, unless the leading edge is delivered perfectly on the downswing so that it contacts the ball first, the leading edge will dig down in the ground, making direct contact with the turf and soil before contacting the ball.

An iron with an excessive bounce sole angle can produce a "thin" or "skulled" shot when the ground is hard or the turf is sparse, because the trailing edge of the sole contacts the ground behind the ball and actually causes the sole to bounce off the hard ground so that the leading edge comes up and makes impact with or just below the "equator" of the ball. However, when a bounce sole iron or wedge is played from normal to long grass, or on moist to wet ground, the bounce sole can help make a slightly "fat" shot become a more solid shot by preventing the sole from digging further downward into the ground.

A huge factor that controls the action of the clubhead through the impact zone is the "angle of descent" of the club down into the ball. The steeper the angle of the clubhead traveling down into the impact zone, the more tendency for the scoop sole to cause a "fat" shot. In addition, when the angle is steep on a shot from wet or very moist ground, if the clubhead is not delivered perfectly at the back of the ball, an excessive bounce sole iron can cause a "fat" shot because the ground is too soft to allow the bounce sole angle to prevent a deep penetration through impact.

The reason sole angle is only a **MINOR** factor is because a bounce sole on the #1 – 9-irons can only help prevent a "fat" shot if the swing was executed well enough to only create a slightly "fat" shot (the club arrives at impact no more than 1/8"-1/4" behind the ball). In the case when a golfer makes such a bad swing move that the club enters the ground 1/2" or more behind the ball, no condition of sole angle can help prevent the shot from being hit considerably "fat."

Scoop Sole Angle causing "fat" shot

Bounce Sole Angle causing thin shot

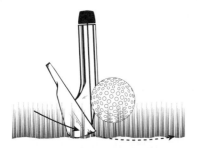

Bounce Sole preventing "fat" shot from tall grass

Fast Fact:
Sole angle is primarily thought of only on the wedges and in particular, on the sand wedge. It is a specification that can be engineered on any iron head and which, depending upon the playing ability of the golfer and the turf conditions of the golf courses being played, can have a moderate effect on reducing the percentage of "fat" or "thin" shots hit by the golfer. As a general rule, the most important points to keep in mind when thinking about the #1 – 9-irons are to never use an iron(s) with

a scoop sole angle and never condemn a set of irons that has a slight bounce sole throughout the set or a progressively increasing amount of bounce from the long irons to the short irons.

• Sole Angle is a **MEDIUM** factor for **Distance** in sand play

The greater the degree of bounce sole angle, the more shallow the sole will penetrate down in the sand. Thus, the greater the degree of bounce, the less a golfer will have the tendency to hit too far under the ball and leave the ball in the sand. If the bounce sole angle is great enough, the sole reacts somewhat like an airfoil in the sand. The sand provides a slight amount of lift on the bottom of the sole to prevent the club from digging too deep in the sand.

However, in addition to a bounce sole angle, the sole width is also very important in achieving success from the bunker. The wider the sole of the wedge, the more the effect of the bounce is magnified. For example, a 12° bounce sole on a narrow sole wedge can dig deeper into the sand than a 7° bounce sole on a very wide sole wedge.

The ability of any bounce sole angle to prevent the club from digging too deep in the sand is as dependent on the swing speed, the angle at which the wedge enters the sand and how far behind the ball the wedge enters the sand, as it is on the actual degree of bounce of the sole angle. In other words, if the golfer has poor swing fundamentals in the bunker, changing from a 6° to a 15° or 20° bounce sole angle will not make the golfer into a good sand player. On the other hand, if the golfer is making a few mistakes in the swing which result in occasional shots left in the bunker, then a change from a 6° to a 15° or 20° bounce sole angle can make a difference in consistency.

Because the golfer's swing ability has so much to do with bunker proficiency, the sole angle is only a **MEDIUM** factor in sand play. However, do not overlook the fact that **MEDIUM** effect factors are very important because there are so few specifications which have a **MAJOR** effect in fitting. In this case, sole angle can make a difference of several shots per round if it is able to prevent the golfer from skulling the ball over the green or leaving the ball in the bunker two to three times per round.

Remember: Those specifications which affect the short game can have much more of a scoring improvement effect than the many golf club specifications which have only to do with hitting the woods and irons. For many golfers with poor athletic ability who are not able to gain noticeable tee to green improvement from fitting, the short game specifications can be the most important in the entire fitting session. (See Chapter 9 - Fitting Wedges and Putters - for more information on this subject.)

Fast Fact:
Sole Angle is a very important specification to fit in the sand wedge because it can help control how the clubhead travels through the sand. For golfers who have a habit of leaving the ball in the sand, an increase in the bounce sole angle over the previous wedge can help prevent the club from traveling

too deep under the ball, which is the primary reason (not cause) the ball does not get out of the sand.

However, sole width is just as important for increasing the gliding effect of the sand wedge through the sand and under the ball. In contrast, decreasing the bounce will help make the clubhead travel deeper under the ball, which in some cases could be a help to the golfer who tends to "skull" the ball from the bunker. Much more information for actually fitting golfers with the correct wedges can be found in Chapter Seven.

■ Effect of Sole Radius on the shotmaking performance factors:

• Front-to-back sole radius is a **MINOR** factor in irons for **Distance** and **Feel**.

With the modern trend toward wider sole irons to keep the center of gravity lower in the head, it is very important to choose an iron head that has at least some front-to-back radius. A very flat sole that has little or no radius from front to back can promote "fat" shots because more of the sole will come in contact with the turf. A flat sole means that the swing must be much more perfect to be able to execute a solidly hit shot.

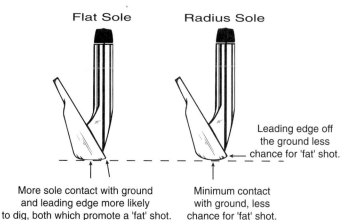

Flat Sole   Radius Sole

Leading edge off the ground less chance for 'fat' shot.

More sole contact with ground and leading edge more likely to dig, both which promote a 'fat' shot.

Minimum contact with ground, less chance for 'fat' shot.

To contrast, an iron with more front-to-back radius can turn a slightly "fat" shot with a flat sole iron into a more solidly hit shot because the radiused sole promotes less surface contact between the sole and the turf. This allows the swing which generates a very slightly "fat" shot to almost bounce or glide into the shot. A club with some front-to-back sole radius also works to prevent "fat" shots on slightly less-than-perfect swings because the presence of the radius keeps the leading edge off the ground and prevents the front edge of the iron from digging into the ground too soon.

NOTE: Fairway wood heads (or any wood hit without a tee) can have a small amount of front-to-back sole radius to assist the less than perfect swing that tends to hit the ground before the ball. For the same reason as with the irons, keeping the leading edge of the wood slightly off the ground coming into impact can prevent "fat" shots on less than perfect swings.

When the front-to-back radius of a wood head is too great (too curved), the leading edge can be so far off the ground coming into impact that a thin shot can result, especially if the ground is firm or hard. However, if this type of fairway wood is used exclusively from tall grass, the increased radius can help prevent the sole from being "grabbed" by the longer turf and increase the chance of hitting a solid shot.

Fast Fact:
    Front-to-back sole radius is a design specification in irons which can promote minimum surface contact between the sole of the clubhead and the turf. A flat sole from front to back can

bring about a slightly higher percentage of "fat" shots because more of the sole has to make contact with the ground.

Front-to-back sole radius is less desirable on the fairway woods because of the width of the sole. The wider the sole, as on a wood, the farther off the ground the leading edge will be for any given front-to-back sole radius. While a slight amount of front-to-back radius is favorable on the fairway woods for the same reason as with the irons, if the radius is too great, "thin" shots can result because the leading edge is too far off the ground. This is primarily a factor to avoid on golf courses with thin turf on harder ground. If the turf is moist or if the shot is played from tall grass, a slight to moderate front-to-back sole radius is acceptable for most golfers.

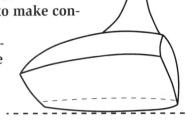

Slight sole radius on wood for minimum surface contact with ground

Excessive sole radius on wood which can promote thin shots, especially on hard ground (Not that bad for tall grass)

• Toe-Heel Sole Radius is a **MINOR** factor in the irons and fairway woods for **Distance** and **Feel**.

The greater the toe-heel sole radius of both the fairway woods and irons, the less the sole will make contact with the ground during impact. However, in this case, a lot of toe-heel radius is worse than having very little because the greater the toe-heel radius, the farther the toe and the heel will be off the ground. For shots that are struck off center toward the toe or heel, this can result in more of a chance the golfer could hit a thin or topped shot, especially if the ground is firm or hard.

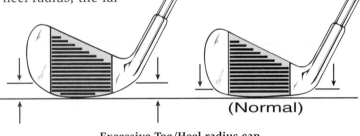

(Normal)

Excessive Toe/Heel radius can promote thin or topped shots on off-center hits

Theoretically, if the golfer hits the ball on center all of the time, it would be possible to say that more toe-heel and front-to-back sole radius would be acceptable. Because golfers are not that consistent, it is important to keep the leading edge off the ground and prevent it from having front-to-back radius, but not too far off the ground in the areas of the clubhead just under the heel and toe.

Fast Fact:
It is more important to prevent the toe-to-heel sole radius on an iron from being excessive than it is to worry about the front-to-back sole radius from being too great. This is because an iron head is much longer from toe to heel than it is from front to back. Therefore, any toe-heel radius is magnified to the point that the toe and heel areas of the face are much farther off the ground and shots hit off the center of the face are much worse than they would have been with less toe/heel sole radius.
An iron design with some toe-to-heel radius is acceptable

but the amount should be kept slight and always be accompanied by enough front-to-back radius to keep the leading edge off the ground when the iron is soled on a hard surface.

Turf, Ground Condition	#1-9 iron Sole Angle	Sole Radius
Bent grass, normal	square to 2° bounce	slight to moderate
Bent, cut short (< 1/2”)	square	moderate
Rye grass, normal	square to 2 bounce	moderate
Bermuda, normal	square to 5° bounce	moderate
Thin, hard	square	moderate
Thin, moist/wet	square to 2° bounce	moderate to heavy
long grass, normal	square to 5° bounce	moderate to heavy
long grass, moist/wet	square to 2° bounce	moderate to heavy

NOTE: See drawing for visual description of slight, moderate and heavy sole radius shapes. Sole radius can be measured in inches or millimeters of radius, but because most golfers do not recognize what the various numerical measurements of radii look like, the descriptions in these drawings should be taken as visual. To compare your irons to the drawings, hold any one of your #1–9- irons in front of your face at eye level, with the grip pointing down, the sole parallel to the ground and the toe pointing away from your face. Check the position of the leading edge and the trailing edge, and ignore any curvature in between. Note whether the leading edge is higher (scoop sole) or if the the trailing edge is higher (bounce sole).

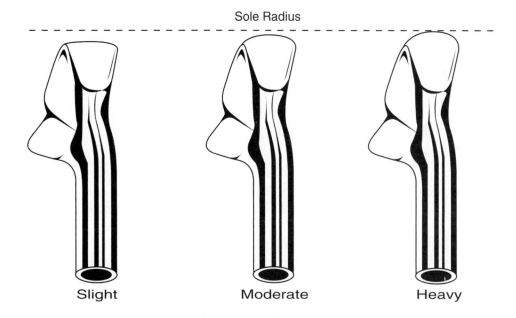

Sole Radius

Slight   Moderate   Heavy

VIII. FACE PROGRESSION/HOSEL OFFSET

Definition:

Face Progression

The distance in inches or millimeters from the centerline axis of the hosel bore to the most forward point of the leading edge on the clubhead. While it is a specification that has chiefly been used in wood head design, face progression can be measured and expressed on wood heads, iron heads, wedges and putters.

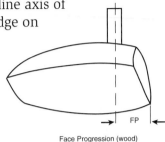
Face Progression (wood)

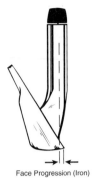
Face Progression (Iron)

Definition:

Hosel Offset

A specification more predominant within iron head, wedge and putter designs, hosel offset is the distance in inches or millimeters from the forward side of the hosel to the most forward point of the leading edge of the clubface. When a wood head is made with offset, it is usually measured in terms of negative face progression or negative onset.

Terminology of Face Progression/Hosel Offset:

While there are not many other terms that are used in association with face progression or hosel offset, it is common for clubmakers to shorten the name and refer to face progression simply as **progression** or just **face**, and talk about hosel offset as being **offset**.

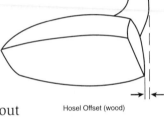
Hosel Offset (wood)

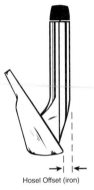
Hosel Offset (iron)

Hosel Onset

Occasionally, irons or putters are designed with the leading edge of the clubface in front of the forward side of the hosel. In this type of iron head, which is the opposite of offset, the distance from the target side of the hosel to the most forward point of the leading edge is called **onset**. In addition, Face Progression on a wood only can be referred to as onset as well.

■ Effect on the shotmaking performance factors:

• Face Progression/Hosel Offset is a **MINOR** factor of **Backspin** and **Trajectory** in the irons, but is a **MEDIUM** factor of **Backspin** and **Trajectory** in the woods.

The greater the face progression of a wood or iron head, the lower the trajectory of the shot and less **Backspin**. The greater the hosel offset, the higher the **Trajectory** and greater the amount of **Backspin**. This is because the farther back the CG is from the shaft centerline, the more the CG tries to align itself with the shaft centerline. This has the effect of bending the shaft forward very slightly and adding loft to the clubhead at impact. (This is the same type of dynamic principle causing the shaft to bow downward, necessitating the need to fit lie angle with the golfer hitting shots from a board in order to note the point of sole impact.)

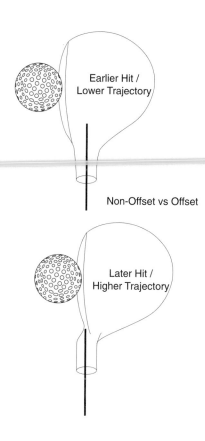

Earlier Hit /
Lower Trajectory

Non-Offset vs Offset

Later Hit /
Higher Trajectory

From a study performed by Titleist Golf Company, for every 1/4" increase in face progression, the launch angle (**Trajectory**) increased by slightly more than 1°, while the **Backspin** increased by over 500rpm, representing nearly a 15 percent increase in **Backspin**. In wood head design, the difference between an offset and a traditional face progression design can be greater than 1/2". This means the effective change in the **Trajectory** and **Backspin** between two woods of the same loft and CG can be as much as 2.5 - 3° in launch angle and as much as 25-30 percent in **Backspin**. Because increased **Backspin** creates more friction in the air, an increase in **Trajectory** and **Backspin** would come at the expense of **Distance**.

In the same study by Titleist, an increase in the irons of 1/4" in hosel offset resulted in an increase of less than 1° in the launch angle. While the **Backspin** also increased by roughly the same number of rpm as the woods, the greater loft in the irons means the additional **Backspin** represented only a 10-12 percent increase, which is significant, but not quite as much as seen in the tests performed on the woods. In addition, it must be noted that the difference between the most and least offset iron designs in the golf industry are much less than with wood heads. In iron design, an offset change of 5/16" is considered to be extreme. Therefore, the effect of changing offset on an iron is much less than it is on a wood. This is the reason face progression/hosel offset is ranked as a **MINOR** factor of **Trajectory** and **Backspin** in the irons but a **MEDIUM** factor in the woods.

Fast Fact:

The greater the face progression or hosel offset, the higher the Trajectory and greater the Backspin. The amount of Trajectory increase is based solely on how much of a change the golfer makes in the face progression/hosel offset of the clubs. For example, if the player changes from a non-offset to the most offset iron (with no change in loft or in CG) the change could only account for a little more than 1° in the launch angle of the ball off the clubface of the iron. It is doubtful that most golfers will notice a 1° change, so this is why offset is considered to be a MINOR factor of Trajectory in the irons.

In contrast, the difference between wood designs with the most face progression to the most offset is quite a bit more than what is seen within the field of iron design. It is entirely possible for the golfer to experience a change of more than 1/2" when changing from an older wood with face progression to a fully offset hosel design metal wood. Therefore, a change in woods can bring more than a 2° change in launch angle and nearly a 30 percent increase in Backspin. This is why face progression and offset are considered a MEDIUM factor in the woods for changing Trajectory and Backspin, but only a MINOR effect change for Trajectory and Backspin in the irons.

• Face Progression/Hosel Offset is a **MINOR** factor of **Accuracy**

The more offset on the clubhead, the more tendency there is for the golfer to either close the face at address, or for the clubface itself to impart a slight hooking sidespin on the ball. After working with many golfers, it has been observed that golfers using an offset clubhead generally address the ball with the face more closed, thus generating almost the same effect as a face angle change on the club. This may be due to the fact that the offset hosel creates an optical illusion so that when the golfer sets the leading edge in the position he/she thinks is square to the target line, the face is actually slightly closed.

The other reason offset has a chance to impart a slight hooking sidespin on the ball is because the ball is hit "later" in the swing than if the golfer were using a non-offset clubhead. The "later" the ball is hit, the more chance there is for the face to rotate closed. Again, because the difference between offset and non-offset models is much greater in woods than irons, this effect is more likely to be seen in woods than irons.

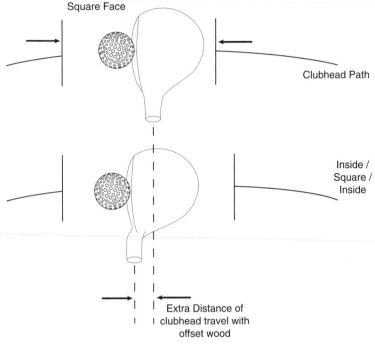

Whether the "later" impact of the offset wood actually results in a less open face angle is totally dependent on how the golfer delivers the clubface to and through the impact area. If the golfer swings on a "pure inside to square to inside" clubhead path with a square face, the face of the offset wood will be slightly more closed when it arrives at impact

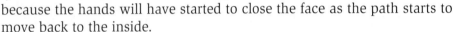

because the hands will have started to close the face as the path starts to move back to the inside.

However, not many golfers are able to swing the club on such a path and deliver the clubhead with a square face through the impact area. As a result, the ability of the offset wood to make any reduction in the slice at all is slight at best.

Fast Fact:
Offset has a very slight tendency to affect Accuracy because many golfers address the ball with the face more closed using an offset clubhead. This is primarily because of the optical illusion created when the hosel is positioned in front of the face. Another, less effective reason that offset can affect Accuracy is because the offset clubhead arrives at impact slightly later than does a non-offset clubhead.

If there is any visible change in Accuracy from using an offset wood or iron, it will almost always be in terms of hitting the ball with slightly less of a push or fade due to the fact that both tendencies result in the face pointing slightly more to the left of the target (For a RH golfer. For a LH golfer the directions are reversed). Therefore, if offset is considered as a way to combat misdirection problems, it should be used only for golfers who slice the ball and only after the golfer has tried a significant change in the face angle.

THE SPECIFICATIONS OF THE SHAFT
IX. SHAFT WEIGHT

Definition:

The mass of the shaft as measured in grams or ounces.

Terminology of Shaft Weight:

As a general accepted principle within the Golfsmith Practical Fitting Program, **heavy weight shafts** are described as any shaft, regardless whether made from a metal or composite material, with a raw, uncut mass of more than 110g (over 3.9 oz). These shafts will result in a Driver total weight of over 12.75oz. and a 5-iron total weight of more than 14.7oz, approximately, when using a standard grip (50-52g) and a standard headweight.

Medium weight shafts are described as any shaft, whether made from a metal or composite material, with a raw, uncut mass between 96g and 109g (3.4oz - 3.9oz). These shafts will result in a Driver total weight of between 12.2oz - 12.75oz. and a 5-iron total weight of between 14.2oz - 14.7oz., approximately, when using a standard grip (50-52g) and a standard headweight.

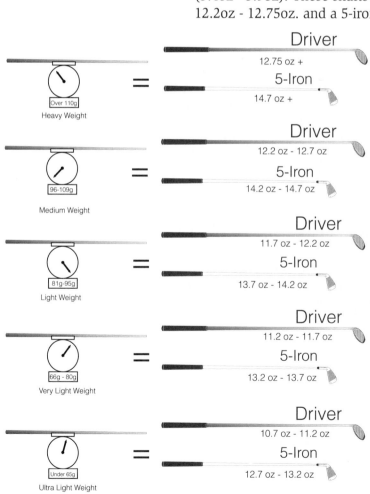

Light weight shafts are described as any shaft, whether made from a metal or composite material, with a raw, uncut mass between 81g and 95g (2.85oz - 3.39oz). These shafts will result in a Driver total weight of between 11.7oz - 12.2oz. and a 5-iron total weight of between 13.7oz - 14.2oz., approximately, when using a standard grip (50-52g) and a standard headweight.

Very light weight shafts are described as any shaft, whether made from a metal or composite material, with a raw, uncut mass between 66g and 80g (2.3oz - 2.84oz). These shafts will result in a Driver total weight of between 11.2oz and 11.7oz. and a 5-iron total weight of between 13.2 - 13.7oz., approximately, when using a standard grip (50-52g) and a standard headweight.

Ultra light weight shafts are described as any shaft, whether made from a metal or composite material, with a raw, uncut mass that is less than 65g (less than 2.3oz). These shafts will result in a Driver total weight of less than 11.2oz. and a 5-iron total weight of less than 13.2oz, approximately, when using a standard grip (50-52g) and a standard headweight.

Classification	Shaft Weight Range	Driver Tot. Wt.	5-Iron Tot. Wt.
Heavy Weight	110g +	> 12.7oz	> 14.7oz
Medium Weight	96-110g	12.2 - 12.7oz	14.2 - 14.7oz
Light Weight	81-95g	11.7 - 12.2oz	13.7 - 14.2oz
Very Light Weight	66-80g	11.2 - 11.7oz	13.2 - 13.7oz
Ultra Light Weight	under 65g	under 11.2oz	under 13.2oz

Note: Average Driver and 5-iron total weights based on standard headweights (200g - Driver, 254g - 5-iron) and standard weight grips (50-52g).

■ **Effect on the shotmaking performance factors:**

• Shaft Weight is a **MAJOR** factor in the **Feel** of a golf club.

The lower the shaft weight, the lighter the total weight of the club. The greater the shaft weight, the heavier the total weight of the club. A change in the total weight will result in a lighter or heavier feel to the golfer.

No other component in the golf club will have as much of an effect on the total weight of the club as the weight of the shaft. While it is true that lighter and lighter weight grips are being developed, as of this printing, the amount of total weight change affected by a change from a standard weight grip to a lightweight grip is approximately 1/2 oz. This is significant when added to the effect of the shaft weight. However, on its own and without a significant change in shaft weight, the grip weight change alone is not that significant in its effect on total weight.

In addition, it is possible to change the total weight of the golf club by changing the head weight. However, drastically increasing or decreasing headweight to change the total weight is not a smart way to create a change in the total weight. Headweight (swingweight) must remain within a somewhat narrow range to retain the proper clubhead feel of the finished golf club.

(**NOTE**: The only exception to this may be when building woods to lengths much longer than standard. When a driver is built to 45" or more in playing length, the head mass is farther and farther away from the golfer, which creates the sensation of greater clubhead **Feel** (the sensation of greater head mass), even if a lighter headweight is used in the building of the club. Therefore, it is only possible to use lighter heads for reducing total weight when the length of the club is to be longer than 45" (driver) or more than 1.5" to 2" longer than old traditional standard lengths.

Therefore, the only way to significantly change the total weight of a golf club in an attempt to effect a **MAJOR** change in **Feel** is to change the shaft weight.

Fast Fact:
Shaft weight is the most significant specification for controlling the total weight of a golf club. Because it is possible to make a change in the shaft weight that can result in a decrease in the total weight of a golf club by more than 2oz (57g) , there

is no doubt that feel will be affected significantly by a change in shaft weight. As of this writing, grip weights were becoming lighter and lighter to the point of contributing significantly to decreasing the total weight of the club. When a golfer uses a new golf club that is lighter than his/her previous club by 2oz or more, there will be an immediate sensation of actually swinging a lighter club. How much this is noticed is dependent on the length and swingweight of the lighter total weight club. Longer clubs with higher swingweights can hide some of the immediate feeling of a total weight decrease when the golfer "waggles" the club. However, when the golfer makes a full swing, the total weight decrease will be noticed.

• Shaft Weight is a **MAJOR** factor of **Distance**

The lower the shaft weight, the lighter the total weight of the club. The lower the total weight, the greater the opportunity for increasing the clubhead speed. The greater the clubhead speed, the greater chance for increasing shot **Distance** (only if the ball is hit solid and on center).

In testing performed at Golfsmith using hundreds of golfers of all abilities, the number who automatically achieved an increase in clubhead speed from a decrease in total weight through a shaft weight change was nearly 50 percent. The testing also revealed that those golfers who did experience an increase in swing speed, the amount of swing velocity increase was almost always less than 6 percent.

However, because there are so few 'sure' ways to increase **Distance**, and because there is a significant percentage of golfers who can and do increase swing speed from decreasing shaft weight, the factor has to be considered as just barely qualifying to be a **MAJOR** factor of **Distance**.

Fast Fact:
Shaft weight is the most significant contributor to the total weight of a golf club. It is important to try and reduce the total weight for golfers in search of more distance because the lighter total weight results in a faster swing using the same effort. Increased clubhead speed can turn into increased Distance only if the golfer is able to hit the lighter total weight club solid and on-center. From a practical fitting standpoint, tests with a variety of golfers have shown approximately 50 percent of all of golfers will realize an increase in swing speed and Distance when shifting to a lighter total weight club. However, testing also showed that for some 50 percent of the golfers who did achieve a swing speed/Distance increase from the shaft weight decrease, the drop in weight had to be at least 1.5oz from the weight of the previous shaft. Changing shaft weight by 1oz. or less resulted in a small percentage of golfers gaining an increase in Distance. Most golfers who experienced a Distance increase from a drop in the shaft weight saw a 10–12 yard increase. It appears that those few who realized a 20 + yard increase did so because their previous club was much too heavy for their individual swing needs. To summarize, not all golfers will gain Distance from decreasing the shaft weight.

Those who do may not realize a significant increase. Still, because there are so few specifications that can result in Distance increases at all, shaft weight has to be considered a MAJOR factor.

• Shaft Weight is a **MINOR** factor of **Accuracy**

The lower the shaft weight, the lighter the total weight of the club. The greater the shaft weight, the heavier the total weight of the club. A change in the total weight of the golf club can change the golfer's tempo and timing, which in turn, can have an effect on **Accuracy**.

It is more common for a golfer to experience an improvement in **Accuracy** from an increase in shaft weight as opposed to a decrease. This is usually the case for a stronger, faster tempo player who has been using clubs which are too light. However, the clubmaker must be aware that this strong player can also experience a slight improvement in **Accuracy** from an increase in swingweight while keeping the total weight low. Like an increase in total weight, higher swingweights can have the effect of "slowing down" the player's tempo due to the player gaining a sense that the head is heavier, thus creating somewhat of a "lagging" effect of the head during the swing.

Most of all, it is important to realize that any effect shaft weight can have on **Accuracy** is very slight because of the fact that **Accuracy** problems result much more from swing errors in the clubhead path and club face angle. Changes in total weight do not normally have any effect on the player's ability to automatically change the face angle or path of the clubhead during the swing. A change of the actual face angle specification of the woods can improve **Accuracy,** but, if the **Accuracy** problem results largely from an error in the clubhead path, the real correction will usually require retraining the direction of the swing (a lesson!).

Therefore, the only way a shaft weight change could affect **Accuracy** is if it allows the golfer to improve his or her tempo and swing timing to the point where they hit the ball more solid and on the center of the clubhead a higher percentage of the time. Hitting the ball solid and on the center of gravity will reduce sidespin, which can then cause the **Accuracy** improvement.

Fast Fact:
Shaft weight can only improve the golfer's Accuracy if the resulting change in total weight allows an improvement in swing timing which in turn changes the clubhead path or allows the golfer to hit the ball on center a higher percentage of the time.

X. SHAFT FLEX

Definition:

The shaft's resistance to bending when subjected to a longitudinal force.

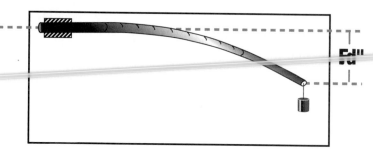

Terminology of Shaft Flex:

Shaft flex is categorized by the shaft manufacturers in five basic classifications; **L-Flex - Ladies; A-Flex- Amateur, Senior or Flexible; R-Flex- Regular; S-Flex- Stiff; X-Flex- Extra Stiff**. In limited use, there are other classifications of shaft flex known as **XL-Flex- Extra Flexible and XX-Flex- Extra Extra Stiff**.

While most shaft manufacturing companies continue to use the same letter codes to label their flexes, few use the same standards for choosing the actual amount of stiffness each flex possesses. In other words, the R flex from one shaft maker may or may not have the same stiffness as the R flex from another shaft producer. This is not an example of a mistake or a lack of quality within the shaft industry, rather it is simply a statement that recognizes each shaft company has the right to design their flex levels to whatever stiffness they feel is appropriate.

What is unfortunate and what all clubmakers must realize is that by continuing to use letter codes as a way to depict shaft flex levels, each shaft manufacturer is not providing enough information to clearly compare the stiffness of one shaft to another. As a result, it is absolutely vital that clubmakers obtain information that enables them to compare the flex of different shafts by means of shaft frequency, shaft deflection or clubhead speed measurements. (See Chapter 7 - the final procedures for fitting for a complete outline of the method for fitting shaft flex.)

■ Effect on the shotmaking performance factors:

• Shaft Flex is a **MAJOR** factor in the **Feel** of a golf club

The more flexible the shaft for the golfer's strength and swing acceleration, the more limber the shaft should **Feel** to the golfer. The more stiff the shaft for the golfer's strength and swing acceleration, the more firm the shaft should **Feel** to the golfer, depending on the golfer's ability to perceive this sensation during the swing.

Although how much this is perceived depends on the sensitivity of the golfer, flex is distinctive enough to generate at least some perception of a bending **Feel** to most golfers. Very few changes in the specifications of a golf shaft can be detected by most golfers, but flexibility is more dominant than others.

The more flexible the shaft, the more the golfer realizes the feeling of a solid impact, while the more stiff the shaft, the less solid the feeling of impact will be perceived. This occurs because the more the shaft bends, the more it can bend backward (loading) and forward (unload) coming into impact. The increased bending, loading and unloading, of the shaft just prior to impact is what creates the sensation of the impact being more solid. Conversely, if the shaft is too stiff, it bends very little. Thus, it cannot load and unload as much so there is little movement of the shaft to transmit the solid **Feel** of impact to the golfer.

This is a description of what many physically stronger golfers want in terms of shaft flex when they tell the clubmaker they prefer not to **Feel** the clubhead "kick too much" and that they prefer a more "firm feeling" of the shaft at impact.

In a case as illustrated above, the shaft is not too stiff for the golfer because it loads or bends a little at the beginning of the downswing, however the unloading is timed so the shaft is in a much straighter position just prior to and at impact.

The difference between the "unloaded C shape" of the shaft just before impact compared to the "unloaded straight shape" of the shaft coming into impact is determined by how firm the shaft is overall for the golfer's type of swing, as well as how firm the tip section is within the design of the shaft (low bend point vs high bend point).

Load

Traditional pattern of bending for proper flex fit for the golfer.

Unload

No Load

Shaft too stiff for the golfer.

No Unload

Fast Fact:

As subtle as this may seem, many golfers can Feel some difference in the amount of bending when the shaft flex is changed. The stiffness of a shaft can create a different sensation of bending, but for most golfers, usually only when the flex is changed by at least two full levels of stiffness, such as from an S- to an A-flex, or an L- to and R-flex.

In general, golfers either have a clear preference for what they like to Feel in terms of how the shaft should bend, or they have no preference at all. For those who have an opinion, the description will usually be that they like to Feel the shaft "kick" coming into impact or they don't want to feel the shaft "kick" coming into impact. Obviously, the more the golfer wants to Feel the shaft "kick," the more flexible the shaft will need to be in relation to that golfer's swing and strength. Conversely, the less the golfer wants to feel the shaft "kick", the stiffer the shaft flex needs to be for that golfer's swing and strength.

If a golfer has no sensation of or preference for the Feel of the shaft stiffness, it is because the golfer does not have the ability to Feel such a difference, or because the golfer has played with shafts which are too stiff, and consequently, has not had the chance to determine if they could Feel the shaft "kick" during the swing. In such cases, it is usually best to fit the golfer into a shaft that "kicks" for their swing strength, or build a test club with the proposed shaft of choice and obtain feedback from the golfer on whether they Feel anything and if it was favorable. In short, choose more flexible shafts for players with little sense of Feel. (Again, much more will be revealed about shaft flex in the shaft fitting section in Chapter 7.)

Load

Shaft too flexible for the golfer.

Unload

• Shaft Flex is a **MEDIUM** factor of **Distance**

The more stiff the shaft, the less energy of the swing is transmitted to impact, reducing the amount the shaft can unload and "kick" coming into impact, as well as slightly decreasing the potential **Distance** of the shot. If a golfer is using a very stiff shaft, a change to a more flexible shaft <u>can</u> give more **Distance**. However, there is a limit as to the increase a more flexible shaft can provide.

Tests with different flex shafts have shown that clubhead velocity can increase slightly when a golfer uses a substantially more flexible shaft. The question then becomes, how flexible can the shaft be for a golfer and still be acceptable in terms of **Feel**? Far too often, even high handicap players reject the **Feel** of a considerably more flexible shaft because they say "they cannot control it (the **Feel**)" or it feels "too much like a buggy-whip." No potential **Distance** increase from using a very flexible shaft is worth the cost of the **Feel** of the club.

However, because shaft fitting in the 1970s and 1980s resulted in so many golfers selecting shafts that were too stiff for their needs, it is possible that a change to a more flexible shaft can result in a slight-to-moderate **Distance** increase. The greater the increase in **Distance** resulting from a change to a more flexible shaft, the more the previous shafts were too stiff for the golfer.

A perception of greater **Distance** often comes with the **Feel** of a more flexible shaft. Often this more flexible **Feel** of the shaft makes the golfer believe they are hitting the ball farther than before. As in all cases with a change in golf equipment, time will tell if the shaft change did result in a permanent increase in **Distance**.

Fast Fact:
While a shaft can be fit to Feel like it is delivering the sensation of a "kick" through impact, when fit properlly to the golfer, it works like a slingshot. This is done through the transmission of physical strength and force from the golfer to the ball. Tests have shown that a shaft can contribute as much as 10 percent to clubhead speed, but the only way a shaft change can increase the clubhead speed is if the golfer's previous shaft was too stiff for their swing speed and downswing acceleration.

It is possible for a golfer to change shafts, usually to a more flexible shaft, and obtain an increase in Distance. In most cases the Distance increase will be slight. Changing shaft weight, club length and clubhead loft are, in most cases, much better ways to increase Distance versus changing the shaft. However, because so many golfers who bought clubs in the 1970s, 80s and early 90s have been using shafts which are too stiff, there will be many cases in which the new, more flexible shaft will result in a Distance increase.

Shaft flex should be fit more for an improvement in Feel rather than Distance. However, to try to satisfy a need for Distance <u>and</u> Feel, the best advice most golfers can receive is to choose the lightest, most flexible shaft they can control.

• Shaft Flex is a **MINOR** factor of **Accuracy**

The more flexible the shaft, the more the shaft bends on the down-swing and the more the face angle of the clubhead rotates coming into impact. If this occurs, the face angle of the club can change at impact. Depending on the amount of clubhead rotation, there is a slight chance for shot misdirection on a shaft that is too flexible for the golfer.

If the golfer's strength, and more particularly, if the acceleration of the downswing causes the shaft to bend forward (unload) just prior to impact, the head will begin to rotate slightly more closed than its position at the top of the backswing. However, this rotation is never enough to turn a sliced shot into a draw or a hook.

Remember, the clubhead path and face angle generated as a result of the golfer's swing movements will dictate **Accuracy** more than the bend-ing of the shaft. For the golfer who slices the ball, changing to a much more flexible shaft will not create a draw, nor will it likely have any noticeable effect on reducing the slice.

Although a golfer who already draws or hooks the ball can slightly increase the drawing action of the ball with a more flexible shaft, the increase in the hooking action of the ball will be slight, at most.

In rare situations when a golfer with a very strong downswing accel-eration is playing with a shaft more flexible than what matches with his/her swing velocity and downswing acceleration, this combination can prevent a flexible shaft from ever unloading. In such an unusual case, the clubface would be rotated more open than it was at the top of the backswing and make the face stay open through impact, thus accentuating a slice in the case of a golfer who normally delivers the clubface in an open or square position at impact.

Conversely, the more stiff the shaft, the less it will bend com-ing into impact and the less the face angle of the clubhead will rotate, creating a slight chance for better **Accuracy**. This is because the shaft does not allow the head to rotate closed or open and delivers the clubface into impact at the posi-tion the golfer created as a result of his/her swing movements.

Remember, if the golfer swings on an outside/in or inside/out clubhead path and has the face open or closed to the path, no matter how stiff the shaft may be the shot direction will not become more accurate from the decreased or completely restricted bending of the shaft. This is a classic example of how the actions and movements in a swing can easily overtake the corrective effects of a change in equipment.

The unloading of the shaft will slightly close the face of the club coming into impact.

Load

Still Loaded

If a very flexible shaft is used by a golfer with a very strong downswing, the shaft could remain in an unloaded state (rare).

Remains Loaded

Using a shaft that is too stiff can prevent the clubface from opening or closing more, but at a cost of distance and feel.

Fast Fact:

The stiffer the shaft for the golfer, the straighter the shot, but only slightly, and at a cost of Distance. In addition, the stiffer the shaft, the less solid the feeling of impact. If a golfer makes slicing or hooking errors in the swing, the stiffer shaft will not correct for these misdirection problems because it does not have that much of an effect on Accuracy.

Because the Accuracy increase is slight and a significant amount of Distance and solid feel at impact can be lost, it is not recommended to increase the shaft stiffness to correct Accuracy problems. The only time a shaft that is more stiff should be used (than what is indicated from the swing speed and downswing acceleration profile) is when the golfer insists on having a very stiff Feel in the shaft. However, even in this case, the golfer should be given the opportunity to hit a club with a shaft that is properly matched for swing velocity and acceleration to be sure that the Distance loss from the stiffer shaft is not significant.

• Shaft Flex is a **MINOR** factor of **Trajectory**

The more flexible the shaft, the higher the shot **Trajectory**. It is possible for a very strong golfer with a high downswing acceleration to use a very flexible shaft and notice a significant change in **Trajectory**. However, it is not likely a strong golfer with a high downswing acceleration would ever play a very flexible shaft. Hence, flex is a **MINOR** factor of **Trajectory**.

Provided most players are matched with a shaft flex that corresponds to their swing speed and rate of downswing acceleration, it is not very likely a change in shaft flex will result in a noticeable change in **Trajectory**.

The only way a change to the proper shaft flex can result in a significant change in **Trajectory** is if the previous shaft used by the player was much too stiff for their needs. While it is true many players have been using shafts that are too stiff, in most cases the player is within at least one flex level of the flex they should be using. For the vast majority of players, considering their ability level, a change of the shaft flex from S to R or from R to A for example, will not likely show up in the **Trajectory** of the shot.

If the player wants to change **Trajectory**, shaft flex is one of the last specifications to address. Shaft flex must be fit with **Feel** and **Distance** in mind before it is ever fit with a change in **Trajectory** as the intent.

Fast Fact:

The more flexible the shaft, the more possibility for an increase in shot Trajectory. However, the only way converting to a more flexible shaft makes a noticeable change in the Trajectory is if the new shaft is much more flexible than the current shaft. To significantly change Trajectory due to a change in flex would, in most cases, require the golfer to move down at least two flex levels below what is considered a proper flex for that golfer's swing speed and swing tempo. This is a factor that might be noticed by more accomplished ball strikers than the average golfer. When changing Trajectory, do so by addressing the specifications of loft, CG and offset before considering shaft flex.

XI. SHAFT TORQUE

Definition:

The resistance of a shaft to twisting when subjected to a specific rotational force.

Terminology of Shaft Torque:

Torque is technically the term which expresses the <u>force</u> of twisting, and is, from an engineering standpoint, the wrong term to describe how much a shaft does or does not resist the twisting forces it encounters during the downswing. **Torsional stiffness** is the proper term associated with describing the shaft's ability to resist the force of twisting. However, because the term has been used in clubmaking and fitting for some time, we will continue to use the word **torque** to describe how torsionally stiff or torsionally flexible a shaft may be.

A **torsionally stiff** shaft is characterized as a shaft with a low number of degrees of torque, while a **torsionally flexible** shaft is known to possess a high number of degrees of torque. **Low torque** is a generic term used to describe any shaft with a greater amount of torsional stiffness (a lower than average measurement of torque, usually less than 4°) and **high torque** is a generic term used to describe any shaft with a lesser amount of torsional stiffness (high degree measurement of torque, usually 4° or higher).

■ Effect on the shotmaking performance factors:

• Shaft Torque is a **MEDIUM** factor in the **Feel** of a golf club

The more torsionally stiff the shaft (the lower the degrees of torque), the more stiff the shaft will **Feel** to the golfer. The less torsionally stiff the shaft (the higher the degrees of torque), the more flexible the shaft will **Feel** to the golfer.

This difference can be difficult for many golfers to perceive because the stiffness **Feel** of a shaft is controlled more by the actual flex than it is by the torque. Therefore, it is possible for a golfer to swing a very stiff flex (high frequency) shaft with a relatively high torque and still **Feel** that the shaft is very stiff.

Because of the research being done to determine how torque contributes to the overall stiffness **Feel** of a shaft, it is now accepted that a driver shaft with a frequency of 250cpm and 2° torque will **Feel** more firm, especially in the tip area, than a 250cpm shaft with a 5° torque measurement, given the fact that the frequencies of the shafts are identical and the shaft in both drivers is the same length. The difference in torque between two shafts of the same flex has to be at least 2° to be perceived by most golfers as a change in the stiffness **Feel** of the shaft.

Fast Fact:
   Golfers who have unknowingly purchased and used a low torque shaft have discovered that torque does make the shaft Feel stiffer.
   However, if the flex of the shaft is carefully matched on its

own to the golfer, the contribution of the torque is largely one of Feel. This is not to say torque is not important to consider in fitting the flex of the shaft. Torque is important because it can make a reasonably correct flex recommendation either result in shots that Feel very solid or very "dead".

Still, because it is a factor that modifies the stiffness of the shaft and does not control it entirely, Torque has to be considered a MEDIUM factor of Feel.

• Shaft Torque is a **MEDIUM** factor of **Accuracy**

The more torsionally stiff the shaft (the lower the degrees of torque), the <u>less</u> the head can rotate during the downswing as the clubhead arrives at impact. The less torsionally stiff the shaft (the higher the degrees of torque), the <u>more</u> the head can rotate during the downswing as the clubhead arrives at impact. Of course, the number of degrees that any shaft can twist during the downswing is totally dependent upon the strength of the golfer using the shaft.

Currently, there are two different schools of thought existing in the shaft industry concerning the role of torque as a factor in **Accuracy**. Some shaft designers believe torque is a definite factor of **Accuracy** and all golfers should use the lowest degree torque shaft that still feels solid. Others feel that torque is not a factor of **Accuracy** because the ball is not on the face of the club long enough for the head to twist and cause the shot to travel off-line.

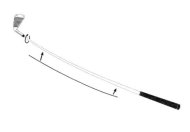

The torsional movement of the shaft under typical downswing motion.

It is true that the ball is on the face of a driver for approximately 5 milliseconds (.0005 secs). This is not enough time for an off-center impact with the ball to cause the head to twist while the ball is still on the clubface. Therefore, the debate over the role of torque in **Accuracy** must focus only on how the shaft torque allows the clubhead to react during the downswing.

Leading one side of the discussion, True Temper's applied research lab believes that torsional stiffness plays no role in the **Accuracy** of a shot. According to them, the amount of torque in a shaft is so slight that the clubhead cannot be twisted open or closed enough before impact to cause an errant shot. If one believes the policy of never fitting physically strong players who have a fast tempo with high degree torque shafts, there is a lot of logic in True Temper's belief.

A number of other industry members believe the lower the torque, the more accurate the shaft will play for any golfer, provided the flex has been modeled to complement a lower torque and keep the shaft from playing too stiff. This philosophy feels the force applied on the shaft by the golfer during the downswing is enough to potentially twist the face open or closed and contribute to misdirection problems.

Golfsmith believes that given the narrow range of torque in shafts (from just under 2° to approximately 8°) **Accuracy** could be negatively affected if a physically strong player used a shaft with a very high degree of torque. However, logic and common sense dictate it is highly unlikely that a strong player would ever be advised to use a shaft with 7° or 8° torque.

Because a very high downswing acceleration can place stress on all the bending properties of a shaft, Golfsmith believes that if it is possible to fit a golfer into a medium to low degree torque shaft (less than 5°) and if the overall stiffness is fit properly to the golfer, the combination can be used to eliminate all of the possible variables relating to **Accuracy**.

In other words, if a shaft with low torque (less than 4°) is used by a slower swing speed golfer who also has a slower downswing acceleration, the frequency (flex) must be kept low to prevent the torque from adding enough stiffness that makes the shaft too stiff in terms of **Feel**.

Fast Fact:
   It is true that the shaft can twist when it is subjected to a strong force during the downswing. Whether the shaft could twist enough to cause the ball to fly drastically off-line is very doubtful. In other words, it is highly unlikely that any golfer will miss fairways and greens simply because of the torque in the shaft being too high (provided the flex/torque interaction is fit properly to the player's swing speed and down-swing acceleration).
   Because the essence of the game is Distance with Accuracy, it is in the best interests of the golfer to use equipment that will allow them to hit the ball as straight as the physical skills allow.
   To that end, specifications such as face angle, swingweight, golf club balance point, length and lie are more important to achieve maximum Accuracy than is torque by itself. Still, it is possible for a clubmaker to be fooled by a slow swing speed into advising a high degree torque shaft for a golfer that has a higher than normal downswing acceleration.
   True Temper Sports Corp. has proven that while swing velocity and downswing acceleration are linked, there are cases in which a golfer with a slow swing velocity can have a high level of downswing acceleration. Downswing acceleration is perhaps a more important factor to consider <u>when fitting torque for the sake of Accuracy</u> than is outright swing speed. This is because the sudden application of a high level of force during the downswing could exert a twisting force on the shaft which might turn the face angle of the clubhead. It is because of this role in downswing acceleration that Golfsmith believes torque is closer to a MEDIUM than a MINOR factor of Accuracy.
   Remember, as long as the range in torque remains between 2° and 8°, the most important role of torque is how it interacts with the flex to determine the overall stiffness of a shaft.

• Shaft Torque is a **MINOR** factor of **Trajectory**
   The more torsionally stiff the shaft (the lower the degrees of torque), the stiffer the overall flex of the shaft. This causes the ball to fly lower for the same given loft on a clubhead. The less torsionally stiff the shaft (the higher the degrees of torque), the higher the ball will fly for the same given loft on the clubhead.

To clarify this point, flex has more of an effect on **Trajectory** than does torque. However, if a golfer were correctly fit for flex in two shafts, one with a low degree of torque and the other with a high degree of torque, the golfer would notice a slightly lower ball flight from the low torque shaft than he would notice a higher **Trajectory** from the higher torque shaft.

Over the years the myth has been perpetuated that a low degree torque shaft is better than a high degree torque shaft. As a result, more golfers have made the mistake of using a lower torque shaft than a high degree torque shaft. However, as long as the torque is factored into the overall stiffness rating for the shaft, and matched to the golfer's swing speed and swing acceleration, torque on its own does not have to be factored into the fitting when making changes in **Trajectory** for the golfer.

Fast Fact:
The lower the torque in a shaft that has been properly fit for flex to the golfer, the lower the Trajectory of the shot will be. Conversely, the higher the torque in a shaft with the flex properly fit to the golfer, the higher the Trajectory of the shot. This is a MINOR factor of Trajectory because there are so many other specifications that have a more visible effect on the launch angle of the shot than torque.

• Shaft Torque is **MINOR** factor of **Distance**

The more torsionally stiff the shaft (the lower the degrees of torque), the more stiff will be the overall flex of the shaft. The stiffer the shaft the less energy of the swing transmitted to impact, thus decreasing the potential **Distance** of the shot. In essence this is the same explanation for why the stiffer the shaft, the shorter it will play. Since torque contributes to the overall stiffness **Feel** of a shaft, it has to be considered a slight factor of **Distance**.

A change to a less torsionally stiff shaft can only provide more distance if the golfer was previously using a shaft too stiff for his needs and is able to hit the ball more on center with the club built with the new shaft. On its own, torque is a very slight factor in terms of its effect on distance. If the flex on its own is too stiff for the player, then the presence of low torque (under 3°) can detract from the distance of the shot.

Fast Fact:
Torque can only have an effect on Distance if it is not factored into the overall shaft flex fitting for the golfer. On one hand, if the torque is low (under 3°) and the flex is matched exactly to the swing speed and acceleration needs of the player, a loss of Distance can occur because the low torque would make the shaft too stiff overall for the player. On the other, if the torque is high (over 6°) and the flex is matched exactly to the swing speed and acceleration needs of the player, it is doubtful if there would be any increase in Distance just from the higher degree torque having softened the Feel of the shaft. This is because it is the softening of the flex itself that can con-

tribute more to an increase of Distance much more than an increase in the torque.

Key point - Torque too low can rob the player of Distance much more than high torque can deliver more Distance.

XII. SHAFT BEND POINT

Definition:

The position of maximum deflection on the shaft when the shaft is subjected to a bending force.

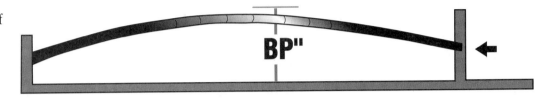

Terminology of Shaft Bend Point:

The shaft's maximum position of bending can be generically described as a **low bend point, mid bend point and high bend point**. These terms are used to describe the general location of this point of maximum bending on the shaft.

Bend point is better described as a term describing the **distribution of flex** throughout the shaft. For example, a **low bend point shaft** is described as being **butt firm and tip flexible**, a **mid bend point shaft** is **butt and tip medium**, and a **high bend point shaft** is **butt flexible and tip firm**, thus indicating the general **Feel** of the shaft as a product of the bend point.

Flex point is an interchangeable term for bend point. **Kick point** is determined by a type of test that finds the shaft's maximum position of bending and is different from the test used to determine the bend point.

■ Effect on the shotmaking performance factors:

• Shaft Bend Point is a **MINOR** factor of **Trajectory**

The lower the bend point, the higher the shot will fly while the higher the bend point, the lower the shot will fly. Because there is little variation in bend point location among all shafts, this is a **MINOR** factor in **Trajectory**.

From independent testing performed on more than 1,000 shafts, it was found that the maximum difference between the lowest and the highest bend points on all the shafts was less than 2". When the shafts with the highest and the lowest bend points were tested using identical clubheads on a hitting machine, it was discovered that the difference in launch angle was just 1°. Therefore, bend point cannot be considered anything but a **MINOR** factor when it comes to affecting a change in **Trajectory**.

Fast Fact:
Among more than 1,000 different shaft designs, the Distance between the highest and lowest bend points is just under 2". Furthermore, when the highest and lowest bend

point shafts were tested, the launch angle difference of shots hit with the two shafts was 1°. Because a change in launch angle of just 1° is very difficult for most golfers to detect, Shaft Bend Point has to be considered a MINOR factor of Trajectory.

• Shaft Bend Point is a **MEDIUM** factor in the **Feel** of a golf club

The lower the bend point, the more tip flexible the shaft. The more flexible the tip of the shaft, the more the clubhead can be felt moving into impact, and the more solid an on-center impact feels to the golfer.

Conversely, the higher the bend point, the more tip firm the shaft. The stiffer the tip of the shaft, the less the clubhead can be felt moving into and through impact and the more the club feels like a firm, "one-piece", non-bending unit to the golfer.

In tests performed with many golfers, those with a more refined sense of **Feel** noted that high bend point shafts felt more firm through impact and low bend point shafts felt more flexible through impact. Through golfer testing it was also found that mid-bend point shafts felt almost identical to high bend point shafts, transmitting a **Feel** to the golfer as if the tip section felt just as firm as the high bend point shaft. As a result, the Golfsmith Practical Fitting Program identifies mid and high bend point shafts as both creating a tip firm **Feel** while the low bend point shafts create a tip flexible **Feel**.

Fast Fact:

In testing players with a more refined sense of Feel for shaft movement during the swing, many noted a difference in Feel between low and high bend point shafts. Low bend point shafts are known for the tip flexible/butt firm distribution of the flex in the shaft, while high bend point shafts are characterized as being tip firm/butt flexible.

This means a low bend point shaft will bend more in the tip section, giving the sensation of the shaft tip "kicking" as it enters the impact area. To contrast, a high bend point shaft will tend to bend less in the tip section, giving the feeling of the shaft tip remaining firm with no sensation of "kick" at impact.

While many golfers can detect a difference in Feel between a low and high bend point version of the same flex, it is normally only very accomplished golfers who are able to note any real difference in Trajectory due to bend point differences in shafts. Extremely good players focus intensely on the "shape" of the shots they hit, so any change in the bending profile of the shaft can make a slight enough change in shot "shape" or Trajectory to be noticed by this level of player.

For all other golfers, shaft bend point should be fit chiefly as a factor of Feel and not with the expectation of making a notice-able change in Trajectory. The only way bend point can make a real difference in Trajectory for average golfers is if the previous shaft was much too tip firm and too stiff overall for the golfer. However, in such a case, the Trajectory change after switching to a low bend point shaft would have to be attributed more to the combination of the effect of the flex <u>with</u> the bend point change instead of the bend point change by itself.

XIII. SHAFT BALANCE POINT

Definition:

The center of gravity of the shaft, or, the point on the shaft at which equal weight distribution is established.

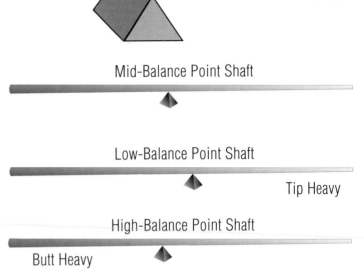

Mid-Balance Point Shaft

Low-Balance Point Shaft

Tip Heavy

High-Balance Point Shaft

Butt Heavy

Terminology of Shaft Balance Point:

The balance point of a shaft can also be expressed as the **weight distribution** or **CG of the shaft**. The balance point can be generically described as a **low balance point, mid balance point or high balance point**. Additionally, a low balance point shaft can be described as being **tip heavy**, and a high balance point shaft can be described as **butt heavy**, thus describing the distribution of weight about the shaft.

■ **Effect on the shotmaking performance factors:**

• Shaft Balance Point is a **MINOR** factor in the **Feel** of a golf club

Provided the stiffness and torque is well matched to the swing speed and downswing acceleration of the player, the lower the balance point of the shaft installed in the clubhead, the more the clubhead will be felt coming into impact. However, because low balance point shafts are heavier in the tip section of the shaft, less headweight is required to make the swingweight of the finished golf club fall within the traditional ranges for men and women (C9-D2 for men, C5-C8 for ladies).

A mid balance point shaft requires more headweight than a low balance point shaft to create a golf club with the same swingweight. What was a "tip- heavy" **Feel** in the raw shaft may not necessarily be a "head heavy" **Feel** when the golf club is assembled with a low balance point shaft. When using a low balance point, tip-heavy shaft, the lower headweight requirement could offset the enhanced clubhead **Feel**, especially if the overall stiffness of the shaft is slightly too firm for the player.

A high balance point shaft can have the effect of increasing the overall stiffness of the shaft to a point that the shaft feels too stiff. From research performed on high balance point, butt-heavy composite shafts, it has been found when the large diameter portion of the shaft (the butt) is also designed to be heavy through an increase in the shaft wall thickness, or by further increasing the diameter of the shaft, the effect of stiffening what is already the firmest portion of the shaft makes the shaft much stiffer overall.

In other words, within any shaft design, the butt is always stiffer than the tip because the butt is much larger in diameter than the tip. Three factors control the stiffness of a shaft – diameter, wall thickness and weight (the last two are related). When you increase wall thickness and weight on a portion of the shaft that already has a larger diameter to begin with, the stiffness of the shaft is magnified to the point that it begins to stiffen the entire shaft, unless the tip section can be made so flexible that it can counteract the stiffness of the butt half.

Clubmakers should check the overall frequency of the shaft when using butt-heavy shafts as a way to avoid providing the golfer with a shaft that is too stiff. For this purpose, the Shaft Appendix section of the Golfsmith Practical Fitting Program has been created to allow you to check the frequency of the industry's more popular shafts and make such a determination.

Shaft balance point is a **MINOR** factor of **Feel** in the Practical Fitting Program because the sensation of tip heaviness in a shaft is extremely subtle. At most, in some tip-heavy shafts, the tip stiffness is increased due to the increased wall thickness in the tip half of the shaft. If the tip-heavy shaft also includes a tip firm profile, the golfer might **Feel** the shaft is too firm or might sense an on-center impact does not **Feel** as solid as it should.

Fast Fact:
Shaft balance point is not to be confused with golf club balance point. Shaft balance point is a specification of the raw shaft while golf club balance point is a specification of the assembled golf club. While they sound similar and related, there is a distinct difference.

The balance point of the golf club directly relates to how much the golfer can Feel the clubhead during the swing. The balance point of the shaft on its own may not. A low balance point shaft does not necessarily create a low balance point golf club because the low balance point shaft does not require as much head weight to achieve a normal range of swingweight. The less the head weight, the higher the balance point of the golf club will be.

The most commonly seen shaft balance point is a mid-balance point shaft, followed by a small number of low balance point shafts. Since the introduction of shafts that imitate the bubble shape, first introduced by Taylor Made in 1994, more high balance point shafts have become available. While in most of these cases, the high balance point is a by-product of the desire to imitate the bubble shape, these shafts do now exist, providing the golfer with a choice between all three types of shaft balance points.

Since the vast majority of shafts are of the mid-balance point type, the effect of shaft balance point on its own still has to be considered MINOR, except in the case of the very high balance point shaft, which can make the shaft Feel more stiff overall, as well as some low balance point shafts which have been designed with more tip flexibility to offset the tip stiffening effect of the lower balance point construction. These exceptions are the only factors relating to shaft balance point that must be kept in mind to prevent this specification from significantly altering the Feel of the shaft.

• Shaft Balance Point is a **MINOR** factor of **Accuracy**

While it has not yet been proven at the time of this writing, it is believed that the higher the balance point, the more accurate the shaft can play. This is possible because the higher the balance point (closer to the grip end of the shaft), the more firm overall the shaft will be and with it, the less the clubhead face angle will change, creating the potential for a slightly straighter shot.

The golfer in search of more **Accuracy** may want to consider using a higher balance point shaft (or using more weight in the grip end of the club), but not at the risk of negatively affecting any of the other golf club specifications. In other words, you would never want to use a high balance point shaft that makes the overall stiffness of the shaft too firm for the player. In that case, the negative effect of using a shaft that is too stiff outweighs the positive effects of a butt-heavy shaft.

The higher the balance point, the more the butt end of the golf club might **Feel** slightly heavier (depending upon the weight of the grip). For players who suffer from hitting the ball off-line to both sides of the fairway, it is possible to use a butt-heavy golf club which could slow the swing tempo down enough to make the swing more consistent, in the process, isolating the misdirection problem to one side of the fairway. If this happens, then the consistency of missing shots more to one side of the hole than the other can be addressed by other specifications such as face angle.

Even though much of this is still largely theoretical, shaft balance point is at best a very **MINOR** factor of **Accuracy** when compared to all of the other factors that effect shot direction. However, in the case of a golfer who hits the ball all over the golf course, it is necessary to try every possible **MEDIUM** and **MINOR** factor of **Accuracy** to help the golfer.

Fast Fact:
Shaft Balance Point can only be a factor of Accuracy if the difference in weight distribution in the shaft makes a change in the tempo and swing timing of the player. For example, sometimes a low balance point shaft might help the player Feel the clubhead more (usually only if the swingweight is higher than normal at the same time, though), which could help the player make a smoother start to the downswing.

A high balance point shaft can make the grip end of the club Feel slightly heavier, which could help the player who hits the ball to the right and left. The heavier grip end of the club might help this type of player find a more consistent and repeating swing by enabling the golfer to make a smoother transition from backswing to downswing.

XIV. GRIP SIZE & TYPE

Definition:

Grip Size

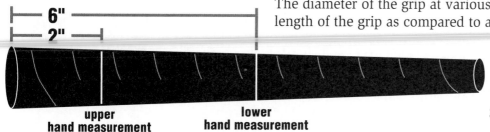

upper hand measurement   **lower hand measurement**

The diameter of the grip at various designated points along the length of the grip as compared to a specific series of standard diameters. The most commonly used diameter for referencing grip size is located 2" down from the edge of the grip cap.

Definition:

Grip Type

The material composition, construction, shape and design of the grip.

Terminology of Grip Size & Type:

Grip Size

Grips are made in **jumbo, midsize, men's, ladies' and junior** sizes, as listed in order of their size from largest to smallest. Because grips are tapered in profile, the actual size of each grip can be compared to a series of designated standard diameters at various points along the grip as it is mounted on a shaft. These standard outside diameters are recognized by virtually every grip manufacturer in the equipment industry.

As a result, it is possible to describe the size of a grip not in its actual series of diameters, but in fractions of inches which may be expressed as **oversize** (larger than the standard) or **undersize** (smaller than standard). Common grip sizes other than standard are **-1/64" undersize, +1/64" oversize, +3/64" oversize, +1/32" oversize and +1/16" oversize**.

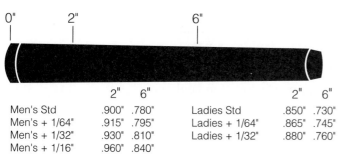

	2"	6"		2"	6"
Men's Std	.900"	.780"	Ladies Std	.850"	.730"
Men's + 1/64"	.915"	.795"	Ladies + 1/64"	.865"	.745"
Men's + 1/32"	.930"	.810"	Ladies + 1/32"	.880"	.760"
Men's + 1/16"	.960"	.840"			

Note: Diameters are for outside grip dimensions only with the grip on the shaft.

The large end of the grip is called the **grip cap**. The point where the grip cap first becomes a part of the side of the grip is the **grip cap edge** and is important as a reference point for measuring club length when a grip is installed. The small open end of the grip is called the **mouth**.

Grips are made with different **core sizes** as well. The core is the size of the open hole inside the grip. The same grip design is commonly made with different core diameters to match the different shaft butt sizes. Jumbo, midsize and men's size grips are produced in .580", .600" and .620" core sizes, while ladies' grips are most commonly produced in .560" and .580" core diameters. Junior grips are commonly produced in .500" and .580" core sizes.

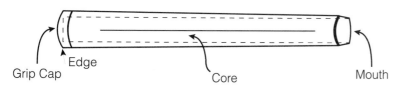

Grip Cap   Edge   Core   Mouth

The core size and outer size may sometimes be expressed in a grip code molded inside the mouth of the grip. For example, a men's .580" core grip may be called an M58 grip. Likewise a ladies' outer size grip with a .560" core may be expressed as an L56 grip.

Grip Type

Grip composition is used to describe the tactile **Feel** of the grip as determined by the material and the inner and outer surface texture or indentations used to make the grip. Grips may be made to **Feel soft, hard, tacky, smooth, rough or spongy**, just to name a few.

Under the USGA Rules of Golf, grips can also be made with or without a **rib**. Ribbed grips have a raised, narrow strip of material which runs up and down the back side of the grip and is intended to act as reference for the golfer to place the hands on the grip in the same way each time. A non-ribbed grip is called a **round grip** because there is no sensation of any portion of the grip protruding out into the hands. Hence, the grip is totally round.

The shape of the grip is greatly regulated by the USGA Rules of Golf. A grip cannot have a **bulge** or a **waist**, a reminder shape or be formed specially for the hands to promote a certain way to grip the club, other than with the rib.

■ Effect on the shotmaking performance factors:

• Grip Size/Type is a **MAJOR** factor in the **Feel** of a golf club

The grip is the only contact the golfer actually has with the golf club. The grip size must be comfortable and create a pleasing **Feel** to allow the golfer to comfortably hold the club. Many golf instructors believe a comfortable grip size keeps the muscles of the forearm relaxed, which in turn allows a more consistent takeaway and accordingly, a more consistent, repeating swing.

In addition, because grips are manufactured from different materials, there is a tactile sensation as well as a surface design or texture surrounding the choice of a particular grip. In addition to the size, golfers must be comfortable with the tackiness, hardness or surface **Feel** of the grip.

Whether a grip is ribbed or round also has a great bearing on the **Feel** of the club. Golfers accustomed to the **Feel** of a rib protruding from the back side of the grip will not usually be as comfortable with a round grip, and vice versa. Therefore, when discussing grips with the golfer, it is important to determine if the golfer has a preference for a particular grip style or grip composition **Feel**.

• Grip Size is a **MINOR** factor of **Accuracy**

The larger the grip, the less the fingers (and/or hand) are able to close around the grip and the smaller the grip, the more the fingers (and/or hand) can close around the grip. It has been said in other clubfitting publications that the more the fingers close around the grip, the more chance the hands have to "turn over" through impact, thus closing the face angle of the club, and in turn, promoting a hook. In addition, the opposite has been said that the larger the grip, the more chance for the hands to "stay open" through impact and keep the face angle of the club open, and in the process, promote a slice.

This is another prime example of how the Practical Fitting Program can set things straight. Whether a golfer has the ability to turn the hands over or not through impact is not solely a product of the grip size, but is determined by the golfer's athletic ability and swing mechanics. In virtually all cases when a golfer is completely comfortable with his/her grip on the club, there is more of a chance for the player to make a full, free swing at the ball, which will improve misdirection problems instead of making them worse.

Therefore, grip size must be fit on the basis of comfort and **Feel** without any worry of affecting the **Accuracy** of the shot. Slicing, hooking and other misdirection problems should be addressed by working on the specifications of the club that have a **MAJOR** to **MEDIUM** effect on **Accuracy**, of which grip size is not included. Grip size should be fit strictly on the basis of **Feel** and comfort.

Fast Fact:

Grip size is much more of a factor of Feel than it is of Accuracy. The old statement about large grips promoting a slice or small grips a hook is untrue. In terms of the golf club, misdirection problems can be remedied by addressing the MAJOR and MEDIUM factors of Accuracy such as face angle, length, lie, swingweight and total weight. First and foremost, Grip size must be fit on the basis of pure comfort. If the grip is comfortable to the golfer, the arm muscles will be more relaxed, promoting a greater chance of executing a repeated golf swing.

XV. GRIP WEIGHT

**Grip Weight
Definition:**

The grip mass, including its installation and build-up tape measured in grams or ounces.

Terminology of Grip Weight:

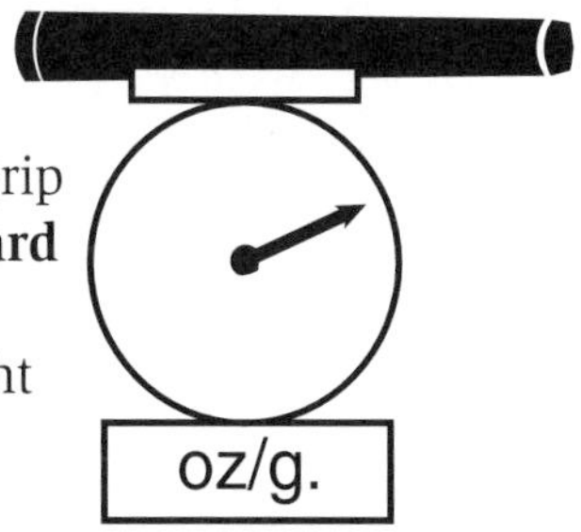

Occasionally, clubmakers refer to a particular grip by its weight range, such as a **light weight**, **standard** or a **heavy weight** grip. In general, the ranges of weight associated with each of the three grip weight categories are as follows:

oz/g.

Grip Weight

Grip Weight	Size	Weight Range
ULTRA LIGHTWEIGHT	Men's	Under 35g
LIGHTWEIGHT	Men's	35g - 45g
STANDARD	Men's	46g - 52g
HEAVYWEIGHT	Men's	53g - up
LIGHTWEIGHT	Ladies'	32g - 42g
STANDARD	Ladies'	43g - 49g
HEAVYWEIGHT	Ladies'	50g - up

Grips do not have a common standard weight because there are so many factors that affect the final mass of the grip. For example, the larger the core of the grip, the lighter the grip. Therefore, the .620" core version of a grip will always weigh less than the .580" version. In addition, the outside diameter of the grip will have a great bearing on the weight of the grip. This is why virtually all ladies' grips weigh less than men's grips. Because most common ladies' grips are sold with a .560" core, this small core is why most ladies' grips are not that much lighter than a men's grip.

In addition, some clubmakers have referred to the lightweight grips as being graphite-weighted grips because this lighter grip increases the swing-weight of golf clubs assembled with graphite shafts.

■ Effect on the shotmaking performance factors:

• Grip Weight is a **MEDIUM** factor in the **FEEL** of a golf club

Grips with the same outside and inside diameter size which are made from conventional grip materials can vary in weight by 14g-18g (+1/2oz). Changing the total weight of the golf club by 1/2oz. is somewhat significant, but not as significant as a total weight change resulting from a shaft weight change, where the weight range can run from 50g up to 130g. However, at the time of this writing, some grip companies were engaged in research to try to produce grips which could weigh as much as 30g or more less than a conventional grip.

In addition, the change from a standard weight grip to a lightweight grip will also change the balance point and swingweight of the club. For example a decrease of 14g in the weight of the grip will increase the swingweight by approximately three swingweight points and lower the balance point by 1/4". This result makes the golfer **Feel** the clubhead more during the swing.

Because the changes in grip weight are not as significant as other component weight to total weight changes that can be made, grip weight is considered a **MEDIUM** factor of **Feel**.

Fast Fact:
Grip weight can vary in the same size grip by up to 18g. While there are non-rubber type grips that weigh less, these are not yet considered because their texture and composition has not yet become popular among clubmakers and golfers. A

change from a 50g standard weight grip to a 35g grip will have the effect of lowering the total weight by about 1/2oz, increasing the swingweight by approximately 3.5 swingweight points and lowering the balance point of the club by 1/4". This has a net result of making the club Feel lighter but with a more noticeable head Feel, both of which are considered to be positive changes for most golfers.

• Grip weight is a **MEDIUM** factor of **Distance**

Because a decrease in grip weight will also decrease the total weight of the club, anything that decreases total weight can be said to have an effect on **Distance**. As stated before, this is because the lighter the total weight, the faster the club can be swung using the same effort. In turn, the faster the swing velocity, the more **Distance** that can be generated, provided the shot can be hit on the CG of the clubhead.

In addition, the lighter the grip weight, the lower the balance point and higher the swingweight of the club can be without actually adding mass to the clubhead. This change, which increases the feeling of mass in the clubhead during the swing, can help some golfers develop better swing timing, which in turn can result in a higher percentage of on-center hits. As has been said many times, the more the golfer hits the ball on center, the more **Distance** will be realized.

Because the total weight change can be as much as 18g (5/8oz.) and the balance point 1/4", the effect on **Distance** from the grip weight change is not as great as what can be realized from a shaft weight change, but is still significant. This is why this factor is ranked as having a **MEDIUM** effect on **Distance**.

Fast Fact:

Changing to a lighter grip will lower the total weight of the golf club. Anytime the total weight is decreased, there is a chance the club can be swung faster, which can result in slightly more Distance. Additionally, the lighter grip can increase swingweight and lower the balance point of the finished golf club, both of which are factors that can make some golfers Feel the clubhead's presence more during the swing. In a few of the golfers, this change in clubhead Feel might have the effect of bringing about better swing timing and tempo, which could help the player hit the ball more on center, a necessity for achieving maximum Distance.

THE SPECIFICATIONS OF THE ASSEMBLED GOLF CLUB
XVI. LENGTH

Definition:

There have been many ways to define the playing length of a golf club. The true definition is — with the center of the clubhead sole touching

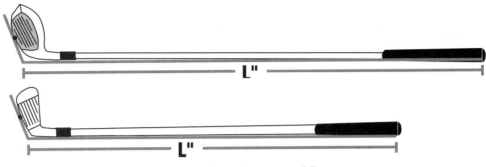

the ground line, the length of the club is the **Distance** from the ground line to the edge of the grip cap. (See the section on Length in Chapter 4 for a list of the standard and most widely seen specifications for length.)

Terminology of Length:

A golf club that is longer than the accepted standard is termed **overlength** and a golf club shorter than the accepted standard is termed **underlength**. Because each clubmaking company is at liberty to set their own standards for playing length, there are many different lengths at use in clubmaking that may be considered standard in one way or another. However, for purposes of making comparisons between clubs, there is a list of **traditional standards** that may be used by clubmakers. (See Chapter 4 - Measuring the Golf Club Specifications – Length).

In testing shafts, there are several other terms used to describe the length of the shaft. **Raw shaft length** is the length of the uncut shaft as it is manufactured before trimming. **Cut shaft length** is the length of the installed shaft in the finished golf club after all trimming has been performed. These terms are important in understanding all the data contained in the Practical Fitting Program Supplement.

■ Effect on the shotmaking performance factors:

• Length is a **MAJOR** factor of **Distance**

The longer the club, the greater the swing arc and thus, the greater the potential for achieving higher clubhead speed with the same swing effort. The greater the clubhead speed, the greater the **Distance** of the shot, providing the shot is hit in line with the CG of the clubhead.

Increases in **Distance** due to length changes are more predictable in the middle and short irons than in the long irons and woods, mainly because the golfer's physical ability to adjust and properly time the swing of a shorter club is better than with a longer club, such as the driver. Golfers who are more physically coordinated have a greater chance of experiencing a swing speed increase from an increase in length in the long irons and woods than golfers who are not as athletic.

Therefore, as length is increased, it is a **MAJOR** factor of distance for all players in the middle and short irons but is only a **MAJOR** factor for the more athletic players in the long irons and woods. To contrast, when length is decreased, it becomes a **MAJOR** factor of **Distance** for all players, but usually with different results. At shorter lengths, golfers with better athletic skills normally will experience a decrease in clubhead speed and usually a decrease in **Distance**.

On the other hand, with a decrease in length, golfers of lesser athletic ability can often experience an increase in **Distance** because the shorter length allows them to hit the ball more on the CG of the clubhead. Hitting the ball on the CG has a greater effect of achieving maximum **Distance** than whatever a length change can do to increase the clubhead speed. More simply, average to high handicap golfers who do not hit the ball very solid with longer woods can normally increase **Distance** by switching to a slightly shorter set of woods because they have a much better chance of hitting the ball on the CG of the clubhead.

Fast Fact:

Increasing the length of the middle and short irons will result in greater Distance for almost all golfers because the shorter clubs in the set are easier to swing for all golfers. A length increase usually only helps more athletically gifted golfers hit the ball farther in the woods and long irons. This is because it is much harder for any golfer to hit the ball solid and on center with the longest clubs in the bag. It is usually only those with a gift of timing and coordination who are able to swing long woods with greater swing velocity <u>and</u> hit the ball on center.

Less athletically inclined golfers who have been using longer woods and long irons without much success can usually achieve greater Distance by decreasing the length of the clubs. This is because the shorter the club, the easier it is to hit the ball on center a higher percentage of the time. No golfer can ever expect to achieve his/her maximum potential Distance unless the ball is hit on the CG of the clubhead.

• Length is a **MAJOR** factor of **Accuracy**

The longer the club, the harder it is to hit the ball solidly and on the CG of the clubhead. The more the ball is hit off center toward the toe or heel, the more sidespin is imparted on the ball and the more off-line the ball can curve. For less athletically inclined golfers, this tendency occurs because it is much more of an athletic endeavor to swing a longer club with repeated consistency, especially if the club has a high total weight as a result of being made with a steel shaft or a heavier graphite shaft (over 90g).

Longer clubs, particularly the woods and long irons, become much more difficult for a less athletically inclined golfer to swing because the increased length places the head mass much farther from the body. As a result, the swingweight becomes too high for the length. In addition, with the total weight being greater than 12.5oz, the club becomes "cumbersome" and actually begins to destroy swing tempo and timing, resulting in mis-hits and problems coordinating the weight shift during the swing. Through field studies, it has been determined that the lighter the total weight, the easier the less skilled golfer has adjusting his/her swing timing to the increased wood length, even if the swingweight is a little higher than what was considered normal.

Longer middle and short irons (up to 1" longer than standard) do not normally present quite the same type of "cumbersome" swing problem because they are shorter to begin with. It is usually easier for a higher handicap player to absorb a length increase in the middle and short irons, than in the woods. Still, if the iron length increase approaches 1 1/2" or more over standard, the fact that the irons have a heavier head weight than the woods can start to cause swing timing problems, which can result in "fat" shots and off-center hits.

The more athletically coordinated the golfer, the more the golfer can absorb a length increase and retain **Accuracy**, even if the total weight is not decreased dramatically. Still, all golfers have their own "point of diminishing return" with regard to length which, when exceeded, immediately results in mis-hits and a loss of **Accuracy** and **Distance**.

A prime example of the Golfsmith Practical approach to clubfitting can be seen with regard to length vs. **Accuracy**. So much has been written about longer clubs creating higher swing speeds and greater **Distance** that many golfers in the 1990s have changed their driver length to 44", 45" and even up to and beyond 48". Permanent increases in **Distance** from longer clubs can only happen if the golfer is able to adjust his/her swing timing to the new length so that a swing speed increase actually occurs and the golfer can hit the ball on center the majority of the time.

Field studies with real golfers have proven repeatedly that many times a decrease in the length of the woods, particularly the driver, can actually increase **Distance** for the single reason that the golfer is able to time his/her swing and hit the ball more solidly, achieving the maximum **Distance** his/her physical skills will allow.

As a result, length is a **MAJOR** factor of **Accuracy**. Not because of imagined automatic increases in swing speed that it is perceived to generate, but because of the fact that the correct length for the golfer will result in the greatest conservation of energy transfer from club to ball.

Fast Fact:
Increasing length will not automatically result in an increase in swing speed and Distance, as many golfers perceive. Only in the middle and short irons can increased length result in a Distance increase for the majority of golfers. This is because golf requires a degree of athletic coordination and timing for success. It will always be true that the longer the club, the harder it will be to hit the ball solidly and on center.

For all golfers in search of greater Distance who wish to try an increase in length as a means of achieving this goal, the lighter the total weight of the club, the more chance for success. Less athletic golfers should never use a shaft weighing more than 90g in a club they plan to play with a 1" or longer increase in length. The lighter shaft helps prevent the longer club from becoming "cumbersome" and disrupting the rhythm of the swing.

However, there is a certain length within all golfers at which the natural timing of the body falls into synchronization with the club length and produces a more repeating consistent swing. This so called "magic length" is not necessarily directly proportional to the golfer's handicap. In other words, it is possible that a tall, but less physically coordinated golfer could find that a 45" or 46" driver is more comfortable to swing than a 43" driver, simply because of the comfort the longer club would create as the golfer stands over the ball.

While this type of situation is rare, what is not so unusual are the number of golfers who can achieve a Distance increase by using a shorter driver length. The shorter the club, the easier it is to hit the club solidly and on center, which is the primary key to Distance and Accuracy. Clubmakers and golfers should approach the fitting of length with the understanding they need to find the greatest length the golfer can hit solidly the highest percentage of the time. For some that may be longer than standard, while for others it may be shorter. (See Chapter 7 - The Step by Step Procedures for Fitting for the methods for fitting length.)

• Length is a **MAJOR** factor in the **Feel** of a golf club

The longer the club, the more "head heavy" the club can feel (unless the headweight is reduced as length increases) and the more "cumbersome," or uncomfortable the club can be to swing for a less athletic golfer. This is because with the longer the club, the farther the clubhead mass is from the hands, giving the club more of a "head heavy" type of **Feel**. To a certain point, a "head heavy" **Feel** in a golf club can be a tremendous benefit to swing rhythm and timing, particularly among golfers with a naturally fast tempo or a quick transition from the end of the backswing to the beginning of the downswing.

Golfers who have a fast tempo, or who are "quick at the top" tend to have a better chance of slowing down or developing better timing in the transition from backswing to downswing if they are able to **Feel** more resistance the moment the force of the downswing is applied. An increased "head heavy" **Feel** that normally comes from longer clubs can enhance this requirement.

On the other hand, as length is increased to the point of being more than 2" longer than the old traditional standard length (45" or more with the driver), for most golfers head weight should be decreased to prevent the club from feeling so "head heavy" that it becomes cumbersome to swing. (See Length vs. **Accuracy** in this section of Chapter 2.)

The shorter the club, the easier it will be to swing with consistent rhythm and timing, with the exception being tall players (over 6'1" men and 5'8" women). The golfer's comfort in fitting club length must also be considered. If the golfer is <u>comfortable</u> with the length of the clubs to start, regardless what that club length may be, there is a greater chance the clubs will **Feel** better during the entire swing.

This is one of the reasons why the Golfsmith Practical Fitting Program begins the actual fitting of length with a measurement of the distance of the golfer's wrist to floor, which is then compared to an initial length recommendation for the driver and 5-iron. With wrist-to-floor dimension as a starting point for fitting length, the golfer or clubmaker can modify the wrist-to-floor recommendation up or down based on the golfer's comfort along with his/her athletic and golfing ability.

Additional note regarding length vs. Feel: From the standpoint of the shaft's flexibility, the longer the club the more flexible the shaft can **Feel** to the golfer; the shorter the length, the more firm the shaft can **Feel** to the golfer, unless the flex is changed to accommodate the effect of the length. When increasing length up to 1 1/2" longer than standard, it is not recommended to alter the original flex recommendation for the golfer. However, the better the player, the more the shaft may need to be installed slightly stiffer to offset the effect of length on the flex.

Fast Fact:
As simple as it may sound, longer clubs do Feel longer to the golfer, simply because the head mass is farther away from the hands, arms and shoulders. This Feel of a longer club can seem to be "cumbersome" and less desirable if the total weight of the club is too high or the swingweight is too high depending on the athletic ability of the golfer.

Therefore, when fitting length, the desire for Distance, the effect of the length on Accuracy and the effect of the length change on the Feel of the club should all be considered. If the length change makes the club Feel worse to the golfer in terms of comfort and ease of swing, then there is no way that length change can result in a consistent Distance increase or consistent Accuracy. That being said, Feel may be the most important aspect of a length change to keep in mind for the golfer.

XVII. SWINGWEIGHT
(ALL CLUBS)

Definition:

The expression of the weight distribution of a golf club about a fixed fulcrum point. Swingweight is not an actual weight but is supposed to be a way to compare the weight distribution of one club to any other.

Because swingweight is an expression of weight distribution about a defined fulcrum point, it is important to know just where that fulcrum point is located. The fulcrum point on the most common swingweight scale is located 14" from the grip end of the golf club.

Swingweight is a much debated point of custom clubmaking. Many clubmakers hold the opinion that swingweight is a good method for matching the swinging feel of clubs to each other, while many others are completely against it. Regardless of the opinion, clubmakers must understand this simple point - it is completely acceptable to develop your own system of club to club matching, whether that be some form of frequency matching, moment of inertia matching, total weight matching, balance point matching or whatever. However, *if you do NOT use one of these or any other method of matching clubs to each other within a set, then you must use swingweight as a method of matching the clubs within a set.*

Therefore, the philosophy of the Golfsmith Practical Fitting Program regarding swingweight is simple - **if you do NOT use some other method of matching clubs to each other within a set which you carefully take the time to explain to the customer, THEN YOU MUST USE LORYTHMIC SWINGWEIGHT AS A METHOD OF BUILDING GOLF CLUBS.**

Terminology of Swingweight:

LORYTHMIC swingweight is a description of the weight distribution of a golf club about a fixed point which is 14" from the butt end of the golf club. The Lorythmic swingweight measurement is expressed in a letter followed by a number, ranging from **A0 to G0.** The higher the letter and number the greater the distribution of weight is in front of the 14" fulcrum point.

PRORYTHMIC is a term used to describe a type of 14" fulcrum swingweight scale which reads swingweight in the A0 through G0 designations but which also has the capability to measure golf club total weight in grams or ounces. **OFFICIAL** swingweight is a designation of swingweight which employs a scale designed with a 12" fulcrum. The Official scale reads the weight distribution in ounces which can then be converted to the A0 through

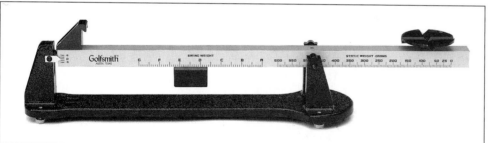

G0 Lorythmic swingweight readings through the use of a reference chart. The Official swingweight scale was invented and sold by the Kenneth Smith Golf Company of Kansas City, Mo. and is very rarely used anymore in clubmaking.

HEAD HEAVY and **HEAD LIGHT** are two terms which describe the relative **Feel** of the clubhead to the rest of the golf club. Head Heavy and Head Light are not precisely defined measurements, rather they are relative and may be different for golfers of different ability and physical strength. A club develops a Head Heavy **Feel** when the amount of head mass, compared to the weight of the grip end of the club, becomes so great the golfer immediately has an increased sense of feeling the weight in the head, regardless of the total weight of the club. Likewise, a club develops a Head Light **Feel** when the amount of head mass compared to the weight of the grip end of the club decreases so that the golfer immediately has an increased sense of weight in the head, regardless of the total weight of the club.

Head Heavy and Head Light conditions in golf clubs are not dependent strictly upon swingweight. It is true that as long as the grip weight is constant and the length does not decrease, the higher the swingweight, the more Head Heavy the club will **Feel**, and the lower the swingweight, the more Head Light the club will **Feel**.

In each of the following discussions of the effect of swingweight on the shot performance factors, swingweight will be referred to as head weight or head weight feel for the express reason that the reader does not become tied to a particular swingweight number. Head weight feel and actual head mass are real factors and can be more definitive for expressing the swinging balance of a golf club.

■ Effect on The Shotmaking Performance Factors:

● Swingweight is a **MAJOR** factor in the **Feel** of a golf club

The higher the swingweight at any given length or total weight, the more the clubhead can be felt during the swing. The lower the swingweight at any given length or total weight, the less the clubhead will be felt during the swing.

The heavier the clubhead **Feel**, the more the resistance to swing motion will be noticed by the golfer on the end of the shaft, and the more effort will be required to swing the club. For golfers who suffer from tempo problems in terms of being too fast, a higher swingweight can help by offering a feeling of resistance to the fast tempo. But, for less physically strong players who possess a smooth tempo, a 'head heavy' **Feel** can promote fatigue later in the round.

Suffice to say that the wrong amount of clubhead **Feel** as expressed through a particular swingweight reading can cause a golf club with the correct shaft, length, clubhead, etc., to perform poorly for the golfer. Head weight **Feel** is a vitally important specification to properly fit to the golfer. Therefore, the custom fitting of swingweight should be done to arrive on a precise lorythmic designation (C9 or D1 or the like) that will achieve a particular head weight **Feel** for the golfer, regardless of what that swingweight reading may be.

> **Fast Fact:**
> **Swingweight is a means of describing the Feel of the clubhead to the rest of the golf club. A change of two or three swingweight points in virtually any golf club can be felt by most golfers. More importantly, a significant change in swingweight can make or break the swing tempo and timing of the golfer. Because swingweight has the very real ability to disrupt or determine the proper swing rhythm and Feel for the golfer, it has to be considered a MAJOR factor of Feel in the golf club.**
>
> **It is very important for all golfers and clubmakers to not become overly swingweight conscious in the sense of restricting their clubmaking to a narrow range of swingweight readings for building clubs. Because length and shaft weight can vary so much in custom clubmaking, the same lorythmic swingweight reading with one choice of shaft and length may never express the same swing Feel as a totally different shaft weight or length of club. For this reason, when building clubs with lighter and lighter shafts to longer or shorter lengths, finding the correct head weight Feel of the club is most important to the golfer, whether that be found at a C2, D2 or E2 swingweight reading.**

• Swingweight (in terms of actual head weight) is a **MEDIUM** factor of **Distance**

Headweight is a major part of the $E = \frac{1}{2}mv^2$, or $F = ma$ formulas (E = Energy, F = Force, m = head weight mass, v = swing velocity and a = downswing acceleration) which attempt to explain the source of the potential **Distance** of any shot. Up to a certain weight, the greater the head mass for a given club length, the greater can be the distance of the shot, providing the shot is hit on center.

Alistair Cochran and John Stobbs, in their 1968 book, *Search for the Perfect Swing*, showed that as driver head weight increased to as much as 224g (8oz) the velocity of the ball off the face continued to increase (Ball velocity off the clubface is a real indicator of shot **Distance**). With most average driver head weights being 200-210g and never as high as 227g, the statement must be accepted that higher head weights can slightly increase **Distance**, as long as the increase in head mass does not create golfer fatigue or contribute to missing the CG of the head.

Clubhead Weight (ounces)	Clubhead Speed (feet/second)	Ball Speed (feet/second)	Length of Carry (yards)
0	203	0	0
1	193	125	< 100
2	185	173	156
4	172	206	206
6	162	214	218
8	153	215	219
10	147	213	216
12	141	209	210
16	132	202	200
24	119	187	178

Source: *The Search for the Perfect Swing*, Alastair Cochran and John Stobbs

The reason swingweight is a MEDIUM factor of Distance and not a MAJOR factor is because the real amount of the Distance increase from increasing head mass is slight at best. After all, in the $E = \frac{1}{2}mv^2$ formula, the mass is halved while the swing velocity (v) is a squared quotient, thus making swing velocity a more important factor of the energy transfer between the clubhead and the ball. The only way a head weight increase can cause a dramatic increase in **Distance** is when the previous club was so 'head light' that it was causing the golfer to hit the ball off center and causing a low velocity of the ball off the face at the same time.

What is much more important to realize, when it comes to building golf clubs, is that forgetting to increase head mass to the proper level for a golfer can cause much more of a **Distance** loss than what any loss in **Distance** could be from using a head weight that was much too heavy for the golfer. In other words, *when installing light graphite shafts into standard weight clubheads, be sure to increase the head mass to a point that the golfer feels a slight* *to moderate 'head heavy' **Feel** during the swing.* To ignore swingweight and build light total weight golf clubs with little or no clubhead **Feel** will rob the vast majority of golfers of **Distance** and **Feel**. The only exceptions may be very slow swinging players and players with limited body mobility.

> **Fast Fact:**
> Up to a certain level that is higher than what might be otherwise thought for all golfers, the greater the swingweight the greater the head weight in the club, the faster the ball will take off from the face and the farther the shot will travel. Clubmakers should always strive to place enough weight in the clubhead to ensure the maximum potential for Distance.
> When building golf clubs with graphite shafts or any very light weight shaft, it is absolutely vital to use more head weight in the golf club than what was used by the golfer in a steel shafted club of the same length. This is because 1) the greater mass does contribute to the actual physics of greater Distance, and 2) the greater mass gives the club more clubhead Feel, which contributes to better swing rhythm and timing, which in turn means hitting the ball more solid and on center.
> The only player types found to play better with lower head weights (low swingweights) are slow tempo, smooth and rhythmic swinging golfers as well as golfers with very limited swing mobility.

• Swingweight is a **MEDIUM** factor of **Accuracy**

The golfer must have the right amount of head weight **Feel** at the top of the backswing to be able to start the downswing on a clubhead path which can enhance **Accuracy** and hit the ball squarely on the CG of the clubhead. While the right swingweight can contribute to hitting the ball more solidly, do not expect that the correct head weight **Feel** will automatically make the golfer swing the club on a square or otherwise more accurate clubhead path.

Outside/In, Inside/Out, Square/Square or any swing path variation thereof is a product of proper instruction combined with the golfer's athletic coordination in the swing. However, because most golfers do consciously try to swing the club consistently in an effort to hit the ball solidly, and because golfers do make genuine attempts to improve swing faults, the proper head weight **Feel** is critical to being able to hit the CG of the clubhead consistently.

When the head weight **Feel** is too heavy or especially when it is too light, it is much more difficult for the golfer to hit the ball consistently on the CG of the head. Whenever the CG of the clubhead misses the CG of the ball, more sidespin is imparted to the ball and greater **Accuracy** problems result.

The ability to hit the ball on-center is dependent on the golfer's head-weight **Feel** preference (along with length, grip size, shaft weight). Once the-length, grip size and shaft weight of the club are selected, then and only then can this optimum head weight **Feel** be identified by a single, particular lorythmic swingweight designation. The higher or lower that swingweight may be compared to the optimum level for the golfer, the less solid and less pleasing will be the **Feel** of the club at impact.

In other words, clubmaker's need to explain to golfers that while they may like the **Feel** of a D1 swingweight in one club, for another club with different length, grip, shaft weight, etc., the same type of comfortable head weight **Feel** won't necessarily be achieved simply by duplicating the same D1 swingweight. Identifying the best clubhead **Feel** for any golfer can be difficult, but on the other hand, it is not a matter of subscribing to one and only one swingweight with no variation up or down.

Fast Fact:

The key point to remember from working with swingweight when using the 14" swingweight scale is that *what we are all looking for is the right head weight Feel in the golf club more than a particular swingweight reading*. In other words, because of differences in shaft weight, grip weight and club length, D7 might provide the same head weight Feel to a player in one type of club as a C9 might in a different type of club. Bottom line – do not be too overly conscious of the swingweight scale reading as much as the golfer's perception of a pleasing head weight Feel.

Once the optimum head weight Feel is found for any golfer, the ball can be hit straighter for two reasons: 1) The amount of sidespin is reduced as a result of hitting the ball on center more often. 2) Swing move changes that can affect Accuracy can be made a little easier because the right head weight Feel can give the golfer a better sense of rhythm and timing.

TIP: Assembling and fitting the correct head weight **Feel** by noting the position of the balance point on a favorite feeling club might be a good alternative to using a swingweight scale. This touches on one of the great points about custom fitting. Experimentation with yourself or with willing subjects is a tremendous way to not only learn new points about fitting, but to build your reputation as a quality, knowledgable clubmaker as well.

XVIII. TOTAL WEIGHT

Definition:

The mass of the fully assembled golf club, as expressed in ounces or grams.

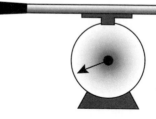

Terminology of Total Weight:

STATIC WEIGHT and **DEAD WEIGHT** are two other terms which clubmakers have used over the years to describe the total weight of the finished club. Both of these terms are competely interchangeable with **TOTAL WEIGHT**. The total weight of a golf club is determined almost entirely by the **GRIP WEIGHT, SHAFT WEIGHT,** and **HEAD WEIGHT** of the club, along with any adhesives for holding the components together such as grip tape and epoxy.

■ **Effect on The Shotmaking Performance Factors:**

• Total Weight is a **MAJOR** factor in the **Feel** of a golf club

The golfer must choose the right total weight in the golf club to be able to swing with the most efficient level of rhythm and swing timing. The correct total weight for any golfer is dependent on the golfer's comfort and preference as well as physical factors such as age, strength, athletic coordination and potential for fatigue. If the total weight is over or under the optimum level for the golfer, the less pleasing will be the feel of the club, the harder it will be for the golfer to establish proper timing and rhythm in the swing and the harder it will be to hit the ball solidly.

However, it is possible to use swingweight to 'mask' or 'hide' the total weight of a golf club and in the process, allow a certain type of golfer to use a different total weight than what had previously been thought was right for that golfer. For example, in the early 1990s, it had been thought that physically strong players would never be able to hit the ball consistently solid with a very light total weight golf club.

Most of this opinion had been based upon fitting strong players with clubs assembled with ultra lightweight shafts (70g or less) that had been built to standard lengths (43 - 43.5" driver) and normal ranges of swingweight (C8-D2). However, it has been discovered through practice and testing that if the length and the swingweight is increased, it is very possible to successfully fit a strong player into a very light total weight golf club.

This is a great example of what is best described as the **low total weight/high swingweight style of clubfitting**. By keeping the swingweight high, a 'head heavy' **Feel** is created which can have the effect of 'hiding' the very light total weight of the club. The strong golfer, who usually ends up swinging a light total weight club too fast and thus starting the downswing too quickly is able to overcome the tendency toward generating a quick and uncontrolled tempo with the assistance of the increased length and 'head heavy' **Feel** of the higher swingweight.

The net result in such a case is a lighter overall **Feel** which still feels to the golfer like there is enough mass in the head to properly time the beginning of the downswing and control the tempo and timing of the swing.

Since it is possible to manipulate length and swingweight to allow strong players to use very light total weight golf clubs, the questions have to be asked - *Should all golfers use very light total weight clubs? Is total weight fitting about to go the route of tennis, in which all players, strong and weak, have made the switch to light total weight racquets?* The answer to that question certainly needs further analysis before making such a generalized statement, but once the flex, torque, flex distribution and balance point characteristics of the very light shaft are properly fit to the golfer, if the clubmaker then understands how to use swingweight and length to provide the right head weight **Feel** for the golfer, it could be said that virtually all players could be effectively fit into very light total weight clubs.

Fast Fact:

The total weight of the golf club is comprised of the weight of the grip, shaft and clubhead all added together. Because shafts can vary from 45g to 130g and grips from 15g to over 60g, total weight may be the single most significant factor of Feel.

In the past, despite the fact that lighter total weight clubs can potentially be swung faster with the same swing effort and result in a Distance increase, it has been felt that physically strong players could not be matched to a very light total weight because their strength would cause them to begin the downswing too fast, thus destroying their sense of rhythm and timing.

But because swingweight is also a very important factor of Feel, it is possible to use a higher swingweight along with a very light total weight to 'hide' or 'mask' the very light Feel of such a club. By creating a 'head heavy' Feel in a very light overall weight club, the strong player can be prevented from becoming too quick at the beginning of the downswing and still retain a good sense of timing and rhythm. Thus the strong player can still have the chance to take advantage of the light total weight for more Distance and better Feel.

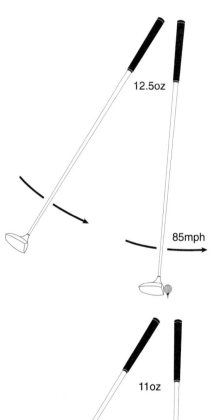

12.5oz

85mph

11oz

88mph

• Total Weight is a **MAJOR** factor of **Distance**

The higher the total weight of the golf club, the slower the club will be swung by the golfer when using the same amount of physical energy. The lower the total weight of the golf club, the faster the club can potentially be swung by the golfer. In turn, the faster the clubhead speed, the greater the possibility for increasing **Distance**, providing the ball is struck on the CG of the clubhead.

This does not mean all golfers who switch to a lighter total weight golf club will experience an increase in **Distance**. Sometimes, when a golfer makes a substantial decrease in the total weight of the club, the change can disrupt the golfer's tempo and timing and thus make it more difficult for the golfer to hit the ball solid. Because hitting the ball solid or making contact with the ball in line with the CG of the clubhead is the most critical factor for achieving maximum **Distance**, hitting the ball farther is only possible if the decrease in total weight allows the golfer to increase clubhead speed AND retain or improve swing timing, rhythm and tempo.

In tests performed on a wide range of golfer types it was discovered that increasing headweight (lowering the balance point of the golf club) on the very light total weight golf club had the effect of helping most of the golfers retain or even improve their swing tempo, rhythm and timing while increasing clubhead speed. Thus, as stated before several times, the combination of a low total weight and a higher swingweight can help to improve the chance of increasing **Distance** from the total weight decrease.

However, the same tests revealed that golfer athleticism and general physical coordination also played a very large part to the point that approximately 60-70 percent of all golfers could be expected to gain a small to moderate **Distance** increase from a drop in total weight, while 30-40 percent did not. Still, because increasing **Distance** is so hard to accomplish, knowing that a reduction in total weight can help increase **Distance** as much as 60 percent of the time, total weight has to be considered a **MAJOR** factor of **Distance**.

> **Fast Fact:**
> The lighter the total weight of the golf club, the faster the club can *potentially* be swung by a golfer using the same swing effort. The reason that not all golfers are able to generate a faster swing velocity with a much lighter golf club is because golf is still an athletic activity; it requires a high degree of physical coordination to be able to make a good golf swing. Not every golfer has this ability so there is no guarantee that a golfer will be able to achieve a faster swing speed with a lighter club.
> In addition, the amount of swing speed increase with a lighter club is also determined by how much of a difference in total weight is made between the new club and the golfer's previous club. If the change to a lighter club does not decrease the total weight by more than 1.5oz, it is unlikely that the swing speed increase will be in more than two or three mph. But because real golfer testing shows that 60% of subjects do experience any swing speed increase from a decrease in golf club total weight, this factor has to be considered as a MAJOR factor of Distance.

• Total Weight is a **MEDIUM** factor of **Accuracy**

Accuracy is really a factor of the clubhead path and face angle on which the golfer swing the club, along with how much sidespin that path and face angle generates on the ball. The more sidespin, the less accurate any shot will be hit. While there are equipment changes that can alter and correct for face angle errors (not related to total weight though), there are no equipment changes that can actually correct for a moderate to severe error in clubhead path.

Because shots hit on center will have less sidespin than shots hit off-center, it is possible to help a golfer hit the ball more on center and as a result, more solidly, through a change in total weight, regardless of the golfer's clubhead path or face angle. To hit the ball solid, the golfer must have the correct amount of total weight feel to be able to swing the club with proper timing and rhythm. What level of total weight that might have an effect on swing consistency and therefore, have an effect on **Accuracy** can be different for each golfer. However, because lighter total weight clubs are more comfortable for so many golfers to swing, it is possible to advise a large segment of golfer types to use a lighter total weight golf club as a way to improve **Feel** and with it, achieve a more solid and more accurate shot.

Physically smaller, physically weaker, slower swinging and smoother tempo players are better off using light total weight clubs at lengths and swingweights closer to standard ranges (43"-44" driver at D0-D1 swingweight), while the stronger, faster swinging players find it much easier to adapt their sense of timing to a light total weight club that has been built to slightly longer lengths and at higher than normal swingweights (44"-45" driver at D4-D7 swingweight).

The golfer that does not usually adapt well to a very light total weight is one who has a very quick transition from the end of the backswing to the beginning of the downswing and does not have much in the way of rhythm or timing established in the swing. This type of player may also be known as a 'slasher'. A 'slasher' is not always physically large or strong, so do not be fooled by this stereotype, as it is possible for a true 'slasher' to be of virtually any size or physique. For this type of player, higher total weight golf clubs made with heavier shafts are usually more effective.

Fast Fact:

The primary factors that control accuracy come from the swing, namely the clubhead path and the face angle of the club as it arrives at impact. Nonetheless, it is possible to help a golfer hit the ball more on center and with it, more accurately by carefully matching the right total weight (and swingweight) to the tempo and rhythm of the golfer. Any golfer that has a problem hitting the ball on center will suffer from more Accuracy problems than the golfer who is able to hit the ball solidly the majority of the time, regardless of the swing path and face angle of the club. This is because any shot hit off center will develop more sidespin than a shot hit solid and on center.

It is possible to find the right total weight for a golfer which will improve the golfer's ability to hit the ball more solid. In addition, it is possible to find the right total weight for a golfer which can even help the golfer to make a change in the clubhead path of his/her swing simply because the club is easier to swing. While Total Weight can have a bearing on the Accuracy of a shot, it is only a MEDIUM factor because it cannot make a significant change in the clubhead path and face angle of the golfer, only how solidly he/she hits the ball.

XIX. GOLF CLUB BALANCE POINT

Definition:

The point on the finished, assembled golf club at which equal weight distribution is established.

Terminology of Golf Club Balance Point:

The **BALANCE POINT** of a golf club can be generically described as a **LOW BALANCE POINT** or a **HIGH BALANCE POINT,** although finished clubs with a balance point closer to the grip than the clubhead are extremely rare and could only be created by excessively weighting the grip. Golf Club Balance Point must NOT be confused with low, mid or high balance point shafts because it is a different specification entirely.

A golf club with a low balance point can be described as having a **HEAD**

HEAVY Feel, and a mid to high balance point golf club can be described as having a **BUTT HEAVY** or **HEAD LIGHT Feel**, thus describing the distribution of weight about the entire club.

Low Balance Point
(Head Heavy)

High Balance Point
(Head Light)

3"

■ Effect on The Shotmaking Performance Factors:

• Golf Club Balance Point is a **MAJOR** factor in the **Feel** of a golf club

By changing the swingweight, the grip weight or adding extra weight to the butt end of the shaft (Butt Weighting), the balance point of the finished golf club can be changed to create either a low balance point **Feel** or a high balance point **Feel**. This does not mean the actual balance point location can move higher up the shaft than the center point of the shaft in the golf club – even in what is considered a high balance point in a finished golf club, the actual location is always on the head side of shaft center. It is usually only on the bare shaft that the balance point can be as high up the shaft so as to be on the grip side of shaft center. Once the head and the grip are attached, the fact that the head is much heavier than the grip pushes the finished club balance point farther down toward the head from what it was on the bare shaft.

The important point to note about balance point is that the lower the balance point of the finished club (not the uninstalled shaft on its own) the more the golfer should be able to **Feel** the clubhead during the swing. The higher the balance point of the finished club (not the uninstalled shaft on its own), the less the golfer should be able to **Feel** the clubhead. The difference between a so called high balance point and a low balance point is normally in the range of 2" to 3", but in rare cases, such as when using very light shafts and grips, can range by as much as 4" to 5".

For most golfers with an average sense of **Feel**, it is possible to note the difference between clubs with different balance points, as long as the balance point difference is at least 2". For the majority of the golfers, the lower the balance point (closer to the head), the more 'head heavy' the golf club will **Feel**, and the higher the balance point, the more 'head light' the clubhead will **Feel**.

The reason a head heavy **Feel** can be important to the golfer is because of how it can help the golfer to properly coordinate or properly time the beginning of the downswing. There is little doubt that properly timing the beginning of the downswing is critical to consistent shotmaking. Therefore, if the balance point of the club creates a **Feel** which allows the golfer to make a more rhythmic transition between the end of the backswing and the beginning of the downswing, the more consistent the golfer will be in striking the ball solidly and on center.

In addition, there are some golfers, regardless of gender, who have very strong hands and arms. These are players who will be able to better transition the start of the downswing by using a club with a lower balance point. These types of golfers normally are not able to hold the angle of release between the shaft and the arms and thus commit the swing error of 'casting off'. This is when the hands push the club out, making the shaft become straight in line with the arms too soon. Ideally, a golfer should try to hold this angle between the arms and the shaft until just before impact, at which time the club is 'released' by the hands and arms to 'snap' down into the ball.

By having a club that *feels* like it has more mass on the end of the shaft, a form of weight resistance can be created which makes it a little bit harder to 'throw' the club out straight away from the hands and arms. For this type of player, lower balance point, *coupled with a low total weight to prevent the club from actually being too heavy,* is a much better fit.

Additionally, the more the player feels the clubhead during the swing, the more the player can sense a solid feeling of impact. This is because most lower balance point golf clubs also tend to **Feel** a little more flexible coming into impact because the higher head weight (lower balance point) actually is making the shaft 'load' and 'unload' more coming into impact. This phenomenon will have the effect of transmitting a more solid feeling of impact back to the golfer when the ball is struck on the center of the clubface.

Fast Fact:
The lower the balance point on the assembled golf club (the farther the balance point is away from the hands), the more the golfer should be able to Feel the mass of the head both at address and during the swing. Golf club balance point can be lowered by increasing the swingweight, by lengthening the club or by reducing the weight of the grip.

When the golfer defintely feels more of a 'head heavy' Feel in the golf club due to a lower balance point, it is a little bit easier to properly time the moment when the downswing should begin. Rushing the beginning of the downswing is a major cause of poor shotmaking, so any change in the golf club that can help to make the transition between the end of the backswing and the beginning of the downswing smoother and better timed to the uncoiling of the shoulders and movement of the weight toward impact will help the golfer to hit the ball more on center.

• Golf Club Balance Point is a **MEDIUM** Factor of **Distance**

If the balance point of the golf club is lower, it usually indicates there is more mass in the clubhead. If greater head mass is the cause of the lower balance point (instead of just using a light grip, in which the balance point is lowered without actually adding mass to the head), the lower balance point can help to increase **Distance**.

Force = Mass x Acceleration (F = ma) and Energy = ½Mass x Velocity² (E = ½mv²) are the two engineering formulas which can be used to predict shot distance. In both formulas, head weight is a very significant part of the total mass (m), so it stands to reason that the greater the mass, the greater the **Distance**. In the book, *The Search for the Perfect Swing,* by Cochran and Stobbs, the two authors proved that even as head weight in a driver increased to as much as 8oz (224g), the velocity of the ball off the face of the driver continued to increase, even as clubhead speed began to slightly decrease!

Clubmakers should know that a 224g driver head is far heavier than what would ever be used to make a golf club, but the point is, when building light total weight clubs, more mass should always be added to the head, not only to create the lower balance point, but to create the possibility for increased **Distance**. (See Cochran & Stobbs', *The Search for the Perfect Swing*, page 206 for further proof of this statement).

It is also possible that a low balance point can be caused by a reduction in grip weight. When the balance point is affected by grip weight, **Distance** will be less likely to increase because the lower balance point has had nothing to do with increasing the mass of the head. The only exception to this would be a rare situation in which the overall combination of the lower balance point balance point, slightly higher swingweight and lower total weight of the club allows the golfer to *accelerate* the club more or to generate greater swing velocity simply because of the decreased total weight and the better **Feel** of the lower balance point.

Because there is no guarantee of this happening with a majority of golfers, and because **Distance** increases from increased head mass are usually slight, balance point can only be considered to be a **MEDIUM** factor of **Distance** at best.

Fast Fact:
   If the lower balance point is created by adding more mass to the head (increasing swingweight) it is possible for the increased head mass to generate more Distance. This is because swing speed and head mass are two important factors which determine how far a shot will travel.
   However, if the lower balance point is created by using a lighter grip or by simply lengthening the golf club, there is much less of a chance for increasing Distance for the simple reason that the lower balance point had nothing to do with increasing the head mass.
   If the golfer is looking for more Distance, using more head weight along with the lighter weight grip are the first two methods of manipulating balance point of the golf club to pursue. Only if the golfer has proven the ability to hit a longer club on center the majority of the time should the increase in length also be incorporated.

• Golf Club Balance Point is a **MEDIUM** Factor of **Accuracy**

Any time that a change in the balance point of a golf club is responsible for improving the consistency of beginning the downswing, **Accuracy** can be improved simply because the golfer would be hitting the ball on the center of gravity of the clubhead a higher percentage of the time.

In other words, a change in golf club balance point can improve the golfer's timing in the swing, which in turn can allow the golfer to hit the ball on center more often. When the ball is hit on the CG of the clubhead, less sidespin will occur and accordingly, an improvement in **Accuracy** will be the result. To contrast, any time the golfer hits the ball off-center, sidespin will be generated on the ball which will add to misdirection problems the golfer already may have.

Whether a low balance point or a higher balance point will generate such a change for the golfer is a matter of the golfer's original swing tempo and overall swing motion. Therefore, for some golfers who are inconsistent in the path the club takes on the downswing (outside/in vs. inside/out), sometimes a heavy grip **Feel** (higher balance point club) can help. For golfers who may be struggling with the problem of starting the downswing too quickly, a heavier head **Feel** (lower balance point club) might help. Which balance point is best for the golfer has to be an evaluation made by the clubmaker using some knowledge of the golf swing (See Chapter 5, The Golf Swing As it Relates to Fitting for more on the importance of clubhead feel in the swing).

> **Fast Fact:**
> **Golf club balance point can be a MEDIUM factor of Accuracy only if the change in the balance point location has the effect of allowing the golfer to gain more control with the beginning of the downswing.**
>
> **If the change in balance point results in helping the golfer to make a smoother transition between the end of the backswing and the beginning of the downswing, it is likely the golfer will hit the ball more solid. The more solid the golfer hits the ball, the less sidespin will be generated from the shot and the less off line the shot will travel.**
>
> **A change in balance point cannot correct an error in swing path (outside to inside path or inside to outside path), or face angle, which stand as the major causes of an off line shot. It is for this reason that a balance point change on the golf club can only be a MEDIUM factor of Accuracy.**
>
> **Trying to correct Accuracy is one of the few times that experimenting with a HIGH balance point might help. For golfers who suffer from hitting the ball off line in both directions, increasing the weight of the grip end of the club (raising the balance point) can be of assistance.**

XX. SET MAKEUP

Definition:

The complement of different golf clubs chosen by the player to comprise the playing set.

Technically, set makeup is not a golf club specification because it adresses the entire set of clubs and not any one part of the club on its own. **However, set makeup is a fitting specification within the Golfsmith Practical Fitting Program because it relates to making equipment changes in order to effect a change in the golfer's score**.

The goal of fitting the set makeup is to replace clubs that are hard to hit with clubs that can be hit the same **Distance** , but with greater **Accuracy** and consistency. The most important aspects of set makeup that must be addressed by clubmakers and golfers in the last decade of the 20th century are loft and length. In the early 1990s, many golf club manufacturers began to decrease the loft and increase the length of their equipment in an attempt to deliver more **Distance** to the golfer.

While increasing length and decreasing loft in the fairway woods and short irons will not harm the shotmaking success of the majority of golfers, doing so in the driver and long to middle irons can have an adverse effect on the player's ability to achieve the proper **Trajectory**, solidness of impact and with it, the maximum **Distance** the golfer hits those clubs.

For example, the following chart illustrates the differences between length and loft changes from the 1960s through the 1990s.

Loft and Length <u>Averages</u> over Time

	1960s		1970s		1980s		1990s	
	Loft	Length	Loft	Length	Loft	Length	Loft	Length
1-wood	11°	43″	11°	43″	10.5°	43.5″	11°	44-45″
3-wood	16°	42″	15°	42″	15°	42.5″	15°	43-44″
5-wood	22°	41″	21°	41″	20°	41.5″	18.5°	42-43″
7-wood	28°	40″	27°	40″	25°	40.5″	22°	41-42″
1-iron	17°	39″	17°	39.5″	16°	39.75″	15°	40″
2-iron	20°	38.5″	20°	39″	19°	39.25″	17°	39.5″
3-iron	24°	38″	23°	38.5″	22°	38.75″	20°	39″
4-iron	28°	37.5″	27°	38″	25°	38.25″	23°	38.5″
5-iron	32°	37″	31°	37.5″	28°	37.75″	26°	38″
6-iron	36°	36.5″	35°	37″	32°	37.25″	30°	37.5″
7-iron	40°	36″	39°	36.5″	36°	36.75″	34°	37″
8-iron	44°	35.5″	43°	36″	40°	36.25″	38°	36.5″
9-iron	48°	35″	47°	35.5″	44°	35.75″	42°	36″
PW	52°	35″	51°	35.5″	48°	35.75″	46°	36″
SW	56°	35″	56°	35.5″	55°	35.5″	54°	35.75″

A quick study of the changes in the loft and length of the driver and long irons quickly reveals the need for a totally new approach to fitting set make up for golfers. While it is true the driver loft has increased on average in the 1990s, the lengths have increased so much to the point that in many cases the change over the past three decades represents more than 2″ in all the woods. For 1996, the vast majority of the major manufacturers' titanium-headed drivers were 45.5″ long, while the stainless headed drivers were 44″ to 44.5″ in length.

Over the same period of time, the average handicap of the nation's golfers has not changed (17hdcp in the 1960s and 17hdcp in the 1990s). Because longer clubs are harder to hit on center, and because golfers still seem to have the same ability as they had when clubs were shorter, it stands to reason that many golfers are probably playing with clubs which are too long and hitting the ball more off-center as a result. However, since all the manufacturers are making clubs that are longer than 30 years ago, the less able golfer has no alternative to use a shorter club, *unless he or she is custom fit for his/her golf clubs by a competent clubmaker.*

One other significant point to note from the average loft and length specifications over the past 30 years concern the loft changes of the long irons, middle irons and wedges. It does not take long to see from the chart that today's 5-iron is closer to a 3 1/2 iron from the 1960s. In the 1960s, most companies built #2-9 irons as their primary eight-piece set make up in the irons. Pitching wedges were just beginning to become popular but had not yet been allowed to become a member of the eight-piece set most commonly shipped to pro shops for sale.

As the PW became more and more popular, but also as the 2-iron became stronger in loft, the typical iron set makeup of the 1970s changed to become the #3-PW. While virtually every golfer does carry a Sand Wedge in his/her bag, manufacturers have not deviated from the now traditional #3-PW iron set as the primary units they ship to retail outlets for sale as sets.

The problem is the vast majority of golfers do not have the physical ability to consistently hit any iron that has less than 24° of loft. Sure, there are high handicap players who do drive with a 1-iron or may see the 4-iron as their favorite iron, but these people are by far in the minority. Any iron with less than 24° loft that happens to also be longer than 38" requires a very precise swing motion to hit the ball solid and achieve the optimum **Trajectory** to make the club perform as it was designed. Yet, most golfers still purchase sets of irons that include a 3- and 4-iron.

At the other end of the set of irons, a real problem in modern set makeup has opened up between the #9 and the PW as well as between the PW and the SW. Due to the decrease in loft throughout the set, the PW has become nothing more than a #8 1/2-iron from the 1960s. This allows the modern PW to be hit farther than older PWs, but it does no good for the golfer who is in search of a soft high **Trajectory** and **Backspin** for the shots from 60 to 100 yards. In addition, golfers who were used to a PW for lofting the ball over bunkers and tall grass, now find the modern PW a lot more difficult to finesse.

Interestingly, most companies have chosen to not change the loft of the SW as much as the PW. While there are companies like PING who have allowed the SW loft to decrease to as little as 51°, the majority have left the SW loft not much more than 2-3° stronger than the old traditional standard SW loft of 56°. This is likely because the club is labeled as a SAND wedge. The manufacturers know that shots from the sand are usually made very close to the green and require **Backspin** to work properly. Because they also know that loft and **Backspin** are directly related, they realize the SW loft cannot decrease as much as the PW loft.

The result is a gap in loft, and with it, a gap in **Distance** that has begun to appear between the PW and SW in most sets of irons. This gap is particularly troublesome for middle to lower handicap players, whose playing ability requires the need for **Accuracy**, finesse, **Backspin**, and variable **Trajectory** for all the little shots around, as well as coming in close to the green. What club does a golfer hit from 60 yards, or use to lob the ball softly over a bunker to a tight pin?

Obviously, this information about the loft of the long irons, middle irons and wedges points toward the need for a significant change in the set makeup of irons for the average to high handicap golfers. Particulary with senior and women golfers, whose clubhead speed and downswing technique are not well matched to low lofted iron clubs and whose abilty to score is directly tied to accurate approach shots, the set makeup of the irons must be changed.

Following are a few suggestions for 'pigeonholing' types of golfers into new recommendations for the selection of the set makeup. These recommendations are intended to only address the set makeup and therefore do not include other additional fitting information such as CG, sole angle, face angle, etc, which would be a part of the other part of the fitting process. These recommendations are only offered as a general guideline for beginning to achieve the goal of finding the proper set makeup – to replace hard to hit clubs with easier to hit clubs.

1. Female player with wood or driver clubhead speed under 50mph, who does not swing athletically or aggressively at the ball.
   WOODS – #5-wood (18°-20° loft), #7-wood, #9-wood, 11-wood (#3-wood only if the loft is no less than 16°).
   IRONS – #7 - PW + 50-51° approach wedge + 56° wide sole SW + 60° lob-type wedge. If desired a chipper/run up club can be used as well.

2. Female player with wood or driver clubhead speed over 50mph but not more than 65mph who is not necessarily well physically coordinated, but who swings with familiarity and experience.
   WOODS – #3-wood(15° loft), 5-wood, 7-wood, 9-wood.
   IRONS – #6 - PW + 49-51° approach wedge + 54-56° wide sole SW + 60° lob-type wedge. If desired a chipper/run-up club can be used as well.

3. Female player with wood or driver clubhead speed over 65mph but not more than 80mph who has some physical coordination, turns the shoulders reasonably well, shifts the weight from back to front on the downswing reasonably well, and who swings with some sense of acceleration and firmness.
   WOODS – #1-wood (13° loft), 3-wood, 5-wood, 7-wood.
   IRONS – #5 - PW + 49-51° approach wedge + 54-56° wide sole SW + 60° lob-type wedge.

4. Female player with wood or driver clubhead speed over 80mph who has good physical coordination, turns the shoulders well, shifts the weight from back to front on the downswing well, and who swings with a definite sense of athleticism.
   WOODS – #1-wood (11° loft), 3-wood, 5-wood, 7-wood.
   IRONS – #4 - PW + 49-51° approach wedge + 54-56° SW + 60° lob-type wedge.

5. Senior player with limited flexibility in the shoulders and legs, swings the driver between 50-65mph, swings the club in somewhat of a frail motion, but with a sense of familiarity of the swing motion gained from having played for a while.
   WOODS – #3-wood (15° loft), 5-wood, 7-wood, 9-wood.
   IRONS – #6 - PW + 49-51° approach wedge + 56° wide sole SW + 60° lob-type wedge. If desired a chipper/run up club can be used as well.

6. Senior player with average flexibility in the shoulders and legs, swings the driver between 65-75mph, swings with average to smooth tempo, does not display a sense of athleticism or firmness in the swing motion, but still swings with a sense of assuredness of the swing motion gained from having played for awhile.
   WOODS – #1-wood (13° loft), 3-wood, 5-wood, 7-wood (could add 9-wood in place of 5-iron if desired).
   IRONS – #5 - PW + 49-50° approach wedge + 56° wide sole SW + 58-60° lob-type wedge.

7. Male player with aggressive swing motion, who does not have accomplished shoulder turn or weight shift through the ball, but swings hard and moves the body around a little during the swing, and has a driver swing speed of 75-85mph.
   WOODS – #1-wood (12° loft), 3-wood, 5-wood, 7-wood.
   IRONS – #5 - PW + 49-51° approach wedge + 54-56° SW + 58-60° lob-type wedge.

8. Male player with smooth to slightly firm swing motion, stays relatively calm during the swing, has average shoulder turn and weight shift but not great, and has a swing speed of 80-90 mph.
   WOODS – #1-wood (11° loft), 4-wood, 7-wood (weak 3-wood and strong 7-wood are OK).
   IRONS – #4 - PW + 49-51° approach wedge + 54-56° SW + 58-60° lob-type wedge.

9. Male player who swings hard with visible force, faster tempo, has some swing fundamentals but not accomplished by any means, whose swing is largely dominated by the aggressive motion of the tempo, with a swing speed of more than 90mph with the driver.
   WOODS – #1-wood(10° loft), 3-wood, 5-wood.
   IRONS – #4 - PW + 49-51° approach wedge + 54-56° SW + 58-60° lob-type wedge.

10. Male player with good fundamental golf swing, who may make mistakes but gives the sense that he has a good swing overall. Firm to slightly aggressive tempo, but not a swinger and not a slasher and has a clubhead speed greater than 90mph with the driver.
    WOODS – #1-wood (9 or 10° loft), 3-wood.
    IRONS – #2 - 9 + 49-50° approach wedge + 54-56° SW + 58-60° lob-type wedge.

In clubmaking there is an old adage that has always proven to be true, "The longer the club, the less the loft, the heavier the club, the stiffer the shaft, the harder the club will be to hit." Keep this statement in mind when discussing set makeup with the golfer.

Fast Fact:
Set makeup could be one of the most effective ways to actually lower the score of the golfer. Virtually all other specifications of the golf club address the ball flight or the Feel of the shot, factors which are important and certainly can have an effect on scoring. Set makeup is different in that its goal is to

replace a hard to hit club with an easy to hit club that does the same thing or adds a club where others are not doing the job. Because of this, set makeup can have more of a direct effect on instantly improving the golfer's score than many of the other golf club specifications.

Over the last 30 years, golf clubs have become longer and have decreased substantially in loft. Both of these changes make the driver, the long irons and the middle irons harder to hit solid and with proper Trajectory. In addition, the decrease in loft in the sets of irons has created a pitching wedge that has too little loft to be used as a finesse club, as well as a gap between the PW and the SW that can leave the golfer without a club to hit certain types of chips, pitches and approach shots.

Chapter Three

THE PLAYER INTERVIEW

DISCOVERING THE PLAYING HABITS AND GAME IMPROVEMENT GOALS OF THE GOLFER

INTRODUCTION

The Player Interview is the part of the Golfsmith Practical Fitting Program in which the playing characteristics of the golfer and the specific areas for game improvement are determined. The clubmaker must devote some time at the beginning of the fitting session to talk to the golfer and ask a certain number of questions specifically intended to determine how the golfer plays, and what specific areas the player wants to change in his/her game.

In addition, the Player Interview is intended to give the golfer a chance to offer his or her opinions on what features of the clubhead, shaft, grip or assembled specifications he/she may like or dislike. With so many different styles and colors of clubhead, shaft and grip designs to choose from, the golfer must be comfortable with the "looks" and general **Feel** of the clubs or else all the effort to choose the right specifications will go for naught. In other words, no matter how correct the loft, lie, face angle, etc., may be, if the golfer does not like the appearance of the clubs, success in changing the shotmaking patterns for the better will be difficult to achieve.

The Player Interview is arguably the most important part of the entire fitting program. It should also be the starting point in the fitting session. This is the only way the clubmaker can obtain the proper information to begin the search for the cause of the shotmaking problems, as well as compile a list of the possible changes in the specifications that might be made to reverse the problem and address the golfer's specific desires for shotmaking improvement.

The relationship between the clubmaker and the golfer must be somewhat like the relationship between the doctor and patient. A doctor cannot begin the checkup with remedies and prescriptions. Neither can a clubmaker begin the fitting session by having the golfer start out by hitting shots with test clubs to determine which action to take.

A doctor takes the time to first discover what problems the patient is reporting, what the symptoms of the problem may be, and what the history of the patient has been. Similarly, the clubmaker must begin the fitting session by talking to the golfer to find out both good and poor shotmaking habits (problems and symptoms) and then analyze the golfer's existing equipment (patient history and vital signs) to find out if the current clubs are a help or hindrance to making the desired changes to hit the ball better (diagnosis and prescription).

There are literally hundreds of questions that can be asked to determine the direction for recommending new fitting specifications. That is why the Player Interview must consist of a carefully selected number of "loaded" questions, each one specifically aimed to contribute some valuable piece of information about a particular specification and how a change in it may or may not help the golfer.

Each clubmaker can determine what questions should make up the Player Interview. As a bit of advice, it is helpful to use a printed form so the clubmaker or golfer can write down their observations. The Player Interview form can become the "doctor's chart" that the clubmaker can refer to at any time during the fitting session to make the decisions about what each specification should be for the golfer.

The Golfsmith Practical Fitting Program has a standard Player Interview form included in this chapter. This form will act as the guideline for following the Golfsmith Practical Fitting Program. As a clubmaker, you are not required to use this fitting form to conduct your Player Interview. You may wish to construct your own form, choosing questions you feel are more revealing and helpful for determining the best combination of fitting specifications.

Whether you use the Player Interview form from the Golfsmith Practical Fitting Program or choose certain questions or parts of this form and supplement it with inquiries of your own is not important. What is important is to pattern the questions you ask the golfer to meet the overall goal of The Player Interview:

1. To discover which of the five shotmaking factors of **Distance, Accuracy, Trajectory, Backspin** and **Feel** the golfer wants to change.

2. To discover which of the golf club specifications you will focus on to help the golfer's desired change in **Distance, Accuracy, Trajectory, Backspin** or **Feel**.

3. To learn the golfer's likes and dislikes about the appearance-related factors of the set such as the shape, size and color of the clubheads, the shaft material, grip style and type, and the characteristics of the golf club the golfer "sees".

4. To keep the information from the Player Interview in mind when analyzing the golfer's current clubs to find out which of those specifications are contributing to or harming the golfer's ability to achieve his or her shotmaking goals.

THE PLAYER INTERVIEW ANALYSIS

PART 1

PLAYER INFORMATION

NAME_____DATE_____

ADDRESS_____CITY_____

STATE_____ZIP_____PHONE_____

HEIGHT	WEIGHT	AGE

YEARS PLAYING GOLF	HANDICAP	AVERAGE SCORE
		18 Holes

AVERAGE GREENS HIT	AVERAGE PUTTS	UP & DOWN IN TWO (%)	
18 Holes	18 Holes	CHIPS	SAND

ROUNDS PER WEEK	PRACTICES PER WEEK		PHYSICAL DISCOMFORT
	LONG GAME	SHORT GAME	

I. PLAYER INFORMATION

1. Name/Date/Address/City/State/Zip/Phone

This information is for organization only and has no bearing on the fitting specifications.

2. Height/Weight

Height

Length, Lie

NOTE: Refer to the chart of Golfer Physical Characteristics and Fitting Guidelines on page 103 to help make these recommendations.

Weight

Total Weight, Swingweight, Shaft Flex and Shaft Weight

NOTE: Refer to the chart of Golfer Physical Characteristics and Fitting Guidelines on page 103 to help make these recommendations.

3. Strength/Physical Coordination/Age

Strength

Swingweight, Golf Club Balance Point and Shaft Flex

NOTE: Refer to the chart of Golfer Physical Characteristics and Fitting Guidelines on page 103 to help make these recommendations.

Physical Coordination

Length, Golf Club Bend Point, Swingweight and Total Weight

NOTE: Refer to the chart of Golfer Physical Characteristics and Fitting Guidelines on page 103 to help make these recommendations.

Age

Swingweight, Total Weight and Shaft Flex

NOTE: Refer to the chart of Golfer Physical Characteristics and Fitting Guidelines on page 103 to help make these recommendations.

Fast Fact:

The player's height can help the clubmaker with information that might help verify the lie angle which will be determined later in the fitting session during the Dynamic Lie Fitting procedure. Height can also offer additional information to make the final decision about length, combining with the player's ability to hit the ball on-center and the wrist-to-floor measurement as other important length fitting factors.

The player's weight can help the clubmaker with information that will help guide the choice of swingweight and might help guide the selection of total weight, shaft weight and shaft flex. Remember though, higher body weight is not necessarily an indicator for higher total weight, heavier shaft weight and stiffer shafts. The less the physical coordination of the heavy person, the lower the total weight, the lower the shaft weight and most certainly, the softer the shaft flex.

The player's strength/age and physical coordination can help the clubmaker with information that might help find the correct total weight, swingweight, length, shaft flex, golf club balance point or bend point specifications.

As general guidelines only, the stronger, younger and more physically coordinated the player, the higher the swingweight, longer the length, lower the balance point, stiffer the shaft, and in some cases, the heavier the total weight of the new clubs. The physically weaker and less coordinated the player, the lower in swingweight (though not too low), the more normal to shorter the length, the lower balance point, the more flexible the shaft flex, and definitely, the lighter the total weight.

The following is a chart that lists some of the general guidelines for starting the fitting recommendations, based strictly on the vital statistics of the golfer. Be sure to understand that in no way can final fitting recommendations be made strictly on the basis of height/weight/age/strength and physical coordination, and that such information in the chart can only be taken as a starting point for directing your fitting decision making.

GOLFER PHYSICAL CHARACTERISTICS AND FITTING GUIDELINES

Height	Weight	Strength	Age	Phys. Coordi.	Guideline
Avg to Short	Light to Avg	Weak to Avg	Young to Old	Poor to Avg	- Total Weight - Swingweight 0/- Length - Balance Point - Shaft Flex 0/- Lie
Tall	Light to Avg	Weak to Avg	Young to Old	Avg	- Total Weight - Swingweight 0/ + Length - Balance Point - Shaft Flex + Lie
Avg to Tall	Light	Strong	Young to Mid	Avg to Good	- Total Weight + Swingweight 0/ + Length 0/- Balance Point 0 Shaft Flex 0/- Lie
Avg to Short	Avg to Hvy	Weak to Avg	Young to Old	Poor to Avg	- Total Weight 0 Swingweight 0 Length - Balance Point 0/- Shaft Flex
Avg to Tall	Avg to Hvy	Strong	Young to Mid	Avg to Good	+ /0/-Total Weight + Swingweight 0/ + Length 0/- Balance Point 0/ + Shaft Flex
Avg to Short	Hvy	Weak to Avg	Young to Mid	Poor to Avg	0/-Total Weight 0/ + Swingweight 0 Length - Balance Point 0/- Shaft Flex
Avg to Tall	Hvy	Avg to Strong	Young to Mid	Avg to Good	0/ + Total Weight 0/ + Swingweight 0/ + Length 0/- Balance Point 0/ + Shaft Flex

The above chart lists some of the general guidelines for starting the fitting recommendations, based strictly on the vital statistics of the golfer. Understand that in no way can final fitting recommendations be made solely on the basis of height/weight/ age/ strength and physical coordination. Under the "Guideline" column, (-) refers to lower than average, (0) refers to average, and (+) refers to greater than average.

4. Handicap/Average Score/Greens Hit in Regulation/Average Number of Putts per Round/Up and Down Percentage

Handicap, Average Score, Greens Hit in Regulation, Average Number of Putts per Round

Length, Center of Gravity, Weight Distribution of the clubhead, Shaft Bend Point, Loft in the short irons and wedges, and Set Makeup

Up and Down Percentage

Sole Angle(wedges), Set Makeup

Fast Fact:

The player's handicap or average score, average greens hit in regulation, and average putts per round can help the clubmaker with information that might be included in making some of the final decisions about the correct length, CG/ weight distribution of the clubhead, bend point, golf club balance point and sole angle specifications, as well as the complement of the set makeup.

The reason for learning this information from the Player Interview is to compare the average greens hit in regulation and average putts per round to the handicap and/or average score to determine whether the player is a better ball striker for his or her handicap or not. That information can make a difference only when the clubmaker is making a final decision between two different measurements of a particular specification; in essence, to "break the tie" and sway the decision to the specification measurement better suited to the player.

5. Years playing golf/rounds per week/practices per week

Total Weight, Swingweight, Shaft Flex, Clubhead Design, Shaft Bend Point, Golf Club Balance Point, Length and Set Makeup

Fast Fact:

The more the golfer plays and practices, the more likely that the MEDIUM and MINOR effect fitting changes will be successful. The less the golfer plays and practices, the less likely the MEDIUM and MINOR effect fitting will be successful, therefore the clubmaker should emphasize the MAJOR effect specifications only.

It is important to ask the golfer if he/she is taking lessons and if the lessons are helping make them a better player. If the golfer does practice and play a lot, it is more likely the lessons will be successful. Therefore, the clubmaker must anticipate what the swing and the game will be like after the swing changes are ingrained in making the final fitting recommendations. In other words, the clubmaker might not make as dramatic of a specification change if it is believed that the swing will be different in the near future.

On the other hand, regardless if the golfer is taking lessons or not, if they do not practice very much, it is not likely that any swing changes from the lessons will be successful. Therefore, if the clubmaker knows the golfer does not have the time or commitment to make the swing changes, it is best to advise the fitting recommendations to address the swing for maximum game improvement.

6. Physical Discomforts

Set Makeup, Shaft Flex, Total Weight, Shaft Weight, Swingweight, Length, Grip Size and Grip Type

Fast Fact:

The clubmaker needs to tactfully inquire if there are any physical discomforts or limitations that prevent the golfer from achieving his or her potential in the game. If the clubmaker does not take the time to ask the golfer about any discomfort or impairment or special physical limitations during the swing, many, if not all of the fitting recommendations, could be of little or no help.

Many adjustments can be made in golf clubs to make up for physical discomforts and impairments from arthritis and joint discomfort to severe physical motion limitations. For the particular fitting remedy for various physical discomforts and limitations, see Chapter 10 – Special Fitting Considerations.

CURRENT SET MAKE-UP

CIRCLE ALL WOODS AND IRONS IN YOUR CURRENT SET; ENTER THE LOFT (IF KNOWN) OF ANY WEDGES IN YOUR SET; SPECIFY THE SOLE-WIDTH OF YOUR WEDGE.

WOODS	IRONS	PITCHING WEDGE (S)		

1   3   5   7   9
  2   4   6   _____
	1 3 5 7 9
	  2 4 6 8
		LOFT	○	WIDE SOLE___
				MED. SOLE___
				THIN SOLE___

SAND WEDGE (S)	**OTHER WEDGE (S)**	**PUTTER**		
LOFT ○ WIDE SOLE___ MED. SOLE___ THIN SOLE___	LOFT ○ WIDE SOLE___ MED. SOLE___ THIN SOLE___	TYPE BLADE___ HEEL/TOE___ MALLET___		
FAVORITE CLUBS	**LEAST FAVORITE CLUBS**	**LONGEST CLUBS HIT WELL**		
		WOOD	IRON	

CURRENT SET MAKEUP

The clubmaker must be aware of the golfer's current set makeup and determine how well certain clubs in the current set are hit as a beginning point for recommending the new set makeup, as well as what clubhead designs may or may not be well suited to the player. It must be stressed that of all the fitting specifications, <u>set makeup may well be the most effective for making an immediate change in the golfer's ability to improve</u>.

While the precise set makeup and head design decisions will not be determined by the current set makeup information from the Player Interview, it does provide the clubmaker with a starting point and helps eliminate particular head design areas or set makeup considerations that would obviously not be a viable choice. For example, let's say the golfer uses a set with 1, 3 and 4 woods, and 1-SW in the irons. In this example, if it is known his/her favorite club is the 4-wood and least favorite are the long irons, the direction to take with the new set make-up becomes much more obvious. This section of the Player Interview will prove to be a very valuable area of information for making effective fitting changes.

1. Woods/Irons/Wedges/Putter

Set Makeup

Fast Fact:
The set makeup of the woods/irons/wedges and type of putter has to be known to help the clubmaker form a beginning point of reference for making new set makeup recommendations. As always with set makeup, the idea is to find out which clubs the golfer cannot hit well and replace them with clubs that will perform the same function in an easier manner and with greater consistency.

In addition, the type of golf course the golfer is predominantly playing and the types of shots the course requires must be considered before the set makeup can be individually tailored. This is information that helps determine if more fairway woods are an advantage or if more wedges of different function might be an advantage. (For more information on this subject see Chapter 2 for Set Make Up and Chapter 7 – The Step by Step Procedures of Fitting for Set Make Up.)

2. Favorite Club(s)/Least Favorite Club(s)/Longest Club Hit Well

Favorite Club(s) and Least Favorite Club(s)
Total Weight, Swingweight, Shaft Flex, Face Angle, Shaft Bend Point, Golf Club Balance Point, Clubhead Design, Length, Set Makeup and possibly Lie Angle

Longest Club Hit Well
Set Makeup, Face Angle, Length, Swingweight, Loft and possibly Lie Angle

PART 2

BALL-STRIKING TENDENCIES

CHECK ANY SHOTMAKING TENDENCIES THAT APPLY TO EACH EQUIPMENT AREA IN YOUR GAME.
ESTIMATE CARRY DISTANCES AS CLOSELY AS POSSIBLE.

	TRAJECTORY			PREDOMINANT POINT OF IMPACT							SHOT PATTERN	EST. CARRY DISTANCE
	HIGH	MED	LOW	TOP	FAT	THIN	SKY	TOE	HEEL	CEN		
DRIVER											A B C D E F G H I	1w
F'WAY WDS.											A B C D E F G H I	5w
1,2,3 IRONS											A B C D E F G H I	3i
4,5,6 IRONS											A B C D E F G H I	5i
7,8,9 IRONS											A B C D E F G H I	7i
WEDGES											A B C D E F G H I	PW

SHOT PATTERN

Where do your shots go?

A B C D E F G H I

II. BALL-STRIKING TENDENCIES

1. Trajectory

Loft, Clubhead Design, Shaft Flex, Shaft Bend Point, Offset and Vertical Roll

Fast Fact:

The golfer's indication of shot Trajectory is important to help make fitting decisions affecting the specifications of loft, clubhead design, shaft flex, shaft bend point, offset and vertical roll. Still, the proper approach is to place more emphasis on whether the golfer wants to change his/her current Trajectory. If he/she wants to hit the ball higher, increase the loft, lower the CG, increase the offset of the clubhead and make the shaft more flexible with a lower bend point.

Be sure to also note the point of impact on the face, high to low, before making any recommendations for the vertical roll change on the woods.

2. Predominant Point of Impact on the clubface – top, fat, thin, sky, toe, heel, center

Total Weight, Swingweight, Golf Club Balance Point, Length, Bulge, Roll and Clubhead Design (Center of Gravity)

Fast Fact:

The most important goal of any fitting session should be to find out how to create a golf club the player can hit on center (or just above or below the CG) the highest percentage of the time. If the ball is hit solid, it will fly with less sidespin and travel its greatest Distance.

In order to help the golfer hit the ball more solid, the most important specifications to be addressed are: total weight, swingweight, golf club balance point and length. Also playing a role in correcting the chronic off-center hitting golfer are bulge and roll and clubhead design.

The heavier and longer the club, the harder it is for any golfer to hit the ball consistently on the center of the clubface and in line with the CG. If it is at all possible, all golfers should try to play with the lightest total weight club he/she can still hit on center, along with the highest swingweight and lowest balance point that they can control. High total weight and high swingweight do not match well together in the same club for any golfers except for those who are the strongest physically and play the most.

3. Shot pattern – Pull-Hook, Pull, Pull-Fade, Straight-Draw, Straight, Straight-Fade, Push-Draw, Push and Push-Slice

Face Angle, Lie, Total Weight, Swingweight, Length and to a lesser extent, Clubhead Design, Shaft Weight and Shaft Flex.

Fast Fact:

Noting the predominant direction the golfer hits the ball with each of the clubs is very important because this informs the clubmaker about what type of accuracy problems are being encountered.

Once the predominant shot direction is known, the clubmaker can then focus on the specifications that have a MAJOR effect on Accuracy, including: the face angle of the woods; the lie angle of the middle and short irons; and the length of the clubs. After that, the clubmaker should note if the golfer is complaining of pulled, pushed or pull-hooked shots, and inspect the combination of total weight and swingweight. A total weight or swingweight that is too low can cause a pulled or pull-hook shot. If the total weight is too high <u>and</u> the swingweight is too high as well, the result can be a pushed shot.

4. Carry Distance - 1w, 5w, 3i, 5i, 7i, PW

Loft, Length, Total Weight, Swingweight, Clubhead Design, Shaft Flex and Shaft Weight

Fast Fact:

The farther the golfer can carry the ball, the more the clubmaker might think that the player should be using clubs that are stiffer in flex, heavier in total weight, higher in swingweight, longer in length, stronger in loft and using clubheads that have a higher center of gravity and less perimeter weighting. This is not the case in many situations because so many of the decisions regarding loft, length, total weight, swingweight, clubhead design, shaft flex and shaft weight have to consider swing tempo and athletic coordination first.

Ball Carry Distance can be a good indicator in some areas, such as:

Loft – The shorter the Distance, the more the loft should be on the driver and long irons and less on the fairway woods and short irons.

Swingweight – The shorter the Distance, the closer to normal or lower than normal the swingweight.

Shaft Flex – The shorter the player's carry Distance, the more flexible the shaft. However, swing speed and down swing acceleration are the best ways to match the player to the right shaft.

Clubhead design – The shorter the player's Distance, the more the player should be using a perimeter-weighted club-head.

Ball carry Distance cannot be a good indicator for the following specifications:

Total weight/shaft weight – Light total weight clubs can be played by both long and short hitters as long as the swing-weight is matched accordingly.

Length – Longer clubs can be played both by long and short hitters as long as the tempo and athletic ability are matched well to the length.

PART 3

P L A Y I N G   G O A L S

CHECK THE BOX OF EACH GOAL YOU WOULD LIKE TO REACH AND CIRCLE IF FOR WOODS, IRONS OR BOTH.

1. I WANT TO HIT THE WOODS/IRONS HIGHER.	12. I WANT TO STOP HITTING THE WOODS/IRONS FAT.
2. I WANT TO HIT THE WOODS/IRONS LOWER.	13. I WANT TO HIT THE WOODS/IRONS MORE SOLIDLY.
3. I WANT TO HIT THE WOODS/IRONS FARTHER.	14. I WANT BETTER CLUBHEAD FEEL IN WOODS/IRONS.
4. I WANT TO HIT THE WOODS/IRONS STRAIGHTER.	15. I WANT TO FEEL MORE KICK IN THE WOOD/IRON SHAFT.
5. I WANT TO STOP SLICING THE WOODS/IRONS.	16. I WANT TO FEEL THE CLUBHEAD MORE AT THE TOP OF
6. I WANT TO STOP HOOKING THE WOODS/IRONS.	THE BACKSWING WITH THE WOODS/IRONS.
7. I WANT TO STOP PUSHING THE WOODS/IRONS.	17. I WANT TO HIT MY CHIPS LESS FAT.
8. I WANT TO STOP PULLING THE WOODS/IRONS.	18. I WANT TO HIT MY CHIPS LESS THIN.
9. I WANT TO STOP TOPPING THE WOODS/IRONS.	19. I WANT TO HIT MY SAND SHOTS LESS FAT.
10. I WANT TO STOP SKYING THE WOODS/IRONS.	20. I WANT TO HIT MY SAND SHOTS LESS THIN.
11. I WANT TO STOP HITTING THE WOODS/IRONS THIN.	21. I WANT A BETTER HOLD ON THE CLUB.

OVERALL GAME IMPROVEMENT DESIRES:

1. I WANT MORE DISTANCE. WOODS/IRONS	4. I WANT A LOWER TRAJECTORY. WOODS/IRONS
2. I WANT MORE ACCURACY. WOODS/IRONS	5. I WANT MORE BACKSPIN. IRONS/WEDGES
3. I WANT A HIGHER TRAJECTORY. WOODS IRONS	6. I WANT BETTER FEEL. WOODS/IRONS

III. PLAYING GOALS

The section of the Player Interview that deals with discovering the specific wants of the golfer is without a doubt, the most important part of the information gathering phase of the fitting session. It is within this section that the golfer tells the clubmaker exactly what it is that he/she wants to change in the way he/she hits the ball and plays the game.

Each of the questions in the Playing Goals section of the Player Interview can be viewed as the golfer making a direct request to change to one of the five shotmaking factors of the Golfsmith Practical Fitting Program. Those are **Distance, Accuracy, Trajectory, Backspin** and **Feel**.

1. I want to hit the ball higher

Game improvement factor being addressed:

Trajectory

Specifications to change:

Loft, Clubhead Design, Shaft Flex and to a lesser extent, Shaft Bend Point, Hosel Offset and Vertical Roll

Minimum corrective remedies to achieve the goal:

• Loft

At least 2° greater in the woods and irons or 1° to 1.5° greater in the wedges.

• Clubhead design

Center of Gravity –

At least 3-4mm lower and 4-5mm farther back from face in the woods and at least 2-3mm lower and 2-3mm farther back from the face in the irons.

Weight distribution –

Greater sole width, longer sole, tall toe height in middle and short irons (pulls CG back, but won't in long irons).

- **Shaft flex**

  More flexible, RSSR at least 10mph lower than swing speed of the player.

- **Shaft bend point**

  Lower.

- **Hosel offset**

  At least 4-5mm greater in the irons and 20mm greater in the woods.

- **Vertical roll**

  At least 4-6" less (straighter face), or more roll on the top of the face and less roll on the bottom of the face (good luck finding this!)

2. I want to hit the ball lower

Game improvement factor being addressed:

Trajectory

Specifications to change:

Loft, Clubhead Design, Shaft Flex and to a lesser extent, Shaft Bend Point, Hosel Offset and Vertical Roll.

Minimum corrective remedies to achieve the goal:

- **Loft**

  At least 2° less for all swing speed players in the woods, irons and at least 1° - 1.5° less in the wedges.

- **Clubhead design**

  Center of Gravity –

  At least 3-4mm higher and 4-5mm closer to the face in the woods and at least 2-3mm higher and 2-3mm closer to the face in the irons.

  Weight Distribution –

  Narrow sole, shorter sole length, normal to mid-size toe height in middle and short irons, taller in the long irons (keeps CG from falling back from the face).

- **Shaft flex**

  More stiff, RSSR equal to or up to 10mph higher than swing speed of the player (Distance could be at risk though).

- **Shaft bend point**

  Higher.

- **Hosel offset**

  At least 4-5mm less in the irons and at least 20mm less in the woods.

- **Vertical roll**

  Less on the top of the face (straighter) and (more rounded) on the bottom of the face.

Fast Fact:

If the player indicates they want to hit the ball higher, the clubmaker must consider increasing the loft, lowering the center of gravity, and recommending a set of woods with an offset hosel. While the other specifications do have some effect on hitting the ball higher, their effect is minimal and can only be a factor if that specification in the previous set was very badly matched to the golfer's needs.

If the player indicates a desire to hit the ball lower, the clubmaker must consider decreasing the loft, raising the center of gravity, and recommending a set of woods with more face progression (non-offset). While the other specifications do have some effect on hitting the ball lower, their effect is minimal and can only be a factor if that specification in the previous set was very badly matched to the golfer's needs.

3. I want to hit the ball farther

Game improvement factor being addressed:

Distance

Specifications to change:

Loft, Clubhead Design, Shaft Weight, Total Weight, Swingweight, Length, Golf Club Balance Point, Grip Size and Shaft Flex.

Minimum corrective remedies to achieve goal:

- Loft

At least 2° less in the driver and longer irons for faster swing speed players; At least 2° more in the driver and long irons for slower swing speed players; At least 2° less in the fairway woods, middle and short irons for all swing speed players.

- Clubhead design

Center of Gravity –

At least 3-4mm higher and 4-5mm closer to the face for faster swing speed players (over 80mph driver swing speed) in the woods ; No more than 2-3mm lower and 3-4mm farther back from the face for slow swing speed players (under 80mph driver swing speed) in the woods;

Weight Distribution –

Greater perimeter weighting for all swing speed players to get more out of an off-center hit.

- Shaft weight

Lighter by at least 30-40g from the player's previous shaft weight.

- Shaft flex

More flexible; RSSR to be 10mph less than player's actual swing speed.

- Total weight

Lighter by at least 1.5oz from the same club number in the previous set.

- Swingweight

At least 3-5 points higher from increasing actual head mass without drastically increasing total weight at the same time from a shaft weight increase; To increase distance, the swingweight increase must come from head weight increase more than from simply increasing length.

- **Length**

  Longer by as little as 1/2" (greater than the previous set) in all the clubs for players who hit the ball on center a high percentage of the time; Shorter by 1" in the driver for players who do not hit the ball on center very often; Longer by 1/2" in the middle and short irons for all players.

- **Golf club balance point**

  Make the club(s) with a lower balance point at the same time the total weight is lowered. This means building the set with swingweight that is higher than normal for the length being advised.

- **Grip size**

  Large enough to be comfortable for the player, regardless of the distance from the fingertips to the heel of the hand.

Fast Fact:

If the golfer wants to hit the ball farther, the specifications to address in order of importance are: decrease the loft in the fairway woods, middle and short irons; decrease the shaft weight in all clubs which results in a drop in total weight; increase in the swingweight with the drop in total weight; and recommend a more flexible shaft.

However, if the golfer swings the driver less than 80mph, the loft of the driver will need to be increased to at least 13°-15° in order to increase the launch angle enough to improve the carry Distance. On the other hand, if the golfer swings the driver more than 90mph, the loft can be decreased to less than 11° in order to increase Distance.

Increasing club length will have a much greater chance of increasing Distance in the fairway woods, middle and short irons than it will in the driver and long irons. Do not advise an increase in driver length as a way to increase Distance unless the golfer has a smooth tempo or is athletically coordinated.

4. I want to hit the ball straighter

Game improvement factor being addressed:

Accuracy

Specifications to change:

Lie in the short and middle irons length, Face Angle, Swingweight, Shaft Weight, Total Weight and to a lesser extent, the Horizontal Bulge, Grip Size and Clubhead Design.

Minimum corrective remedies to achieve the goal:

- **Lie in the short and middle irons**

  Dynamically fit to the player to ensure center of sole contact with the ground.

- **Length**

  At least 1" shorter for all players, but longer only for those very tall, short armed players who have been very crouched and uncomfortable with the previous length.

- **Face angle**

  At least 2° more open or more closed from the previous woods to be noticed; direction of face angle change to opposite direction of flight, e.g. more closed for slice; more open for hook. Another reference is 1° change from the previous face angle for every 5-7 yards of desired accuracy change.

- **Swingweight**

  At least 2-3 swingweight points higher, more if the previous set was greatly underweighted for the player.

- **Shaft weight/total weight**

  Lighter, but there is no hard, fast rule of the amount required to make a change in accuracy because the swingweight must be properly matched to the total weight for the strength, playing ability and athletic coordination of the player. Normally, if the previous shaft was so heavy it was causing accuracy problems, the shaft weight would have to be reduced by at least 30-40g to show improvement. On the other hand, if the previous shaft was so light it was causing accuracy problems, the swingweight would be increased by at least 3-5 points before increasing the shaft weight to correct the problem so the total weight would not increase so much and cause a distance decrease.

- **Horizontal bulge**

  Greater radius if previous face too flat; less radius if previous face too much bulge. Amount of bulge to be within normal ranges for all woods.

- **Grip size**

  Large enough to be comfortable for the player regardless of the distance from fingertips to the heel of the hand.

- **Clubhead design**

  Weight distribution —

  More perimeter weighting regardless if the player hits the ball off center a high percentage of the time. Less perimeter weighting if the player wants to intentionally hook or slice the ball more.

Fast Fact:

   If the golfer wants to hit the ball straighter, the specifications to address in order of importance are: a change in the face angle of the woods (driver in particular); a decrease in club length; an increase in swingweight with a decrease in total weight; and a properly fit lie angle, especially in the middle and short irons. After those changes, anything else done to improve accuracy will be minimal at best, unless any of the other specifications of horizontal bulge, clubhead design or shaft flex were very poorly fit to the golfer's current set.

5. I want to stop slicing the ball

Game improvement factor being addressed:

Accuracy

Specifications to change:

Face Angle and to a lesser extent, the Swingweight, Shaft Weight, Total Weight, Horizontal Bulge, Length, Shaft Flex, Lie, Grip Size and Clubhead Design.

Minimum corrective remedies to achieve goal:

- Face angle

  1° more hooked than the previous face angle for each 5-7 yards of slice to be corrected.

- Swingweight

  At least a 3-point decrease if previous clubs are above D4 (based on men's traditional length). It is also possible for a slice to come from a swingweight that is way too low for the golfer, in which case the swing-weight should be increased by at least 3-5 points.

- Shaft weight/total weight

  If previous clubs are very light in total weight, try increasing swing-weight at least 3-5 points before increasing total weight. If swingweight is already at normal to high level, increase shaft weight by at least 30-40g. It is also possible for the slice to come from a club in which the total weight is too high.

- Horizontal bulge

  Less bulge (flatter face) if the golfer hits the ball off the toe of the woods regularly and the current woods have excessive bulge (inches of radius less than 8").

- Length

  Shorten by at least 1".

- Shaft flex

  More flexible shaft. Choose shaft with RSSR as much as 20mph below and never higher than the golfer's swing speed.

- Lie

  Lie should be fit in one of the two dynamic fitting methods to be correct for the golfer. In some cases, the lie could be made at least 2-3° more upright than proper for the golfer in the woods to help correct a slice.

- Grip size

  Grip size should be comfortable for the golfer regardless of the distance from fingertips to the heel of the hand.

- Clubhead design

  Weight Distribution –

  More heel weighting in the woods and perimeter weighting overall.

Fast Fact:

If the golfer wants to stop slicing the ball, the specifications to address in order of importance are: a change in the face angle of the woods (driver in particular) to be more closed than that of the current set, in addition to a switch to a significantly heel-weighted club (again, the driver in particular).

After those changes, an increase in the swingweight at the same time the total weight is decreased, in addition to a decrease in length and a check on the horizontal bulge can offer some limited chance of preventing a slice. After those changes, anything else done to decrease the slice will be minimal at best, unless any of the other specifications such as shaft flex were poorly fit to the golfer in the current set.

6. I want to stop hooking the ball

Game improvement factor being addressed:

Accuracy

Specifications to change:

Face Angle, and to a lesser extent, the Swingweight, Shaft Weight, Total Weight, Shaft Flex, Lie, Grip Size and Clubhead Design.

Minimum corrective remedies to achieve the goal:

- Face angle

  1° more open than the previous face angle for each 5-7 yards of hook to be corrected.

- Swingweight

  At least a 3-5 point increase if previous clubs are below C8 (based on men's traditional length).

- Shaft weight/total weight

  If previous clubs are very light in total weight, try increasing swingweight at least 3-5 points before increasing total weight. If swingweight is already at normal to high level, increase shaft weight by at least 30-40g.

- Shaft flex

  Slightly stiffer shaft but not enough to cause a loss in distance. Choose shaft with RSSR that is no more than 10mph above the golfer's swing speed.

- Horizontal bulge

  More bulge radius (rounder face) by at least 4" if the golfer hits the ball off the toe of the woods regularly and the current woods have too little bulge. (See Bulge in Chapter 4 for standard specification ranges for each wood head.)

- Lie

  Lie should be fit in one of two dynamic fitting methods to be correct for the golfer. In some cases, the lie could be at least 2-3° more flat than proper for the golfer in the woods to help correct a hook. However, it is not usually as effective to help a someone who hooks with a flatter lie as it is to help a slicer with a more upright lie because of the manner the club appears in the address position. A wood head that sits on the toe end of the sole (more flat than what player needs) is perceived by most players as being too awkward to swing comfortably.

- **Grip size**

  Grip size should be comfortable for the golfer regardless of distance from the fingertips to the heel of the hand.

- **Clubhead design**

  Weight Distribution –

  More toe weighting in the woods although the result is not nearly as effective as heel weighting is for correcting a slice. More perimeter weighting overall.

Fast Fact:

    If the golfer wants to stop hooking the ball, the specifications to address in order of importance are: a change to a more open face angle of the woods (driver in particular), and an increase in the swingweight (head Feel) of the clubs. After those changes, checking to see if the player is strong, with a fast tempo and changing to a shaft that is stiffer could be another way to help slightly reduce the hook. The golfer who hooks should also stay completely away from any heel-weighted club-head designs.

7. **I want to stop pushing the ball.**

   Game improvement factor being addressed:

   Accuracy

   Specifications to change:

   Face Angle, Lie (particularly in the middle and short irons), Swingweight, Shaft Weight, Total Weight, Grip Size, Shaft Flex, Horizontal Bulge and Clubhead Design.

   Minimum corrective remedies to achieve the goal:

   - **Face angle**

     1° more closed than the previous face angle for each 5-7 yards of push to be corrected.

   - **Lie (particularly in the middle and short irons)**

     Lie should be fit in one of two dynamic fitting methods to be correct for the golfer.

   - **Swingweight**

     At least a 2-point decrease if swingweight of previous clubs is believed too high for the strength of the player.

   - **Shaft weight/total weight**

     If previous clubs are believed too heavy in total weight for the player, decrease shaft weight by at least 30-40g.

   - **Lie**

     Lie should be fit in one of two dynamic fitting methods to be correct for the golfer. If the golfer pushes the ball, look to make the clubs more upright, especially in the middle and short irons where greater loft magnifies the push problem for each degree the clubs are too flat for the player.

- Grip size

  Grip size should be comfortable for the golfer regardless of the distance from the fingertips to the heel of the hand.

- Shaft flex

  More flexible. Choose shaft with RSSR equal to, but no more than 20mph lower than the golfer's swing speed.

- Horizontal bulge

  Less bulge (flatter face) if the golfer hits the ball off the toe of the woods regularly and the current woods have excessive bulge (inches of radius less than 8").

- Clubhead design

  Weight distribution –

  More heel weighting in the woods. More perimeter weighting overall.

Fast Fact:

   If the golfer wants to stop pushing the ball, the specifications to address in order of importance are: the lie angle of the clubs, especially in the middle and short irons, making sure the lie is not too flat for the player; a change of the face angle on the woods (driver in particular) to be more closed than the face angle of the current set; and a decrease of swingweight and total weight on the clubs. In addition, some relief from a pushed shot can come from changing to a more flexible shaft.

8. I want to stop pulling the ball.

Game improvement factor being addressed:

Accuracy

Specifications to change:

Face Angle, Lie (particularly in the middle and short irons), Swingweight, Shaft Weight, Total Weight and Grip Size

Minimum corrective remedies to achieve the goal:

- Face angle

  1° more open than the previous face angle for each 5-7 yards of pull to be corrected.

- Lie

  Lie should be fit in one of two dynamic fitting methods to be correct for the golfer. If the golfer pulls the ball, look to make the clubs more flat than what they are, especially in the middle and short irons, where the greater loft magnifies the pull problem for each degree the clubs are too upright for the player.

- Swingweight

  At least a 3-5 point increase if swingweight of previous clubs is believed too low for the strength of the player (3 for steel, 5 for graphite).

- Shaft weight/total weight

  If previous clubs are believed too light in total weight for the player, try to increase the swingweight by at least 3-5 points. If swingweight is already at normal to high range, increase shaft weight by at least 30-40g.

- **Grip size**

Grip size should be comfortable for the golfer regardless of the distance from fingertips to heel of the hand.

Fast Fact:

If the golfer wants to stop pulling the ball, the specifications to address in order of importance are: check the lie angle of the clubs, especially in the middle and short irons, to see if the lie is too upright for the player; change the face angle of the woods (driver in particular) to be more open than the face angle of the current set; and increase the swingweight and total weight of the clubs. In addition, some relief from a pulled shot can come from changing to a slightly stiffer shaft.

9. I want to stop topping the ball

Game improvement factors being addressed:

Distance, Trajectory, Backspin, Feel

Specifications to change:

Swingweight, Shaft Weight, Total Weight, Grip Size and Length

Minimum corrective remedies to achieve the goal:

- **Swingweight**

Increase by at least 3-5 points if the problem clubs are C8 or less for men (based on men's traditional length).

- **Shaft weight/total weight**

Usually, increase by at least 30g. If the player wants a lighter total weight for potential distance increase, raise the swingweight by at least 3-5 points.

- **Grip size**

Grip size should be comfortable for the golfer regardless of the distance from the fingertips to heel of the hand.

- **Length**

Increase length by at least 1" in the woods and at least 1/2" in the irons.

Fast Fact:

If the player indicates a need to stop topping the ball, the clubmaker has to determine if the problem is frequent or not. If the player is a relative newcomer to the game, lessons are the first choice to help them learn how to swing down and through impact while preventing the upper body from raising up off the ball.

If the golfer has some experience and still tops the ball several times a round, the clubmaker needs to check that the clubs causing the problem are not too short, and identify if the swingweight and total weight are too low for the player. Remember, it is best to look at a slight increase in the swingweight first, because increasing total weight alone can do more damage with average to lesser ability players.

10. I want to stop skying the ball.

Game improvement factors being addressed:

Distance, Trajectory, Backspin, Feel

Specifications to change:

Clubhead Design, Length and possibly the Swingweight and the Shaft Weight/Total Weight.

Minimum corrective remedies to achieve the goal:

- Clubhead design

  Deeper face height driver.

- Length

  At least 1" shorter length

- Swingweight

  Increase by at least 3 points if swingweight is felt to be too light for the player.

- Shaft weight/total weight

  Increase shaft weight/total weight only after trying to increase the swingweight with the lighter total weight.

Fast Fact:

If the player indicates a need to stop skying the ball off the tee, the clubmaker must check the obvious point that has nothing to do with fitting - whether the golfer simply tees the ball up too high. If the golfer does not tee the ball too high or refuses to tee the ball any lower for confidence reasons, the only equipment solution the clubmaker can offer is an increase in the face height of the wood(s).

After that, changes in length or the swingweight and total weight of the club could make some difference since clubs which are too long and too light for the player could promote the chance of skying the ball.

11. I want to stop hitting the ball thin.

Game improvement factors being addressed:

Distance, Trajectory, Backspin and Feel

Specifications to change:

Swingweight, Shaft Weight/Total Weight, Vertical Roll, Length and Hosel Offset.

Minimum corrective remedies to achieve the goal:

- Swingweight

  Increase by at least 3 points if swingweight is believed too light for the player.

- Shaft weight/total weight

  Increase shaft weight/total weight only after trying to increase the swingweight with the lighter total weight.

- **Vertical roll**

  Decrease radius (to be more flat) by at least 4" so bottom of face has more loft.

- **Length**

  Increase by 1" in the woods and 1/2" in the irons only if the player is very crouched over the ball in the address position.

- **Hosel offset**

  Increase the offset in the irons by at least 4-5mm and the woods by at least 20mm (changing from a traditional face progression to an offset hosel).

  Fast Fact:

  When the player hits the ball thin, the best ways to reduce the problem through an equipment change are to consider making the clubs longer, increasing the swingweight, and, for very big and strong fast swinging players, increasing the total weight. In addition, the clubmaker should think about checking the existing woods for excessive vertical roll, as well as advising a change to woods and irons with more offset.

12. I want to stop hitting the ball fat

Game improvement factors being addressed:

Distance, Trajectory, Backspin and Feel

Specifications to change:

Length, Swingweight, Shaft Weight/Total Weight, Sole Angle of the irons and Hosel Offset

Minimum corrective remedies to achieve goal:

- **Length**

  Decrease the length of the woods by 1/2" to 1" but not shorter than traditional standard. Decrease the length of the irons by 1/2", but not shorter than traditional standard.

- **Swingweight**

  Increase the swingweight by at least 3 points and do not let the swingweight fall below D0 (based on men's traditional standard lengths - See Length section of Chapter 4 for traditional standards chart).

- **Shaft weight/total weight**

  Increase shaft weight/total weight only after trying to increase swingweight with a lighter total weight.

- **Sole angle of the irons**

  Choose a square to 3-4° bounce sole angle on the #1-9 irons. Increase to a 6-7° bounce sole on the PW. Never allow a scoop (negative) sole angle to be present on any of the irons.

- **Hosel offset**

  Decrease the offset on the irons by 4-5mm and 20mm on the woods (changing from an offset hosel to a traditional face progression wood head model).

Fast Fact:
When the player indicates a problem of hitting behind the ball, the clubmaker should first consider increasing the swingweight or decreasing the length of the clubs. Because so many golfers are better off playing with lighter total weight clubs, the total weight should only be increased as a way to combat fat shots if the player is physically strong and swings with a very fast tempo. Even high swing speed players with light total weight clubs should not increase the total weight until the swingweight is increased as a first solution to reduce the tendency to hit behind the ball. In addition, the clubmaker should always check the sole angle of the current set to see if the 1 - PW irons have a scoop sole angle. If so, the new set should be selected with a square or slight bounce sole angle in mind.

13. I want to hit the ball more solid

Game improvement factors being addressed:

Distance, Feel and Accuracy

Specifications to change:

If the player is having difficulty hitting the ball in the center of the club-face (in line with the CG of the clubhead) – Length, Swingweight, Shaft Weight/Total Weight, Grip Size and possibly the Clubhead Design.

If the player hits the ball on center but the feeling of impact is not solid – Shaft Flex, Shaft Bend Point, Swingweight, Shaft Weight/Total Weight, Clubhead Design and possibly Loft.

Minimum corrective remedies to achieve goal:

<u>For not making contact on-center</u>

- Length

  Decrease length of the woods at least 1". Decrease the length of the irons by 1/2" - 1".

- Swingweight

  Increase by at least 3 points and do not allow to fall lower than D0 (based on men's traditional standard length).

- Shaft weight/total weight

  Match to tempo of player starting with lower total weight but with normal to slightly higher than normal swingweight. If this fails, increase the total weight without allowing the swingweight to fall below normal levels.

- Grip size

  Increase to make the grip feel more comfortable and disregard the fingertip to heel of hand distance as a sizing factor.

- Clubhead design

  Match the clubhead size to the desire of the player. In many cases a larger head shape can help by increasing confidence.

When contact is on-center but feels unsolid

- •Shaft flex

  More flexible shaft. Choose shaft with RSSR that is equal to, or lower than the actual swing speed of the player by 10mph.

- • Shaft bend point

  Choose a shaft with a lower bend point.

- • Swingweight

  Increase by at least 3 points and do not allow to fall lower than D0 (based on men's traditional standard length).

- • Shaft weight and total weight

  Match to tempo of player starting with lower total weight but with normal to slightly higher than normal swingweight. If this fails, increase the total weight without letting the swingweight fall below normal levels.

- • Clubhead design

  Center of gravity –

  Make sure clubhead design of choice has the CG located in the center of the face scoring area. Make sure the CG is not too high.

- • Loft

  Increase loft by at least 2° but only if the golfer's need for more solid feel outweighs the possible distance loss.

Fast Fact:

If the golfer is hitting the ball off of the clubface center, the most effective way to help most average players hit the ball more on center is by shortening the length of the club(s) and changing to clubs with a combination of light total weight and higher swingweight. In addition, it can be helpful to recommend a larger-than-normal grip size for comfort as well as a clubhead design that possesses the maximum in perimeter weighting for less of an unsolid Feel when the ball is hit off the toe or heel.

When the player can hit the ball in the center of the clubface but reports a feeling at impact that is not as solid as he/she feels it should be, the clubmaker needs to address the specifications of shaft flex, shaft bend point, swingweight and total weight, clubhead design and possibly loft.

One of the most effective ways to make an on-center hit **Feel** more solid is to fit the player into a much more flexible shaft that also has a lower bend point. The increased flexibility, combined with the greater tip flexibility of a low bend point will make the shaft bend forward more, just before impact. Such a bending action of the shaft will tend to transmit a more solid feeling of impact up the shaft to the hands of the player.

In addition, the change to a golf club with a light total weight along with a slightly higher than normal swingweight can make the on-center shot **Feel** more solid to the player. The higher swingweight has a tendency to lower the balance point and improve the feel of the club coming into impact. The lower balance point makes the head more likely to retain momentum through the ball, in the process, transmitting a more solid **Feel** up the shaft to the player's hands.

Finally, it is possible for the less able player to improve the **Feel** of impact on the driver by increasing the clubhead loft. The greater the loft, the more glancing of a blow imparted to the ball and the less the ball is compressed against the face. For a lesser ability player, this can provide the sensation of a slightly more solid feeling at impact. Normally this type of adjustment would be done to help improve the launch angle and carry **Distance** for players with slower clubhead speeds (< 80mph driver) and not for the **Feel** of impact.

Fast Fact:
   When a player complains of a less than solid impact when the ball is hit on the center of the face, the clubmaker should first recommend a softer flex shaft with a lower bend point. If the more flexible shaft has a low degree of torque, the change in Feel will not be as noticeable unless the torque is above 3° for the better player and above 4.5° for the average player.
   After the shaft change, the next best way to help the player obtain a more solid Feel from an on-center hit is to be sure the swingweight is high enough to promote better clubhead Feel during the swing. This can be done by recommending a light total weight combined with a higher than normal swingweight. The stronger the player, the higher the swingweight for the light total weight.

14, 15. I want better clubhead Feel/I want to Feel more kick in the shaft

Game improvement factors being addressed:
Feel

Specifications to change:
Swingweight, Shaft Flex, Shaft Bend Point, Length, Grip Weight and Golf Club Balance Point.

Minimum corrective remedies to achieve the goal:

- **Swingweight**
  Increase by at least 3 points and do not allow to fall lower than D0 (based on men's traditional standard length).

- **Shaft flex**
  More flexible shaft. Choose shaft with RSSR that is at least 10-15 mph lower than the actual swing speed of the player.

- **Shaft bend point**
  Choose shaft with lower bend point.

- **Length**
  Increase length of woods by at least 1" and irons by at least 1/2" to 1", only if the player can hit the ball on-center a high percentage of the time with the longer lengths.

- Grip weight

Decrease the grip weight by at least 10-12g.

- Golf club balance point

Assemble the clubs to a lower balance point by using a higher swing-weight, lighter grip, lighter shaft or longer length.

Fast Fact:

Clubhead Feel and shaft kick are subtle but related factors of Feel in the golf club during the swing that not very many players can perceive. However, clubs with enhanced clubhead Feel (through greater head weight or lighter grips) and shaft kick are better for average-to-higher handicap players than clubs with little feeling of mass in the head or kick in the shaft, because increased clubhead Feel helps the player develop an improved sense of rhythm and swing timing. With a considerable number of experienced players who actually know and want such a Feel, it is important to be aware of clubhead Feel and shaft kick and know how to create such a sensation in the golf club.

The best way to make a golf club with increased clubhead Feel is to increase the swingweight _and_ select a shaft that is slightly more flexible with a lower bend point (more tip flexibility) than what the player has been using. More subtle variations of this type of Feel can be created by using lightweight grips on the club. Using a grip that is 12-15g or more lighter than standard will cause the balance point to move farther from the hands.

Be aware that some players will not want such a Feel in the club(s). In these cases, the player will normally make that statement in the Player Interview, thus informing the clubmaker to slightly decrease the swingweight and recommend a shaft that is slightly stiffer and/or with a mid-to-high bend point (less tip flexibility).

16. I want to Feel the clubhead more at the top of the backswing

Game Improvement Factors Being Addressed:

Distance, Accuracy and Feel

Specifications to change:

Swingweight, Shaft Flex, Shaft Weight/Total Weight, Grip Weight, Balance Point of the golf club, and possibly the Length

Minimum corrective remedies to achieve the goal:

- Swingweight

Increase by at least 3 points and do not allow to fall lower than D0 (based on men's traditional standard length).

- Shaft flex

More flexible shaft. Choose shaft with RSSR that is at least 10-15 mph lower than the actual swing speed of the player.

- Shaft weight/total weight

Decrease shaft weight and total weight by at least 30-40g and build with a "head-heavy" feel, achieved by using a swingweight that is at least D3-D4 based on men's traditional standard length.

- Grip weight

Decrease the grip weight by at least 10-12g.

- Golf club balance point

Assemble the clubs to a lower balance point by using a higher swing-weight, lighter grip, lighter shaft or longer length.

- Length

Increase length of woods by at least 1" and the irons by at least 1/2" to 1", only if the player can hit the ball on-center a high percentage of the time with the longer lengths.

Fast Fact:

To make a smooth transition from the end of the backswing to the beginning of the downswing, it can be very helpful if the golfer can Feel the "heft" of the clubhead. Clubhead Feel, particularly at the top of the swing, can be improved by increasing the swingweight, or by changing to a light total weight club at the same time the swingweight is increased.

Using lightweight grips will also have the effect of lowering the balance point of the club(s), which in turn will give the clubhead a more hefty feeling at the top of the swing. Finally, increasing the playing length of the club(s) can give more club-head Feel because the mass of the head is placed farther from the hands. However, this is risky in the case of the player who already has a hard time hitting the ball on the center of the clubface. This is why increasing swingweight or using the combination of light total weight and higher swingweight is a better way to help the player Feel the clubhead and improve swing timing and rhythm.

17. I want to hit my chip and pitch shots less fat

Game improvement factors being addressed:

Distance, Trajectory, Backspin and Feel

Specifications to change:

Swingweight, Total Weight and Swingweight, Grip Size, Grip Weight, Golf Club Balance Point or possibly from the Sole Angle

Minimum corrective remedies to achieve the goal:

- Swingweight

Increase by at least 3 points or try to increase the swingweight of the PW to at least 2 points higher than the Nos. 1- through 9-irons.

- Total weight/shaft weight

Lower the total weight at the same time the swingweight is increased to try and feel the clubhead more noticeably.

- **Grip size**

  Increase in size or at least increase to make the grip feel more comfortable and disregard the fingertip to heel of hand distance as a sizing factor.

- **Grip weight**

  Decrease the grip weight by at least 10-12g.

- **Golf club balance point**

  Assemble the PW to have a lower balance point by using a higher swingweight, lighter grip, lighter shaft or longer length.

- **Sole angle**

  Use a slight to moderate bounce sole angle from 4-7° in the PW and never allow a scoop (negative) sole angle.

18. I want to hit my chip and pitch shots less thin

Game improvement factors being addressed:

Distance, Trajectory, Backspin and Feel

Specifications to change:

Swingweight, Total Weight/Swingweight, Grip Size, Grip Weight, Golf Club Balance Point or possibly from the Sole Angle

Minimum corrective remedies to achieve the goal:

- **Swingweight**

  Increase by at least 3 points or try to increase the swingweight of the PW to be at least 2 points higher than the Nos. 1- through 9-irons.

- **Total weight/shaft weight**

  Lower the total weight at the same time the swingweight is increased to feel the clubhead more noticeable.

- **Grip size**

  Disregard the fingertip to heel of hand distance as a sizing factor and increase the grip size to make it feel more comfortable.

- **Grip weight**

  Decrease the grip weight by at least 10-12g.

- **Golf club balance point**

  Assemble the PW to have a lower balance point by using a higher swingweight, lighter grip, lighter shaft or longer length.

- **Sole angle**

  Use a slight to moderate bounce sole angle from 4-7° in the PW and never allow a scoop (negative) sole angle or an excessive bounce sole angle on the PW of more than 7°.

19. I want to hit my sand shots less fat

Game improvement factors being addressed:

Distance, Trajectory, Backspin and Feel

Specifications to change:
Swingweight, Total Weight/Swingweight, Grip Size, Grip Weight, Golf Club Balance Point, Sole Angle and Sole Radius
Minimum corrective remedies to achieve the goal:

- **Swingweight**
  Increase by at least 6 points or try to increase the swingweight of the SW to be at least 6-7 points higher than the Nos. 1- through 9-irons.

- **Total weight/shaft weight**
  Lower the total weight at the same time the swingweight is increased to make the clubhead more noticeable.

- **Grip size**
  Disregard the fingertip to heel of hand distance as a sizing factor and increase the grip size to make it feel more comfortable.

- **Grip weight**
  Decrease the grip weight by at least 10-12g.

- **Golf club balance point**
  Assemble the SW to have a lower balance point by using a higher swingweight, lighter grip, lighter shaft or longer length.

- **Sole angle/sole radius**
  Use a moderate bounce sole angle from 12-15° in the SW and never allow a scoop (negative) sole angle. Use a wider sole (3/4" to 1" or more) with more front-to-back radius.

20. I want to hit my sand shots less thin

Game improvement factors being addressed:
Distance, Trajectory, Backspin and Feel
Specifications to change:
Swingweight, Total Weight/Swingweight, Grip Size, Grip Weight, Golf Club Balance Point or possibly from the Sole Angle.
Minimum corrective remedies to achieve the goal:

- **Swingweight**
  Increase by at least 6 points or try to increase the swingweight of the SW to be at least 6-7 points higher than the Nos. 1- through 9-irons.

- **Total weight/shaft weight**
  Lower the total weight at the same time the swingweight is increased to make the clubhead more noticeable.

- **Grip size**
  Disregard the fingertip to heel of hand distance as a sizing factor and increase the grip size to make it feel more comfortable.

- **Grip weight**
  Decrease the grip weight by at least 10-12g.

• Golf club balance point

Assemble the SW to have a lower balance point by using a higher swingweight, lighter grip, lighter shaft or longer length.

• Sole angle/sole radius

Use a bounce sole angle from 8-12° in the SW and never allow an excessive bounce sole angle of greater than 15°. Use a more narrow sole (less than 3./4") with less front-to-back radius.

Fast Fact:

Chips, pitches and sand shots are all related in that they are shots that are almost always hit with the club swinging at much less than the full swing speed. Because of this, helping the golfer reduce the number of fat or thin shots with a change in the equipment is best done by increasing the swingweight, or by decreasing total weight and increasing the swingweight at the same time. It is always necessary to check the sole angle of the player's current short irons and pitching wedge to see if a scoop sole angle (cause of fat chips, pitches) is present for some reason. For a full discussion on short game fitting, see Chapter 9 - Fitting Putters and Wedges.

21. I want a better hold on the club

Game improvement factors being addressed:

Feel

Specifications to change:

Grip Size/Type

Minimum corrective remedies to achieve the goal:

• Grip size/type

Disregard the fingertip to heel of hand distance as a sizing factor and increase the grip size to make it feel more comfortable. Choose a grip with a tackier texture or one made from a softer molding compound.

Fast Fact:

By asking the player if he/she is having any problems holding on to the club, the clubmaker is trying to find out information to guide the search for proper grip size and type. The larger and the tackier the grip, the easier it will be to hold on to the club. It is a good idea to recommend a slightly larger than normal grip for average-to-less able players as well as for people who do not play or practice very much (< 2 times/week during the season).

PART 4

EQUIPMENT PREFERENCES

MARK ANY OF THE EQUIPMENT DESIGN FEATURES YOU PREFER. LEAVE BLANK IF YOU HAVE NO OPINION.

1. I PREFER A PERSIMMON WOOD.	16. I PREFER L A R S X SHAFT FLEX. (circle)
2. I PREFER A LAMINATED MAPLE WOOD.	17. NO PREFERRED SHAFT FLEX.
3. I PREFER A METAL WOOD.	18. I PREFER A STANDARD GRIP.
4. I PREFER A GRAPHITE WOOD.	19. I PREFER A HALF-CORD GRIP.
5. I PREFER A TITANIUM WOOD.	20. I PREFER A FULL-CORD GRIP.
6. I PREFER AN INVESTMENT-CAST IRON HEAD.	21. I PREFER A TACKY RUBBER GRIP.
7. I PREFER A FORGED IRON HEAD.	22. I PREFER A LEATHER GRIP.
8. I PREFER A GRAPHITE IRON HEAD.	23. I PREFER A SOFT (CUSHION) GRIP.
9. I PREFER A STANDARD-WEIGHT SHAFT.	24. I PREFER A HARD (NON-CUSHION) GRIP.
10. I PREFER A LIGHTWEIGHT SHAFT.	25. I PREFER A RIBBED GRIP.
11. I PREFER A VERY LIGHTWEIGHT SHAFT.	26. I PREFER A ROUND GRIP.
12. I PREFER A GRAPHITE SHAFT. WOODS/IRONS	27. I PREFER AN OVERSIZE GRIP.
13. I PREFER A TITANIUM SHAFT. WOODS/IRONS	28. I PREFER AN UNDERSIZE GRIP.
14. I PREFER A STEEL SHAFT. WOODS/IRONS	29. I PREFER A STANDARD-SIZE GRIP.
15. I PREFER A _____ SHAFT.	

CIRCLE EQUIPMENT DESIGN FEATURES YOU LIKE OR DISLIKE FOR THE CHOICES OFFERED; LEAVE BLANK IF YOU HAVE NO OPINION.

1. I LIKE/DISLIKE AN OFFSET HOSEL ON THE IRONS.	14. I LIKE/DISLIKE A LONGER THAN NORMAL DRIVER.
2. I LIKE/DISLIKE AN OFFSET HOSEL ON THE WOODS.	15. I LIKE/DISLIKE COMPACT SIZE IRONHEADS.
3. I LIKE/DISLIKE AN OVERSIZE DRIVER.	16. I LIKE/DISLIKE STANDARD SIZE IRONHEADS.
4. I LIKE/DISLIKE OVERSIZE FAIRWAY WOODS	17. I LIKE/DISLIKE OVERSIZE IRONHEADS.
5. I LIKE/DISLIKE A MID SIZE DRIVER.	18. I LIKE/DISLIKE A CAVITY BACK IRONHEAD DESIGN.
6. I LIKE/DISLIKE MID SIZE FAIRWAY WOODS.	19. I LIKE/DISLIKE A MUSCLEBACK IRON DESIGN.
7. I LIKE/DISLIKE A STANDARD SIZE DRIVER.	20. I LIKE/DISLIKE WIDE SOLE IRONS/WEDGES.
8. I LIKE/DISLIKE STANDARD SIZE FAIRWAY WOODS.	21. I LIKE/DISLIKE THIN SOLE IRONS/WEDGES.
9. I LIKE/DISLIKE A HOOK FACED DRIVER OR WOODS.	22. I LIKE/DISLIKE A FERRULE ON MY WOODS.
10. I LIKE/DISLIKE AN OPEN FACED DRIVER OR WOODS.	23. I LIKE/DISLIKE A FERRULE ON MY IRONS.
11. I LIKE/DISLIKE A DEEP FACE DRIVER OR WOODS.	24. I LIKE/DISLIKE COLORFUL GRAPHITE SHAFTS.
12. I LIKE/DISLIKE A STANDARD FACE HEIGHT DRIVER.	25. I LIKE/DISLIKE A SHINY CLUBHEAD SURFACE.
13. I LIKE/DISLIKE A SHALLOW FACE DRIVER.	26. I LIKE/DISLIKE A SATIN CLUBHEAD SURFACE.

IV. EQUIPMENT PREFERENCES

Plain and simple – the golfer must have a positive perception about whatever clubs the clubmaker builds or recommends to help his/her game or many of the remedial features of the club specifications will be clouded by bad swings. As with any other discretionary purchase, people have to like their golf clubs, feel confident in using them, and like the "look of the club behind the ball." Otherwise, doubts, tension and many other negative thoughts and feelings will overcome the ability to make a relaxed, repeating golf swing.

The questions included in the equipment preferences section of the Player Interview Form cover most of the different equipment features about which a golfer may have an opinion. In reality, most of the questions in this section will probably be left blank, either because the golfer has no preference or no knowledge of the design feature. Expect for some golfers to be more curious about the various design preferences than others. If a golfer asks about any particular feature mentioned in the equipment preferences section, be prepared with an answer to explain the factor in question. Remember, the less experienced the golfer, the fewer of these golf club design preferences he/she will have and the more the player may need to be educated.

There are equipment features for which a golfer may indicate a preference that are based in myth or on incorrect information. For example, the quest for more **Distance** is powerful and many golf consumer publications are filled with articles and advertisements that "guarantee" **Distance** from an increase in the club length. The Golfsmith Practical Fitting Program knows that lengthening the short irons and high lofted woods will almost always guarantee an increase in yardage, but not so with the driver and long irons. Because the driver is almost always the club in focus when it comes to a desire for more **Distance**, many golfers might indicate that they want a longer club.

Your job as a clubmaker is to help each player get the most out of their game. By allowing the player to go ahead with a preference when you have reasons to believe such a change may be counterproductive for their game is not doing anyone a favor; not the golfer who may desperately be clutching at every straw to get more **Distance**, or the clubmaker, whose reputation might be stained by making and selling a golf club that does not bring improvement.

When trying to fulfill a golfer's desire for game improvement, most of the time the clubmaker will achieve success by changing the specifications that have a **MAJOR** and **MEDIUM** effect on the playing goals sought by the player. However, once in a while, the clubmaker may have to go beyond using **MAJOR** and **MEDIUM** effect specifications of the Practical Fitting Program and rely on a **MINOR** effect specification change to try and fulfill the golfer's game improvement goal.

A good doctor who knows that some medications have more of a predictable effect on a disorder will always explain to the patient what to expect from each medication. Similarly, explaining to the golfer the reasons for **MAJOR**, **MEDIUM** or **MINOR** specification changes in a golf club is to try everything possible to successfully achieve a particular playing goal. The clubmaker should not only tell the golfer which changes can be expected to work and those that may not, but why they are being included as a part of the new set.

For example, if a golfer wants to hit the ball lower, the clubmaker who is familiar with the principles of the Golfsmith Practical Fitting Program is certain that decreasing loft can make a difference in **Trajectory**. After the decrease in loft, the clubmaker could continue to try and lower the shot height by decreasing the shot **Trajectory** through a recommendation of a higher center of gravity, less vertical roll on the woods, less offset on the clubheads, a slightly stiffer shaft flex, a slightly lower torque and a higher bend point. In the end, the real change in **Trajectory** will likely come from the loft change, but the clubmaker and the golfer who explore <u>all</u> options will know that everything with any possible effect on shot **Trajectory** will have been tried in an effort to help the golfer achieve that playing goal.

If the golfer is informed to the best of the clubmaker's ability in a positive but realistic way about what to expect from the new club(s), no one gets hurt. The golfer receives a realistic prediction of the outcome and in turn knows they have received value for the money they will be spending on the new clubs, while the clubmaker gains a bit of image for being honest and accurate. If the golfer were fortunate enough to achieve a lower **Trajectory** from one of the **MEDIUM** or **MINOR** effect specifications, no negative response will have occurred. In fact, the golfer and clubmaker would be thrilled that a change they did not entirely expect did in fact have some effect.

However, if the clubmaker who is trying to lower the shot **Trajectory** indicated that each of the proposed specification changes – stronger loft, higher center of gravity, reduction in offset, slightly stiffer shaft flex, lower torque and higher bend point – were all going to equally allow the player to hit the ball lower, the player would probably expect more of a change to take place than would actually happen. The result would be when the ball flight does not decrease that much, the golfer might feel a bit "cheated" or misinformed and not have the same positive feeling about the clubmaker and his abilities. In the process, whose reputation gets enhanced, regardless of what happens to the ball flight of the golfer's shots? The honest clubmaker gains respect, the one who was able to predict what was and was not likely to happen.

Not only with the desire for improving one of the five shotmaking factors of **Distance, Accuracy, Trajectory, Backspin** and **Feel** can there come a large incidence of myth and misinformation, this can also occur with the golfer's individual perception of particular specification changes. For example, the golfer may believe that using a 47" driver with 8° of loft will result in greater **Distance**. Let's say in the player analysis and from the Player Interview, the clubmaker discovers the golfer has a 79mph swing speed with the driver, shoots 95 with fewer than 30 putts a round, only plays or practices twice a week at the most and is not well physically coordinated. Does the clubmaker keep his/her mouth shut and make the super long, super strong club of request, or should the clubmaker sit down with the player and explain what is likely to happen should the golfer insist on using such a golf club?

Quite obviously, the more the clubmaker educates the golfer, the better off both parties will be. In order to educate the golfer and clearly explain why a 47" driver with 8° of loft won't help this 79mph, less athletically coordinated golfer hit the ball as far as he thinks, requires knowledge on behalf of the clubmaker – knowledge that is contained within the pages of this book that may take a long time to sink in.

There may be times the clubmaker is not able to use any level of knowledge to convince a golfer regarding the potential outcome of changing a particular specification(s) in the clubs. Stubborn personalities, even a conflicting comparison by another source of technical information with the clubmaker's knowledge, can contribute to a disagreement between golfer and clubmaker.

There are no winners in a disagreement that turns into an argument, particularly when one party is about to pay money to the other for a service. If the clubmaker has confidence that the golfer's request is going to be a mistake, the clubmaker can only state his/her reasons why such a club would not likely bring about the desired improvement, and then let the golfer decide whether to request the club or not.

There are also likely to be strong psychological reasons why a golfer may like or dislike any particular design feature on a golf club. For example, it is very common for some players to attach a sense of self image to the flex of a shaft and insist on using a shaft flex that may be stiffer than what the clubmaker would recommend. Or, a golfer may think that playing with "standard length" clubs is a sign of lesser ability and might insist that the clubs be "overlength." Golfers are as different as fingerprints, not only in their swings, but in their customs and behavior. The clubmaker must be able to read and react in the proper way for each situation and deliver the best combination of specifications for the golfer.

For example, because the overall stiffness of any shaft can be ranked by a swing speed index, it is possible to find a shaft that matches the swing speed of the player and carries the desired flex letter code. In this case, the clubmaker who realizes that shaft flex has little to do with its letter code can give the golfer what he/she wants and what he/she needs at the same time without changing the golfer's mind.

Still, as in the case of the overlength example, there will be times when it is necessary to convince the golfer that the clubmaker's advice is better than the golfer's wants. Pure facts, a thorough knowledge of the principles of practical fitting and an open and sincere attitude of wanting to help the golfer will prove to be the most successful combination in getting the golfer to agree with the correct specifications, whatever they may be, for the new clubs. Ultimately, the goal is for the golfer to indicate equipment preferences in the Player Interview so that the clubmaker can provide the golfer with what he/she wants in addition to the specifications that will help his/her game the most.

CONCLUSION:
OVERALL GOAL OF THE PLAYER INTERVIEW

There are many different questions that can be used in a Player Interview. However, the key point of any Player Interview is to discover how the golfer plays the game, what their playing tendencies may be, what they want to change or achieve in his/her game, and what types of equipment he/she would like to use. This is the information the clubmaker needs to determine the fitting specifications that will help the golfers achieve what they want.

By combining information from the Player Interview with the knowledge obtained through measuring the specifications of the player's current set, the clubmaker should be able to create an actual list of specifications for the new set – a list of preliminary fitting recommendations – without performing one single ball-striking drill.

This is how simple the Golfsmith Practical Fitting Program can be –

1) Learn the specifications of the golf club that have a MAJOR, MEDIUM and MINOR effect on Distance, Accuracy, Trajectory, Backspin and Feel.

2) Learn the specifications that have a MAJOR and MEDIUM effect on the golfer's playing goals.

3) Analyze the player's current set and determine how much the MAJOR and MEDIUM specifications need to be changed in order to achieve the golfer's desires for change.

4) Compile the list of preliminary fitting recommendations for the new clubs.

5) Complete the fitting by measuring the player for a few parameters that will finalize the list of fitting recommendations (Chapter 7).

This chapter includes a copy of the Golfsmith Player Interview Form to compare the explanations that have been written in the chapter and act as a guide for making your own Player Interview Form, should you desire. Later in the book, at the end of Chapter 6 – Compiling the Preliminary Fitting Recommendation, a sample of this Player Interview Form will be filled out, using an example. Along with the sample Player Interview Form is a sample Equipment Analysis Form that will also be filled out with information taken from measuring the necessary specifications of the example golfer's clubs.

The information from both forms will then be analyzed to demonstrate how an example preliminary fitting recommendation can be compiled. Clubmakers are urged to take the time and learn from this chapter what the Player Interview questions mean in terms of making actual changes to the golf club specifications before studying the sample fitting at the end of Chapter 6.

The next chapter, Performing the Equipment Evaluation, will explain how to measure the different specifications of golf clubs that could have a bearing on making fitting recommendations. Later, in Chapter 6, the explanation will be made to reveal exactly how to conduct the Equipment Evaluation in a "Practical" manner, to save time, and still come up with the vital information necessary to discover what needs to be learned from the player's current set of clubs. Chapter 6 will also explain how to combine the Player Interview data with the necessary information from the Equipment Evaluation to compile a list of the Preliminary Fitting Recommendations – the actual specifications of the new golf clubs to help the player achieve his/her playing goals.

Fast Fact Conclusion to the Player Interview:
As long as the clubmaker is fully aware of the MAJOR, MEDIUM and MINOR effect specifications and their effect on Distance, Accuracy, Trajectory, Backspin and Feel, it is possible to make 80-90 percent of the decisions about what specifications of the new set should be solely by analyzing the information from the Player Interview.

It is extremely important to thoroughly study the MAJOR, MEDIUM and MINOR points thoroughly and always keep a copy of the chart that lists them close at hand when analyzing the Player Interview form. With them, all of the information a golfer may reveal about his/her playing habits and goals will be easily translated into an initial fitting recommendation.

Chapter Four

THE EQUIPMENT EVALUATION

ANALYZING THE GOLFER'S CURRENT EQUIPMENT TO DETERMINE THE NEED FOR CHANGE

> **NOTE FOR CHAPTER 4:** Even though there are 20 different specifications which could be measured in the golfer's existing set of clubs, it is only necessary to measure a handful to combine with the information in the Player Interview to make the Preliminary Fitting Recommendation. This chapter will offer instruction on how to measure <u>all</u> of the specifications of a set of golf clubs, but at the same time, it will also teach that there are only a few specifications which must be determined to satisfy the requirement for fitting information. To use this chapter most effectively, first read the section under each specification titled "Importance of Measuring the (specification)." These sections will reveal whether the specification needs to be measured and which clubs in the set will need to be measured. For the clubmaker wishing to learn only the Fast Facts about the Equipment Evaluation, at the end of the chapter will be found a review of all 20 specifications along with an overview of which do and do not need to be measured.

INTRODUCTION

The Player Interview is an important segment in the Golfsmith Practical Fitting Program because it provides the clubmaker with information regarding how the golfer plays the game and wants to improve. That information alone, combined with the knowledge of the golf club specifications which have a **MAJOR**, **MEDIUM** or **MINOR** effect on **Distance, Accuracy, Trajectory, Backspin and Feel,** can be enough to do a credible job of fitting. That, in essence, is what the Golfsmith Practical Fitting Program is all about – reacting to the game improvement wishes of the golfer with knowledge of which particular changes on the golf clubs will make those desires come about.

However, unless the clubmaker knows some of the key specifications in the player's current set of clubs, it becomes very difficult to know exactly what to change and how much of a change to make in the new club(s). For example, by now every clubmaker should be aware that the best way to correct **Accuracy** with the driver is by making a change in the face angle. Slice the ball and recommend a hook-faced wood; hook the ball and recommend an open-faced wood... *but how much hook or open should the face angle change be?*

Unless the clubmaker knows the face angle of the driver that the golfer is using to hit the ball off-line, there is no sure way of knowing what the new face angle should be. What if the player is currently using a 2° closed face angle driver but still slices the ball? If the clubmaker simply interprets the Player Interview that the person wants to stop slicing the ball, it might seem logical for the golfer to change to a driver with a 2° closed face angle. After all, most component supply companies offer at least one or more drivers with a 2° closed face angle. Such ignorance of the golfer's current driver specifications could cause the clubmaker to make an error in judgment. Taking a moment to note the face angle of the player's existing driver would help the clubmaker avoid an embarrassing mistake and help determine the correct face angle.

The Golfsmith Practical Fitting Program realizes it is not practical to measure every specification of each club in the golfer's current set because this would require a number of expensive measuring gauges or machines, not to mention the time to record the measurements. The clubmaker needs to understand a few critical measurements of the golfer's current set or there will be no point of reference for making fitting recommendations on the new club(s).

The efficient way to approach the Equipment Evaluation phase of the Golfsmith Practical Fitting Program is to **analyze only the specifications of the existing set that have a MAJOR or MEDIUM effect on the shotmaking factors being considered for change**. Consider the example of a golfer who wants to improve **Distance** and **Accuracy**, two of the five shotmaking factors in great demand in the fitting session. The Practical Fitting Program identifies the following **MAJOR** effect specifications for generating a change in **Distance** and **Accuracy**:

Distance – Loft; Clubhead Center of Gravity; Total Weight; Shaft Weight; Length

Accuracy – Length; Face Angle; Short Iron Lie Angle

Although there are several **MEDIUM** effect specifications which affect **Distance** and **Accuracy** that can make a difference and should be addressed in a fitting session, the philosophy of the Practical Fitting Program is to first concentrate the initial focus on **MAJOR** effect specifications. For example, before recommending any alterations to **MAJOR** effect specifications for a golfer desiring an increase in **Distance**, such as decreased loft, wider sweet spot (higher moment of inertia), light total weight, light shaft weight, or longer length, it would be wise for the clubmaker to look at the same five specifications on the golfer's existing clubs.

If the clubmaker is reasonably proficient, it would only take 2-3 minutes to read the loft of the woods with a protractor, evaluating the overall weight distribution of a wood head and its ability to enhance **Distance**, and take a total weight measurement of the existing driver. But why not take a total weight measurement of all the woods? How would the weight of the shafts in a set of finished clubs be obtained from a total weight measurement? And when would the **MEDIUM** effect specifications for **Distance** be considered and measured in the existing set?

First of all, if the shafts in the woods or the irons are the same, as is common in most sets, it is only necessary to measure total weight of the driver and 5-iron to determine the shaft weight. By measuring only one wood and an iron, the clubmaker can save time and acquire the necessary information for determining the shaft weight to be used in fitting all the clubs.

How is a golf club total weight converted into shaft weight? That, and many other "tricks" are the purpose of this chapter. But the main focus of Chapter 4 is to teach clubmakers how to perform the equipment evaluation and use the information along with the Player Interview and make accurate fitting recommendations. **Remember, the goal of the Golfsmith Practical Fitting Program is to note** the game improvement desires of the golfer through the Player Interview, measure only the specifications of the existing equipment which are pertinent to the changes desired, and to use the knowledge of what specifications have a MAJOR, MEDIUM or MINOR effect on the area of desired shotmaking improvement to prescribe the correct fitting recommendation. Without the ability to perform an Equipment Evaluation to note how the golfer's current equipment helps or hinders the desire for shotmaking improvement, the fitting recommendation will never be accurate.

The Equipment Evaluation Form created for use with the Golfsmith Practical Fitting Program is designed to allow the clubmaker to list only the golf club specifications that must be known to combine with the Player Interview information to make the correct fitting recommendation. It is not necessary to use just this form, as clubmakers can create their own form or simply write down the measured specifications. The following Equipment Evaluation Form is offered as a guide for following the explanations of how to measure each of the specifications.

The outlined boxes on the Equipment Evaluation Form represent the minimum number of specifications that need to be measured in the golfers existing set. This chapter will teach how to measure only those specifications of the golfer's current set which are necessary to make an accurate decision of how much to change each specification to meet the golfer's needs for improving **Distance, Accuracy, Trajectory, Backspin** and/or **Feel**. This will keep the clubmaker from having to spend any more time than is absolutely necessary to learn what is necessary from evaluating the golfer's current equipment.

THE GOLFSMITH
Practical CLUBFITTING PROGRAM
EQUIPMENT EVALUATION FORM

NAME _____ HEIGHT _____

ADDRESS _____ WRIST TO FLOOR LENGTH RECOMMENDATION 1w: _____ 5 i: _____

CITY _____ STATE _____ ZIP _____ SWING SPEED 1w (3w): _____ mph 5 i: _____ mph

PHONE Home: ( )_____ Work: ( )_____ DYNAMIC LIE FITTING ☐ Center of Sole ☐ _____ " Toward Heel

☐ RH ☐ LH ☐ _____ " Toward Toe

CURRENT WOODS

Brand/Model: _____ ☐ Traditional Size ☐ Offset ☐ Non-offset ☐ Oversize ☐ Mid-oversize ☐ Mid-size

SET MAKEUP	LOFT	FACE ANGLE	TOTAL WEIGHT	SWING WEIGHT	LENGTH	SHAFT MODEL /FLEX	BEND POINT	FREQ.	EST. TORQUE°	RSSR mph
1										
2										
3										
4										
5										
6										
7										
9										
__										
__										

SHAFT WEIGHT DRIVER
☐ Heavy 110g + ☐ Medium 96-110g ☐ Light 81-95g ☐ Very Light 66-80g ☐ Ultra Light 50-65g

WOODS GRIP SIZE
☐ Undersize __/__ " ☐ Std. Men's/Ladies ☐ + 1/64 ☐ + 1/32 ☐ + 1/16 ☐ _____
Grip Type: _____

CURRENT IRONS

Brand/Model: _____ ☐ Offset ☐ Non-offset ☐ Prog.Offset ☐ Oversize ☐ Mid-size ☐ Compact ☐ Cavity Back ☐ Muscle Back

SET MAKEUP	LOFT	TOTAL WEIGHT	SWING WEIGHT	LENGTH	SHAFT MODEL /FLEX	BEND POINT	FREQ.	EST. TORQUE°	RSSR mph
1									
2									
3									
4									
5									
6									
7									
8									
9									
PW (10)									
SW									
PT									

SHAFT WEIGHT 5-IRON
☐ Heavy 110g + ☐ Medium 96-110g ☐ Light 81-95g ☐ Very Light 66-80g ☐ Ultra Light 50-65g

IRONS GRIP SIZE
☐ Undersize __/__ " ☐ Std. Men's/Ladies ☐ + 1/64 ☐ + 1/32 ☐ + 1/16 ☐ _____
Grip Type: _____

SOLE ANGLE
____° ☐ Sq. ☐ Bounce
____° ☐ Sq. ☐ Bounce
____° ☐ Sq. ☐ Bounce

Because the Equipment Evaluation is critical to **Accuracy** of the fitting recommendations, this chapter will reveal not only how to measure each specification of any golf club, but whether the measurement is necessary or not as a way to be efficient and save time in the overall fitting session. In addition, because all clubmakers do not have, nor wish to invest in a full array of measuring equipment, this chapter will also outline different ways to perform measurements in an economical manner as well. These different methods are identified in the following manner:

($) - Least expensive, tool costs less than $20

($$) - Moderately expensive, tool costs $20-$100

($$$) - Most expensive, tool costs more than $100

After the following section, which explains every detail on measuring the various specifications, the chapter will include a shortened outline of the necessary specifications to measure as an easy-to-use reference.

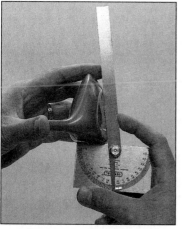

The long arm of the machinist's protractor touches the center of the sole while the scale touches the vertical center of the middle of the face.

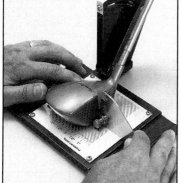

The measuring protractor must be held perpendicular to the face to obtain an accurate loft reading.

MEASURING SPECIFICATIONS OF THE CLUBHEAD
I. MEASURING LOFT ANGLE
A. Wood Loft

Importance of Measuring Wood Head Loft in the Equipment Evaluation:

From the standpoint of performing the Equipment Evaluation, it is important to know the exact loft of the driver and 5-wood, in order to know if the new wood heads will hit the ball farther or shorter, or higher or lower than the wood heads in the previous set. Therefore, it is important the clubmaker learns how to quickly perform loft measurements on the woods, preferably using the machinist's protractor for speed. The only reason to measure the loft of all wood heads is if the entire set is to be custom fit so the clubmaker can confirm that each fairway wood does not hit the ball shorter than the same head in the previous set.

Tools required:
Machinist's protractor ($)

Golf club specifications measuring machine ($$$)

Procedure for measuring loft angle with the machinist's protractor ($)

STEP 1 — Place the long arm of the protractor flat on the sole perpendicular to the face. If the sole is radiused from front to back, the point of contact for the protractor arm will be in the center of the sole.

STEP 2 — Position the scale end of the protractor so it touches the vertical center of the face (the middle scoreline).

STEP 3 — Read the loft angle of the wood head directly off the protractor scale in degrees.

Procedure for measuring loft angle with a golf club specifications machine ($$$):

STEP 1 — Insert a shaft or mandrel into the hosel bore and secure the wood head in the shaft clamp of the machine so the center of the sole touches the base of the machine.

STEP 2 — Press down on top of the wood head so it is soled properly on the base of the machine. If the sole is radiused from front to back, rotate the wood head so it is contacting the base of the machine in the center of the sole from front to back as well as toe to heel.

STEP 3 — Hold the protractor perpendicular to the face so it touches the vertical center of the face (middle scoreline). Read the loft angle of the wood head directly off the protractor scale in degrees.

Standard loft angle specifications for woods

There are no standard loft specifications for wood heads that are accepted universally by the golf industry. Each clubmaking company is free to determine the loft angle for any wood head they manufacture. However, in the past, there were generally accepted standards for loft that did exist. Following is a chart of the traditional loft standards for wood heads along with a list of the current average loft specifications.

	Traditional	Average		Traditional	Average
1-wood -	11°	10.5°	7-wood -	28°	25°
2-wood -	13°	13°	8-wood -	31°	not common
3-wood -	16°	15°	9-wood -	34°	29°
4-wood -	19°	18°	11-wood -	37°	33°
5-wood -	22°	21°	13-wood -	40°	37°
6-wood -	25°	23°	15-wood -	43°	40°

Fast Fact:
When checking loft angle on wood(s) to determine if it can be altered and make a change in distance, the clubmaker must remember that decreasing driver loft can only increase distance for players who already have a high trajectory or swing speeds in excess of 80mph. For golfers with swing speeds of less than 80mph using the driver, an increase in loft is normally more successful in increasing Distance.

When checking loft angle on wood(s) to determine if it can be altered and make a change in trajectory or backspin, the clubmaker must question whether the anticipated change will cause a decrease in distance.

B. Iron, Wedge and Putter Loft

Importance of Measuring Iron, Wedge or Putter Loft in the Equipment Evaluation:

From the standpoint of performing the Equipment Evaluation, it is important to know the loft of the 5- and 7-irons, as well as all the wedges. Without at least a limited knowledge of the lofts of the current set, it is impossible to know if the new set of irons or wedges will hit the ball higher or lower, farther or shorter. This will likely be the part of the Equipment Evaluation that will require the most time, because the iron and wedge lofts cannot be measured like the woods using a protractor. Therefore, the clubmaker really needs to obtain some means of measuring loft and learn how to make the necessary measurements as quickly and accurately as possible.

Tools required:

Bench vise and magnetic protractor ($)

Golf club specifications measuring machine ($$$)

While not as accurate as the Golf Club Specifications Measuring Machine, using a bench vise to hold the iron while the protractor is tilted against the face is the most inexpensive way to measure iron loft.

Procedure for measuring loft angle with the bench vise and magnetic protractor ($):

STEP 1 — Rotate the vise so the jaws are parallel to the front of the workbench. Place a shaft vise clamp around the shaft, about 2" up from the hosel. Secure the shaft in the vise by the clamp so the center of the sole of the iron head touches the top of the bench. The scorelines should be parallel to the top of the bench.

STEP 2 — Rotate the face square to the edge of the workbench. Place the non-magnetic side of the protractor flat against the center of the face.

STEP 3 — Read the loft angle of the iron head in degrees directly off the protractor scale. Note: If the magnetic side of the protractor is placed on the face, the loft will be subtracted from 90°.

Procedure for measuring iron, wedge or putter loft angle with a golf club specifications machine ($$$):

STEP 1 — Insert a shaft or mandrel into the hosel bore and secure the iron head in the clamp of the machine so the center of the sole from toe to heel touches the base of the machine. In virtually all modern iron designs, the scorelines will be parallel to the base of the machine when positioned correctly.

STEP 2 — Rotate the iron head so the face is square. In the square position, the leading edge of the iron will be parallel to the offset measuring lines that are commonly on the base of such machines.

STEP 3 — Hold the protractor perpendicular to the face so it is flat on the center of the face. Read the loft angle of the iron head directly off the protractor scale in degrees.

Standard loft angle specifications for irons:

There are no standard loft specifications for iron heads accepted universally by the golf industry. Each clubmaking company is free to determine the loft angle for any iron head they manufacture. However, in

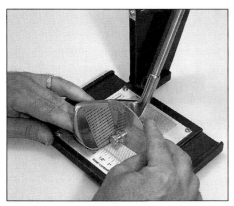

The measuring protractor must be held perpendicular to, and flat against the face to obtain an accurate loft reading of an iron head or wedge.

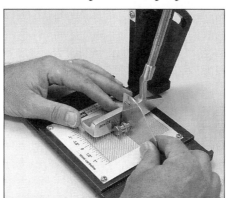

For measuring the loft of a putter, the same procedures used to measure iron or wedge loft are employed.

the past, generally accepted standards did exist for loft of irons. Following is a chart of the traditional loft standards for iron heads along with a list of the current average loft specifications. These traditional specifications are used when making references to loft alterations using terms such as the strong or weak. For example, a 3° weak 8-iron would have a loft of 47°, while a 1° strong 1-iron would have 16° of loft. Of course, other clubmakers and companies have their own standards which they may have adopted.

	Traditional	Average		Traditional	Average
1-iron -	17°	16°	7-iron -	40°	35°
2-iron -	20°	18°	8-iron -	44°	39
3-iron -	24°	21°	9-iron -	48°	43°
4-iron -	28°	24°	PW -	52°	47°
5-iron -	32°	27°	SW -	56°	55°
6-iron -	36°	31°	Putter	3°	2.5°

Fast Fact:

More than with the woods, iron lofts have become much stronger since the 1980s. When fitting a full set of irons, it is very important to know the lofts of at least the 5- and 7-irons in both the new and current set to determine if the new set will hit the ball farther, shorter, higher or lower. In addition, because wedges are such personal clubs for most golfers, it is important for the clubmaker to know the loft of all the wedges in the current set before recommending new wedges.

Iron loft cannot be measured with a machinist's protractor using the same method as measuring wood loft. Iron loft must be measured with the clubhead held in the square hit position.

II. MEASURING LIE ANGLE

Importance of Measuring Lie Angle in the Equipment Evaluation:

From the standpoint of performing the Equipment Evaluation, it is not necessary to measure lie angles of the current set. If one of the two existing methods for dynamic lie fitting is used to fit the player to the proper lie angle, the fitting procedure will determine the exact degrees of lie required for the player, not the measurement of lie angles on the former set. Thus it is only necessary to know the lie angle and length of the club(s) used in the dynamic lie test.

Knowing the length of the lie angle test club is vital because if the length of the new set is different than the length represented by the lie test club, the lie angle will require an adjustment to accommodate the different length. This simple adjustment of 1° more flat for each 1/2" increase in length and 1° more upright for each 1/2" decrease in length is easy to make if the length of the club used in determining the lie is known. (See Chapter 7 - The Final Fitting Procedures for Compiling the Preliminary Fitting Recommendation - Lie Angle.)

While not as accurate as the golf club specifications measuring machine, using a bench vise to hold the iron while the protractor is placed flat on the shaft is an inexpensive way to measure lie.

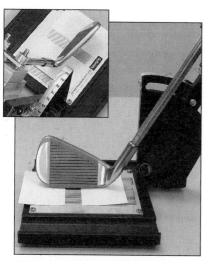

Virtually all golf club specifications measuring machines will have a protractor built into the machine for reading the lie.

Tools required:

Bench vise and magnetic protractor ($)

Golf club specifications measuring machine ($$$)

Procedure for measuring lie angle with the bench vise and magnetic protractor ($):

STEP 1 — Rotate the vise so the jaws are parallel to the front of the workbench. Place a shaft vise clamp around the shaft, about 2" up from the hosel. Secure the shaft in the vise by the clamp with the sole touching the top of the workbench at the center of the face scoring area.

STEP 2 — With a wood head, press down on top of the head to position the sole properly. With an iron head, rotate the face square to the edge of the workbench. Place the magnetic side of the protractor flat on the shaft. Note: If the clubhead is assembled with a steel shaft, try to avoid placing the protractor on top of the step downs. To do so will tilt the protractor and adversely affect the accuracy of the lie reading.

STEP 3 — Read the lie angle of the clubhead directly off the protractor scale in degrees. Note: If the non-magnetic side of the protractor is placed on the face, the lie will be subtracted from 90°.

Procedure for measuring lie angle with a golf club specifications machine ($$$):

STEP 1 — Insert a shaft or mandrel into the hosel bore and secure the clubhead in the clamp so the center of the sole from toe to heel touches the base of the machine. In most modern iron designs, but not necessarily in the wood heads, the scorelines will be parallel to the base of the machine when positioned correctly.

STEP 2 — With a wood head, press down on top of the head to position the sole properly. With an iron head, rotate the face square. In the square position, the leading edge of the iron will be parallel to the off-set measuring lines that are commonly on the base of the machine.

STEP 3 — Read the lie angle of the clubhead directly off the protractor scale in degrees.

Standard lie angle specifications:

There are standard lie angle specifications for all clubheads that are generally accepted by the golf industry. However, standards or not, each clubmaking company may determine the lie angle for any set of clubheads, wedge or putter they manufacture. Following is a chart of the traditional lie standards for all clubheads.

Standard Lie		Standard Lie	
1-wood -	55°	7-wood -	58°
2-wood -	55.5°	8-wood -	58.5°
3-wood -	56°	9-wood -	59°
4-wood -	56.5°	11-wood -	59.5°
5-wood -	57°	13-wood -	60°
6-wood -	57.5°	15-wood -	60.5°

Standard Lie		Standard Lie	
1-iron -	56°	7-iron -	62°
2-iron -	57°	8-iron -	63°
3-iron -	58°	9-iron -	64°
4-iron -	59°	PW -	64°
5-iron -	60°	SW -	64°
6-iron -	61°	Putter -	72°

Fast Fact:

It is not necessary to measure the lie angle of the golfer's existing set of irons as long as the clubmaker uses the Dynamic Lie Fitting Board or the Lie Detector methods for fitting lie. (See Chapter 7 - The Final Fitting Procedures for Compiling the Preliminary Fitting Recommendation - for more about these two methods of dynamically fitting the lie angle.) This is because both methods of dynamically fitting the lie angle do not depend on the lie angles of the previous clubs to determine the correct lie angle for the player. This is important to remember in order to help save time in the fitting session. To save time, it is acceptable to perform the dynamic lie fitting with only a 3-wood, 3-iron, 6-iron and 9-iron and then "fill in the gaps" for the lie angles of the other clubs based on what the dynamic lie fitting method revealed for the clubs tested.

III. MEASURING FACE ANGLE (WOODS ONLY)

Importance of Measuring Face Angle in the Equipment Evaluation:

From the standpoint of performing the Equipment Evaluation, it is critical to measure the face angle of the existing driver or club used most often off the tee. As mentioned in the introduction to this chapter, it is impossible to prescribe a new face angle without knowing the same specification on the existing set of woods. Without knowing the current face angle, the clubmaker cannot be certain the new recommendation would help meet the player's request for a change in **Accuracy**. Therefore, it is necessary for the clubmaker to have a means of measuring the face angle, even if only the tile floor or benchtop methods described in this section.

Tools required:

A tile floor ($)

Bench vise and drafting protractor ($)

Golf club specifications measuring machine ($$$)

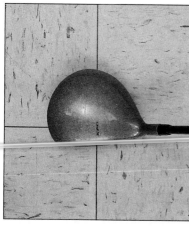

The face angle of any wood head can be identified as open, square or closed using a simple exercise of comparing the face with the lines in a tile floor. (Exampe pictured is 2° closed.)

The top of the workbench can be used to approximate the face angle of any wood head as long as the jaws of the vise are parallel to the front edge of the benchtop.

Procedure for measuring face angle on a tile floor ($):

STEP 1 — The wood must have a full shaft inserted into the head in order to judge the face angle on the tile floor. Sole the wood on the floor so the center of the sole is the point of contact. Hold on to the grip end of the shaft with the right hand.

STEP 2 — Position the wood head so a line between two tiles can represent the "target line." This target line should run under the center of the wood head from front to back. Move the wood forward on the target line until the hosel and shaft are positioned directly over a line in between tiles that is perpendicular to the target line.

STEP 3 — Hold the shaft steady while leaning over to look directly down on top of the wood head. Note the direction the face is pointing with respect to the "target line" running under the head from front to back. If the face is pointing directly down this tile line, the face angle is square. If the face is pointing to the left of the line, the face angle is closed for a right-handed wood head. If the face is pointing to the right of the line, the face angle is open. **NOTE:** This method is only for identifying the face angle as open, square or closed and cannot accurately measure the number of degrees it may be open or closed.

Procedure for measuring face angle with the bench vise and drafting protractor ($):

STEP 1 — Draw a series of lines 1/4" apart on top of the bench on either side of the vise (for making RH and LH observations). Take caution to draw the lines perpendicular to the front of the bench. Rotate the vise so the jaws are parallel to the front of the workbench. Place a shaft vise clamp around the shaft, about 2" up from the hosel. Secure the shaft in the vise with the sole touching the top of the workbench under the center of the face scoring area.

STEP 2 — Press down on top of the wood head to seat the head properly on its sole. Note the angle of the face with respect to the parallel lines and determine if the face is open, square or closed.

STEP 3 — If the face is open or closed, lie the drafting protractor on the workbench with its straight side toward the clubface. Slide the edge of the protractor toward the center of the face. Turn the protractor so it is parallel to the very center of the leading edge of the face. Make a mark at this point on the center of the leading edge.

STEP 4 — Place a mark on the bench where the protractor indicates a point of 90°. Draw a line between the point at the center of the face and point at 90°. Measure the angle between this line and the closest of the lines perpendicular to the front of the bench and determine the number of degrees the face angle is open or closed.

Procedure for measuring face angle with a golf club specifications machine ($$$):

STEP 1 — Insert a shaft or mandrel into the hosel bore and secure the wood head in the clamp so the center of the sole from toe to heel touches the base of the machine.

STEP 2 — Press down on top of the wood head to sole the head properly. Place the face angle indicator on the machine and slide it toward the face of the wood head.

STEP 3 — Position the face angle indicator so the two sides of the arrow are equidistant from the center of the face. Hold the clubhead steady while pressing the indicator against the face. The face angle is read as 0° square or in the number of degrees open or closed.

The only way to accurately measure the actual degrees of a face angle is to use a special golf club specifications measuring gauge, such as the Golfsmith gauge shown above.

Standard face angle specifications:

There is no accepted standard measurement for the face angle of a wood head. In the past when "wooden" woods were the predominant wood head, a measurement of 2° open was most widely seen as a face angle standard by most manufacturers. Modern metal wood head design has changed that dimension to be closer to 0° square on average. However, it must be understood that face angle is a specification that is up to each clubmaking company to decide for its woods.

> **Fast Fact:**
>
> **It is not possible to accurately gauge the face angle of a wood by simply placing the club on the ground and looking at it from the playing position, although many clubmakers and golfers attempt to. (Refer to tile floor measuring method in this section.) To note the real face angle of a wood requires a form for more accurate referencing measurement such as the descriptions in this section.**
>
> **Simply advising a hook face angle for a person who slices the ball or an open face wood for someone who hooks the ball is not accurate fitting. The existing face angle must be noted before making any recommendation for a new face angle.**

IV. CLUBHEAD DESIGN — PART 1
MEASURING CENTER OF GRAVITY

Importance of Measuring Center of Gravity in the Equipment Evaluation:

From the standpoint of performing the Equipment Evaluation, it is not necessary to measure center of gravity on the existing clubs. First, CG cannot be measured with the clubhead attached to the shaft, and second, it is not worth the effort to remove the head from the shaft in order to measure it. After looking at the chart on average CG measurements, it is apparent that wood heads and their CG have more of an effect on shot **Trajectory** than iron heads. For that reason, a golfer requiring the maximum help in getting the ball higher, it is more important for the clubmaker to use CG for help with loft in the wood heads, and more important to use the loft, itself, to help in the iron heads.

It is necessary for the clubmaker to get an idea of whether the new clubheads are about the same or are different with respect to CG than the golfer's current set. This can be done by simply performing the quick visual evaluation described in this section.

Tools required:

Eyes and judgment($)

1/8" pin punch with ruler ($)

Procedure for measuring center of gravity using the eyes in judgment ($):

It is not possible to pinpoint the CG of a clubhead simply with the eyes. However, because **Trajectory** is the main shotmaking factor affected by CG, the clubmaker should have the ability to make a judgment on the difficulty or ease any clubhead may have in getting the ball airborne.

Higher **Trajectory** (low center of gravity) clubheads are characterized by the following visual characteristics: wide sole iron, thick soleplate wood, brass soleplate wood, shallow face height wood, short toe height iron, broad front-to-back wood head, a hollow iron, a deep cavity-back iron or a long blade-length iron.

Lower **Trajectory** (high center of gravity) clubheads are characterized by the following visual characteristics: narrow sole iron, thin soleplate wood, aluminum soleplate wood, deep face height wood, tall toe height iron, narrow or compact wood head, a muscleback iron or a short blade-length iron.

Procedure for measuring center of gravity with a 1/8" pin punch with ruler ($):

STEP 1 — Mount the pin punch vertically in the vise.

STEP 2 — With the clubhead off the shaft, balance the clubhead with the face on the pin punch. Use a marking pen to note the point of balance.

Note: Clubhead center of gravity can only be measured with the shaft removed from the head.

STEP 3 — Balance the clubhead sole on the pin punch. Note: This will be all but impossible with an iron or wedge, but much easier to do with a wood head or putter.

STEP 4 — Using the ruler, measure the CG location on the X, Y and Z axes as indicated in the drawings.

Standard center of gravity specifications:

There is no accepted standard measurement for the center of gravity of a clubhead. In fact, there is no definition for what might be considered a high or a low CG clubhead. As a general guideline from measurements taken by the author, the following chart of average CG locations for different types of heads can be estimated.

The center of gravity of any clubhead can only be measured when the shaft is removed. The easiest and most accurate way to measure CG in the shop is to balance the clubhead on a pin punch and note the points of balance.

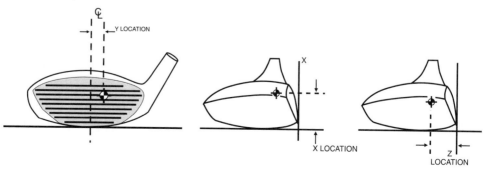

AVERAGE CENTER OF GRAVITY LOCATIONS

WOOD HEADS (1-wood)

	X axis	Y axis	Z axis
Low CG	23mm	0mm	29mm
High CG	31mm	0mm	37mm

IRON HEADS (5-iron)

	X axis	Y axis	Z axis
Low CG	20mm	0mm	13mm
High CG	22mm	0mm	11mm

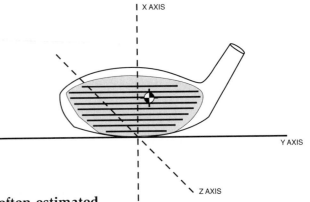

Fast Fact:

The center of gravity of a clubhead is most often estimated by the clubmaker or golfer based on visual keys. If the wood head has a shallow face height (<36mm driver), brass sole-plate, thick soleplate (>3/16"), or is broad from front to back (>80mm driver), it will be easier to get the ball airborne and hit it higher. If the wood head has a deep face height (>42mm driver), thin soleplate (<1/8"), or is more narrow from front to back (<75mm driver), it will be more difficult to get the ball airborne and will hit it lower.

If the iron head has a shallow toe height (<56mm 5-iron), wide sole (>22mm 5-iron), long blade length (>87mm 5-iron) or has a deep cavity-back with thin topline, it will be easier to get the ball airborne and increase the Trajectory. If the iron head has a deep toe height (>59mm 5-iron), a narrow sole (<18mm 5-iron), a short blade length (<84mm 5-iron) or is made with a muscleback design or thick topline, it will be more difficult to get the ball airborne and will hit it lower.

IV. CLUBHEAD DESIGN — PART 2
MEASURING WEIGHT DISTRIBUTION

Importance of Measuring Weight Distribution in the Equipment Evaluation:

From the standpoint of performing the Equipment Evaluation, and because there is no way to do so in the workshop, it is not necessary to measure weight distribution of the existing clubs.

It is only necessary for the clubmaker to use a visual judgment and get an idea of whether the new clubheads are about the same or different, with respect to weight distribution, compared to the clubheads in the golfer's current set. This can be done by performing the quick visual evaluation described in this section.

Tools required:

Eyes and judgment($)

Procedure for measuring weight distribution with the eyes, using judgment ($):

It is not possible for clubmakers to measure the weight distribution of a clubhead, but only estimate it in a general sense. While engineers can use sophisticated computer design programs to measure the clubhead's moment of inertia to obtain a numerical description of clubhead forgiveness when the clubhead is struck off center, this type of analysis is not available to clubmakers. However, because feel is the main shotmaking factor most affected by the selection of weight distribution, the clubmaker should learn how to make a judgment about how much the clubhead could prevent excessive vibration from an off-center hit.

Game improvement clubheads that are more forgiving when hit off center (high moment of inertia) are characterized by the following visual characteristics: wide sole iron, thick sole wood, shallow face height wood, oversize wood, broad front-to-back wood, hollow iron, deep cavity-back iron with a substantial amount of mass on the toe, heel or back of sole, or a long blade-length iron.

Clubheads that are not as forgiving on off-center shots (lower moment of inertia) are characterized by the following visual characteristics: narrow sole iron, thin sole wood, deep face height wood, traditional size wood, more narrow front-to-back wood, muscleback-type of iron with no cavity on the back, or a short blade-length iron.

Fast Fact:
Weight distribution of a clubhead cannot be measured in the workshop; it can only be gauged and estimated only in a general sense by inspecting the design of the clubhead. The design features with the most shot forgiveness are a wide sole on an iron, thick sole on a wood, oversize wood (> 200cc driver), shallow face height on a wood or iron, or a very deep cavity-back iron with a great deal of mass positioned on the toe, heel or back of sole.
The design features with the least shot forgiveness are a very thin sole iron, a deep face height wood or iron, and a small muscleback type of iron.

V. MEASURING HORIZONTAL FACE BULGE

Importance of Measuring Bulge in the Equipment Evaluation:

From the standpoint of performing the Equipment Evaluation, it is not necessary to measure the bulge of the existing woods. One of the only reasons for inspecting the old woods for bulge is to get an idea if there is anything wrong with the bulge on the current set that might be causing any of the **Accuracy** problems the golfer may have indicated on the Player Interview.

It is necessary for the clubmaker to get an idea of whether the various bulges of the new clubheads are approximately the same or different, with respect to the golfer's current set. This can be done by quickly measuring with the gauges or through a visual evaluation.

Tools required:

Radius gauges ($)

Procedure for measuring horizontal bulge with radius gauges($):

There are a number of different radius gauges available in the club-making industry which measure the bulge of a wood head. The most common gauge is a four-sided radius gauge designed to measure 8", 10", 12" and 14" radii. In addition, a four-sided radius gauge is also available for precisely measuring 9", 11", 13" and 15" radii. Some companies offer a much larger radius gauge that includes each 2" incremental radius from 8" up to 22".

The procedure for determining the actual bulge of a wood head is to hold the different radii of the gauge on the clubface from toe to heel until a radius is found that most closely matches the toe-to-heel radius of the clubface. The ends of the radius gauge should be positioned an equal distance from the end of the clubhead's toe and heel in order for the club-maker to compare the radius of the wood head face to the gauge.

Clubmakers should be aware of, and not too critical of the fact that most wood heads, particularly those that are investment cast, will not conform perfectly to the radius of the gauge. It is a normal part of the casting process for very small areas of the face to be slightly flat or rounded so that a little bit of "daylight" shows between the face and radius gauge. As long as the face radius is reasonably consistent in its curvature and conforms within the accepted standards listed for each wood head in this section, the bulge radius will be considered acceptable. (See standard bulge measurements.)

By looking down the face from the top of the clubhead while moving the radius gauge up and down the face, the clubmaker can identify which side of the radius gauge most closely conforms to the bulge (toe-to-heel radius of the face).

Standard horizontal bulge specifications

There is no single standard bulge measurement for each wood head. However, there are ranges of bulge radius that each wood head should produce or the bulge is considered poorly designed for that particular loft and head size. Following is a chart of the acceptable range of bulge along with the industry average for each wood head.

Head	Bulge Range	Average Bulge
1-wood	8" to 12"	10"
2-wood	8" to 12"	11"
3-wood	10" to 14"	12"
4-wood	12" to 16"	12"
5-wood	12" to 16"	14"
6-wood	14" to 18"	14"
7-wood	14" to 18"	14"
9-wood	14" to 20"	16"

If a wood head has more bulge (a greater curvature, i.e. lower number of inches of radius) than the standard bulge chart indicates for the particular wood head, it does not necessarily mean the greater bulge is the cause of the golfer's **Accuracy** problems. Only if the golfer consistently pushes the ball when impact is made on the toe, or consistently pulls the ball when impact is made on the heel should an excessive bulge radius be considered a possible cause. However, in such a case, the clubmaker must also check if the swing path could also be the most likely reason for a push or pull. (See Chapter 5 - The Swing as it Relates to Fitting - Swing Path.)

On the other hand, if the bulge is much flatter than the standard range for any wood head (less curvature, i.e. a higher number of inches of radius), it is not a good situation from an **Accuracy** standpoint. The results of the bulge being too little are an excessive hook from a shot hit off the toe, or a low, dramatic slice off the heel. If the head has a very flat face compared to bulge standards, it should be replaced with a head designed to fall within the acceptable standards.

Fast Fact:
   Bulge, the toe-to-heel curvature of the face, is measured by comparing the face curvature to a gauge designed to a series of specific radii. When the bulge gauge is held against the face of the wood head, the radius of the gauge that most closely matches the toe-to-heel radius of the head will be the bulge of the head.
   Only when the bulge is very rounded or flat compared to the standard ranges of each head is it considered a potential shotmaking problem. Therefore, clubmakers must realize that it is practical to be lenient when measuring and noting wood head bulge because it does not create any real harm to the shotmaking efforts if the bulge is a little less than perfect, as long as it is within the acceptable range for each wood head number.

VI. MEASURING VERTICAL FACE ROLL

Importance of Measuring Roll in the Equipment Evaluation:

From the standpoint of performing the Equipment Evaluation, it is not necessary to measure the roll of the existing woods. However, one reason for inspecting the roll on older woods might be to get an idea if anything is wrong with the roll on the current set that might be the cause of **Trajectory** or **Distance** problems from hitting the ball too high or low as indicated on the Player Interview.

It is only necessary for the clubmaker to inspect the new clubheads and determine if they have the same or less curvature (not more rounded) than the old set. This can be done by measuring with the gauges or performing a quick visual evaluation of the roll.

Tools required:
Radius gauges ($)

Procedure for measuring vertical roll with radius gauges($):
The same radius gauges employed to measure horizontal bulge are also used to measure vertical roll. The most common gauge is a four-sided radius gauge designed to measure an 8", 10", 12" and 14" radius. In addition, a four-sided radius gauge is available for precisely measuring 9", 11",

13" and 15" radii. Some companies also offer a much larger radius gauge that includes each 2" incremental radius from 8" to 22".

The procedure for determining the roll of a wood head is to match the radii on the gauges to the vertical radius on the face of the wood head. Hold the gauge on the face, from top to bottom, until the radius that most closely matches the up and down radius of the clubface is found. The ends of the radius gauge will hang over the top and bottom of the face, with the clubhead held so the clubmaker can look across the plane of the face, from the toe to heel end of the club.

Standard vertical roll specifications:

As with bulge, there is no single standard roll measurement for each wood head. However, there are ranges of roll that each wood head should be within for the loft and size of the head. Following is a chart of the acceptable range of vertical roll along with the industry average for each wood head.

By looking across the face from the toe end of the club-head while moving the radius gauge back and forth across the face, the clubmaker can identify the side of the radius gauge that most closely con-forms to the roll (up and down radius of the face).

Head	Roll Range	Average Roll
1-wood	10" to 14"	12"
2-wood	10" to 14"	13"
3-wood	12" to 16"	14"
4-wood	12" to 18"	14"
5-wood	12" to 18"	14"
6-wood	12" to 18"	14"
7-wood	12" to 18"	14"
9-wood	12" to 18"	16"

If a wood head has more roll (a greater curvature, i.e. lower number of inches of radius) than what the standard roll chart indicates for the particular wood head, it does not necessarily mean the greater roll is the cause of the golfer's shotmaking problems. Only if the golfer consistently hits the ball with a very low **Trajectory** when impact is made low on the face, or hits the the ball much higher than desired when impact is made on the upper third of the face, should an excessive roll radius be considered a possible cause.

On the other hand, if the roll is much flatter than the standard range for any wood head (less curvature, i.e. a higher number of inches of radius), which is rare, it would be a good situation from a **Trajectory** standpoint. As mentioned in Chapter 2, roll is not really needed on the face of a wood. If the roll of the wood head is completely flat and the bulge is correct, it would be slightly harder to sky the ball and the wood head would yield a slightly higher **Trajectory** on shots hit low on the face. However, clubmakers must remember that the advantage of a flat roll vs. a radiused roll is slight.

Fast Fact:
Roll is measured by comparing the top-to-bottom curvature of the face to a gauge made with a series of specific radii. When the radius gauge is held against the face of the wood head, the curvature of the gauge that most closely matches the top-to-bottom radius of the head is the roll of the head.

Only if the roll is extremely rounded compared to the standard ranges for each head (a much lower number of inches of radius) would it be considered a potential shotmaking problem. Therefore, clubmakers must be aware that it is completely acceptable to be a little lenient when measuring and noting wood head roll. This is because most of the time, there is no real harm to shotmaking if the roll is a little less than perfect.

VII. SOLE DESIGN
MEASURING SOLE ANGLE

Importance of Measuring Sole Angle in the Equipment Evaluation:

From the standpoint of performing the Equipment Evaluation, it is not necessary to measure the actual degrees of the sole angle on the existing irons. However, it is important to visually inspect the nos. 1 – 9 irons to make sure the irons do not have a scoop or negative sole. To do this, follow the procedure outlined previously for visually identifying whether an iron has a bounce, square or scoop sole angle. A scoop or negative sole angle should never be present on any iron, wedge or putter.

With regard to the golfer's current wedges and the importance of sole angle, it might be important to have an idea of the exact number of degrees of the sole angle.

Tools required:

Sole Angle

1. Machinist's protractor and a way to measure iron loft ($ to $$$).

(See Loft Angle - Irons, in this chapter for the procedures to measure iron loft angle.)

2. Visual inspection ($).

Procedure for visually identifying sole angle ($):

STEP 1 — Hold the iron, wedge or putter in one hand with the grip down and the toe of the club facing away. Hold the shaft as straight up and down as possible. If necessary, use a vertical reference in the distance such as a door frame, a window frame, the seam on a paneled wall, etc. to help hold the shaft vertical.

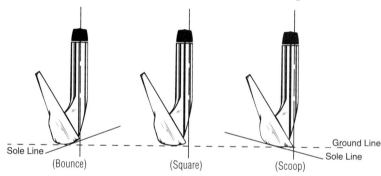

(Bounce)   (Square)   (Scoop)

Ground Line
Sole Line

Sole Line

The sole line is the line touching the center of the sole. The ground line is a horizontal line touching the lowest part of the sole when the clubhead is placed in the playing position. The angle between the two is the sole angle.

STEP 2 — Keeping the shaft vertical, hold the club so that the sole is precisely at eye level. Look across the sole from heel to toe while being aware of the vertical alignment of the shaft. Look at the leading edge, then the trailing edge and form a mental picture of a line across the sole from leading edge to trailing edge. Note if this line is perpendicular to the shaft line.

STEP 3 — Compare the line across the sole to the vertical position of the shaft. If the line across the sole is perpendicular to the shaft, the sole angle is square. This is how most irons and all putters should be manufactured. If a putter is identified without a square sole angle, the hosel should be bent to correct the problem or else the putter should be replaced. One sure symptom of a putter with a poor sole angle is when it automatically turns left or right of the target when soled on the green.

When looking across the sole with the shaft vertical to the ground, if the trailing edge of the iron head is higher than the leading edge, the iron has a bounce or a positive sole angle. On the nos. 1 – 9 irons, if this angle is slight, the clubs are considered to be acceptable. It is also acceptable if the 7-, 8- and 9-irons have more bounce than the rest of the set. However, if the set has inconsistent bounce sole angles where the long and middle irons have more bounce than the short irons, or if any of the long and middle irons have severe bounce sole angles, the set should be replaced.

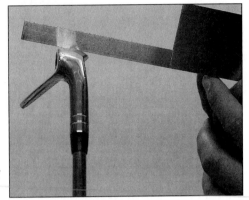

Finally, when looking across the sole with the shaft vertical to the ground, if the leading edge of the iron head is higher than the trailing edge, the iron has a scoop or a negative sole angle. If any of the irons has a scoop sole, the set is poorly made or has been incorrectly bent for a loft change and should be replaced with a correctly designed set in which the sole angles of the nos. 1 – 9 irons are all square, all have a slight bounce sole or progress from square in the long irons to a slight bounce sole in the short irons.

From a fitting standpoint, it is more important to visually identify the difference between a bounce, square and scoop sole angle than it is to actually measure the number of degrees of the sole angle. This picture illustrates a moderate bounce sole angle.

NOTE: Do not be fooled by the front-to-back sole radius of the iron. Only focus on the position of the leading edge with respect to the trailing edge for identifying the sole angle.

Procedure for measuring sole angle with a machinist's protractor and the loft angle ($ to $$$):

STEP 1 — Secure the iron head or wedge in a clubhead specification measuring machine (or bench vise, as outlined in the loft section of this chapter), with the center of the sole touching the base of the machine just below the middle of the scoreline area. Square the face by rotating the head so that the leading edge is parallel to the offset measuring lines on the base of the machine.

STEP 2 — Hold the face in the square position and measure the iron or wedge loft with a half protractor or magnetic protractor. Lie the zero edge of the protractor flat

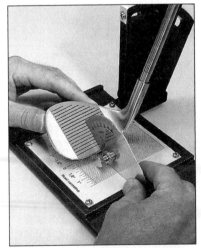

The first step in determining the sole angle is measuring the real loft of the iron or wedge.

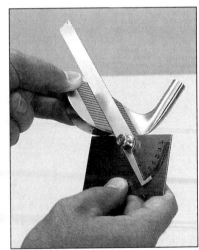

By measuring and comparing the angle between the sole and face to the real loft angle, it is possible to determine the sole angle of the iron or wedge.

on the middle of the face, perpendicular to the scorelines and read the loft in degrees. Note: When using a magnetic-sided protractor, for direct loft, lie the non-magnetic side flat on the face.)

STEP 3 — Remove the iron head or wedge from the clubhead specs measuring machine. Using the machinist's protractor, measure the angle between the center of the sole and the face plane. This is accomplished by positioning the long arm of the protractor flat on the face while the scale touches the very center of the sole from front to back. (The sides of the protractor can be reversed if it allows the center of the sole to be touched by the shorter side of the protractor scale.)

STEP 4 — If the angle between the sole and the face is less than the loft, the iron has a scoop or negative sole angle. If the angle between the sole and the face is greater than the loft, the iron has a bounce or positive sole angle. The difference between the angle of the sole to the face and the loft angle determines the number of degrees of the sole angle.

Standard sole angle specifications:

There are no precisely defined standards for sole angle on a set of irons. While there are ranges for sole angle on the wedges, there are no set individual standard sole angle specifications. Following is a chart that lists the range in sole angle for each iron and wedge as well as the approximate industry averages for each.

Head Number	Sole Angle Range	Average Sole Angle
1-iron	0-2°	0°
2-iron	0-2°	0°
3-iron	0-2°	0°
4-iron	0-2°	0°
5-iron	0-3°	0°
6-iron	0-3°	0°
7-iron	0-4°	0°
8-iron	0-4°	0°
9-iron	0-4°	0°
10-iron	0°	0°
11-iron	0°	0°
PW	1° - 7°	5°
SW	1° - 20°	12°
UW	0° - 20°	8°

VII. SOLE DESIGN
MEASURING SOLE RADIUS

Importance of Measuring Sole Radius in the Equipment Evaluation:

From the standpoint of performing the Equipment Evaluation, it is not necessary to measure the actual radius of the sole on the existing irons. However, it is important to look at the sole radius while evaluating the sole angle and determine if the clubhead has no radius, a little or a lot of radius. Remember, in an iron, the flatter the sole is from front-to-back or more curved from toe to heel, the less desirable the design (if drastically radiused). In a fairway wood, the more rounded the sole from front-to-back as well as from heel-to-toe, the less desirable the design.

Tools required:

Set of radius gauges normally used for drafting ($)

Procedure for measuring sole radius ($):

While sole radius can be identified as a fitting specification, it is really more of a design specification. To the clubhead designer and tooling manufacturer, sole radius is measured by using a series of precise acrylic or metal radius forms that can be purchased from drafting supply companies. While clubmakers can acquire and use the same equipment to precisely measure both toe-to-heel and front-to-back sole radius in inches or millimeters much like roll or bulge, there is no need to do so from a fitting standpoint.

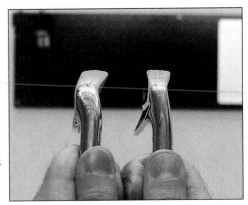

The only fitting requirement to determine sole radius is identifying if the clubhead has toe-to-heel and/or front-to-back radius and, approximately, whether it is a lot, a little or none. Remember, a little sole radius from toe-to-heel is acceptable, a range of 250mm to 1000mm radius. To have a toe-to-heel radius of less than 250mm (more curvature) can cause the average-to-less able player problems with hitting the ball solid from all lie conditions.

Chapter 2 also indicates that some front-to-back sole radius is more desirable compared to none in order to prevent the golfer from hitting the ball "fat." Therefore, if the golfer is complaining of hitting behind the ball, not only should the applicable swing movements be checked (See Chapter 5), but so too should the sole to determine if the club has a negative sole angle or if the front-to-back radius is too flat. All golfers will run less risk of hitting fat shots if the front-to-back radius is between 25mm and 250mm.

The iron on the left has much more front-to-back sole radius than the iron on the right. While both are very playable sole radius designs, the greater radius will be a little more forgiving on chip shots from short grass and full shots from tall grass.

Within wood head designs, it is most common for the clubhead to possess a moderate to severe toe-to-heel radius but with very little front-to-back radius. While the traditional toe/heel sole radius was 6" in the days of wooden woods, modern oversize metal wood design has created a preponderance of triple level sole designs, a configuration where the sole has three distinctly separate sections from toe to heel.

Standard sole radius specifications:

There are no standard dimensions on a wood, iron, wedge or putter for sole radius, either from toe-to-heel or front-to-back.

Modern sole design on metal woods calls for a three level sole "radius," with only the center section contacting the ground.

Fast Fact:

While sole radius could be measured in inches or millimeters like roll or bulge, there is no reason to do so as a part of the fitting process. For fitting purposes, it is only necessary to determine whether the sole radius from toe-to-heel is excessive, which should cause the leading edge of the head to "stab" itself into the ground promoting more of a "fat" or "thin" shot.

With the front-to-back sole radius, wood heads and putters should have a minimal radius because otherwise the broad nature of the wood head sole from front-to-back would make the leading edge come off the ground and cause thin or topped shots from firm ground. However, it is OK for a putter to have the leading edge off the ground by as much as 1/4" (6mm) to help prevent scuffing putts.

For irons and wedges, it is important to have some front-to-back radius for preventing "fat" shots and help the sole travel smoother through longer grass. However, it should not be so much that the leading edge is 1/4" or more off the ground at address. A completely flat sole from front to back on an iron or wedge is not a good situation for any type of player.

VIII. FACE PROGRESSION/HOSEL OFFSET
MEASURING FACE PROGRESSION

Importance of Measuring Face Progression in the Equipment Evaluation:

From the standpoint of performing the Equipment Evaluation, it is not necessary to measure the actual face progression on the existing woods. However, it is important for the clubmaker to visually inspect the golfer's existing woods and get a general idea of the approximate amount of face progression in order to recommend a new wood head design that will not be drastically different. If the golfer is asking for help in getting the ball airborne with the woods, recommending a fully offset set of woods can be very helpful. In this case, there would be no need to measure or assess the face progression of the existing set of woods.

Tools required:

Bench vise, machinist's protractor and ruler ($)
Golf club specifications measuring machine ($$$)

Procedure for measuring face progression with a bench vise, machinist's protractor and ruler ($):

STEP 1 — Draw a series of lines 1/8" apart on top of the bench on either side of the vise, making sure the lines are drawn parallel to the front edge of the bench. Rotate the vise so the jaws are parallel to the front of the workbench. Place a shaft vise clamp around the shaft, about 2" up from the hosel. Secure the shaft in the clamp of the vise with the sole touching the top of the workbench on the center of the face scoring area.

By noting the position of the center of the bore in relation to a series of parallel lines drawn on the workbench, the face progression can be inexpensively measured.

STEP 2 — To measure the face progression of a wood head, press down on top of the head to seat the head properly on its sole. If measuring an iron, wedge or putter head, rotate the face so the leading edge and face is square. For an iron, wedge or putter head, the square face position will be achieved when the leading edge is parallel to the lines drawn on the top of the bench. Use a pencil to mark the position of the furthest forward point of the leading edge of the face with respect to the parallel lines.

STEP 3 — Approximate the location of the center of the bore on the bench top. One way is to adjust the machinist's protractor so it is in the 90° measurement position, standing straight up under the center of the shaft. Turn the measuring scale parallel to the face's leading edge with the flat side of the long arm touching the center on the bottom side of the shaft. Use a pencil to make a mark on the bench where the center of the shaft falls with respect to the lines on the benchtop.

STEP 4 — Draw a line through each mark that is parallel with the original lines drawn parallel to the front edge of the bench. The distance in inches or millimeters between the center of the shaft and the leading edge of the clubhead is the face progression.

Procedure for measuring face progression with a golf club specifications machine ($$$):

STEP 1 — Insert a shaft or mandrel into the hosel bore and secure the clubhead (wood, iron, wedge or putter) in the machine clamp so the center of the sole, from toe to heel (in the case of a wood or putter), or center of the face scoring area (in the case of an iron or wedge) touches the base of the machine.

STEP 2 — Press down on top of the wood head to sole the head properly, or rotate the face to a square position in the case of an iron, wedge or putter.

STEP 3 — Use a pencil to mark the most forward area of the leading edge on the measuring scale on the base of the machine. In the case of an iron, wedge or putter, this will be at the center of the face.

The distance from the center of the bore, indicated by the 0 (zero) line on the base of the machine, to the farthest forward point on the leading edge of the clubhead is the face progression of the clubhead, regardless of whether it is a wood, iron, wedge or putter head.

STEP 4 — Almost every clubhead specifications measuring machine will be made with a series of lines parallel to the front edge of the machine. These lines are the reference lines for measuring face progression or hosel offset. There will be one line that will be labeled as 0 (zero) representing the center of the shaft bore. The distance from the 0 (zero) line to the mark representing the leading edge will be the measurement of face progression.

Standard face progression specifications:

There are no standard dimensions for face progression, especially in a wood. Among wood heads with a traditional hosel design, face progression is more of an appearance-related specification than it is one that can change ball flight.

The only exception is an offset wood head, in which the hosel is positioned in front of the shaft. An offset wood can be a good design for golfers looking to increase **Trajectory**, particularly from fairway lies. When a wood head is inspected for face progression as part of the Equipment Evaluation, the clubmaker should only think in terms of whether the golfer likes the look of more or less progression and whether or not he/she needs an offset wood head to hit the ball higher.

While standard club-to-club face progression can be measured within irons, it is far more common to talk about this condition in irons and wedges as hosel offset. (See hosel offset following this section.)

Fast Fact:
Although face progression has an effect on Trajectory, it is very slight in woods, unless the wood is designed with offset. In this case, a fully offset wood head can make a difference in trajectory because of its dramatically different measurement of face progression compared to the traditional face progression.

In fitting, clubmakers should not think of irons in terms of face progression. Irons should be thought of in terms of hosel offset, even though the two specifications are somewhat similar. For example, we can relate better to an iron with 6-7mm of hosel offset better than the same iron with a face progression of 0.5mm. (In irons, face progression = the hosel offset minus 1/2 the diameter of the hosel. Therefore, an iron with 7mm of hosel offset with a 13mm diameter hosel would have a face progression of 7mm - 6.5mm = 0.5mm.)

VIII. FACE PROGRESSION/HOSEL OFFSET
MEASURING HOSEL OFFSET

Importance of Measuring Hosel Offset in the Equipment Evaluation:

From the standpoint of performing the Equipment Evaluation, it is not important to know the exact amount of hosel offset. It is helpful to note if old the set of irons has consistent offset and what type, (heavy, moderate or non-offset), or whether it is made with progressive hosel offset. This determination can be made by placing the clubs in the address position and looking at the relationship to the hosel.

When a clubhead is inspected for hosel offset as part of the Equipment Evaluation, the clubmaker should think in terms of the golfer's preferences. Whether the golfer prefers the look of more or less offset, whether offset is necessary to help get the ball up better, and if the golfer wants help getting the ball up only with the longer irons, in which case progressive offset is a better choice for the player.

Tools required:
Bench vise, machinist's protractor or block, and ruler($)

Golf club specifications measuring machine, protractor or block($$$)

Procedure for measuring hosel offset with a bench vise, machinist's protractor or block, and ruler ($):

STEP 1 — Draw a series of lines 1/8" apart on the top of the bench on either side of the vise, making sure the lines are drawn parallel to the front edge of the bench. Rotate the vise so the jaws are parallel to the front of the workbench. Place a shaft vise clamp around the shaft, about 2" up from the hosel. Secure the shaft in the clamp with the sole touching the top of the workbench at the center of the face scoring area.

An inexpensive way to measure hosel offset is holding the iron head in the bench vise with the face squared to the front of the bench. The protractor can reference the front of the hosel.

STEP 2 — If measuring an iron, wedge or putter, square the face so the leading edge is parallel to one of the reference lines drawn on the benchtop. Use a pencil to mark the position of the most forward point of the leading edge on the face with respect to the parallel lines.

STEP 3 — Adjust the machinist's protractor so it is standing straight up directly in front of the hosel. Turn the measuring scale parallel to the leading edge of the face with the flat side of the long arm touching flat against the front edge of the hosel. Use a pencil to mark where the front of the hosel is located, with respect to the lines on the benchtop.

OPTIONAL STEP 3 — It can be difficult using a machinist's protractor to reference the position of the front of the hosel on the benchtop because it is hard to confirm that the protractor is standing vertically straight. Any rectangular block of wood or metal, no longer than 4" – 5", can be placed on the end and pushed against the front side of the hosel. When the block is touching flat against the face side of the hosel, a mark can be made on the bottom of the block at the neck, to note the front of the hosel position.

STEP 4 — Draw a line through each of the two marks, parallel to the lines drawn on the bench. The distance in inches or millimeters between the front edge of the hosel and the leading edge of the clubhead is the hosel offset.

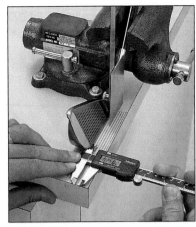

After making marks at the leading edge and the front of the hosel with respect to the benchtop, the distance between the two marks is the hosel offset of the clubhead.

Procedure for measuring hosel offset with a golf club specifications machine ($$$):

STEP 1 — Insert a shaft or mandrel into the hosel bore and secure the clubhead (wood, iron, wedge or putter) in the clamp so the center of the sole, from toe to heel (in the case of a wood or putter), or the center of the face scoring area (in the case of an iron or wedge), touches the base of the machine.

STEP 2 — Press down on top of the wood head to sole the head properly, or rotate the face to a square position in the case of an iron, wedge or putter.

STEP 3 — Make a mark on the base of the machine with a pencil at the most forward point of the leading edge. In the case of an iron, wedge or putter, this will be at the center of the face.

STEP 4 — Almost every clubhead specifications measuring machine will be made with a series of lines parallel to the front edge of the machine. These lines are the reference lines for measuring hosel offset. Place the protractor arm or the side of the block against the front of the hosel. Mark the position on the base of the machine that references the front of the hosel.

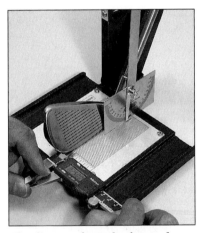

The distance from the front edge of the hosel to the forward point of the leading edge on the clubhead is the hosel offset for the clubhead, regardless of whether it is a wood, iron, wedge or putter head.

STEP 5 — Note the distance between the mark representing the front of the hosel and the mark representing the leading edge of the clubhead. The difference between the two marks is the hosel offset of the clubhead.

Standard hosel offset specifications:

There are no standard dimensions for hosel offset, whether in a wood, iron, wedge or putter. In general, irons and wedges are noted as being heavily offset (offset greater than 5mm), moderately offset (offset from 2mm to 5mm), or non-offset (offset less than 2mm).

In addition, sets of irons are made to be consistently offset (all irons have the same amount of offset) or progressively offset (the long irons have the most offset, graduating down to the least amount of offset on the short irons and wedges).

Fast Fact:

Hosel offset is normally only thought about in regard to irons, wedges or putters. It is measured as the distance from the front of the hosel to the leading edge. In the set of irons, hosel offset will either be consistent (the same in each head in the set) or progressive (changing from more in the long irons to less in the short irons and wedges).

From the standpoint of fitting, hosel offset does not need to be measured precisely. It only needs to be recognized on the basis of what the player needs or wants. If the player wants help getting the ball airborne or in improving the ability to hit down on the ball, a set of offset woods and irons can help, but only slightly. Therefore, hosel offset has to be discussed with the player as a part of the appearance of the clubs, such as the player liking the look of offset or not.

MEASURING SPECIFICATIONS OF THE SHAFT

IX. MEASURING SHAFT WEIGHT

Importance of Measuring Shaft Weight in the Equipment Evaluation:

When performing the Equipment Evaluation, it is important to know the total weight of the golfer's current driver and/or 5-iron in order to know the shaft weight and make fitting recommendations that can help with regard to **Distance** and **Feel**. If the clubmaker has no idea what shaft weight will correspond to a certain total weight, it then becomes impossible for the clubmaker to fulfill a total weight recommendation in the fitting.

The only way a clubmaker can achieve a specific total weight in the new club recommendation is knowing the shaft weight and grip weight, which when added to the head weight, will yield the particular total weight. Therefore, it is important for the clubmaker to obtain a total weight measurement of the driver in order to estimate the current shaft and grip weight of the golfer's existing clubs.

Tools required:

Gram or ounce weight scale (+/-1g) ($$)

Procedure measuring shaft weight using gram weight scale +/-1g ($$):

NOTE: It is certainly not practical to disassemble the golfer's current set in order to determine the shaft weight. Because shaft weight is the primary factor of total weight, with grip weight playing a small part as well, all that is necessary to estimate shaft weight closely is to know the total weight of the current driver and 5-iron along with the approximate grip weight. With that information, it is possible to use the chart in this section to determine the shaft weight.

There are many different types of scales available for measuring the total weight of a golf club to help determine the weight of the shaft. It may be preferable for a workshop to possess a scale with +/-1g accuracy, but for fitting analysis it is not necessary to be that accurate. For that reason, the +/-5g accuracy of most swingweight scales is sufficient for determining shaft weight.

The first step to measuring shaft weight from the finished golf club is obtaining the total weight, followed by estimating the weight of the grip based on its size.

STEP 1 — Use the driver to determine the approximate shaft weight of the woods and the 5-iron for the irons. Place the club on the scale and obtain a total weight reading in grams or ounces.

STEP 2 — Measure the size of the grip using a grip size gauge or calipers. (See Grip Size section of this chapter for procedures in measuring grip size.) Estimate the weight of the grip from the following information:

Grip Size	Weight	Grip Size	Weight
Ladies' Standard	47g (1.65oz)	Men's Standard	50g (1.76g)
Men's + 1/64"	52g (1.83g)	Men's + 1/32"	54g (1.90oz)
Men's +1/16"	57g (2.01g)	Men's Jumbo	64g (2.25oz)

NOTE: Determine if the grip being used is a lightweight grip. The Golfsmith catalog lists the weight of each grip and is a good reference to use. At the time this book was published, the only lightweight grips commonly used by clubmakers were the Griptec Series 38/46, the Golf Pride Tour Velvet Lite 39g and Golfsmith's PosiLite 36g grip. To identify these grips, utilize the following information:

Griptec 38g - Gold 'G' on front + number 38 on the end cap

Griptec 42g - Gold 'G' on front + number 42 on the end cap

Griptec 46g - Gold 'G' on front + number 46 on the end cap

Tour Velvet Lite 39g - Has the name Tour Velvet 'Lite' on front.

Posilite 36g - PosiLite name on front, PosiTrac name on grip cap.

At the time of publication, a number of brand name manufacturers were in the process of changing their finished clubs to use grips weighing much less than standard. In successive years, it will be more difficult to identify all the different brand name lightweight grips, but as a general rule, if the driver weighs less than 10.5oz (295g), or the 5-iron weighs less than 12.75oz (360g), the grip is more than likely a lightweight model weighing in the range of 38g or less.

STEP 3 — Compare the driver or 5-iron total weight reading to the chart below in order to estimate the shaft weight. The column titled "catalog shaft weight" represents the shaft weight before installation into the club, and is the weight range the clubmaker needs to refer when selecting a new shaft in order to achieve the corresponding total weight listed.

Driver Total Weight Range	Shaft Weight	Catalog Shaft Weight	5-Iron Total Weight Range	Shaft Weight	Catalog Shaft Weight
10.65-11oz(300-310g)	50-60g	55-65g	12.8-13.15oz(365-375g)	50-60g	55-65g
11-11.3oz(310-320g)	60-70g	65-75g	13.15-13.5oz(375-385g)	60-70g	65-75g
11.3-11.65oz(320-330g)	70-80g	75-85g	13.5-13.85oz(385-395g)	70-80g	75-85g
11.65-12oz(330-340g)	80-90g	85-95g	3.85-14.2oz(395-405g)	80-90g	85-95g
12-12.35oz(340-350g)	90-100g	95-105g	14.2-14.55oz(405-415g)	90-100g	95-105g
12.35-12.7(350-360g)	100-110g	105-115g	14.55-14.9oz(415g-425g)	100-110g	105-115g
12.7-13.05oz(360-370g)	110-120g	115g-125g	14.9oz-15.25oz(425g-435g)	110-120g	115-125g
>13.05oz(>370g)	>120g	>125g	>15.25oz(>435g)	>120g	>125g

NOTE: Total weights of less than 10.65oz. can be achieved on a driver with a normal weight grip because of the availability of a limited number of shafts weighing less than 50g. However, it is more likely that the driver with a total weight of less than 10.65oz. has been made with a much lighter grip. For any driver total weight of 10oz. or less, the grip would have to weigh less than 25g.

Measuring total weight of the golfer's current driver and 5-iron is the only way to determine the shaft weight the player has been using in the woods and irons.

Standard shaft weight specifications:

There are no standard specifications for shaft weight. However, for the purpose of fitting shaft weight, The Golfsmith Practical Fitting Program identifies five different classifications for shaft weight, all based on the catalog uncut shaft weight. This chart is not to be confused with the previous chart that is more detailed and identifies shaft weight based on a wider range of driver and 5-iron total weights. The following chart is a shortened, condensed version of the larger chart that is constructed for the purpose of awarding a classification to each range in shaft weight.

Classification	Shaft Weight Range	Driver Tot. Wt.	5-Iron Tot. Wt.
Heavy Weight	110g +	>12.7oz	>14.7oz
Medium Weight	96-110g	12.2 - 12.7oz	14.2 - 14.7oz
Light Weight	81-95g	11.7 - 12.2oz	13.7 - 14.2oz
Very Light Weight	66-80g	11.2 - 11.7oz	13.2 - 13.7oz
Ultra Light Weight	50-65g	10.7 - 11.2oz	12.7 - 13.2oz

NOTE: Based on 50g grip weight. If using 38g lightweight grips, subtract 0.4oz from the total weight in the range for each classification of shaft weight.

IX. MEASURING SHAFT FLEX

Importance of Measuring Shaft Flex in the Equipment Evaluation:

When performing the Equipment Evaluation, it is not that important to calculate the RSSR (Recommended Swing Speed Requirement) of the driver (3-wood is OK) and 5-iron shafts in the golfer's current set. This is because the new shaft flex (RSSR) will be determined from scratch by measuring the clubhead speed of the player assessing the player's downswing acceleration and comparing that information to the swing speed rating (RSSR) of the shafts in consideration.

However, if the player indicates he/she wishes to keep the same flex in a new shaft or wishes to duplicate the flex **Feel** of a particular shaft in the new club(s), it will be necessary to calculate the RSSR of that shaft. Once the RSSR of the current or selected shaft is determined, the new shaft can be chosen from a list of shafts which have the same RSSR.

To determine how to calculate the RSSR of any driver or 5-iron shaft, refer to that section found on page 168 of this section on shaft flex.

Tools required:

Golfsmith Catalog or Golfsmith Practical Fitting Book($)

Shaft deflection board ($$$)

Shaft frequency analyzer ($$$)

NOTE: When evaluating the golfer's current flex it is more important to know the RSSR (Recommended Shaft Speed Rating) of the golfer's driver and 5-iron shafts (3-wood is OK in lieu of driver), than it is to know the deflection or frequency by itself. If the RSSR of the golfer's current wood and iron shafts can be determined, that mph rating of the shafts can be

compared to the golfer's swing speed for the driver and 5-iron and determine if the current shafts are too stiff, too flexible or correctly matched in terms of stiffness.

Procedure for measuring shaft flex using Golfsmith Catalog or Golfsmith Practical Fitting Book ($):

In the shaft section of each Golfsmith catalog, the RSSR (Recommended Swing Speed Ratings) can be found on each shaft available for distribution. The RSSR is an estimation of the clubhead speed required to correctly match the mph rating of stiffness for the shaft, based on measurements of frequency and torque.

However, if the golfer's current set is not manufactured with a shaft listed in the Golfsmith catalog, the only way to determine RSSR of a shaft will be using a frequency machine along with the shaft swing speed charts for driver and 5-iron shafts. The shaft swing speed calculation tables are printed in this section of the book for men's and ladies' driver and 5-iron shafts. (See Importance of Measuring Shaft Flex in the Equipment Evaluation later in this section for an explanation of how to find the RSSR for any shaft.)

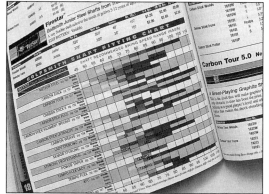

The Golfsmith Catalog can be used to determine the recommended swing speed range (RSSR) of a number of the most popular shafts.

Procedure for measuring shaft flex using shaft deflection board ($$$):

STEP 1 — For normal tip deflection, secure the butt of the shaft or grip end of the finished club in the clamp. Level the shaft or club so the shaft is in line with the 0" horizontal deflection line. For the ASTM proposed standard, the butt of the shaft shall be clamped at 5".

STEP 2 — Hang the deflection weight from the tip end of the shaft or just above the hosel of the finished club. For the ASTM proposed standard, a 5-lb. weight is to be suspended from a clamp attached 1.5" up from the tip end of the shaft.

STEP 3 — Note the distance the center of the shaft tip has deflected in inches or millimeters under the influence of the hanging weight.

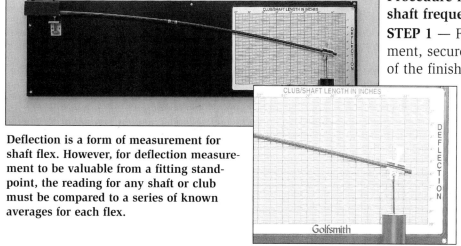

Deflection is a form of measurement for shaft flex. However, for deflection measurement to be valuable from a fitting standpoint, the reading for any shaft or club must be compared to a series of known averages for each flex.

Procedure for measuring shaft flex using shaft frequency analyzer ($$$):

STEP 1 — For normal frequency measurement, secure the butt of the shaft or grip end of the finished club in the clamp. For the ASTM standard, the shaft butt or grip end of the club shall be clamped at 5".

STEP 2 — If testing a bare shaft, attach the prescribed weight to the tip. For the ASTM standard, a 205g weight must be secured to the tip, with the tip insertion depth at 1.5".

STEP 3 — Pull the weight or the clubhead down at least 3" and release, which will set the shaft in motion, oscillating up and down. Note the reading of the frequency on the machine in cycles per minute. It is customary to repeat the frequency test three times and average the readings.

Average shaft flex measurements:

Shaft deflection

There are no standard specifications for shaft flex using deflection as a form of flex comparison and measurement. While most shaft deflection boards operate the same in principle, the differences that will affect the comparison of measurements are the amount of

Shaft frequency is another form of measurement for noting the flex of a shaft. Again, for frequency measurement to be valuable from a fitting standpoint, the reading for any shaft or club must be compared to a series of known average frequency readings for each flex

shaft clamped, the length of the shaft or club being tested, and the amount of weight used to deflect the shaft. It was anticipated in 1996 that the ASTM (American Standard Testing Methods) would approve standard test procedures for shaft deflection, shaft frequency and shaft torsional stiffness (torque).

Currently, there are deflection measurements published for individual shafts. There are only averages for deflection with the five basic flexes of L, A, R, S and X for woods and irons in both steel and graphite shafts. However, being aware of the average deflection for graphite and steel shafts for drivers and 5-irons, it is then possible to perform deflection measurements and discern whether the shaft being tested is more flexible, average or more stiff compared to its average flex. Following are a series of average deflection readings for steel and graphite shafts for drivers and 5-irons for each shaft flex:

Club	Flex	For Finished Club (1w-42"/5i-36,5")	For Finished Club (1w-43"/5i-37.5")
Steel	L	5.4"/3.2"	—
Steel	A	—	5.6"/3.2"
Steel	R	—	5.2"/3.0"
Steel	S	—	4.7"/2.8"
Steel	X	—	4.3"/2.5"
Graphite	L	4.6"/3.2"	—
Graphite	A	—	4.9"/3.0"
Graphite	R	—	4.7"/3.0"
Graphite	S	—	4.4"/2.7"
Graphite	X	—	3.7"/2.5"

Average shaft flex measurements:

Shaft frequency

There are no standard specifications for shaft flex using frequency as a form of flex comparison and measurement. The main difference among all frequency analyzers that affects the comparison of measurements is the amount of shaft clamped, the mass attached to the shaft tip, and the length of the shaft or club being tested. Again, it was anticipated that the ASTM (American Standard Testing Methods) would approve standard test procedures for shaft deflection, shaft frequency and shaft torsional stiffness (torque).

Currently there are only averages of the frequency with the five basic flexes of L, A, R, S, and X for woods and irons in both steel and graphite shafts. Being aware of the average frequency for graphite and steel shafts on drivers and 5-irons makes it possible to perform frequency measurements and discern whether the shaft being tested is more flexible, average or more stiff compare to its average flex. Following are a series of average frequency readings for steel and graphite shafts for drivers and 5-irons for each shaft flex:

Shaft Material	Flex	Avg. Frequency For Finished Club (1w-43"/D1)	(5i-37.5"/D1)
Steel	L	237cpm	282cpm
Steel	A	239cpm	283cpm
Steel	R	250cpm	294cpm
Steel	S	260cpm	306cpm
Steel	X	270cpm	320cpm
Graphite	L	239cpm	277cpm
Graphite	A	243cpm	280cpm
Graphite	R	253cpm	289cpm
Graphite	S	262cpm	303cpm
Graphite	X	275cpm	317cpm

NOTE: The above chart represents averages only for a large sampling of different steel and graphite shafts of each flex. This chart is NOT to be taken as an indication of a standard frequency measurement for each flex of steel and graphite shafts. However, it will provide a good comparison for noting the frequency of any shaft in relationship to what is considered the average for that flex of wood/iron in a steel or graphite shaft. Averages are subject to change as industry trends in flex design may change.

How to calculate the RSSR for any shaft:

To calculate RSSR for the driver and 5-iron shafts in the golfer's current set requires the frequency and torque of the shafts to be determined. If the frequency can be measured on a frequency analyzer and the torque either measured, approximated from a shaft/component company catalog, or by calling Golfsmith, those readings can be applied to the following driver and 5-iron swing speed tables. In addition, this book also includes a separate chart of specifications including the RSSR for many popular brand name drivers and 5-irons from the 1996 equipment season which can be found in the supplement which is provided with this book. In succeeding years, Golfsmith will make measurements of popular brand name driver and 5-iron shafts available to clubmakers. These charts of popular brand name finished golf clubs will enable the clubmaker to reference an RSSR if the golfer being fit owns clubs listed in the charts.

Find the frequency of the club in the left hand column. Find the torque of the shaft in the club at the top of the chart. Referencing the two measurements across and down the chart will reveal the estimated swing speed of the shaft in the club (the RSSR rating).

RSSR Swing Speed Table – Driver (43.5"/D1)

Frequency	Torsional Stiffness (T°)										
	2.0°	2.5	3.0	3.5	4.0	4.5	5.0	5.5	6.0	6.5	7.0
200cpm	60	59	57	55	53	51	50	49	48	47	47
205	61	60	59	57	55	53	51	50	49	48	48
210	63	62	61	59	57	55	53	52	51	50	50
215	66	65	63	61	59	57	55	54	53	52	52
220	70	69	67	65	62	60	58	56	55	54	54
225	74	73	71	69	66	63	61	59	58	57	57
230	78	77	75	72	69	66	64	63	61	60	60
235	83	82	79	76	73	71	69	68	66	65	64
240	87	86	83	80	77	75	73	72	70	69	68
245	91	89	86	84	82	79	77	75	73	72	72
250	94	92	89	86	83	81	79	78	77	76	76
255	97	95	92	89	86	84	83	82	81	80	80
260	101	100	97	93	90	88	87	86	85	84	84
265	104	103	100	97	95	93	92	91	90	89	89
270	107	106	104	101	99	97	96	95	94	93	93
275	110	109	106	104	102	101	100	99	98	97	97
280	113	112	109	107	105	104	103	102	101	100	100
285	116	115	112	110	108	107	106	105	104	103	103
290	119	118	116	114	112	110	109	108	107	106	106
295	121	120	118	116	114	112	111	110	109	108	108
300	123	121	119	117	115	114	113	112	112	111	110

RSSR Swing Speed Table – 5-Iron (38"/D1)

Frequency	Torsional Stiffness (T°)									
	1.5°	2.0	2.5	3.0	3.5	4.0	4.5	5.0	5.5	6.0
240cpm	56	53	50	47	45	43	41	41	40	40
245	56	53	50	47	45	43	41	41	40	40
250	57	54	51	49	47	45	43	43	42	42
255	58	55	52	50	48	46	45	45	44	44
260	60	57	54	52	50	48	47	47	46	46
265	62	59	56	54	52	50	49	49	48	48
270	64	61	58	56	54	52	51	51	50	50
275	66	63	60	58	56	54	53	53	52	52
280	68	65	62	60	58	56	55	55	54	54
285	70	67	64	62	60	58	57	57	56	56
290	72	69	66	64	62	60	59	59	58	58
295	74	71	68	66	64	62	61	61	60	60
300	76	73	71	69	67	65	64	64	63	63
305	78	75	73	71	69	68	67	67	66	66
310	80	77	75	73	72	71	70	70	69	69
315	83	80	78	76	75	74	73	73	72	72
320	85	82	80	78	77	76	76	76	75	75
325	88	85	83	81	80	79	79	79	78	78
330	91	88	86	85	84	83	82	82	81	81
335	94	92	90	88	87	86	85	85	84	84
340	96	94	93	91	90	89	88	88	87	86
345	98	96	94	93	92	91	90	90	89	88
350	100	99	97	95	93	92	91	91	90	90

Note: for both driver and 5-iron RSSR calculation charts, frequency is measured by clamping 5 inches of the grip end of the club, with a 50g grip (men's flexes) or 47g grip (L flex) installed.

Procedure for determining the RSSR for any shaft using shaft frequency analyzer and torque rating ($$$):

STEP 1 — Obtain a frequency reading for the driver and 5-iron in the golfer's current set. Be sure to clamp 5" of the grip in the frequency machine so the measurement is compatible in the manner the charts for calculating the RSSR were created.

STEP 2 — Measure, reference or search out the approximate torque for the shaft in the golfer's current driver and 5-iron. For R, S, and X flex steel shafts, use an approximate torque of 2.5° for the driver shafts and 2.0° for the 5-iron shaft. For L and A flex steel shafts, use an approximate torque of 3° for the driver shaft and 2.5° for the 5-iron shaft. If the shafts in the golfer's current driver and 5-iron are graphite, an approximate torque will have to be found by measuring the torque on a torque machine, by referring to the torque listings in a shaft/component company catalog (or by calling Golfsmith Technical service for the information).

STEP 3 — If the golfer's current driver and 5-iron have a different length and swingweight than the standards upon which the swing speed tables were created, re-calculate the frequency for the clubs based on a simple math conversion technique. The standards for which the RSSR entries in the tables were created are:

For A, R, S and X flex shafts:	**For L flex shafts:**
driver - 43.5"/D1	driver - 42.5"/C6
5-iron - 38"/D1	5-iron - 37"/C6

Any driver or 5-iron that is different from the above specifications for length and swingweight will require converting back to these above standards using simple math before using the RSSR tables. Follow these conversion factors and instructions to learn how to convert the golfer's existing driver and 5-iron length/swingweight specifications back to the standards used for creating the tables.

Conversion factors:

+1/2" = -3.5cpm
- 1/2" = +3.5cpm
+1/2" = +3 swingweight points
- 1/2" = -3 swingweight points
+1" = +0.25° Torque (approximately)
-1" = -0.25° Torque (approximately)
+1 swingweight point = -1cpm
- 1 swingweight point = +1cpm

First, determine the effect a change in length back to the standard has on the swingweight and frequency, using the conversion factors listed above. The clubmaker must then complete the conversion by determining the final adjusted frequency after converting the swingweight.

Example 1:

Golfer's current driver -	44.5"/D8/R-Flex/249cpm/4.8°
Convert to -	43.5"/D1 and determine the CPM to use the tables.
Current driver -	44.5" / D8 / 249cpm / 4.8°
Change length and solve for 43.5" -	43.5" / _?_ / _?_ cpm / _?_ torque
	43.5" / D2 / 256cpm / 4.5° torque

Shortening to 43.5" is a decrease of 1" in length. That will decrease the swingweight by 6 points (1/2" = 3 points), lower the torque by @0.5°, and increase the frequency by 7cpm.

	43.5" / D2 / 256cpm/4.5° torque
Change swingweight and solve for D1 -	43.5" / D1 / _?_ cpm
	43.5" / D1 / 257cpm

Decreasing the swingweight from D2 to D1 will increase the frequency by 1cpm.

Remember, you must convert drivers to 43.5"/D1 to use the RSSR tables.

Therefore, the clubmaker would use the 257cpm/4.5° entry on the RSSR swing speed tables to obtain the correct mph rating (RSSR) for the golfer's 44.5"/D8/R-Flex/249cpm driver.

Example 2:

Golfer's current 5-iron -	37.5"/D0/S-Flex/310cpm/2°
Convert to -	38"/D1 and determine the CPM to be able to use the tables.
Current 5-iron -	37.5"/D0/310cpm/2°
Change length and solve for 38" -	38" / _?_ / _?_ cpm/ _?_ °
	38" / D3 / 306.5cpm/2.10°

Lengthening to 38" is an increase of 0.5" in length. That will increase the swingweight by 3 points (1/2" = 3 points), increase torque by @0.25°, and decrease the frequency by 3.5cpm.

	38" / D3 / 306.5cpm / 2..10°
Change swingweight and solve for D1 -	38" / D1 / _?_ cpm
	38" / D1 / 308.5cpm

Decreasing the swingweight from D3 to D1 will increase the frequency by 2cpm.

Remember, you must convert 5-irons to 38"/D1 to use the RSSR tables.

Therefore, the clubmaker would use the 308cpm/2.25° entry on the RSSR swing speed tables to obtain the correct mph rating (RSSR) for the golfer's 37.5"/D0/S-Flex/310cpm driver.

Example 3:

Golfer's current driver -	45"/D2/S-Flex/251cpm/4°
Convert To -	43.5"/D1 and determine the CPM to use the tables.
Current driver -	45"/D2/251cpm/4°
Change length and solve for 43.5" -	43.5" / _?_ / _?_ cpm/ _?_ °
	43.5" / C3 / 261.5cpm/3.7°

Shortening to 43.5" is a decrease of 1.5" in length which will decrease the swingweight by 9 points (1/2" = 3 points) and will increase the frequency by 10.5cpm.

	43.5" / C3 / 261.5cpm / 3.7°
Change swingweight & Solve for D1 -	43.5" / D1 / _?_ cpm
	43.5" / D1 / 254.5cpm

Increasing the swingweight from C3 to D1 will lower the frequency by 7cpm..

Therefore, the clubmaker would use the 254cpm/3.7° entry on the RSSR swing speed tables to obtain the correct mph rating (RSSR) for the golfer's 45"/D2/S-Flex/251cpm driver.

Note: torque values rounded down to tenth of degree in all calculations.

Fast Fact:

    The optional importance of measuring the shafts in the golfer's current driver and 5-iron is not to note the deflection or frequency, but to convert the frequency along with an approximation of the torque into an RSSR (swing speed rating) for the shafts being used. When the RSSR of the golfer's current woods and irons is compared with the golfer's actual driver and 5-iron swing speed, it is then possible to discover if the current shafts are too stiff, too flexible or a good match. Remember, compare the driver only to a driver clubhead speed as well as the 5-iron measurements only for the 5-iron clubhead speed. Do not try to fit the iron shafts using only a wood shaft swing speed. Wood shaft flex and iron shaft flex are fit as if they are completely separate from each other.

    Be aware that tempo/downswing acceleration also have a bearing on whether the current shafts fit the golfer. If the golfer has a very fast tempo or is quick in the transition from backswing to downswing, it will be OK for the RSSR of the current shafts to be as much as 10mph higher than the golfer's actual clubhead speed. On the other hand, if the golfer has a very slow or smooth tempo or a definite pause in the transition from backswing to downswing, it will be OK for the RSSR of his/her current shafts to be as much as 10mph lower than their actual clubhead speed. In general, it is better for the RSSR of the current shafts for an average-to-higher handicap golfer to be lower than the golfer's actual swing speed. (More will be covered on tempo and downswing acceleration during the shaft fitting instruction in Chapter 7 - The Final Fitting Procedures.)

XI. MEASURING SHAFT TORQUE

Importance of Measuring Shaft Torque in the Equipment Evaluation:

    <u>When performing the Equipment Evaluation, it is not necessary to measure torque as long as the RSSR of the current shafts can be evaluated.</u> (Review the preceeding Shaft Flex section in this chapter before this section.) It is more important to know how torque combines with flex to determine RSSR of the shafts than it is to evaluate the torque as an individual fitting factor.

Tools required:

Golfsmith Catalog or suitable reference book($)

Shaft Torque Measuring Machine ($$$)

    The main contribution of torque in the fitting process is how it combines with the shaft flex (frequency) to determine the overall stiffness of the shaft. It is more important to know how torque interacts with frequency in determining the RSSR (Recommended Shaft Speed Rating) of the golfer's driver and 5-iron shafts (3-wood in lieu of driver) than it is to view torque as an independent fitting factor for the golfer.

    After evaluating the RSSR of the current set and the swing speeds of the golfer's driver and 5-iron, the only reason to evaluate the golfer's current torque is to see if it is too high for the golfer's tempo and downswing acceleration. This would be if the golfer has a high swing speed, fast tempo and strong downswing acceleration, and the shafts are higher than 6° in torque. (If the RSSR of the current set is matched well to the golfer's swing speed, the torque cannot be too low because it is a part of the RSSR.)

Procedure for measuring shaft torque using the Golfsmith Catalog or Golfsmith Practical Fitting Book ($):

The shaft section of each Golfsmith catalog provides the torque of each available shaft. If the golfer is using a shaft listed in one of the clubmaker's published resources, it will not be necessary to actually measure the torque.

However, if the golfer's current set is built with a shaft not listed in the Golfsmith catalog or any other printed resource, the only way to determine the shaft torque will be to call Golfsmith or to use a torque machine.

Procedure for measuring shaft torque using torque measurement device ($$$):

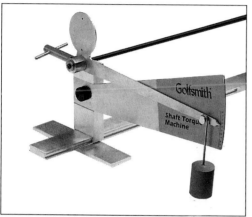

STEP 1 — Clamp the grip end of the shaft in the butt clamp of the machine. To conform with anticipated ASTM standards, 5" of the butt of the bare shaft must be clamped. (In the case of a finished club, the grip and grip tape must be removed before the torque can be measured.)

STEP 2 — Install the tip clamp 1.5" up from the tip of the shaft. Hang the 1-lb. weight from the torque arm that extends 12" out from the tip end of the shaft.

STEP 3 — The torque can be read in degrees of rotation on the shaft. If desired, the shaft can be tested in the opposite direction of rotation and the two readings can be averaged.

Torsional stiffness measuring machines are available to clubmakers for an affordable price and can measure the torque of any golf shaft accurately.

Standard shaft torque specifications:

There are no standard specifications for torque. Torque is a shaft design specification created by the shaft manufacturer to match the intended playing characteristics of the shaft.

Because torque is part of determining the RSSR for the current shafts, the torque must be estimated at a minimum, or the RSSR of the shafts cannot be pinpointed. Because it is not practical for the majority of clubmakers to own a torque machine, the best way to determine shaft torque in the golfer's current set is by looking up the torque in a component company catalog or another printed resource, or by calling Golfsmith and making an inquiry for the torque of the shaft(s) in question. Keep in mind that among steel shafts, the torque will not vary by more than a degree or so. Average torque cannot be approximated for graphite shafts because of its wide range in composite shaft designs. However, the average torque for steel shafts is as follows:

L - flex steel woods - 3.2°	L-flex steel irons - 2.5°
A - flex steel woods - 2.9°	A-flex steel irons - 2.3°
R - flex steel woods - 2.7°	R-flex steel irons - 2.1°
S - flex steel woods - 2.5°	S-flex steel irons - 2.0°
X - flex steel woods - 2.3°	X-flex steel irons - 1.8°

Fast Fact:

It is important to know the shaft torque in the golfer's current set of woods and irons only as a factor in the calculation of their RSSR (Recommended Shaft Speed Rating). If the torque of the golfer's current shafts can be found listed in the shaft section of a component company catalog, in another printed reference, or by contacting a knowledgeable resource, the torque for the golfer's shafts can be obtained. Once the torque of a shaft is known, it can be combined with the shaft's frequency to determine the RSSR of the shaft using the tables found in the Shaft Flex section of this chapter.

Other than the contribution of torque to shaft flex, the other reason to estimate the torque of the current shafts is to determine if it may be too high for the golfer and thus a partial contributor to problems indicated by the golfer including Accuracy, or a shaft Feel that is too limber in the tip half of the shaft. The only way this can happen is if a high swing speed golfer (+100mph) also with a fast tempo <u>and</u> strong downswing acceleration is using shafts with a torque greater than 6° or 7°.

While it might be suggested that it is more important to find out if a slow swinging player is using shafts with too low of torque, keep this logical point in mind – As long as the RSSR (swing speed rating) of the golfer's current shafts is equal to or less than the golfer's swing speed, the torque cannot be too low for the golfer. This is because the RSSR incorporates the torque in its determination of overall shaft stiffness.

If the RSSR is matched to the golfer's swing speed and the torque is as low as 2°, the only way the RSSR could be equal or greater than the golfer's swing speed is if the frequency of the shaft is very low. In such a case, the low frequency would offset the stiffening effect of the low torque to make the overall shaft fit well to the golfer.

XII. MEASURING SHAFT BEND POINT

Importance of Measuring Shaft Bend Point in the Equipment Evaluation:

<u>When performing the Equipment Evaluation, it is not necessary to know the bend point of the shafts in the golfer's current set. It is only important to know what bend point the golfer needs in future clubs</u>. This decision will be based on the golfer's desire or need for a particular Feel in the new shafts.

A low bend point is for golfers who want to Feel the clubhead more in the swing, who complain about a lack of a solid Feel at impact, or who have no preference or cognition of the Feel of the shaft during the swing. A mid or high bend point is for the golfer who actually requests a firm Feel at impact or who possesses strong downswing acceleration. The Golfsmith Practical Fitting Program believes there is so little difference in performance between a mid and high bend point shaft that they could be classified the same in terms of performance. Bend point should be considered only for Feel purposes.

Tools required:
Golfsmith Catalog or other published references ($)
Shaft bend point measuring machine ($$$)

Procedure for determining shaft bend point using Golfsmith Catalog or other published references ($):

In the shaft section of each Golfsmith catalog is a description of the bend point for each family of shafts available. In addition, the RSSR x Shaft Weight tables found in the supplement to this book also lists the bend point for each of the shafts. If the golfer is using a shaft that is listed in one of the clubmaker's published sources, it will not be necessary to attempt to measure or probe further for the bend point determination.

However, because bend point is not listed in terms of an actual location on the shaft in inches from the tip of butt, it is hard to guarantee that the written descriptions of Low, Mid or High bend point will be comparable to each other. For example, the low bend point from True Temper steel shafts is often in the same position on the shaft as the high bend point of Apollo's steel shafts. This is a case of different internal company standards that clubmakers have no control.

However, if the golfer's current set is built with a shaft that has a bend point not listed in the Golfsmith catalog, this book or in any of it future supplements, the only way to determine the bend point of the shaft will be to call Golfsmith Technical Service.

Courtesy: Grafalloy Shaft Corporation

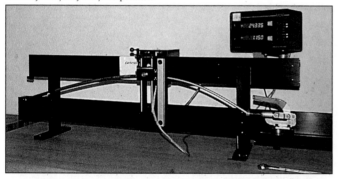

Bend point is a specification that attempts to identify the location of the shaft's maximum point of deflection when subjected to a cantilever force. At best, the measurement is suspect as a fitting specification because the shaft is never subjected to this type of force application during the golf swing.

Procedure for measuring shaft bend point using bend point measurement device ($$$):

Currently, there are no devices for measuring bend point commercially available to clubmakers. Shaft companies manufacture their own machine for determining the bend point of their shafts. Because of that, it is not practical to tell clubmakers they have the ability to actually measure the bend point of shafts. As a result, the only way to determine the bend point of the shafts in a golfer's current set is to find a written or published description for the bend point of shafts.

It is not possible for any person to determine the bend point of a shaft by simply applying a bending force on the shaft and looking at the shaft with the naked eye. The author has seen individuals who claim they can determine bend point by pushing down on the grip shaft and watching the shaft bend in response to the force applied. This is nonsense and any clubmaker who encounters such a display of ignorance should not believe any information coming from this individual.

Standard shaft bend point specifications:

There are no standard specifications for bend point. While bend point can be measured with custom made machinery, at the time of this book's publication, not enough bend point measurements have been made to determine any type of average or standard.

Fast Fact:
    Knowing the bend point of the shafts in a golfer's current set can determine if the specification may be the cause of a lack of clubhead Feel or a lack of a solid Feel at impact. However, from a truly practical sense, it is not necessary to know the bend point a golfer has been using. It is only important that the clubmaker know enough about bend point to know how to choose the bend point that would help alleviate problems such as lack of clubhead Feel or solid Feel at impact for the golfer. From that standpoint, it is only important the clubmaker has a reference source to find the bend point of the shaft(s) being considered for use by the golfer. Again, clubmakers are always urged to call Golfsmith for such information whenever needed.

XIII. MEASURING SHAFT BALANCE POINT

Importance of Measuring Shaft Bend Point in the Equipment Evaluation:

    When performing the Equipment Evaluation, it is not necessary to know the balance point of the shafts in the golfer's current set because the shaft balance point has very little effect on the fitting recommendation of the shaft. (Not to be confused with the golf club's balance point.)

Tools required:

Index finger ($)!

Shaft balance point measuring device ($$$)

Procedure for determining shaft balance point using index finger or shaft balance point measurement device ($) ($$$):

    The easiest and fastest way to measure balance point is to simply balance the shaft horizontally on your index finger. Measure the distance from the butt or tip of the shaft to the point of balance on the shaft.

    While at the time of publication there are no mechanical devices available for measuring shaft balance point, any object the shaft can be horizontally balanced on can be used, along with a 48" ruler for making the actual measurement of the shaft's balance point.

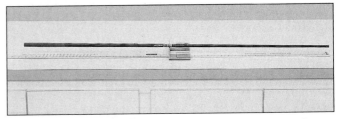

Any object on which the shaft can balance can be used to determine the balance point of the shaft.

    However, this discussion concerns the shaft's balance point and not the golf club balance point. (See XIX. Measuring Golf Club Balance Point in this chapter) Therefore, to measure shaft balance point of the golfer's current set would require removing the grip, grip tape and clubhead, an exercise not worth the effort considering the information revealed.

Standard shaft bend point specifications

    There are no standard specifications for shaft balance point. While the majority of shafts are manufactured with a mid shaft balance point, there are many produced with the balance point on the tip or butt side of the shaft center. There is no reason to standardize shaft balance point because it is simply a part of the shaft design.

Fast Fact:

The balance point of a shaft is the point on the shaft (not the assembled club) where it can be balanced horizontally. In short, it is the center of gravity of the shaft. From a practical sense, it is not necessary to know the balance point of the shafts used in the golfer's current set.

If the clubmaker considers making a new set with low balance points in the finished clubs, it should be known that a low balance point shaft will not ensure the finished club will have a low balance point. This is because a shaft with a lower balance point requires less head weight to achieve a normal to higher range swingweight. Increasing the head weight is one important way to create a lower balance point on a finished club. The fact that a low shaft balance point means less headweight also means a low balance point shaft is not likely to yield a finished club with as low of a balance point as a mid-balance point shaft. As a result, low balance point shafts are not really related to low balance point golf clubs.

MEASURING THE SPECIFICATIONS OF THE GRIP
XIV. MEASURING THE GRIP
MEASURING GRIP SIZE

Importance of Measuring Grip Size in the Equipment Evaluation:

When performing the Equipment Evaluation, it is not necessary to measure grip size of the golfer's current set because a grip sizing device or actual grip size samples will be used to determine the new grip size. It is only necessary to measure the golfer's existing grip size if the golfer declares that the size on the new set "needs to be the exact size of my old grips".

It is also unnecessary to measure the 6" diameter of any grip, unless the golfer indicates that they have a special grip size that may be customized for the lower hand as well.

Tools required for measuring grip size:

Grip size gauges ($)

Calipers and grip size references($$)

Procedure for using grip size gauges to measure grip size:

There are a number of different grip size gauges available for measuring grip size. The most common gauges are made with a series of different size openings that check the grip for a specific diameter at a point 2" down from the edge of the grip cap. This gauge is used to measure the diameter at the top half of the grip for fitting the golfer's upper hand on the grip.

In addition, there is also a grip size gauge for measuring the diameter of the bottom half of the grip at a point 6" down from the edge of the grip cap. With these two gauges, clubmakers have the opportunity to check for a series of different diameters on the grip as it would be felt by both hands.

| 6" |
| 2" |

upper hand measurement

lower hand measurement

STEP 1 — Starting with the Standard size cut-out on the upper hand grip gauge, slide the opening onto the front of the grip, starting at the bottom of the grip. (Never try to

The designations in this illustration show the position of measurement for upper and lower hand positions for grips.

measure grip size from the side of the grip. The presence of a "rib" on the back side of many grips will confuse the measurement.) Move the gauge up the grip until both sides of the gauge opening just begin to rub against the sides of the grip.

STEP 2 — Mark the point on the grip that the gauge begins to experience the slightest amount of friction. Measure the distance from this point to

the edge of the grip cap. If this distance is 2" when tested with the standard size cutout on the gauge, the grip is standard size. If the distance is greater than 2", the grip is larger than standard and the test should be repeated with successively larger openings on the gauge until one is found that touches the sides of the grip at a point 2" down from the edge of the grip cap is found.

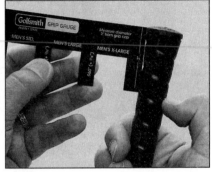

One at a time, the different grip gauge openings are slid up the <u>front</u> of the grip to determine the point where the grip touches the sides of the gauge.

The gauge opening that touches both sides of the grip at a point 2" down from the edge of the grip cap identifies the size of the grip

If the distance from the edge of the grip cap and the gauge's point of contact with both sides of the grip is less than 2", the grip is smaller than standard and the gauge sizing test should be repeated with successively smaller openings on the gauge until one is found that touches the sides of the grip at a point 2" down from the edge of the grip cap.

NOTE: The top edge of most grip gauges is made to be 2" long so it can be used as a ruler to measure the required 2" down from the edge of the grip end cap.

Procedure for using calipers to measure grip size ($$):

STEP 1 — Open the calipers to a distance of 2" to find the point on the grip 2" down from the edge of the grip cap. Mark this point with the thumb, a piece of tape, or the eye.

STEP 2 — Use the calipers to record the diameter of the grip at this point, measuring the grip from side to side, not from front to back. Do not pinch the grip between the jaws of the calipers; the diameter is found when the calipers just begin to touch both sides of the grip.

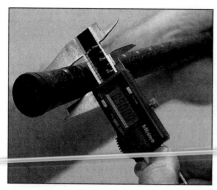 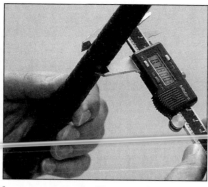

STEP 3 — Compare the diameter reading obtained with the calipers to the decimal equivalent sizes listed in the Standard grip size specifications table following this section of the chapter to determine the grip size.

STEP 4 — If desired, the lower hand grip size can be determined following the same procedures listed, but taken at a point 6" down from the edge of the grip cap. This size can also be identified by comparing the reading of the calipers to the standard size table that follows.

The most professional way to measure the common grip diameter is to use calipers and reference the measurement to the chart for standard size specifications in this section. If desired, measurements can be made at the 2" (above) and 6" (below) positions on the grip to note the sizes of the grip in both hands.

Standard grip size specifications

The size specifications for men's and ladies' grips are listed in the following chart. The sizes represent actual diameters at the point down from the edge of the grip cap listed in ( ) following the diameter.

Designated Size	Men's Grips	Ladies' Grips
-1/64" undersize	.885" (2")	.835" (2")
	.765" (6")	.705" (6")
Standard	.900" (2")	.850" (2")
	.780" (6")	.720" (6")
+1/64" oversize	.915" (2")	.865" (2")
	.795" (6")	.735" (6")
+1/32" oversize	.930" (2")	.880" (2")
	.810" (6")	.750" (6")
+3/64" oversize	.945" (2")	.895" (2")
	.825" (6")	.765" (6")
+1/16" oversize	.960" (2")	.910" (2")
	.840" (6")	.780" (6")

Fast Fact:

Grip size can be measured as the diameter of the grip at two different points along the grip, 2" and 6" down from the edge of the grip cap. It is not important to measure the golfer's existing grip size because the method of fitting grip size for the new clubs does not require any prior knowledge of the previous grip size. (See the Grip Size Fitting section of Chapter 7 - The Final Procedures for Fitting for a complete description of the methods for fitting grips.)

XIV. MEASURING THE GRIP
NOTING GRIP TYPE

Importance of Grip Type in the Equipment Evaluation:

It is not important to note the type of grip the golfer is currently using unless the golfer requests the same type or model of grip on the new clubs. In that case, the clubmaker would want to take a few seconds and identify the type and brand of the grip for future use. It is only necessary to be aware of different types of grips as well as having samples of the different types for the golfer to make a fresh decision.

Tools required:

None

Procedure for identifying grip type:

There is no measurement procedure for identifying the type of grip the golfer has been using other than looking at the old grips. The different types of grips currently available are:

1. Natural rubber compounds
   E.G. - Golf Pride Victory, Avon Nexus, Lamkin Sure Tac, etc.
2. Leather
   E.G. - R. Neumann or Lamkin leather wraps
3. Thermoplastic
   E.G. - Tacki Mac grips
4. EPDM
   E.G. - Royal grips, Griptec grips, Golf Pride Tour Wrap
5. Synthetic leather
   E.G. - Winn wrap-on grips

Standard specifications for grip type

There are no standard specifications for the type of grip. However, there are trends that may be popular at the time of the fitting session the clubmaker may wish to inform the golfer. At the time of publication, the popular grip types were EPDM and thermoplastic grips because of their tackiness and feel.

XV. MEASURING GRIP WEIGHT

Importance of grip weight in the Equipment Evaluation

It is not important to determine the weight of the golfer's current grips because in the process of determining the total weight, swingweight and grip size of the new club(s), the clubmaker will decide the grip weight as well. In short, it is only necessary for the clubmaker to know the swingweight and shaft weight that will be recommended before deciding on the weight of the grip on the new clubs.

For example, if the clubmaker is thinking about making the new club(s) to a normal swingweight range with a very light graphite shaft, low balance point, or total weight as light as possible, each of these conditions would be easier to achieve through the use of a lighter grip. To contrast, none of these conditions would require the clubmaker to know the weight of the grips on the golfer's previous set.

Tools required:

Gram weight scale + /-1g ($$)

Procedure for measuring grip weight ($$):

There is no method for measuring the weight of a grip installed on the golfer's current clubs without removing the grip. Only if the golfer's current clubs are extremely light in total weight, could it be deduced with any certainty that the grips are lighter than normal. (See IX. Shaft Weight in this chapter for guidelines in identifying the grip weight.)

Standard specifications of grip weight:

There are no standard specifications for the weight of a grip. This is because there are many different compounds of materials used in the making of various grip models that can bring about different weights in grips produced to the same size. In addition, most grips are produced in different core sizes to accommodate the different size shaft butt diameters in use. As the core size of the grip changes, so too will the weight of the grip even though the outside diameter remains the same.

Those conditions being understood, the <u>average</u> weight for a .580" core men's grip is 50g, while the <u>average</u> for a .560" core ladies size grip is 45g.

At the time of publication, many grip companies had begun to create lighter weight grips in an effort to help clubmakers build golf clubs with even lighter total weights. While many of these first generation light weight grips currently average 38-39g for a men's size grip, work continues on behalf of many companies to produce lighter and lighter grips with an eye toward manufacturing grips as light as 10-15g.

Grip Weight Size	Weight Range	Average
LIGHTWEIGHT	Men's 35g - 45g	38g
STANDARD	Men's 46g - 52g	50g
HEAVYWEIGHT	Men's 53g - up	65g
LIGHTWEIGHT	Ladies 32g - 42g	35g
STANDARD	Ladies 43g - 49g	45g
HEAVYWEIGHT	Ladies 50g - up	60g

Fast Fact:

While grip weight can be measured by removing and weighing one of the grips from the golfer's current clubs, it is not necessary for the clubmaker to do so as part of the Equipment Evaluation. All that is required for the clubmaker is knowing the proper time when to use a light or heavy grip to achieve a specific total weight, golf club balance point or swingweight on the new clubs.

MEASURING THE SPECIFICATIONS OF THE FINISHED GOLF CLUB
XVI. MEASURING LENGTH

Importance of Measuring Length in the Equipment Evaluation:

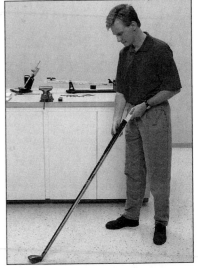

It is important to measure the length of the driver, 5-iron, putter and all wedges in the golfer's current set. From the driver and 5-iron it will be possible to quickly note the length of the set, assuming the incremental change from club to club is the normal 1/2" standard among the adjacent irons and 1" between the 1, 3, 5, 7 woods. Because the wedges and putter are so often individually chosen by the golfer, it is very important to note their lengths and check with the golfer to see if any oddities in their lengths, compared to the 9-iron, exist intentionally or by mistake.

In addition, it is important to note the incremental change in length between the woods and irons. This can be done quickly by arranging the woods and irons next to each other and visually identifying if the incremental change from club to club is the same or if it varies. If the incremental change from club to club is not the usual 1/2" standard, the clubmaker must ask the golfer if this is a specification that is intentional (and must be followed on the new set) or, in the case the golfer is not aware of the variation, if it is simply a mistake in the building of the set. For example, it is possible that a person might have their woods cut in 3/4" increments from the driver to the 3, 5, and 7 woods, or the irons cut in 3/8" increments between each club. If so, this would need to be noted to prevent a mistake from being made in creating the lengths of the new set.

Taking care to hold the club in the proper lie position with the center of the sole touching the ground, the length is measured with the 48" ruler from the floor to the edge of the grip cap.

Tools required:

48" clubmaking ruler ($)

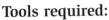

Procedure for measuring the length of woods, irons and wedges with the 48" clubmaking ruler ($):

STEP 1 — Hold the club with the center of the sole from toe to heel touching the floor, in the correct lie angle position.

STEP 2 — Slide the 48" clubmaking ruler up behind the back of the shaft so the flat measuring side of the ruler touches the back of the grip, the back of the shaft and the back of the hosel. The 0" end of the ruler is touching the floor below the heel of the clubhead.

STEP 3 — Read the length in inches to the edge of the grip cap.

Procedure for measuring the length of putters with the 48" clubmaking ruler ($):

STEP 1 — Hold the putter with the center of the sole from toe to heel touching the floor, in the correct lie angle position.

STEP 2 — Position the 48" clubmaking ruler to touch the side of the shaft and the side of the hosel. The 0" end of the ruler is touching the floor below the hosel of the putter.

STEP 3 — Read the length in inches to the edge of the grip cap.

Because most putters have a substantial portion of the clubhead protruding behind the shaft, it is necessary to position the ruler to touch the side of the shaft and the hosel to obtain an accurate reading of the length.

Standard specifications for length:

In the 1990s, many golf club manufacturers began to increase their existing standards for club length. As a result, no particular overall standard exists within the golf equipment industry for club length. However, there is a traditional standard for length that existed prior to the 1990s. For purposes of making comparisons to traditional length only, as well as noting the average length being followed in the equipment industry at the time of publication, this chart of men's and ladies' traditional standard length dimensions is offered.

Club	Men's Traditional Length	Men's Average Length (1996)
1-wood	43″	44″
2-wood	42.5″	43.5″
3-wood	42″	43″
4-wood	41.5″	42.5″
5-wood	41″	42″
6-wood	40.5″	41.5″
7-wood	40″	41″
9-wood	39″	40″
11-wood	38.5″	39″
13-wood	38″	38.5″
15-wood	37.5″	38″

Club	Men's Traditional Length	Men's Average Length (1996)
1-iron	39.5″	40″
2-iron	39″	39.5″
3-iron	38.5″	39″
4-iron	38″	38.5″
5-iron	37.5″	38″
6-iron	37″	37.5″
7-iron	36.5″	37″
8-iron	36″	36.5″
9-iron	35.5″	36″
PW	35.5″	36″
SW	35.5″	36″

Club	Ladies' Traditional Length	Ladies' Average Length (1996)
1-wood	42″	43″
2-wood	41.5″	42.5″
3-wood	41″	42″
4-wood	40.5″	41.5″
5-wood	40″	41″
6-wood	39.5″	40.5″
7-wood	39″	40″
9-wood	38″	39″
11-wood	37.5″	38″
13-wood	37″	37.5″
15-wood	36.5″	37″

Club	Ladies' Traditional Length	Ladies' Average Length (1996)
2-iron	38″	38.5″
3-iron	37.5″	38″
4-iron	37″	37.5″
5-iron	36.5″	37″
6-iron	36″	36.5″
7-iron	35.5″	36″
8-iron	35″	35.5″
9-iron	34.5″	35″
PW	34.5″	35″
SW	34.5″	35″

Fast Fact:
Length is measured fastest and most efficiently by building the club with the center of the sole touching the floor, and using a 48" clubmaking ruler to measure up the back of the shaft, from the floor to the edge of the grip cap. Because so many putter heads are designed with a substantial portion of the heel protruding behind the shaft, it can be difficult obtaining an accurate length measurement on putters. This 48" ruler can also measure the length of any putter by manipulating it so the ruler remains parallel to the entire shaft from floor to the edge of the grip cap.

Knowing the length of the golfer's existing clubs is important in the Equipment Evaluation phase of the Practical Fitting Program. However, to save time, it is not necessary to measure the length of every club in the set, but only the driver, 5-iron, wedges and putter. In addition, it is helpful to line up the woods and irons side by side to note any oddities in the incremental changes in length from club to club. Any variations or unusual findings should be discussed with the golfer to find if they are by intention or are a mistake in the building of the previous set.

XVII. MEASURING SWINGWEIGHT

Importance of Measuring Swingweight in the Equipment Evaluation:

It is important to have a general idea of the average or most predominant swingweight in the golfer's existing set of clubs. (Due to variations in equipment quality, swingweight can vary in a set.) To save time in the equipment evaluation, it is not necessary to measure the swingweight of each golf club, but at least two of the woods and two or three of the irons. From those measurements, the clubmaker can gain a clear picture of the set swingweight and whether the set was built to a reasonable degree of accuracy with regard to it.

From a fitting recommendation standpoint, the only reason to know swingweight of a golfer's current set is if the person prefers this same particular headweight **Feel**, in which the clubmaker would want to use that measurement as a possible starting guideline for the new set. Otherwise, the clubmaker will select a swingweight for the new set based on the feedback received from the player interview questions dealing with **Feel**.

Tools required:

14" fulcrum swingweight scale ($$)

Note: It is possible to use the total weight and balance point of a golf club to calculate swingweight, but since clubmakers are advised to possess a swingweight scale to accurately assemble clubs, it is not worth the time or effort to learn this total weight/balance point system of swingweight determination.

Procedure for measuring swingweight using a 14" fulcrum swingweight scale ($$):

STEP 1 — Set the swingweight scale on a level surface. If the scale has a self-leveling feature, take the time to level the scale itself.

STEP 2 — Place the grip end under the end of the scale and rest the shaft in the shaft holding fixture on the forward end with the toe of the club pointing down. Make sure the end of the grip is pushed up against the end of the scale.

STEP 3 — Move the weight to whatever posi-

The 14" fulcrum prorhythmic swingweight scale is the most widely used scale for measuring standard swingweight in the clubmaking industry.

tion that will cause the scale to move into equilibrium. The mark on the slide weight will point to the letter/number swingweight designation.

Standard specifications for swingweight:

There is no recognized standard specification for swingweight of a golf club. However, the informal standard has been a swingweight reading of D1 for men's average length golf clubs and C6 for ladies. In addition, most sand wedges have been traditionally built to swingweights much higher than the informal standard for golf clubs. In general, the average swingweight for a men's sand wedge has been D7.

> **Fast Fact:**
> Every clubmaker must have a 14" swingweight scale in the shop. It is not possible to perform accurate clubmaking or club repair without one. Therefore, measuring the swingweight of the clubs in the golfer's current set is a simple matter of measuring a few of the clubs to get a general idea of what the swingweight averages in the woods and irons. It is not necessary to measure the swingweight of all the clubs during this part of the Equipment Evaluation, but only enough to give the clubmaker a clear idea of what the predominant swingweight may be.
>
> The swingweight in the new set will only be copied from the old set if the player indicates a preference for that clubhead feel and the same approximate length and shaft weight are being used in the new set. However, if the clubmaker is contemplating a change of shaft weight/total weight in the range of 20g or more, and/or a length change of more than 1/4", a new swingweight should be recommended on the basis of those changes.

XVIII. MEASURING TOTAL WEIGHT

Importance of Total Weight in the Equipment Evaluation:

It is very important to know the total weight of a golfer's current driver and/or 5-iron or it will be impossible for the clubmaker to know how much potential help can be given to the golfer in search of more distance and swing comfort. To avoid wasting time, if the woods are all made with the same shaft, it is only necessary to measure the total weight of the driver to obtain enough information and help make accurate fitting decisions. Likewise, if the irons are all made with the same shaft, it is only necessary to measure the total weight of the 5-iron.

The main reason for measuring the total weight of the driver and 5-iron is to know how much the shaft and grip weight might need to be changed in the new clubs to effectively make a difference that will help increase swing speed and distance. For most golfers, the total weight has to be decreased by at least 1.5oz before a noticeable increase in distance can be realized. (To translate total weight measurements into shaft weight estimates, see the chart in the Shaft Weight section of this chapter.)

Tools required:

Swingweight scale that measures total weight ($$)

Gram weight scale +/-1g ($$)

Procedure for measuring total weight with a swingweight scale ($$):

STEP 1 — Most of the 14" swingweight scales available to clubmakers can also measure total weight within +/-5g, which is close enough to make accurate fitting decisions. Level the scale and place the golf club on the total weight holding fixture that is generally found on the front half of the balance arm. Adjust the club so it rests horizontally on the scale.

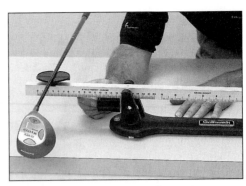

Virtually all 14" swingweight scales are designed to measure the total weight of the golf club in either grams or ounces. For fitting decision making it is usually easier to refer to total weight in ounces.

STEP 2 — Move the slide weight toward the front of the scale where the total weight can be measured in either grams or ounces. Position the weight so the scale arm achieves equilibrium. Note the total weight in ounces at this point.

Procedure for measuring total weight using a gram weight scale ($$):

STEP 1 — If the clubmaking shop has a gram weight scale, it will be more accurate to use this tool to measure the total weight of the golf club. Zero the scale (manually or electronically, depending on the type of scale) and lie the club on top of the plate until it rests without moving.

If the shop has a gram weight scale, it will be more accurate to use for measuring the total weight of the club. Remember to convert the total weight measurement in grams to ounces by dividing grams by 28.35.

STEP 2 — If the scale is electronic, read the total weight in grams directly from the display. If the scale is manual, move the slide weights until the point of equilibrium is found, then note the weight of the club in grams.

STEP 3 — Convert the gram measurement of the total weight to ounces by dividing the grams by 28.35. For purposes of making total weight comparisons, ounce measurements are more generally used.

Standard specifications for total weight:

Because total weight is dependent on shaft weight and shaft weight has decreased so much since the popularity of graphite in the late 1980s, average total weights for clubs in a set have decreased as well. In addition, the 1990s have also brought the development of the lightweight grip, an achievement that is moderately affecting the total weight of the golf club.

Prior to these developments, there was a time when a chart of standard total weights could have been established for each club. However, this chart was based using only 125g steel shafts with 50g+ grips.

So clubmakers have a measure of comparison, the following chart of total weights is offered. The chart lists average total weight for each club based on three different shaft weights, 120-gram steel or heavy graphite, 90-gram conventional graphite or very light steel, and 60-gram ultralight graphite.

Chart of Average Golf Club Total Weight based on Different Shaft Weights

Club	Based on 120g shaft	Based on 90g shaft	Based on 60g shaft
1-wood	13 1/8oz	12 1/16oz	11oz
2-wood	13 3/8oz	12 5/16oz	11 1/4oz
3-wood	13 5/8oz	12 9/16oz	11 1/2oz
4-wood	13 7/8oz	12 13/16oz	11 3/4oz
5-wood	14 1/8oz	13 1/16oz	12oz
6-wood	14 3/8oz	13 5/16oz	12 1/4oz
7-wood	14 5/8oz	13 9/16oz	12 1/2oz
9-wood	14 7/8oz	13 13/16oz	12 3/4oz
11-wood	15 1/8oz	14 1/16oz	13oz
13-wood	15 3/8oz	14 5/16oz	13 1/4oz
15-wood	15 5/8oz	14 9/16oz	13 1/2oz
1-iron	14 5/8oz	13 9/16oz	12 1/2oz
2-iron	14 7/8oz	13 13/16oz	12 3/4oz
3-iron	15 1/8oz	14 1/16oz	13oz
4-iron	15 3/8oz	14 5/16oz	13 1/4oz
5-iron	15 5/8oz	14 9/16oz	13 1/2oz
6-iron	15 7/8oz	14 13/16oz	13 3/4oz
7-iron	16 1/8oz	15 1/16oz	14oz
8-iron	16 3/8oz	15 5/16oz	14 1/4oz
9-iron	16 5/8oz	15 9/16oz	14 1/2oz
PW	16 5/8oz	15 9/16oz	14 1/2oz
SW	17 1/8oz*	16 1/16oz*	15oz*

* Based on swingweight increasing to D7. SW's are traditionally built to a much higher swingweight than the rest of the irons, so the total weight will reflect a greater incremental increase from the PW.

Note: Above chart based on traditional length with 50g grip weight. If grip weight is decreased and headweight left constant, the total weight values in all columns will decrease by approximately 7/16oz (12g) based on using 38g grip.

Additional Note: For ladies average total weights, subtract 1/4oz from each entry in the chart. This reflects a change of 1" in length and a decrease of 5g from the grip weight. If swingweight is within normal ladies range, head weight in a ladies set is the same as in a men's length set.

Fast Fact:

Total weight is a very important specification to measure in the golfer's existing set because it is a MAJOR factor of Distance. Because so many golfers are in search of more distance, the clubmaker has to know the total weight of the old set in order to determine how much the new shaft has to weigh before providing the golfer with a real chance of gaining more yards.

Total weight has to be decreased by a minimum of 1.5oz before the swing speed can be increased enough to yield a noticeable increase in distance. Unless the clubmaker knows the precise total weight of the current clubs, it will be difficult to comprehend the amount of total weight decrease that will be possible with the new shaft selection for the golfer.

Total weight can easily be measured using a swingweight scale with a total weight fixture attached, or a gram weight scale. In terms of total weight measurements for drivers, 13oz. is considered heavy, 11oz. is considered light. For a driver total weight to be 11oz., the shaft cannot weigh more than 60g (based on a 50g traditional grip weight). To make total weight (and shaft or grip weight) decisions, the only clubs the clubmaker must measure are the total weight of the golfer's driver and 5-iron. As long as the new set is built to a matched swingweight and 1/2" incremental changes in length throughout the set, the rest of the clubs will fall into a proper sequence of total weight.

XIX. MEASURING GOLF CLUB BALANCE POINT

Importance of Measuring Balance Point in the Equipment Evaluation:

It is not important for the clubmaker to measure the balance point of the golfer's existing clubs unless the golfer really likes the particular clubhead feel of the current club(s) and wants to have this duplicated in the new club(s). However, in that case, because balance point is controlled mainly by length, shaft weight, grip weight and swingweight, the chances are likely to duplicate a balance point will require duplicating the club. Still, it is possible to shift from one shaft to a totally different shaft design of the same weight and retain the same balance point, to allow the golfer to try a different shaft feel with the same type of swing feel.

Balance point is not that important in the equipment evaluation, but it can be in the recommendation of the fitting specifications for new clubs. Be aware that to achieve a specific balance point in the new clubs, it is not necessary to know what the balance point was in the old clubs.

Tools required:
Index finger or small piece of angle iron ($)
Balance point scale ($$)

Procedure for measuring golf club balance point with index finger or small piece of angle iron ($):

STEP 1 — The simplest way to measure balance point is positioning the club so it rests horizontally on some object. That object can be anything such as an index finger or a small piece of angle iron.

STEP 2 — Mark or note the exact position of balance on the shaft. Measure the distance from the edge of the grip cap to the balance point in inches.

Procedure for measuring golf club balance point with balance point scale ($$):

At the time of publication, devices that could accurately measure the balance point of a finished golf club were in the

Finding the balance point of the golf club can be very simple. However, the smaller the object the club is balanced on, the more accurate the measurement.

development stage. Because balance point is becoming more and more important as a way to estimate clubhead feel, clubmakers can expect devices to be available so such measurements can be made.

Standard specifications of golf club balance point:

There are no set of standard specifications for balance point because it is dependent on shaft weight, grip weight, head weight and club length.

As a point of reference so that other golf club balance point measurements may be compared, the following chart lists a series of balance point measurements for different drivers and 5-irons.

Average Balance Point Locations for Assembled Golf Clubs					
Club	Shaft Weight	Length	Swingweight/ Grip Weight	Balance Point From Grip	From Sole
1-wood	125g	43.5″	D1/50g	30 1/2″	12 1/2″
1-wood	90g	43.5″	D1/50g	32″	11 1/2″
1-wood	60g	43.5″	D1/50g	34″	10″
5-iron	125g	38″	D1/50g	28 3/4″	9 1/4″
5-iron	90g	38″	D1/50g	29 1/2″	8 1/2″
5-iron	60g	38″	D1/50g	30 1/4″	7 3/4″

Fast Fact:

The balance point of the finished golf club is becoming a more important specification to be aware of in building new clubs. It is controlled by length, swingweight, grip weight and shaft weight. Many golfers are discovering a golf club can yield more favorable clubhead Feel and even more Distance if the balance point is farther from the hands. However, because shaft weight is a big contributor to the actual balance point location, clubmakers must never Feel they can duplicate an actual balance point location when a switch is made from steel to graphite, or vice versa.

The balance point of a golf club can easily be measured by resting the club horizontally on almost any small object and measuring the distance from the edge of the grip cap to the club's point of balance.

XX. MEASURING SET MAKEUP

Importance of Measuring the Set Makeup in the Equipment Evaluation:

Noting the golfer's current set makeup is one of the most important parts of the Equipment Evaluation. If the golfer has indicated on the Player Interview form that there are clubs that are hit well, the clubmaker must decide if the distances those clubs represent are needed in the new set. The most common situation in set makeup analysis is to encounter a golfer with a set of three woods and eight irons who hits the fairway woods and short irons well but cannot hit the driver, 3-iron and 4-iron very well in addition to not having a very good short game.

In this case, the information from the Player Interview about which clubs are hit well and which are not from the Player Interview would tell the club-maker that a higher lofted driver and a #7- and 9-wood should replace the driver plus the 3- and 4-irons, and additional wedges or wedges with different sole width and sole angle should be recommended. Of course other variations in set makeup can be recommended as guided by the Player Interview information.

Tools required:

Common sense

Procedure for measuring the set makeup:

The only procedure for measuring set makeup of a golfer's current clubs is to note what clubs are in the bag and relate that observation to the information about what clubs the golfer hits well and poorly, in addition to the longest iron and wood the golfer hits well as described in the Player Interview. The idea is then to replace the clubs that are not hit well with clubs not in the current set that will perform the same function from a **Distance** standpoint.

Standard specifications for set makeup:

While there are no standard specifications for set makeup, it is a fact that most sets are sold in a very usual combination of 1, 3, 5 woods with 3, 4, 5, 6, 7, 8, 9, PW, SW and putter. Observing this type of set makeup in the golfer's current set is an indication the golfer has probably not given any thought to using other clubs that might perform better. On the other hand, if the golfer is using a set that is made up of a complement of clubs that are quite different, it is an indication the golfer has been experimenting with clubs to replace the other clubs they don't hit well, or they are consciously trying to use clubs to help make the most out of their ability for the type of course they play.

> **Fast Fact:**
> Noting the set makeup of the golfer's current set is one of the most important parts of the entire Equipment Evaluation because the clubmaker must always be conscious of replacing hard to hit clubs with clubs that will hit the ball the same Distances which are easier to hit. The most common replacements are: a change from the standard driver to a driver with a lighter, more flexible shaft and greater loft; to get rid of long irons and replace them with higher lofted fairway woods; to add wedges eliminating any gaps in yardage close to the green; and to change to a sand wedge with a swingweight, sole width and sole angle that make it easier to get the ball closer to the hole from the sand.

QUICK REFERENCE FOR PERFORMING THE EQUIPMENT EVALUATION FOR THE GOLFSMITH PRACTICAL FITTING PROGRAM

I. LOFT

√ It is only necessary to measure the loft of the player's current driver, 5-wood, 5-iron, 7-iron and wedges.

II. LIE

√ It is not necessary to measure the lie angle of any of the existing clubs, unless the golfer indicates the current lie and length of the set are exactly what is wanted in the specifications of the new set.

III. FACE ANGLE

√ It is important to measure the face angle of the player's current driver or tee shot club, if not a driver.

IV. CLUBHEAD DESIGN - Center of Gravity and Weight Distribution

√ It is important to perform a visual inspection of the woods and irons to see if the current heads have a relatively low center of gravity or not, and whether they are perimeter weighted or not.

V. HORIZONTAL BULGE

√ It is not necessary to measure the exact inches of bulge on old woods.

VI. VERTICAL ROLL

√ It is not necessary to measure the exact inches of roll on old woods.

VII. Part I - SOLE ANGLE

√ It is not necessary for the clubmaker to note the sole angle of the existing #1 — 9 irons because the player's current sole angles usually have little relevance to what is used in the future. However, it is important to perform a visual inspection of the new iron heads to see if they have a scoop, square or bounce sole.

VII. Part II - SOLE RADIUS

√ It is not necessary to measure either the toe/heel or the front/back sole radius of the existing irons. It is important for the clubmaker to look at the sole radius of the new clubheads to determine if the clubhead has no radius, a little or a lot.

VIII. Part I - HOSEL OFFSET of the Irons
√ It is not important to measure the exact amount of hosel offset on the player's existing irons to make a recommendation for the new set. Only if the player indicates a desire to keep the same amount of offset on the new set of irons would the clubmaker have to inspect the old set for the type of, and amount of hosel offset.

IX. SHAFT WEIGHT
√ Shaft weight is determined by recording the total weight and comparing the measurements to a chart (see below). It is important to measure the total weight of a golfer's current driver and 5-iron to determine the shaft weight.

X. SHAFT FLEX
√ It is only necessary to measure the exact flex or know the RSSR of the shafts in the player's current set if the player indicates a desire to have the same shaft (if no identification exists on the shaft), or the same stiffness **Feel** in the new set. If the shafts in the player's current set are not to be duplicated in the new set, it is not necessary to measure the flex or calculate the RSSR of the previous shafts.

XI. SHAFT TORQUE
√ It is not necessary to reference or measure torque of shafts in the new set unless the player indicates they want the same shaft (if no identification exists on the shaft), or the same stiffness **Feel** in the new shafts. If the shafts in the player's current set are not to be duplicated in the new set, it is not necessary to determine the torque of the previous shafts.

XII. SHAFT BEND POINT
√ It is not necessary to know the bend point of the shafts in the new set unless the player indicates they want the same shaft or the same **Feel** in the new shafts. If the shafts in the player's current set are not to be duplicated in the new set, it is not necessary to measure or try to determine the bend point of the previous shafts.

XIII. SHAFT BALANCE POINT
√ As with all of other shaft specifications, it is only necessary to know the balance point of the shafts in the new set if the player indicates they want the same shaft in the new clubs.

XIV. Part I - GRIP SIZE
√ It is not necessary to measure the size of the grips in the old set unless the player indicates they want the same exact size grips in the new set.

XIV. Part II - GRIP TYPE
√ If the player wants the same type of grips as installed on the current set, the clubmaker should look at the grip on the golfer's favorite club and note the brand and style.

XV. GRIP WEIGHT
√ While grip weight can be measured by removing and weighing one of the grips from the golfer's current clubs, it is not necessary for the clubmaker to calculate the grip weight.

XVI. LENGTH
√ It is important to measure the length of the driver, 5-iron, putter and all wedges in the golfer's current set.

XVII. SWINGWEIGHT
√ It is only necessary to measure the swingweight of at least two of the woods and at least two or three of the irons. From a fitting recommendation standpoint, the only importance of knowing the swingweight on the golfer's current set is if the person prefers a particular head weight **Feel**, in which case the clubmaker would want to use the measurement as a possible starting guideline in the new set.

XVIII. TOTAL WEIGHT
√ It is only necessary to measure total weight of the golfer's current driver and 5-iron. However, if the golfer has been using a different shaft in the driver compared to the fairway woods, and wants this to be the same in the new set, the clubmaker will need to measure the 3-wood in addition to the driver.

XIX. GOLF CLUB BALANCE POINT
√ It is not important for the clubmaker to measure the balance point of the golfer's existing clubs unless the golfer indicates a desire to keep the particular clubhead **Feel** of the current club by duplicating it in the new set or clubs. Be aware that to establish a particular balance point in the new clubs, it is not necessary to know what it was in the old clubs.

XX. SET MAKEUP
√ Noting the golfer's current set makeup is one of the most important parts of the Equipment Evaluation. Comparing the information in the Player Interview about longest wood/iron hit well in addition to the least and most favorite clubs are a starting point for ideas about possible changes in set makeup.

Chapter Five

THE GOLF SWING AS IT RELATES TO THE FITTING DECISIONS

LEARNING THE KEY MOVEMENTS IN THE GOLF SWING THAT INDICATE PARTICULAR CLUBFITTING REQUIREMENTS

> **NOTE FOR CHAPTER FIVE:** An optional part of the Practical Fitting Program is to observe the golfer's swing to observe motions which indicate a need or a strong tendency toward a particular specification(s) on the new club(s). This chapter is offered as a brief guide to certain movements in the golf swing which can send a message to the clubmaker as to whether a particular change in the golf clubs may or may not be required to bring about improvement. It is certainly not a required part of the Practical Fitting Program and is only offered as additional information for the club-maker who wishes to broaden his/her education to learn as much as possible about whether a change in golf equipment will bring about a change in the game. If you feel this is an aspect of clubfitting is not applicable nor appropriate to your approach to fitting, you are urged to skip ahead to Chapter 6 where you will learn how to combine the information obtained from both the Player Interview and the Equipment Evaluation to compile the Preliminary Fitting Recommendation.

INTRODUCTION

This optional segment of the Golfsmith Practical Fitting Program involves learning different movements in the golf swing and translating those movements into fitting decisions. For example, the input obtained from a golfer during the Player Interview is intended to be the primary guide for helping the clubmaker identify the specifications on the new set of clubs that need to be customized in order for the player to achieve his/her playing goals. In addition it can be helpful to observe the golfer to see the actual swing movements to develop the confidence to make the fitting recommendations you have envisioned and *know* whether the changes will make a difference in helping the golfer improve through a change in equipment.

When learning how the mechanics of the golf swing affect the fitting recommendations, the clubmaker must first accept one very important point about the golf swing and how it reacts with a set of golf clubs...

The golf swing has the ability to overcome any change the club-maker can create through a change in the golf clubs.

The best way to explain the humbling importance of this statement is to create the following example. There is no doubt that one of the most powerful specifications the clubmaker has at his/her disposal in trying to create a real improvement in shotmaking is the face angle of the woods. If the face angle of the golfer's current set of woods is altered by more than 2°, it is safe to say that 99 percent of the time the golfer will notice some change in shot direction after just 3 to 5 shots. It could be actually said that face angle may very well be the single most dramatic specification because its effect can be noticed sooner by the golfer than any other specification change.

Despite the fact face angle is such an important specification, there are golfers who regularly hit the ball so far off-line that the maximum change in face angle available on a wood head will have little corrective effect. What's more, even if a new face angle specification has successfully resulted in a significant improvement in a golfer, it is entirely possible that the player can unleash an occasional swing which is so bad that the newly corrected face angle cannot prevent the shot from going out of play.

Therefore, it is important the clubmaker realize even the most accurate fitting prescription cannot work miracles for players with extremely poor swing mechanics or for players who lack at least a minimum level of swing consistency and swing repeatability. In fact, the more repeatable the swing, no matter how high the handicap, the more the clubmaker can assure a change in shotmaking will occur from a change in specifications. It is the very inconsistent golfer that poses the greatest problem to the clubmaker in terms of trying to provide some type of permanent change or improvement to their game.

This is not to say that fitting cannot help the majority of players. On the contrary, the higher the handicap of the player, the more certain it is that changes in different golf club specifications will create a noticeable level of game improvement. Because one of the goals of the Golfsmith Practical Fitting Program is to be practical and uncomplicated, it is extremely important for the clubmaker to determine how much help any particular change in the specifications can provide the player. In some cases, if the swing mechanics are very poor and/or inconsistent, the club-maker may need to diplomatically inform the player that it may not be possible to achieve a certain playing goal because of the limitations imposed by the swing. This is one reason why it is helpful to know the effect some of the movements of the golf swing have on the possible changes in the golf club specifications.

If the clubmaker believes that the recommended changes in the golf club(s) might not bring about the desired changes in shotmaking, the clubmaker might inform the player that the custom fitted clubs may need to be accompanied by a swing change before the desired playing goals can be achieved. Therefore, the purpose of this chapter is to help the clubmaker learn more about the golf swing and some of its mechanics, not only to identify limitations of the fitting, but to also determine if a particular golf club change is required and whether it has the chance to truly help the player.

As a final word before learning some of the mechanics of the golf swing, there is a "chicken or egg" relationship between clubfitting and lessons that troubles many clubmakers – should the clubmaker fit the specifications of the clubs to correct the swing as it is? Or, should the clubmaker tell the golfer to take lessons before performing the fitting?

Part of the answer to this question was covered in Chapter 3 during the discussion pertaining to the Player Information segment of the Player Interview. If the player is taking lessons, the clubmaker has to determine if the player has the commitment to actually make the swing change(s) before deciding the final recommendation for the fitting specifications.

In the case of the golfer who is demonstrating such a severe problem with the swing to the point there is doubt the fitting specifications could be of real help, the clubmaker might want to recommend the player take lessons in order to fully benefit from the changes being made in the golf clubs. If so, and if the golfer is going to take lessons while the custom clubs are being made, how should the clubmaker determine what the specifications should be?

In the case of the golfer who is already taking lessons, the determination is a little more clear. Remember, in Chapter 3 the Golfsmith Practical Fitting Program teaches if the player is taking lessons, and has the commitment to see the lessons through to a positive change in the swing, the clubmaker should fit the clubs for what the golfer's playing ability will be after the swing changes become a permanent part of their game. However, if the clubmaker determines the player's commitment to the lessons are such that the swing changes are not likely to come about, then the clubs should be fit to address the current needs of the player.

At best, these are philosophical points about the clubmaker's overall approach to the fitting session, but points that can allow you to become an expert clubmaker offering the best possible service along with the best possible fitting assistance. To learn enough about the golf swing, its mechanics, and help make better fitting decisions for the player, The Golfsmith Practical Fitting Program recommends the clubmaker take some time learning the following parts of the swing and how they relate to some of the specifications that are a key part of the clubfitting process.

Fast Fact:
There is no doubt the key to playing good golf is to develop the most sound swing fundamentals possible. There is no such thing as a good golfer with very poor swing movements, no matter how good the set of clubs. Some changes in golf club specifications will not elicit their desired effect on shotmaking if the swing movements are very poor.

One of the requirements of a good clubfitter is to predict how the changes in the golf club specifications are going to affect the flight of the ball. If the clubmaker knows absolutely nothing about the golf swing and what swing movements are related to the fitting specifications, it becomes very difficult to predict what a change in any specification will do to the flight of the ball.

For this reason, it is very helpful for the clubmaker to add to his/her full education in clubfitting by learning about some of the golf swing movements and the clubfitting specifications they affect.

MOVEMENTS IN THE GOLF SWING AND THEIR RELATIONSHIP TO THE FITTING SPECIFICATIONS

I. ADDRESS POSITION AND SET UP TO THE BALL
A. The Grip

The grip is one of the most important parts of the swing to consistently hit the ball with **Accuracy**. However, the grip is <u>not</u> the most common reason for misdirectional problems. The swing path and delivery of the clubface into the impact area (face angle) have more of an effect on **Accuracy** than the grip. Still, many golfers hit the ball off-line because of a poor grip. Poor **Accuracy** with a good grip will likely indicate that the swing path and face angle are more the cause of the **Accuracy** problem. On the other hand, poor **Accuracy** with a poor grip might indicate that the swing path and face angle might not be as much of the cause of the **Accuracy** as previously thought. With this knowledge, in addition to an advised grip change, the clubmaker might not advise as much a change in face angle or other specifications which affect **Accuracy**.

It should not be the role of the clubmaker to change a player's grip unless the clubmaker is also a qualified teacher. However, if the clubmaker has the ability to recognize whether a portion of the player's **Accuracy** problems result from the grip, awareness of the grip can be helpful when it comes to recommending the degree of the changes in specifications that have an effect on **Accuracy**.

 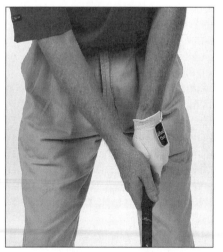 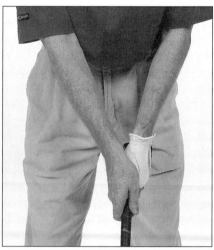

"Strong" Grip. The V's between the thumb and index finger are pointing well to the right of the chin (RH player) or well to the left of the chin (LH player)

'Normal' Grip. The V's between the thumb and index finger are pointing between the chin and the right shoulder (RH player) or between the chin and the left shoulder (LH player).

'Weak' Grip. The V's between the thumb and index finger are pointing straight up at the chin or even to the left of the chin (RH player) or just to the right of the chin (LH player).

Study the illustrated examples of the grip. If the clubmaker observes a player with a very "strong" grip, there is a pretty good chance the player will pull or hook the ball. Therefore, if the player has this type of grip, the clubmaker is advised to think in terms of a more open face angle. If the player has a very "weak" grip, there is a likelihood the player will slice the ball, necessitating the move to a more closed face angle.

However, it should be recognized that grip is not the best swing indicator for face angle because it is entirely possible to slice the ball with a "strong" grip when the club is swung on an outside to inside swing path, just as it is possible to hook the ball with a "weak" grip when the club is swung on an inside to outside path.

Fast Fact:
The grip is a primary key to Accuracy in the swing because it helps determine the angle of the clubface at impact. The grip is not as much a contributor to Accuracy as is the swing path, but it is still very important. If the clubmaker notices from the Player Interview that the golfer wants to hit the ball with better Accuracy but later observes the player has a poor grip, the clubmaker may want to counsel the player and determine if a grip change could be made along with changes in specifications that have a MAJOR or MEDIUM effect on Accuracy.

However, if the golfer is comfortable with the grip, has no plans to take lessons, does not play or practice very much and is not very athletic or physically coordinated, the clubmaker must address the changes for Accuracy strictly in the club specifications.

B. Gripping the Club in the Fingers as Opposed to Gripping More in the Palm

Gripping the club in the palm of the hand. This type of grip will make the grip sizing method result in a grip size that might be too large.

Gripping the club in the fingers will allow the traditional method of grip fitting to work properly. If the player is gripping the club in the palm, the clubmaker will need to adjust the grip in his/her hands to this finger gripping position.

The traditional method for determining the proper size of the grip is to ask the golfer to hold, in succession, a series of different grip size samples. Clubmakers have then been taught to choose the grip with a slight clearance between the fingertips and heel of the upper hand (the left hand for a right-handed player and the right hand for a left-handed golfer).

In theory, this system works well, <u>if the golfer grips the samples in the fingers and not the palm</u>. After observing the different ways that golfers hold the club, it becomes obvious that some people grip the club in the fingers while many hold the grip in the palm. When the golfer grips the club in the palm, the traditional method of size fitting by noting the distance of the fingertips to the heel of the hand will not yield the same result as a grip held in the fingers.

To ensure an accurate fit, the clubmaker must first observe if the golfer normally holds the club in the fingers or the palm. If the golfer grips the club in the palm, the clubmaker could ask the player to temporarily grip the club in the fingers for the purpose of performing the fitting only. By doing this, the golfer is not being asked to permanently change his/her grip, but only change the way they hold the club during the grip size fitting session.

Fast Fact:
Fitting the proper grip size is important to assure the golfer has a comfortable hold on the club. The traditional method of fitting grip size only works if the golfer grips the club in the fingers and not the palm. Therefore, if the golfer holds the club in the palm the clubmaker must move the grip into the fingers before using the traditional grip fitting method of noting distance from the fingertips to the heel on the upper hand.

This requires the clubmaker to initially observe whether the golfer's normal grip is held in the fingers or the palm. If the golfer is asked to simply pick up a club and make a few practice swings, the clubmaker can quickly make this observation.

C. Ball Position at Address

One of the most important points the clubmaker should note is where the golfer positions the ball in their stance. In most cases, the farther forward the ball in the stance, the higher the **Trajectory**, while the farther the ball is back in the stance, the lower the **Trajectory**.

Therefore, if the golfer wants a change in **Trajectory**, the ball position has to be identified before advising a change in loft or center of gravity. For example, if the player wants to hit the ball lower, all of the fitting changes that might decrease **Trajectory** will not be successful if the golfer already plays the ball considerably forward in the stance. In the same light, making fitting changes that enable the player to hit the ball higher will be all but impossible if the ball is played well back of the normal position for that club in the stance.

Increasing the **Trajectory** of a shot through a change in equipment without sacrificing **Distance** is very difficult. In the Golfsmith Practical Fitting Program, the only **MAJOR** factor that affects **Trajectory** is the loft of the clubhead. However, because loft is also a **MAJOR** factor of **Distance**, any change in loft for the purpose of altering **Trajectory** will also change **Distance**.

For the player who wants to change **Trajectory** but uses a ball position in opposition to the desired **Trajectory** change, the clubmaker must identify this dilemma to the

With the ball farther up in the stance it is harder for any change in the loft or other specifications to lower the shot trajectory.

With the ball farther back in the stance it is harder for changes in the loft or other specifications to increase the shot trajectory.

With the ball farther up in the stance it is harder for changes in loft or other specifications to lower the shot trajectory.

With the ball farther back in the stance it is harder for changes loft or other specifications to increase the shot trajectory golfer. From that observation, it is then the player's decision to determine if making a ball position change can be done without disrupting some other aspect of their shotmaking.

Fast Fact:

The ball position in the stance is a key swing point that has a definite effect on shot Trajectory. Therefore, if the golfer wants to make a change in shot Trajectory, the ball position must be identified before making any change in golf club specifications.

Making a real change in shot trajectory through a change in fitting specifications is very difficult to do because the only specification with a MAJOR effect on shot height also has a MAJOR effect on shot Distance. If the golfer wants to hit the ball higher and is not willing to accept the loss in Distance that is likely to result from the change(loft), the ball position must then be addressed. If the golfer wants to hit the ball lower, the recommendation of less loft will probably not bring about the desired decrease in Trajectory unless the ball position is moved at the same time.

The 'classic' address position with a straight line from the shoulder to the clubhead. While there is no assurance of the proper action, this position can encourage golfers to keep the hands low on the takeaway and in front of the ball at impact.

A 'break' in the straight line from the shoulder to the clubhead at the hands. While there is no assurance of the improper action, this position can cause some golfers to 'pick the club up' too soon on the takeaway and to allow the clubhead to pass the hands prior to impact, possibly causing a variety of poor shots such as topped, thin, fat, pulled, hooked or heeled.

E. Forward Arm and Hand Position at Address with the Ball

Many teachers profess that the golfer should set up to the ball with a straight line from the top of the forward shoulder, through the hands, the shaft, and all the way down to the ball. (In the right-handed golfer, this would be an imaginary straight line from the top of the left shoulder down the club to the ball.) The idea behind this "perfect" setup is to make it easier to retain the same position of straight left arm, hands and shaft through impact with the ball. This, in turn, helps ensure that the hands lead the clubhead through the ball, causing the clubhead to hit properly down and through the ball, thus getting the ball airborne.

When the straight line "breaks" at the hands, the result is a clubhead that could pass the hands before impact and result in less favorable type of shots, including topping the ball or hitting a pull-hook. While no human can actually see if the hands remain in front of the ball through impact, the flight of the ball can act as an indicator of such a swing error. If the golfer tops the ball, hits the ball thin, pulls the ball, hooks the ball or hits the ball severely on the heel of the clubface, it can be an indication that the clubhead passed the hands prior to impact.

During takeaway (moving the club the first 2-3 feet away from the ball), retaining a straight line from the front shoulder to the clubhead can encourage the golfer to take the club back in "one-piece," thus avoiding the problem of "picking the club up" and "breaking the wrists" too soon. Like all swing moves that are less than perfect, picking the club up too soon on the backswing can cause a number of different types of mishits ranging from topped to fat shots.

If the clubmaker believes that the golfer is having a problem retaining the straight line from the top of the lead shoulder down to the clubhead during takeaway, as well as recovering this straight line through impact, it can be an indication to try a slightly longer club length, a heavier swingweight or a larger grip size.

Fast Fact:
It is an ideal situation if the swing of the club comes into impact with the forward shoulder, arm and club all in a straight line. It is a common swing fault for many golfers to not achieve this impact position because they hinge the wrists too soon during the takeaway instead of sweeping the club away from the ball, thus retaining the straight line from the top of the forward shoulder down to the clubhead.

This is not to say it is impossible to hit the ball well with an early wrist break. Some golfers who pick the club up too soon instead of sweeping it back with the clubhead low to the ground can make an unconscious correction on the downswing to get back to the desired straight forward arm and club position at impact. An early wrist break only becomes a problem if this movement causes the clubhead to pass in front of the hands or stay well behind the hands before impact.

However, if the golfer complains of topping the ball, hitting the ball thin, hitting the ground behind the ball, pulling the ball or hitting the ball on the heel side of the clubface, the clubmaker should observe if the golfer is setting up to the ball with a straight line formed from the top of the forward shoulder all the way down to the clubhead. This straight-line position can help prevent an early wrist break, as can a slightly longer club length, slightly higher swingweight and/or a slightly larger grip size.

II. THE BACKSWING
A. Tempo of the Backswing

How fast is fast in the golf swing? This is a difficult question to answer unless the clubmaker has had a chance to observe many different golfers hitting shots. Clubmakers who do not have the confidence to make a decision regarding what is a fast tempo compared to a smooth, slower tempo should go to a busy driving range to study and compare as many different swings as possible. After a while, it will become apparent even to a higher handicap clubmaker just what constitutes a fast versus a slower swing tempo.

The tempo of the backswing can have a bearing on the length, total weight and swingweight of the clubs. When the clubmaker determines a golfer's backswing tempo is too fast and might be causing certain shotmaking problems such as hitting the ball fat, thin, off-line in either direction, or unsolid, the first specifications to consider for a change in tempo are total weight and swingweight.

Obviously, it makes sense that a higher total weight can help a player slow the swing. But because heavy total weight is not recommended for the vast majority of players due to its negative effect on swing speed and overall swing timing, the clubmaker should first consider advising a light total weight with a slightly higher than normal swingweight to see if the "head heavy" nature of the club might make it easier for the golfer to slow down the backswing.

Increasing the swingweight on its own can be effective as long as the total weight does not become too high or is not too high in the beginning. For most average-to-less-able players, a good rule is for clubs made with a shaft weight under 90g, an increase of at least 3 swingweight points over normal steel shaft swingweight levels can bring about enough of a "head heavy" **Feel** to make it slightly easier to slow the backswing. Only in the case of a very strong player with a fast tempo should the option of increasing total weight be considered, but only after trying an increase in swingweight by itself.

For a better-than-average player, a fast backswing tempo can also be controlled by an increase in length accompanied by a higher-than-normal swingweight. However, as with all situations of length increase, this should only be considered if the player demonstrates the ability to hit the longer club on-center. A length change that also incorporates a decrease in swingweight from using a lighter head is not advised for fast backswing tempo players because the decrease in head weight usually has the effect of offsetting the tempo moderating influence of the greater length.

Fast Fact:
    If the golfer has a fast backswing, the primary reason is because the golfer is very strong or possesses a faster natural sense of rhythm. Simply advising this type of golfer to just "slow it down" is extremely difficult because the tempo is so much of an "inherent" trait. When the clubmaker is working with a golfer that possesses a fast backswing, several changes in the golf club such as an increase in swingweight, decrease in total weight accompanied by an increase in swingweight or possibly an increase in club length, can help the golfer make it slightly easier to "slow it down."

B. The Swing Plane

The plane of the swing is the position of the club and the angle of the shoulders compared to the ground. A flat swing plane appears to the observer as if the club is being swung "around" the player on the backswing. At the end of the backswing on a flat swing plane, the clubhead will be much closer to the ground than the golfer swinging on an upright plane. In addition, an upright swing plane will make the observer sense that the club is moving to the top on a much steeper angle to the ground.

A final point of reference to identify a flat versus upright swing plane is watching the position of the hands at the end of the backswing. The closer the hands are to the ground at the top of the backswing, the flatter the swing plane; the higher the hands are from the ground at the top of the backswing, the more upright the swing plane. Additionally, the farther the golfer stands from the ball, the more tendency there will be to swing on a flatter plane, while the closer the player stands to the ball, the more likely the golfer will have an upright swing plane.

The Flat swing plane. Hands are 'lower', closer the ground as the club is swung more around the body with the hands either even with, or below the shoulder.

The Normal swing plane. Hands are closer to being directly over the shoulder as the club is swung to the top.

The Upright swing plane. Hands are 'higher, further away from the ground as the club is swung up into position between the shoulder and the head.

Swing plane is a part of the swing that can help verify decisions made about lie and sometimes, club length. As an obvious point, the more upright the swing plane, the more likely the lie angle of the clubs will need to be upright; the flatter the swing plane, the more flat the lie of the clubs.

It is not possible from observing the swing plane to determine how many degrees upright or flat the lie of the clubs should be. That is the role of the dynamic lie fitting procedure or the lie detector fitting device, both of which will be outlined in detail in Chapter 7.

If the player is contemplating a length increase, the clubmaker must first consider the key points of athletic ability, ball-striking ability and tempo, along with physical size to determine if the longer clubs might disrupt swing timing and tempo so much that it causes the golfer to hit the ball off center.

Swing plane is another point that can help the clubmaker decide if the length increase can be successfully accomplished. Among two people of the same height, the golfer with a flatter swing plane will have an easier time accommodating an increase in length. This does not mean all golfers with a flat swing plane need longer clubs. However, if a golfer wants to increase **Distance** or complains of feeling uncomfortable in the address position with their current club length and is only average to slightly less-than-average in ball-striking ability, a flatter swing plane could indicate to the clubmaker that a length increase might have a slightly better chance of being successful.

At the same time, some clubmakers and swing teachers believe a player with an upright swing plane needs a longer club while a golfer with a flat swing plane needs a shorter club. This is a myth that has been created because so many tall people swing upright and many short people swing flat.

Think of the situation this way – if two players are 6'3" tall, possess only average athletic ability and are about to increase the length of the clubs the same amount, the player with the flatter swing plane would likely have a slightly easier time making the adjustment to the new length.

This is because longer clubs automatically force the swing into a flatter plane. Therefore, the golfer who swings on a flatter plane to begin with will have less of a plane change to adjust to when using longer clubs.

> **Fast Fact:**
> One of the main differences from one swing to another is the swing plane, or whether the golfer swings the club on an upright, normal or flat angle to the ground. To the clubmaker, an upright swing plane usually indicates the need for an upright lie angle on the clubs, just as a flat swing plane indicates a necessity for a flatter lie angle. However, lie angle must be determined by one of the two dynamic lie fitting methods and should not be determined solely by observing the swing plane.
> While it is true that most tall golfers swing the club on a more upright plane than shorter players, the swing plane cannot be an indicator on its own for recommending the proper length for a golfer. The swing plane can, however, help provide the clubmaker with an idea of how easy or difficult it may be for the golfer to accommodate the length change.
> While player comfort and athletic ability are the primary determinants of length, a flatter swing plane can make it easier for the golfer to accommodate a length increase because a longer club forces the golfer to swing flatter at the ball. This is not to say that a golfer with an upright plane cannot effectively swing a longer club. It only means a player with the upright swing should also have adequate athletic ability or be tall enough to make the length increase comfortable.

C. Position of the Clubface at the Top of the Backswing

By learning to identify whether the face of a club is open, square or closed at the top of the backswing, it is possible for the clubmaker to predict how well a change in face angle will work in correcting **Accuracy** problems. However, this is only one of the various swing movements that can indicate a need for a face angle change in the woods.

While almost anything can happen in the golf swing, for most players, a clubface closed at the top of the backswing will result in the player hooking or pulling the ball, while an open face at the top will result in a push or a slice. In the end, the clubmaker's most important point to identify for recommending face angle is the flight of the ball itself. An obvious fitting point: the more the ball is pushed or sliced, the more closed the face angle will need to be and the more the ball is pulled or hooked, the more open the face angle.

To identify the face position at the top of the backswing requires a quick eye, but with a little experience, it is relatively easy to make this evaluation. At the very end of the backswing, just before the club begins its path down to impact, the clubmaker needs to focus on the position of the toe or face of the clubhead with respect to the ground.

If the toe of the club is pointing down at a slight angle to the ground, the clubface is considered to be square. If the toe of the club is pointing straight toward the ground, the face is open. If the clubface is pointing up to the sky, the clubhead is said to be closed.

Remember, the position of the face at the top of the backswing is not the only, nor is it the primary indicator of shot direction. However, it is a good indicator and can be used to determine whether it is the face angle or lie angle that might be the cause of an off-line shot. For example, if the golfer pulls or pushes the ball with the irons but has a clubhead with a square face angle at the top of the backswing, this is reason to check and see if the lie angle is correct for the golfer.

On the other hand, if the golfer pulls or pushes the ball and has the clubface closed or open at the top of the backswing, there is a slight chance the lie angle might be incorrect, but it will not be as obvious as a push or pull occurring with the face square.

Fast Fact:
Identifying the face angle of the clubhead at the top of the backswing as either open, square or closed can help the clubmaker determine if a face angle or lie angle change is necessary. If the toe of the club is pointing straight down at the ground at the end of the backswing, the face of the club is open. If the toe is pointing down to the ground at a slight angle toward the golfer, the face is square. If the face of the club is pointing toward the sky, the face is closed.

The obvious recommendation for the face angle would be to choose a face angle opposite to the position of the clubhead at the top of the backswing. However, because the face angle of the clubhead during the swing is not the only factor controlling the shot direction, it is wise to note the direction of the shot in comparison with the face angle of the club at the top of the backswing before making a final recommendation.

If the face angle is square at the top of the backswing but the player hits the ball to the right or left with the irons, a change in the lie angle may be indicated.

The Open Clubface position. When observing the clubhead with the toe pointing almost straight down at the top of the swing, it is a strong indication of the need for a more closed face angle on the woods.

The Square Clubface position. When observing the clubhead with the toe pointing down at an angle to the ground at the top of the swing, it is a strong indication of the need for a square face angle on the woods.

The Closed Clubface position. When observing the clubhead with the face pointing more to the sky at the top of the swing, it is a strong indication of the need for a more open face angle on the woods.

D. Length of the Backswing and Shoulder Turn

The length of the backswing can have an effect on making decisions about shaft flex, shaft bend point, total weight and swingweight of the golf club. While there are many variations among golfers in the length of backswing, in general, three basic backswing lengths are recognized – the three-quarter backswing, the parallel backswing and the past-parallel backswing.

The 'three/quarter' length backswing. If accompanied by a full shoulder turn, this shorter backswing will generate more bending of the shaft than a longer backswing.

The normal backswing length with the shaft approximately parallel to the ground When the shaft is just short of or just past this parallel position, it is considered to be the same backswing condition.

The 'Past Parallel' backswing. This type of backswing usually generates more bending force on the butt end of the shaft as the hands pull down on the club.

When the golfer swings the club with a shorter backswing, there can be more acceleration force exerted on the shaft during the beginning of the downswing. For most golfers with a short backswing, the shoulders act more as the starting mechanism for the downswing. Because the shoulders occupy a more powerful role in the swing than do the hands and arms, a shorter backswing can dictate the need for a slightly stiffer shaft within the golfer's swing speed range, a higher bend point version of the golfer's proper shaft flex, and a higher than normal swingweight (lower golf club balance point) to complement the greater force generated on the tip half of the shaft.

The clubmaker must also look for the amount of shoulder turn that accompanies the backswing. If the shoulders are turned at a full 90° and the front shoulder is under the chin (left shoulder for RH golfers; right shoulder for LH golfers), more power will be generated by the shorter backswing than if the shoulder turn is not as fully rotated. Remember, the shoulders are much stronger than the arms and hands in the swing. Whenever the downswing is initiated by the shoulders rather than the arms, more bending stress is placed on the shaft, necessitating the selection of a stiffer shaft for the golfer in addition to a need for greater headweight.

In contrast, the longer the backswing, the farther past the point of parallel to the ground and generally a reduced amount of force is applied to the shaft on the downswing. This is because the club actually has to be released sooner (the wrists have to unhinge earlier) in order to return back around to parallel and the impact area. In other words, for most golfers with a past parallel backswing, the arms have to move the club first on the downswing before the more powerful shoulders can bring the club into the ball.

Whenever the arms become the dominant way to move a club from the top of the backswing rather than the shoulders, less overall bending force will be applied to the shaft, which in turn will require a slightly more flexible shaft for the golfer. In addition, because the initial downswing force in a long backswing is generated by the arms, more stress is placed on the butt end of the shaft, illustrating a need for a lower bend point (tip flexible) pattern of shaft selection within an overall flex that is correct for the golfer.

If the golfer is physically strong and generates a strong shoulder move into the ball with a shorter backswing length, it might require a higher total weight to offset the force at the beginning of the downswing. Remember the golfer's strength alone is not an automatic indicator of a need for a higher total weight. It is possible on a short backswing to counteract the force of the downswing start by using a light total weight accompanied by a higher than normal swingweight. Again, the light total weight/high swingweight **Feel** provides some resistance at the beginning of the downswing to the force generated by the short backswing.

Whether or not a heavier total weight (heavier shaft + normal weight grip) is offered to the golfer should be as much a request by the golfer as it is a recommendation from the clubmaker, since it has been determined that light total weight and high swingweight can often achieve the same goal of offsetting a strong person with a full shoulder turn and a short backswing.

For the golfer with the long backswing that goes "past parallel," the recommendation is usually for a lighter total weight with a normal to slightly higher than normal swingweight. This is due to the longer the backswing and additional distance the clubhead has to travel back to the ball. The heavier the head feels for this type of golfer, the harder it will be for the golfer to get the club back to the ball with a high amount of swing velocity.

Fast Fact:
There are many variations in the length of a backswing and the amount of rotation the golfer's shoulders turn. Backswing length and shoulder turn have a bearing on the choice of shaft flex, shaft bend point, total weight and swingweight of the clubs.

The shorter the backswing, the more initial force will be placed on the tip end of the shaft at the start of the downswing. On a shorter backswing, powerful shoulders play a greater role in starting the downswing. Therefore, a short backswing with a full shoulder turn can indicate the need for a stiffer than normal shaft, with mid to high bend point (tip firm), higher swingweight and occasionally, a higher total weight.

A long backswing that extends past parallel can indicate a need for a slightly more flexible than normal shaft with lower bend point (tip flexible), lighter total weight and a normal range of swingweight. This is due to the fact that a longer swing causes the arms to play a greater role of initiating the downswing. With the arms not as strong as the shoulders, the force is less on the shaft and more on the butt.

III. The Downswing Move Through to Impact

A. Tempo of the Downswing/Beginning of the Downswing

The speed or tempo at the beginning of the downswing has a great bearing on the clubmaker's recommendation for shaft flex, total weight and most importantly, the swingweight. This is the movement in the golf swing that establishes how much the golfer will "load" or deflect the shaft.

Simply stated, this is the motion in the golf swing that establishes whether the golfer is a "hitter" or a "swinger." The faster the transition between the end of the backswing and beginning of the downswing, the more the golfer might accelerate the club on the downswing and the greater amount of load might be placed on the shaft.

For example, if two golfers have the same clubhead speed, but arrive at impact at different times, the golfer who gets to the ball sooner will have to accelerate the club more on the downswing

While both golfers have the same swing velocity, the golfer to the right has a faster downswing motion, thus allowing him to reach impact sooner than the golfer above. Even though the velocity is the same, the golfer with the faster downswing acceleration is applying more force to the shaft. As a result the shaft flex, bend point, total weight and swingweight need to be adjusted accordingly.

and in the process, will have placed more force on the shaft. This faster tempo player will require a slightly stiffer shaft than normal usually with a higher swingweight (lower balance point in the finished club) compared to the slower tempo player.

In past fitting instruction it was also believed that a faster downswing tempo required an increase in total weight. Since the introduction of ultra lightweight shafts, it has been discovered that even fast tempo players can use the much lighter total weight as long as the swingweight is high enough to create a "head heavy" **Feel** in the swing. For the stronger, faster tempo player, a "head heavy" **Feel** in the club will create enough of a resistance feeling at the beginning of the downswing to prevent the golfer from swinging too fast and disrupting swing timing and rhythm.

The only swing type still advised to use a high total weight is a big, physically strong player, who happens to also be very fast in the transition between the backswing and start of the downswing. In addition, if this type of player has already tried a low total weight/high swingweight combination with little success, it is more of an indication to use a higher total weight as a means to simply help the player slow down.

If the clubmaker observes a smoother or slower transition between the end of the backswing and beginning of the downswing, it is an indication for the clubmaker to advise a slightly more flexible shaft than what the swing speed might indicate. This is because less force is applied to the shaft during the slower tempo at the start of the downswing which in turn, reduces the amount of loading or bending force on the shaft. In addition, the slower tempo and slower accelerating type of downswing also indicates the need for a lighter total weight and with it, more of a normal swingweight range for the club.

Another specification that can be indicated by the action of downswing tempo is the shaft bend point. The Golfsmith Practical Fitting Program does not recognize shaft bend point as a contributor to shot **Trajectory**, but instead identifies bend point as a contributor to the "**Feel**" of the shaft.

The lower the bend point of the shaft, the more flexible the tip of the shaft will **Feel**. The higher the bend point of the shaft, the more firm the tip half of the shaft will **Feel**. If the golfer does not indicate a preference for a tip flexible or tip firm **Feel** from the Player Interview (most golfers will not indicate a preference), the clubmaker could observe the player's downswing motion to make the recommendation. For players with a faster downswing tempo, a mid to high bend point shaft (tip firm **Feel**) might be indicated, while those who have a slower downswing acceleration, a lower bend point shaft (tip flexible **Feel**) would be best.

It should be noted that regardless of the golfer's strength and downswing tempo, a player that indicates no preference for shaft tip **Feel** is almost always better off with a lower bend point version of the shaft flex that best matches the golfer's swing speed and acceleration. (All shaft fitting procedures are explained fully in Chapter 7 - The Final Procedures for Fitting).

Fast Fact:
The speed at which the golfer begins the downswing can be an indicator of the shaft flex, shaft bend point, total weight and swingweight of the club. The faster the transition between the end of the backswing and beginning of the downswing, the more the golfer is advised to use a stiffer than normal shaft with a mid to high bend point, along with a higher than normal swingweight to help slow down the faster downswing move.

In contrast, the smoother the transition between the end of the backswing and beginning of the downswing, the more the golfer would be advised to use a more flexible than normal shaft with a low bend point, along with a lower total weight and a normal swingweight range to complement the more controlled downswing.

B. Holding the Angle Between the Shaft and the Arms vs 'Casting Off' with the Club at the Start of the Downswing

One of the most significant swing movements that has an effect on shaft selection is how well the player can retain the angle between the arms and shaft of the club during the downswing. More accomplished ball strikers are better able to hold this angle through most of the downswing while most average to below average ball strikers cannot.

The 'Hold the Angle' swing move. The player has developed the ability to start the downswing with the shoulders or body, which allows the hands to remain more passive, thus retaining more of an angle between the shaft and the arms.

This is because the more skilled player has learned to start the downswing more with either the shoulders, hips, or body, thus allowing the hands to remain more passive at the beginning of the downswing. With the body providing the initial movement of the downswing, the hands will not pull the club out away from the body. Thus, the golfer is better able to retain the angle between the shaft and arms during the phase of the downswing when the most force is applied to the club.

For the less skilled player who has not learned how to use the body to start the downswing, the first move is usually made by pulling with the hands and causing the club to extend out away from the body, in the process losing the angle between the shaft and arms. This dissipates the loading force on the shaft sooner and causes the club to accelerate into the ball at much more of a decelerating rate than a club which the angle has been retained.

The golfer who cannot hold the angle during the downswing is said to be "casting off" the club, an action in which the arms and club are similar to the way a fisherman unhinges the wrist and "casts" the fishing rod straight away from the body. On the other hand, the golfer who is able to hold the angle between the arms and shaft through the downswing is said to be either "holding the angle" or achieving "a late release" in the swing.

"Casting off" the club at the beginning of the downswing places more bending force on the butt end of the shaft, less on the tip end, and dissipates the force applied to the entire shaft much sooner than the swing which is able to retain the angle between the shaft and forearm. Therefore, when the clubmaker observes the golfer who casts the club from the top of the downswing, the fitting points to consider are: choosing a lighter weight and more flexible overall shaft with a lower bend point (tip flexible shaft). To contrast, if the golfer is able to hold this angle on the downswing, the clubmaker should think more in terms of a stiffer shaft with a mid or high bend point (tip firm shaft). (The Golfsmith Practical Fitting Program regards mid and high bend point shafts as virtually the same with respect to tip firmness.)

The 'Casting Off' swing move. The player starts the downswing more with the hands instead of the shoulders or body, which causes the wrists to 'unhinge' and straighten out the club.

Clubmakers should note from this observation that a lighter shaft is recommended for the player who casts the club, while no overall shaft weight recommendation is made for the player with the later release. A golfer who is able to hold the angle is not automatically a candidate for a heavier shaft because of the fact that lighter total weight clubs are generally better for most players. Even if the clubmaker thinks a particular golfer might be better suited with a heavier shaft due to tempo and physique, it is best to first try and increase the swingweight on a lighter shafted club to create a head-heavy **Feel** which likely will achieve the same tempo slowing result as a heavy shaft.

Usually the clubmaker will be better off recommending a heavier shaft along with a higher swingweight only for the big, strong golfer who possesses a very jerky and quick tempo in addition to hitting the ball off-line in both directions. If the clubmaker has experienced little or no success using the low total weight/high swingweight combination for the faster tempo player, the only alternative, regardless of off-line tendencies, is a move to a heavier shaft (higher total weight) along with a higher swingweight.

Because the golfer with a later release is almost always retaining more of a flex bending force on the shaft than a player who casts the club off at the top, there will naturally be more times that the player with the late release might be better fit into a heavier shaft or a heavier swingweight than the less skilled player. The best procedure with this type of player is to outline the option for a light or heavier shaft and let the golfer provide input as to whether they prefer the **Feel** of a lighter or heavier club. Still, lighter shafts are better for most players, regardless of the downswing movement as long as the swingweight is fit to the tempo – normal swingweights for smoother, slower tempos and higher swingweights for faster tempos.

In addition, the golfer who casts the club off as the first move toward impact may have a tendency to hit the ball "fat," contacting the ground before the ball. This indicates a recommendation for a wide sole iron with more front-to-back radius in order to prevent the club from digging down into the ground as much.

Fast Fact:
The way a golfer starts the downswing can have a bearing on the shaft flex, bend point, total weight, swingweight and sole width/radius of the club. If the golfer can start the downswing by holding the angle between the arms and the shaft, this is an indication they will be better off with a slightly stiffer than normal shaft and a mid to high bend point (tip firm).

In addition, this type of golfer will be better with a slightly higher than normal swingweight. While it might be believed this swing move is better matched to a higher total weight along with the higher swingweight, this is not the case. Only if this "hold the angle from the top" type of golfer has an extremely fast tempo and hits the ball off-line should the clubmaker consider increasing the total weight as an additional fitting factor.

In contrast, if the golfer "casts the club off" at the beginning of the downswing (throws the club away from the body, losing the angle between the arms and the shaft in the process), the clubmaker should recommend a more flexible shaft than normal, with a lower bend point (tip flexible), built into a club with a lower total weight. In addition, the "casting off" move from the top can also cause the golfer to hit a higher percentage of "fat" shots with the irons. Because of this, an iron with a wider and more radiused sole from front to back will be better for this type of player.

C. The Transfer of Weight During the Downswing

Another key swing move typical of the better ball striker is the ability to transfer the weight to the front foot during the downswing and through impact. The classic pose of the golfer ending the swing with the belt buckle facing the target and the sole of the back foot facing away from the target is a dream for many golfers who suffer from the swing flaw called "fire and fall back."

"Fire and fall back" is a term describing the golfer who finishes the swing with the weight on the back foot because of an inability to coordinate the movement of the weight toward the target on the downswing. The golfer who finishes the swing on the forward foot will generate more power through impact, usually resulting in greater **Distance**.

From a clubfitting standpoint, the golfer who is not able to move the weight to the forward foot through impact will be better off with clubs that feature a much lighter total weight, a swingweight within the normal range, a shaft more flexible than normal for the golfer, and a lower bend point for more tip flexibility. In addition, this player will have a harder time swinging longer clubs and most likely will slice the ball due to an outside to inside swing path, thus indicating a need for a face angle that is more closed.

On the other hand, just because the golfer has the ability to properly transfer the weight to the forward foot does not mean the opposite in equipment specifications from the player who "fires and falls back." It is true that in all likelihood the player can play, with a higher swingweight, but if he/she has a very smooth tempo along with the proper weight shift, they do not necessarily need more of a "head heavy" **Feel** in the clubs. In short, a good weight shift through the ball does not point to any particular fitting specification that is indicated by the weight shift only. Only with the "fire and fall back" type of player does the weight shift point to particular fitting needs.

Fast Fact:
The less the player moves the weight to the front foot through the downswing and impact, the more beneficial it is for the player to use clubs with a more flexible shaft, lower bend point for more tip flexibility, normal range of swingweight and lower total weight. In addition, any golfer who ends the swing with the majority of the weight on the back foot will probably have swung the club across the ball from the outside to the inside, causing a slice. Therefore, a player who "fires and falls back" is also a candidate for a more closed face angle in the woods as well.

IV. THE SWING PATH

The swing path is the direction the club travels on the downswing through the ball. The swing path is traditionally described in terms of the direction the clubhead travels into impact when compared with the target line. Swing path is described using terms such as outside to inside, inside to outside or square (inside to inside). The first term describes the path the clubhead is traveling on the downswing while the second term indicates where the clubhead is traveling after impact.

A swing path that travels from outside to inside (normally called an outside/in path) describes a swing with the downswing beginning on the outside of the target line and traveling through impact to the inside of the target line. In contrast, an inside/out swing path starts with a downswing on the inside of the target line and proceeds to travel through impact to the outside of the target line. The least common of the three basic swing paths is the inside to inside path, also referred to as the square path because it describes the most desirable direction of clubhead travel – at the target.

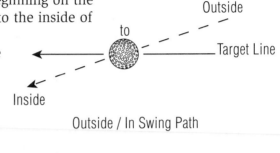

Outside / In Swing Path

To identify the swing path, the clubmaker should stand behind the golfer, looking straight down the target line. To see the movement of the club on the downswing and through impact is difficult for the untrained clubmaker. To learn to spot the different types of swing path, follow these techniques:

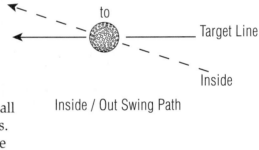

Inside / Out Swing Path

1. Stand behind the golfer directly in line with the ball and the target and watch the golfer hit a few shots. Take note only of the movement of the club on the downswing and through the ball. Do not watch the flight of the ball because the focus must remain on the downswing and the club as it passes through impact. After a few shots, try to decide if the club has been traveling from the outside of the line to inside, from inside to the outside, or from the inside directly down the target line.

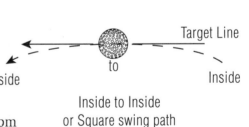

Inside to Inside
or Square swing path

2. Another way to identify the swing path is to stand behind the golfer looking down the target line holding a club or long ruler in a vertical position directly on top of the target line. Hold the shaft or ruler so it appears to be directly on top of the ball with the line of the shaft or ruler traveling from the ball to the target. This will look as if the clubmaker is reading a putt using the "plumb bob" method. Alternate switching the focus from the shaft or ruler to the golfer. Watch the club on the downswing to see if it moves from one side of the shaft/ruler to the other. Noting the swing path is a great way to determine and verify the fitting recommendation for the face angle of the woods.

A. Outside-to-Inside Swing Path

When the club travels from outside the target line and crosses to the inside at the time of impact, the golfer will most likely slice the ball. In fact, the outside/in path is by far the most commonly seen swing path in the game. It is characterized by a movement of the hands away from the body at the beginning of the downswing, causing the club to shift "over" to the outside plane of the target line before it swings across the body, eventually crossing to the inside of the target line at impact. In short, the outside/in swing path for the RH golfer should look like a RH baseball batter who deliberately hits the ball into left field.

From watching the flight of the ball, it is also possible to determine how the golfer is delivering the face angle of the club into impact. (Note: All of the following shot patterns are described for a right handed golfer. For the left handed golfer, simply reverse the direction of the ball in the diagrams.)

For an outside/in swing path, if the ball starts its flight initially to the left or the right of the target, and then curves right in a slicing direction, the face angle of the clubhead is open to the outside/in swing path. If the ball starts

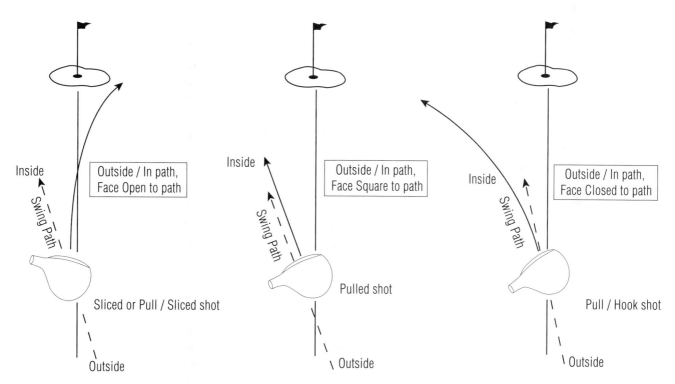

its flight at or to the left of the target and flies straight to the left of the target, the face angle of the clubhead is square to the swing path. If the ball starts its flight to the left of the target and then curves left in a hooking shot, the face angle of the clubhead is closed to the outside/in swing path.

Watching the golfer's swing path and the resulting flight of the ball can determine how open or closed the golfer delivers the face into impact and also help determine how much to change the face angle of the woods. By general estimates, a one degree change in the face angle of the golf club will cause the ball to change in flight direction by approximately 5-7 yards left or right at 200 yards of carry (side spin due to degree of face angle error by the golfer also enters into the final amount).

This means if the clubmaker sees the ball curve 20-25 yards in the air in one direction or the other, it would theoretically require a change of 4° in face angle compared to the original driver to get rid of most of the ball curvature. Therefore, 20-25 yards of slice would call for a change of at least 4° more closed than the previous driver to correct the slice.

If the clubmaker is lucky enough to see the golfer hit the ball, this becomes one of the areas of swing analysis that can be more precise in its ability to identify a fitting decision.

Fast Fact:
In an outside/in swing path, the golfer begins the downswing by moving the club farther away from the body to go outside the target line. As the club moves down toward the ball, the clubhead is now traveling on a path to the left of the target (this is a RH golfer example). At impact the club crosses the target line and continues the follow through toward the left of the target.

The outside/in swing path is the most common cause of a sliced or even pushed shot and almost always indicates a need for a change to a face angle in the woods that is more closed than the golfer's current driver (woods). The amount of face angle change is recommended to be 1° to offset each 5-7 yards of curving ball flight.

B. Inside-to-Outside Swing Path

When the club travels from inside the target line and crosses to the outside at the time of impact, the golfer will most likely push, 'push-hook' or 'snap-hook' the ball. It is characterized by a dropping of the hands either straight down or closer to the body at the beginning of the downswing which causes the club to drop to the inside plane of the target line before it swings out away from the body, eventually crossing to the outside of the target line at impact. In short, the inside/out swing path for the RH golfer should look like a RH baseball batter who tried to deliberately hit the ball into right field.

From watching the flight of the ball, it is also possible to determine how the golfer is delivering the face angle of the club into impact. (Note: All of the following shot patterns are described for a right handed golfer. For the left-handed golfer, simply reverse the direction of the ball in the diagrams.)

For an inside/out swing path with the ball starting its flight initially to the right or just slightly to the left of the target, and then curves left in a hooking direction has a clubhead face angle that is closed to the inside/out swing path. If the ball starts its flight at or just to the right of the target and then flies straight, or to the right of the target, the face angle of the clubhead is square to the inside/out swing path. If the ball starts its flight to the right of the target and then curves farther right in a slicing shot, the face angle of the clubhead is open to the inside/out swing path.

Since a one degree change in the face angle of the golf club will cause the ball to change in flight direction by approximately 5-7 yards left or right at 200 yards of carry (side spin due to degree of face angle error by the golfer also enters into the final amount), it would require the clubmaker who sees the ball curve 20-25 yards from right to left on a right-handed golfer to change the face angle some 4° more open compared to the golfer's original driver in order to eliminate most of the ball curvature.

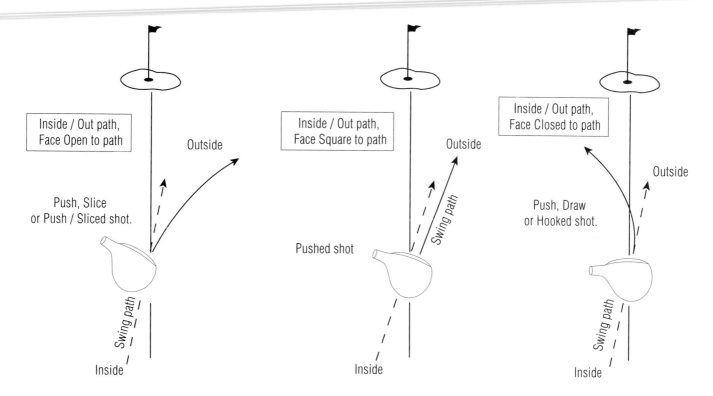

Fast Fact:

In an inside/out swing path, the golfer begins the downswing by dropping the hands with the club closer to their body to go inside the target line. As the club moves out toward the ball the clubhead is now traveling on a path to the right of the target (this is a RH golfer example). At impact the club crosses the target line and continues the follow through to the right of the target.

The inside/out swing path is the most common cause of a duck hook or even a pushed shot and requires careful analysis on behalf of the clubmaker to determine the degree and direction of change. If the ball flight is a push with the inside/out path, a change to a more closed face angle would be necessary. On the other hand, if the ball flight is a hook, the indication would be for a more open face angle than the golfer's current driver (woods). The amount of face angle change is recommended to be 1° to offset each 5-7 yards of curving ball flight or 5-7 yards to the side of the intended target.

C. Inside-to-Inside or Square Path

When the club travels from inside the target line, reaches the target line and remains on it until impact, then crosses back to the inside at the time of impact, the golfer will most likely hit the ball straight or with a slight fade or draw, any of which will be in play. It is characterized by the shoulders and arms moving back down to the ball on the same plane that the shoulders turned back on during the backswing. Theoretically, the inside-to-inside path is also called a square path because it is the closest to traveling directly on the target line. In short, the inside/inside or square swing path for the RH golfer should look like the RH baseball batter who hit the ball into dead center field.

From watching the flight of the ball on an inside/inside swing path, it is possible to determine how the golfer is delivering the face angle of the club into impact. (Note: All of the following shot patterns are described for a right-handed golfer. For the left handed golfer, simply reverse the direction of the ball in the diagrams.)

On an inside/inside or square swing path, a ball that starts its initial flight at or slightly to the right of the target, and then curves slightly to the right of the target indicates a face angle is open to the square swing path. If the ball starts its flight at or slightly to the right of the target and then flies straight or draws back slightly, the face angle of the clubhead is square to the square swing path. If the ball starts its flight at or slightly to the left of the target, and then fades back toward the center, the face angle of the clubhead is closed to the square swing path.

When the clubmaker observes the inside/inside path, the golfer should first be congratulated for having such a controlled swing motion! All kidding

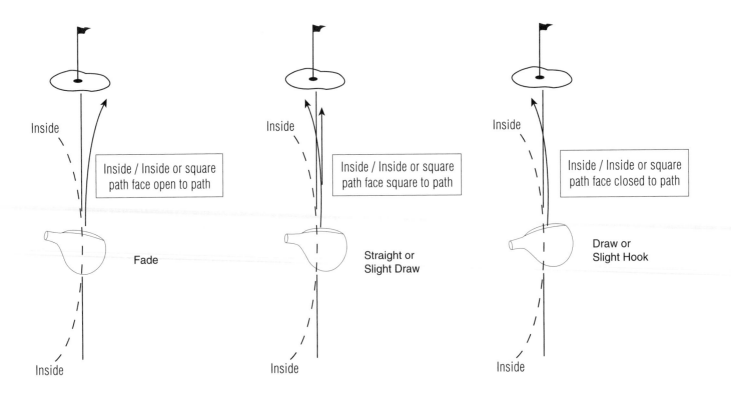

Inside

Inside / Inside or square
path face open to path

Fade

Inside

Inside

Inside / Inside or square
path face square to path

Straight or
Slight Draw

Inside

Inside

Inside / Inside or square
path face closed to path

Draw or
Slight Hook

Inside

aside, rarely will the clubmaker have to advise any face angle change for this type of player. However, in any new set of woods for such a player, the club-maker should take the time and determine the current face angle of the inside/inside player's path to ensure the same directional control.

Fast Fact:

In an inside/inside swing path, the golfer begins the down-swing by rotating the shoulders directly at the ball with the hands, arms and club following on the same plane. The club will appear as if it is flying directly at the target if the player were to let go of the club at impact.

Obviously, the inside/inside path is a very desirable swing path for any golfer to possess. However, it is possible for a player to hit the ball off-line with an inside/inside path if the face angle is too far open or closed. This condition would be rare because most players who have developed the ability to swing the club on path at the target will have also developed the ability to keep the angle of the face relatively close to square. If the player slices or hooks the ball with an inside to inside path, the change in face angle would still be 1° in the opposite direction of the ball flight for each 5-7 yards of misdi-rection curvature.

Despite what teachers or golf professionals might believe, it is not possi-ble to perform a complete fitting from seeing a golfer swing the club. However, with a strong knowledge of the golf swing and the movements that reveal information that supports certain fitting recommendations, it is possi-ble to analyze the golfer's swing. It also provides the clubmaker with greater certainty on whether a fitting decision made as a result of combining infor-mation from the Player Interview, Equipment Analysis, and knowledge of the specifications with a **MAJOR**, **MEDIUM** or **MINOR** effect on ball flight will be right for the golfer.

In particular, the clubmaker who sees the actual flight of the ball will be more certain about the symptoms of poor shotmaking rather than just read-ing or hearing about them from the Player Interview. Often a player will not have as accurate of an indication of their ball-striking tendencies as might be indicated on the Player Interview Form. How high is high? How much on the heel is "on the heel?" How much of a slice is the slice? Golfers with little experience often over or under exaggerate certain ball-striking tendencies when asked to write them down. As a result, the clubmaker sees the flight of the ball and knows whether the player really has a problem hitting the ball high, severely or slightly hitting the ball on the heel, or needs a slight or a significant change in face angle.

Many clubmakers may worry about a lack of access to a driving range for performing the swing analysis will damage their ability to issue an accurate fit-ting recommendation. This is not true at all. Even if the clubmaker only makes some observations of the swing using this information while the golfer is going through the dynamic lie fitting procedure or hitting shots into a net, this would still be enough to reveal the additional information that the swing can provide.

At best though, the swing analysis is seen only as a support of the original Golfsmith Practical Fitting Program procedures of using the Player Interview, Equipment Evaluation and a thorough knowledge of the specifications having a **MAJOR**, **MEDIUM** or **MINOR** effect on ball flight to make the actual fitting recommendations. Remember, the goal of the Practical Fitting Program is just that, a practical approach. Because of this, the swing analysis has to be seen as a luxury addition to make it to the Practical Fitting Program.

Chapter 6

COMPOSING THE PRELIMINARY FITTING RECOMMENDATION

COMBINING THE PLAYER INTERVIEW WITH THE EQUIPMENT EVALUATION TO DETERMINE THE SPECIFICATIONS OF THE NEW SET

NOTE FOR CHAPTER SIX: Chapter 6 is the most important part of the instruction in how to use the Practical Fitting Program because it teaches the clubmaker how to use the information obtained from the golfer to compile the Preliminary Fitting Recommendation. To this point, the golfer will have completed the Player Interview Form and the clubmaker will have completed the golfer's Equipment Evaluation. Because it is efficient to do so, the clubmaker may also have already measured the golfer's clubhead speed, downswing acceleration and wrist to floor dimension, and have put the golfer through the dynamic lie board and grip size fitting. (Measuring and reacting to the golfer's clubhead speed, downswing acceleration, wrist to floor dimension, dynamic lie and grip size parameters will be covered in detail in Chapter 7, but, to save time, the actual measurements may be done when the golfer is in the shop filling out the Player Interview Form).

To use this chapter efficiently, the clubmaker will need to have reduced the information from the Player Interview down to the most basic feedback - does the golfer want more Distance, better Accuracy, a higher or lower Trajectory, more Backspin or better Feel? With those goals in mind, the clubmaker can turn to page 229 and reference what the specification changes will help the golfer achieve those goals.

To help the clubmaker see how a Practical Fitting Program actually works, turn to page 280 and follow the example fitting for an imaginary golfer. Through this example, it will be possible to learn exactly how the Practical Fitting Program can help a golfer with real game improvement desires to achieve his/her goals.

USING THE PLAYER INTERVIEW AND EQUIPMENT EVALUATION TO COMPILE A PRELIMINARY FITTING RECOMMENDATION

There is no doubt every clubmaker (and golfer) would prefer clubfitting to be a cut-and-dried activity with the right specifications for the player to come down to making a series of very simple "black and white" decisions. Unfortunately, this is not the case because there is a human element involved. While it is easy to think, for example, that all tall players need longer and more upright clubs, several other factors may enter into the decision which make such an assumption incorrect. For example, if the tall player has very long arms, is not athletically coordinated, or swings the club on a flat swing plane, longer clubs with an upright lie might likely be far from the preferred recommendation. Even if it could be said that all tall players need longer, more upright clubs, what determines how long or how upright?

The goal of the Preliminary Fitting Recommendation phase of the Golfsmith Practical Fitting Program is to use the information obtained from the Player Interview and Equipment Evaluation, in conjunction with knowledge of the specifications that have a MAJOR, MEDIUM and MINOR effect on the game improvement changes desired by the player, to compile a list of proposed fitting specifications for the new clubs.

This is why the Golfsmith Practical Fitting Program is structured in a way so the fitting session focuses first on discovering how the golfer wants to improve (**Distance, Accuracy, Trajectory, Backspin** and **Feel**), and then explains which of the specifications have a **MAJOR, MEDIUM** or **MINOR** effect on those five areas of game improvement. **If the clubmaker knows which of the five game improvement factors the golfer wants to change, knows the specifications that will and will not make such changes take place, and is aware of a few important specifications in the player's current set for making comparisons, it is possible to compile an accurate fitting recommendation for the specifications the golfer needs without putting the golfer through a long series of ball-striking tests with an array of test clubs.**

To make a Preliminary Fitting Recommendation from the Player Interview and Equipment Evaluation requires the clubmaker to learn how to properly analyze the information and convert it into specifications for the new clubs. **The purpose of this chapter is to teach the clubmaker the specific parts of the Player Interview information that are important to note and the measurements from the player's current set that need to be made in order to address the game improvement factors (Distance, Accuracy, Trajectory, Backspin and Feel) the golfer wants to improve.**

Chapter 6 continues with a chart review of the Player Interview and Equipment Evaluation, which teaches the clubmaker what each of the responses to the questions means with regard to making a fitting decision.

In short, all the clubmaker has to do is to reduce every part of the Player Interview to a simple overview of whether the golfer wants to increase

MAJOR or MEDIUM effect on **Distance** and **Feel**. Remember, the key to compiling the Preliminary Fitting recommendation is to address the game improvement needs of the player.

I. DISTANCE

MAJOR Effect Specifications — The Specifications to Address First to Increase Distance

A. CHOOSING LOFT ANGLE TO INCREASE DISTANCE

1. DRIVER

√ The driver loft for increasing **Distance** cannot be determined until the player's swing speed is known. When this is measured, the following chart can be applied:

Driver Swing Speed	Recommended Driver Loft
under 70mph	15°
70-80mph	13°
80-90mph	12°
90-100mph	10 or 11°
100mph +	10° or less

√ If the player indicates he/she hits the ball on a medium or a low **Trajectory** with the driver, follow the loft recommendation of the above chart to select a new driver loft. If the player is already a high ball hitter with the driver because of certain swing movements, identify his/her current driver loft from the Equipment Evaluation and decrease it by a minimum of 2° (or more, based on a discussion with the player) on the new driver.

2. FAIRWAY WOOD LOFTS

√ Deciding which fairway woods are to be chosen is based on the set makeup recommendation. Once the set makeup of the fairway woods is determined, check the loft of the original 5-wood from the Equipment Evaluation and select the lofts for the new fairway woods to be stronger so they will not hit the ball shorter than the previous fairway woods. Strive to keep a minimum of 3° between each wood in the set for proper difference in distance. (Remember - not all fairway woods of the same number have the same loft! Check the lofts of the new woods before selecting.)

3. IRON LOFTS

√ Selecting iron lofts for greater **Distance** is based on knowing the loft of the previous irons as well as from choosing which irons are to make up the new set. Check the lofts of the 5- and 7-irons in the player's current set. If the current 5- and 7-iron are not less than 27° and 34° respectively, and the longest club hit well from the Player Interview is as long as the 4- or 5-iron, select the lofts for the set of new irons to be 2° less than the current 5- and 7-iron lofts. If the lofts of the current 5- and 7-iron are 26° and 33° respectively (or less), do not decrease the lofts of the #1 through #5 irons unless the player is already a high ball hitter.

4. WEDGE LOFTS

√ Note the loft of the PW and SW in the new set being considered and compare them to the lofts of the PW and SW in the old set. If there is 8° or more between the loft of the PW and SW, recommend a third wedge to be selected with a loft halfway between the PW and SW lofts. If the set makeup allows for it, discuss the benefits of using a lob-type wedge with 3° or more loft than the SW.

NOTE: All of the above recommendations are assuming the player wants to increase distance. Should the clubmaker encounter the unlikely situation of a player wishing to decrease distance, the opposite recommendations to these suggestions should be followed.

FAST FACT:

The actual loft angle decisions for the new set to achieve greater Distance will be chosen primarily as a result of the Preliminary Fitting Recommendation which comes from the Player Interview and especially from reacting to loft measurements of the old set that are made in the equipment analysis. The decision on new lofts will not require any ball-striking tests, other than to obtain the player's swing speed to determine driver loft (using the chart in this section) and set make up related to the long irons/fairway woods.

B. CHOOSING THE CLUBHEAD DESIGN TO INCREASE DISTANCE

All of the questions in the Player Interview related to choosing a club-head design are intended to help the clubmaker determine if the golfer is having trouble hitting the ball on center with his/her current clubs. From the Player Interview, **a player who does not score very well does not normally hit the ball very well, does not play or practice very much and doesn't hit a club longer than the 5-iron very well. The only thing that can be done is to advise a forgiving type of clubhead design with a low CG and more perimeter weighting.**

To help the golfer hit the ball on-center a higher percentage of the time, the clubmaker must focus on comfort and swing timing-related specifications that affect how solidly the player hits the ball including

**Major Factors
of Distance**

total weight, shaft weight, swingweight, grip size, length, shaft flex and golf club balance point. Focusing on these specifications will help the golfer hit the ball more on center – a function of CG and a **MAJOR** determinant of **Distance**.

The player with a slower swing speed must use low center of gravity clubheads to achieve their optimum launch angle for Distance.

The player with a high swing speed who still hits the ball on a low or medium Trajectory must also use a low center of gravity clubhead design to achieve their optimum launch angle for Distance.

If the player hits the ball off-center a high percentage of the time, he/she must have the utmost in perimeter weighting to recover for the Distance loss from the off-center impacts.

If the player hits the ball very high but does not sky the ball, a decrease in loft will be the first specification to address in addition to a higher CG. Be careful with a high-ball hitter who hits the ball off center a lot and uses a high CG combined with a maximum perimeter weighted design. If the high-ball hitter hits the ball relatively solidly, the choice will be easier such as a deeper face set of woods and a stronger lofted, high toe, thinner sole iron that is still perimeter weighted.

1. WOOD HEAD DESIGN

√ **Jumbo oversize wood heads (driver > 240cc) are better for slow swing speed, low-ball hitters to improve launch angle and increase Distance. If jumbo woods are chosen for the high swing speed player, choose no more than 10° loft on the driver to prevent high shots that can lose Distance.**

√ **Oversize wood heads (driver 200-230cc) are OK for all player types, but choose the loft to complement the player's swing speed in order to retain maximum Distance.** (Refer back to the chart of recommended driver loft vs. swing speed in the previous section that pertains to fitting loft for achieving **Distance**.)

√ **Standard and midsize wood heads are better for players who hit the ball solidly most of the time, and are not as good a choice for those who do not practice a lot, or hit the ball on-center half the time.**

√ **Deep face oversize, midsize and standard size (not jumbo) woods (driver > 43mm) are better for high-ball hitters who hit the ball lower for better distance. However, if enough loft can be found on a deep face driver or set of woods, it is OK to recommend for the medium Trajectory player as well.**

√ **The shallow face driver (< 38mm) is usually not a good choice for the high or medium Trajectory player who wants more Distance.** The only way a high or medium **Trajectory** player who wants more **Distance** can use a shallow face driver is if he/she tees the ball very low. It is a much better choice for the low ball hitter and slower swing speed player to improve launch angle.

2. IRON HEAD DESIGN

√ **A compact size iron head is better for the low-ball hitter because the CG is lower. Caution must be taken with the weight distribution because as a general rule, compact size iron heads do not normally have much perimeter weighting**, so the higher handicapper who plays once a week or less might lose confidence with a small head. Compact size iron heads are a good choice for the low-ball hitter who hits the ball solidly most of the time, and almost always a bad choice for the high-ball hitter.

√ **Oversize iron heads can have a lower CG than many clubmakers might think because of their longer sole**. Therefore, if the set makeup starts with the 4- or 5-iron, oversize irons can be good for the lower ball hitter, especially if the sole is a little wider than normal. Be careful when selecting an oversize iron head for a high-ball hitter for this reason. Remember, many oversize iron heads have a lower CG than what is believed.

√ **The best choice for an infrequent player, higher handicapper or any player who hits the ball off-center more than half the time are the wide sole, cavity-back iron heads**, because the overall combination of low CG and weight distribution brings about greater perimeter weighting.

√ **Regardless of clubhead speed, muscleback iron head designs are only for good ball-strikers who hit a lot of greens, play and practice a lot, hit the ball on-center a high percentage of the time, and have confidence in their games**. However, be careful the loft on a muscleback iron head is not too weak for the higher ball hitter because most musclebacks have a lower CG compared to cavity-back irons due to their shorter blade height.

√ **Virtually all wide sole irons have a low CG so they, along with the long blade, oversize iron heads, will be the best choice for the low-ball hitter and slow clubhead speed player. The wide sole iron design is a poor choice for the high-ball hitter who has a high clubhead speed.**

√ **It is important to keep a compact or midsize iron with a thin sole out of the hands of a player who hits the ball fat**. However, most thin-sole irons have a little lower CG than what is thought, because traditionally, the thin sole iron has a shallow face height, resulting in a low CG. Even though these heads have a low CG, the thin sole and muscleback weight distribution together make this type of design a poor choice for the less able player. **On the other hand, if the thin sole is on a very large iron (5-iron toe height > 61mm), it may likely have a low CG**. This is because the sole will likely be long enough on such a large head to comprise a high percentage of the head's mass and keep the CG low.

**Major Factors
of Distance**

FAST FACT:

The goal in choosing the right clubhead design for Distance is to find a clubhead design that has the desired loft angles, necessary CG and weight distribution for the player, all of which are within a design that is pleasing to the golfer's eye.

While it is nice to have test club examples of the heads to recommend for the player, it is not practical to do so due to all the possible different designs that could be considered. Therefore, after the head design with its proper loft and weight distribution characteristics is selected, the Golfsmith Practical Fitting Program recommends the clubmaker purchase the driver (or 3-wood) and 5-iron (or 7-iron) in the recommended model and build these clubs for the golfer to try before finishing the set. This way, the golfer has an opportunity to be certain of the design before the entire set is committed.

C. CHOOSING TOTAL WEIGHT/SHAFT WEIGHT TO INCREASE DISTANCE

All decisions for the total weight of the new clubs have to pinpoint the shaft weight, since the weight of the shaft is most responsible for the total weight. Therefore, think of the two specifications of total weight and shaft weight as one in the fitting recommendation. As grips become available which weigh substantially less than the norm, their contribution to the total weight becomes more important. **The lighter the total weight, the faster the player may be able to swing the club. The faster the swing speed, the greater the Distance, if the player can hit the ball on center**.

In general, every player who is trying to maximize his/her potential for Distance should play with a light total weight club. However, the lighter the total weight of the golf club, the more the golfer could speed up the tempo, causing a higher percentage of off-center hits and as a result, an actual loss of **Distance**. **The key to control for a faster tempo player using a light total weight golf club to increase Distance is a higher swingweight and lower balance point in the finished golf club.** Big, strong, fast tempo players become too quick and have problems with light total weight golf clubs if the club feels light. The key to preventing this is to increase the swingweight and/or length of the club as the total weight is decreased. By creating a 'head-heavy' **Feel** in the golf club for the higher swing speed, faster tempo type of player, it is possible to "hide" or "mask" the lightness of the total weight behind a feeling of heaviness in the head. The result is a club or set that does not cause a total disruption of the player's tempo and rhythm, while enhancing the chance of hitting the much lighter club on-center.

In order for a change in total weight/shaft weight to help increase swing speed enough to increase Distance, the total weight decrease has to be a minimum of 1.5oz (45g) lighter than the previous club. It follows accordingly that the greater the total weight decrease, the greater potential for increasing the swing speed, and with it, **Distance**. Therefore, if the total weight could be changed by two or more ounces, there is a chance for an even greater **Distance** increase, if the player's timing and rhythm are not disrupted by the decrease in the lightness **Feel** of the clubs. Because grip weight also affects the total weight (but to a lesser extent than the shaft weight) all the decrease in total weight does not have to come from the shaft. It is best to decrease total weight as much as possible through shaft weight, and then use a grip weight decrease to drop another 12 + g from the total weight.

To make the total weight/shaft weight recommendation, the clubmaker must first decide if the decrease in total weight is to be made in all the clubs, woods only, or just the driver. Because very lightweight shafts are more expensive, the clubmaker must discuss with the player which clubs are candidates for a shaft weight/total weight decrease. **Remember, it is possible to get more Distance by changing the loft than it is from reducing the total weight of the clubheads**. The player has to understand that the expense of paying for very light graphite shafts in all the clubs may not justify the cost. Reducing total weight does help increase swing speed and can be responsible for a significant **Distance** increase. Still, it is far more likely that clubmakers will perform more shaft weight reductions in the driver than in the full set of woods, and even more in the woods than they will in the full set of the irons. Do not expect to obtain a **Distance** increase from a shaft weight/total weight decrease of less than 1.5oz. In other words, a switch from standard weight steel to lightweight steel will be a waste of time to the player in search of greater **Distance** because the total weight of the golf club will not be reduced enough to have a significant effect on increasing the player's swing speed.

A lighter shaft weight in the hands of a stronger, faster tempo player requires a higher swingweight in the finished club. In contrast, a lighter shaft weight for the slow, smooth tempo player could be built to a swingweight that is within a normal range on the finished club. (See swingweight recommendations in this section of the chapter.)

While there is a considerable amount of evidence indicating that all players should use very lightweight shafts and with it, very light total weights in all their golf clubs, it is a fact that many shafts weighing as much as 130g (4.6oz) continue to be made and used. **Who should be playing with very light shafts? Who should be playing with the heavy shafts? Regardless of tempo and strength, the player desperate to recover lost distance must be using a very light total weight which is at least 1.5oz lighter than the golfer's previous club.**

Within this general guideline, it must be understood that if the RSSR, torque, balance point and bend point of the shaft do not fit the player's swing speed and downswing acceleration/tempo, the reduction in shaft weight will not likely have the desired effect of improving **Distance**. **Do not select a shaft for a player in search of Distance based solely on its weight. The playing characteristics as indicated by the RSSR, torque, balance point and bend point of the shaft must also fit the player before the lighter shaft weight can help increase Distance**. If the player uses a 55g shaft to create a golf club with a very light total weight in hopes of increasing **Distance** but the flex is too stiff, torque is too low, and

Major Factors of Distance

bend point and balance point are too high, there is no way the shaft can help increase **Distance**.

Because the actual choice of which particular shaft will be made during the Step-by-Step Fitting Procedures which are yet to come in chapter 7, **the clubmaker's task in making a decision on shaft weight for the Preliminary Fitting Recommendation is to first list a weight classification for the shaft**. Following is a chart of the five shaft weight classification areas within the Practical Fitting Program that are identified by total weight ranges, each created in an assembled driver and 5-iron. **If the clubmaker has measured the total weight of the driver and 5-iron in the golfer's current set, this chart can be used to note which classification the new shaft weight must come from in order to recommend a 1.5oz (45g) lighter weight and make a significant difference in swing speed.**

Shaft Wt. Classification	Shaft Wt. Range	Driver Tot. Wt.	5-Iron Tot. Wt.
Heavy Weight	110g +	> 12.7oz	> 14.7oz
Medium Weight	96-110g	12.2 - 12.7oz	14.2 - 14.7oz
Light Weight	81-95g	11.7 - 12.2oz	13.7 - 14.2oz
Very Light Weight	66-80g	11.2 - 11.7oz	13.2 - 13.7oz
Ultra Light Weight	50-65g	10.7 - 11.2oz	12.7 - 13.2oz

NOTE: Based on 50g grip weight. If using 38g lightweight grips, subtract 0.4oz from the total weight in the range for each classification of shaft weight.

FAST FACT:
The actual shaft weight/total weight decisions to achieve greater Distance will be chosen primarily as a result of first properly fitting the flex and torque of the shaft (See RSSR shaft flex fitting in section of this chapter), and then by determining if a shaft of that stiffness can be found in a shaft weight at least 1.5oz lighter than the previous shaft being used by the player. This is a fitting specification that will be determined by a request for more Distance made by the golfer in the Player Interview and compared to the total weight of the golfer's previous driver (full set). There will be no need to ask the golfer to use a series of test clubs as long as the RSSR of the shaft has been properly matched to the swing speed and swing acceleration needs of the player as well.

However, once the shaft and clubhead design are chosen, the Golfsmith Practical Fitting Program recommends the clubmaker build a driver (or 3-wood) and 5-iron (or 7-iron) for the golfer to try before finishing the full set. This way, the golfer can be certain of the shaft before the entire set is committed.

D. CHOOSING SET MAKEUP TO INCREASE DISTANCE

Set makeup is one of the most important overall specifications in the fitting process that affects Distance. **The ability to change from clubs that are hard to hit to clubs that are much easier to hit which still hit the ball the same Distance is a different way to look at the goal of increasing Distance.** In short, if the player couldn't hit the longer irons very well, they were losing **Distance.** Replacing the longer irons with higher lofted fairway woods then becomes a way to increase **Distance** through set makeup.

The best way to make a Preliminary Fitting Recommendation of the set makeup is to note the appropriate parts of the Player Interview – longest wood/iron hit well, most and least favorite clubs, the carry distance for the clubs noted on the form – **and comparing them with the golfer's answers to the questions in the Player Interview about the current set makeup.** If there are gaps in carry **Distance** between any areas in the current set (driver to 5-wood, 5-wood to 3-iron, 3-iron to 5-iron, etc.), or if there are areas of the set that are very close together in yardage (< 10), it is a tip for the clubmaker to look at replacing those short yardage clubs with another type of club that can hit the ball farther.

The most obvious set makeup change to recommend for increasing distance is to eliminate all long and middle irons that are not being hit well and to replace them with fairway woods, even if it means starting the irons with the 6 or 7-iron and extending the fairway woods through the 11-wood or higher.

The second most obvious set makeup change to recommend is to compare the lofts of the wedges to the Distance they are being hit and recommend more wedges with loft specifications that create an even Distance between all the wedges. This way the golfer will not have to overhit a SW for example, when the PW goes too far.

FAST FACT:
Changing set makeup can increase distance by replacing clubs that the golfer can't hit very well with clubs that can still hit the ball a comparable yardage. The most obvious set makeup change to increase Distance is replacing any long and middle irons not being hit well with higher lofted fairway woods. Fairway woods are normally easier to hit for most golfers because they have a lower and much more rearward located CG.

E. CHOOSING LENGTH TO INCREASE DISTANCE

The actual recommendation for length of the woods and irons starts with the measurement of the player's wrist to floor distance using the Golfsmith Length Fitting Ruler. Because this is a part of the Step-by-Step Procedures covered in Chapter 7, **the only reference to playing length the clubmaker will enter on Preliminary Fitting**

Major Factors of Distance

Recommendation is an estimate of whether the recommendation is for longer, the same, or shorter than the player's previous clubs. Then, once the wrist to floor measurement is taken, the clubmaker can reference back to the Preliminary Fitting recommendation and determine the actual final length for each club.

It is true that "the longer the club, the harder it is to hit the ball solidly and on-center." It is also true that the player with better physical coordination has an easier time adapting his/her swing to a longer club and hitting the ball solidly on the center of the clubface. It is also true that the lighter the total weight of the longer golf club, the easier it is to swing. **However, this is a point that is more important than the goal of using an increase in length to increase shot Distance – the golfer must Feel comfortable standing over the ball at the address position in order to make a rhythmic, repeating swing that has the greatest chance of hitting the ball solidly and on-center.**

Since the early 1990s, major manufacturers of golf clubs have increased the "standard" length of clubs to a point where there are far more drivers longer than 44" than there are shorter drivers. In fact, at the time of publication, the "norm" has jumped to 45" for driver length. In the irons, far more sets are now made with a 5-iron length of 38" than under 38". When it is understood that 43" used to be the standard for driver length and 37" the old standard length for 5-irons for many years, it is not hard to see that the problems many golfers could be encountering in hitting the ball solidly and on-center could simply be because their clubs might be too long. **No length increase for the purpose of increasing shot Distance is worth the effort if the golfer cannot hit the ball on-center a higher percentage of the time.**

Since this increase in playing length "standards," many golfers have also bought into the belief that longer clubs automatically hit the ball farther. Longer clubs do not hit the ball farther unless two things happen as a result of the length increase:

1) The clubhead speed increases as the length is increased, and;

2) The golfer can hit the longer club solidly and on-center a majority of the time and not just some of the time.

The Golfsmith Practical Fitting Program has discovered that the success of increasing clubhead speed and retaining the ability to hit the ball on-center with longer clubs is chiefly dependent upon the player's individual athletic and physical coordination along with the total weight and swingweight of the club.

To deliver more **Distance** for an average ability to higher handicap player, length cannot be high on the list of fitting specifications to change unless the length change makes the player more comfortable standing over the ball. This normally only happens if the golfer is tall and/or has longer legs with short arms. Therefore, the clubmaker should always be aware of this "comfort" situation. This is one of the most important functions of Golfsmith's playing length measuring ruler. **The Playing Length Measuring Ruler references a Distance from the golfer's wrist to the floor (not fingers, as hand size has nothing to do with judging length)** to give clubmakers an initial length guideline for making the final length recommendation.

Therefore, arriving at the Preliminary Fitting Recommendation for length as a way of increasing distance is not simply a matter of using the length fitting ruler, or measuring the player's current driver and 5-iron, or increasing the length in comparison to the known dimensions. **For an increase in playing length to result in hitting the ball farther, the club-maker needs to determine the longest length the golfer can still hit solidly and on center the highest percentage of the time.**

Other fitting systems call for the clubmaker to apply impact sensitive labels or tape on the clubface and ask the golfer to hit enough shots to determine the greatest length that can be hit on center the highest percent-age of the time. Seriously, how can this be done from a practical stand-point? Several different test clubs, not only of different lengths but with dif-ferent swingweights and total weights, combined with repeated hitting ses-sions over a period of weeks, would be required to realistically make such a procedure successful. In other words, such a method is not practical.

To fit length from the standpoint of increasing Distance, the club-maker must begin with a simple wrist-to-floor measurement to find the "comfort length" for the player based on his/her height, torso size, and arm length. From this starting length, the clubmaker has to look at the current length of the driver and 5-iron, noting from the Player Interview whether the golfer is hitting these clubs solidly and on-cen-ter, and determine if any problems of unsolid contact with the clubs are for reasons other than length (e.g., poor swingweight, total weight, shaft weight to name the more important factors). Finally, the physical coordination of the player must be evaluated to maximum playing length for the player, i.e. the more coordinated the player, the longer the clubs <u>could</u> be.

Longer clubs are an interesting situation for both the clubmaker and golfer. Longer drivers are hard to hit on center while longer fairway woods are usually not. Longer Nos. 1-, 2-, 3- and 4-irons are hard to hit on center while longer middle and especially longer short irons are usual-ly not. This is because of two facts:

1) The greater the loft, the easier it is to hit the longer club;

2) Increasing length for a club that is shorter to begin with does not tend to create problems hitting the ball on-center.

In other words, when a 7-iron, a club that is short compared with the rest of the set, is increased in length to be as long as the old 5-iron, it is not difficult to hit because it was relatively short compared to the long irons. On the other hand, **when a driver is increased from 43.5" to 45", it seems the only players who can successfully adapt are those who are:**

1) **Better ball strikers with good swing fundamentals;**

2) **Tall, short-armed, long-legged individuals who were uncomfort-able with the previous length, or;**

3) **Smooth tempo swingers with a decent sense of rhythm and swing timing, even though they may not have a high clubhead speed to start.**

Major Factors of Distance

These three conditions represent the points to look for in a golfer before recommending significant increases in length for more **Distance**. Clubmakers should remember that it is common for many golfers trying to hit the ball farther, who have switched to longer drivers, to hit maybe one shot out of ten longer and farther than before. Unfortunately, because these golfers have "seen" the **Distance** increase, they continue to try to hit the longer club with hope that they will "catch another one." It is at this point the clubmaker must intervene and make the golfer realize that golf is a game of percentages. As a result, all golfers can achieve their "maximum consistent **Distance**" with the club they can hit the most solidly and on-center the highest percentage of the time.

In addition, just because a golfer cannot achieve a **Distance** increase with a longer driver does not mean that **Distance** cannot be increased by increasing the length of the other clubs within the set. In other words, **it is perfectly acceptable to deviate from the usual 1/2" to 1" incremental change in length between clubs in the set to gain more Distance in the fairway woods and middle and short irons**. There is no hard and fast rule that says the driver, 3-wood and 5-wood have to be 1" different in length, or that the irons have to be 1/2" different in their lengths. Certainly some consistent incremental length change has to be established from club to club, combined with a consistent difference in loft angles, to ensure a consistent separation in shot **Distance**.

But, clubmakers should think of exploring the option of making the set of woods with a change of 5/8" to 3/4" between the driver, 3-wood, 5-wood, 7-wood and 9-wood or, an incremental change of 3/8" between the irons. This will make the fairway woods progressively longer in relationship to the standard driver while the middle and short irons will be longer in relationship to the standard in the long irons. The result is normally greater **Distance** in the fairway woods, middle and short irons – all clubs which are used frequently by the golfer.

This changing of the normal incremental length between clubs in the set is also a great way to make a tall player with shorter arms **Feel** more comfortable standing over the ball in the address position and deliver more **Distance** in the scoring clubs (fairway woods, middle and short irons) without putting the player in harm's way using the driver and longer irons and making them long enough to hit off-center.

FAST FACT:
Making length decisions for the new clubs to achieve greater Distance must follow these priorities: 1) Measure the wrist to floor dimension of the golfer and reference the length indicated by the measuring tool as a starting point. 2) Evaluate the golfer's athletic ability and physical coordination to judge if the length increase will allow the golfer to hit the ball on center a high percentage of the time, or not. 3) Note the length of the golfer's previous driver and 5-iron and refer to the Player Interview to note how solidly the golfer can hit these clubs. 4) To use length as a way to increase Distance, the new woods will need to be at least 1" longer than the previous set and the irons at least 1/2" longer. However, if the clubmaker determines that this amount of length increase would harm

the player's ability to hit the ball on-center, the clubmaker should not make the recommendation for length increase as a way to gain more Distance.

The other option the clubmaker has to help increase Distance within the set is to progressively increase the length down through the woods and irons by changing the increment of trimming length from club to club. Instead of the traditional trim of 1" in the woods and 1/2" in the irons, trim to 3/4" in the woods and 3/8" in the irons and it will make each club progressively longer as the set descends to the fairway woods, through the middle irons and to the short irons. Although many golfers want to hit the driver farther, in most cases it is not possible. The second best alternative is to help the player hit the fairway woods, middle and short irons longer. At least this way the golfer can still experience some game improvement through a Distance increase in some other part of the set.

MEDIUM Effect Specifications – The Next Specifications to Address to Increase Distance

Medium Factors of Distance

F. CHOOSING VERTICAL ROLL TO INCREASE DISTANCE

In Chapter 3 and earlier in this chapter, the Practical Fitting Program outlined how changes in the **vertical roll could help increase Distance. In the actual practical application of the information, it has to be understood that this applies <u>only</u> to the player who hits the ball low or high on the face of the wood head**. If the golfer hits the ball in the center, toe or heel area of the clubface, a change in roll will have no effect on the **Distance**. For the player who hits the ball high or low on the face of the woods, it is possible to make a **MEDIUM** change in improving the quest for more **Distance**, if more options for wood heads with very little roll are available from the supplier of clubheads.

Unfortunately, there are not many metal woods being made with little or no roll. **There are some with the roll 4" or more less than the horizontal bulge. In the case of a golfer who hits the ball high or low on the face and wishes to increase Distance, these should be the wood heads of choice, as long as the other design features indicated in the Equipment Preferences section of the Player Interview can also be met.** Understand that if certain requested appearance related features such as size, color, etc. cannot be met, the improvement of the roll might not overcome the potential negatives the golfer may have playing with a design to which he/she is opposed.

Bottom Line – If a straighter vertical faced wood head can be found that satisfies all other requirements for shape and style as well as face angle and loft, it could help the golfer experience an improvement in Distance when the ball is hit higher or lower on the face.

**Medium Factors
of Distance**

FAST FACT:
The actual decisions for choosing roll to achieve greater Distance will be to try to find wood heads that have as little roll as possible which also satisfy the other design features the golfer indicated in the equipment preferences section of the Player Interview. If this combination can be found, it is not necessary to take the golfer through any type of ball-striking tests to verify the recommendation. If it is not possible to find a wood head that satisfies all of the shape and style preferences of the golfer in addition to having much less vertical roll, there are other more important specifications than roll that can deliver more Distance. In the end, it is more important for the golfer to like the shape and style features of the clubhead design, have the proper loft on the design, along with the best shaft, than it is to worry about the roll.

G. CHOOSING SWINGWEIGHT/GOLF CLUB BALANCE POINT TO INCREASE DISTANCE

Although they are considered to be separate specifications, the swingweight and balance point of the finished clubs are directly related and therefore, from the standpoint of determining the Preliminary Fitting recommendation, will be addressed together. **In the physics of achieving more Distance, clubhead mass is a very important factor – increase head mass and Distance increases, decrease it and the Distance of the shot decreases. However, increase the head mass too much for the player and the club feels too heavy and cumbersome, and becomes difficult to swing. As a result, if the swingweight is too great or too low, the golfer can lose either clubhead speed or the ability to hit the ball solidly and on center.** The result would be a significant **Distance** decrease for the golfer.

Observations of golfers have shown that the lower the total weight of the club along with the higher the swingweight, the better the club feels and the more solidly the golfer hits the ball with more potential for an increase in Distance. This low total weight/higher swingweight combination is also the combination that creates a low balance point on the golf club. When combined, a decrease in total weight and an increase in swingweight will provide the golfer with two chances for gaining more **Distance**:

1) The lower total weight increases the golfer's swing speed;

2) The greater headweight increases the mass behind the ball as well as enhances the ability of the player to hit the ball on center.

To make the recommendation of the proper swingweight for Distance requires the clubmaker to judge the strength, tempo, smoothness of transition between the end of the backswing and the beginning of the downswing, swing speed, and the comfort of the golfer with whatever swingweight of the previous set may have been. At the same time, the clubmaker must keep the total weight/shaft weight in mind because the higher the shaft and grip weight, the less the swingweight can be increased before the club begins to "**Feel**" too heavy for the golfer.

Because different weight shafts (i.e. – different total weight golf clubs) **Feel** heavier or lighter to the golfer, it is important to realize that a swing-weight which may "**Feel** good" to the golfer in a club made with a 60g shaft will probably not in a club built with a 90g or heavier shaft. This is because swingweight is not an actual weight but rather an expression of the club's weight distribution. With a heavy shaft, more mass resides in the tip half of the golf club to begin with, making the swingweight read higher when less weight is actually in the clubhead.

Should a golf club be built so the balance point is the same regardless of the shaft weight/total weight of the club? Emphatically, the answer is NO. For example, to create the same balance point in a 44" driver made with a 60g shaft compared to a 44" driver built with a 120g shaft, the heavier shafted club would require a swingweight that is approximately 20 points higher than the lighter shafted club. Clearly a heavy total weight with a very low balance point would create a golf club that is far too heavy and cumbersome for all but a very small number of players.

The key to judging starting point for the swingweight of clubs is to first know the length and the shaft weight/total weight of the club(s), The clubmaker's job is to provide a starting swingweight based on guidelines for different lengths and different weight shafts. **Following is a chart to help recommend a beginning swingweight for different classifications of shaft weight, based on different lengths, for different types of golfers.**

NOTE: For longer lengths with all shaft weight ranges, allow the swingweight to increase by two swingweight points for each 1/2" increase in length up to a maximum length of 45" on the driver and 39" on the 5-iron. For shorter lengths, decrease the swingweight by two swingweight points for each 1/2" decrease in length down to a minimum length of 41.5" on the driver and 36" on the 5-iron. For lengths greater than 45" on the driver and 39" on the 5-iron, head weight will have to decrease more to prevent the clubs from feeling too "head heavy" due to the fact the greater length places the mass farther from the hands and accentuates the feeling of the head weight. This is for fitting and clubhead feel and should not be confused with the effect of length changes on a swingweight scale, which is a different subject.

Swingweight Recommendations Based on Using a Shaft Weight of 70g or less:

TEMPO	SWING SPEED with Driver	43.5"-1w/38"-5i Swingweight	42.5"-1w/37"-5i Swingweight
Fast, quick, a golfer who is more of a "Hitter"	under 50mph	D1	C9
	50-65mph	D2	D0
	65-80mph	D3	D1
	80-90mph	D4	D2
	90-105mph	D5	D3
	105+mph	D7	D5
Slow, smooth tempo, a golfer who is more of a "Swinger"	under 50mph	C8	C6
	50-65mph	D0	C8
	65-80mph	D1	C9
	80-90mph	D2	D0
	90-105mph	D2	D0
	105+mph	D4	D2

Swingweight Recommendations Based on Using a Shaft Weight of 71-95g:

TEMPO	SWING SPEED with Driver	43.5"-1w/38"-5i Swingweight	42.5"-1w/37"-5i Swingweight
Fast, quick, a golfer who is more of a "Hitter"	under 50mph	D0	C8
	50-65mph	D1	C9
	65-80mph	D1	C9
	80-90mph	D2	D0
	90-105mph	D2	D0
	105+mph	D3	D1
Slow, smooth tempo, a golfer who is more of a "Swinger"	under 50mph	C8	C6
	50-65mph	C9	C7
	65-80mph	D0	C8
	80-90mph	D0	C8
	90-105mph	D0	C8
	105+mph	D1	C9

Swingweight Recommendations Based on Using a Shaft Weight of 95g +:

TEMPO	SWING SPEED with Driver	43.5"-1w/38"-5i Swingweight	42.5"-1w/37"-5i Swingweight
Fast, quick, a golfer who is more of a "Hitter"	under 50mph	C8	C6
	50-65mph	C8	C6
	65-80mph	C9	C7
	80-90mph	D0	C8
	90-105mph	D1	C9
	105+mph	D1	C9
Slow, smooth tempo, a golfer who is more of a "Swinger"	under 50mph	C6	C4
	50-65mph	C6	C4
	65-80mph	C7	C5
	80-90mph	C8	C6
	90-105mph	C9	C7
	105+mph	D0	C8

FAST FACT:
The correct swingweight for any golfer is the highest swing-weight that can be used before the golfer perceives the club as being too 'head heavy' and too difficult to swing repeatedly with comfort. While statements such as this all sound well and good, they fall short because they do not give the clubmaker an actual formula for choosing an actual swingweight for any particular type of golfer. The charts included with this section will form a good starting point for the clubmaker to make a recommendation for swingweight.

From recent testing, it has been determined that the combination of a low total weight (using a very light shaft) with a higher than normal swingweight is good for increasing Distance as well as improving the clubhead Feel. It also appears from testing that all types of players can benefit from a low total weight, as long as the distinction is made between how to swingweight the light total weight club for the slower vs. faster swing speed players and the smoother vs. quicker tempo players. To match a fast swing speed, fast tempo player with a low total weight/low swingweight is a sure ticket to a poor feeling golf club that will lose Distance and destroy Feel for the player overall.

As with many cases in the fitting process, it is always smart to first build the driver (or 3-wood) and the 5-iron (or 7-iron) for the player as a test before finishing the set. Because swingweight is such a personal choice based on the feel of the individual player, it is very difficult to expect to pinpoint the correct swingweight from the start, especially given the variables in custom fitting from different lengths to different weight shafts.

H. CHOOSING SHAFT FLEX TO INCREASE DISTANCE

The proper choice of shaft flex cannot be made from the information provided on the Player Interview Form or the Equipment Evaluation.

The shaft flex is fit by determining swing speed of the player with the driver (3-wood is OK) and 5-iron and combining that data with an evaluation of the player's downswing acceleration. Separate swing speed readings for the wood and iron must be taken because golfers tend to swing the irons and woods differently, no matter how hard they try to prevent it from happening. When fitting the shaft flex, one of the worst mistakes a clubmaker can make is fitting the iron shafts based on a driver swing speed or fitting the wood shafts based on an iron swing speed.

Unless the swing speed and downswing acceleration is known, the clubmaker will not make an initial flex selection on the the Preliminary Fitting Recommendations. However, to prevent leaving the clubmaker from 'feeling in the dark' during this time of compiling initial fitting recommendations for so many of the clubs' other specifications, the procedure for fitting shaft flex will be comprised of the following steps:

Medium Factors of Distance

Step 1 - Determine the swing speed separately for the driver and the 5-iron using a clubhead speed measuring unit.

Step 2 - Choose the shaft weight for the player based on the player's Distance and Feel needs (See Shaft Weight recommendations in this section).

Step 3 - Use the chart of shafts as categorized by shaft swing speed rating (RSSR) vs. the shaft weight found in the supplement to this book to narrow down the selection of the possible shafts for consideration by the player.

Step 4 - Evaluate the downswing acceleration and tempo of the player. A simple judgement of fast vs. smooth tempo may be used, or the clubmaker may choose to use an acceleration measurement device such as The Determinator by True Temper. Adjust the RSSR from which the shaft is to be selected based on the tempo and downswing acceleration rating of the player.

Step 5 - Note the player's handicap, ball-striking ability, strength, physical coordination and desire for feeling the club at impact before selecting the bend point for the shafts still in contention.

Step 6 - Ask for the player's input for color, price range and flex.

Step 7 - Choose the shaft that matches the swing speed of the player after adjusting for the downswing acceleration factor with the shaft weight, bend point and player's desires.

If the player is desperate for more **Distance**, the shaft should be selected so that its RSSR is at least 10 mph less than the actual swing speed of the player. Whenever **Distance** is a consideration in choosing the flex of the shaft, never choose the RSSR to be equal to or higher than the swing speed of the player. From a **Distance** standpoint it is far better for the player to be fit into a shaft that is too flexible for his/her strength and swing speed than a shaft that is the slightest bit too stiff.

Remember, the shaft flex can only be determined after making the swing speed and downswing acceleration measurements. This part of the fitting process can be done along with the few other swing tests or measurements (grip size, wrist to floor, dynamic lie fitting) at the same time the player fills out the Player Interview Form. The complete procedures for selecting the correct shaft will be revealed in chapter 7.

FAST FACT:
    The only way shaft flex can contribute to an increase in Distance is: 1) If the golfer's previous flex was too stiff and the new flex will be much more flexible and allow the shaft movement to increase clubhead speed slightly, and, 2) If the golfer can get used to the feeling of a shaft that bends more during the swing than before.
    Many golfers have no sensation of the shaft bending or moving during the swing, so a change to a much more flexible shaft in an effort to increase distance is not usually difficult. However, some golfers with more of a refined sensation might not feel as much in control of the shot if faced with swinging a substantially more flexible shaft.

II. ACCURACY

MAJOR Effect Specifications – The Specifications to Address First to Improve Accuracy

A. CHOOSING LENGTH TO IMPROVE ACCURACY

The same clubmaking guideline first referenced in the Length vs. Distance section in this chapter can be expanded to say, "the longer the club, the harder it is to hit the ball solidly and on center, and therefore the harder it is to hit straighter." There is no doubt that countless tests with actual golfers have shown that the higher the handicap and less accomplished the ball-striking skills of the player, the more difficult it is to hit a longer club with **Accuracy**. However, because so many golfers perceive greater club length as one of the major keys to **Distance**, there are more golfers than ever before interested in increasing club length in an effort to increase **Distance** rather than tempering their perception of club length to consider the importance of **Accuracy**.

It is also a fact that the more off-center the golfer hits the ball, not only will the ball fly a shorter Distance, but the more sidespin will be imparted on the ball, creating a shot that flies farther off line. From a clubfitting standpoint, the same guidelines the clubmaker should use to fit length for distance also apply to fitting length for Accuracy as well. The goal of the clubmaker when fitting length as a key toward **Accuracy** is to *fit the player into the longest club they can hit on-center the highest percentage of the time.* By doing so, not only will the golfer hit the ball farther, but they will also hit the ball straighter.

Unlike **Distance**, which is a sheer product of swing speed and solidness at impact, **Accuracy** is a product of the solidness at impact along with several human factors over which club length has little control — swing path and the face angle of the golf club as it is swung into impact. If the club is traveling toward impact on an inside/out or outside/in path and the face angle is significantly open or closed, no matter how solidly or on-center the golfer makes contact with the ball, it will still fly severely off line. In following, **if the swing path and face angle errors that cause the Accuracy problem are severe enough, there is no change in length that will help improve Accuracy. This is why for severe cases of Accuracy problems, changing the face angle of the wood head is the only recommendation that can have any remedial effect.** (See face angle in this section.)

If the player needs definite help improving Accuracy and has not indicated a desire to also increase Distance, the clubmaker should first measure the player's wrist-to-floor dimension with the Golfsmith Fitting Ruler and compare that recommendation for length to the length of the golfer's previous driver and 5-iron. Keeping that comparison in mind,

Major Factors
of Accuracy

the following guidelines can be followed:

√ If the driver and 5-iron lengths recommended by the measurement of the wrist-to-floor fitting ruler are **greater** than the length of the player's current driver and 5-iron by 1" or more, the clubmaker should keep the length for the new set the same as the current set and focus the **Accuracy** improvement on either the face angle or lie angle recommendations.

√ If the driver and 5-iron lengths recommended by the measurement of the wrist-to-floor fitting ruler are **equal** to the length of the player's current driver and 5-iron, reduce the driver (and other woods) length by 1" and the 5-iron (and other irons) length by 1/2" in an effort to help with the **Accuracy** problem. No more than this amount should be reduced in order to prevent the golfer from losing too much **Distance** or ending up with a length that forces him/her to crouch uncomfortably over the ball.

√ If the driver and 5-iron lengths recommended by the measurement of the wrist-to-floor fitting ruler are **less** than the length of the player's current driver and 5-iron, make the length of the driver 1" shorter (with the other woods in accordance) and the 5-iron 1/2" shorter (with the other irons in accordance) than the lengths recommended by the ruler in an effort to help with the **Accuracy** problem.

√ If the golfer's previous driver and 5-iron are 1" or more longer than the driver and 5-iron lengths recommended by the measurement of the wrist-to-floor fitting ruler, for the sake of **Accuracy**, the new lengths should be no longer than the recommendation of the ruler.

As a general guideline for Accuracy, the golfer has to be comfortable in the address position and the length cannot be shortened to the point where the golfer has to crouch over the ball making it uncomfortable.

If the player has indicated on the Player Interview Form that they desire an improvement in both **Distance** and **Accuracy** at the same time, the length should be chosen with **Accuracy** as the premier guideline, meaning the club lengths will likely be shorter than the golfer might anticipate. **As a result, when the clubmaker hears the dual request for Distance and Accuracy, the recommendation should be to keep the length as short as possible to strive for the improvement in Distance to come from a higher percentage of on-center impacts.**

For the sake of Accuracy, it is completely acceptable for the clubmaker to change from the normal 1" increments between each of the woods as well as the usual 1/2" increments between the irons. By trimming the lengths of the woods in 3/4" increments and irons in 3/8" increments, the clubmaker can keep the length of the driver and longer irons at standard (avoiding overlength situations on the harder to hit clubs in the set), but then progressively increase the length on the clubs which already are easier to hit by virtue of their greater loft and shorter lengths to begin with. This is particularly helpful in the case of taller golfers with shorter arms who happen to have an **Accuracy** problem. The clubs that are harder to hit straight are kept at relatively shorter lengths, while the clubs that are not hard to hit straight are allowed to progressively become longer, in the process making the taller golfer more comfortable over the ball.

FAST FACT:

For fitting Accuracy, the correct length should be the minimum length that makes the golfer Feel comfortable when assuming his/her normal stance while addressing the ball. Any shorter than this and the golfer might make mistakes resulting in mishits simply because he/she is uncomfortable standing over the ball. Any longer than this might accentuate the errors in clubhead path and face angle the golfer makes causing the Accuracy problem. Because the maximum Distance and supreme Accuracy comes from hitting the ball on-center, and, because swing path errors are easier to correct with a shorter length golf club, it is completely acceptable for the clubmaker to fit length a little shorter than what have been the traditional standards without much fear of losing Distance in an effort to hit the ball straighter.

As Harvey Penick stated in his Little Red Book, "The woods are full of long drivers." As applied to clubfitting, Mr. Penick's definition of long drivers has to be understood not as people, but as the clubs which are longer than standard. In other words, when in doubt when it comes to fitting for Accuracy, go shorter rather than longer and Distance will not suffer as much.

B. CHOOSING FACE ANGLE TO IMPROVE ACCURACY

Face angle is one of the easier specifications to determine in the fitting session. Without a doubt, **face angle is the single most powerful specification at the disposal of the clubmaker for helping the golfer improve Accuracy.** This is because there is no other golf club specification that can directly address the types of errors that are the primary cause of **Accuracy** problems.

To make the proper face angle recommendation, the clubmaker has to know the face angle of the golfer's existing driver (or set of woods) from the Equipment Evaluation and the lateral distance the golfer is hitting the ball off line (from the Player Interview or Swing Analysis). By using a face angle correction of a 1° change for every 5-7 yards of slice or hook, the clubmaker can decide exactly how much the face angle has to change to make a distinct correction on the Accuracy problem. For example, if the golfer's current driver has a 1° open face angle and the golfer slices the ball approximately 35 yards off line, the face angle of the new driver should be at least 4° closed (hook), representing a total change of 5° to correct the problem.

The key point in making a face angle recommendation is that **the clubmaker has to come up with an accurate measurement of the face angle on the existing wood(s) and an assessment of how far off-line the golfer is hitting the ball.** Without these two bits of information, offering a recommendation that provides the most help is impossible. Therefore, it is

**Major Factors
of Accuracy**

absolutely vital for the clubmaker to measure the face angle as a part of the Equipment Evaluation.

In addition, the clubmaker has to realize two other important points concerning the recommendation of the face angle:

1) The human golf swing has the ability to change the degree of error it creates, which makes the correction of a face angle change look effective some of the time and ineffective at others, and;

2) Wood heads are not manufactured in every conceivable degree of open or closed face angle, thus imposing a limit to the amount of **Accuracy** improvement available to the golfer.

Obviously, more golfers with **Accuracy** problems slice rather than hook the ball. As a result, there are more hook than open face angle wood heads available to clubmakers. Of those hook face angle wood heads, few are available closed more than 2°. As a result, clubmakers have to realize they may only be able to help a golfer reduce his/her slice to a controlled fade.

FAST FACT:

Face angle is one of the easiest golf club specifications to determine for the Preliminary Fitting Recommendation. By knowing the face angle of a golfer's existing driver (woods) along with the fact that a 1° change in the face angle is worth approximately 5-7 yards of lateral movement on the shot, the clubmaker has the ability to make an accurate recommendation. There is a limit to how much a face angle change can be made because of the availability of wood heads with a variety of different face angles. However, because most golfers slice the ball and most custom wood head options are created in closed rather than open face angle dimensions, clubmakers can still offer quite a bit of correction for those seeking an improvement in Accuracy.

The face angle change that is advised in the Preliminary Fitting Recommendation will be the final decision for face angle in the new set of clubs. No further ball-striking tests will be necessary to verify the new face angle as long as the clubmaker can make an accurate measurement of the golfer's existing face angle.

C. CHOOSING LIE ANGLE (SHORT IRONS) TO IMPROVE ACCURACY

Lie angle is a MAJOR factor in the improvement of Accuracy in the short irons but not in the middle or long irons and woods. (See Chapter 2 for a complete explanation.) This is because the greater the loft angle of the clubhead, the more off line the shot can travel when the face is tilted at impact due to an incorrect lie angle. **The exact lie angle specification cannot be determined as a part of the Preliminary Fitting Recommendation. For the lie to be fit properly to the golfer, it must be determined through one of the two different methods for dynamic lie fitting,** such as noting the point of impact on the sole from hitting shots off a lie board, or using the Lie Detector from Golftek Inc. (See chapter 7 for a full explanation of the methods of dynamic lie fitting.)

While the information from the Player Interview can possibly give the clubmaker an indication of whether the player might be more likely to use an upright or a flat lie angle, the lie can only be fit during the ball-striking test so there is no use in wasting time trying to make an educated guess.

FAST FACT:

Lie is more important in the short irons for the sake of Accuracy than within any other club in the set. There is no recommendation for a correct lie angle can be made as a part of the Preliminary Fitting Recommendation because lie can only be properly fit using one of the two existing dynamic lie fitting methods. This will be done as a part of the ball-striking tests yet to be performed as a part of the Step-by-Step Procedures for Fitting to be explained in Chapter 7.

D. CHOOSING SET MAKEUP TO IMPROVE ACCURACY

The same principle that allows set makeup to be considered as a way to increase **Distance** also applies to improving **Accuracy**. By studying the answers in the Player Interview that pertain to longest wood/iron hit well, most/least favorite clubs, as well as the shot pattern for the clubs in the ball striking tendencies section, it is possible for the clubmaker to discern a pattern of **Accuracy** improvement that might be specific to certain areas of the set.

Most golfers do not hit fairway woods as far off-line as the Nos. 1-, 2-, 3-, and 4-irons because the center of gravity of the fairway woods is so much farther behind the face than it is on the irons. Therefore, if the golfer complains of hitting the longer irons off-line, changing to higher lofted fairway woods can offer some relief. Still, because **Accuracy** is a product of the swing path and how square, open or closed the face angle is delivered to the ball, it is possible that the golfer will not gain as much **Accuracy** improvement from a set makeup change as **Distance** and **Trajectory** improvement.

FAST FACT:

Set makeup can also be used to improve Accuracy in the same way it can improve Distance – by replacing clubs that are being hit off-line with clubs designed to hit the ball the same distance but are easier to hit straight. Again, the most obvious way to use set makeup to improve Accuracy is to replace the Nos. 1-, 2-, 3-, 4- and occasionally the 5-iron with higher lofted fairway woods. Noting the longest club hit well along with the shot pattern for each group of clubs from the Player Interview is the best way to determine where to make the break between fairway woods and irons.

Medium Factors of Accuracy

MEDIUM Effect Specifications – The Next Specifications to Address to Improve Accuracy

E. CHOOSING SWINGWEIGHT/GOLF CLUB BALANCE POINT TO IMPROVE ACCURACY

The same procedures and guidelines that were used to determine the swingweight for helping the golfer achieve a maximum in Distance will suffice for Accuracy as well. There is no such thing as an optimum swingweight for **Distance** and a separate optimum swingweight for **Accuracy**. In other words, swingweight is a very important specification for helping the player hit the ball more consistently on the center of the clubface. **Because hitting the ball on-center is key to both Distance and Accuracy, the same chart of recommended swingweight based on length and shaft weight/total weight that was established in the Distance section of this chapter will apply for Accuracy.** For that reason, please review the swingweight guidelines and charts on page 243 of this chapter to establish the initial swingweight recommendation as for the Preliminary Fitting Recommendation.

FAST FACT:
The swingweight that is determined to be the optimum level for achieving the maximum distance is also best for achieving the optimum in Accuracy. Therefore, the guidelines established in the fitting swingweight for Distance section of this chapter recommending the proper starting swingweight for the player will suffice for the needs of Accuracy as well.

The reason is because slightly higher swingweights normally indicate a slightly greater head feel and an actual increase in head mass. The greater the clubhead Feel, the better rhythm and timing of the player and generally the better the accuracy. On the other hand, the greater the head mass while the clubhead feel is still comfortable for the player, the greater the Distance.

F. CHOOSING LIE ANGLE (MIDDLE IRONS) TO IMPROVE ACCURACY

While lie angle is a MAJOR factor of Accuracy in the short irons, it is a MEDIUM factor in the improvement of Accuracy in the middle irons. (See Chapter 2 – Lie Angle for a more complete explanation of why the lie angle becomes less important to **Accuracy** as the loft gets stronger.) The primary reason for this difference in **Accuracy** importance is because the middle irons (Nos. 4-, 5-, 6-irons) have more loft than the woods and long irons, and less than the short irons. As mentioned before, **the greater the loft angle of the clubhead, the more offline the shot can travel when the incorrect lie causes the face to be tilted at impact.** Therefore, the lie of the middle irons is still very important because the Nos. 4-, 5- and 6-irons have enough loft to cause the ball to travel moderately off-line when the lie is incorrect at impact.

Once again however, **the proper lie angle for the player on any club in the set cannot be determined as a part of the Preliminary Fitting Recommendation because the lie angle can only be fit through the use of a dynamic lie fitting method**. The two methods are one that notes the point of impact on the sole from hitting shots off a lie board, or the Lie Detector by Golftek, Inc. (See Chapter 7 for a full explanation of the two methods of dynamic lie fitting.)

FAST FACT:
The clubmaker should not waste any time trying to determine lie for the player from the Player Interview and Equipment Evaluation information. Lie can only be fit correctly to the player using one of the two methods for dynamic lie fitting, both of which will be outlined in Chapter 7.

G. CHOOSING SHAFT TORQUE TO IMPROVE ACCURACY

It has been said that golfers should use a shaft with the lowest degree of torque in order to improve **Accuracy**. **Since the early 1990s, it has been discovered that a low degree of torque does not ensure Accuracy**. Instead it has been discovered that a low degree of torque increases the stiffness **Feel** of a shaft. **Torque is more important in its contribution to the overall stiffness of a shaft than it is to the Accuracy of the shot**. As a result, the shaft flex fitting segment of the Practical Fitting Program has been structured to take torque into account when the golfer's swing speed is matched to the swing speed requirement of the shaft. Therefore, torque is fit as a part of the shaft flex fitting, which is described in detail in Chapter 7.

There is some evidence provided by a number of shaft companies to substantiate a claim that **among two shafts which both fit the golfer for overall flex Feel, the shaft with the lower degree of torque will help the golfer hit the ball slightly straighter**. This fact is more important for high swing speed players with strong downswing acceleration than it is for slow swing speed players. For the narrow range in which torque exists within the shaft industry (1.5° to 8° among traditionally designed metal or composite shafts), only the strongest downswing move could possibly apply enough twisting force to the shaft to cause the head to turn open or closed and affect the **Accuracy** of the shot. **A slow swing speed player, or even a medium to high swing speed player with a low level of acceleration on the downswing cannot generate enough twisting force on the shaft to turn the clubhead open or closed enough to affect Accuracy.**

Torque only has to be independently fit to the player with a driver swing speed greater than 95mph, who also has a very high downswing acceleration or fast tempo. For this stronger player, of the shafts which meet their swing speed and downswing acceleration requirements, the ones with a torque of 5° or less should be chosen over the ones which have an RSSR equal to the player's swing speed which have a torque of 5.5° or higher.

Medium Factors of Accuracy

FAST FACT:
The fitting procedures for shaft flex in the Practical Fitting Program involve measuring the swing speed and downswing acceleration of the player and matching that information to the RSSR (Recommended Shaft Speed Rating) of the shafts. The RSSR for each shaft is computed as a product of the stiffness and torque of the shaft combined together. Hence, the torque is factored into the flex fitting procedure.

However, in the case of the player with a driver swing speed of 95mph or more who also possesses a high level of downswing acceleration, should the torque also be fit independently to its role in the RSSR of the shaft? In this case, the clubmaker will first pick a group of shafts with an RSSR that matches the swing speed and acceleration of the player. From that group of compatible shafts, the clubmaker would choose the one with the lowest torque.

H. CHOOSING HORIZONTAL BULGE TO IMPROVE ACCURACY

Most component supply companies do not offer a very wide range of bulge on the wood heads they distribute or design. For that reason, making the Preliminary Fitting Recommendation for bulge does not involve much decision making. However, should wood heads with a range in bulge be available, the following **Accuracy** enhancing guidelines should be followed:

√ **If the player has a tendency to hit the ball on the toe and slices the ball, choose less bulge** radius (higher number of inches of bulge) on the woods to help generate more hooking sidespin on the ball.

√ **If the player slices the ball and tends to hit the ball on the heel most of the time, choose more bulge** radius (lower number of inches of bulge) on the woods to start the ball more to the opposite side of the fairway.

√ **If the player hooks the ball and hits the ball off the toe, choose more bulge** radius on the woods to start the ball more to the opposite side of the fairway.

√ **If the player hooks the ball and hits the ball off the heel, choose less bulge** radius on the woods to generate more slicing sidespin on the ball.

FAST FACT:
There is not a lot that fitting bulge to the player can do for Accuracy because there is not much variation in the bulge designs on wood heads offered for custom clubmaking. However, within the range of bulge for each head number that is available, keep the bold face guidelines mentioned above in mind when advising the clubhead for the player.

III. TRAJECTORY

MAJOR Effect Specifications – The Specifications to Address First to Increase/Decrease Trajectory

Trajectory is the only game improvement factor in the Golfsmith Practical Fitting Program for which the clubmaker may receive opposite requests for changing in the player's game. While every golfer wants more **Distance**, better **Accuracy** and **Feel**, there are some players who want to hit the ball higher and others who want to hit it lower. This section, which explains how to compile the Preliminary Fitting Recommendation for meeting the **Trajectory** requirements of the player, will cover both sides of **Trajectory** – how to use the specifications that have a **MAJOR** and a **MEDIUM** effect to either increase or decrease the **Trajectory**.

A. CHOOSING LOFT TO INCREASE TRAJECTORY

To make a noticeable increase in Trajectory through loft, the club-maker has to increase the loft angle on the woods and irons by a minimum of 2° compared with the loft of the golfer's current clubs, or more if the requirement for elevating the height of the shot is greater. To recommend the exact loft angle per club requires the clubmaker to refer to the loft measurements of the key clubheads (1w, 5i, 7i, wedges) from the Equipment Evaluation and make a minimum 2° loft increase in relation to these readings.

Clubmakers must understand a golfer who complains of topping the ball and has indicated on the Player Interview Form a desire to hit the ball higher is a completely different fitting situation. In other words, increasing the loft for a person who tops the ball will do nothing to help this player get the ball airborne. If the clubmaker wishes to address the aspect of topping the ball for the player through an equipment change, see the reference to "I want to stop topping the ball" found in Chapter 3.

The only difficulty in recommending an increase in loft to increase Trajectory is to consider whether there will be a potential Distance loss for the player and how it will affect his/her game. In other words, before increasing the loft of the clubheads to increase the **Trajectory**, the clubmaker has to ask the golfer if the potential loss in **Distance** is worth the sacrifice.

However, for slow clubhead speed players, an increase in driver loft can often result in both an increase in Trajectory and Distance. This is because the slower the swing speed of the player, the less **Backspin** and in turn, the less lift on the ball, which in the end results in a lower **Trajectory** and a shorter carry **Distance**. **When increasing loft to increase Trajectory, expect most players with a driver swing speed under 80mph to increase Distance at the same time they increase**

Major Factors of Trajectory

Trajectory with the driver. For clubs other than the driver and long irons, any increase in loft will result in an increase in Trajectory at the sacrifice of some Distance.

Because most players do not wish to sacrifice **Distance** to increase **Trajectory**, it is best to increase only the driver loft on sub 80mph players and high handicappers, while not increasing the loft on any other of the player's clubs unless they believe that the increase in **Trajectory** is more important than the resulting loss of **Distance**. However, it is possible to offer some **Trajectory** increase to the slower swinging, higher handicap player by changing the set makeup. By eliminating the long irons and replacing them with high lofted woods, the person can hit the ball higher without losing **Distance**. This is the purpose of the question in the Player Interview, "What is the longest iron hit well." By knowing the longest iron the player can hit successfully, in terms of **Trajectory**, the set makeup can eliminate all irons up to that iron and replace them with high lofted woods. Remember, fairway woods are available up to a 15 wood.

Should the clubmaker encounter a good player who indicates a request to increase **Trajectory**, it must be discovered if the player is willing to sacrifice some **Distance** to hit the higher shot. While there may be a few long hitters who might, it is doubtful most players would agree to such a trade-off. In the case of the good ball striker in search of a higher shot pattern, it would be acceptable to combine an increase in loft with an increase in club length to offset the potential **Distance** loss from such a combination. Remember, this would be a recommendation for the player who has the athletic ability to retain his/her swing tempo and rhythm while still being able to hit the longer club on-center.

The wedges are one area of the game the clubmaker will likely receive the most requests for increasing Trajectory. It is far more important to stop the ball quickly than it is to hit the ball farther with the wedges. **Clubmakers should be prepared to recommend a change in the set makeup of the wedges at the same time they are called upon to increase the loft and in turn, Trajectory.** For example, many sets of irons are made with much stronger lofts such that the PW of today is equivalent in loft to the 8- or 9-iron of ten or twenty years ago. At the same time though, the SW has not decreased nearly as much in loft over the past two decades.

Depending on the loft of the short irons and PW, a golfer may need to fill in the gap in yardage between a strong lofted PW and a traditional lofted SW. This can be done either by increasing the loft of the present PW or by leaving its loft the same and adding a third "gap" wedge with a loft angle halfway between the PW and SW. **If the difference in loft between the PW and SW is 7° or less, the PW loft could be increased by 1° and the SW loft decreased by 1° to "close the yardage gap" created by the original loft difference without widening the yardage difference between the 9-iron and PW or requiring another wedge.** In this way, any additional wedges being considered in the set makeup could be reserved for lofts greater than the SW. However, **if the loft difference between the PW and the SW is 8° or more, any increase in** the PW loft or decrease in the SW will create a gap between the 9-iron and PW, or make the SW Trajectory too low. In this case of an 8° loft angle gap, a third wedge should be added with a loft angle in between the two existing wedges. Then, if a higher loft wedge (a fourth wedge) is considered, the golfer can decide whether to eliminate another long iron or fairway wood to remain within the 14 club maximum limit. (See Chapter 9 for more information on fitting wedges.)

FAST FACT:

Normally, clubmakers only receive a request from slower swinging and higher handicap golfers to increase the Trajectory with the woods and irons. Because a potential loss of Distance in the fairway woods and irons can come from increasing the loft, the best way to increase Trajectory for the slower swinger, middle to higher handicapper or weaker player is to increase loft of the driver, eliminate all the long irons and some of the middle irons, and replace them with high-lofted fairway woods. Remember, fairway woods do exist up to a 15-wood.

When the better player wants to hit the ball higher, the clubmaker must find out if the player is willing to sacrifice some Distance to gain the Trajectory. If the better player cannot afford the Distance trade-off, the clubmaker can work with the other factors affecting Trajectory yet to be discussed in this section, including suggesting lower center of gravity clubheads, or clubheads designed with more offset. However, the CG and offset will not have as much of an effect on Trajectory as will loft. The only other alternative that can work with the better player is to increase the loft and offsetting the potential Distance loss through an increase in length and swingweight or a decrease in the total weight.

A. CHOOSING LOFT TO DECREASE TRAJECTORY

To make a noticeable decrease in shot Trajectory through loft, the clubmaker has to decrease loft angle of the woods and irons by a minimum of 2° or more over the loft of the golfer's current clubs. To recommend the exact loft angle per club requires the clubmaker to refer to the loft measurements as determined from the Equipment Evaluation and make a minimum of a 2° loft decrease in relation to these readings.

It is a lot easier for the clubmaker to increase Trajectory than it is to decrease the height of the shot. When a player complains of hitting the ball too high, frequently a change in loft of 2°-3° will not end up satisfying the player. Most of the time, the only way the clubmaker can help a golfer who hits the ball really high to bring the ball down to an optimum Trajectory, is to recommend a change in the swing or ball position. This is one example in fitting where the swing has the power to overcome any change made in the equipment to offset the shot-making condition.

While it is not the intent of the Practical Fitting Program to teach clubmakers to be swing instructors, **trying to help a player lower the**

Major Factors of Trajectory

Trajectory is one of the few cases it is quite helpful for the clubmaker to observe the player's ball position. If the player indicates a desire to hit the ball lower and the clubmaker notices the ball is being played much farther forward in the stance, the clubmaker should know that any loft angle or center of gravity hosel offset changes prescribed in the Preliminary Fitting Recommendation will not likely bring the ball down enough to satisfy the player. In this case, the clubmaker should tell the player the equipment changes will not likely overcome the effect of the forward ball position on **Trajectory**, and suggest the player consider a change in ball position.

Theoretically, it is possible to think about decreasing the loft on clubs by more than 2-3° to decrease **Trajectory**, but this is not really a practical solution. If the clubmaker were to find a set of clubheads with loft angles that were at least 4° less than the lofts of the clubheads in the current set, more problems might appear when addressing the short game requirements that might require even more creative solutions. **In short, unless the player is using a very weak lofted set of clubs by modern standards, if the golfer hits the ball too high, the swing or ball position needs to be changed. However, if the golfer hits the ball just slightly too high, the change can be made through the equipment.**

The solutions of decreasing the loft or choosing higher center of gravity clubsheads are best advised for the player who wants a *slight* decrease in **Trajectory** for the purpose of controlling the ball better in cross-wind conditions, or to "work" the ball better when trying to hit draws or fades. In this case, which is normally restricted to the better ball striker, the **MINOR** effect factor of increasing the stiffness of the shaft by additional tip trimming or by selecting a shaft with a slightly higher RSSR can also help. This is because the better player does not usually want to increase his/her **Distance**, particularly with the irons, because they have built their game around a confidence in knowing exactly how far they hit the ball with each club. To decrease loft will solve the player's problem and bring the ball down effectively, but it will also cause the player to hit the ball farther, which he/she may not want to do.

FAST FACT:
Decreasing loft is the most effective way to decrease shot Trajectory. However, the clubmaker must make an evaluation of how high the player hits the ball before determining if the solution is best served by a change in loft or a change in swing habits. With average-to-higher handicap players, the main cause of hitting the ball too high is a ball position that is too far forward in the stance. When the clubmaker hears of an average-to-higher handicap player who hits the ball too high, the first thing to do is look at the ball position and recommend a change before changing the loft. The reason? A decrease in loft can only help so much and can easily be outweighed by a ball position that is too far forward.

For the better ball striker in search of a slight Trajectory decrease, the clubmaker can help decrease Trajectory through a change in loft or other factors such as CG or offset (or the MINOR effect factors as well).

B. CHOOSING SET MAKEUP TO INCREASE/DECREASE TRAJECTORY

Set makeup can have an influential effect on changing the **Trajectory** of the player's shot pattern. **There are two areas a set makeup change can offer game improvement in Trajectory – long irons and wedges**.

It is very common for a golfer to have problems hitting any iron longer than a 5-iron high enough to achieve maximum **Distance** and be able to stop the ball on the green. **By replacing any of the long and even some middle irons with higher lofted fairway woods, the clubmaker can make a significant difference in increasing the height of the shots that were intended to carry the Distance of a well hit long iron**. The reason is because the CG on a fairway wood is much lower and farther back from the face than on any long iron.

The other area of the set that is advantageous to hit the ball higher is with the wedges. **Because so many golfers have a hard time developing the "soft hands" and smooth tempo required to hit soft, high, floating wedge shots that can stop the ball on the green, changing the type of, and the complement of the wedges can help the player hit the ball higher and with more control**. By noting the lofts of the player's current wedges and responding by changing to wedges with greater loft or a wider sole (lower CG) or more or less bounce on the sole angle, it is possible for the golfer to hit the ball higher with more backspin and stop it better on the green. (See Chapter 9 for more specific information about wedge fitting.)

FAST FACT:
Long irons are hard for most players to hit high enough to carry their maximum Distance and still stop the ball on the green (or short of a hazard). High-lofted fairway woods are easy to hit higher because the CG is lower and much farther back from the face than on a long or middle iron. Repeating the same set makeup technique of eliminating long irons and replacing them with higher-lofted fairway woods is a great way to make a big difference in hitting the ball higher with clubs that are intended to carry the Distance of a long iron.

With the tremendous selection in styles and loft angles of the various types of wedges, it is possible to change the player's wedge set makeup to make it easier to hit the higher, softer landing shots that save strokes around the green. Choosing higher lofted wedges with less of a bounce sole angle is a great way to help the golfer hit high, soft shots from grassy lies. Choosing higher lofted sand wedges with more bounce and a wider sole is a good way to help the player not only get out of the bunker more often, but hit softer landing shots from the sand as well. (See chapter 9 for more information on fitting wedges.)

**Medium Factors
of Trajectory**

MEDIUM Effect Specifications – The Next Specifications to Address to Increase/Decrease Trajectory

C. CHOOSING CLUBHEAD DESIGN TO INCREASE TRAJECTORY

For the player who is consistently getting the ball airborne, but wants to hit the ball higher, a clubhead design with a lower and more rear located CG is a must. In the woods, this can be accomplished by advising the golfer to **choose wood heads which are larger in size from front to back, and which have a slightly more shallow face height (40mm or less on the driver face height) and are designed with an offset hosel.** (See the section following Center of Gravity in this section which explains Face Progression/Hosel Offset for changing Trajectory.)

In the irons, the clubmaker will need to advise the golfer in search of greater **Trajectory** to **select a set of iron heads that have a shorter blade height, a wider sole and a longer blade or sole length.** Do keep in mind that **loft is more influential in creating a change in Trajectory. A low CG cannot overcome a stronger set of loft angles in a set of iron heads to increase Trajectory.**

Perhaps the best way to help a player increase Trajectory through a change in clubhead design is by changing the set makeup. By eliminating the long irons and as many middle irons as the player still indicates a desire to hit higher, the clubmaker can replace the lower-lofted irons with high-lofted fairway woods that hit the ball the same Distance. This way, the golfer can achieve the goal of a higher **Trajectory** without losing **Distance**.

Many players in search of increased Trajectory are much better served with a set of woods that may extend down to the 9- and 11-woods, matching to a set of irons that starts with the 5- or 6-iron as the longest club.

Following is a chart of equivalent fairway woods to long irons, and is intended for use when trying to replace a hard to hit iron with a higher hitting fairway wood that can fly the same **Distance**. Be sure and check the lofts and know the lengths to assemble any high lofted wood to ensure the **Distance** trade-off is even.

Iron	Avg Loft Range	Avg Length	Equivalent Fwy Wood	Avg Loft Range	Avg Length
1-iron	16-17°	40"	4-wood	17-18°	42"
2-iron	18-20°	39.5"	5-wood	19-21°	41.5"
3-Iron	21-23°	39"	7-wood	23-25°	41"
4-iron	22-24°	38.5"	9-wood	26-28°	40"
5-iron	25-28°	38"	11-wood	29-31°	39"
6-iron	29-32°	37.5"	13-wood	32-34°	38"
7-iron	33-36°	37"	15-wood	35-37°	37"

As a last point, remember, the player who is struggling with topping the ball will not find their troubles solved with a change to a clubhead with a lower or more rear located CG. While this is obviously the clubhead to recommend for this type of player to provide all the help possible, the real difference in topping the ball compared to getting the ball consistently airborne is in the swing, not the club. Once the golfer acquires the ability to get the ball airborne, then and only then can the CG help.

FAST FACT:

To help the player increase Trajectory through the clubhead design, the clubmaker will need to advise a set of wood heads that are larger in size, lower in profile/face height and if possible, designed with an offset hosel. For the irons, the clubmaker will want the player to choose a set that has a shorter blade height and wider sole. If it has both, then a longer-than-normal blade length is necessary so that the sole is longer and carries more mass to keep the CG low.

The key to increasing Trajectory as much as possible through clubhead design is to seek out clubheads with a low CG as well as a more rearward located CG.

D. CHOOSING CLUBHEAD DESIGN TO DECREASE TRAJECTORY

The players who indicate a desire to lower the Trajectory of their shots are not likely to be helped that much by simply making a change in the CG. The clubmaker can try to help this player by recommending a clubhead with a CG that is higher and closer to the face, but the loft will also have to be changed to have any real effect on lowering the height of the shot.

As with the loft recommendations, **anytime the player talks about hitting the ball too high, the clubmaker should analyze the ball position and make a suggestion to move the ball back to the traditional address position if it is too far forward in the stance.**

FAST FACT:

To decrease shot Trajectory requires all of the specifications working together, including loft, CG and offset, in order to have a chance of affecting the height of the shot from a player who complains of hitting the ball too high. More times than not, the only way the average player can reduce Trajectory is by making a ball position change in the stance.

E. CHOOSING VERTICAL ROLL TO INCREASE/DECREASE TRAJECTORY

As with the horizontal bulge of wood heads, the range of vertical roll selection for each wood head number is limited because most companies do not try to change the roll to be different than the normal range seen in the golf industry. However, it is a fact that many of the metal woods in the golf industry are made with too much vertical radius for the standard

Medium Factors
of Trajectory

specification of the head number. It will be wise for the clubmaker to check this specification on all woods that might be headed for the bags of players who either sky the ball or hit the ball thin. The greater the radius of the roll, the higher the shot will be hit when contact is made on top of the face (sky shot) and, the lower the shot will be when contact is made on the bottom of the face (thin shot).

Again, being practical, regardless if there is extra roll curvature or not, any player who hits the ball high on the insert will hit the ball high and any player who hits the ball low on the face will hit the ball low. Theoretically, the clubmaker should look for wood heads with a minimum of 4 inches of radius difference between the bulge and roll (with roll being a higher number by 4 inches) for virtually all players, but especially the players who complain of either hitting the ball too high or too low with the woods. (And then check their ball position and how high they are teeing the ball!)

FAST FACT:
Inspect the face of the woods being considered for the player to be sure the roll is not too great (too much curvature). The greater the radius of the roll, the higher the shot will be hit when contact is made on top of the face (sky shot) and the lower the shot will be when contact is made on the bottom of the face (thin shot). The clubmaker should look for wood heads which have a minimum of 4 inches of radius difference between the bulge and the roll (with roll being a higher number by 4 inches) for virtually all players, but especially the players who complain of hitting the ball too high or too low with the woods.

F. CHOOSING FACE PROGRESSION/HOSEL OFFSET TO INCREASE/DECREASE TRAJECTORY

The better the player, the more that an offset clubhead design will affect the Trajectory of the shot in both woods and irons. Among average to higher handicap players, a change in offset of the woods will have a much more dramatic effect on Trajectory than will a change in offset in the irons.

To increase the Trajectory through a change in offset, the clubmaker would need to recommend more offset in the woods and irons, while to decrease the Trajectory would call for an decrease or a substantial reduction of the offset in the woods and irons.

If the average to higher handicap player wants to hit the ball higher, recommend changing to a set of woods and irons with maximum offset. In the case of the woods there is really only one style of offset wood head that is usually offered by most companies. However, because there are variations in the amount of offset in irons, a maximum amount of iron offset would be 6-8mm of 'constant' offset in each head in the set.

If the average to higher handicap player wants to hit the ball lower, the only way that a non-offset design can help is if the player was previously using a set of offset woods. It is not as likely that a change from an offset to a non-offset set of irons would have very much of an effect on changing the **Trajectory** with the irons as it would in changing from an offset to a non-offset set of woods.

If the better ball-striking player wishes to hit the ball a little higher with the woods, a change to an offset wood head design would likely cause the Trajectory to increase too much. However, this would have to be judged by the player after hitting several shots comparing the offset to the non-offset wood head design. **Should the better ball-striking player wish to hit the ball a little higher with the irons, a change to an offset iron design could provide just the slight amount of Trajectory increase the better player desires.**

If the better ball striker is already playing with a set of irons which has 6-8mm of hosel offset, and wants to hit the ball higher, the change will have to come from specifications other than offset such as the CG or loft angles of the clubheads.

For assistance in hitting the long irons only slightly higher but leaving the Trajectory of the middle and short irons the same, the clubmaker could recommend a set of irons with "Progressive Offset" where the long irons are made with 5-8mm of offset, middle irons with 3-5mm and short irons with 1-3mm.

When making the Preliminary Fitting recommendation it is only necessary to note "non-offset," "progressive offset," or "maximum offset" in the listing of the recommended specifications rather than to try to list an actual amount of offset.

FAST FACT:
The clubmaker can use hosel offset to increase the Trajectory in the woods more than in the irons. By advising a change from a non-offset to an offset wood head design, the player can acquire a noticeable increase in Trajectory. However, the increase in Trajectory that comes from changing from irons with no offset to irons with offset is much less noticeable, with the only exception being the better ball striker. The better ball striker, who is more sensitive to noticing flight change, will likely see what he/she believes to be a more substantial increase in Trajectory from a maximum offset hosel iron design (6-8mm) than will the higher handicap player.

Likewise, if the better player wants to decrease the Trajectory and the player has been using a set of irons with offset, the conversion to a non-offset (1-3mm) design will normally cause a change slight enough in shot height to satisfy the better player. In the case of the average player who hits the ball too high, the change to a non-offset iron will not afford enough of a change. Once again, the higher handicap players who hit the ball too high are best served by a change in loft or by moving the ball back in their stance.

IV. BACKSPIN

MAJOR Effect Specifications – The Specifications to Address First to Increase Backspin

A. CHOOSING LOFT TO INCREASE BACKSPIN

Trajectory and Backspin are very much interrelated in the Golfsmith Practical Fitting Program because in general, the higher the shot, the greater the backspin. The reason the Practical Fitting Program addresses Backspin as a separate game improvement factor is because a player usually wants to increase **Backspin** only in the short irons and wedges. Occasionally, the clubmaker will hear from a player who uses the fairway woods to hit a lot of his/her shots into the greens and also wishes to increase his/her ability to stop the ball on the green with these clubs.

To make a noticeable increase in Backspin through a change in loft, the clubmaker has to increase the loft angle by a minimum of 2° to 3° more than the loft of the current clubs, or even more if the requirement for Backspin is greater. To recommend the exact loft angle for each club to increase **Backspin** will require the clubmaker to refer to the loft measurements from the previous set determined in the Equipment Evaluation and make the minimum 2° loft increase in relation to these readings.

Even though loft is the only specification which has a **MAJOR** effect on **Backspin, when loft is increased to enhance Backspin, the clubmaker has to evaluate if the resulting possible loss of Distance is worth the increase in Backspin.** In some cases it will not be, especially if the player discovers he or she has to hit a longer club into the green.

When the player wishes to increase loft only in one part of the iron set to increase Backspin, the loft change must be made in a progressive manner to prevent gaps in yardage between any of the clubs. Learn from the example created in the following chart for a player wishing to increase **Backspin** in the middle and short irons but who does not want to lose **Distance** or create a gap in yardage between any two clubs in the set.

Head	Current Loft (for example)	Desired Loft for Backspin	Compromise Lofts for Backspin with little Distance loss	Current Lengths	New Lengths
1-iron	16°	no change	no change	40″	40″
2-iron	19°	no change	no change	39.5″	39.5″
3-iron	22°	no change	no change	39″	39″
4-iron	25°	no change	no change	38.5″	38.5″
5-iron	28°	30°	29°	38″	38 1/8″
6-iron	32°	34°	33.5°	37.5″	37 3/4″
7-iron	36°	39°	38°	37″	37 3/8″
8-iron	40°	43°	42°	36.5″	37″
9-iron	44°	47°	46.5°	36″	36 5/8″
PW	48°	51°	51	35.5″	36 1/4″
SW	54°	56°	56°	35.5″	36″
60° wedge	new club	60°	60°	35.5″	35 3/4″

Remember, **it is completely acceptable to alter the length to help overcome the potential loss of Distance or gap in yardage between clubs when the loft is increased**. In addition, this procedure of manipulating the lofts and lengths will increase the **Trajectory** and can be added to the discussion in this chapter about using loft to change **Trajectory**.

If the golfer has the ability to hit the ball on-center a higher percentage of the time, it is acceptable for the clubmaker to recommend a 2° minimum increase in loft along with a 1/2" increase in length to allow the golfer to gain more Backspin on the fairway woods.

For the higher handicap player, the preferred method for increasing Backspin in the fairway woods will be switching to a set of offset woods with the same loft or even 1-2° less loft than the player's current fairway woods. This fitting recommendation will prevent a loss in **Distance** as the offset will increase **Trajectory** and make the stronger loft easy enough to hit higher and achieve the desired result of stopping the ball on the green faster.

The primary area the clubmaker will receive a request for more **Backspin** will be in the wedges. Because most golfers do not (and should not) hit the wedges for maximum **Distance** each time they are used, **the preferred method for increasing Backspin on the wedges is to increase the loft. If the player is concerned about losing Distance in the wedges even though there is a desire for more Backspin, the length of the wedges can be increased by 1/2" to 3/4"**. To offer the most help in stopping the ball on the green with the wedges, a set makeup change in the number of different wedges, one or more of which may incorporate a loft increase, should be combined together.

Points for the clubmaker to consider when changing the set makeup and lofts of the wedges to increase Backspin should be noted as follows:

√ First, note the 9-iron loft. The PW loft should not be more than 5° greater than the loft of the 9-iron.

√ The loft difference between any two wedges should not be more than 7° to prevent problems with too much of a yardage gap between the wedges.

√ Three wedges is the traditional set makeup to follow if the loft of the PW is not less than 48° and the golfer does not want to change the lofts of the short irons. (E.G. PW = 48°; SW = 55°; High-Loft Wedge = 60°.)

√ If the loft of the PW is 47° or less and the golfer does not want to change the lofts of the short irons, the clubmaker should consider recommending 4 wedges in total. (E.G. PW = 46°; 'Gap' wedge = 50°; SW = 55°/56°; High-Loft Wedge = 60°.)

FAST FACT:

The main way to increase Backspin is to increase loft. For the Backspin to be increased enough to make a real difference in stopping the ball on the green, the loft will have to be increased by at least 2-3° over what the loft of the same club was in the current set. To prevent such a loft increase from causing a problem with a loss of Distance, it is acceptable to

**Medium Factors
of Backspin**

change the length increment between clubs so the shorter clubs get progressively longer in length, and in the process help pick up some of the Distance lost by the loft increase.

The best way to increase Backspin on the woods is to determine if the player can make a switch to a set of fairway woods with an offset hosel design. If this style of wood head does not appeal to the player, the other method for increasing Backspin is an increase in loft at the same time as the length is increased, but only if the player can still hit the longer woods on-center the same percentage of the time.

Backspin increases are most often sought on the wedges. To increase Backspin, increasing loft is always the best procedure because in the wedges most players can adjust to the potential Distance loss. Should the loss of Distance not be acceptable with the increase in loft/Backspin, the clubmaker could increase the length of the wedges or instruct the player to lengthen the swing slightly to offset the loss of Distance.

B. CHOOSING SET MAKEUP TO INCREASE BACKSPIN

Because set makeup can be influential in changing the **Trajectory** of the player's shot pattern, it can also be helpful in increasing **Backspin** and the ability of the player to stop the ball on the green. **Again, there are two obvious areas where the set makeup can offer game improvement in Backspin – long irons and wedges.**

It is very common for a golfer to have problems hitting any iron longer than a 5-iron with enough **Trajectory** and **Backspin** to stop the ball on the green. **By replacing any long and even some middle irons with higher lofted fairway woods, the clubmaker can make a significant difference in increasing the height, and accordingly the ability of the ball to stop on the green for shots that are supposed to carry the same Distance of a well-hit long iron.** Once again, the reason is because the CG on a fairway wood is much lower and farther back from the face than on any long iron.

The other area of the set that a change in the set makeup can improve the ability to stop the ball on the green is with the wedges. **By changing the type and loft of the wedges, the golfer can hit the ball higher and generate more Backspin.** By noting the lofts of the player's current wedges and changing to wedges that have greater loft, it will be possible to allow the golfer to use the same swing and hit the ball higher with more **Backspin** and better stop the ball on the green. (See Chapter 9 for more specific information about wedge fitting.)

FAST FACT:
Long irons are hard enough for most players to hit in the air at all, and even harder to hit high enough to generate enough Backspin to stop the ball on anything but a 10,000 sq. ft. green! In addition, when a long iron is required to 'lay up' in front of a hazard, it is also advantageous to hit the ball high with more Backspin. High-lofted fairway woods normally stop much faster

than long irons when they land because the CG is lower and much farther back from the face.

With the tremendous selection in styles and lofts of wedges, it is possible to change the player's wedge set makeup to enable him/her to generate more Backspin on the ball. Choosing higher, lofted wedges with less bounce sole angle is a great way to help the golfer hit high, soft landing shots from grassy lies. Choosing higher-lofted sand wedges with more bounce and a wider sole is a good way to help the player not only get out of the bunker more often, but to hit softer landing shots from the sand as well.

MEDIUM Effect Specifications – The Next Specifications to Address to Increase Backspin

Medium Factors of Backspin

C. CHOOSING FACE PROGRESSION/HOSEL OFFSET TO INCREASE BACKSPIN

The greater the amount of offset on both the fairway woods and the irons and wedges, the slightly higher the **Trajectory** of the shot and the better the ball will stop on the green. The greater the amount of offset change from the player's current set design, the more improved the player's ability is to stop the ball on the green. Keeping this in mind, it must be understood that the difference between a non-offset and a fully offset design is much greater in a wood head design than an iron head design. That means the player looking for help in stopping the ball on the greens with the woods can expect to get more help from the offset than is possible to offer with the irons. If the golfer is regularly hitting fairway woods for the approach shots into par-3 and par-4 holes, and needs help stopping the ball on the green, the clubmaker should recommend the golfer use a set of offset woods.

While more offset can generate a slightly higher **Trajectory** with the irons, it is usually only the better player that can work the increase in offset into enough of a **Trajectory** and **Backspin** increase to make the ball stop better on the green. Better ball-striking players are more critical of the look of the clubheads they select. If the better player can get used to the look of the offset hosel on a new set of irons and particularly with the wedges, it will be possible to generate an increase in **Backspin**.

FAST FACT:

Increasing the offset of the clubhead will have a more dramatic effect on stopping the ball on the green with the fairway woods than it will with the irons. Slower swinging players who hit the ball shorter and accordingly, hit a high percentage of fairway woods into greens should consider changing to an offset wood head design to improve their ability to stop the ball.

While increasing offset on the irons can increase Trajectory and make it a little easier to stop the ball, this effect is slight. However, for the better player looking for that extra holding power on the green, a change to fully offset wedges can make a difference in how soft he/she can land the ball on the green.

Major Factors of Feel

V. FEEL

MAJOR Effect Specifications – The Specifications Addressed First to Improve the Feel of the Golf Club

A. CHOOSING SHAFT WEIGHT/TOTAL WEIGHT TO IMPROVE FEEL

It has been stressed many times that the weight of the shaft controls the total weight. Therefore, **anytime the shaft weight is being considered for the player, the total weight is automatically being chosen at the same time. In addition, from the standpoint of the weight of the club and how it affects its Feel, the swingweight must also be considered at the same time.** The same procedures that are used to recommend the correct shaft weight/total weight for **Accuracy** are the same procedures used in selecting the shaft weight/total weight that will **Feel** best for the player. This is because the overall weight of the golf club must **Feel** good to the player to allow him/her to generate a more consistent swing tempo and rhythm.

The proper shaft weight/total weight for offering the best Feel is the one that allows the golfer to swing with the most comfort and least effort during the swing, and allowing the golfer to control his or her tempo without consciously thinking about it. If the golfer says, "These clubs are OK but they're just a little bit heavy (or just a little bit light)" then that shaft weight/total weight is not the right choice to generate the best **Feel** for the golfer.

As far as the shaft weight/total weight to choose for improving **Feel** of the new clubs, the clubmaker has to start with a cardinal rule of clubmaking which states that, **"Unless the player has enough experience to tell the clubmaker what type of shaft weight/total weight (and swingweight) would Feel the best, the clubmaker has to fit the player into the lightest shaft weight/total weight they can control." To think in terms of light over heavy means the club would be more comfortable to swing, which in turn means the club would Feel better.**

Some guidelines to help the player make the shaft weight/total weight decision for Feel are as follows:

STEP 1 - **Ask the player, "Do the current clubs Feel too heavy or too light in any way?" Do they Feel too heavy or light in general, or do they Feel too heavy or too light in the clubhead?"** The player will either respond with a yes, no or not too sure. If the player thinks his/her current clubs are too heavy or too light, ask if he/she is talking about the overall weight or head weight. From that answer, the clubmaker can advise a higher or lower shaft weight and higher/lower swingweight from reacting to the measurement of the total weight and swingweight of the current clubs.

STEP 2 - If the player is not sure if their clubs **Feel** heavy or not, or they are not sure if the heaviness or lightness is from the overall weight or head weight, the clubmaker must find out if the player wants to have graphite or steel shafts in the new set. In other words, **the clubmaker has to diplomatically inquire whether the golfer wants to spend the money for graphite or steel**.

STEP 3 - If the golfer wants graphite but wants to keep the cost as low as possible, the clubmaker has to wait until the shaft flex fitting segment in the Practical Fitting Program before determining if there are inexpensive graphite shafts that fit the player for the right flex, torque and bend point which are also available in a weight lighter than the shafts of the current set. (Remember, if the player is not sure if his/her current clubs are too light or too heavy, the logical reaction for the clubmaker to believe is that the clubs are in all likelihood not too heavy or else the golfer surely would have noticed that. In that case, the clubmaker can react to the current total weight of the golfer's clubs and look for a shaft that is lighter.)

STEP 4 - **If the golfer wants steel shafts to save money and doesn't have an opinion of whether his/her current clubs are too heavy or too light, the clubmaker should choose a lightweight steel shaft in the range of 95-110g in weight**. The comfort portion of the shaft weight/total weight fitting for **Feel** will have to come from choosing the right flex to match the player's swing speed and downswing acceleration, which will come later in the session.

STEP 5 - If the player wants graphite in the woods (or just the driver) and steel shafts in the irons, the clubmaker should choose from the group of lightweight steel shafts in the range of 110g for the irons. The shaft weight for the woods should be chosen using the following general guidelines:

√ If the player is more interested in gaining **Distance** than **Accuracy** along with having better **Feel**, the shaft should weigh less than 70g and preferably less than 60g, making sure the new shaft weighs at least 45g less than the player's current shaft weight.

√ If the player is interested in gaining **Distance**, **Accuracy** and better **Feel**, the clubmaker has to look at the player's strength, tempo and downswing acceleration, following accordingly:

> **Fast tempo swing seeking better Distance, Accuracy and Feel**
> **Shaft weight under 85g with slightly higher swingweight**; Swingweight increasing proportionately as shaft weight decreases from 85g.

> **Smooth tempo swing seeking better Distance, Accuracy and Feel**
> **Shaft weight under 70g with normal swingweight range.**
> Swingweight slightly decreasing for players with slower swing speeds within this type of player.

> **Slow to normal backswing tempo, much faster downswing seeking better Distance, Accuracy and Feel**
> **Shaft weight 75-90g with slightly higher swingweight.**
> Swingweight higher for players with higher swing speeds within this type of player.

Major Factors of Feel

Fast backswing fast downswing seeking better Distance, Accuracy and Feel

Shaft weight 85-95g with slightly higher swingweight. Swingweight higher for players with higher swing speeds within this type of player.

Powerful swing but not overly fast tempo seeking better Distance, Accuracy and Feel

Shaft weight 75-90g with normal to very slightly higher swingweight. Swingweight slightly higher for players with higher swing speeds within this type of player.

Weaker swing with very little sense of power seeking better Distance, Accuracy and Feel

Shaft weight under 70g with slightly lower than normal swingweight range. Swingweight slightly decreasing for players with slower swing speeds within this type of player.

Very fast wild swing tempo and physically strong player seeking better Distance, Accuracy and Feel

Shaft weight 100g + with higher than normal swingweight. Swingweight slightly higher for players with higher swing speeds within this type of player.

FAST FACT:

When choosing the shaft weight/total weight with the best Feel in mind, the swingweight must also be considered because all three combined are what controls the golfer's comfort level in swinging the club. Accomplished, experienced players will most likely tell the clubmaker the shaft weight range they want to use by referring to the total weight of a particular club. The clubmaker can then measure the total weight of the favorite club and calculate the shaft weight requirement to follow for the new set.

For all other players with a moderate amount of playing experience, the clubmaker should select the lightest shaft weight the player can control. The control part of the shaft weight selection will be determined by the swingweight that is chosen to go with the shaft weight selection. In general, tests have shown that virtually any player can successfully use ultra light shafts to obtain better Feel as long as the length and swingweight (clubhead Feel) match the tempo and Feel needs of the player.

However, shafts that weigh less than 70g are among the most expensive shafts. Therefore, if the player is not that concerned with the cost of the equipment, the clubmaker should consider the possibility of using a sub 70g shaft for virtually all players using the length and swingweight to make the shaft weight/total weight fit the swing tempo and timing of the player.

The only players who are better off using heavy total weight clubs for better Feel are: 1) Those who specifically request a heavier weight. Traditionally, these will be more accomplished players who are aggressive hitters of the ball. 2) Physically big, strong players who "muscle" the ball with what is described as an "arm type swing." 3) Strong players who either pull the ball severely or suffer from Accuracy problems in both directions.

B. CHOOSING SWINGWEIGHT/GOLF CLUB BALANCE POINT TO IMPROVE FEEL

The same procedures and guidelines that were used to determine swingweight and achieve the player's Distance and Accuracy goals will suffice for Feel as well. There is no such thing as an optimum swingweight for **Distance** and **Accuracy** and a separate optimum swingweight for **Feel**.

However, by observing the answers to the questions from the Playing Goals section of the Player Interview, "I want to **Feel** the clubhead more at the top of the backswing", "I want to **Feel** more kick in the shaft", or "I want more clubhead **Feel**", the clubmaker can get a general idea of whether the golfer wants a "head heavy" type of swingweight **Feel** or more of a "head light" **Feel** in the clubhead.

When fitting the golfer into a lighter total weight golf club, it is very important to note the tempo, rhythm and strength of the golfer in order to determine if the swingweight should be recommended to create a "head heavy" (higher than normal swingweight) or "head light" (normal to slightly lower than normal swingweight) type of clubhead **Feel. If the player indicates even just one of the following from the Player Interview - a desire for more clubhead Feel, a feeling of more shaft kick or to Feel the clubhead more at the top of the backswing, the clubmaker has to opt for a swingweight higher than normal for the length of the clubs.** Again, refer to the following chart of recommended swingweights as the starting point for making the swingweight recommendation for better **Feel**.

Swingweight Recommendations Based on Using a Shaft Weight of 70g or less:

TEMPO	SWING SPEED with Driver	43.5"-1w/38"-5i Swingweight	42.5"-1w/37"-5i Swingweight
Fast, quick, a golfer who is more of a "Hitter"	under 50mph	D1	C9
	50-65mph	D2	D0
	65-80mph	D3	D1
	80-90mph	D4	D2
	90-105mph	D5	D3
	105+mph	D7	D5
Slow, smooth tempo, a golfer who is more of a "Swinger"	under 50mph	C8	C6
	50-65mph	D0	C8
	65-80mph	D1	C9
	80-90mph	D2	D0
	90-105mph	D2	D0
	105+mph	D4	D2

Major Factors of Feel

Swingweight Recommendations Based on Using a Shaft Weight of 71-95g:

TEMPO	SWING SPEED with Driver	43.5"-1w/38"-5i Swingweight	42.5"-1w/37"-5i Swingweight
Fast, quick, a golfer who is more of a "Hitter"	under 50mph	D0	C8
	50-65mph	D1	C9
	65-80mph	D1	C9
	80-90mph	D2	D0
	90-105mph	D2	D0
	105+mph	D3	D1
Slow, smooth tempo, a golfer who is more of a "Swinger"	under 50mph	C8	C6
	50-65mph	C9	C7
	65-80mph	D0	C8
	80-90mph	D0	C8
	90-105mph	D0	C8
	105+mph	D1	C9

Swingweight Recommendations Based on Using a Shaft Weight of 95g +:

TEMPO	SWING SPEED with Driver	43.5"-1w/38"-5i Swingweight	42.5"-1w/37"-5i Swingweight
Fast, quick, a golfer who is more of a "Hitter"	under 50mph	C8	C6
	50-65mph	C8	C6
	65-80mph	C9	C7
	80-90mph	D0	C8
	90-105mph	D1	C9
	105+mph	D1	C9
Slow, smooth tempo, a golfer who is more of a "Swinger"	under 50mph	C6	C4
	50-65mph	C6	C4
	65-80mph	C7	C5
	80-90mph	C8	C6
	90-105mph	C9	C7
	105+mph	D0	C8

NOTE: For longer lengths with all shaft weight ranges, increase the swingweight by 2 swingweight points for each 1/2" increase in length up to a maximum length of 45" on the driver and 39" on the 5-iron. For shorter lengths, decrease the swingweight by 2 swingweight points for each 1/2" decrease in length down to a minimum length of 41.5" on the driver and 36" on the 5-iron. For lengths greater than 45" on the driver and 39" on the 5-iron, head weight will have to decrease more to prevent the clubs from feeling too "head heavy" due to the greater length placing mass farther from the hands and accentuating the feeling of head weight.

FAST FACT:

The swingweight that is identified as the optimum level for achieving an improvement in Distance and Accuracy will also be the best swingweight for achieving the utmost in Feel. Therefore, the guidelines established in the Fitting for Distance section of this chapter that recommended the proper starting swingweight for the player will also suffice for the needs of Feel.

C. CHOOSING SHAFT FLEX TO IMPROVE FEEL

The actual flex of the shaft must be determined by measuring the player's swing speed and rate of downswing acceleration and comparing those evaluations to an RSSR listing of the shafts.

However, to improve clubhead Feel for the player, the choice of the shaft will need to be slightly more flexible than what the swing speed and downswing acceleration of the player might normally indicate. In other words, it is necessary for the shaft to be slightly more flexible than what is considered a normal RSSR match to the golfer.

FAST FACT:
If the player wants the utmost in solid clubhead Feel and a sensation of feeling the shaft kick, the shaft should be slightly more flexible. In short, the RSSR rating of the shaft will need to be 10-15mph lower than the clubhead speed of the player.

D. CHOOSING LENGTH TO IMPROVE FEEL

For the best **Feel**, the length of the club must match the athletic ability and physical coordination of the player while allowing him/her to swing with the most ease and comfort, yet still hit the ball on-center the highest percentage of the time. If the player is saddled with clubs that can only be hit solidly once in a while, or **Feel** too cumbersome or awkward to swing, the length is too long. If the player's clubs force him/her to crouch over the ball in an uncomfortable stance, the clubs are too short. For the best **Feel** from the length of the clubs, the player should **Feel** comfortable addressing the ball and be able to swing with ease and comfort.

For that reason the guidelines established for recommending the proper club length for the utmost **Accuracy** are the same guidelines to follow for recommending proper length for the best **Feel**.

√ Measure the golfer with the wrist-to-floor ruler to determine the recommended length for the comfort of the golfer. The wrist-to-floor ruler will take into account the physical size of the player including height, arm length and leg length, and can should be used only as a starting point for making the length recommendation.

If the player has indicated a desire for more **Distance** and/or better **Accuracy** on the Player Interview Form, the length requirements for **Feel** must also satisfy the desire for **Distance** and **Accuracy** as follows:

√ If the driver and 5-iron lengths recommended by the measurement of the wrist-to-floor fitting ruler are **greater** than the length of the player's current driver and 5-iron by more than 1", the clubmaker should keep the length the same in the new set and focus the **Accuracy** improvement on either the face angle or lie angle recommendations.

√ If the driver and 5-iron lengths recommended by the measurement of the wrist-to-floor fitting ruler are **equal** to the length of the player's current driver and 5-iron, reduce the driver (and other woods) length by

**Major Factors
of Feel**

1" and the 5-iron (and other irons) by 1/2" in an effort to help with the **Accuracy** problem. No more than this amount should be reduced in order to prevent the golfer from losing too much **Distance** or ending up with a length that forces him/her to crouch uncomfortably over the ball.

√ If the driver and 5-iron lengths recommended by the measurement of the ruler are **less** than the length of the player's current driver and 5-iron, make the length of the driver 1" shorter (with the other woods in accordance) and the 5-iron 1/2" shorter (with the other irons in accordance) than the lengths recommended by the ruler to help with the **Accuracy** problem.

√ If the golfer's previous driver and 5-iron are 1" or longer than the driver and 5-iron lengths recommended by the ruler measurement, the new lengths should be no longer than the recommendation of the ruler.

As a general guideline for the best Feel, the golfer has to be comfortable in the address position, so the length cannot be shortened so much that it makes the golfer crouch over the ball in an uncomfortable manner.

For the sake of comfort and Feel, it is completely acceptable for the clubmaker to change from the normal 1" increments between each of the woods as well as the usual 1/2" increments between the irons. By trimming lengths of the woods in 3/4" increments and irons in 3/8" increments, the clubmaker can keep the length of the driver and longer irons at standard (making the longer woods and longest irons more comfortable to swing), while progressively increasing the length on the clubs that are easier to hit in the first place. This is particularly helpful in the case of the tall golfer with shorter arms or longer legs – the clubs that are harder to swing comfortably are kept at relatively shorter lengths while the clubs that are not as hard to hit are allowed to progressively become longer, in the process making the tall golfer **Feel** more comfortable over the ball.

FAST FACT:
The correct length for the best Feel should be the length that makes the golfer Feel the most comfortable when assuming his/her normal stance at address. Any shorter than this and the golfer might make mistakes resulting in mishits from the uncomfortable feeling. Any longer than this might accentuate the errors of the clubhead path and face angle that can cause an Accuracy problem. Because maximum Distance and Accuracy come from hitting the ball more on-center, and because swing path errors are easier to correct with a shorter length, it is completely acceptable for the clubmaker to fit the length slightly shorter than traditional standards, as long as the golfer is still comfortable.

E. CHOOSING GRIP SIZE TO IMPROVE FEEL

As obvious as it may sound, the grip is the only physical contact the player has with the golf club. If the grip is not comfortable, there is no way a player can make a swing with a consistent tempo and rhythm.

However, the grip size will not be listed in the Preliminary Fitting Recommendation because proper grip size fitting requires the clubmaker to ask the player to select a size from a series of sample grip sizes or to use a measuring device such as the Golfsmith Grip Sizer to determine the actual grip size. Despite the techniques that exist for checking the size of the grip in accordance with the distance of the fingers from the heel of the hand, the primary guideline for recommending proper grip size to the player for the purpose of developing the best **Feel** will be comfort. (See Chapter 7 for fitting grip size.)

FAST FACT:

   Grip size cannot be listed in the Preliminary Fitting Recommendation because it requires the clubmaker to take measurements of the golfer's hands. Therefore, grip size will be fit along with proper lie, shaft flex and the wrist-to-floor length measurement for length.

   Above all else, the grip size is determined on the basis of comfort first.

MEDIUM Effect Specifications – The Next Specifications to Address to Improve the Feel of the Golf Club

Medium Factors of Feel

F. CHOOSING THE CLUBHEAD DESIGN TO IMPROVE FEEL

The two different factors involved in recommending the proper clubhead design for the player from the standpoint of **Feel** are CG and weight distribution. **CG is more important in its effect on Distance, Accuracy, Trajectory and Backspin, while weight distribution is more important with regard to the Feel of the clubhead.**

To make the proper choice of weight distribution on the clubhead with regard to **Feel** in the Preliminary Fitting Recommendation, the clubmaker must focus primarily on how solid and how much of the time the player hits the ball on-center. **The more the player has a tendency to hit the ball off-center, the more the clubmaker will want to recommend a clubhead with the maximum in perimeter weighting. If the player has the ability to hit the ball on-center most of the time, the clubmaker can recommend either a perimeter weighted or non-perimeter weighted clubhead design, whatever the player prefers.**

Therefore, the clubmaker has to note the responses the player makes to questions from the Playing Goals section of the Player Interview such as "I want to hit the ball more solidly," "I want better clubhead **Feel**," "I want to stop hitting the ball thin," or "I want to stop skying the ball." If the player indicates a desire to hit the ball more solidly and the ball-striking tendencies from the Player Interview indicate the player hits the ball off-center enough to be noted as a chronic problem, the clubmaker has to recommend a perimeter-weighted design. The more perimeter weighted

Medium Factors of Feel

the clubhead, the more solidly the shot will **Feel** when it is hit off-center, and the better the club will **Feel** to the player overall.

Because a muscleback, non-perimeter-weighted club tends to Feel very unsolid when hit off-center and considering the fact that no golfer hits the ball on-center all the time, the clubmaker has to leave the decision of muscleback vs. perimeter weighted in the hands of the player who is the better ball striker.

~~FAST FACT.~~

From analyzing the ball-striking tendencies and the playing goals parts of the Player Interview, the clubmaker has to recommend a perimeter-weighted clubhead design for any golfer who indicates a desire to hit the ball more solidly, or who reports any tendency of hitting the ball off-center.

The player who hits the ball on-center the majority of the time is free to choose any type of weight distribution in the clubhead, with the understanding a muscleback style of weight distribution does not improve the on-center hit as much as it makes the off-center hit Feel very unsolid, in comparison to the perimeter-weighted clubheads.

G. CHOOSING SHAFT BEND POINT TO IMPROVE FEEL

The primary contribution of shaft bend point is a slight change in the Feel of the shaft. While some accomplished players can perceive a slight change in **Trajectory** from a change in bend point, more than 95 percent of all golfers cannot. Therefore, **the selection of bend point from among the shafts that fit the player will be made on the basis of meeting the Feel needs of the player**. Although the shaft industry identifies low, mid and high bend points on the shafts they design, **the Golfsmith Practical Fitting Program believes the difference in Feel between high and mid bend point shafts is so slight they must be classified as the same in terms of Feel**. Therefore, the clubmaker will only have to make a recommendation for the player between a low bend point shaft and a high or mid bend point shaft.

Remember, the actual shaft choice is not going to be made in the **Preliminary Fitting Recommendation**. That will be performed after the clubmaker compiles the Preliminary Fitting Recommendation. **For now, the clubmaker only has to indicate whether the golfer should have a low or a mid/high-bend point shaft in the Preliminary Fitting Recommendation.**

Recommending the bend point is very simple. The player will either tell the clubmaker the Feel he/she desires in the shaft, which can then be translated into a choice between a low or mid/high bend point, or the player will have no idea of what Feel he/she would like in the shaft at which point the clubmaker will choose a low bend point for the player.

To help clarify the selection, the clubmaker can ask the player, "Do you like to **Feel** the shaft kick as it comes through impact, or do you like to **Feel** the shaft as if it were not bending at all through impact, as if it were more of a "one-piece," firm action through impact?" **If the golfer tells the clubmaker he/she likes to Feel a "kick" or "'snap" in the shaft, the clubmaker will indicate a low-bend point on the Preliminary Fitting Recommendation**. On the other hand, it is more common for the accomplished golfer with a sense of **Feel** to prefer a shaft that does not kick too much through the ball. In this case, **when the golfer indicates he/she wants the shaft to Feel like it exhibits a "one-piece action" through the ball with no kick, the clubmaker should write down a recommendation for a mid/high-bend point shaft.**

When the clubmaker asks the golfer for a preference in the kick action of the shaft or not and the reply is one of confusion or bewilderment, the clubmaker should always indicate low-bend point on the Preliminary Fitting Recommendation. Finally, if the player answers yes to one or more of the following questions on the Player Interview, "I want to Feel more kick in the shaft," "I want to hit the woods/irons more solid," or "I want better clubhead Feel," the clubmaker should indicate a low bend point shaft on the Preliminary Fitting Recommendation.

FAST FACT

The Golfsmith Practical Fitting Program believes the primary contribution of bend point is to enhance the feeling of a solid shot, and not to increase or decrease Trajectory. In addition, The Golfsmith Practical Fitting Program believes there is not enough difference in Feel between a mid- and high-bend point shafts to merit treating them as different shafts as far as bend point is concerned.

While the actual shaft fitting will be determined when the clubhead speed and downswing acceleration of the golfer are measured, the clubmaker can determine enough from the Player Interview and talking to the golfer to make an initial recommendation whether the golfer will be better off with a shaft and a low-bend point or a mid/high-bend point.

If the player wants a firm Feel through impact and is not comfortable with the feeling of the shaft "kicking" through the ball, the clubmaker will recommend a mid- or high-bend point shaft. If the player desires a feeling of the shaft kicking through impact, or if the golfer has no idea of the Feel of the shaft, the clubmaker will recommend a low-bend point shaft.

H. CHOOSING SHAFT TORQUE TO IMPROVE FEEL

As mentioned earlier in this chapter in the fitting of shaft torque for **Accuracy, when the flex of the shaft is chosen by matching the RSSR of the shaft to the swing speed of the player, the torque is automatically factored into the selection at the same time.** As it will be explained in Chapter 7, the flex and torque of all shafts can be combined to determine the overall stiffness of the shaft. The lower the degrees of torque, the greater resistance of the shaft to any twisting force, so the stiffer the

**Medium Factors
of Feel**

shaft will **Feel**. The higher the torque in degrees, the more soft the shaft will **Feel**.

Chapter 7 will explain how the flex and torque of a shaft can be combined in such a way as to reference the shaft in terms of a swing speed requirement, called the RSSR of the shaft (Recommended Shaft Speed Rating). As long as the shaft flex fitting is performed in a way to match the swing speed rating of the shaft to the swing speed and downswing acceleration of the player, the torque will be properly fit to the player for **Feel**.

Beyond that, it is possible to select a shaft with an RSSR compatible to the player's swing speed that has a slightly lower or higher torque measurement to "fine tune" the shaft for **Feel** (and **Accuracy**). In such a case, **among two shafts with the same swing speed rating, the one with the lower degree of torque will make the tip end of the shaft Feel slightly more firm while the one with the higher degree of torque will make the tip end Feel slightly more flexible**.

This is a very slight factor in the **Feel** of a shaft that does not have to be accounted for in the overall shaft fitting process if the player or the clubmaker chooses not to do so. Other factors such as bend point, swingweight/golf club balance point and the flex itself will have as much or more of an effect on the **Feel** of the shaft than trying to individually choose a different torque within a number of shafts that match the swing speed of the player. In other words, **don't worry about trying to fit torque for Feel as a separate matter from its role in determining the swing speed requirement of the shaft**.

FAST FACT:
The torque of the shaft does have an effect on the stiffness Feel of the shaft. The lower the degrees of torque, the stiffer the tip section of the shaft will Feel and the higher the degrees of the torque, the softer the tip section of the shaft will Feel. As a Feel factor, torque is not usually fit independently for the player because it is already included as part of the shaft flex fitting. Therefore, unless the clubmaker wishes to experiment with Feel for the player with a very refined sense of Feel for the shot, it is not necessary to worry about trying to choose a torque outside of its role in determining the swing speed requirement of the shaft.

I. CHOOSING GRIP WEIGHT TO IMPROVE FEEL

One of the most beneficial developments in the clubmaking industry in the 1990s has been the introduction of lighter weight grips. **A lightweight grip can be installed to increase the sensation of feeling the clubhead during the swing, and reduce the total weight of the club at the same time.** The result is a higher swingweight and more clubhead **Feel** without actually adding any weight to the head.

If the player answers yes to any of the following questions from the Playing Goals section of the Player Interview, "I want to Feel more kick in the shaft," "I want to hit the woods/irons more solid," or "I

want better clubhead Feel," the clubmaker should make every attempt to urge the golfer to choose a grip style from among the available lightweight grip models to enhance the sensation of feeling the club-head more during the swing. The benefits of feeling the clubhead more without increasing the total weight are so positive to the majority of golfers that the clubmaker should almost automatically recommend the use of lightweight grips.

Another very beneficial reason for using lightweight grips is to enhance the Feel of the club whenever the golfer requests or requires oversize grips. When oversize grips are installed using a normal weight grip, the balance point of the club moves away from the clubhead and the total weight of the club is increased, both of which can rob the player of clubhead **Feel. By starting with a lightweight grip, an oversize grip can be created that will be much lighter than the same oversize diameter created using a standard weight grip.**

The only potential problem in recommending lightweight grips is their current lack of available styles. As of this printing, lightweight grips are available in a limited selection of grip types, so it is possible the golfer may not be able to find a lightweight grip that suits his/her taste in style or texture. Undoubtedly this situation will improve through the late 1990s, as the popularity of light grips becomes more established through-out the golf equipment industry.

FAST FACT:
Grips are manufactured in a variety of different weights. By using a lightweight grip, the clubmaker can create clubs that have greater clubhead Feel for improving the consistency of the golfer's swing tempo and rhythm, and are lighter in total weight. Whenever possible, lighter weight grips should be recommended.

A REVIEW OF THE SPECIFICATIONS TO CONSIDER IN MAKING THE PRELIMINARY FITTING RECOMMENDATION

The previous section was created to teach the clubmaker the thought processes to go through to turn information from the Player Interview and Equipment Evaluation into the Preliminary Fitting Recommendation. To complete the Preliminary Fitting Recommendation, the clubmaker has to think in terms of the player's desires for game improvement by creat-ing a list of as many correct specifications as possible for the player by directly addressing his/her desire to increase **Distance**, improve **Accuracy**, increase or decrease **Trajectory**, increase **Backspin** and improve the **Feel** of the golf club. Remember, the Practical Fitting Program is intended to focus on those specifications that have a **MAJOR** or **MEDIUM** effect on increasing **Distance**, improving **Accuracy**, increas-ing or decreasing **Trajectory**, increasing **Backspin** and improving **Feel** of the golf club.

This is a departure from other fitting systems in the past that have trained the clubmaker to approach a fitting recommendation by going

Part II – Ball-Striking Tendencies

PART 2

BALL-STRIKING TENDENCIES

CHECK ANY SHOTMAKING TENDENCIES THAT APPLY TO EACH EQUIPMENT AREA IN YOUR GAME.
ESTIMATE CARRY DISTANCES AS CLOSELY AS POSSIBLE.

	TRAJECTORY			PREDOMINANT POINT OF IMPACT					HEEL	CEN	SHOT PATTERN	EST. CARRY DISTANCE	
	HIGH	MED	LOW	TOP	FAT	THIN							
DRIVER			X					X	X		A B C D E / F G (H) (I)	1w	200
F'WAY WDS.		X	X					X	X		A B C D E / F (g) H I	5w	185
1,2,3 IRONS			X								A B C D E / F G (H) I	3i	165
4,5,6 IRONS		X									A B C D (E) / F (g) H I	5i	155
7,8,9 IRONS		X									A B C D (E) / F G (H) I	7i	135
WEDGES	X	X									A (B) C D E / F G H I	PW	100

SHOT PATTERN

Where do your shots go?

A, B, C, D, E, F, G, H, I

If he was honest in his evaluation of his carry distances, Mr. Johnson has an average carry distance for his strength and handicap with his driver, but has a very short 15-yard difference between the driver and his favorite club, the 5-wood. He does not hit the long irons very far, which is why he indicated he does not like the 2- and 3-iron, while his middle and short iron distances are fairly typical for most 20 handicap players.

He says he hits the driver off-center, pushes or slices the ball with the driver most of the time and does not achieve much **Trajectory** with the club. He must not be much of a high-ball hitter because he indicates his shots travel on a medium to low **Trajectory** with his favorite club, the 5-wood. Because he indicates that he fades the ball with his favorite club, as well as the middle to short irons, Mr. Johnson might have somewhat of an outside-to-inside swing path and may also be leaving the face open at impact.

The short irons appear to be pushed, while the wedges are pulled to the left, so there could be a lie angle problem causing the tendency to hit the ball off-line with these clubs. Mr. Johnson did not indicate his predominant point of impact with the irons or wedges, but because his longest iron hit well is the 5-iron, he probably mishits the long irons while hitting the rest of the irons in the center of the face most of the time.

Ball-Striking Tendency Analysis

It can easily be seen that Mr. Johnson needs help with the driver as well as the fact he needs to replace the long irons with higher lofted fairway woods. He appears to be a slicer so there is an indication of a need for a face angle change that is more closed than his current woods, particularly on the driver. In addition, the total weight, length, swingweight, loft and possibly the shaft are probably suspect in the driver because he hits the ball short, low and off-center. Because Mr. Johnson is not a high-ball hitter, a lower CG clubhead with maximum perimeter-weighting must be the first choice.

The Accuracy problems of leaving the middle and short irons slightly to the right could be an indication of a lie angle that is too flat. However, the fact that he pulls the ball with the wedges might point to these clubs being too upright, as well as the possibility the swingweight may be too light. The Distance of the middle and short irons is typical for a 20 handicapper, but they are not that long. As a result, because Mr. Johnson seems to hit the ball well with these clubs, the loft or length could be altered to give him more Distance.

Part III – Playing Goals

PART 3

PLAYING GOALS

CHECK THE BOX OF EACH GOAL YOU WOULD LIKE TO REACH AND CIRCLE IF FOR WOODS, IRONS OR BOTH.

X	1. I WANT TO HIT THE (WOODS) IRONS HIGHER.			12. I WANT TO STOP HITTING THE WOODS/IRONS FAT.
	2. I WANT TO HIT THE WOODS/IRONS LOWER.	X		13. I WANT TO HIT THE WOODS/IRONS MORE SOLIDLY.
X	3. I WANT TO HIT THE (WOODS) IRONS FARTHER.	X		14. I WANT BETTER CLUBHEAD FEEL IN WOODS/IRONS.
X	4. I WANT TO HIT THE (WOODS) IRONS STRAIGHTER.	?		15. I WANT TO FEEL MORE KICK IN THE WOOD/IRON SHAFT.
	5. I WANT TO STOP SLICING THE WOODS/IRONS.	?		16. I WANT TO FEEL THE CLUBHEAD MORE AT THE TOP OF
	6. I WANT TO STOP HOOKING THE WOODS/IRONS.			THE BACKSWING WITH THE WOODS/IRONS.
X	7. I WANT TO STOP PUSHING THE WOODS (IRONS.)			17. I WANT TO HIT MY CHIPS LESS FAT.
X	8. I WANT TO STOP PULLING THE WOODS (IRONS.) PW SW			18. I WANT TO HIT MY CHIPS LESS THIN.
	9. I WANT TO STOP TOPPING THE WOODS/IRONS.	X		19. I WANT TO HIT MY SAND SHOTS LESS FAT.
	10. I WANT TO STOP SKYING THE WOODS/IRONS.			20. I WANT TO HIT MY SAND SHOTS LESS THIN.
	11. I WANT TO STOP HITTING THE WOODS/IRONS THIN.	X		21. I WANT A BETTER HOLD ON THE CLUB.

OVERALL GAME IMPROVEMENT DESIRES:

X	1. I WANT MORE DISTANCE. WOODS/IRONS			4. I WANT A LOWER TRAJECTORY. WOODS/IRONS
X	2. I WANT MORE ACCURACY. WOODS/IRONS	X		5. I WANT MORE BACKSPIN. IRONS/WEDGES
X	3. I WANT A HIGHER TRAJECTORY. WOODS IRONS	X		6. I WANT BETTER FEEL. WOODS/IRONS

Mr. Johnson appears desperate to obtain help with the driver because he has indicated a desire to hit the driver higher, farther, straighter, without a slice. In addition, he is aware of the problems of pushing and pulling the ball with the irons and wants to stop pushing the ball with the middle and short irons as well as pulling the ball with his wedges.

Mr. Johnson noted he does not hit the ball as solidly as he would like, adding that he cannot **Feel** the clubhead as much as he would like. The question marks indicate he is a bit confused by the questions of whether he wants to **Feel** the shaft kick during the swing or not and whether he should **Feel** the clubhead at the top of the swing, so he probably does not have much of a sense of **Feel** during the swing – something that is completely normal for a 20 handicap player. Mr. Johnson recognizes he has a need for improvement with his sand play, considering he has a problem getting the ball out of the bunker. Finally, he mentioned that he is having difficulty maintaining his grip on the club, possibly due to the hand discomfort problem or the condition and/or type of grip on his clubs.

In the overall game improvement desires, Mr. Johnson checked boxes 1, 2, 3, 5 and 6, indicating he wants the fitting to address matters of greater **Distance**, **Accuracy**, a need for higher **Trajectory**, more **Backspin** and better **Feel**. The real purpose of including these overall game improvement desires is for golfers who do not take the time to fill out the entire Player Interview Form, as well as to allow the clubmaker to clearly focus on the sections of the **MAJOR**, **MEDIUM** and **MINOR** effect list of specifications to reference when making the Preliminary Fitting Recommendations.

Playing Goals Analysis:

In the Player Interview, the Playing Goals section is the one that "pulls the whole interview information together" and allows the clubmaker to know exactly which specifications will be targeted for change in the new set. As a tip for using the Player Interview information most efficiently, it is a good idea for the clubmaker to study the Playing Goals before looking at the rest of the information. By doing this, the clubmaker will know what specifications are likely to be targeted while the analysis of the other interview information is being done.

In Mr. Johnson's case, the driver should be made with more loft, a lower CG, an offset hosel for more Trajectory, a face angle that is more closed than the current driver, a lower total weight and probably, a slightly higher than normal swingweight. Because Mr. Johnson hits the Nos. 3- and 5-woods well and wants more overall Distance, stronger lofted fairway woods can be recommended. Because he also wants more Trajectory but does not complain of hitting the ball thin with the woods, a wood head design should be chosen with more vertical roll curvature to help increase the Trajectory. In addition, Mr. Johnson should be fit into a slightly more flexible shaft than his clubhead speed might indicate because of his desire for a more solid Feel and an ability to Feel the shaft and clubhead during the swing.

Because of the desire to stop pushing and pulling the ball, the lie angles of all the new irons should carefully fit using one of the two dynamic lie fitting methods. Remember, it was not necessary to measure the existing lie angles of Mr. Johnson's clubs because the dynamic fitting procedure will automatically ensure the correct fit in the new clubs. In addition, to help the player hit the ball farther with the irons, the lofts will need to be a little stronger and the length might be a little longer. In fact, Mr. Johnson is a good candidate for altering the normal 1/2" length increment between the irons and even fairway woods to make the set become progressively longer through the high-lofted woods and fairway woods. This would have the effect of allowing him to achieve better Accuracy with the driver and greater Distance with the fairway woods.

To prevent the Trajectory from being too low, the new iron head lofts should not be more than 2° stronger than the current set, while the iron head design should have a low CG with slightly more offset. Delivering more Distance and increasing Trajectory is not easy to do in the same iron design. Often one will have to be sacrificed slightly in favor of what the golfer believes to be more important. To ensure a more solid Feel at impact as well as better clubhead Feel in the rest of the clubs, the clubmaker should be sure and consider lowering the total weight while probably increasing the swingweight in the same manner as the driver.

As mentioned before, a completely new sand wedge should be advised that would possibly have a little less bounce sole angle and slightly more narrow sole to possibly help get the wedge through the sand and the ball out more consistently. Finally, either new grips of a tackier, softer grip texture as well as a larger grip size would be advised to help Mr. Johnson maintain a better hold on the club and help alleviate some of the hand discomfort.

Part IV – Equipment Preferences

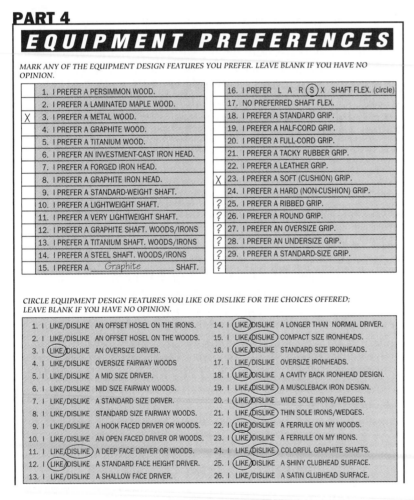

From analyzing the equipment preferences Mr. Johnson indicated in the Player Interview, it appears that while he has some distinct likes and dislikes, he is very much open to what the clubmaker thinks would make a better playing golf club. He does want oversized metal woods, and in particular, a driver with a face height that is not too deep.

Mr. Johnson also knows that he would be better off with a cavity-back iron design, as long as the iron head is not too large. However, there might have to be a compromise if he wishes to have any chance to increase **Trajectory** at the same time he increases **Distance**. For cosmetic purposes, he likes the look of a ferrule on his clubs, would rather have a black graphite shaft with a conservative logo, and would be more comfortable with a shiny type of finish on the clubheads. Because he thinks it will give him more **Distance**, he indicated that he wants to use a longer than standard driver.

Equipment Preference Analysis:

The clubmaker is going to have to try to find all of the anticipated wood head specifications of more loft (driver), less loft (fairway woods), closed face angle, low CG and slightly higher headweight, all on a set of oversize, offset metal woods with a standard face height. On the irons, the clubmaker will have to match up the need for heads which can be bent for a lie angle adjustment, slightly higher head weight for achieving a higher swingweight, less loft, low CG and more offset all in a standard size cavity-back design, with a square hosel (ferrule), medium width sole and satin finish.

GOLFSMITH PRACTICAL FITTING PROGRAM EXAMPLE

SECTION 2 – Equipment Evaluation Example - Bob Johnson

General comments:

After completing the Player Interview, the clubmaker will need to perform a brief Equipment Evaluation to determine a few key specifications from Mr. Johnson's current set of clubs.

From inspecting only the necessary specifications of Mr. Johnson's current set of golf clubs, a number of interesting points have surfaced that can explain some of the problems as well as some of the positive statements made on the Player Interview Form. The comments regarding the evaluation of the equipment will be categorized in terms of the driver, fairway woods, irons and wedges. After the specific comments regarding the equipment evaluation are completed, the Preliminary Fitting Recommendation for Mr. Johnson will be compiled.

CURRENT WOODS

Brand/Model: _Driver-BF-10 Stainless_____ ☐ Traditional Size ☐ Offset ☐ Non-offset ☐ Oversize ☒ Mid-oversize ☐ Mid-size

SET MAKEUP	LOFT	FACE ANGLE	TOTAL WEIGHT	SWING WEIGHT	LENGTH	SHAFT MODEL /FLEX	BEND POINT	FREQ.	EST. TORQUE°	RSSR mph	SHAFT WEIGHT DRIVER	WOODS GRIP SIZE
1 ☒	9	1° open	12.4 oz	E1	45	Graphite Power/5	?	268	3°	108	☐ Heavy 110g +	☐ Undersize ___/___ "
2 ☐											☐ Medium 96-110g	☒ Std. (Men's)/Ladies
3 ☒	16										☒ Light 81-95g	☐ + 1/64
4 ☐											☐ Very Light 66-80g	☐ + 1/32
5 ☒	21	1° open	13.6 oz.	D2	41	Steel Shadow/ ?	Low	262	2-5°		☐ Ultra Light 50-65g	☐ + 1/16
6 ☐												☐ _____
7 ☐												Grip Type: _Rubber_
9 ☐												___Composition___
☐												
☐												

Equipment Evaluation – Driver

Considering Mr. Johnson's strength and swing speed of 81mph with the driver and after noting the general specifications of the driver, it is no wonder he is requesting a driver that he can hit farther, higher and with better **Accuracy**. The reason for the problems with the driver are as follows:

√ Too little loft at 9°, which for his swing speed is not allowing him to get the ball airborne to achieve his optimum **Trajectory** for carry **Distance**, and is an explanation for the low **Trajectory** in general;

√ Too much length at 45" which could be a reason for hitting the ball off-center;

√ A face angle of 1° open that is a cause of the fading shot pattern;

√ A shaft frequency of 268cpm that when combined with a torque of 3° creates a shaft with a swing speed requirement of over 105mph, which is much too stiff for Mr. Johnson's 81mph swing speed;

√ A total weight of 12.4oz that is slightly heavy for generating any clubhead speed increase. This total weight indicates an approximate shaft weight of 85-90g;

√ The head is a stainless metal wood that is a basic oversize model, estimated to be about 200cc in volume. It has a relatively low CG because the face height is not too deep and the CG is relatively far back from the face due to the 200cc moderate oversize nature of the head. In short, the head style is not too bad, but some of its specifications are just not right for Mr. Johnson, as noted.

√ It is not necessary to measure the lie, bulge, roll, face progression or balance point of the head. Enough is known from the **MAJOR** and **MEDIUM** effect specifications for **Distance**, **Accuracy** and **Trajectory** to explain why Mr. Johnson is having a hard time achieving those playing goals with this club.

EQUIPMENT REASONS FOR PROBLEMS ACHIEVING DISTANCE:

Loft too strong (9°); total weight combined with swingweight too heavy for the player type (12.4oz/E1); shaft much too stiff (108mph RSSR); torque too low (3°); length too long (45").

EQUIPMENT REASONS FOR PROBLEMS ACHIEVING ACCURACY:

Face angle is open (1°) and the player slices the ball; shaft much too stiff (108mph RSSR); length too long (45"); total weight combined with swingweight (12.4oz/E1) too heavy for the player type (20 hdcp).

EQUIPMENT REASONS FOR PROBLEMS ACHIEVING HIGHER TRAJECTORY:

Loft too strong (9°); shaft much too stiff (108mph RSSR).

Equipment Evaluation – Fairway woods

Mr. Johnson plays with a 5-wood that is the traditional standard length (41") built with a low bend point steel R-flex shaft. When carrying out the frequency of the 5-wood to a driver swing speed (See Chapter 7 for this procedure), the shaft of the 5-wood has an RSSR of approximately 90mph. When compared to his driver shaft, this is much more closely matched to Mr. Johnson's 81mph swing speed, although it is still slightly stiff for him. The 1° open face angle is likely one of the reasons for the fading shot pattern, but the increased loft on the 5-wood is why the fade is not as bad as the driver. The fact that the 5-wood loft is naturally easier to hit, combined with its standard length, more traditional swingweight and low bend point shaft (even though a little stiff) are the main reasons this is Mr. Johnson's favorite club.

CURRENT IRONS

Brand/Model: __858 C Stainless__   [X] Offset ☐ Non-offset ☐ Prog.Offset ☐ Oversize [X] Mid-size ☐ Compact [X] Cavity Back ☐ Muscle Back

SET MAKEUP	LOFT	TOTAL WEIGHT	SWING WEIGHT	LENGTH	SHAFT MODEL /FLEX	BEND POINT	FREQ.	EST. TORQUE	RSSR mph	SHAFT WEIGHT 5-IRON	IRONS GRIP SIZE
1 ☐										[X] Heavy 110g +	☐ Undersize __/__ "
2 [X]										☐ Medium 96-110g	[X] Std.(Men's)/Ladies
3 [X]										☐ Light 81-95g	☐ + 1/64
4 [X]										☐ Very Light 66-80g	☐ + 1/32
5 [X]	28	15.1 oz.	D3	37 3/4	Dynamic / R	High	315	2	80	☐ Ultra Light 50-65g	☐ + 1/16
6 [X]											☐ _____
7 [X]	35	15.4 oz.	D0	36 1/4	Dynamic / R	High	326	2			Grip Type: _____
8 [X]										**SOLE ANGLE**	Thermoplastic
9 [X]										4 °☐Sq. [X] Bounce	Wrap Style
PW [X] (10)	46		D3	35 1/2						6 °☐Sq. [X] Bounce	
SW [X]	56		D4	35 1/2						___°☐Sq. ☐ Bounce	
__ ☐											
PT ☐			D1	35							

Equipment Evaluation – IRONS

√ From the 5- and 7-iron measurements, it appears the lofts are fairly standard as far as late 1980s specifications are concerned. However, they are certainly weaker than most mid-1990s iron lofts. This means it is possible to decrease the lofts a little without them becoming too strong for a 65 mph 5-iron swing speed player. (The stronger the loft, the greater the swing speed needs to be to gain enough **Trajectory**.)

√ The swingweights are different enough on the 5- and 7-irons to show the current set might not have been very well made, but this is not a problem in the fitting because the new set will correct the swingweights on each club. It appears that because Mr. Johnson has no real complaints about his middle and short irons, he has simply adjusted to any swingweight variations that may exist in the new clubs. However, if the new set of irons is to be made with steel shafts, the starting swingweight should be no less than D0 and no more than D3 as a general guide.

√ The lengths are not consistent, but again, this is a specification that will be corrected on the new set. The important point to take from the 5- and 7-iron lengths is the old irons are not that long to begin with, so Mr. Johnson's wrist-to-floor recommendation of a 38" 5-iron will allow for a slight length increase in the new irons to achieve greater **Distance** without making them too long for Mr. Johnson's ability or comfort.

√ The shafts are Dynamic R, which is a tip firm, heavy shaft with a 5-iron swing speed rating of nearly 80mph. The new shafts will be fit using Mr. Johnson's 65 mph/5-iron swing speed as a guideline and a way to deliver more clubhead **Feel** and a more solid feeling at impact. Also, even though the new shafts will probably be steel for cost consideration, the choice should be at least to choose lighter weight steel to drop the total weight of the irons slightly.

√ Because the grips on the irons are standard, and because Mr. Johnson talks about wanting a better hold on the club and does have some hand discomfort, the new grips will need to be larger and softer with enough tacky texture to provide a good grip on the club.

√ Mr. Johnson's current iron head model is basically what he wants to use based on the equipment preferences. However, the new set will have slightly stronger lofts to help grant his request for a little more Distance.

Equipment Evaluation – WEDGES

									SOLE ANGLE		
PW [X] (10)	46		D3	35 1/2					4 ° □Sq. [X] Bounce
SW [X]	56		D4	35 1/2					6 ° □Sq. [X] Bounce
□									___° □Sq. □Bounce

√ The lofts of the two wedges are 10° apart, probably making it a little difficult for Mr. Johnson to gauge how hard to swing when hitting short shots into the green. Because the trend is toward stronger lofts in most available wedge designs, the PW loft will not likely be much different in the new set. A change in the set makeup for the wedges should include a gap wedge with a loft between the current PW and SW.

√ The lengths of the wedges will likely be increased as part of the desire to increase **Distance**, as well as to accommodate the comfort fitting of the length which will be indicated by the wrist-to-floor recommendation for length. This might help Mr. Johnson with the short game by preventing him from crouching over the wedge shots as much as he probably has done in the past due to his height.

√ The swingweight of the SW appears to be lighter than what is normal. Along with the length, this could be one of the reasons he is having problems with leaving the ball in the sand. Also, because he indicates his current SW has a medium sole width, the new sand wedge will be recommended with a wider sole and more of a bounce sole angle to keep the wedge from digging too deep and leaving the ball in the sand.

THE PRELIMINARY FITTING RECOMMENDATION FOR MR. BOB JOHNSON:

THE GOLFSMITH
Practical
CLUBFITTING PROGRAM

PRELIMINARY FITTING RECOMMENDATION

NAME __Bob Johnson__   ADDRESS __123 Main Street__
PHONE Home: (___)____ Work:(___)____   CITY__Key West__   STATE __FL__ ZIP____

SET MAKEUP	Circle & write in recommended set makeup	LOFT ANGLES	Enter recommended loft angles for each
WOODS	① 2 ③ 4 ⑤ ⑦ 9 ___ ___ ___	WOODS	#1 _12_° #3 _16_° #5 _20_° #7 _24_°
IRONS	1 2 3 4 ⑤ ⑥ ⑦ ⑧ ⑨ ___ ___	IRONS	#3 _X_ ° #5_26.5_° #7_34_° #9_42.5_°
WEDGES	☐ PW ☑ SW _PW2_ Other wedges	WEDGES	PW _47_° SW _54_° PW2 _50.5_°

CLUBHEAD DESIGN Check all recommended features
WOODS   ☐ Jumbo ☑ Oversize ☐ Mid-size ☐ Traditional
☐ Steel ☐ Aluminum ☐ Titanium ☐ Graphite ☐ Other____
☐ Deep Face ☑ Standard Face ☐ Shallow Face ☑ Offset ☐ Non-offset ☑ Low CG ☐ Mid-high CG

IRONS   ☑ Cavity Back ☐ Muscle Back   ☐ Compact ☑ Std ☐ Oversize
☑ Offset ☐ Non-offset   ☑ Wide Sole ☐ Std ☐ Thin Sole

WEDGES   PW – ☑ Wide Sole ☐ Medium ☐ Thin Sole   PW2 – ☑ Wide Sole ☐ Medium ☐ Thin Sole (for 3rd or 4th wedge)
SW – ☑ Wide Sole ☐ Medium ☐ Thin Sole

LENGTH List each length; indicate incremental change in length between irons
WOODS   1w _44_" 3w _43_" 5w _42_" #7 w _41_" (for 7w, 9w or other)
IRONS   5I _38_" Incremental Change _⅜_"   WEDGES PW_36½_" SW _36½_" Other PW2 _36½_"

SWINGWEIGHT List swing weight for woods & irons
WOODS _D4_   IRONS _D2_   WEDGES PW _D2_ SW _D7_ Other PW2 _D2_

TOTAL WEIGHT Check driver range; indicate Fairway woods to match or other by listing shaft weight
WOODS   1w – ☑ < 11.25 oz. ☐ 11.25 - 11.75 oz. ☐ 11.75 - 12.25 oz. ☐ 12.25 - 12.75 oz. ☐ > 12.75 oz.
Fairway Woods – ☑ To match to 1w Other____
IRONS   ☐ Match Wood Range Other _match to steel shaft total wt. & light grips_

FACE ANGLE Check angle
WOODS   1w – _2_° ☑ Hook ☐ Square ☐ Open   Fairway Woods – _0_° ☐ Hook ☑ Square ☐ Open

BULGE/ROLL
WOODS   1w – Bulge____" Roll____" ☑ Std   Fairway Woods – Bulge____" Roll____" ☑ Std

GRIP SIZE Check size or indicate other size for woods/irons
WOODS   ☐ Jumbo ☐ +1/16" ☑ +1/32" ☐ +1/64" ☐ Std. ☐ –1/64" ☐ Other____
IRONS   ☐ Jumbo ☐ +1/16" ☑ +1/32" ☐ +1/64" ☐ Std. ☐ –1/64" ☐ Other____

GRIP TYPE/WEIGHT Write in grip name and check weight range
WOODS   Type – _Golfsmith wrap rubber_   Weight – ☑ < 40g ☐ 40-50g ☐ >50g
IRONS   Type – _Golfsmith wrap rubber_   Weight – ☑ < 40g ☐ 40-50g ☐ >50g

SHAFT WEIGHT Check shaft weight range and material for each
WOODS   1w – ☑ < 65g ☐ 66 - 80g ☐ 81 - 95g ☐ 96 - 110g ☐ > 110g ☑ Graphite ☐ Steel ☐ Other
Fairway Woods – ☑ < 65g ☐ 66 - 80g ☐ 81 - 95g ☐ 96 - 110g ☐ > 110g ☑ Graphite ☐ Steel ☐ Other
IRONS   5I – ☐ < 65g ☐ 66 - 80g ☐ 81 - 95g ☑ 96 - 110g ☐ > 110g ☐ Graphite ☑ Steel ☐ Other

SHAFT FLEX (RSSR) & BEND POINT Enter swing speeds - check downswing acceleration; indicate mph range for shaft
WOODS   1w – Swing Speed – _81_ mph Downswing – ☐ Fast ☐ Avg ☑ Slow RSSR – _75_ – _85_ mph
IRONS   5I – Swing Speed – _65_ mph Downswing – ☐ Fast ☐ Avg ☑ Slow RSSR – _55_ – _65_ mph
WOOD BEND POINT ☑ Low ☐ Mid/High   IRON BEND POINT ☑ Low ☐ Mid/High

The final decisions for the specifications for the sample exercise based on the Player Interview and the Equipment Evaluation

Loft

12° on the driver to increase **Trajectory** and to increase **Distance** by matching with his 81mph clubhead speed, 16° on the 3-wood and 20° on the 5-wood. Add a 7-wood with 24° or 25° loft to change the set make-up and complete the fairway woods. Choose the set of irons with lofts stronger in the middle and short irons, as well as including a 50° "gap wedge" to fit in between the PW and SW.

Head #	Loft	Head #	Loft
1-wood	12°	5-iron	26.5°
3-wood	16°	6-iron	30°
5-wood	20°	7-iron	34°
7-wood	24°	8-iron	38°
		9-iron	42.5°
		PW	47°
		PW2	50.5
		SW	54°

Lie

Lie will be fit dynamically as one of the swing tests that will follow. The lie will be fit in the irons because the lie of the woods has a **MINOR** effect on **Accuracy**.

Face Angle

Driver - 2° closed (Because he slices the ball more with the Driver)

3-wood - 0° Square

5-wood - 0° Square

7-wood - 0° Square

The fairway wood face angles will be square because he fades the ball less than the driver due to their greater loft angles. However, because the difference in Accuracy between a 0° and 2° closed face angle would not be more than 10-15 yards in right to left ball flight with fairway woods, it would be acceptable to choose all the woods to have a 2° closed face angle.

Clubhead Design

The woods should have a low CG and be oversized (with an offset hosel) but with standard face height. Cavity-back, offset hosel, standard size, low CG, wide sole irons will be best with the ability to be altered for lie (431 steel or with a thin crotch area to make bending easier). The set of woods to match the CG and weight distribution requirements in Mr. Johnson's equipment preferences, as well as the required lofts and face angles will be the XPC Plus 2° closed face angle metal woods. The set of irons to match the CG and weight distribution requirements for Mr. Johnson's equipment preferences, as well as to conform to the required lofts, will be the RMC-270 stainless irons.

Horizontal Bulge and Vertical Roll

The bulge and roll of the XPC Plus closed face woods will meet Mr. Johnson's needs. While it might be ideal if the XPC Plus woods had less roll, the effect on increasing his **Trajectory** would not be that great.

Sole Angle/Sole Radius

The sole angle and sole radius of the RMC-270 iron heads chosen are a match to Mr. Johnson's requirements. The RMC-270 SW has a bounce sole angle of 12° and is moderately wide to help get the ball out of the sand better. The wedges also have more of a rounded sole radius from front to back to help with chipping, which is another area in which Mr. Johnson needs help.

Hosel Offset/Face Progression

The face progression of the woods is normal and adequate for Mr. Johnson's **Trajectory** needs. The offset of the RMC-270 irons however, is progressive, but it is not believed it will harm the achievement of Mr. Johnson's playing goals of **Distance** and **Accuracy**.

Shaft Weight

The shaft for the woods will be chosen from those shafts which weigh less than 65g to decrease the total weight in an effort to increase swing speed and with it, **Distance**. Since Mr. Johnson did not wish to invest in graphite shafts for the irons, the weight of the iron shaft will be as light as possible, with the expectation that it will be at least 12-15g lighter than the current Dynamic pattern used in his existing irons. (One of the existing 95g steel shafts can also be considered, which would decrease shaft weight by some 30g below his current Dynamic pattern.)

Shaft Flex

The shafts for the woods will be matched to Mr. Johnson's 81 mph driver swing speed and his measured downswing acceleration. The shafts for the irons will be matched to Mr. Johnson's 65 mph swing speed for the 5-iron. NOTE: See Chapter 7 for an example of how the shaft fitting procedure is performed based on Mr. Johnson's information as the example.

Shaft Torque

Torque will be automatically incorporated into the RSSR swing speed requirement of the shaft to match with Mr. Johnson's driver and 5-iron swing speeds.

Shaft Bend Point

When the actual shafts for the woods and irons are chosen during the shaft fitting procedures, a low bend point will be selected to make the shaft more tip flexible and contribute to the clubhead **Feel** and a feeling of obtaining a more solid impact **Feel**.

Shaft Balance Point

When the actual shaft is chosen, the balance point will be selected in the middle of the shaft to allow for using more head weight to increase the clubhead **Feel** and potentially help increase Distance. (Remember, mid balance point shafts require more head weight to achieve any swingweight than do low balance point shafts.)

Grip Size/Type

The grips will be chosen to be tackier in **Feel** and slightly larger in size to improve Mr. Johnson's hold on the club as well as to help alleviate his hand discomfort. Mr. Johnson will be shown a series of grip samples mounted on cut shaft butt sections to make the selection for the type of grip. The actual size will be determined using the Golfsmith Grip Sizer gauge.

Grip Weight

A lighter grip (36-38g) will be chosen to enhance the slightly higher swingweight requirements with the ultra lightweight shaft, and to further decrease the total weight of the shaft for better comfort and **Feel**.

Length

The length indicated by the wrist-to-floor ruler was a 44" driver and a 38" 5-iron. This represents the length required to ensure comfort for Mr. Johnson based on his height and arm length/leg length. The real length will be as listed below, with the decision made to give more **Distance** and comfort on the fairway woods and middle and short irons. This length recommendation includes a different incremental length decrease on the irons, and comes about by changing the club to club length change increment from 1/2" to 3/8". This has the effect of making the shorter irons progressively longer, so the chance of increasing their **Distance** is much greater. It is not necessary to do this on the woods because the 1" difference between woods still gives Mr. Johnson more length than he had on the previous fairway woods.

Head #	Length	Head #	Length
1-wood	44"	5-iron	38"
3-wood	43"	6-iron	37 5/8" (+1/8")
5-wood	42"	7-iron	37 1/4" (+1/4")
7-wood	41"	8-iron	36 7/8" (+3/8")
		9-iron	36 1/2" (+1/2")
		PW	36 1/2" (+1/2")
		PW2	36 1/2" (+1/2")
		SW	36 1/2" (+1/2")

Swingweight

Because of the light total weight resulting from the sub-65g shaft weight, and in order to provide Mr. Johnson with more clubhead **Feel** and enough head weight to help increase **Distance**, the starting swingweight for the woods will be D4. On the irons, because they are remaining as steel shafts, the swingweight will be D2 on the 5-iron through PW2, with the SW swingweight at least D7 to get the head through the sand. The use of the lighter weight grips will help achieve this swingweight in the woods. (Due to the progressive length increase in the irons, it may be necessary to use a standard weight grip to achieve the swingweights, if the iron shaft weight ends up being 110g instead of 95g.)

Total Weight

The total weight of the driver will be about 11oz. due to the sub-65g shaft weight and lightweight grips. Each fairway wood with the same shaft will be approximately 1/4oz. heavier due to the requirement to make the swingweight of these shorter clubs the same D4 as the driver. The total weight of the irons should end up about 3/4 to 1oz. lighter than Mr. Johnson's current steel-shafted irons because of the use of lightweight steel and lightweight grips, with an estimated 5-iron total weight of 14 to 14.25oz. (May be at 3/8oz. higher if standard weight grips have to be used.)

Golf Club Balance Point

The increase in the club length, swingweight and the use of the light grip will all contribute to making the balance point of the finished clubs lower and farther from the hands than the current clubs for a much better overall clubhead **Feel**. Nothing should be done to independently enhance this specificaion because it is a by product of the chosen shaft weight, grip weight and swingweight.

Set Make-Up

The new set make-up will consist of a 1-, 3-, 5-, 7- and possibly a 9-wood if Mr. Johnson desires with 5-, 6-, 7-, 8-, 9-, PW, SW and a PW2 with a loft in between the PW and SW. NOTE: Mr. Johnson's putter fitting will be explained as a sample exercise in Chapter 9 - Fitting Wedges and Putters.

Conclusion to the Preliminary Fitting Recommendation

Learning how to use the information from the Player Interview with the measurements obtained during the Equipment Evaluation and compiling the Preliminary Fitting Recommendation for the player is the most important part of the entire Practical Fitting Program. With this skill, the clubmaker can avoid the use of countless test clubs and make fitting recommendations that react directly to the wants and needs of the golfer. In short, the clubmaker can create the fitting recommendation from information about the player and his/her clubs and have the confidence that real changes are being made such as: an increase in **Distance**, an improvement in **Accuracy**, an increase or decrease in **Trajectory**, an increase in **Backspin** and an improvement in the **Feel**.

The clubmaker has to remember that the information from the Player Interview and Equipment Evaluation will allow the chance to make the Fitting Recommendations for every golf club specification except for those which require performing an actual measurement of the golfer – Grip Size, correct Shaft Flex, final Length recommendation, and dynamic lie fitting. In the next chapter, the Practical Fitting Program will teach the clubmaker exactly how to complete the total compilation of the golfer's Fitting Recommendation by making measurements that determine these few remaining specifications of Grip Size, Length, Shaft Flex and Lie.

Chapter 7

THE FINAL FITTING PROCEDURES FOR COMPILING THE PRELIMINARY FITTING RECOMMENDATION

PERFORMING THE PLAYER TESTS THAT DETERMINE THE FINAL CHOICE OF THE SHAFT LENGTH, GRIP SIZE AND LIE ANGLE

NOTE FOR CHAPTER SEVEN: Chapter 7 covers the step by step fitting procedures for the four specifications, the Shaft, Length, Grip Size and Lie Angle, which cannot be pinpointed by using the information from the Player Interview.

To best use this chapter, first understand that each of these four specifications require some form of measurement to be obtained from the golfer; a driver/5-iron swing speed and an evaluation of the downswing acceleration for the shaft fitting, a wrist to floor measurement for finalizing the length recommendation, a hand measurement for fitting grip size, and finally, the hitting of shots to determine the dynamic lie angle fitting.

In the actual fitting session, each of these measurements should be obtained at the same time the golfer is filling out the Player Interview Form. This way, the clubmaker can determine the shaft, grip size, length and lie at the same time the other specifications are being compiled on the Preliminary Fitting Recommendation.

Look for each of the four sections in this chapter which pertain to each of the remaining fitting procedures. Skim over the high points of the procedures that are listed in step by step form to become familiar with fitting the shaft, the grip size, the length and the lie. Pay particular attention to the steps for fitting the shaft and to understand the RSSR (Recommended Shaft Speed Range) and how to use it. Of utmost importance for fitting the shaft using the RSSR method will be the chart found in the book supplement. This RSSR x Shaft Weight Range chart lists every shaft in the Golfsmith component catalog by a 10mph range of its swing speed rating, cross referenced by its weight and bend point. With the swing speed, an estimation of the golfer's downswing acceleration and this chart, an accurate selection of the proper shaft can be made.

INTRODUCTION

To this point in the Golfsmith Practical Fitting Program, it has been stressed that the goal of the program is to provide clubmakers with enough truthful and practical information about the effects of the various specifications on the ball flight that it will be possible to compile a list of correct playing specifications for any golfer without using an arsenal of test clubs and without requiring the golfer to hit any shots. This can be accomplished because the Golfsmith Practical Fitting Program identifies the various golf club specifications that have a **MAJOR, MEDIUM** or **MINOR** effect on the playing goals of the golfer.

If the clubmaker knows the golf club specifications that have a **MAJOR, MEDIUM** or **MINOR** effect on increasing **Distance**, improving **Accuracy**, increasing or decreasing **Trajectory**, increasing **Backspin** and improving **Feel** of the golf club, it is easy to use the information the player reveals about his/her playing tendencies in the Player Interview with minimal measurements of his/her existing clubs and arrive at a recommendation for all of the fitting specifications except for the grip size, actual shaft selection, final decision on length and the correct lie angle.

The reason that grip size, shaft selection, length and lie cannot be pinpointed from the Player Interview and Equipment Evaluation is because each of these remaining specifications demand the clubmaker to perform measurements of the golfer that require swinging the club or undergoing a static measurement procedure.

Perhaps the real benefit of the Practical Fitting Program is the fitting aids required to obtain these measurements are the only items the clubmaker needs to complete an accurate, total fitting of the player. In other words, there is no requirement for a vast arsenal of test clubs and fitting devices as is the case with all other fitting systems.

THE PROCEDURES FOR DETERMINING THE FINAL FITTING SPECIFICATIONS FOR LIE, LENGTH, GRIP SIZE, AND THE SHAFT

A. LIE ANGLE FITTING

As of this writing, there are two different methods for dynamically fitting the lie angle to the player – the Dynamic Lie Board and the Lie Detector system, developed by Golftek Inc. Dynamic lie fitting refers to fitting of the lie angle so all of the dynamic factors of shaft bending and the golfer's swing are taken into account to finish with a truly customized set of lie angles for the player.

The ideal condition is to determine the lie angle for each club which will allow it to arrive at impact with the center of the sole in contact with the hitting surface, thus preventing the club from contacting the ground on the toe or heel areas of the sole. As explained in Chapter 2, when the club comes into impact and the center of the sole is not in contact with the ground, the face will be tilted to one direction or the other and cause the shot to fly off line.

During the golf swing, depending on the length of the club, swing plane of the golfer, swingweight of the club, stiffness of the shaft, and strength of the

golfer in comparison to the shaft's stiffness, the shaft will deflect or "bow downward" in what is best described as a "toe down" type of bending.

In addition, the golfer is prone to making a variety of different movements during the downswing that can change the position of the clubhead with respect to the ground upon the club's arrival at impact.

Because of this shaft bending action and the swing variations of the golfer, it is impossible to determine the correct lie for the player's clubs by simply noting the position of the club sole when the golfer addresses the ball in a stationary position.

At some point in the fitting session, preferably after the Player Interview and Equipment Evaluation have been conducted, the clubmaker needs to fit the golfer for lie using one of the two dynamic methods of fitting the lie angle.

Address   Impact

1. Dynamic Lie Board Method of Fitting

This method of determining the correct lie will be the most familiar to clubmakers. To perform the dynamic lie board fitting, the clubmaker will need to have an area, either indoors or outdoors, where the golfer can hit shots from a hard surface with a club that has a lie and length already known.

A variety of different lie fitting boards are commercially available from clubmaking supply companies for performing the test. In the absence of one of these products, the clubmaker can make his/her own lie fitting board from a 4' X 4' X 3/4" piece of plywood. While it is preferable for the golfer to hit real golf balls from the lie board into a hitting net, it is not absolutely necessary. Plastic practice golf balls can be substituted in place of the real golf balls.

For the most accuracy in fitting the lie, the hitting surface must not be lower or higher than the golfer's standing position. When using a hard surface hitting board that is large enough for the golfer to stand and hit the required shots, the golfer must not wear golf shoes with spikes. Advise the person to wear tennis shoes or another type of flat-soled shoe that does not have a raised heel. Rubber sole shoes are idea when using a hard surface hitting board because they prevent the golfer from slipping and losing his/her balance while hitting the shots.

If the dynamic lie fitting board is made so the standing area for the golfer is artificial turf, the golfer may wear golf shoes with spikes (such as when using the Golfsmith large lie fitting board).

Setting up for the Dynamic Lie Fitting

PROCEDURES FOR DYNAMIC LIE BOARD FITTING

FITTING AIDS REQUIRED:

1. Lie hitting board.

2. Golf balls or plastic practice golf balls.

3. 1/2" wide paper masking tape or impact sensitive sole labels.

4. Marking pen or pencil.

5. Small ruler with at least 1/4" increments.

6. One 5-iron (minimum) about which the lie and length are precisely known.

7. (optional) - a 3-wood, 3-iron, 5-iron, 7-iron and 9-iron about which lie and length are precisely known.

STEP 1

Ask the golfer to warm up by performing a few stretching exercises. After loosening the upper torso muscles, have the golfer hit four or five shots using a 9-iron to get used to the **Feel** of hitting the ball from a hard surface.

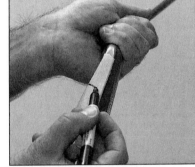

After applying the masking tape, mark the position of the center of the face

If the golfer is hesitant about hitting the board with the clubhead when hitting the shots, stop the procedure and take a moment to explain that the test will not hurt them or the club and that contact with the board at impact is necessary to perform the test. Assure the golfer that a normal swing is all that is required.

STEP 2

Apply a strip of masking tape lengthwise to the sole, making sure it is long enough to cover the entire sole area. Press the tape firmly on the sole to eliminate loose edges. Use a felt tip pen or pencil to mark the location of the center of the face scoring area across the middle of the sole.

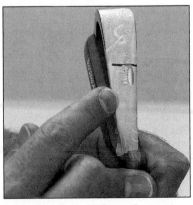

Note the distance from the <u>center</u> of the impact mark to the center line.

STEP 3

The golfer should hit a minimum of 3-5 shots with the test 5-iron. It is very common for a wide section of the tape to be torn from the impact, particularly if the iron has a relatively flat sole from toe to heel. After each shot, mark the center of the portion of the scarred or torn area of the tape. In some cases it may be necessary to replace the tape after each shot in order to accurately note the point of impact on the board.

After 3-5 shots, determine the average point of impact on the sole for all shots. Measure and note the distance of the average point of impact from the center of the sole.

STEP 4

Calculate the lie of the new clubs as follows. For each 1/4" the point of sole impact is <u>on the toe side</u> of the sole center, the correct lie will be <u>1° more upright</u> *than the lie of the club used in the test.* For each 1/4" the sole impact is <u>on the heel side of sole center, the correct lie will be 1° more flat</u> *than the lie of the club used in the test.*

When using only the 5-iron to test for lie, the lie of the other clubs will have to be determined in 1° increments up or down from the 5-iron, while the lie of the woods will be determined in accordance to the irons.

STEP 5

Note the length of the 5-iron as determined by the Preliminary Fitting Recommendation. If the recommended length of the 5-iron in the new clubs is different than the length of the 5-iron used in the lie test, the correct lie angle will have to be adjusted for the difference in length:

If the new 5-iron length is to be longer than the 5-iron used in the test, <u>the final correct lie will be 1° more flat for each 1/2" the new 5-iron is longer than the club used in the test.</u> If the new 5-iron length is to be shorter than the 5-iron used in the test, <u>the final correct lie will be 1° more upright for each 1/2" the new 5-iron is shorter than the club used in the test.</u>

Fitting examples follow to explain the procedure.

DYNAMIC LIE FITTING EXAMPLE 1:

Lie/length of 5-iron being used in the test = 60°/38"

Average point of impact on the sole - 1/2" toward the toe

Correct lie of 5-iron for the golfer = 62°

5-iron length determined for the golfer = 38 1/2"

Correct 5-iron lie adjusted for final length = 61°

Lie Angles for the rest of the new set of clubs:

WOODS	Lie	Length	IRONS	Lie	Length
1-wood	56°	44"	1-iron	57°	40.5"
3-wood	57°	43"	2-iron	58°	40"
5-wood	58°	42"	3-iron	59°	39.5"
7-wood	59°	41"	4-iron	60°	39"
			5-iron	61°	38.5"
			6-iron	62°	38"
Note for woods: Because the 61° 5-			7-iron	63°	37.5"
iron lie is 1° more upright than the			8-iron	64°	37"
industry's standards, so too will the			9-iron	65°	36.5"
lie of the woods.			PW	65°	36.5"
			SW	65°	36.5"

DYNAMIC LIE FITTING EXAMPLE 2:

Lie/length of 5-iron being used in the test = 60°/38"

Average point of impact on the sole - 3/4" toward the heel

Correct lie of 5-iron for the golfer = 57°

5-iron length determined for the golfer = 37 1/2"

Correct 5-iron lie adjusted for final length = 58°

Lie angles for the rest of the new set of clubs:

Woods	Lie	Length		Irons	Lie	Length
1-wood	54°	43"		1-iron	54°	39.5"
3-wood	55°	42"		2-iron	55°	39"
5-wood	56°	41"		3-iron	56°	38.5"
7-wood	57°	40"		4-iron	57°	38"
				5-iron	58°	37.5"
				6-iron	59°	37"
Note for woods: Because the 58° 5-				7-iron	60°	36.5"
iron lie is 2° flatter than the indus-				8-iron	61°	36"
try's standards, so too will the lie of				9-iron	62°	35.5"
the woods.				PW	63°	35"
				SW	63°	35"

ADDITIONAL COMMENTS ON DYNAMIC LIE BOARD FITTING

The examples used to explain the techniques for dynamic lie board fitting were based on using only a 5-iron of known lie and length for the test. While this provides the set with customized lies that are close enough to prevent any real accuracy problems, some clubmakers will want to perform the test using more clubs to account for variations in the way the golfer might swing with different length clubs. By using a 3-wood, 3-iron, 5-iron, 7-iron and 9-iron, the clubmaker can obtain a more accurate fitting of the lie for each individual club in the set. Because golfers swing different clubs in different ways, the correct lie angle may not progress in the traditional 1° increments of change from club to club.

Like the dynamic lie fitting with the 5-iron, performing the lie fitting test with multiple clubs requires the clubmaker to know the lie and length of each of the clubs being used.

The same adjustments for lie and length will be made no matter how many clubs are used in the test. To make sure this technique is understood, the following example will show how the final lie progression for the player may not fall within the traditional 1° incremental change.

A point to note when performing a lie test with a wood. Because the traditional change in lie among woods is 1° for each change in length of 1" (not 1° for each 1/2" as with the irons), the adjustment in the lie to allow for the final length will be 1° for each change in length of 1". (See the following example).

DYNAMIC LIE FITTING EXAMPLE 3:

3-wood test

Lie/length of 3-wood being used in the test = 56°/42.5"

Point of impact on the 3-wood sole - 1/2" toward the toe

Correct lie of 3-wood for the golfer = 58°

3-wood length determined for the golfer = 44"

Correct 3-wood lie adjusted for final length = 56.5° (allowing for a 1.5" increase in length = 1.5° more flat than the lie determined by the test club at its 42.5" length)

3-iron Test

Lie/length of 3-iron being used in the test = 58°/39"

Point of impact on the 3-iron sole - 1/4" toward the toe

Correct lie of 3-iron for the golfer = 59°

3-iron length determined for the golfer = 40"

Correct 3-iron lie adjusted for final length = 57°

5-iron Test

Lie/length of 5-iron being used in the test = 60°/38"

Point of impact on the 5-iron sole - 1/4" toward the toe

Correct lie of 5-iron for the golfer = 61°

5-iron length determined for the golfer = 39"

Correct 5-iron lie adjusted for final length = 59°

7-iron Test

Lie/length of 7-iron being used in the test = 62°/37"

Point of impact on the 7-iron sole - 1/4" toward the heel

Correct lie of 7-iron for the golfer = 61°

7-iron length determined for the golfer = 38"

Correct 7-iron lie adjusted for final length = 59°

9-iron Test

Lie/length of 9-iron being used in the test = 64°/36"

Point of impact on the 9-iron sole - 1/2" toward the heel

Correct lie of 9-iron for the golfer = 62°

9-iron length determined for the golfer = 37"

Correct 9-iron lie adjusted for final length = 60°

Lie angles calculated for the rest of the new set of clubs:

Woods	Lie	Length	Irons	Lie	Length
1-wood	55.5°	45"	1-iron	55°	41"
3-wood	56.5°	44"	2-iron	56°	40.5"
5-wood	58°	42.5"	3-iron	57°	40"
7-wood	59°	41.5"	4-iron	58°	39.5"
			5-iron	59°	39"
			6-iron	59°	38.5"
			7-iron	59°	38"
			8-iron	59.5°	37.5"
			9-iron	60°	37"
			PW	61°	36.5"
			SW	61°	36.5"

(Note: The change in length of woods for this example was not the traditional 1" increment between the 3-wood and 5-wood. Therefore, the lie angles for the 1-wood, 5-wood, 7-wood were calculated from the 3-wood lie and adjusted for the length differences from the 3-wood test club length. Lie angles for the 1-iron, 2-iron, 4-iron, 6-iron, PW, SW were calculated from the 3-, 5-, 7-, 9-iron lies and adjusted for the length differences from each test club length)

2. The 'Lie Detector' Method of Fitting Lie

The other method for dynamically fitting lie angle to the golfer is to use a device invented by Golftek, Inc. called the 'Lie Detector.' This lie fitting method is designed to show the "tilt" of the clubface to identify the lie angle, instead of relying on the point of impact on the sole.

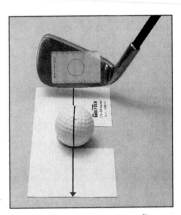

The Lie Detector employs the use of an impact label applied to the face of the club which shows the orientation of a line that appears on the label as a result of impact with a grooved golf ball. The golfer positions the ball so that the groove is in a vertical position before hitting the ball into a net. If the line recorded on the face from the ball is perpendicular to the scorelines, the lie of the club is correct for the player, based on the club's length. If the line on the impact label is tilted to either side of vertical, the lie of the test club is not correct for the golfer. The correct lie angle is then determined by comparing the tilt of the impact line to a series of incremental lines printed at the top and bottom of the label.

To use the Lie Detector, first align the ball so its groove is perpendicular to the center of the club face.

PROCEDURES FOR LIE DETECTOR FITTING
FITTING AIDS REQUIRED:

1. Lie hitting board or hitting mat with net

2. The Lie Detector system (which consists of...)
   a. Grooved golf balls
   b. Impact-sensitive labels
   c. Ball position alignment template

3. Small ruler or straight edge

4. One 5-iron (minimum) about which the lie and length are precisely known

5. (optional) - a 3-wood, 3-iron, 5-iron, 7-iron and 9-iron about which the lie and length are precisely known

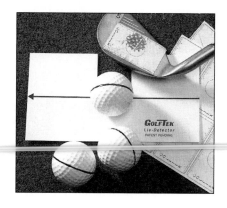

STEP 1

Apply an impact label to the face of the club being used to conduct the test. Make sure the bottom edge of the label is parallel to the bottom scoreline or leading edge of the face.

STEP 2

Place the plastic alignment plate on the hitting surface with the arrow pointing to the imaginary target. Position the golf ball so the groove is aligned with the target line on the plate. When looking straight down on top of the ball, the groove should be perfectly in line with the target line indicating that the ball is properly aligned. Remove the alignment plate before hitting the ball.

STEP 3

After the golfer hits the ball, note the position of the line on the face label. If it is straight up and down, the lie of the club used in the test is correct for the golfer based on the length of the test club.

If the line is not straight up and down, the correct lie for the golfer can be calculated using the measurement marks on top and bottom of the label. Use a ruler to draw a line through the groove mark on the label so it intersects the measurement lines. Count the number of measurement lines between the top and bottom points of intersection. A 4-line difference from top to bottom is equal to a change of 2° in the lie of the club used in the test.

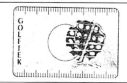  

If the mark is tilted in this manner from lower left to upper right, the lie angle of the club being used in the test is too FLAT for the golfer, at that length.

If the mark is straight up and down, the lie of the club being used in the test is correct for the golfer, at that length. (NOTE: The impact mark does NOT have to be in the exact center of the circle)

If the mark is tilted in this manner from lower right to upper left, the lie angle of the club being used in the test is too UPRIGHT for the golfer, at that length.

STEP 4

Make any adjustments in the lie angle to allow for the final length to be used in the same manner as the Dynamic Lie Board Test. For each 1/2" the irons are to be longer than the test club, the lie will have to be 1° more flat than the correct lie determined in the test. For each 1/2" the irons are to be shorter than the test club, the lie will have to be made 1° more upright than the correct lie determined in the test.

For each 1" the woods are to be longer than the test club, the lie will have to be made 1° more flat than the correct lie determined in the test. For each 1" the woods are to be shorter than the test club, the lie will have to be made 1° more upright than the correct lie determined in the test.

Because of the very precise nature of the Lie Detector's degree markings and how different the average golfer can swing the club, it is recommended the clubmaker determine the lie from a minimum of five hits with the 5-iron test club. In short, a poor swing made by a golfer with the Lie Detector will indicate a much more extreme lie angle than will the lie board method. This is because the lie board's adjustment is 1/4" per degree of change while the Lie Detector uses much smaller degree increments.

B. FITTING LENGTH

The question of whether to rely on some type of measurement device to determine club length has long been debated in the clubmaking industry. For years, the more serious clubmaker has ignored measurements that tried to relate the golfer's fingertip-to-floor and hands-to-floor height to a recommenda-tion of length for the golfer because it is believed the golfer's ability is more important for determining length than is his/her physical size. This type of length fitting philosophy has defended its position based on the premise that a longer club is much harder to hit on-center, and hitting the ball on-center is the most important goal of any fitting session. Thus, the method for fitting length under this type of philosophy is to "choose the length the golfer can hit on-center the highest percentage of the time."

While it is certainly true that much longer clubs are harder to hit on-center, especially for the average-to-higher handicap golfer, there are two practical aspects of length fitting that support the need for some type of measurement. First, it would be ideal if the clubmaker had many test clubs and the golfer had enough time and energy to find a length, total weight, swingweight, grip size and clubhead style, all through hitting test clubs. Because of the number of test clubs and time necessary to perform such a test, this is simply not a practical way to fit length.

Second, to hit the ball solid a high percentage of the time, the golfer has to be comfortable in the address position as well as during the swing, regardless of abil-ity. If the golfer's ability is the only factor taken into account, this practice falls short in the case of the less skilled player, who because of certain physical differ-ences such as height, shorter or longer than normal arm length, or stance and address position variations, may need a longer club simply to be comfortable.

If the golfer is not comfortable standing in the address position, the chance of making consistent swings which achieve a relatively consistent tempo and rhythm is greatly reduced. The Golfsmith Practical Fitting Program believes that golfer comfort is much more important than handicap or ability when it comes to fitting length.

But like the case of the ability-only method of fitting length, there is a point when the clubmaker must decide when the true adage of "the longer the club, the harder to hit on center" has to allow for a compromise in the face of com-fort fitting for length.

As a result, the Practical Fitting Program teaches that the recommendation of club length must start with a measurement of the golfer's wrist-to-floor dimension to first determine the proper length for comfort. After this is complete, modifications can be made on the basis of golfer ability and how length might need to be used to achieve such playing goals as more **Distance** and better **Accuracy** as indicated by the golfer on the Player Interview Form. The reason the Practical fitting Program chooses to use a wrist-to-floor dimension rather than a finger tip-to-floor measurement is because the size of the golfer's hands has nothing to do with what length is required. In fact, abnormally large hands or long fingers can negatively affect the accuracy of the measurement so much that the goal of finding an initial length with comfort in mind cannot be achieved.

PROCEDURES FOR FITTING LENGTH

FITTING AIDS REQUIRED:

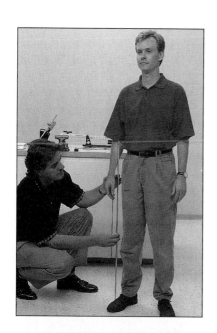

1. Golfsmith wrist-to-floor fitting ruler, a clubmaking ruler or a yardstick.

STEP 1

Ask the golfer to stand comfortably erect, shoulders perfectly level and arms hanging comfortably at the sides. The measurement should be performed with the golfer standing on a hard surface, wearing flat sole shoes without heels. Do not try to obtain this measurement with the golfer wearing golf shoes with spikes or standing on grass. However, if the measurement is performed at a golf course, the golfer can wear golf shoes and the measurement can be performed on the putting green.

STEP 2

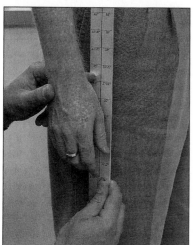

Holding the fitting ruler or yardstick straight up and down, measure the distance from the major crease of both golfer's wrists to the floor. If using the Golfsmith Length Fitting Ruler, the length of the driver and 5-iron will be indicated on the ruler itself. If one wrist position on the ruler indicates a different length than the other, take the shorter of the two. If the position of the wrist is on the line between two different club lengths, take the longer of the two measurements for the sake of comfort. The half inch difference is hardly enough to cause the golfer to hit the ball off-center.

If the wrist-to-floor measurement is being performed with a common yardstick or a clubmaking ruler, add both measurements in inches and divide by two to obtain an average wrist-to-floor measurement. Compare the measurement to the chart below and obtain the initial length recommendation for the driver and the 5-iron.

Wrist to Floor Dimension Avg.	Driver Length Recommendation	5-iron Length Recommendation
25"-27"	41½"	36"
27"-29"	42"	36½"
29"-32"	42½"	37"
32"-34"	43"	37½"
34"-36"(Driver only)	43½"	—
34"-37"(Iron only)	—	38"
36"-38"(Driver only)	44"	—
37"-39"(Iron only)	—	38½"
38"-40"(Driver only)	44½"	—
39"-41"(Iron only)	—	39"
40"-42"(Driver only)	45"	—
over 41"(Iron only)	—	39½"
over 42"(Driver only)	45½"	—

Making the Final Length Recommendation After the Wrist-to-Floor Measurement

Refer back to the sections in Chapter 6 that outline the considerations to be made when determining the final length recommendation of the golf clubs. In chapter 6 there are two sections, one that deals with fitting length for the sake of **Distance** while the other pertains to fitting length for the sake of **Accuracy**. Both have to be considered by the clubmaker before making the final length determination for the golfer.

After measuring the golfer for the wrist-to-floor length recommendation, the clubmaker must refer to the Playing Goals section of the Player Interview to determine if the golfer is in search of greater **Distance** or better **Accuracy** in the new set of clubs.

Procedure for Fitting Length with Distance as the Primary Goal

Keeping in mind that no increase in **Distance** is worth a loss of **Accuracy**, the clubmaker must also remember that the only people for whom a significant increase in club length results in any increase in clubhead speed are:

√ Golfers who have been playing with clubs that were too short and causing the golfer to **Feel** uncomfortable during the swing.

√ Golfers who are well-coordinated physically and who have above average athletic ability.

√ Better players who have the ability to hit the ball on-center a high percentage of the time.

√ Golfers, regardless of handicap, who possess a smooth tempo and a rhythmic, well-timed golf swing.

Fitting Length for Distance

1) Measure the wrist-to-floor dimension of the golfer and note the length indicated by the measuring tool as a starting point.

2) Evaluate the golfer's athletic ability and physical coordination from the Player Interview to judge if the length increase would still allow the golfer to hit the ball on-center a high percentage of the time, or not.

3) Note the length of the golfer's previous driver and 5-iron from the Equipment Evaluation and note from the Player Interview how solidly the golfer hit these clubs.

4) To use length as a way to increase **Distance**, the new woods will need to be at least 1" longer than the woods in the previous set and in the irons, at least 1/2" longer than the previous set. However, if the clubmaker judges this amount of length increase would harm the player's ability to hit the ball on-center, the clubmaker cannot make the recommendation for the length increase as a way to increase **Distance**.

Procedure for Fitting Length with Accuracy as the Primary Goal

If the player needs more help improving **Accuracy** than **Distance**, the clubmaker should first measure the player's wrist-to-floor dimension and check the length of the golfer's previous driver and 5-iron. With both measurements in mind, the following guidelines can be followed to fit the golfer for length with an eye toward **Accuracy**:

√ If the driver and 5-iron lengths recommended by the measurement of the wrist-to-floor fitting ruler are <u>greater</u> than the length of the player's current driver and 5-iron by 1" or more, the clubmaker will have to make the length of the new set the same as the current set and hope for the **Accuracy** improvement to come from face angle and/or lie angle recommendations.

√ If the driver and 5-iron lengths recommended by the measurement of the wrist-to-floor fitting ruler are <u>equal</u> to the length of the player's current driver and 5-iron, reduce the driver (and other woods) length by 1" and the 5-iron (and other irons) by 1/2" in an effort to help with the **Accuracy** problem.

√ If the driver and 5-iron lengths recommended by the measurement of the wrist-to-floor fitting ruler are <u>less</u> than the length of the player's current driver and 5-iron, make the length of the driver 1" shorter (with the other woods in accordance) and the 5-iron 1/2" shorter (with the other irons in accordance) than the lengths recommended by the ruler in an effort to help with the **Accuracy** problem.

Choosing the Increment of Length Change for the Rest of the Set of Woods and Irons

Clubmakers are aware that once the driver and 5-iron lengths are decided, most sets are then made with the golf industry's usual incremental change in length of 1" between the 1-, 3-, 5-, 7-, 9-woods and 1/2" between the 1- through 9-irons. **While a 1/2" difference is how most sets of golf clubs are made, the clubmaker does not have to follow this traditional incremental change in length for the set of woods and irons**.

For reasons of achieving comfort, **Accuracy** and **Distance** at the same time, **when the clubmaker senses an increase in driver length might cause the golfer to hit the ball more off-center and off-line, deviating from the normal incremental changes in length among the clubs is a must**. By starting the driver and the longest iron at standard or even a little shorter length, and then decreasing the difference in length between clubs, the club-maker can offer the golfer control in the longer, less-lofted clubs and the chance of more **Distance** in the fairway woods and shorter irons. In addition, such a recommendation can offer the golfer more comfort in the middle and shorter irons, the clubs with which tall and/or short-armed people are normally the most uncomfortable.

Example of How to Change Playing Lengths to Increase Distance in the Fairway Woods, Middle & Short Irons, Retain Accuracy with the Driver and Long Irons, and Offer Comfort to the Golfer by Changing the Incremental Length Difference Between Clubs.

WOODS	Length[1]	Length[2]	IRONS	Length[1]	Length[2]
Driver	43½"	42½"	3-iron	38¾"	38¼"
3-wood	42¾"	41¾"	4-iron	38⅜"	37⅞"
5-wood	42"	41"	**5-iron**	**38"**	37½"
7-wood	41¼"	40¼"	6-iron	37⅝"	37⅛"
9-wood	40½"	39½"	7-iron	37¼"	36¾"
			8-iron	36⅞"	36⅜"
			9-iron	36½"	36"
			PW	36½"	36"
			SW	36½"	36"

Length[1] - *Suggestion for lengths within the full set for an average golfer who is tall with short arms or long legs who wants more Distance, but cannot sacrifice Accuracy.*
Length[2] - *Suggestion for lengths within the full set for a higher handicap golfer who is tall with short arms or long legs who has real Accuracy problems but wants more Distance.*
Low total weight would be recommended in both cases for the driver (woods) to help increase Distance but make the clubs easier to swing.

C. Fitting Grip Size

As is the philosophy behind fitting length, __fitting for the correct grip size should be done primarily on the basis of comfort, regardless of how close or far the fingers may be from the palm when the hands are closed around the grip__. Traditional grip fitting theory has taught that a proper grip size is achieved when the upper hand is closed around the grip and the fingers are barely able to touch the palm.

While this grip fitting technique has been used by clubmakers for decades, there is one basic problem that can cause it to be a less than perfect guideline for matching the golfer with the grip size best for his/her game – many golfers who are fit in this manner simply do not **Feel** comfortable with the grip size indicated by this procedure.

If the golfer is not comfortable with the size of the grip, the muscles of the forearm will contract and tighten in response to the lack of comfort. When the forearm muscles are tight before the swing begins, it becomes much more difficult for the golfer to take the club away from the ball in a smooth, well-timed manner. While many golfers use many different "swing keys" to try and make a consistent, rhythmic swing, a smooth takeaway is a must for virtually all golfers to generate consistent swing tempo.

This section will explain the two methods of fitting grip size and outline how to ensure the golfer ends up with the most comfortable grip for his/her game.

1. Traditional Method of Fitting Grip Size – Noting the Fingers to Palm Dimension

Noting the distance from the fingertips to the palm to choose the correct grip size is the most widely used method for fitting grip size because it has been taught for the longest time. As long as the golfer is asked for his or her opinion of the comfort during the fitting, this method is acceptable for matching the golfer with the correct grip size.

In outlining the need for sample grips in the overall fitting of the grip, clubmakers should think in terms of preparing two separate sets of grip samples:

1). Grip-type samples, and

2). Grip-size samples.

Fitting the type of grip (the style, texture, color, etc.) was outlined in Chapter 6. In that section it was mentioned that the clubmaker should choose to invest in a buying a number of different styles of grips to mount on cut off shaft sections. This way the golfer can actually **Feel** the grip, which is the most critical requirement for matching type of grip to the golfer's desires. A set of sample grip types is distinctly separate from the set of grip size samples that will be required to traditionally fit grip size.

The most common way for setting up grip-size samples is to purchase separate men's and ladies' size grips of the same style/model and mount each on cut-off shaft butt sections to the usual assortment of sizes. In doing this, the clubmaker will have created approximately 8-10 different grip-size samples.

Another approach is to create a "non-gender specific" set of grip-size samples, using one single grip model that is available in both men's and ladies' sizes. (For example, some golf companies make a men's and ladies grip model in the same color.) By understanding the relationship in size between men's and ladies' grips (i.e. A men's standard size grip [.900"] = a ladies +3/64 oversize grip [.895"]), one uniform set of grip-size samples which actually consists of some ladies' and men's grips, but all of the same color and style, can be used to fit all golfers.

Among the advantages in using this unisex approach would be that the men who need smaller grips would not feel as if they had to use a ladies' grip and the ladies who need larger grips would not feel as if they had to jump up to a men's grip. Both options for sample grip size collections will be outlined in the procedures for fitting grip size.

PROCEDURES FOR TRADITIONAL GRIP SIZE FITTING

FITTING AIDS REQUIRED:

1. Option #1 - Separate men's and ladies samples

    a. Men's grip-size samples

    i) - 1/64" undersize

    ii). Standard men's size

    iii). + 1/64" oversize

    iv). +1/32" oversize

    v). +1/16" oversize

    vi). Jumbo (usually +3/32" to +1/8" oversize)

    b. Ladies' grip-size samples

    i) - 1/64" undersize

    ii). Standard ladies' size

    iii). + 1/64" oversize

    iv). +1/32" oversize

2. Option #2 - Non-gender specific grip-size samples

    a. Grip-size samples (listed in reference to men's sizes and decimal equivalent size for purposes of explanations only)

    i) - 1/64" undersize ladies' (.835")

    ii). Standard ladies' size (.850")

    iii). + 1/64" oversize (.865")

iv). +1/32" oversize (.880")

v). Standard men's size (.900")

vi). + 1/64" oversize (.915")

vii). +1/32" oversize (.930")

viii). +1/16" oversize (.960")

ix). Jumbo (.990" to 1.025")

STEP 1

Ask the golfer to take their normal grip with a standard size sample grip (men's std./.900" for men and ladies' std./.850" for ladies) and compare to the photos illustrated below to make the initial determination for size. The golfer should try different grip sizes until the clubmaker observes an acceptable space between the fingertips of the upper hand in the grip (the right hand for left-handed players; the left hand for right-handed players) and the base of the heel of the palm.

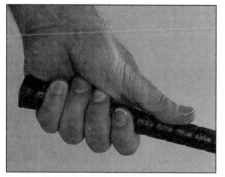

When the golfer takes his/her normal grip, if the fingers dig into or touch the base of the palm, the grip is considered to be too small by traditional fitting methods.

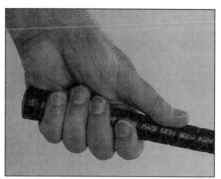

When the golfer takes his/her normal grip, if the fingers just barely do not touch the base of the palm, the grip is considered to be the correct size by traditional fitting methods.

When the golfer takes his/her normal grip, if the fingers are significantly far from the base of the palm, the grip is considered to be too large by traditional fitting methods.

STEP 2

When the sample grip size is reached which prevents the fingers of the upper hand from touching the base of the palm, ask the golfer if the size is comfortable. Tell the golfer to take a minute to grip and re-grip the sample before responding. If the golfer is not sure or does not reply right away, replace the grip in their hands with one that is at least 1/64" larger and ask the question once more, "How does this grip feel?" Many times, moving back and forth between another grip size will help the golfer make up his/her mind about comfort of the grip.

If the golfer indicates he/she likes a grip that does not satisfy the guidelines for fingers to palm distance described for a proper size grip, the clubmaker must realize that the choice will likely have been made because of comfort only.

Ladies with long fingernails should be fit with their nail length in mind. As the various sample sizes are given to the lady to try, ask about the comfort of the grip, especially with respect to the possibility of the fingernails touching or digging into the base of the hand. While long fingernails can result in the golfer using a much larger grip size, the clubmaker will still have satisfied the most important aspect of grip size fitting – the comfort of the golfer's hands on the club. Remember, this grip is the only direct physical contact the golfer has with the club. As such, the grip size has to be comfortable to the player.

NOTE: **A grip found to be too large or too small for a golfer under the guidelines of traditional fingertip to hand fitting method will not cause a hook or a slice by itself**. Likewise, changing to a smaller grip to cure a slice, or a larger grip to cut down on a slice does not solve the **Accuracy** problem. Comfort helps more, so do not worry about altering the **Accuracy** of the golfer's shot pattern in a negative way from allowing him/her to choose a grip larger or smaller than his/her finger to hand dimension might indicate.

STEP 3

(Optional) Some players may want to be custom fit for the grip diameter of the lower hand as well. It is fairly common for some golfers to ask for one particular grip size condition for the upper hand, but yet a different one (usually a little larger) for the lower hand. Even though it is primarily low handicap players who are aware of the benefit of fitting the lower hand grip size separately from the upper hand, the clubmaker can ask any golfer if they **Feel** the diameter of the grip where the lower hand is holding on to the grip is acceptable, too small or too large. If the golfer indicates a desire to custom fit the lower hand, this size should be determined after a discussion between clubmaker and golfer rather than by creating a set of grip samples for testing the lower hand grip size.

STEP 4

(Optional) Take a few minutes to install a grip on an actual club that is the type and the size the golfer chose. Making a decision about a particular grip size from a sample mounted on a cutoff piece of shaft is very different than holding a grip mounted on a real golf club.

For the small investment in one grip, the golfer will have the chance to really **Feel** what the new grips will be like. Additional points of service such as this can go a long way toward making the final sale, which easily covers the expense of a single grip sacrificed as a sample to help in the fitting.

2. Using the Golfsmith Grip Sizer to Fit Grip Size

Hands come in all shapes and sizes. Some people have large palms and short fingers, others small palms and long fingers, while some have a combination of both. Because the hands wrap around the grip so that the palm and fingers are both involved, then both the fingers and palm have to be considered in choosing the right grip size for the player.

The Golfsmith Grip Sizer is designed to fit grip size by separately measuring the size of the golfer's fingers and palm, then combining the two dimensions to come up with a compatible grip size for the golfer. While the sizing gauge can do an accurate job of advising the correct grip size, the clubmaker should still utilize a set of grip size samples to allow the golfer to actually touch and **Feel** the grip being recommended. In addition, because the golfer's comfort is still the best guide for matching the right size, the clubmaker must ask the golfer for his/her input before making the final decision for grip size.

PROCEDURES FOR GRIP SIZE FITTING USING THE GOLFSMITH GRIP SIZER

FITTING AIDS REQUIRED:

1. Golfsmith Grip Size Fitting Gauge

2. Grip-Size Samples

Option #1 - Separate men's and ladies' samples

    a. Men's grip-size samples

        i) - 1/64" undersize

        ii) Standard men's size

        iii) + 1/64" oversize

        iv) + 1/32" oversize

        v) + 1/16" oversize

        vi) Jumbo (usually + 3/32" to + 1/8" oversize)

    b. Ladies' grip-size samples

        i) - 1/64" undersize

        ii) Standard ladies' size

        iii) + 1/64" oversize

        iv) + 1/32" oversize

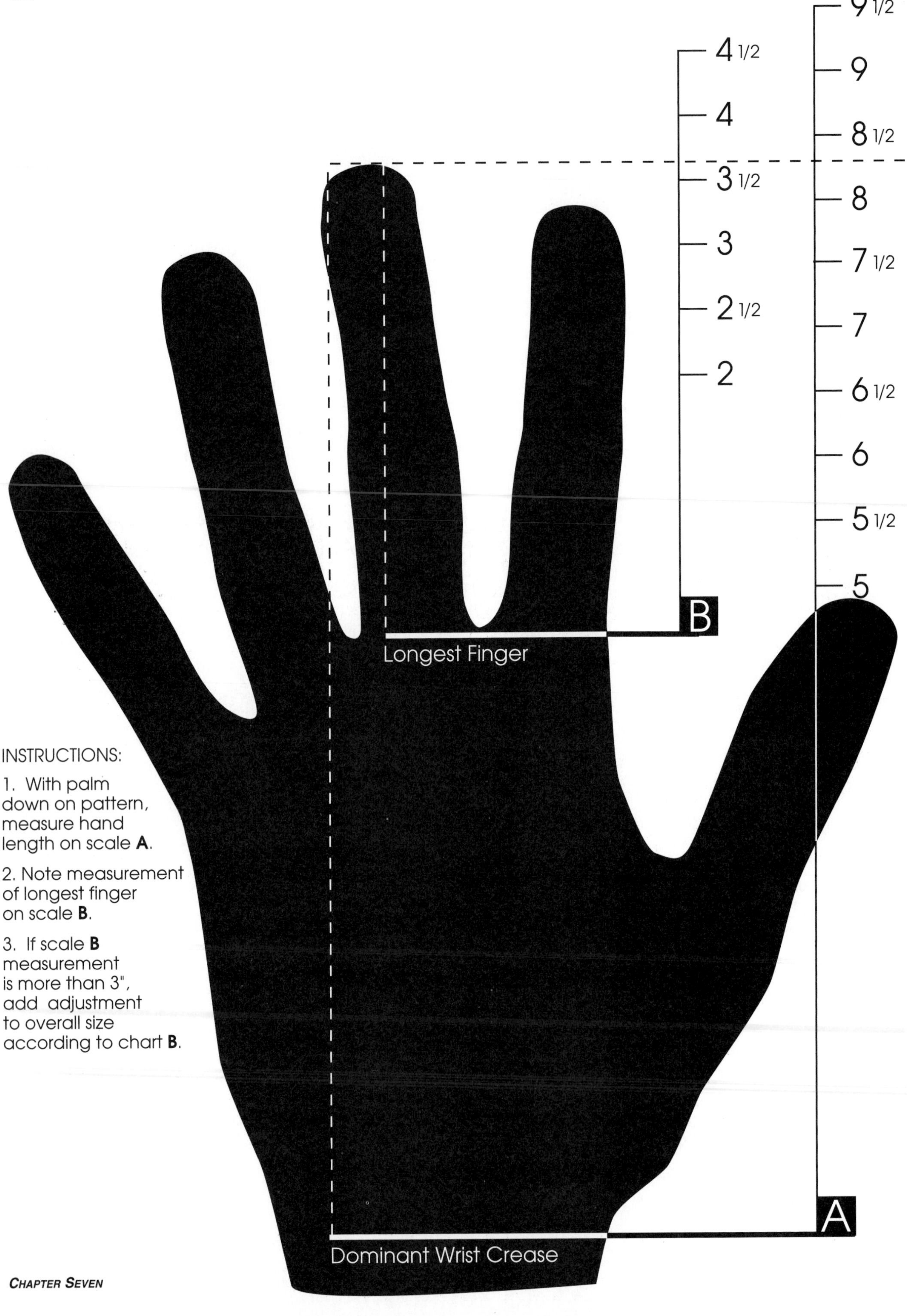

9 1/2
9
8 1/2
8
7 1/2
7
6 1/2
6
5 1/2
5

4 1/2
4
3 1/2
3
2 1/2
2

B
Longest Finger

INSTRUCTIONS:

1. With palm down on pattern, measure hand length on scale **A**.

2. Note measurement of longest finger on scale **B**.

3. If scale **B** measurement is more than 3", add adjustment to overall size according to chart **B**.

A
Dominant Wrist Crease

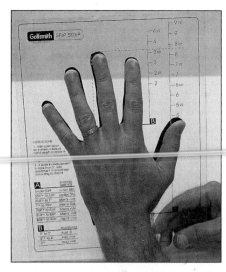

A	STARTING GRIP SIZE
Under 5 3/4"	Junior Std.
5 3/4"+ to 6 1/2"	Ladies' Std.
6 1/2"+ to 7"	Men's -1/64
7"+ to 7 3/4"	Men's Std.
7 3/4"+ to 8 1/4"	Men's +1/64
8 1/4"+ to 8 3/4"	Men's +1/32
8 3/4"+ to 9 1/4"	Men's +1/16

B	ADJUSTMENT
2" to 3"	Add 0
3"+ to 4"	Add +1/64
4"+	Add +1/32

Option #2 - Non-gender specific grip-size samples

   a. Grip-size samples (listed in reference to men's sizes for explanation plus decimal equivalent size)

      i) - 1/64" undersize ladies' (.835")

      ii) Standard ladies' size (.850")

      iii) + 1/64" oversize (.865")

      iv) +1/32" oversize (.880")

      v) Standard men's size (.900")

      vi) + 1/64" oversize (.915")

      vii) +1/32" oversize (.930")

      viii) +1/16" oversize (.960")

      ix) Jumbo (.990" to 1.025")

STEP 1

Lay the grip sizer on the workbench or table so the black hand silhouette corresponds to the golfer's upper hand on the grip. (The right hand is the upper hand for a left-handed golfer and the left hand is the upper hand for a right-handed golfer.) Ask the golfer to place the upper hand flat on the hand outline. Be sure the major crease of the golfer's wrist is in line with the zero (0) measuring line at the base of the hand outline.

STEP 2

Using the measurement gradations on the Grip Sizer, note the length of the palm and length of the middle finger. Compare these dimensions to the sizes indicated on the tables printed on the Grip Sizer. The palm size will give the clubmaker an initial indication of the grip size. Then the length of the middle finger will be used as a modifier for the initial grip size. The longer the fingers in addition to the palm size, the larger the grip will be advised while the shorter the fingers in addition to palm size, the smaller the grip that the gauge will advise.

STEP 3

Select a sample grip-size the same as indicated by the Grip Sizer measurements. Have the golfer take his/her normal grip with the sample and ask the golfer for input with regard to comfort. Make the final size recommendation based on the golfer's feedback. Again, it is a nice professional touch to actually mount a grip of the golfer's type and size selection onto a real club to give them a real **Feel** for how the new grips will **Feel**.

D. Fitting The Shaft – making the actual selection of the shaft for the player

Even though the information from the Player Interview and the Equipment Evaluation of the golfer's driver and 5-iron have already determined a number of general points about the fitting of the shaft, the clubmaker does not yet know which actual shaft will be installed in the new set. The shaft comprises five separate fitting specifications – flex, torque, weight, bend point and balance point. Several of these shaft fitting specifications are **MAJOR** to **MEDIUM** contributors for **Distance**, **Accuracy** and **Trajectory**. Because of the multiple importance of shaft specifications, **the Golfsmith Practical Fitting Program treats the final shaft fitting determination almost as if it were a separate fitting process within the overall fitting**.

To pinpoint the selection of the shaft, the clubmaker will have to measure the golfer's swing speed and assess the golfer's downswing acceleration force. From these two swing tests, the clubmaker can use shaft fitting data provided in the charts in the supplements to this book, along with the shaft weight, shaft bend point and shaft balance point recommendations which have already been determined from the Player Interview/Equipment Evaluation to make the selection of the shaft.

Many clubmakers are well aware of the fact that the shaft cannot be fit by a flex, torque or bend point description that comes from the shaft manufacturer. At the time of this writing, no standards were yet in existence for measuring the flex, torque and bend point of a shaft. In addition, the shaft manufacturers are free to determine for themselves what they feel should constitute an L, A, R, S or X flex, what the torque may be or where a low or high bend point should be on the shaft. As a result, there is no way the shaft descriptions provided by the various shaft makers can be used to identify the right shaft for any player.

Most of the time, the level of stiffness that identifies an R-flex to one company is not the same stiffness which indicates an R-flex to another. What's more, in most cases, the R-flex of one design is not even the same stiffness as the R-flex of another shaft design, sometimes even within the same shaft manufacturing company! While changes will come about in the very near future which will standardize the testing procedures for a few of the different shaft specifications, even when they are adopted, each shaft company will still be free to define what they feel should constitute an L, A, R, S or X flex, the torque, or the bend point of the shafts they design.

As a solution to this and all the other problems which make it impossible to make meaningful comparisons of shaft specifications, **the Golfsmith Practical Fitting Program has established the RSSR Shaft Fitting System. In the RSSR Shaft Fitting System, each golf shaft is individually measured for flex and torque. Based on the comparison of the flex and torque, which together control the overall flex and stiffness of any shaft, a rating can be determined for each shaft and expressed in the speed the golfer must swing the club to be considered well matched to the stiffness of the shaft**. As a result, the Golfsmith Practical Fitting Program does not recognize or use flex letter codes to identify whether the stiffness of any shaft matches well to the golfer. Regardless of the letter code designation of flex, each shaft is rated by how many miles per hour the golfer needs to swing the driver or 5-iron to be matched to the overall flex and stiffness of the wood or iron shaft.

Once the compatibility of the golfer's swing speed is matched with a group of shafts that are known to possess the same swing speed requirement, the other shaft fitting factors of the shaft weight, bend point and balance point can be brought into the shaft selection process to narrow the field of compatible shafts and make the selection of the actual shaft for the player.

The Beltronics SwingMate is an example of a reasonably accurate method of recording clubhead speed.

Because each shaft is ranked by a swing speed requirement, the clubmaker first needs some way to accurately determine the swing speed of the player to then be able to match the shaft's swing speed requirement (RSSR) to the golfer's swing speed. The type of swing speed analyzer will depend on the volume of work being done by the clubmaker and level of commitment to clubmaking. Reasonably accurate electronic swing speed measuring devices can be purchased for as little as $70-150. More accurate, high-end units can cost from $400 up to as much as tens of thousands of dollars.

Never try to fit the wood and iron shafts on the basis of the driver swing speed only. Golfers do not swing the woods and irons the same. It is very common for two golfers with the same driver swing speed to have completely different 5-iron swing speeds, or vice versa. Therefore, the decision for an iron shaft cannot be made on the basis of a driver swing speed. In addition, wood and iron shafts of the same pattern (same flex and brand name shaft) do not always fall in the same progression of, or relationship of stiffness to each other. For example, two different R-flex shafts for woods might both be rated at 90mph, but the matching iron shaft of one might require a 65mph, 5-iron swing speed while the matching iron shaft of the other might be rated at 75mph, 5-iron swing speed. **Simply stated, when fitting the golfer for a full set of clubs, fit the shafts for the woods on the basis of a driver (or 3-wood) swing speed and the shafts for the irons on the basis of a 5-iron swing speed**.

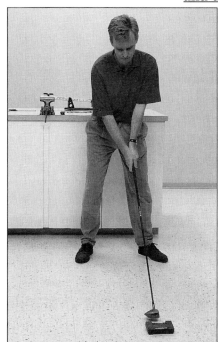

The swing speed measurement should be conducted by having the golfer hit real golf balls, whether at a driving range or into a net. While plastic practice balls will work in the absence of a hitting net, it is more accurate to work with real balls to give the golfer the sense of making a real swing. Unless the Equipment Evaluation has shown the length of the golfer's own existing clubs are very poorly matched to the golfer, the swing speed tests can be conducted with the golfer's existing driver (3-wood is OK in the absence of a driver) and 5-iron. Even though the new clubs will probably be different in many respects, these are clubs with which the golfer is most familiar, and therefore more likely to make a typical, representative swing.

If the golfer's existing driver and/or 5-iron have been determined to be too long and are a source of problems with swing rhythm and tempo, the clubmaker might want to keep a couple of drivers and 5-irons in the shop for the golfer to use to perform the swing speed measurement. The "substitution clubs" could be made up with a flexible lightweight steel shaft to standard lengths (43.5" driver and 38" 5-iron for men to use and 42" driver and 37" 5-iron for the ladies to use).

The shaft fitting procedure consists of measuring the golfer's driver and 5-iron swing speeds, noting the shaft weight recommendation, judging the downswing acceleration of the golfer for making modifications to the swing speed requirement of the shaft, referring to the Player Interview to note any **Feel** requirements of the player as they relate to the shaft, and finally, referencing the shaft(s) of choice from the data listings of shafts found in the book supplement.

In short, the shaft fitting phase of the Practical Fitting Program is really a process of elimination, using the swing speed and RSSR data, along with the information already compiled in the Player Interview to quickly sort through the hundreds of possible shafts, discarding those which do not meet each of the player's needs, until the clubmaker is left with two or three shafts that satisfy all the requirements for making the final selection. Shaft fitting the practical way is simple and only requires the clubmaker to know where to look in this book for information to help perform the process of shaft selection through the process of shaft elimination.

In the supplement supplied with this book, there are a number of charts to help the clubmaker identify the swing speed requirement, weight and bend point of virtually any shaft. It is necessary to have the golfer's swing speeds, shaft weight range, and bend point requirements in mind before turning to the charts for sorting out the proper shaft(s) for the player.

DOWNSWING ACCELERATION AND ITS EFFECT ON THE SHAFT FITTING PROCESS

Because it is common to find two golfers with the same swing speed who possess a different swing tempo, it is possible that two golfers with the same swing speed can place a different amount of bending force on the shaft at the beginning of, and during the downswing. **Among two golfers with the same swing speed, the one who accelerates the club more and in turn, places more bending stress on the shaft during the downswing, will need to have a shaft with a slightly higher RSSR rating (needs to be fit with a slightly stiffer shaft)**.

For example, this means a golfer who has an 85mph driver swing speed and possesses a high downswing acceleration will be better fit into a shaft with an RSSR that is higher than his/her actual 85mph swing speed. In the RSSR shaft rating system, the higher the rating in mph, the stiffer the shaft. Likewise, the lower the RSSR rating for a shaft, the more flexible the shaft. When the RSSR of the shaft is greater than the swing speed of the player, the shaft is a little stiffer than what the golfer should normally use, and is not a good fit, unless, like this example illustrates, the golfer places a higher amount of bending stress on the shaft.

A higher than normal downswing acceleration for any particular swing speed, or what may be called "greater than normal loading of the shaft," can be measured with a fitting device specially made to identify such forces in the swing, or it may be evaluated using visual evaluation of the golfer's downswing movement.

Swing Movements to Look for Which Indicate a Higher Than Normal Rate of Downswing Acceleration

√ A fast swing tempo in general.

√ The sense or judgment that the golfer is a "hitter" or a "slasher" rather than a "swinger".

√ A quick transition between the end of the backswing and beginning of the downswing; when the club never comes to a stop at the top of the backswing before starting back down, usually with a sense of quickness.

√ Even in the case of a rhythmic swing, the overall sense of a powerful downswing move to the ball.

Swing Movements to Look for Which Indicate a Lower Than Normal Rate of Downswing Acceleration

√ A smooth or slower swing tempo in general.

√ The sense or judgment that the golfer is a "swinger" rather than a "hitter" or "slasher".

√ A smooth transition between the end of the backswing and beginning of the downswing; when the club actually pauses or comes to a stop at the top of the backswing before starting back down.

√ The overall sense of a weak or non-athletic looking movement down to the ball.

After obtaining a swing speed measurement, ask the golfer to swing The Determinator at least five times. Compare the predominant reading to the chart on page 328 to determine if the golfer should use a shaft with an RSSR lower than, equal to or higher than his/her swing speed.

In 1994, the True Temper Corp. developed a shaft fitting tool intended to provide the clubmaker with a way to identify the loading force a golfer placed on the shaft to determine if the golfer needs a shaft with a higher RSSR than his/her swing speed might indicate. The shaft fitting tool, The Determinator, is a simple comparative accelerometer that records a measurement in response to the force of the downswing. The measurement scale on the Determinator reads from 0 to 26; the higher the number, the greater the downswing acceleration and the greater the bending force being applied to the shaft.

The Determinator's measurement scale is not a true quantitative measurement for the rate of downswing acceleration, but is a comparative scale. The Determinator can be used to identify whether a golfer needs a shaft with a higher RSSR than his/her swing speed, a slightly more flexible shaft such that the RSSR is lower than the golfer's swing speed, or a shaft with an RSSR rating equal to his/her swing speed.

THE STEP-BY-STEP PRACTICAL PROCEDURES FOR SHAFT FITTING

SHAFT FITTING AIDS REQUIRED:

1. Swing speed recording device

2. RSSR shaft fitting tables from this section of the book

(OPTIONAL FITTING AIDS):

3. Downswing acceleration measuring device

4. Hitting net and hitting mat

5. A men's length driver and 5-iron made with an R-flex version of a lightweight steel shaft

6. A ladies' length driver and 5-iron made with an L-flex version of a lightweight steel shaft

(While not necessary, these clubs would be for recording the swing speed when the clubmaker determines the golfer's existing clubs would yield an inaccurate measurement.)

STEP 1

After the golfer has warmed up sufficiently, record the driver and 5-iron swing speeds of the golfer. Note and retain the swing speed as the most frequently seen swing speeds obtained with each club.

Shaft fitting example:

Swing speed with driver = 85mph
Swing speed with 5-iron = 65mph

STEP 2

Refer back to the Preliminary Fitting Recommendation for the shaft weight recommendation to obtain the weight range from which the shaft is to be selected. The shaft weight range is determined by the golfer's total weight requirements, which are based on the golfer's need for **Distance**, **Accuracy** and **Feel**.

Combine the swing speed and shaft weight classification range for the player's wood and iron shafts to begin the process of elimination of unsuitable shafts for the player.

Shaft Weight Classification	Shaft Weight Range	Resulting Driver Tot. Wt.	Resulting 5-Iron Tot. Wt.
Heavy Weight	110g +	>12.7oz	>14.7oz
Medium Weight	96-110g	12.2 - 12.7oz	14.2 - 14.7oz
Light Weight	81-95g	11.7 - 12.2oz	13.7 - 14.2oz
Very Light Weight	66-80g	11.2 - 11.7oz	13.2 - 13.7oz
Ultra Light Weight	50-65g	10.7 - 11.2oz	12.7 - 13.2oz

NOTE: Based on 50g grip weight. If using 38g lightweight grips, subtract 0.4oz from the total weight in the range for each classification of shaft weight.

Shaft fitting example (Continued):

From STEP 1 –
Swing speed measurement with driver = 85mph
Swing speed measurement with 5-iron = 65mph

From STEP 2 –
Recommended shaft weight range from Preliminary Fitting
Recommendation = 66g to 80g for wood shafts;
96g for Iron shafts

STEP 3

Use the data chart "RSSR X Shaft Weight Range" to find the group of eligible shafts that conform to the swing speed requirement and shaft weight range for both woods and irons. The "RSSR X Shaft Weight Range" tables can be found in the book supplement. Following is a section from the chart to help explain the fitting of the example golfer with an 85mph driver swing speed and 65mph 5-iron swing speed, who is in need of a 66-80g graphite shaft for the woods and a 96-110g steel shaft for the irons.

Shaft Fitting Example (Continued):

From STEP 1 -
Swing speed measurement with driver = 85mph
Swing speed measurement with 5-iron = 65mph

From STEP 2 -
Recommended shaft weight range from preliminary fitting
Recommendation = 66g to 80g for wood shafts;
110 + g for iron shafts

From STEP 3 -
Looking through the chart of RSSR x Shaft Weight Range, locate the shafts which are rated 80-90mph, which weigh between 66-80g.

80-90mph/66-80g
(L/M) Golfsmith Carbon Stick Ultralite • R-flex
(M) Aldila SpeedFit-80
(H) True Temper Dynamic Lite graphite • R-flex
(L) Aldila Low Torque 5.0 • Firm flex
(M) True Temper TT Lite graphite • R-flex

Locate iron shafts rated at 65mph within a weight range of 96-110g.

60-70mph/96-110g
(L) Ti-Tour Titanium 140
(M) True Temper Stratus • A-flex
(H) True Temper Dynamic graphite • R-flex
(M) True Temper TT Lite taper tip • L-flex

Note: (L) = Low Bend Point; (M) = Mid Bend Point; (L/M) = Low to Mid Bend Point; (H) = High Bend Point.

Note: Eliminate any possible shafts from the list of eligible shafts found in Step 3 that do not conform to the price the golfer is willing to pay for the set of clubs. How the golfer's cost requirements are handled is a matter to be discussed between the clubmaker and golfer, based largely on how much the clubmaker is going to charge for clubs made with shafts of different costs.

STEP 4

Determine the golfer's downswing acceleration capability using either simple judgment or a test device created to make such an assessment. Adjust the golfer's RSSR requirement based on the measurement or judgment of his/her downswing acceleration force. (See following procedures for learning how to use the True Temper Determinator to modify the swing speed fitting of the shaft. Following the Determinator procedures, the steps in the overall total shaft fitting procedure will be continued.)

PROCEDURES FOR USING THE TRUE TEMPER DETERMINATOR TO MEASURE DOWNSWING ACCELERATION

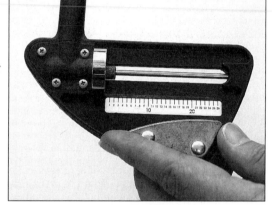

'Zero out' the Determinator to start the test by pushing the foam piece against the slide weight.

Determinator Procedure #1 – Push the foam cylinder back against the circular sliding weight before starting the test.

Determinator Procedure #2 – Make sure the golfer is warmed up, either by stretching or hitting a few shots. Explain to the golfer that the goal is to make swings with the Determinator as close to the golfer's real swing as possible. Caution the golfer against hitting the ground with the "head" of the device.

Determinator Procedure #3 – Allow the golfer to make 2 or 3 practice swings with the Determinator to get used to the feel of the device. During these swings, the clubmaker must watch the position of the clubhead at the top of the backswing to verify that the golfer is swinging the device on the proper swing plane to obtain reliable reading. The Determinator must be swung in a square face position so that the toe of the clubhead is pointing down at the ground at the top of the backswing.

If the golfer closes or opens the face of the Determinator during the swing, the unit will not provide a reliable measurement because the spring-loaded circular weight will not be able to slide down the rod when the force of the downswing is initiated. Visually observing the position of of the head of the Determinator at the top of the backswing will indicate if the unit needs to be adjusted to make allowances for the swing mistakes the golfer might be making on the backswing.

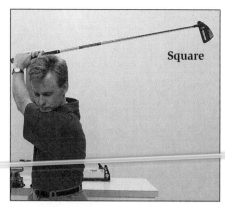

When the Determinator clubhead is in the SQUARE face position at the top of the backswing, the unit will give an accurate reading when the golfer grips the unit square in the address position.

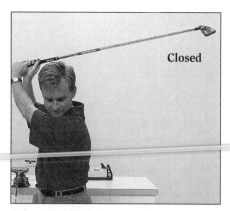

When the Determinator clubhead is in the CLOSED face position at the top of the backswing, the golfer will have to turn the unit so the clubhead is OPEN in the address position to be able to obtain an accurate reading.

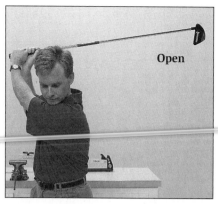

When the Determinator clubhead is in the OPEN face position at the top of the backswing, the golfer will have to turn the unit so the clubhead is CLOSED in the address position to be able to obtain an accurate reading.

If the toe of the clubhead is pointing away from the back of the golfer, the device is in an open position. If the toe of the clubhead is pointing away from the front of the golfer, the device is in an closed position. To overcome these problems, the golfer should grip the unit so the clubhead is turned in the appropriate direction at address so when the unit is swung to the top of the backswing, the toe of the clubhead is pointing to the ground.

IF THE DETERMINATOR'S TOE POSITION AT TOP OF BACKSWING IS:	THE GOLFER MUST GRIP THE DEVICE WITH THE 'CLUBHEAD':
1. Down to ground	Square or normal
2. Face to sky, toe points away from the front of the golfer	Turned @ 30° open
3. Face to ground, toe points away from the back of the golfer	Turned @ 30° closed

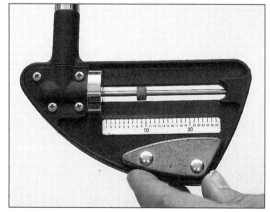

In this example, the golfer has swung the Determinator to a reading of 8. The reading is always taken from the rear end of the foam slide piece.

Determinator procedure #4 – Have the golfer make five to six full swings with the Determinator. Note the position of the foam cylinder in relation to the numerical scale. Reset the foam cylinder back to zero after each swing.

Determinator procedure #5 – After five or six swings, throw out the high and the low readings and note the measurement most often repeated. This will be the Determinator reading for the clubmaker to use in the fitting.

Determinator procedure #6 – Refer to the Determinator Chart which follows. Compare the golfer's predominant Determinator reading to the chart columns for low, mid and high Determinator readings for the golfer's driver swing speed.

True Temper DETERMINATOR Ranges per Golfer Swing Speed

Driver Swing Speed Range	Low Determinator Measurement	Medium Determinator Measurement	High Determinator Measurement
40-50	0-6	7-12	13 and higher
50-60	0-7	8-14	15 and higher
60-70	0-8	9-15	16 and higher
70-80	0-8	9-15	16 and higher
80-90	0-8	9-16	17 and higher
90-100	0-10	11-17	18 and higher
100-110	0-10	11-18	19 and higher
	Choose Shaft with RSSR less than the Golfer's Swing Speed by 5-10mph	Choose Shaft with RSSR equal to the Golfer's Swing Speed	Choose Shaft with RSSR greater than the Golfer's Swing Speed by 5-10mph

Determinator procedure #7 – Make the adjustment in the RSSR for the golfer based on the column that the predominant Determinator reading is located. If the golfer's Determinator reading is considerably lower or higher than the top end of the low range or bottom end of the high range, the clubmaker can adjust the RSSR up or down by as much as 10mph.

For example, if the golfer with an 85mph driver swing speed achieved a 4 or 5 on the Determinator, the reading would be very low even within what is considered to be the low range of Determinator readings for an 85mph swing speed. In that case, the RSSR should be shifted down by 10mph so the clubmaker would now be looking among shafts rated at 75mph (70-80mph range).

On the other hand, if the golfer with the 85mph driver swing speed achieved a 21 or higher on the Determinator, the reading would be very high within the high column of Determinator readings for that 85mph swing speed. In that case, the RSSR should be shifted up by 10mph so the clubmaker would be looking for a shaft rated at 95mph (90-100mph range).

Shaft Fitting Example (Continued):

From STEP 1 –
Swing speed measurement with driver = 85mph
Swing speed measurement with 5-iron = 65mph

From STEP 2 –
Recommended shaft weight range from Preliminary Fitting
Recommendation = 66g to 80g for the wood shafts;
96-110g for the iron shafts

try the new fitting specifications and report back to the clubmaker. If the specifications of the clubs need to be modified or changed in any way, the clubmaker can make the changes on the sample clubs before the rest of the set is built. When the golfer is pleased with the initial clubs, the rest of the set should then be ordered and built.

CONCLUSION

By identifying the path to game improvement by working only with the specifications which have a **MAJOR** or **MEDIUM** effect on **Distance, Accuracy, Trajectory, Backspin** and/or **Feel**, and then setting about to identify the necessary changes in only those specifications that could possibly bring about the desired game improvement change, the Practical Fitting Program can shorten the fitting session, avoid the extensive use of test clubs, will not exhaust the golfer with an endless series of test clubs and ball-striking tests, and best of all, will provide a more accurate fitting.

If the Practical Fitting Program remains confusing in any way to this point, it is strongly suggested the clubmaker go back through chapters 1, 2, 3, 4, 6 and 7 and read the **bold type entries** to review the highlights of the program. Remember, the purpose of any book is to explain the subject to its full extent, but still allow the reader to understand the subject from a practical standpoint. Each chapter contains the most complete explanation of every single point in the Practical Fitting Program so there can be no doubt as to why a particular decision or conclusion is made. However, the book is also designed to explain the same points in a shorter format through the use of the **bold type** sections as well as the **FAST FACT** segments.

When all else fails, always remember the simplicity of the Practical Fitting Program is in the fact that the clubmaker needs only to find out how the golfer wants to improve **Distance, Accuracy, Trajectory, Backspin** or **Feel** and then proceed to change only the specifications which have a **MAJOR** or **MEDIUM** effect on those factors the golfer wishes to change.

The following chapter, The Fitting Priorities, is designed to help clubmakers view the Practical Fitting Program from a truly common sense approach. In virtually all fitting sessions there will be times when the clubmaker is a bit confused with regard to the direction to go in choosing a particular specification. What will happen if the shaft is a little too stiff compared to being a little too flexible for the golfer? What if the lie angle is off by a degree; is that going to throw everything off? In the choice of length, especially for a golfer in search of more **Distance**, when will the clubmaker know if the club is too long vs. too short for the golfer? In short, until the clubmaker has had enough experience to gain the confidence in making the right choice between two directions in the fitting, what should be done?

The information contained in Chapter 8 is completely new, and is designed to help the clubmaker learn enough about the priorities of the fitting specifications to help make that final fitting decision for any golfer with the confidence that the recommendation will actually help, and will never harm the player's quest for game improvement.

Chapter 8
THE PRIORITIES IN MAKING ACCURATE FITTING RECOMMENDATIONS

KNOWING THE CHANGES IN GOLF CLUB SPECIFICATIONS WHICH COULD HELP OR HINDER THE PLAYER'S QUEST FOR GAME IMPROVEMENT

> NOTE FOR CHAPTER EIGHT: Chapter 8 is best described as the confidence building section of the book. In this chapter can be found a world of information to help clubmakers gain the confidence to make the final selection of any fitting specification for a golfer. There will be many times the clubmaker may not be sure how much to change a certain specification. The following chapter is designed to be the 'voice of experience' for the clubmaker, the mentor to which to turn when there is doubt about what to recommend.
>
> To use this chapter effectively, first review the information from Chapter 2 which identifies the specifications which have a MAJOR effect on Distance and Accuracy. Many golfers will indicate a desire for more Distance and better Accuracy long before they ask for a change in Trajectory, Backspin or Feel. If the clubmaker is aware of the pros and cons of making changes in the specifications which pertain the most to changing Distance and Accuracy, more confidence can be gained when it comes time to compiling the Preliminary Fitting Recommendation.
>
> The specifications which have a MAJOR effect on both Distance and Accuracy which should be studied first in this chapter are Loft, CG, Total Weight, Shaft Weight, Face Angle, Length and Lie Angle in the short irons.
>
> The other way this chapter can best be utilized in the fitting session is to use it as a reference after the Preliminary Fitting Recommendation (PFR) is compiled. With the PFR filled out, the clubmaker can open Chapter 8 and look for the specifications that are a major part of the game improvement goals of the player to determine if the recommendations need to be modified.

INTRODUCTION

To this point, The Golfsmith Practical Fitting Program has taught the clubmaker how to use the **MAJOR, MEDIUM** and **MINOR** rankings of the specifications, the Player Interview, the Equipment Evaluation, the Swing Analysis and the Final Swing Measurements to determine the specifications for the new clubs to help the player improve. However, during the time the clubmaker is sorting through all of the fitting information and thinking about what changes to make in the specifications, there are going to be times when the decision of exactly what the new specification should be is not crystal clear. Should the loft of the driver be 11, or 12 degrees? Should the face angle be 2, or 3 degrees closed? Should the 85mph swing speed player use an 80-90mph shaft, a 75-85mph shaft or an 85-95mph rated shaft?

Decisions like these bother many clubmakers because they are unsure just what the difference in the specification will actually do for the golfer. One of the unfortunate things about clubfitting is that a clubmaker or a golfer cannot usually find out how helpful a change in one specification could be until after the change is made.

Certainly, knowing the specifications in terms of whether they have a **MAJOR,** a **MEDIUM** or a **MINOR** effect on the **Distance, Accuracy, Trajectory, Backspin** or the **Feel** of the club is a vitally important step in this direction. But during the time the actual degrees or inches or mph of each golf club specification are being selected for the player, how can the clubmaker be sure if enough of a change, or too much of a change is being made?

For those reasons, this chapter, which outlines the priorities within the selection of the fitting specifications, is very important in the clubmaker's development of an accurate clubfitting program. The information which follows can be used by the clubmaker whenever there is doubt in making the final selection of a fitting specification. In short, the information in Chapter 8 will reveal whether to make the specification in question a 'little more' or 'a little less' to be sure the player will gain the maximum benefit from the change and will not be harmed by the selection of any fitting specification. The Golfsmith Practical Fitting Program thinks of this chapter as its 'common sense' or 'logical' element; a way for the clubmaker to develop more confidence and be sure the fitting specifications selected create the best set of golf clubs the player has ever owned.

THE SPECIFICATIONS OF THE CLUBHEAD

1. LOFT

What happens if the loft angle is too strong for the player?

* Will lower **Trajectory,** making it harder to stop the ball, making it easier for the ball to 'run' into trouble spots on the course.
* Will decrease carry **Distance** and with it, decrease overall **Distance** in the longer clubs, particularly the driver, for medium to slower swing speed players.
* Could make it harder to get the ball airborne for players of lesser ability.
* Could make the original set makeup obsolete for certain players by making certain longer irons even harder to hit, thus creating gaps in yardage between the fairway woods and irons.

* Could also make the set makeup obsolete by making the gap in yardage between the 9-iron, PW and a current SW too far apart.
* Could confuse the golfer when deciding what club to hit from familiar landmarks on the golf course.
* Could add yardage to the golfer's game, but likely only in the short irons and higher lofted fairway woods, because the longer and middle irons as well as the driver and lower lofted fairway woods would just become harder to hit and get airborne.

What happens if the loft angle is too weak for the player?

* Will increase **Trajectory**, making it easier to stop the ball, but at the same time, could decrease **Distance** for higher swing speed players.
* Will increase carry **Distance** in the longer clubs, particularly the driver, for players with slower swing speeds.
* Could also confuse golfer's sense of **Distance** on his/her home course
* Could make it easier to get the ball airborne for players of lesser ability.
* Could change the set makeup for certain players by making certain longer irons slightly easier to hit, thus possibly making some fairway woods and irons hit the ball the same **Distance**. Could also make the set makeup different by making the 9-iron and a current PW hit the ball similar distances.
* Could confuse the golfer when deciding what club to hit from known landmarks on the golf course.
* Could decrease yardage from the golfer throughout the set.

FAST FACT Conclusion for Loft:

<u>Too weak is better than too strong in the driver, however, too strong is better than too weak in the high lofted fairway woods, the middle irons and the short irons</u>. If the lofts are made stronger than the old clubs, be sure to re-check the set makeup to determine if the loft change will create a gap in yardage or make two clubs hit the ball the same Distance.

Because Distance is so important to all golfers, it is better to err on the side of being too weak with the driver loft but a little too strong in the irons and fairway woods for all but the strongest swing speed players. If going stronger in the loft within the set all of a sudden makes one or more of the long irons impossible to hit, that 'lost' club can be replaced by selecting a high lofted fairway wood, a club that would have been easier to hit than any of the long irons in the first place. At the same time, it is not likely that stronger lofts in the short irons will cause a problem for the average to higher handicappers, because higher loft angles are easy to hit for virtually all golfers. However, for average to lesser ability players it could be very damaging to make the Driver too strong. For stronger, faster swing speed players, it is OK to err slightly too strong on the driver.

2. LIE

What happens if the lie angle is too flat for the player?

* Could cause the player to push the ball – the greater the loft <u>and</u> the more the lie is too flat for the player, the more off line the pushed shot will be.
* Could cause the golfer to make swing changes to accommodate the lie error, thus creating an array of other swing problems, including low hands at address and a flatter swing plane.

What happens if the lie angle is too upright for the player?

* Could cause the player to pull the ball – the greater the loft <u>and</u> the more the lie is too upright for the player, the more off line the pulled shot will be.
* Could cause the golfer to make swing changes to accommodate the lie error, thus creating an array of other swing problems, including higher hands in the address position and a more upright swing plane.

FAST FACT Conclusion for Lie:

<u>No deviation should be allowed in the correct fitting of the lie angle in the middle and short irons. However, it is not as important to be perfectly fit for lie in the woods and long irons.</u>

The shotmaking error of an incorrect lie is magnified as loft increases. Hence, fitting the lie properly in the short irons and middle irons is more important than it is in the long irons and woods. As a tip, it is conceivable that a lie angle which is much too upright for the player could help to correct for a slice in the driver. However, the driver would have to be at least 4-5° too upright to effect the slice because the driver has the least loft of any club in the bag. Face angle still remains the number one way to correct a slice or a hook in the woods.

3. FACE ANGLE

What happens if the face angle is too open for the player?

* Will cause the golfer to push or slice or push/slice (both together) the ball off line.
* Could cause the golfer to hit the ball slightly lower.
* Could possibly cause the golfer to alter his/her stance, grip or hand position in an effort to re-align the clubface to a more familiar position at address, thus negating the corrective effect of the face angle change.

What happens if the face angle is too closed for the player?

* Will cause the golfer to pull or hook or pull/hook the ball off line.
* Could cause the golfer to hit the ball slightly higher.
* Could possible cause the golfer to alter his/her stance, grip or hand position in an effort to re-align the clubface to a more familiar position at address, thus negating the corrective effect of the face angle change.

FAST FACT Conclusion for Face Angle:
<u>No deviation should be allowed in the correct fitting of the face angle of the woods, particularly in the driver.</u> Both situations of deviation in the face angle, when the wood head is either too open or too closed, can be damaging to the golfer. Face Angle has to be considered one of the most important fitting specifications for which every effort should be made to match it correctly to the golfer's swing habits.

The less the loft on the wood head, the more pronounced the effect of the face angle change will be, so expect face angle corrections to be both more needed and more evident in the driver than in the high lofted woods, for example. When making the decision about the amount of face angle to change, remember a change of 1° in face angle is roughly equivalent to five to seven yards of sideways ball movement at 200 yards of carry.

4. PART I – CLUBHEAD DESIGN (CENTER OF GRAVITY)

What happens if the center of gravity is too high for the player?

* Could cause a little more difficulty in getting the ball airborne, but only in the driver, long and perhaps middle irons.
* Could cause a slightly lower **Trajectory**, thus making it a little more difficult to stop the ball on the green with the middle and longer irons.
* Will not have a pronounced effect on the **Trajectory** or **Distance** of the short irons for average players, but could lower the shot height for more skilled, higher swing speed golfers.
* Could slightly increase carry **Distance** for the more skilled, higher swing speed golfers, but not likely for the higher handicapper. Some **Distance** increase can be expected from a slightly enhanced roll, but usually only if the turf is dry and hard.
* Could slightly decrease driver **Distance** among golfers with slower swing speeds (Driver < 80mph) due to creating a lower shot **Trajectory** that generates much less carry **Distance**.
* Could promote a more unsolid **Feel** when the CG of the ball makes contact below the CG of the clubhead.
* Could bring more control in strong wind conditions, due to the lower **Trajectory**.

What happens if the center of gravity is too low for the player?

* Could make it a little easier to get the ball airborne, more so in the driver and 3-wood, as well as the long and middle irons, than in the high lofted fairway woods and the short irons.
* Could cause a slightly higher **Trajectory**, making it a little easier to stop the ball on the green with the middle and longer irons.
* Will not have a pronounced effect on the **Trajectory** or **Distance** of the short irons for average players, but could noticeably increase the shot height for more skilled, higher swing speed golfers.

* Could slightly decrease carry **Distance** for the more skilled, higher swing speed golfers, but could increase carry **Distance** for the slow swing speed players (less than 80mph driver swing speed). Some **Distance** decrease could be expected from slight decrease in roll, especially if the turf is lush and moist.
* Could slightly increase driver **Distance** among golfers with slower swing speeds (Driver < 80mph) due to a higher shot **Trajectory** that generates a little more carry **Distance**.
* Could promote a more solid **Feel** when the CG of the ball makes contact just slightly above the CG of the clubhead.
* Could bring less control in strong wind conditions, due to a higher **Trajectory**.

FAST FACT Conclusion for Clubhead Design - Center of Gravity:
Too low is better than too high because a CG that is too low could always be offset for the player with changes in loft. For all players, the Feel of impact is more solid if the CG of the ball is slightly above the CG of the clubhead at impact. If this impact occurs because the head happens to have a lower CG rather than because of the way the player swings the club, it does not matter – the Feel will still be the same. Conversely, for all players, the Feel of impact is much less solid if the CG of the ball is below the CG of the clubhead at impact. For that reason it is better to err on the side of a lower CG than a higher CG. Still, the golfer has to like the look of the clubhead design he/she uses. More shotmaking errors will result from the negative perception of the clubhead than what could possibly be overcome by the positive location of the CG.

The net result is if the clubmaker is trying to increase Trajectory for the average to higher handicapper, a low CG will help, but not as much as an increase in loft. Also, when trying to increase Distance for the average to higher handicap golfer, a low CG will help a little, but again, not as much as an increase in loft, nor as much as a decrease in total weight.

A low CG clubhead could hurt a strong player more than it could help a weaker player, but a high CG clubhead could hurt a weaker player more than it could enhance the shot making of a stronger player.

4. PART II – CLUBHEAD DESIGN (WEIGHT DISTRIBUTION)

What happens if the weight distribution has too little perimeter weighting for the player?

* Will generate a much more unsolid feeling at impact when the ball is hit off-center by ¾" or more.
* Will cause more of a **Distance** loss for the player when the ball is hit off-center by ¾" or more.
* Could cause the ball to fly a little lower on off-center hits because of head vibration.

What happens if the weight distribution has too much perimeter weighting for the player?

* Will generate a slightly more solid feeling at impact when the ball is hit off-center by as much as 1".
* Will cause a little bit less of a **Distance** loss for the player when the ball is hit off-center by as much as 1".
* Could cause the ball to fly a little higher on off-center hits because of reduced head vibration.

FAST FACT Conclusion for Clubhead Design - Weight Distribution:

<u>More perimeter weighting is better than less perimeter weighting (Because even good ball striking players hit the ball off-center some of the time).</u>

In the mid 1990s, some better ball strikers began to switch back from the cavity back iron to a non-perimeter weighted iron because of the perception the non-perimeter weighted head will give them more 'feedback' when they hit the ball off-center. This is largely a belief that is being created more out of ego than common sense. No perimeter weighted head feels as solid when hit off-center. Thus, the better player would still know he/she has missed the shot.

There is no reason a good player should want to suffer the feeling of an unsolid impact even though he/she hits the ball off-center fewer times in a round than the average player. In short, the better player who wants to use a non-perimeter weighted (muscleback) head should make that decision based on the shape and style features of the clubhead, not because the clubhead will 'teach' or 'punish' them when he/she hits the ball poorly.

After all, how many good players want to go back to a persimmon or laminated wood head and give up the metal wood? While some good ball strikers are staying away from the super jumbo driver shapes, most are still playing with wood heads with far more perimeter weighting than persimmon or laminated woods. The fact this player type is using a perimeter weighted wood is another indication of a lack of common sense associated with the choice of a muscleback design.

As long as the specifications of the clubhead are fit correctly to the needs of the player, and as long as the player can safisfy his/her shape and style desires in a perimeter weighted clubhead design, then all players should be using clubheads with maximum perimeter weighting.

5. HORIZONTAL BULGE

What happens if the horizontal bulge of the woods is too great (too rounded) for the player?

* Could hit the ball in much more of a push or push/slice type of shot (for both inside/out and outside/in swing paths) when shots are hit off the toe.

* Could hit the ball in much more of a pull, pull/hook (inside/out swing path), or pull/fade (outside/in swing path) when shots are hit off the heel.

What happens if the horizontal bulge of the woods is too little (too flat) for the player?

* Could hit the ball in much more of a low, hooking type of shot (inside/out swing path), or low with slightly less fade/slice (outside/in swing path), when shots are hit off the toe.
* Could hit the ball in much more of a low slicing type of shot (for both types of swing paths) when shots are hit off the heel.

FAST FACT Conclusion for Horizontal Bulge:
<u>No deviation should be allowed in the correct fitting of bulge (Because both too much and too little bulge are not helpful in any way to the player).</u>

A case could be made for trying to fit the golfer who slices the ball with an outside/in swingpath, and hits the ball off the toe, with a set of woods with less bulge (flatter face). However, the amount the bulge would have to be flattened would be significant to help this type of player hit toe shots with a draw or with much less fade. Such a wood head design would be very difficult to find because all clubhead suppliers make their woods within a fairly narrow range of bulge. In the end, it is far better to use face angle changes to correct a slice than to use a flatter bulge.

Beyond this, the better player might have a visual desire for one bulge radius as opposed to another which would be born out of his/her experience with previous wood head designs. It is not uncommon for the more experienced player to quickly note a difference between two woods which have a 2" radius difference in the bulge. In that case, bulge becomes more of a psychological factor in meeting the golfer's equipment preference which has to be taken into account in the selection of the wood head design.

6. VERTICAL ROLL

What happens if the vertical roll of the woods is too great (too rounded) for the player?

* Will hit the ball in a noticeably higher **Trajectory** when the shot is hit off the top half of the clubface.
* Will hit the ball slightly shorter when the shot is hit off the top half of the clubface. However, could generate slightly more **Distance** for the slow swing speed player.
* Will make the ball roll less when the shot is hit off the top half of the clubface.
* Will hit the ball in a slightly lower **Trajectory** when the shot is hit off the bottom half of the clubface.
* Will make the ball fly slightly shorter and roll a little more when the shot is hit off the bottom half of the clubface (net **Distance** still less than average for the player).

* Will make the ball more difficult to control in windy conditions when the shot is hit off the top half of the clubface.

What happens if the vertical roll of the woods is too little (too flat) for the player?

* Will make the ball fly in a higher **Trajectory**, although slight, when the shot is hit off the top half of the clubface.
* Will hit the ball slightly shorter when the shot is hit off the top half of the clubface.
* Will make the ball stop only slightly faster when the shot is hit off the top half of the clubface.
* Will hit the ball in a slightly lower **Trajectory** when the shot is hit off the bottom half of the clubface, but not as low as if the face has too much roll.
* Will make the ball fly slightly shorter and roll a little more when the shot is hit off the bottom half of the clubface, but not as low as if the face has too much roll.
* Will make the ball slightly easier to control in windy conditions when the shot is hit off the top half of the clubface.
* Will give a slightly more consistent shot pattern for players who hit the ball off-center up to down.

FAST FACT Conclusion for Vertical Roll:
Too little vertical roll is far better than too much roll. A flatter roll is better than a more rounded roll because the loft is closer to being the same on the top, middle and bottom of the clubface when the wood head has less roll.

However, this is more of a theoretical fitting factor to contend with because once more, there are very few wood head makers who offer no-roll or significantly less roll on the wood heads they manufacture. Less roll, if offered on the selected wood head design, is better for all types of players as long as all of the more important fitting specifications of the wood head can be properly matched to the needs of the golfer.

7. PART I – SOLE ANGLE (#1-PW IRONS)

What happens if the sole angle of the #1-PW irons is too great (too much bounce sole angle) for the player?

* Could cause a thin or 'skulled' shot, although usually only when the ball is struck from hard ground or very short grass on hard ground.
* Could help to clear the iron through tall grass, or through creeping types of grasses like Kikuyu or Bermuda, and thus prevent or slightly lessen the effects of a 'fat' shot, giving the shot a little more **Distance**.

What happens if the sole angle of the #1-PW irons is too little (a scoop sole angle) for the player?

* Will increase the chances of hitting a 'fat' shot for all players with all the irons, but much more with the long and middle irons than with the short irons.

FAST FACT Conclusion for Sole Angle (#1-PW Irons):
<u>A little too much bounce on the sole is far better than too little</u>. A slight bounce sole angle is not going to harm any player on any type of turf conditions, but a scoop sole angle is not good for any player in any type of turf condition.

Sole angle on the #1-9 irons will likely vary only slightly among the majority of head designs. However, it is possible for lower quality clubhead producers to make iron heads in which there is a scoop sole angle on some of the irons. This is why it is necessary to at least perform a cursory visual check of the sole angle of the #1-9 iron heads the golfer has chosen before assembling the set.

Sole Angle on the PW is a different matter than it is on the #1-9 irons because virtually all PWs are designed to have a slight to moderate amount of bounce. If the PW has more than 7° bounce or be produced with a scoop sole angle, it will not be a good choice for any player. However, it is still far better for the PW to have a little more bounce than normal than it is to have a scoop sole angle.

7. PART II – SOLE ANGLE (SAND WEDGE)

What happens if the sole angle of the sand wedge is too great (too much bounce sole angle) for the player?

* Could cause the sand shot to be hit slightly more thin than the player intended, causing the ball to fly farther than intended.
* Could help the wedge move a little easier through tall grass, or through creeping types of grasses like Kikuyu or Bermuda, and to prevent or slightly lessen the effects of a 'fat' shot around the greens.
* Could cause a thin or 'skulled' shot when the ball is struck from hard ground or from very short grass on top of very hard ground.
* Will prevent the wedge from traveling too deep in the sand under the ball.

What happens if the sole angle of the sand wedge is too little (too little bounce sole angle) for the player?

* Could cause the sand shot to be hit slightly more 'fat' than the player intended, causing the ball to fly short or stay in the bunker.
* Might prevent the wedge from traveling easily through tall grass, or could cause the sole to get 'hung up' through creeping types of grasses like Kikuyu or Bermuda.
* Could make it slightly easier to hit the ball solid from a very thin lie or a hardpan lie.
* Will help the wedge travel deeper under the ball in the sand.

FAST FACT Conclusion for Sole Angle (Sand Wedge):
<u>Sole angle in the sand wedge must be matched to the general ability of the player</u>. The ability to hit the ball properly out of the sand is more a product of the player's swing skills than the

club. Because of that, whether the player has the ability to get the ball out of the sand successfully is an initial skill that must be evaluated by the clubmaker before the sole angle can be termed to be too great or too little for the player. However, with that understanding and given the fact most players are of average ability, it is better to recommend more bounce on the sole angle of the sand wedge (> 10°) than less bounce.

8. Part I – Face Progression (woods)

What happens if the face progression of the woods is too great for the player?

* Could cause a slight decrease in **Trajectory**, although very little, given the slight difference in face progression between non-offset woods.
* Could have a negative effect on the appearance preference of the golfer, since woods with more face progression than normal are rare, and tend to be a bit odd looking to most golfers.

What happens if the face progression of the woods is too little for the player?

* Could cause a slight increase in **Trajectory**, although very little, given the slight difference in face progression between non-offset woods. The golfer would have to use a fully offset set of woods to have an effect on increasing **Trajectory**.
* Could have a slight negative effect on the appearance preference of the golfer, since woods with less face progression than normal give the general impression that part of the face is "missing".

FAST FACT Conclusion for Face Progression of the Woods:
Because there is little difference between the amount of face progression in woods being manufactured today, there is no performance advantage to recommending more or less face progression. However, this is not to say that offset woods should be ignored (see Part II – Hosel Offset-Woods). The face progression of the wood heads is more a part of the appearance factors which have to satisfy the golfer in the selection of the wood head design.

8. Part II – Hosel Offset (irons)

What happens if the offset of the irons is too great for the player?

* Could cause the player to pull the ball (because the offset has caused the shoulders to turn in the address position and thus aim to the pull side of the target).
* Could cause the player to hit the ball 'fat' a slightly higher percentage of the time.
* Could cause the player to hit the ball slightly higher, and with it, slightly shorter (depending on the loft angle of each head in the set and the swing speed of the player).

* Could cause the player to set up to the ball in the address position with the hands farther in front of the ball, thus encouraging the clubhead to come into impact at a steeper angle. This can both help the player get the ball airborne more consistently as well as cause the slightly higher incidence of hitting the ball fat.

What happens if the offset of the irons is too little for the player?

* Could cause the player to hit the ball 'thin' a slightly higher percentage of the time.
* Could cause the player to hit the ball slightly lower, and with it, very slightly farther (depending on the loft angle of each head as well as the swing speed of the player).
* Could cause the player to set up to the ball with the hands not as far in front of the ball (This could possibly cause the angle of the clubhead's descent into the ball to be more shallow, which is one of the possible reasons for a slightly higher incidence of hitting the ball thin).

FAST FACT Conclusion for Hosel Offset of the irons:
   Because there is little effect of the offset of irons on the Trajectory and Distance of a shot, there is no real performance advantage to recommending more vs less offset to the player who already is able to get the ball adequately airborne. For the player who is hitting the ball thin a high percentage of the time, more offset could help by making the angle of attack of the clubhead into impact steeper, but at the risk of slightly increasing the incidence of hitting the ball fat as well. For the most part, iron hosel offset is largely an appearance factor which has to appeal to the equipment preference of the golfer in the selection of the iron head design.

8. Part III – Hosel Offset (woods)

What happens if the offset of the woods is too great for the player?

* Could cause the player to pull the ball (because the offset has caused the shoulders to aim to the pull side of the target).
* Could cause the player to hit the ball 'fat' a slightly higher percentage of the time.
* Will cause the player to hit the ball slightly higher, and with it, very slightly shorter (depending on the loft angle of each wood head as well as the swing speed of the player).
* Could cause the player to set up to the ball in the address position with the hands farther in front of the ball, thus possibly promoting more of a downward angle of the clubhead coming into impact (this can both help the player get the ball airborne more consistently as well as could cause the slightly higher incidence of hitting the ball fat).

What happens if the offset of the woods is too little for the player?

* Could cause the player to hit the ball 'thin' a slightly higher percentage of the time.
* Could cause the player to hit the ball slightly lower, and with it, very slightly farther (depending on the loft angle of each wood head).
* Could cause the player to set up to the ball with the hands not as far in front of the ball (possibly causing the angle of the clubhead's descent into the ball to be more shallow, leading to a slightly higher incidence of hitting the ball thin).

FAST FACT Conclusion for Hosel Offset of the woods:
    More offset is better for the golfer who has been struggling to get the ball airborne consistently or for the golfer who has hit the woods on a very low Trajectory and wants to hit the ball higher. The increase in Trajectory, which comes from a change from a non-offset set of woods to an offset set of woods is almost always greater than the increase in Trajectory which comes from switching to a fully offset set of irons.

9. SHAFT WEIGHT/TOTAL WEIGHT

What happens if the shaft weight is too heavy for the player?

* Could help control and slow down the tempo which could bring a fast tempo swing more under control.
* Could cause a golfer to become tired during a round and bring about poor swings from fatigue.
* Could slow down swing speed, thus decreasing **Distance**.
* Could bring a very slight improvement in **Accuracy** by slowing down the swing, or could cause the golfer to push the ball as a result of a lack of strength to square the clubface on the downswing.

What happens if the shaft weight is too light for the player?

* Could have a negative effect on **Accuracy** by causing the swing to become more uncontrolled. The result is usually a pull, but could be a low slice hit off the heel of the club.
* Could increase swing speed, thus increasing **Distance** (but only if the swingweight is standard to high).
* Could promote a quick swing tempo (but normally only if the swingweight is too low).

FAST FACT Conclusion for Shaft Weight:
    Neither extreme for the player is acceptable. However, a light weight shaft would be better than heavy as long as the swingweight is kept at standard to high levels to allow the golfer to feel the clubhead during the swing and gain a sense of timing and rhythm.

10. SHAFT FLEX

What happens if the shaft flex is too stiff for the player?

* Will cause a slight to moderate loss in **Distance**.
* Will cause a decrease in clubhead **Feel**.
* Will cause a decrease in the feeling of solid impact with the ball.
* Could cause a shot that is slightly straighter, but could also cause the golfer to push the ball.
* Could cause the ball to fly on a slightly lower **Trajectory**.

What happens if the shaft flex is too flexible for the player?

* Could cause the golfer to hit the ball slightly less to the slice side of the fairway.
* Could cause the ball to fly on a slightly higher **Trajectory**.
* Could cause the golfer to increase **Distance**, possibly with a very slight decrease in **Accuracy**.
* Will cause an increase in the ability to **Feel** the clubhead during the swing and through impact.
* Will cause an increase in the sensation of a solid feeling of impact.

FAST FACT Conclusion for Shaft Flex:
<u>Too flexible is better than too stiff because it is far better to increase clubhead Feel and gain the feeling of a solid impact than it is to lose this feeling during the swing.</u> The loss of Distance and Feel that comes from a shaft being too stiff is far more damaging to the golfer than is the possible slight increase in Trajectory and the slight loss of Accuracy that could come with a shaft that is too flexible.

11. SHAFT TORQUE

What happens if the shaft torque is too low for the player?

* Will cause a slight to moderate loss in **Distance** from the stiffening effect on the shaft.
* Could cause the golfer to hit the ball slightly straighter, but with the loss of **Distance**.
* Could cause a slightly lower **Trajectory**.
* Could cause a decrease in clubhead **Feel** and a decrease in the sensation of solid impact with the ball, especially if the low torque is combined with a shaft flex that is also too stiff for the player.
* Will increase the overall stiffness of the shaft.

What happens if the shaft torque is too high for the player?

* Could cause a slight decrease in **Accuracy** but only in the case of a very aggressive, fast swing speed player using a very high degree torque shaft.

* Could cause a slightly higher **Trajectory**.
* Could promote an increase in clubhead **Feel** and an increase in the sensation of making solid impact with the ball.
* Will make the overall feeling of the stiffness of the shaft more flexible.

FAST FACT Conclusion for Shaft Torque:
A slightly lower torque is better than a torque that is much too high, but only as long as the flex of the shaft is not too stiff for the swing speed needs of the player. The decision of torque for the player is determined by the RSSR (Recommended Swing Speed Rating) of the shaft, which is a ranking of the overall stiffness of a shaft based on its frequency (flex) and its torque combined together. If the selected stiffness is slightly more flexible than what the swing speed of the golfer would normally indicate, a low degree of torque can improve Accuracy without sacrificing Distance and Feel. However, if the shaft flex chosen is slightly more stiff than what the swing speed of the golfer would normally indicate, a lower torque will result in a loss of Distance and Feel that cannot be overcome by any improvement in Accuracy.

12. SHAFT BEND POINT

What happens if the shaft bend point is too low for the player?

* Could bring an increase in clubhead **Feel** and a slight increase in the sensation of a more solid impact with the ball.
* Could cause the golfer to hit the ball slightly higher, but normally only among higher swing speed players.

What happens if the shaft bend point is too high for the player?

* Could bring a decrease in clubhead **Feel** and a slight decrease in the feeling of making a solid impact with the ball, especially if the shaft flex/shaft torque is too stiff.
* Could cause the golfer to hit the ball slightly lower.

FAST FACT Conclusion for Shaft Bend Point:
Too low is better than too high, because the so called significant Trajectory increases directly attributed to bend point are unsubstantiated for the vast majority of players. The choice in bend point should be made on the basis of trying to give the golfer more of a chance to experience a solid feeling of impact with the ball. A low bend point shaft will help transmit a feeling of a more solid impact with the ball to a much higher percentage of players than will a mid or a high bend point shaft.

13. SHAFT BALANCE POINT

What happens if the shaft balance point is too low for the player?

* Could bring about slightly less clubhead **Feel** from the decreased head weight required to achieve normal swingweight levels. (Note: A low balance point on a shaft, not the golf club, means that less head weight is required to achieve any swingweight. The less the head weight in the club, the less the clubhead **Feel**).

* Could make the tip of the shaft slightly more stiff feeling (unless shaft is especially designed to offset this tendency).

* Could help the player achieve a normal range of swingweight when using standard weight clubheads.

What happens if the shaft balance point is too high for the player?

* Could make the butt end of the shaft much more stiff, which could have the effect of making the entire shaft more stiff in its overall **Feel**.

* Could make the golf club **Feel** more butt heavy.

* Could make the swingweight much lower than normal when using standard weight clubheads, which would result in a loss of clubhead **Feel**.
  Note: This refers only to the balance point of the shaft and is not to be confused with the balance point of the assembled golf club.

FAST FACT Conclusion for Shaft Balance Point:
   Too low is better than too high, although mid balance point shafts are a safer selection for most players. This is because some (not all) low balance point shafts could be tip stiff from the added shaft material in the tip required to make the balance point lower.
   For those low balance point shafts which are made with a more flexible tip, the lower balance point results in better clubhead Feel. This is one reason lower balance point shafts could be better than higher balance point shafts for many players. The other reason is that in the case of lightweight graphite shafts, it is common for some clubmakers to forget to increase the swingweight to near normal or higher levels to ensure proper clubhead Feel. In this case, the low balance point shaft would always be preferable for its ability to prevent the club from being swingweighted too low to Feel the clubhead during the swing.
   As a general rule, very strong, high swing speed players can play with both low and high balance point shafts, while the majority of average to less able players cannot play with a high balance point shaft.

14. PART I – GRIP SIZE

What happens if the grip size is too large?

* Could make it slightly more difficult to teach the proper release of the hands through impact.

* Could decrease clubhead **Feel** by shifting the club's balance point toward the grip end (only if large grip was heavy, > 55g).
* Could increase total weight of the club.
* Could make the golfer **Feel** more comfortable and relaxed with the club.
* Could help relax the forearm muscles at address and during the takeaway.

What happens if the grip size is too small?

* Could accentuate the release of the hands through impact.
* Could increase clubhead **Feel** by shifting the club's balance point toward the head end (only if small grip was light, < 42g).
* Could decrease total weight, although only slightly.
* Could make the golfer **Feel** more uncomfortable and have a much harder time holding on to the club.
* Could increase tension in the forearm muscles at address and during the takeaway.

FAST FACT Conclusion for Grip Size:
A grip that is too large is better for the majority of golfers than a grip that is too small. However, attention must be paid to the swingweight to retain adequate clubhead Feel when the grip is made larger than 1/32" oversize.

The grip is the golfer's only physical contact with the club. It must Feel comfortable in the golfer's hands in order to promote a consistent, repeating golf swing. Because slicing and hooking are primarily caused by errors in swing path and face angle, fears of further slicing being caused by a large grip are unsubstantiated. Because comfort is more important than the absolute correct traditional fit, a grip that is too large is better than one which is too small for the player.

14. Part II – Grip Type

FAST FACT Conclusion for GRIP TYPE:
<u>Because the player must be the sole judge of the type of grip with which he/she will play, the only grip type that is acceptable is the one which is comfortable to the player</u>. Try to set up the fitting session with samples to allow the player to handle and touch the various types of grips to make a selection which will be pleasing in terms of Feel to him/her.

15. Grip Weight

What happens if the grip weight is too heavy for the player?

* Will decrease the clubhead **Feel** due to the heavy weight on the grip end of the club. This moves the balance point of the club closer to the grip, creating the sensation of a golf club with a light clubhead.
* Will increase the total weight of the golf club, in turn slowing down the player's swing speed.

What happens if the grip weight is too light for the player?

* Will increase the clubhead **Feel**. The light grip shifts the balance point of the golf club down toward the head, thus creating the sensation of a 'head heavy' golf club.
* Will decrease the total weight of the golf club, as a result slightly increasing the player's swing speed.

FAST FACT Conclusion for Grip Weight:
  <u>Too light is much better than too heavy because the lighter the grip, the more the clubhead can be noticed during the swing, while the lighter the total weight will become.</u>
  If it is necessary to make a larger grip for the player, by all means the lighter weight grips should be used to prevent the larger size from weighing too much and negatively affecting the total weight and clubhead Feel.

16. LENGTH

What happens if the length of the golf club is too long for the player?

* Could cause the golfer to hit the ball more off the center of the clu face, thus decreasing **Distance** and **Accuracy**.
* Could allow the golfer to hit the ball farther, but only if the ball is hit on center.
* Could make the shaft **Feel** more flexible to the player.
* Could make the club **Feel** heavier and more cumbersome. Could force the player to make swing plane changes to accommodate the longer length; the longer the club, the flatter the swing plane could become.

What happens if the length of the golf club is too short for the player?

* Could allow the golfer to hit the ball more on center, thus increasing **Distance** and **Accuracy** (only if the player was hitting the ball off center a high percentage of the time with the previous longer club).
* Could cause the golfer to hit the ball shorter, but only if the player's previous club was longer <u>and</u> the player was able to hit this longer club solidly and on-center.
* Could make the shaft **Feel** more stiff to the player.
* Could make the club **Feel** slightly lighter.
* Could force the golfer to make swing plane changes to accommodate the shorter length; the shorter the club, the more upright the swing plane could become.

FAST FACT Conclusion for Length:
  <u>Too short is better than too long, but if you try long, be sure the shaft is lighter and the player is athletically coordinated enough to hit the ball on center a high percentage of the time.</u>
  Shorter clubs are always easier to hit for all levels of player ability. It is true that in virtually all cases a player will be better off with a shorter club, because the shorter the club, the greater

the chance of hitting the club on-center. In following, the more on-center a player can hit the ball, the straighter and longer the shot will be. Yet, the lure of Distance is great, so all options for increasing Distance should be tried. Since the longer the club, the greater the *chance* for Distance, all golfers should seek the longest club they can hit solidly a high percentage of the time.

17. SWINGWEIGHT

What happens if the swingweight is too high for the player?

* Could cause an increase in **Distance**, as long as the total weight of the club is not too high for the golfer. If the total weight is high and the swingweight is high, a slight loss of clubhead speed could develop from the overall weight of the club being too heavy. From that could come a slight loss of **Distance**. If the total weight is low and the swingweight is too high, the golfer could experience the feeling of the club being too 'head heavy,' which could disrupt rhythm and tempo.
* Could cause an increase in clubhead **Feel** and a slight increase in the feeling of solid impact with the ball.
* Could cause the golfer to become tired during the round, especially if the total weight of the club is too high as well.
* Could slow down a quick swing tempo and help prevent 'hitting from the top'.
* Could increase **Distance** just from a simple increase in head mass.

What happens if the swingweight is too low for the player?

* Could cause an increase in **Distance**, but only if the total weight of the club is just right for the golfer. If the total weight is too low and the swingweight is too low, this could cause unsolid impact, off-center hits and a general loss of **Distance** and **Feel**. If the total weight is too high and the swingweight is too low, this could also cause unsolid impact, off-center hits and a general loss of **Distance** and **Feel**.
* Could cause a decrease in **Distance**, particularly if the total weight of the club is not correct for the golfer.
* Could cause a decrease in clubhead **Feel** and a noticeable decrease in the feeling of solid impact with the ball.
* Could help prevent the golfer from becoming tired during the round.
* Could increase swingspeed.
* Could promote a faster tempo, and could accentuate 'hitting from the top'.
* Could possibly decrease **Distance** because of the decrease in head mass.

FAST FACT Conclusion for Swingweight:
<u>Too high is better than too low, as long as the total weight is not too high at the same time</u>.
While the issue of swingweight may be debated, there are two main facts that support erring on the side of making clubs with higher swingweights; 1). Standard shaft trimming is

based on standard swingweight. Ignore swingweight and you
destroy good clubhead Feel. 2). Clubhead mass is an important
part of the Distance formula ($E = 1/2mv2$ or $F = ma$). Ignore
clubhead mass and you lose Distance.

18. SET MAKEUP

Should the player carry more woods or more wedges?

* Long irons are tough to hit for a lot of players; fairway woods which
hit the ball the same **Distance** are much easier to hit for a larger range
of golfers.

* Adding wedges is a way to improve the short game, an area of fitting
that is often overlooked. So much of what is written about fitting pertains only to the woods and irons. When you think that woods and irons
only constitute half of the game's strokes, you can understand that any
type of short game fitting has a good chance of positively affecting the
player's score.

* The key to fitting set makeup is to first find the longest iron the golfer
can hit solidly a high percentage of the time, then eliminate all irons
longer than that one. Fill in with high lofted woods. Then look at the
golfer's short game and analyze the short game requirements of the
courses played the most. Make wedge recommendations based on individual needs to make up for problem areas around the green.

FAST FACT Conclusion for Woods vs Wedges:
   More woods and more wedges is better than fewer woods
and more irons.

   Be aware that once in a while the clubmaker may
encounter a player who hits irons better than woods. In this
case do not force the fairway woods on the player under the
assumption they will be easier to hit. In addition, for wedge fitting learn the different types of wedge specifications and what
type of golf course conditions call for what type of wedge specification. See Chapter 9 for guidance in this area.

Chapter 9

FITTING FOR THE SHORT GAME

THE PRINCIPLES INVOLVED IN THE ACCURATE FITTING OF WEDGES AND PUTTERS

NOTE FOR CHAPTER NINE: Chapter 9 represents the most complete discussion ever published on the fitting of clubs which comprise the short game – the wedges and putter. Because such a complete discussion of the vital part of the game has never been revealed, clubmakers are advised at some point to take the time to read all of this chapter in an effort to become as familiar as possible with the full complement of short game information contained within. However, to gain the high points from this section on short game fitting, we recommend clubmakers study the following main parts of the chapter.

1. The section which outlines the recommended set makeup of wedges for all types of golfers from scratch to high handicapper. In this section can be found the receommendations for how many wedges each type of golfer should carry, along with what their specifications should be.

2. The step by step procedures for fitting the wedges, found at the end of the wedge section of the chapter on page 377.

3. The step by step procedures for fitting the putter, found at the end of the putter section of the chapter on pages 380-381 and 384-385.

From these sections can be gained enough information to do a credible and accurate job of recommending ways to cut strokes from any golfer's game.

INTRODUCTION

One of the most interesting points about clubfitting is that virtually all of its instruction has been focused on trying to make accurate fitting decisions for the woods and irons. Yet the shots hit with the woods and irons comprise only some 50 to 65 percent of the total number of shots in a round of golf. As a result, can it be said that any fitting session really has the ability to lower the golfer's handicap if it completely ignores the short game?

In the same light, when people practice, what do the majority of them do? They head to the driving range to hit full shots with the woods and irons, most of the time focusing on hitting the driver as soon as possible. How many golfers go to the golf course strictly for the purpose of practicing their short game? While most people do 'hit a few putts' just prior to teeing off, most of this time cannot really be considered a practice session designed to improve the putting stroke, but rather is best described as an action primarily taken to occupy those last few minutes before taking the tee to start the round.

In Harvey Penick's various books, the late and great teacher advised golfers who did not have adequate practice time before a round of golf to never waste their time at the driving range. Instead, Mr. Penick urged his students to spend the 15-20 minutes before teeing off hitting chip shots and putting on the practice green, instead of pulling the driver out of the bag to hurriedly hit a few shots before play began. It was his belief, and correctly so, that if scoring was the primary focus of the game, the golfer has a much better chance of positively affecting his/her score by sharpening the short game, rather than hoping to hit longer, more accurate shots from tee to green.

There is no doubt that keeping the ball in play off the tee and hitting greens in regulation is a key to better scoring. Realistically though, how many more fairways and greens will a properly fit set of woods and irons allow the golfer to hit? Will a well fit set of clubs double the number of fairways and greens the golfer can hit over the number they did before? As much as everyone would like that to be the case, it is doubtful such a dramatic ball striking change will occur, no matter how well the new clubs fit the player. Yet, that is approximately the ball striking change that would be required to lower a handicap by five or six shots.

However, if the golfer has indicated on the Player Interview Form a low Up & Down Percentage for chipping and sand shots, as well as a high Number of Putts Per Round, the clubmaker should focus his/her clubfitting skills on improving the golfer's short game. For example, if the golfer can change the Up & Down percentage from 20 to 50 percent, get the ball out of the bunker 100 percent of the time instead of 50 percent of the time, and reduce the Number of Putts by three or four per round, the handicap could go down by as many as seven to ten shots!

One of the main reasons short game fitting, particularly with the wedges, has become so important is due to the change in loft and length specifications among iron sets that has taken place in the 1990s. The current 'standard' specifications for loft and lie have 'strengthened and lengthened' drastically over the last 10-20 years so that problems have been created within the short game clubs which are not being addressed as much as they should to help the player score better.

While the traditional iron set makeup of #3-9, PW & SW is essentially the same as it has been for years, the loft angle of the sand wedge has not changed as much as the lofts of the short irons and the pitching wedges. Thus, when a more traditional lofted SW is matched with a stronger lofted set of #3-PW irons, the result can be a frustrating 'gap' in yardage between the PW and the SW.

Note the following chart, which compares short iron lofts since the 1970s.

Comparison of Short Iron Lofts Over Time

Club	Avg Loft 1970s	Δ	Avg Loft 1980s	Δ	Avg Loft 1990s	Δ
8-iron	44°	—	40°		38°	—
9-iron	48°	4°	44°	4°	42°	4°
PW	52°	4°	48°	4°	46°	4°
SW	56°	4°	55°	7°	55°	9°

The most obvious point that can be seen from the chart is the gap in loft that has evolved between the PW and the SW as the lofts of the irons has become stronger. Some of the problems this evolution of loft within the irons has created in the short game can be outlined as follows:

Possible problems created by a strong loft angle on the pitching wedge

* Player has a harder time hitting the ball high with pitch shots from 80 yards or less to stop the ball on the green.

* Player has a harder time hitting chip shots from the grass around the green which can land softly and stop quickly.

* Player is forced to use the sand wedge for more shots from grass lies that need higher **Trajectory**, shots for which the SW may not be well suited due to its much greater bounce sole angle.

Possible problems created by a strong loft pitching wedge and a strong loft angle on the sand wedge

* The player is forced to use the SW for more short chip shots around the green in an effort to hit the ball high enough, but the greater bounce sole can cause a higher percentage of 'fat' shots, 'schlaffed' shots (bouncing the wedge off the ground into the ball), or 'bladed' shots from the much shorter grass around the green.

* If the player is forced to use a SW for pitch and chip shots close to the green, the much greater loft on the SW compared to the PW can cause the player to leave the shots short of the target.

* The player does not have enough loft for hitting higher, soft landing shots from the sand because the SW has had to be strengthened to prevent its loft from being so far away from the PW.

* A 'gap' in yardage opens up between the PW and SW which forces the player to overhit the SW and risk a loss of **Accuracy** with inconsistent **Distance**. (Hitting a full shot with a club which has a high degree of bounce can cause inconsistent shotmaking because the trailing edge of the sole makes the initial contact with the turf).

The net result is that because the lofts of irons as well as the PW and SW have become so much stronger over the past 20 years, the wedges are not as well suited for the shots for which they are being called upon to play.

In addition to the loft angle differences, there is also one other important specification which makes a wedge different from the short irons - the sole angle. The two most predominant shotmaking problems from which average to high handicap players suffer are hitting the chips and pitches either 'fat' or 'thin'.

Since professional golfer Tom Kite was credited with the evolution of the so called 'third wedge', a vast assortment of wedges with different combinations of loft, sole angle and sole widths have been made available to golfers to help fine tune their short games. What has not been provided along with the modern assortment of different wedges, has been adequate information to educate the golfer about what combination of wedge specifications will best suit which types of playing circumstances.

One of the factors which makes the recommendation of a 'family' of wedges even more confusing for the clubmaker is that not all players use wedges in the same manner. Some people prefer to chip the ball low, some want to hit the same distance of shot high; some are more creative and rely on using different wedges for different types of shots while others want to rely on one club for hitting all short shots around the green. Once more, the human factor enters into the decision making process to make the selection of the wedges more than simply a matter of recommending loft, sole angle and sole width.

The Golfsmith Practical Fitting Program is pushed to its limit devising a practical method to streamline all of the possible ways in which golfers can be properly matched with the different specifications which make up the various wedges. Since so little has been written about short game fitting, this chapter will attempt to provide a complete reference for short game fitting along with a more simple and efficient way to make general recommendations for wedges and putters which will enhance the golfer's ability to score.

To realize such a dual goal in short game fitting, this chapter will be set up in two basic sections. In the first section of this chapter, the Practical Fitting Program will identify the key specifications which affect the performance of wedges and putters and will explain the general use for each type of wedge or putter specification.

In the second section of the chapter, The Golfsmith Practical Fitting program will offer recommendations for general wedge specifications for different golfer types. This will give clubmakers a general starting point for advising the best set of wedges for each type of golfer. In addition this section of the chapter will conclude by directly addressing some of the problem areas with wedge play which come from the Player Interview Form. Individual fitting recommendations are made in several areas to directly address the problems of hitting chips, pitches and sand shots thin or fat.

FITTING THE WEDGES – THE KEY FITTING SPECIFICATIONS

I. LOFT

Loft is a **MAJOR** Specification of Wedge Fitting.

> * **For the average player, the separation in the loft angle between any of the wedges, whether there be two, three or four different wedges, should not be less than 4° and not greater than 6°, as a general guideline. Better players, or golfers who are more skilled at shortening the swing to hit half, or three-quarter length wedge shots, can play with as much as a 7° difference between two of the wedges, but as a general guideline, such a great loft separation should be avoided even for the better player.** Clubmakers do have to remember that the total number of clubs the golfer is allowed to use is 14, so the complement of wedges must be selected with that limitation in mind. If clubmakers keep in mind that the long irons are practically worthless in most golfer's bags, it can be possible to manipulate the set makeup to allow for as many as four wedges.

II. SOLE ANGLE

Sole Angle is a **MAJOR** Specification of Wedge Fitting.

<u>**Descriptions and Specifications for Sole Angle:**</u>
SHALLOW Bounce Sole Angle - 0° to 4° bounce
MEDIUM Bounce Sole Angle - 5° to 9° bounce
MODERATE Bounce Sole Angle - 10° to 14° bounce
HEAVY Bounce Sole Angle - 15° to 20° bounce

* The greater the sole angle (Moderate and Heavy bounce sole angles), the more shallow the wedge will travel though the sand or the turf, and the higher the leading edge will arrive at impact with respect to the ball. **Wedges with a greater bounce sole angle are a better choice for:**
- Players who have had a problem leaving the ball in the sand trap due to the wedge digging too deep under the ball.
- Players who have had a problem hitting the ball fat on pitch shots and chip shots from normal fairway grass or light rough.
- Hitting pitch and chip shots from fluffy, thick, tall grass.
- Hitting pitch and chip shots from creeping, broad leaf types of grass, such as Bermuda, Kikuyu or St. Augustine. Broadleaf grasses are used primarily in the southern parts of the United States.
- Hitting bunker shots from traps in which the sand is fluffy, aerified or not packed densely, and very deep.

* **Wedges with a greater bounce sole angle (Moderate and Heavy bounce sole angles) are not recommended for:**
- Hitting shots from thin grass, hard ground or hardpan.
- Short chip and run shots close to the green.
- High lob shots which need to land softly and stop quickly on the green.
- Use in sand traps in which the sand is very coarse, grainy, pebbly, of a gravel type consistency, in which the sand is very shallow, in which the sand is very heavy, tightly packed or consistently wet.

* The less the sole angle (Shallow to Medium bounce sole angles), the deeper the wedge will travel though the sand or the turf, or, the less chance the sole has to hit behind the ball and literally 'bounce' into the ball. **Wedges with less bounce sole angle are a better choice for:**
- Hitting normal pitch and chip shots from regular length fairway grass or the fringe/apron of the green.
- Players who have had a problem 'skulling' the ball out of the sand trap due to the wedge not digging deep enough under the ball.
- Players who have had a problem hitting the ball thin on pitch shots and chip shots from normal fairway grass or light rough.

- More skilled players who do not hit the ball fat or thin for hitting pitch and chip shots from normal fairway grass or light rough.

- Hitting normal pitch and chip shots from thin leaf types of grass, such as Bentgrass, Ryegrass, Fescue or Bluegrass. Thin leaf grasses are used primarily in seasonal climate areas where it is cold in the winter, cool in the spring and fall and warm in the summer, i.e. the northern parts of the United States.

- Hitting bunker shots from traps in which the sand is very coarse, grainy, pebbly, of a gravel type consistency, in which the sand is very shallow, in which the sand is very heavy, tightly packed or consistently wet.

- High lob shots which need to land softly and stop quickly on the green.

A more complete listing of the possible uses of different sole angle specifications follows as a reference for clubmakers:

SHALLOW BOUNCE SOLE ANGLE - Sole Angle from 0° - 4°

- Best used from grass that is of fairway length and light rough up to about 2" in length (Bent grass, Ryegrass, Fescue, Bluegrass, any narrow bladed type of grass that is not a creeping type of turf and any type of dried grass).

- Good for thin lies, hardpan or dirt.

- Good for standard pitch shots from the fairway or light rough up to about 2" in length (Bent grass, Ryegrass, Fescue, Bluegrass, or any narrow bladed type of grass that is not a creeping type of turf).

- Good for chip shots from fairway grass or light rough up to about 2" in length (Bent grass, Ryegrass, Fescue, Bluegrass, or any narrow bladed type of grass that is not a creeping type of turf).

- Not good for use in sand for virtually all players. The only sand from which this low of a bounce sole angle can work for the average player is very coarse 'pebble' type sand or 'dirt' traps in which the loose dirt material is not more than 1" deep.

- Not that good from heavy rough of more than 2" deep, or from light rough on golf courses which are planted with creeping, broadleaf grasses such as Bermuda, Kikuyu, St. Augustine, etc., seen mostly in the South in the spring, summer and fall.

- Good for use on wedges which will be used to hit soft, high shots from normal fairway grass or light rough up to about 2" in length (Bent grass, Ryegrass, Fescue, Bluegrass, or any narrow bladed type of grass that is not a creeping type of turf).

- Not good for use on pitch and chip shots from wet fairway lie conditions (wet enough that water can be seen when the foot is pressed down firmly on the fairway).

MEDIUM BOUNCE SOLE ANGLE - Sole Angle from 5° - 9°

- Good for use from fairway lies and light rough on golf courses which are planted with creeping, broadleaf grasses such as Bermuda, Kikuyu, St. Augustine, etc., seen mostly in the South in the spring, summer and fall.

- Good for use on northern golf courses from medium to heavy rough longer than 2" (Bent grass, Ryegrass, Fescue, Bluegrass, or any narrow bladed type of grass that is not a creeping type of turf).

- Good for chip shots from longer Ryegrass or Bluegrass fairway turf which is allowed to grow up to 1" around the green (not rough).

- Good for chip shots around the green from fairway grass or light rough on golf courses which are planted with creeping, broadleaf grasses such as Bermuda, Kikuyu, St. Augustine, etc., seen mostly in the South in the spring, summer and fall.

- Good for sand shots, but only for very skilled bunker players who like to try to 'skim' the shot from sand or who are able to successfully use a soft, slower tempo from the bunker.

- Good for average ability bunker players (people who can at least get the ball out of the sand with little problem) but only when used in bunkers with coarse sand, heavy river bottom type sand, bunkers with normal sand which are shallow (less than 2" of sand depth), or normal sand which is wet.

- Good for long distance sand shots (over 30yds) for above average ability bunker players from normal sand traps.

- Not good for use on pitch and chip shots from thin grass or hardpan.

- Good for use on shots from soft underbrush, i.e. pine needles, a bed of leaves, etc.

MODERATE BOUNCE SOLE ANGLE - Sole Angle from 10° - 14°

- Good for normal sand conditions for golfers with average ability from the bunker (people who can at least get the ball out of the sand with little problem) with normal swing speed velocities.

- Good for poor ability bunker players (people who cannot consistently get the ball at least out of the bunker) who swing hard at the ball, but only when used in bunkers with coarse sand, heavy river bottom type sand, bunkers with normal sand which are shallow (2" or less of sand depth).

- Good for short pitch and chip shots from heavy rough of 4" or more or rough of 2-3" which is thick and lush in which the ball tends to sink down.

- Not good for use on normal pitch or chip shots from fairways which are cut to normal length (less than 3/4") unless the golfer sets the hands well in front of the ball or plays the ball near the back foot in the stance.

- Definitely not good for pitch and chip shots from thin grass or hardpan.

HEAVY BOUNCE SOLE ANGLE - Sole Angle from 15° - 20°

- Good for use by poor ability bunker players (people who struggle to get the ball at least out of the bunker) but who also swing hard at the ball.

- Not that good for the very slow swinging, poor bunker player (players who struggle to get the ball at least out of the bunker). For this player in normal sand conditions, the 10-14° bounce sole angle is a little better, or a 5-9° bounce sole angle when combined with a wide sole (1" or wider).

- Not good for any wedge used from grass lie conditions.

III. Sole Width

Sole Width is a **MEDIUM** Specification of Wedge Fitting.

Descriptions and Specifications for Sole Width

NARROW SOLE (Sole Width from .700" - .800")

MEDIUM SOLE (Sole Width from .850" - .950")

WIDE SOLE (Sole Width from 1.00" - 1.25")

SUPER SOLE (Sole Width from 1.30" - over 2")

Sole Width and Sole Angle are almost interchangeable in the wedges. For example, the wider the sole, the more pronounced the effect of the bounce sole angle. If the player wishes to gain the maximum game improvement effect from a bounce sole angle, combining a Medium, Wide or Super sole on the wedge design with the bounce sole angle will literally double the effect of the bounce sole angle.

A Narrow to Medium sole width combined with a Shallow bounce sole angle is a good combination for:

- Most pitching wedges. For hitting a wide assortment of chip and pitch shots around the green and back from the green as far as 100 yards (depending on the loft and the player's strength).

- Hitting chip and run or pitch and run shots.

- Hitting high lob shots which require the face to be laid open (depending upon the loft of the wedge).

- Hitting 'knock down' shots or 'punch' shots from 80 yards or less into the green (depending on the loft and the player's strength).

- A high lofted wedge for the player who wants to use such a club only from normal fairway grass or shallow rough.

A Narrow to Medium sole width combined with a Shallow bounce sole angle is not a good combination for:

- A sand wedge which is intended to be used primarily from the sand. This type of SW could only be used by the highest skilled sand players.

- Hitting soft, short distance shots from tall, lush, moist grass.

A Narrow to Medium sole width combined with a Medium bounce sole angle is a good combination for:

- Most pitching wedges which would be used in the southern part of the country on Bermuda type, broadleaf grasses.

- A sand wedge for more skilled players who do not have much of a problem hitting quality shots from the bunker.

- A player (usually of better than average ability) who likes to use the sand wedge also from the fairway or light rough.

A Medium sole width combined with a Moderate bounce sole angle is a good combination for:

- Most sand wedges which would be used in the sand for average ability bunker players who do not have much of a problem in getting the ball out of the sand.

- Hitting pitch and chip shots from normal length grass fairway lies as well as tall grass which do not have to land soft and stop very quickly.

- Golfers who always chip the ball with the hands well in front of the ball in the address position. This type of action reduces the effect of the bounce sole angle on the ground. However, this also reduces the loft so it will not be possible to hit high trajectory shots with this hand position.

A Medium sole width combined with a Moderate bounce sole angle is not a good combination for:

- Hitting pitch or chip shots from thin grass or 'hard pan' lies when using a normal chipping or pitching swing technique. (Hands would have to be well in front of the ball to hit this shot with this type of wedge, and the ball would fly lower).

Most players should be careful to avoid the situation of a Wide to Super sole width combined with a Moderate or Heavy amount of bounce sole angle. Such a combination in a wedge is only good for:

- Hitting pitches and chips from tall, lush, moist grass, usually more than two to three inches long.

- Hitting sand shots from bunkers in which the sand is very deep and in which the sand is very fluffy and light.

- Players who have tried everything to prevent leaving the ball in the sand trap as a result of the wedge digging too deep under the ball.

A Wide to Super sole width combined with a Shallow bounce sole angle is a good combination for:

- Hitting high lob-type shots from normal fairway grass or light rough to tight pin placements, to undulating, small greens or over hazards close to the green (depending upon the loft).

- Hitting normal short pitches and chip shots from longer fairway grass or moderate rough (up to 2" to 3" deep grass).
- Hitting pitch and chip shots from soft under growth such as pine needles, leaf beds, mulch, grass clippings, etc.
- Average ability bunker players to improve their ability to change tempo with the swing and hit more finesse shots from the sand trap without fear of leaving the ball in the bunker.
- Lesser skilled players looking to hit short to medium distance shots from thin lies or hard pan.

A Wide to Super sole width combined with a Shallow bounce sole angle is not a good combination for:
- Hitting longer distance shots from the fairway or light rough into the green (more than 50-60 yds, depending upon the loft).
- Hitting chip and run shots which are expected to hit on the green or just short of the green and roll most of the distance to the target.

IV. SET MAKEUP

Set Makeup is a **MAJOR** Specification of Wedge Fitting.

The first concept in selecting a complement of wedges for any golfer is to realize that wedges are simply clubs which have a different combination of loft, sole angle and sole width. In the most open minded, custom fitting philosophy for wedges, the clubmaker can virtually choose any combination of loft, sole angle and sole width, as well as length and swingweight/total weight to make up the wedges. **In short, the wedges should be thought of as fitting a separate set of golf clubs within the full set of golf clubs, because they can be so individual in their use and function**.

Because the possible combinations of loft, sole angle, sole width, length and swingweight/total weight are virtually limitless, and because virtually limitless fitting situations are not the ideal situation for a PRACTICAL approach to fitting, **the following section covering the set makeup of wedges will identify a number of possible combinations of three-wedge and four-wedge sets which can prove to be helpful for different player types**.

Factors to Consider When Recommending the Number of Wedges

1) The number of wedges chosen must still allow the golfer to have all of the necessary woods, irons and putter and still not exceed the 14 club limit as ordained by the USGA Rules of Golf.

2) The ball striking skills of the player. In general, the lower the handicap, the better the ball striking ability will be, and with it, the tendency to use two or three wedges as opposed to four wedges will be far more predominant. This is because the good ball striker hits more greens in regulation.

The better player's needs are generalized into two categories - a pitching and chipping club and a reliable sand club.

3) The higher the handicap, the more wedges will likely be needed to help improve the game. Not only do higher handicap players find themselves chipping or pitching into greens more often, but also, these golfers tend to have a greater number of shotmaking situations as well. This means a minimum of three wedges and, if the player does not hit any iron longer than a 5-iron very well, a four-wedge complement should be considered.

SET MAKEUP COMBINATIONS FOR WEDGES FOR DIFFERENT PLAYER TYPES

NOTE: The following recommendations for wedge set makeup do not actually pinpoint a precise loft angle for each wedge, only the difference in loft between the clubs. With all of the different loft specifications for sets of irons, a specific loft for each wedge cannot be recommended unless the clubmaker knows the actual loft of the #9-iron in the set. For that reason, all of the following set makeup recommendations for each player type will require the clubmaker to know the loft of the 9-iron in the set before the precise loft of the wedges can be identified.

TWO-WEDGE SET MAKEUP

A two-wedge set makeup combination is getting to be more and more rare in the game, even among lower handicap players. About the only type of player who should still be using a two-wedge complement is a good player who really likes to use the long irons, in which case the number of woods and irons plus putter will only allow for two wedges to stay within the 14-club limit.

Even good players who hit long irons reasonably well should be made aware of the advantages of using a three-wedge system to improve shotmaking. After all, it was a PGA Tour player, Tom Kite, who, after analyzing where he was losing shots, decided to drop one of the long irons in favor of adding a third wedge.

A low handicap player who relies on the long irons to play the game to the point that his/her set makeup is driver, fairway wood, #1-9 + PW, SW and putter = 14 clubs.

PITCHING WEDGE
Loft	5° greater than #9-iron (if the 9-iron is ≥44°)
Length	Same length as #9-iron
Sole Angle	Shallow bounce sole angle
Sole Width	Narrow sole width
Swingweight	Medium swingweight (D1-D3)
Total Weight	Same shaft weight as irons

SAND WEDGE
Loft	5°-6° greater than PW
Length	Same length to 1/2" shorter than #9-iron
Sole Angle	Medium to Moderate bounce sole angle
Sole Width	Wide sole width
Swingweight	Medium to High swingweight (D4-D6)
Total Weight	Same shaft weight as irons

THREE-WEDGE AND FOUR-WEDGE SET MAKEUPS

There are two general options for creating three-wedge, or four-wedge combinations within the set of golf clubs.

1) To create an additional wedge to fall between the PW and the SW to offset a gap in loft (distance) which has been created by a strong lofted set of irons. In this case, the golfer has to agree that the need to cover the yardage gap between the PW and SW is more important than creating the third wedge with more loft than the SW to hit short, high, soft landing shots. Traditionally, this type of three-wedge combination is only recommended for the better than average player who will be able to hit the ball high and soft either with the SW or the wedge with a loft angle which falls in between the PW and the SW.

2) To create a higher lofted wedge than the SW for high, soft lob type shots. This type of three-wedge system is the most commonly used complement of three wedges in the game, but it requires the separation in loft between the PW and SW to be no greater than 5-6° to prevent a yardage gap from opening up between the two primary wedges.

3) To combine both options into a four-wedge complement. This typically consists of the PW and SW, a 'gap' wedge to bridge the yardage gap between the PW & SW, and a 'lob' wedge with at least 3-4° more loft than the SW.

Examples of Three and Four-Wedge Systems for Different Player Types:

1. Recommended Wedge Set Makeup Combinations for Low Handicap Player (0-8 hdcp); Avg to Faster Tempo; Avg to Greater Strength:

PITCHING WEDGE

Loft	+5° greater than the #9-iron
Length	-1/2" to same as the #9-iron
Sole Angle	Shallow; 0° to 4° (depending on grass)
Sole Width	Narrow to Medium (match the short irons)
Swingweight	+2 points more than the irons

SAND WEDGE

Loft	+6° greater than the PW
Length	-1/2" to same as the #9-iron
Sole Angle	Medium to Moderate; 5° to 14° (depending on type of sand)
Sole Width	Medium to Narrow (match to bounce)
Swingweight	+3 to +6 points more than the irons (player's feel)

UTILITY WEDGE

Loft	+4° to 5° greater than the SW
Length	-1/2" shorter than the #9-iron
Sole Angle	Medium; 5° to 9° (to be used also in sand as option)
Sole Width	Narrow to Medium (match the short irons)
Swingweight	+2 to +4 points more than the irons

2. Recommended Wedge Set Makeup Combinations for Low Handicap Player (0-8 hdcp); Slower Tempo; Lower Strength:

PITCHING WEDGE

Loft	+5° greater than the #9-iron
Length	Same as the #9-iron
Sole Angle	Shallow; 0° to 4°
Sole Width	Medium
Swingweight	Same as the irons

SAND WEDGE

Loft	+6° greater than the PW
Length	-1/2" shorter than the #9-iron
Sole Angle	Moderate; 10° to 14°
Sole Width	Medium to Wide (match to bounce)
Swingweight	+4 to +7 points more than the irons

UTILITY WEDGE

Loft	+4° to 5° greater than the SW
Length	-1/2" shorter than the #9-iron
Sole Angle	Medium; 5° to 9° (to be used also in sand as option)
Sole Width	Medium
Swingweight	+1 to +2 points more than the irons

3. Recommended Wedge Set Makeup Combinations for Mid-Low Handicap Player (9-15 hdcp); Avg to Faster Tempo; Avg to Greater Strength:

PITCHING WEDGE

Loft	+4° to 5° greater than the #9-iron
Length	Same as the #9-iron
Sole Angle	Shallow; 0° to 4°
Sole Width	Medium
Swingweight	0 to +2 points more than the irons

SAND WEDGE

Loft	+5° to 6° greater than the PW
Length	Same as the #9-iron
Sole Angle	Moderate; 10° to 14°
Sole Width	Medium
Swingweight	+5 to +7 points more than the irons

UTILITY WEDGE

Loft	+4° to 5° greater than the SW
Length	-1/2" shorter than the SW
Sole Angle	Medium; 5° to 9° (to be used also in sand as option)
Sole Width	Medium to Wide
Swingweight	+2 to +4 points more than the irons

4. Recommended Wedge Set Makeup Combinations for Mid-Low Handicap Player (9-15 hdcp); Slower Tempo; Lower Strength:

PITCHING WEDGE

Loft	+5° greater than the #9-iron
Length	Same as the #9-iron
Sole Angle	Shallow; 0° to 4°
Sole Width	Medium
Swingweight	Same as the irons

SAND WEDGE

Loft	+6° greater than the PW
Length	Same as the #9-iron
Sole Angle	Moderate; 10° to 14°
Sole Width	Medium to Wide (match to bounce)
Swingweight	+5 to +7 points more than the irons

UTILITY WEDGE

Loft	+5° greater than the SW
Length	-1/2" shorter than the SW
Sole Angle	Medium; 5° to 9° (to be used also in sand as option)
Sole Width	Medium to Wide
Swingweight	0 to +2 points more than the irons

5. Recommended Wedge Set Makeup Combinations for Middle Handicap Player (16-25 hdcp):

At this level, it is possible to think in terms of a four-wedge system as well. The following options for fitting the middle handicap player will include both a three-wedge and a four-wedge option for the clubmaker to consider. Remember, the more short game help the player needs, the more the four-wedge system should be considered.

Three-Wedge Option for 16-25 hdcp. player

PITCHING WEDGE

Loft	+4° to 5° greater than the #9-iron
Length	Same as the #9-iron
Sole Angle	Medium; 5° to 9°
Sole Width	Medium to Wide
Swingweight	+1 to +2 points more than the irons

SAND WEDGE

Loft	+6° greater than the PW
Length	Same as the #9-iron
Sole Angle	Moderate to Heavy; 10° to 20° (depending on sand skill)
Sole Width	Wide to Medium (match to the bounce)
Swingweight	+6 to +8 points more than the irons

UTILITY WEDGE

Loft	+5° to 6° greater than the SW
Length	-1/2" shorter than the 9-iron
Sole Angle	Shallow to Medium; 0° to 9° (to be used from grass/rough)
Sole Width	Wide to Medium (match to the bounce)
Swingweight	+2 to +3 points more than the irons

Four-Wedge Option for 16-25 hdcp. player

PITCHING WEDGE

Loft	+4° greater than the #9-iron
Length	Same as the #9-iron
Sole Angle	Shallow: 0° to 4°
Sole Width	Medium to Wide
Swingweight	Same as the irons

SAND WEDGE

Loft	+9° greater than the PW
Length	-1/2" shorter than the #9-iron
Sole Angle	Moderate to Heavy; 10° to 20° (depending on sand skill)
Sole Width	Wide to Medium (match to the bounce)
Swingweight	+6 to +8 points more than the irons

UTILITY WEDGE #1 (Gap Wedge)

Loft	+4° to 5° greater than the PW
Length	-1/2" shorter than the 9-iron
Sole Angle	Shallow to Medium; 0° to 9° (to be used from grass/rough)
Sole Width	Wide to Medium (match to the bounce)
Swingweight	+1 to +2 points more than the irons

UTILITY WEDGE #2 (Lob Wedge)

Loft	+4° greater than the SW
Length	-1/2" shorter than the 9-iron
Sole Angle	Shallow to Medium; 0° to 9° (to be used from grass/rough)
Sole Width	Wide to Medium (match to the bounce)
Swingweight	0 to +2 points more than the irons

6. Recommended Wedge Set Makeup Combinations for Higher Handicap Player (26 + hdcp):

NOTE: This is the level of player that can also start to benefit the most from a Super Wide sole width. If the Super Wide sole width wedge is chosen as a Utility Lob Wedge, be sure the sole angle is Shallow. The recommendation would also be to make this type of super wide sole/shallow sole angle wedge to be +2 to +4 swingweight points higher than the set of irons.

It is also possible to think in terms of a four-wedge system for the higher handicap player as well. The following options for fitting the higher handicap player will include both a three-wedge and a four-wedge option for the clubmaker to consider. Remember, the more short game help the player needs, and the less skilled the long game, the more the clubmaker would consider the four-wedge system over the three-wedge system.

Three-Wedge Option for 26 + hdcp. player

PITCHING WEDGE

Loft	+4° greater than the #9-iron
Length	Same as the #9-iron
Sole Angle	Medium; 5° to 9°
Sole Width	Medium to Wide
Swingweight	+2 to +3 points more than the irons

SAND WEDGE

Loft	+5 to +6° greater than the PW
Length	Same as the #9-iron
Sole Angle	Moderate to Heavy; 10° to 20° (depending on sand skill)
Sole Width	Wide to Medium (match to the bounce)
Swingweight	+6 to +8 points more than the irons

UTILITY WEDGE

Loft	+5° to 6° greater than the SW
Length	-1/2" shorter than the 9-iron
Sole Angle	Medium; 5° to 9° (to be used from grass/rough)
Sole Width	Wide
Swingweight	+2 to +3 points more than the irons

Four-Wedge Option for 26 + hdcp. player

PITCHING WEDGE

Loft	+4° greater than the #9-iron
Length	Same as the #9-iron
Sole Angle	Shallow to Medium; 0° to 9°
Sole Width	Wide to Medium (match to the bounce)
Swingweight	Same as the irons

SAND WEDGE

Loft	+9° to +10° greater than the PW
Length	Same as the #9-iron
Sole Angle	Moderate to Heavy; 10° to 20° (depending on sand skill)
Sole Width	Wide to Medium (match to the bounce)
Swingweight	+6 to +8 points more than the irons

UTILITY WEDGE #1 (Gap Wedge)

Loft	+4° greater than the PW
Length	-1/2" shorter than the 9-iron
Sole Angle	Medium; 5° to 9° (to be used from grass/rough)
Sole Width	Medium to Wide (match to the bounce)
Swingweight	+2 to +3 points more than the irons

UTILITY WEDGE #2 (Lob Wedge)

Loft	+4° greater than the SW
Length	-1/2" shorter than the 9-iron
Sole Angle	Medium; 5° to 9° (to be used from grass/rough)
Sole Width	Medium to Wide (match to the bounce)
Swingweight	0 to +2 points more than the irons

NOTE: This is also the level of player that can benefit from a Super Wide sole width. If the Super Wide sole width wedge is chosen as a Utility Lob Wedge, be sure the sole angle is Shallow. The recommendation would also be to make this type of super wide sole/shallow sole angle wedge to be +2 to +4 swingweight points higher than the set of irons.

V. LENGTH

Length is a **MEDIUM** Specification of Wedge Fitting.

Traditionally, all wedges have been created to be the same length as the #9-iron. However, as this is a matter of custom clubfitting, the length of the wedges can be altered to suit certain playing habits or comfort needs of the player. **When thinking about the length of the wedges keep the following points in mind:**

* If the player grips down on the wedges a lot, the length can be cut shorter to accommodate the comfort of the player. However, remember that in many cases when a player grips down on the club, he/she does so to create a certain clubhead and comfort **Feel** that can only be duplicated when the hands are closer to the head, or when there is a portion of the grip protruding from the back of the hands. If the wedge(s) are made shorter for the primary reason the player grips down on a traditional length wedge, be sure to swingweight the clubs for the shorter length (do not let the swingweight go lower just because of the shorter length) to keep the swingweight at the levels recommended in the preceding player charts, with the length taken into account to prevent the wedges from losing clubhead **Feel**.

* The modern trend of longer lengths in the irons will normally make the length of the wedges longer as well. The wedges are the scoring clubs. Because of that, most wedges should not be hit with a full swing. If that principle is understood, the golfer will also understand that **Accuracy** is far more important with the wedges than **Distance**. The shorter the length of the wedges, the easier most golfers will be able to hit the ball straight.

* The higher the loft on the wedge, the shorter its length may be. Many golfers like to make the PW the same length as the 9-iron, but cut the SW to be 1/2" shorter than the PW, and a high lofted utility wedge to be 1/4" or even 1/2" shorter than the SW. when this is done, the golfer is admitting that he/she will never hit the high lofted wedge as hard as the SW, and the SW never as hard as the PW. The principle is this - the shorter the most predominant swing length with the wedge, the shorter the length can be for **Feel** and **Accuracy**.

* It is not a good idea to make the length of the wedges longer than the 9-iron. For one, the head weights of most wedges are intended to be heavier to allow for making a higher swingweight or for creating more clubhead **Feel** on these clubs which are not to be hit with a full swing. When wedges are made longer, **Accuracy** could suffer as a result, unless the golfer makes it a rule to never use a full swing with a wedge.

* Earlier in the book, the Practical Fitting Program introduced the idea of trimming the length of the irons in 3/8" increments instead of the usual 1/2" increments, especially for the taller player with shorter arms or longer legs who desires more comfort in the address position. If such a club to club incremental length difference is used, realize that the wedges will end up being much longer than standard. In such a situation, it is still acceptable to shorten the SW and any other wedges for **Accuracy** sake, as long as the golfer is still comfortable when setting up over the ball.

* As a general rule, do not make the length of any of the wedges more than 1" shorter than the #9-iron. This is because such a short length could force the golfer to bend the knees much more than desired or make the golfer bend more over the ball, both situations could affect the golfer's comfort and with it, **Accuracy**. In addition, making one or more of the wedges too short, usually in an effort to try to generate better **Accuracy**, will have an adverse affect on **Distance**. The goal of **Distance** with the wedges is not to hit the ball far, but to hit the ball far enough. If the golfer is confused about how hard to swing the wedge to carry the ball over hazards between the golfer and the flag, many more strokes will be lost rather than saved.

VI. SWINGWEIGHT

Swingweight is a **MEDIUM** Specification of Wedge Fitting.

Swingweight should be thought of as a very individual specification in the wedges. While most sets have traditionally been made with the Pitching Wedge the same swingweight as the #1-9 irons and the sand wedge swingweight considerably higher than the irons, there are advantages to recommending a different swingweight for each of the wedges.

In addition, because the length can be varied for each of the wedges, the swingweight has to be thought out carefully for each wedge with the length in mind to create the best clubhead **Feel** for the player. Swing timing and rhythm with the wedges are without a doubt the most important keys to **Accuracy**. By carefully considering the swingweight individually for each wedge, the clubmaker can help the player generate the best timing, rhythm, and **Accuracy**.

* The more often the golfer uses a full swing with the pitching wedge, gap wedge or lob-type wedge, the more the swingweight of each of these clubs should be the same as the swingweight of the full set of the irons.

* If the golfer uses less than a full swing with the Pitching Wedge, Gap Wedge or Lob type wedge, what are called the 'grass wedges', the swingweight should be a little higher than the rest of the irons to create better clubhead **Feel** and help the golfer swing with better timing and rhythm. Half and three-quarter length wedge shots generate less swing speed than the full swing. The slower the clubhead speed, the less the golfer can **Feel** the clubhead as a key to swinging with proper timing and rhythm. If the golfer has a habit of never swinging the 'grass wedges' full, the swingweight of each of these wedges should be from two to four swingweight points higher than the rest of the set of irons. (See wedge set makeup recommendations for individual wedge swingweight guidelines).

* If the wedges are made shorter in length than the 9-iron, the swingweight should still be raised to at least the level of the 9-iron or higher to ensure the best clubhead **Feel** for the shorter length. For example, a Pitching Wedge with a D2 swingweight which is 1/2" shorter than a #9-iron with a swingweight of D2, will have better clubhead **Feel** because it actually has a greater head mass to create the same D2 swingweight. Again, this is helpful for retaining the proper swing rhythm and timing for **Accuracy**.

* Never let the swingweight of the 'grass wedges' fall below the swingweight of the rest of the set of the irons. To do so will create wedges with less than desirable clubhead **Feel** and will promote the tendency to pull or hit the ball thin.

* The swingweight of the SW is traditionally four to six points higher than the rest of the set of irons. This is a custom which has evolved over the years as a way to help the golfer generate more momentum with the sand wedge through the sand.

The most common sand trap mistake is for golfers to leave the ball in the bunker. This shotmaking error is usually the result of the golfer not maintaining the acceleration of the clubhead through the ball or swinging the club on a steep angle so that it digs too deep into the sand under the ball. While the swing technique of the bunker shot is more important to the success of the shot than the club itself, using a much higher SW swingweight than the rest of the irons can help keep the clubhead moving through the sand and get the ball out of the bunker on the swings which are slightly less than perfect.

In other words, if the golfer sees the ball pop into the sand only a few feet in front of the point of impact, a heavier swingweight will not cure the problem. But if the golfer sees the ball hit just below the lip of the trap and trickle back down, a higher swingweight in the Sand Wedge could help.

* Avoid making the swingweight too high on the Sand Wedge. If the swingweight is much more than the customary five to six swingweight points higher than the PW for the average player, and the club has a higher total weight (any SW with a steel shaft), the club could be too cumbersome to generate the proper swing timing to coordinate the movement of the wedge through the sand at the same time the weight is shifting from the back leg to the front. Of great help to most average to higher handicap players would be a sand wedge with light total weight with a high swingweight. In this case, using a 80g or lighter graphite shaft with a swingweight of at least D5 to D8, the sand wedge would actually have more mass in the head than a D7 steel shafted club, yet would be easier to swing because of the lighter total weight.

* As a general starting rule, based on 35 1/2" to 36" wedge lengths, if the swingweight of the 9-iron was D1, the pitching wedge and 'gap' wedge should be D3, the sand wedge D7 and the high lofted lob wedge D4. (See the three-wedge/four-wedge recommendation tables in this chapter for more swingweight guidelines based on player ability).

VII. LIE ANGLE

Lie Angle is a **MAJOR** Specification of Wedge Fitting.

The Golfsmith Practical Fitting Program identifies Lie Angle as a **MAJOR** specification for **Accuracy** in the short irons. This is because as the loft of a clubhead is increased, the more the clubface will point off-line when the leading edge of the clubface and the scorelines are not parallel to the ground at impact. Since the wedges are the most lofted irons in the entire set, it stands to reason that fitting the lie of the wedges correctly is the most critical factor of **Accuracy**, outside of the swing itself.

As a practical fitting tip, the wedges are the only clubs in the set for which it may be advisable to fit the lie angle to the player using the static lie fitting method as opposed to the Lie Board method of dynamically fitting the lie. This is because of two primary reasons. 1) In the case of wedges which have a medium to heavy bounce sole angle, the wedge will make contact with the lie board on its trailing edge, not on the leading edge. However, if the

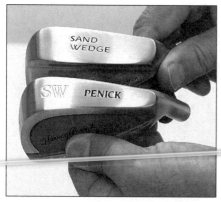

Some wedges, primarily sand wedges, are designed with a tapered sole width. When fitting lie either in the static position or through Dynamic Lie fitting, it is possible for the clubmaker to be fooled into recommending the wrong lie angle with a tapered shape sole width because the wider part of the sole will tend to show the point of contact with the fitting board. Hence a lie angle can be correct when the point of sole contact is toward the toe.

wedge is designed in such a way that the sole is the same width all the way across the bottom of the club, or so that the center of the sole is the widest part of the sole, the Dynamic Lie Board Fitting method will work well to match the proper lie to the golfer.

2) Many wedges with a bounce sole angle are designed so the sole is wider at the toe area than at the heel or center (see picture). Whenever the wedge has a bounce sole angle and the sole width is tapered, the point of contact shown through the lie board fitting method can be 'fooled' by the tapered bounce sole and will show the sole contact mark for a correctly fit lie angle to be more toward the toe side of sole center. For wedges with a tapered sole width, the static lie fitting approach will be more accurate.

The proper lie for any wedge, with or without a bounce sole and with or without a tapered sole width, is achieved when the leading edge or the scorelines of the wedge are parallel with the hitting surface when the wedge arrives at the impact position, or when the golfer sets up in his/her most natural address position. Identifying such a position is very difficult using the dynamic lie board fitting method for the reason that whenever the wedge has a medium to heavy bounce sole angle, and has a tapered sole width, the point of impact will tend to be on the toe side of the trailing edge when the wedge has the proper lie for the golfer.

NOTE: Although it may take more time to perform than the Lie Board method, the Lie Detector method of dynamically fitting the lie angle will not be fooled by a tapered bounce sole wedge because it does not depend upon a sole impact mark to determine the proper lie. (See Chapter 7 for using the Lie Detector fitting device)

It was mentioned previously that the static lie fitting method is preferable to use in fitting the lie of the wedges compared to the lie board fitting method. Therefore, the clubmaker will have to be sure that the leading edge is parallel with the ground/board/floor even though it will be the toe side of the trailing edge that will be the point of contact on the ground or floor. The other reason the lie of the wedges can be fit statically is because the shafts in the wedges will not likely exhibit much (if any) downward bending due to their shorter length and level of stiffness compared to the other shafts in the set.

When the wedge has a bounce sole angle and a tapered shape sole width, static fitting the lie is best done by kneeling down to focus at the leading edge and scorelines of the wedge in relation to the floor. When the scorelines are parallel to the floor and the center of the leading edge appears as if it would contact the floor were it not for the presence of the bounce sole angle, the wedge will be considered to be statically fit to the golfer.

To statically fit the lie of the wedges, have the golfer assume the address position with the wedge on a hard surface (floor will suffice; definitely not on turf any longer than the putting green) with a wedge of the same length which he/she will be using. The proper wedge lie angle will be achieved when the wedge sits on the floor so that the scorelines are parallel with the floor, and the center of the leading edge appears as if it would be the point of contact with the floor, if the wedge did not have a bounce sole angle. (Remember, due to the bounce sole angle, the wedge will actually touch the floor on its trailing edge. Therefore, the clubmaker may have to kneel down to be able to spot the position of the center of the leading edge with respect to the floor. (See the two photographs which compare the static fitting of two wedges, one with bounce and a consistent sole width, the other with a bounce sole angle and a tapered sole width).

As a last point of caution to clubmakers when fitting lie using the static fitting method, the technique of using two business cards slid under the sole, one from the toe and one from the heel, to determine when the center of the sole is in contact with the floor, will not work as a reference for wedges with a bounce sole angle and a tapered sole width. Because the tapered sole touches the floor on the toe side of the center of the sole, the cards would show the wedge touching on the toe side of the center of the scoreline area, and would make most clubmakers believe the lie was too flat for the player.

For any wedge with a bounce sole angle which has a consistent sole width, the proper lie angle position for the golfer will be achieved when the leading edge and the scorelines are parallel to the hitting surface AND the center of the trailing edge is making contact with the hitting surface as well. Any bounce sole angle wedge with a CONSISTENT sole width can be fit to the golfer using one of the Dynamic Lie Fitting methods as well as using a static lie fitting method.

For any wedge with a bounce sole angle which has a TAPERED shape sole width, the proper lie angle position for the golfer will be achieved when the leading edge and the scorelines are parallel to the hitting surface BUT the toe side of the trailing edge is making contact with the hitting surface. Any bounce sole angle wedge with a TAPERED sole width is best fit to the golfer using a static lie fitting method instead of a Dynamic Lie Fitting Method.

This method of static fitting using the two business cards as reference points to identify when the center of the sole is in contact with the floor can only be used when the wedge does not have a tapered shape sole width. For that reason, static fitting of bounce sole, tapered sole width types of wedges will have to be done by eye, looking at the face and leading edge of the wedge from the level of the floor.

VIII. Clubhead Design – Center of Gravity and Weight Distribution

Center of Gravity is a **MINOR** Specification of Wedge Fitting.

Just as there are a variety of different clubhead designs in the irons, so too are there different clubhead designs which exhibit different CG locations in the wedges. The primary reason that CG is not that important in the fitting of the wedges is because the much greater loft is a more important contributor to the **Trajectory** needs of a wedge than is the CG.

There is no doubt a golfer needs to have the ability to hit the wedges high when the shot calls for it. Likewise there is no doubt that the lower the CG, the higher will be the shot **Trajectory** for a shot hit with any clubhead. However, when loft exceeds 40°, the CG does not have the ability to increase the **Trajectory** by a significant amount. Another reason this is true is because most wedge shots are hit with far less than a full swing and as such, with far less than maximum swing speed. The faster the swing speed, the greater will be the effect of the center of gravity on the **Trajectory** and the **Backspin**. Therefore, wedges gain their real **Trajectory** far more from their loft than their CG.

When the clubmaker makes the selection of the clubhead design, there is nothing wrong with choosing a low CG design, but it is much more important for the heads to have the correct loft to meet the **Trajectory** needs of the player.

Weight Distribution is a **MINOR** Specification of Wedge Fitting.

The level of shot forgiveness and the Feel of an off-center hit is not affected to any great extent on the wedges by perimeter weighting. How much a clubhead transmits the feeling of vibration from an off-center hit to the golfer is affected greatly by the loft of the clubhead. In other words, the more the loft, the less the club vibrates from an off-center hit. Since wedges are the highest lofted clubheads in the set, there is very little difference in the **Feel** of an off-center hit when struck by a cavity back, perimeter weighted wedge compared to a non-perimeter weighted wedge.

In addition, the less solid feeling of an off-center shot is also controlled by the clubhead velocity at impact. The less the clubhead speed when the ball is hit off-center, the less the shot will tend to **Feel** unsolid. Make no mistake - there is no doubt a chip shot hit off center still feels like it was not hit as solid as if it were hit in the middle of the clubface, but whether the off-center shot was hit with a perimeter weighted wedge vs a non-perimeter weighted wedge will have little effect on the outcome of the chip shot.

As a result, it is completely acceptable for the golfer to choose either perimeter weighted or non-perimeter weighted wedges to match with the set of irons and not have to worry about any loss of shot performance as a result.

THE STEP BY STEP PROCEDURE FOR FITTING THE WEDGES

STEP 1 – IDENTIFY THE NUMBER OF WEDGES TO BE RECOMMENDED

* Based on the loft of the irons and how they create 'gaps' in yardage between the PW and SW.
* Based on the types of shots the golfer needs to be able to hit to get the ball up and down a greater percentage of the time.
* Based on the way the golfer prefers to hit pitch shots, chip shots and sand shots.
* Refer to the section on pages 365-371 in this chapter which outlines the possible wedge set makeups for the various player types.

STEP 2 – CHOOSE THE LOFT OF EACH OF THE WEDGES

* Note the loft of the 9-iron.
* Refer to the section on pages 365-371 in this chapter which outlines the loft differences between the wedges for each particular set makeup for each type of player.

STEP 3 – CHOOSE THE SOLE ANGLE OF EACH OF THE WEDGES

* Based on the chipping, pitching and sand play abilities of the player.
* Based on the soil and ground conditions, the types of turf and the length of the grass on the golf course.
* Based on the type of and the consistency of the sand in the bunkers on the golf course for which the wedges are being advised.
* Refer to the section on pages 365-371 in this chapter for set makeup recommendations by player type. Follow the guidelines for sole angle and sole width based on the player type and the type of shots the player is required to hit.

STEP 4 – CHOOSE THE LENGTH AND SWINGWEIGHT OF THE WEDGES

* Based on the physical size, the set up to the ball and the playing ability of the golfer.
* Based on the tempo of the player.
* Based on the maximum swing length used the majority of the time for each wedge by the golfer.

STEP 5 - FIT THE LIE ANGLE OF THE WEDGES

* Based on determining if the Dynamic Lie Fitting techniques are advised due to the sole angle of the wedges, as opposed to using the static lie fitting method.

FITTING THE PUTTER – THE KEY FITTING SPECIFICATIONS

There is an old saying in the game, "Good putters are born, not made." When it comes to custom fitting the putter, a good putter can be produced for any golfer, but it must be accompanied by a good putting stroke before any real improvement in putting can be realized.

A good putting stroke consists of the golfer seeing the line to the hole, accelerating or maintaining the velocity of the putter through the ball, and keeping the face of the putter square to the target line through impact. While these swing mechanics must be learned and practiced and cannot be bought, the right combination of putter specifications can make them easier to learn and retain. In other words, **putting is definitely one area of the game in which the wrong putter can do much more to harm the golfer than the right putter can do to help**. For that reason alone it is important for the clubmaker to include putter fitting as an important part of the overall fitting session.

One of the first secrets to improving a golfer's putting has nothing to do with the putter itself, but with the woods, irons and wedges. If the clubmaker can create a set of clubs which allows the golfer to hit more fairways, hit more greens in regulation, chip or pitch the ball closer to the hole, the number of putts per round can drop simply because the golfer is able to encounter more 'makeable' putts. For this reason, the clubmaker can take heart in the fact that if a good job is done in fitting the golfer with a better set or clubs, especially including the wedges, putting should automatically improve because the ball will be closer to the hole a greater number of shots.

That being said, eventually the goal of improving the golfer's ability to putt will come down to identifying and fitting the specifications of the putter which have an effect on its performance. As with all other parts of the Practical Fitting Program, there are specifications which have a **MAJOR**, **MEDIUM** and a **MINOR** effect on putter fitting which must first be identified and learned by the clubmaker.

Comfort, comfort, comfort. If there is one section of the game in which the golfer is completely dependent upon being totally comfortable in the preparation and set up for the shot, it is putting. While there are a few critical putting stroke mechanics which were mentioned in the introductory paragraphs of this section on fitting putters, every single specification the clubmaker addresses in the fitting of the putter must be made with the single goal of making the golfer as comfortable and relaxed, while standing over the ball and during the stroke, as is possible. To do so will make it far easier for the golfer to then master the swing mechanics which are the secret to successful putting.

I. LENGTH

Length is a **MAJOR** Specification for Putter Fitting.

Not too long and not too short is the common sense rule for the length of the putter. Over the years of clubmaking, manufacturers of putters have adopted a standard for length which still stands at 35" for men and 34" for ladies. While a general guideline is a start, a much more specific recommendation is necessary to adequately pinpoint the putter's length for the player.

When the golfer stands over the putt, no matter how much he/she bends over or how erect he/she stands, the eyes must be directly over the ball. Therefore, a good check for whether the golfer's existing putter length is right or not is to stand behind the golfer while he/she addresses the putt and see if a straight line can be drawn down from the eyes to the ball.

If the eyes are beyond or past the ball, the putter could be too short for the player, while if a line straight down from the eyes falls short of the ball, the putter might be too long. Of course making an adjustment to the length which results in the golfer having to bend over more (with a shorter putter) or stand more erect (with a longer putter) must be discussed with the golfer to determine if the change will still allow the golfer to be comfortable in taking his/her stance.

When the golfer assumes his/her normal putting stance, if the eyes are beyond being directly over the ball, the putter could be recommended to be a little longer.

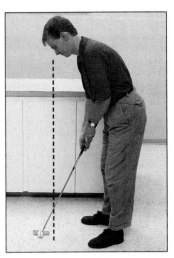

When the golfer assumes his/her normal putting stance, if the eyes are short of being directly over the ball, the putter could be recommended to be a little shorter.

If the golfer does not wish to bend over more nor stand more erect than his/her current stance, then the clubmaker should carefully point out the swing fundamental which states the golfer's eyes should be directly over the ball in the address position. At this point, the golfer can make the decision whether to keep the length of the putter the same and simply move the ball closer or farther away to enable the eyes to fall directly over the ball. By all means, if the golfer indicates he/she is used to his/her current putting stance and address position he/she displays in the fitting, the putter should be made to fit the stance and position of the golfer, not the other way around.

Using a Putter Fitting Device for Recommending Putter Length and Lie

Golfsmith manufactures a handy putter fitting aid, which can be quite helpful in identifying the actual length and lie for the golfer. The Putter Fitting Aid is made with a telelscoping 'shaft' for determining the most comfortable lengths and an adjustable 'clubhead' for determining the correct lie at the chosen length. To use such a device, use the following procedures:

STEP 1

Adjust the putter fitting device to the same length as the golfer's current putter. Give the golfer the fitting device and ask them to set up over the ball. Adjust the 'clubhead' on the fitting device so the 'sole' sits completely flat to the ground or floor. Have the golfer aim the ball at the intended target with the 'clubhead' on the fitting device. Move the golfer until his/her eyes are directly over the ball. Ask the golfer how comfortable he/she feels over the ball. If the player feels good over the ball and does not make any changes in the set up or how he/she grips the fitting aid, this length is correct.

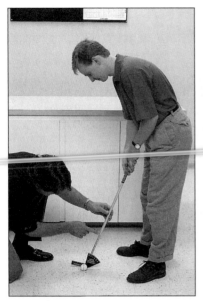

A putter fitting aid can be very helpful for pinpointing the exact length and lie angle of the putter for the golfer.

STEP 2

If the golfer indicates a lack of comfort, fidgets, grips down on the putter fitting aid or immediately shifts his/her body position so the eyes are no longer over the ball in an effort to try to become comfortable with the length, change the length of the fitting device so it is 1" longer his/her current putter length. Ask the golfer if this length is comfortable. Check also to see if the golfer's eyes are directly over the ball.

If the length is still not correct, give back the fitting device and ask the golfer to set up over the ball once more. Again, adjust the length of the fitting device so it is 1" shorter than the current putter length and tilt the 'clubhead' on the fitting device so the 'sole' sits completely flat on the floor. Have the golfer aim the fitting device behind the ball at the intended target. Move the golfer until his/her eyes are directly over the ball. Ask the golfer how comfortable he/she feels over the ball. If he/she feels good over the ball, if does not make any changes in the set up or how he/she grips the fitting aid, this length is correct.

If this length is not comfortable to the player, continue to adjust the telescoping length of the shaft until the player indicates he/she is comfortable setting up over the ball, and the golfer's eyes are directly over the ball.

Once the length is comfortable to the golfer, adjust the 'clubhead' on the fitting device so the 'sole' sits completely flat to the ground or floor. Have the golfer aim the ball at the intended target with the 'clubhead' on the fitting device. Move the golfer until his/her eyes are directly over the ball. If he/she feels good over the ball and does not make any changes in his/her set up or how he/she grips the fitting aid, this length and lie is correct.

Symptoms of the putter length being wrong for the player

- Scuffing the sole of the putter on the green during the takeaway or just prior to contacting the ball - (Putter too long).
- Topping or hitting a high percentage of putts low on the face of the putter - (Putter too short. But be careful with this assessment as moving the body around during the stroke is just as much a cause of topped/thin putts as is a putter which is too short).
- Eyes are not directly over the ball when the golfer sets up over the putt. (Eyes beyond ball = putter possibly too short; eyes short of ball = putter possibly too long).
- Golfer fidgets and moves around a lot while setting up to the putter, as if giving the impression he/she is working hard at trying to get comfortable - (Putter too long or too short).

II. SWINGWEIGHT

Swingweight is a **MAJOR** Specification for Putter Fitting.

The woods and irons within virtually all sets of golf clubs are fit and built to a specific swingweight for the purpose of achieving the proper clubhead feel for the player. Why not the putter? Why not the putter indeed!

A putter must have the proper clubhead feel for the individual needs of the golfer or it will be very difficult for the player to accomplish what is perhaps the most important of all the swing principles of putting – to keep the putter square to the target and the path of the stroke moving on a line straight at the target. In addition, a putter with an improper head weight (swingweight) for the player is much harder to keep moving through the ball so the putter does not decelerate through impact. 'Quitting' on the putting stroke, as this is called, is one of the most common reasons for inconsistency on the greens.

If the putter head is too light for the player, it is much more difficult for the player to keep the putter face square and to stroke the putter on a path which is square to the target. Much like a wood or an iron with too little head weight (too low of a swingweight) with which it becomes much more difficult to control and swing the club consistently, so too is the case with the putter. In addition, for some player types, a putter with too little head weight is very difficult to consistently control the swing speed through the ball. Sometimes the player will hit the putt too far past the hole, while the next time the putt falls well short.

On the other hand, if the putter is too head heavy for the player (swingweight too high) it can be very difficult to comfortably coordinate the timing of the end of the backstroke in rhythm with the beginning of the forward stroke. This in turn also results in putts which can either roll far past the hole on one stroke and fall well short on another. **To put it in the most simple terms, the swingweight of the putter must be chosen for the comfort of the player so that the stroke can be as smooth, consistent and rhythmic as possible**.

When a company manufactures a line of putters, the same grip weight and shaft weight will normally be used on every putter produced. Very few companies will offer the same putter in a graphite vs a steel shaft or with a light vs a heavy grip, as is the more common case with woods and irons. As a result, most putter manufacturers will choose one common head weight for each of the putters they make, which in turn, will make the clubhead **Feel** of all putters the same, with slight exceptions for the different lengths in which they may offer their putters.

Some companies will choose the putter head weight based on achieving a particular swingweight. But the majority do not for the simple reason that with all the different putter grip shapes, and the variation in the amount of offset of the shaft or the putter hosel, it is rare if the putter is able to rest in the required measurement position in the swingweight scale with the toe of the head pointing straight down. Therefore, most putter makers do not publish a standard swingweight for their putters and in fact, do not mention swingweight in the literature accompanying the sales of their putters. However, the average putter swingweight based on a 35" steel shaft length with a non-jumbo putter grip is approximately D2 to D3.

Because so many putters are manufactured with steel shafts, which all weigh virtually the same, it is definitely possible to fit the clubhead feel of the putter by also noting a particular balance point of the putter. Using an actual balance point location as a method of fitting for the proper clubhead feel can only be done if the shaft weight in the previous club with the favorite balance point is the same as it will be in the new club to be built.

Because the vast majority of putters are made with steel shafts, putter balance point becomes a viable way to identify, and then duplicate a particular clubhead feel. By measuring the balance point of a favorite putter, the clubmaker can try a new putter model and still be able to enjoy the same clubhead feel, provided the length, head weight and grip weight are retained in the new putter model.

Clubmakers who are faced with using a variety of different putter head designs, a variety of different putter grip shapes and sizes, a variety of different types of shafts, all which can be assembled to a variety of custom lengths, must adopt a different approach to putter building than do the major manufacturers. How many clubmakers build putters to a specific swingweight or a specific balance point? Very few, yet it is a common practice to build the woods and irons to a particular swingweight specification. **To truly help the golfer putt as well as his/her physical coordination will allow, clubmakers must become accustomed to building putters to set swingweights based on the needs of each player they fit**.

Fitting for swingweight (clubhead feel/balance point) in the putter is very much a judgment call which the clubmaker must determine, based on the following information:

1. Measuring the swingweight or balance point of any putter for which the golfer has indicated a positive feel, or with which the golfer has had some success in the past.

2. Noting the tempo and type of putting stroke used by the player and matching the player's style to a higher or lower swingweight (balance point).

3. The length and the grip weight to be used on the putter and how they affect the amount of head weight which will be required to achieve that specific swingweight or balance point.

4. The player's tendencies for errors on the green, such as hitting the putt thin or scuffing the ground/hitting the putt too far (swingweight too high.)

Step by Step Procedures for Fitting Putter Swingweight

STEP 1

Start by choosing the length for the putter using a putter length fitting aid such as the Golfsmith Putter Length/Lie Fitting Device.

STEP 2

Fit the player for the desired putter grip style and size using grip samples mounted on cut off shaft butt sections. If the clubmaker does not employ grip samples in the fitting session, the player will have to make this decision based on previously used grips with which he/she was comfortable, or by choosing from a selection of putter grips illustrated in a clubmaking supply catalog.

STEP 3

Observe the golfer stroke a few putts with his/her existing putter or with a putter in the clubmaker's workshop. (Any putter will do as long as it is the same length as the putter length specification advised by the clubmaker for the golfer). Match the player's putting stroke style to the descriptions in the table below and choose the recommended swingweight.

Swingweight Recommendation Table for Traditional Length Putters

Putting Stroke or Tendency	Swingweight Range	Based on Length
Stroke Long and Slow Tempo	D4-D7	36"
	D2-D5	35"
	D0-D3	34"
	C8-D1	33"
Short and Firm; Faster Tempo	D1-D5	36"
	C9-D3	35"
	C7-D1	34"
	C5-C9	33"
Quits on the Putting Stroke	D4-D7	36"
	D2-D5	35"
	D0-D3	34"
	C8-D1	33"
Leaves Putts Consistently Short	D4-D7	36"
	D2-D5	35"
	D0-D3	34"
	C8-D1	33"
Strokes Putts Consistently Long	D1-D5	36"
	C9-D3	35"
	C7-D1	34"
	C5-C9	33"
"Arm and Shoulder" Stroke Motion	D4-D7	36"
	D2-D5	35"
	D0-D3	34"
	C8-D1	33"
"Wristy" Stroke Motion	D1-D5	36"
	C9-D3	35"
	C7-D1	34"
	C5-C9	33"

Note: Based on normal size putter grip of 55-60g weight.

If the golfer wishes to use a long pendulum style putter (46"-50"+), advising a swingweight will not be possible due to the much greater length of the putter, but the head weight should be much higher than average. The average putter head weight range is 310g - 325g for traditional length putters. The headweight range for long pendulum style putters is 370g - 425g.

When fitting the head weight/swingweight for long pendulum style putters, the same general rules exist for when to choose the higher head weight vs when to choose the lower head weight as is indicated in the recommended swingweight table for traditional length putters.

III. GRIP TYPE AND SIZE

Grip Type and Size is a **MAJOR** Specification for Putter Fitting.

The grip is the only contact the golfer will have with the putter. Because successful putting depends so much on finding the best feel and comfort for the player, the putter grip must be comfortable to the golfer or else there is very little chance of the golfer being able to develop a smooth, rhythmic, repeating stroke through the ball.

Within the USGA Rules of Golf, there do exist rules which govern the shape of the putter grip. While the putter is the only club which is allowed to use a grip designed with a flat section, the putter grip cannot be designed with what is described in the rules as a 'bulge or a waist'. More simply stated, this restriction means golfers who may engage in competitive events which are conducted under the auspices of the United States Golf Association or the Royal and Ancient of St. Andrews cannot use any grip which transitions in diameter from large to small and back to large again. The grip may be tapered in cross-sectional shape from small to large and back to small, but not in the opposite manner.

In addition, the rules also state in the case of putters which are designed to have two separately installed grips (such as the long pendulum style putters), the bottom grip must be circular in cross section and cannot have a flat side or shape intended to help align the hands better for the execution of the stroke. In short, the lower grip of a long putter must be round in cross section.

Fitting the Putter Grip to the Player

In selecting the putter grip, there is no 'fitting method' employed other than to present the golfer with enough options to be able to find the grip which feels the most comfortable. Because golfer comfort rules all when it comes to putter grip fitting as well, if the clubmaker wishes to make a concerted effort to fit putters as accurately as possible, the group of fitting aids used in the fitting session should include an array of different putter grip samples, mounted on cut off shaft butt sections.

The golfer should take a few minutes to grip each sample with the goal being to choose the putter grip which feels the most comfortable. The main point the clubmaker can ask the golfer to note is whether the grip makes the golfer **Feel** as if the pressure of the hands on the grip is lighter than with other grips. Calm hands which hold onto the putter with a minimum of tension and pressure tend to make better putting strokes than if the grip tension is tight.

Size and shape are the two **MAJOR** factors in making the selection of the putter grip for the player. A few tips to keep in mind when choosing the size of the grip for the player are as follows:

* The larger the grip, the more tendency there can be to help the player keep the putter head low to the ground and square to the target line. This is because the larger the grip, the less tendency there may be to unhinge the wrists during the backswing or prior to impact.

* The larger the diameter of the grip, the less the chance exists for the player to be affected by the 'Yips'. 'Yipping', as it is called, is an involuntary twitching type of reflex of the wrist(s), causing severe miss-hits and miss-direction, which can occur occasionally or chronically to a small percentage of golfers including, unfortunately, the author! Greatly increasing the size of the putter grip can cause the hands, wrists and forearms to relax and thus help reduce the chance of the condition from occurring.

* Any putter grip should give the player a feeling of being able to align and keep the back of the upper hand and the palm of the lower hand square to the hole and moving on the path toward the hole. When fitting grip size, it is helpful to ask the player if the grip makes him/her **Feel** more able to make the stroke with the palm and back of the hand square to the hole through impact.

IV. SOLE ANGLE

Sole Angle is a **MAJOR** Specification for Putter Fitting.

Most clubmakers and golfers are not aware that it is possible for a putter to be manufactured with a bounce, square or scoop sole angle. On a putter, the angle between the bore and the sole should always be 90°, or square. The angle of the bore with respect to the sole angle is not to be confused with the lie angle. To clarify, when the putter is viewed from the face, and angle of the hosel bore is termed the lie angle. However, if the putter is viewed from the heel or the toe, the angle of the bore into the head or into the hosel should always be 90° to the sole.

When viewed from the toe or the heel of the putter head, the angle of the bore to the ground line or sole should be 90° to prevent the putter from having a sole angle. If the putter has a sole angle, when it is set on the ground, the putter face can turn open or closed to the target line, or the golfer will be forced to move his/her hands forward or back in an effort to keep the face square to the target.

Another way to identify if the putter has a sole angle is to hold the putter with the sole pointing up and the shaft pointing straight down to the ground. This is the same club holding position which was described in Chapter 4 to identify the sole angle of an iron. While holding the putter with a shaft installed and held perfectly vertical, an imaginary line touching the center of the sole should be at a 90° angle to the shaft. If the line across the center of the sole is not 90° or perpendicular to the shaft, the putter is considered to have a sole angle.

This illustration shows a traditional hosel design putter and a non-hosel style putter both with a scoop sole angle, in which the angle between the shaft and the sole line is not 90°. In this case, when the putter is allowed to sit flat on its sole, if the golfer forces the face to be square to the target line, the shaft will tilt back away from the face. If this putter is allowed to sit flat on its sole with the golfer holding the shaft at a 90° angle to the ground, the face will turn open and point to the right of the target line for a RH golfer. In either case, the fact that the putter has a negative or scoop sole angle is a bad situation which makes it extremely difficult for the golfer to properly align the putter to the target line.

This illustration shows a traditional hosel design putter and a non-hosel style putter both with a bounce sole angle, the other case in which the angle between the shaft and the sole line is not 90°. In this case, when the putter is allowed to sit flat on its sole, if the golfer forces the face to be square to the target line, the shaft will tilt forward from the face. On the other hand, if this putter with the bounce sole angle is allowed to sit flat on its sole with the golfer holding the shaft at a 90° angle to the ground, the face will turn closed and point to the left of the target line for the RH golfer. In either case, the fact that the putter has a bounce sole angle is a bad situation which makes it extremely difficult for the golfer to properly align the putter to the target line.

If the putter is made with a scoop or bounce sole angle, when the putter is set down flat on its sole behind the ball, the face can turn 'open' or 'closed' to the intended target line. If the golfer then rotates the face of any putter with a sole angle to be square to the target line, then the shaft will move forward or back, in the process causing the golfer to either 'press' the hands forward or hold the grip back of the face just in an effort to keep the face square to the target line.

The ideal situation is for the putter to always be designed and produced with a square sole angle. This way the golfer can set the putter down behind the ball with the sole sitting flat on the ground, and the orientation of the shaft allowing the golfer to keep the hands square to the target line. This condition of a possible putter sole angle is not a specification the clubmaker has to custom fit to the golfer. Rather, this is a situation the clubmaker must inspect on the new putter by inserting a shaft into the head and performing the previously illustrated inspections to determine if such a condition exists.

If the putter has a permanently attached hosel as a part of its design (traditional style design, intended to accept a straight shaft) and is produced with a sole angle, the hosel will need to be bent either to the right or the left of the face until the bore is 90° to the ground line to remove the sole angle. This will require the clubmaker to know the material from which the putter is manufactured and if that material

Shown from the golfer's view over the ball, this shows the two conditions which can happen to the golfer if the putter is made with a scoop sole angle. Of the two different styles of putters, for the ones on the left, if the golfer sets the putter square to the target line, the sole angle will cause the shaft to extend back away from the face, in the process forcing the golfer to keep the hands behind the face. On the right, if the golfer sets the putter down so that the shaft is 90° to the ground line (holds the putter so the hands are perpendicular to the target line), the putter tends to 'sit' open. Neither situation is good for proper putter fitting.

can be bent. Following is a list of the predominant putter head materials and whether they can be bent to correct such a situation. Remember, this is only in the case that the design has a conventional hosel which is intended to accept a straight shaft.

Head Material	Hosel Bendability
Stainless Steel	Yes, but with some effort
Aluminum	Not normally
Zinc	No, it will break
Brass	Yes, easily
Bronze Alloys	Yes, easily
Beryllium Copper	Yes, but with some effort

If the putter is designed to accept a curved or double bend style of shaft, the correction for a bounce or scoop sole angle must be made by bending the shaft. This can easily be done in the case of steel double bend shafts, but not in the case of a graphite double bend shaft. To bend the shaft will require a shaft bending block or a specially made putter shaft bending tool.

> NOTE: It must be understood that some putter manufacturers do intentionally design more loft on the face of the putter and design the hosel to force the angle of the shaft back away from the face. This is usually done to try to force the golfer using the putter to position his/her hands is a particular manner which expresses the putting technique the manufacturer would like the golfer to use. This is not to be confused with a sole angle. Remember, if the shaft is 90° to the sole, the putter has a square sole. It is possible for the putter to have loft and still be made with a square sole angle. (See Effect of Loft on Putter Fitting in this chapter for more information).

V. LIE

Lie is a **MEDIUM** Specification for Putter Fitting.

If the lie angle of the putter were so critical, how could a player as good as Senior Professional Isao Aoki putt so well, given the fact his putter sits on the ground on the extreme end of the heel of the blade? Because putters have the least amount of loft, if the toe or the heel of the putter is sticking up at the moment of impact, the face is tilted off line far less than any other club in the bag. On the other hand, given the fact the hole is but 4 1/4" in diameter, it would also seem logical that while minimal, the face of a putter with an average loft of 2.5° - 3° would still point off-line when the lie is incorrect. Even though it is entirely possible for golfers to get used to aiming slightly right or left of the hole to account for such an errant lie angle situation with the putter, it is not a good situation and one that certainly should be avoided. The goal of the clubmaker is to fit the lie angle of the putter so that the sole of the putter sits absolutely flat on the green when the golfer addresses the putt.

In addition, a putter which comes into the impact position with the toe or the heel more in contact with the ground has more of a chance of 'scuffing', possibly affecting the **Distance** and the **Accuracy** of the putt at the same time. While the off-line alignment of the putter face is certainly minimal when the lie angle is not correct for the player, there is no reason to take the chance of the face being even slightly aimed off-line, or the sole 'scuffing' the surface of the

While putter lie should be correct, even if the lie is off by a significant degree, the very low loft of the putter will only result in an off line shot at the longest distance.

ground by allowing the lie to be incorrect for the player. For this reason, lie is considered to be a **MEDIUM** factor of putter fitting.

The standard lie angle for a putter manufactured in the golf industry is 72°. However, this is of little significance to the clubmaker because putter lie fitting is a specification which needs to be addressed individually with each player.

The lie of the putter should be fit statically at the same time the length is being fit. The best way to fit for the lie of the putter is to make the determination at the same time the length is being fit using a Putter Lie/Length Fitting Aid, such as the one described in Section I earlier in this chapter.

VI. TOTAL WEIGHT

Total Weight is a **MEDIUM** Specification for Putter Fitting.

As with the woods and the irons, because head weight is somewhat constant, the total weight of the putter is controlled largely by the shaft and then by the weight of the grip. Total weight is only a **MEDIUM** factor in the fitting of the putter for two primary reasons:

1) There are very limited performance advantages to be gained by varying the total weight of the putter compared to varying to the total weight of the woods and irons. It is generally agreed that the lighter the total weight of the putter, the more tendency there is for the golfer to develop a faster, less controlled putting stroke. **Because putting requires a methodical, repeating tempo in the stroke, decreasing the total weight of the putter is not generally considered to be a key to success on the greens.** It is much easier to develop the proper stroke tempo with a higher total weight than with a very light total weight in the putter. For that reason, most putters are manufactured with steel shafts to keep the total weight of the putter heavy. With a higher total weight, the golfer will have less of a tendency to swing the putter too fast or too jerky and therefore may find it a little easier to keep the stroke on line toward the target.

2) Unlike the woods and irons, for which the total weight and the swingweight are both important, **the swingweight (balance point) of the putter is far more important than total weight**. This is because the speed of the putting stroke is so much less than the speed of the swing used with the woods and the irons. At such slow swing speeds the stroke tempo is affected far more by the head weight **Feel** (swingweight) than the total weight.

If the player wishes to use a lightweight shaft in the putter, it is most important that the head weight be kept heavy enough (swingweight higher) to give the player a more definite sense of clubhead feel to be more conducive to generating a methodical, repeating stroke. Recommended swingweight ranges for putters assembled with very light shafts such as lightweight graphite are the same as for putters which are assembled with steel shafts for the purpose of ensuring the golfer feels the clubhead during the stroke. (See putter swingweight chart on pages 384).

Even though the possible pitfalls of making the total weight of the putter too light have been exposed, the clubmaker must also exercise caution to be sure the putter does not become too heavy as well. If the golfer chooses a jumbo oversize putter grip for comfort and feel, care should be taken not to increase the head weight too much to offset the effect the large and heavy grip has on decreasing the swingweight. If the total weight of the putter is too high, there is a small chance the golfer could experience problems with the rhythm and timing of the stroke. However, as a point of comparison, **it is far worse for the putter to be made with a very light total weight and light swingweight than a heavy total weight and a heavy swingweight at the same time**.

The type of player who traditionally can benefit from a much higher than normal total weight is a person who suffers from the 'yips' with the putting stroke. This frustrating malady which causes the putter to 'jerk' or 'jump' just prior to impact can be reduced for some through the use of a very heavy total weight. The idea is the much heavier total weight will almost pull the hands through the impact zone, thus eliminating the need of the golfer to consciously make a forward stroke with the hands, arms or shoulders.

Methods of creating a very heavy total weight putter to combat the 'yips' range from using a jumbo putter grip with high swingweight to actually filling the shaft completely with sand before installing the grip.

The final rule of thumb for total weight in the putter is to be conscious of the head weight **Feel** first and the total weight second.

VII. LOFT

Loft is a **MEDIUM** Specification for Putter Fitting.

Very few golfers are even aware that a putter is made with a slight degree of loft. Most people think putters are made with 0° loft because the function of the putter is to roll the ball on the green.

The average loft for a putter is 2.5 to 3°. However, there are a number of putters which have been intentionally produced with as much as 6° loft depending upon the design intent of the manufacturer.

The reason putters have loft is because the vast majority of all golfers deliver the putter to impact with the hands slightly in front of the clubhead. Whenever the hands are 'ahead' of the putter, the real loft of the head is decreased. If the putter arrives at impact with a negative loft angle (when the putter face has been pushed forward past 0° loft), the ball will hop or skip off the face, adversely affecting the roll and the **Distance** of the putt.

Ideally, the clubmaker should fit the player for putter loft by having the person set up over the putt with the hands positioned just as they would be at impact. This may require the clubmaker to observe a number of putting strokes to see if the player's hands are in a different position with respect to the clubhead than they were in the address position.

With the golfer's hands holding the putter as close to the position they will be at impact, the clubmaker can bend down and measure the loft of the putter on the floor, using a special 'half-protractor' similar to the type sold by Golfsmith for use with the Golfsmith Specification Measurement Machine.

The idea of this method is to provide the golfer with a putter which, at the the proper length and lie for the golfer, would have a loft angle of 0° in the impact position. Theoretically, this method of putter loft fitting will perfectly match the golfer to the correct loft. However, such a method can be very difficult to assure **Accuracy** with because of the variables of how the player simulates the position of the hands with the putter.

Therefore, the practical guidelines for fitting putter loft are as follows:

* If the player places the hands at least 4-5" forward in front of the ball in the address and impact position, the loft should not be less than 6°. This would be characterized as an extreme forward press with the putter.

* If the player places the hands at least 2-3" forward in front of the ball at address and impact position, the loft should not be more than 4° or less than 2°. This would be characterized as an average forward press with the putter.

* If the player places the hands directly on top of the ball in the address and impact position, the loft should not be greater than 3° nor less than 1°.

* No putter should be fit to the golfer with a loft of 0° or a negative loft.

VIII. CLUBHEAD DESIGN – PUTTERS

Center of Gravity is a **MINOR** Performance Specification but a **MAJOR** Appearance Factor for Putter Fitting.

Putters are not designed with a significant range in the vertical position of the CG because within the realm of traditional putter face height (1" average), the CG will have no real effect on the shot.

Occasionally, a putter will be designed and marketed as having 'top-weighting' or a high CG to supposedly make the ball leave the putter face with immediate overspin. Because the speed of the putting stroke is so much slower than with a wood or iron, and because the difference between a so-called high and low CG putter is so slight, such claims have to be considered false. The loft of the putter will have a far greater effect on the ability of the putter to quickly generate the desired overspin roll than will the CG.

However, because putters are made in a tremendous variety of sole widths, shapes and sizes, all of which make the golfer think they are using a low or a high CG putter, the appearance factor becomes a very important part of the psychology of the putt. In short, the golfer has to like the appearance of the putter to putt successfully. Because there is no such thing as an improperly fit CG in a putter, the golfer should be free to select any putter on the basis of its 'psychologically perceived' CG location.

Weight Distribution is a **MEDIUM** Performance Specification but a **MAJOR** Appearance Factor for Putter Fitting.

Weight distribution is a completely different factor in the design of a putter than is the center of gravity. Heel and Toe weighting, the primary means to improving the **Feel** and **Distance** of a putt hit off-center, was originated for putter designs long before it was incorporated in iron or wood head design.

Unless the golfer has a definite appearance preference for a blade style putter, or happens to possess a very consistent putting stroke, the clubmaker should always advise golfers to try to look for a confidence building putter which has heel/toe weighting. Between a blade and a heel/toe style putter head, a putt hit 1/2" to 1" to the right or left of the CG will travel farther and therefore more consistently when struck by the heel-toe weighted design.

IX. HOSEL OFFSET

Hosel Offset is a **MINOR** Performance Specification but a **MAJOR** Appearance Factor for Putter Fitting.

There are two primary ways in which hosel offset is incorporated in a putter design. 1) The traditional method of creating offset in the putter is to design the hosel with an angle which causes the shaft to be aligned in the hosel in front of the face. (In some rare cases, putters have been designed with the hosel bore behind the face, a condition called onset). 2) The most recent method of incorporating offset into the design of a putter is through the use of an intentionally curved or bent shaft, in which the particular bend of the shaft places the center of the shaft in front of the putter face.

The primary goal of creating offset putters is to encourage the golfer to present his/her hands ahead of the ball at impact. This is said to enhance the ability of the golfer to keep the speed of the putter head constant, or accelerating slightly, through the ball, which is a key fundamental to hitting the putt consistently solid and on-center.

If the golfer's putting stroke is such that the wrists 'break' or unhinge before impact, increasing the amount of offset in the putter could help the golfer achieve a little more consistency in striking the putt on-center. On the other hand, if the golfer uses an 'arm and shoulder style putting stroke' in which the wrists are completely eliminated from the putting stroke, it is strictly up to the golfer whether to select a putter with or without offset.

Because the amount of offset cannot have a dramatic effect on cutting down the amount of unhinging of the wrists through the impact zone, putter offset is considered to be far more of an appearance related factor in the selection of the putter than a performance related factor. As such, the golfer should be free to choose whichever putter he/she likes, free of a great deal of outside influence from the clubmaker.

As a last point of putter offset fitting, because there are so many variations in the types of bent putter shafts, the clubmaker might be well advised to keep an array of the different bent shafts in the shop. When the golfer is considering a new putter, the shafts can then be test inserted into the putter head without epoxy, allowing the golfer to see the different options before making a decision as to which looks the best, is easiest to align the putter square to the target and which makes him/her **Feel** the most comfortable over the putt.

NOTE: Not all bent putter shafts will fit in the same putter head because of the angle of the bore in the putter head. Be sure to take the time to learn the difference between a bent shaft which is designed to be installed only 90° bore angle putter heads vs. bent shafts which are intended to be used only with 71-72° bore angle putters. Again, this is strictly an appearance related matter of the fitting which can only be determined by the golfer.

Chapter 10
SPECIAL FITTING CONDITIONS

GUIDELINES FOR FITTING JUNIORS, LADIES, SENIORS, LOW HANDICAP AND PHYSICALLY CHALLENGED PLAYERS

I. FITTING JUNIOR GOLFERS – THE KEY SPECIFICATIONS

A. LOFT

Loft is a **MAJOR** Factor in Fitting Junior Players.

* Choose wood and iron heads with lofts which are weaker than adult loft angles. The smaller and lighter the junior player, the more loft on the woods, unless the youngster has already exhibited the ability to easily get the ball airborne. (Driver not less than 13° to 16° of loft).

* Lofts on irons should not approach the standards on adult iron heads. (Not stronger than 29-30° loft on the #5-iron).

B. LENGTH

Length is a **MAJOR** Factor in Fitting Junior Players.

* The longer the clubs, the harder they will be to successfully use, especially for the younger, smaller and lighter weight junior players.

Recommended Lengths for Junior Players by Height and Weight

Height	Weight	Driver	5-iron	9-iron
42"	Under 35 lbs	32"	28"	26.5"
	Over 35 lbs	33"	29"	27.5"
44"	Under 38 lbs	32"	28"	26.5"
	Over 38 lbs	33"	29"	27.5"
46"	Under 42 lbs	34"	29"	27.5"
	Over 42 lbs	35"	30"	28.5"
48"	Under 50 lbs	34"	29"	27.5"
	Over 50 lbs	35"	30"	28.5"
50"	Under 58 lbs	36"	31"	29"
	Over 58 lbs	37"	32"	30"
52"	Under 66 lbs	36"	31"	29"
	Over 66 lbs	37"	32"	30"
54"	Under 74 lbs	37"	32"	30"
	Over 74 lbs	38"	33"	31"
56"	Under 80 lbs	38"	33"	31"
	Over 80 lbs	39"	34"	32"
58"	Under 86 lbs	39"	34"	32"
	Over 86 lbs	40"	35"	33"
60"	Under 94 lbs	39"	34"	32"
	Over 94 lbs	40"	35"	33"
62"	Under 104 lbs	40.5"	35"	33"
	Over 104 lbs	41.5"	36"	34"

C. TOTAL WEIGHT/SWINGWEIGHT

Total Weight/Swingweight is a **MAJOR** Factor in Fitting Junior Players.

* The heavier the clubs, the harder they will be for the junior player to successfully use.

* Because of the shorter length needs of junior players, fitting to a total weight is more important than fitting to a swingweight. This is because shorter lengths make it impossible to use a conventional 14" swingweight scale. However, **any addition of weight required to meet the recommendations for total weight should be added to the clubhead in an effort to create as much clubhead Feel as possible when building clubs to the shorter lengths**.

* When financially possible, try to use junior graphite shafts to keep the total weight light.

* The following chart of recommended total weights for junior clubs is offered as a starting point for clubmakers. It is based upon using lighter weight junior clubheads with junior steel shafts and junior weight grips.

Chart of Total Weight Recommendations for Junior Golf Clubs

Height	Weight	Driver	5-iron	9-iron
42"	Under 35 lbs	32"/11.25-11.5oz	28"/12.5-12.75oz	26.5"/13.25-13.5oz
	Over 35 lbs	33"/11.5-11.75oz	29"/12.75-13oz	27.5"/13.5-13.75oz
44"	Under 38 lbs	32"/11.25-11.5oz	28"/12.5-12.75oz	26.5"/13.25-13.5oz
	Over 38 lbs	33"/11.5-11.75oz	29"/12.75-13oz	27.5"/13.5-13.75oz
46"	Under 42 lbs	34"/11.25-11.5oz	29"/12.5-12.75oz	27.5"/13.25-13.5oz
	Over 42 lbs	35"/11.5-11.75oz	30"/12.75-13oz	28.5"/13.5-13.75oz
48"	Under 50 lbs	34"/11.25-11.5oz	29"/12.5-12.75oz	27.5"/13.25-13.5oz
	Over 50 lbs	35"/11.5-11.75oz	30"/12.75-13oz	28.5"/13.5-13.75oz
50"	Under 58 lbs	36"/11.5-11.75oz	31"/12.75-13oz	29"/13.75-14oz
	Over 58 lbs	37"/11.75-12oz	32"/13-13.25oz	30"/14-14.25oz
52"	Under 66 lbs	36"/11.5-11.75oz	31"/12.75-13oz	29"/13.75-14oz
	Over 66 lbs	37"/11.75-12oz	32"/13-13.25oz	30"/14-14.25oz
54"	Under 74 lbs	37"/11.75-12oz	32"/13-13.25oz	30"/14-14.25oz
	Over 74 lbs	38"/12-12.25oz	33"/13.25-13.5oz	31"/14.25-14.5oz
56"	Under 80 lbs	38"/11.75-12oz	33"/13.25-13.5oz	31"/14.25-14.5oz
	Over 80 lbs	39"/12-12.25oz	34"/13.5-13.75oz	32"/14.5-14.75oz
58"	Under 86 lbs	39"/12-12.25oz	34"/13.5-13.75oz	32"/14.5-14.75oz
	Over 86 lbs	40"/12.25-12.5oz	35"/13.75-14oz	33"/14.75-15oz
60"	Under 94 lbs	39"/12-12.25oz	34"/13.5-13.75oz	32"/14.5-14.75oz
	Over 94 lbs	40"/12.25-12.5oz	35"/13.75-14oz	33"/14.75-15oz
62"	Under 104 lbs	40.5"/12.25-12.5oz	35"/13.75-14oz	33"/14.75-15oz
	Over 104 lbs	41.5"/12.5-12.75oz	36"/14-14.25oz	34"/15-15.25oz

NOTE: Total Weight Ranges based upon using lighter weight junior clubheads (1w - 190g; 5i - 236g; 9i - 264g) with Junior Grip Weight (36g) with Golfsmith Firestar Junior Steel Shaft for Woods and Irons. These total weight recommendations do not apply when using standard adult headweights, with normal L through X flex steel shafts. For the recommended total weight ranges for using junior graphite shafts for each club within each size group, subtract a minimum of 1oz from the ranges listed. Remember – any weight addition to meet the recommendations should be added to the clubhead.

D. SET MAKEUP

Set Makeup is a **MAJOR** Factor in Fitting Junior Players.

* Follow the same rule for fitting set makeup for adult players - Eliminate the hard to hit clubs in favor of easier clubs to hit.

* Until the junior demonstrates the ability to easily get the ball airborne, the strongest loft wood should not be less than 15-16° and the strongest iron should not be less than a 5-iron.

* Whenever possible, add a PW for chipping and use in the sand in addition to the 9-iron. Most junior PWs have enough bounce to work from sand.

Recommended Set Makeup Examples for Juniors

Height Range	Set Makeup
42" - 50"	20° wood + 5-iron, 9-iron or PW & Putter
50" - 54"	16° wood, 20° wood + 5-iron, 9-iron, PW & Putter
56" - 62"	16° wood, 20° wood, 25° wood + 5-iron, 7-iron, 9-iron, PW & Putter (add driver only when player develops skill)

E. CLUBHEAD DESIGN/CENTER OF GRAVITY/WEIGHT DISTRIBUTION

Clubhead Design/Center of Gravity/Weight Distribution are **MEDIUM** Factors in Fitting Junior Players.

* Choose junior clubhead designs expressly made to lighter head weights and weaker lofts whenever possible, especially for junior players shorter than 4'10" tall, or who weigh less than 90lbs, or who have not developed very much body strength.

* If the junior player is more than 5" tall or weighs more than 90lbs or is strong for their age and size, adult clubheads may be selected. The key then will be to choose the proper set makeup to avoid giving the junior any strong lofted and oversize shaped clubheads.

* Slightly oversize woods are acceptable as long as the lofts are weaker than normal. Try to avoid oversize irons at all times because of the increased sole area and the difficulty that may present in trying to move the clubhead through the turf.

* Key design features to look for in the clubhead design:

    • Low center of gravity.

    • Shallow woodhead face height (Driver not more than 36mm tall).

    • Wide, radiused sole from front to back on the irons to facilitate low center of gravity and the ease of moving the iron through the turf.

    • Square to Closed face angle on the woods (unless the junior definitely has developed the ability to hit the ball with a pronounced draw or hook).

    • Compact, smaller profile to standard size iron heads.

F. GRIP SIZE

Grip Size is a **MEDIUM** Factor in Fitting Junior Players.

* Junior grips to be used whenever possible for the advantage in size fitting and in helping to achieve the lighter total weights which are recommended for the junior player.

* It is far better to err on the side of making the grips too large than to make them too small. Whenever in doubt, always make the size of the junior grip larger rather than smaller.

* For fitting grip size, it is acceptable to use the method of having the junior to grip a sample junior size grip and noting the distance from the fingertips of the upper hand in the grip to the palm. If the fingertips of the upper hand (the RH for LH players and the LH for RH players) are at least 1/4" from the palm, the grip is acceptable for size. If the fingertips are closer to the palm than 1/4", make the grip larger.

* The following chart is offered as a rough guideline for creating the junior grip size when it is not possible to fit the grip in person.

Recommended Grip Size for Junior Fitting

Child Height	Grip to Use	Installed Size
42" - 50"	.500" or .580" core Jr. grip	Jr. Standard size
52" - 54"	.500" or .580" core Jr. grip	+1/32" over Jr.
56" - 62"	.500" or .580" core Jr. grip or .560" core Ladies grip	Ladies Standard size

G. Shaft Flex

Shaft Flex is a **MEDIUM** Factor in Fitting Junior Players.

* Use flexible Junior shafts whenever possible in lieu of trimming adult flex shafts shorter. Be careful in evaluating the flex of the junior shaft. At the time of this printing, the Golfsmith Firestar and Harvey Penick Future Classic steel shafts were expressly designed to be substantially more flexible than the junior steel shafts offered by the major shaft companies.

* Loft, Length, Total Weight and Set Makeup are far more important for helping the junior begin to develop competent ball striking skills than is the flex of the shaft. While it is always preferable to use as much flexibility in the shaft as is available to the clubmaker, a shaft that is too stiff will not prevent the junior from developing the proper skills to get the ball airborne.

* The ideal junior shaft is a very light graphite shaft designed with much more flexibility. Again, the Golfsmith Firestar and Harvey Penick Future Classic graphite shafts were designed with substantially more flexibility to meet this need. However, because economy must be taken into consideration, it is likely that most parents will request steel shafts be used in the junior set. However, clubmakers should try to convince the parents to allow the use of a graphite shaft in the "driver" or tee shot club to help facilitate a lighter total weight in the longest club.

H. Other Specifications Considered in Fitting Junior Players

Lie Angle

The lie angle is not that important in fitting juniors for two reasons – 1) Most junior woods are manufactured from aluminum alloys while most junior irons are made from zinc. Neither can be bent to custom fit the lie. 2) Juniors do not hit the ball far enough to have the tilt of an improper lie angle cause the ball to fly far enough off-line to cause a significant **Accuracy** problem. However, as the junior begins to achieve greater **Distance** (> 125yds/5-iron), lie should be considered as an **Accuracy** factor.

Face Angle (Woods)

Because variations in face angle are not likely to be available in junior wood heads, clubmakers cannot count on using this specification to help correct any **Accuracy** problems being experienced by the junior player. If the junior hits the ball far enough off line with the wood(s) to show a need for a custom face angle, the clubmaker should make every effort to urge the parents to have the child seek proper instruction to correct the **Accuracy** problem before it becomes ingrained into the swing. Swing changes are far easier for a junior player to make than an adult because of the age and lack of playing experience of the child.

II. FITTING FEMALE AND SENIOR GOLFERS

The Golfsmith Practical Fitting Program does not recognize gender or age among adults as a fitting factor. Golfers are golfers and should always be approached in the fitting process as being either shorter or taller, athletic or non-athletic, weaker or stronger, etc., rather than as men or women and younger or older.

In short, this philosophy means the clubmaker must learn to ignore the fact that the golfer being fit is either a man or a woman, or a senior vs. a younger player, and focus instead on the individual abilities and fitting needs of the player as dictated by size, strength and physical coordination, with no regard to gender or age.

Every aspect of the Golfsmith Practical Fitting Program has been created with this philosophy in mind to discover the best fitting recommendation for any player regardless of gender or age. In the Player Interview, the golfer will reveal most of the information upon which the fitting specifications are to be chosen. It is upon that information, along with the equipment evaluation, the swing analysis and the step by step fitting procedures that the new set of golf clubs must be built.

Not all women need to use L-flex shafts installed into clubs built to lower swingweights and shorter lengths, just as there are seniors who do not need to be fit into sets made with greater loft and A-flex shafts. While an exception rather than a norm, it is possible to encounter a 35-year-old man who swings the driver 60mph with very little athletic coordination, just as it is possible to find a woman with a 90+ mph swing speed and a keen sense of rhythm and swing timing. To pigeonhole golfers into particular 'assumed' fitting specifications simply because of their gender or age is a mistake which should be avoided at all times.

It should be noted that age is recognized as a separate fitting factor in juniors because children have not yet developed the muscularity or often the coordination to be considered only as a shorter player in the fitting process. However, as a junior begins to develop more adult characteristics of strength and swing coordination, the philosophy governing his/her fitting has to be changed to the point he/she should be considered nothing more than a younger golfer.

III. FITTING LOW HANDICAP GOLFERS

It has been said many times by experienced clubmakers that the person they least want to see walk into their shop is the low handicap golfer. This is because of the fact the better the player, the harder it will be to make changes in the equipment which will make a substantial change in ball flight and performance. The good player has gotten to that point because of his/her experience, 'savvy on the course' and primarily, his/her ability to swing the club consistently with good swing fundamentals. As a result, the clubmaker's goal in fitting the more accomplished player is to make a positive change in the **Feel** of the golf club which in turn can help the player to **Feel** better psychologically in his/her perception of the club and what it can do for his/her game. In other words, while there may be an occasional time in which the clubmaker can help the low handicap player achieve more **Distance**, better **Accuracy**, or a change in **Trajectory** and **Backspin**, the vast majority of the time, success in the fitting of a better player will be measured in terms of **Feel** more than shot performance.

In addition, it is worth mentioning that it is very common for the very skilled player to adopt somewhat of a 'know it all' attitude in the fitting, especially if the player is well aware he/she has a much lower handicap than the clubmaker. It is not the purpose of this section in the Practical Fitting Program to establish a stereotype of all good players as being arrogant, but simply to offer a number of points and tips of which the clubmaker must be aware when working with the low handicap golfer. Keeping these points in mind will help ensure the fitting session will be helpful to the golfer and satisfying to the clubmaker. After all, one of the most powerful forms of advertising any clubmaker can hope to develop is to have low handicap players touting his/her skills and excellence to the golfing community.

Tips for Fitting Low Handicap Golfers
Focus on Feel

Learn and be especially aware of the factors in the Practical Fitting Program which have a **MAJOR** effect on the **Feel** of the golf club. Even though the good player might make a request for achieving greater **Distance**, better **Accuracy** or a specific change in **Trajectory** or **Backspin**, in large part, most of the changes made in the specifications to try to achieve those goals will end up having more of an effect on the **Feel** of the club. This is because the better player will probably already hit the ball about as far or as straight as he/she is ever going to hit it with the swing he/she has – in short, dramatic changes in **Distance** and **Accuracy** are not likely to occur for the better player as much as a change in the **Feel** of the club can come about. **Real improvements in scoring for the better player are more likely to come from a careful fitting change in the short game than in the woods and irons**.

Of particular importance to the better player in terms of the specifications which control the Feel of the golf club are Length, Shaft Flex, Swingweight and Total Weight/Shaft Weight. In other words, not to say the other specifications which have a **MAJOR** effect on the **Feel** of the golf club are less important, slight to moderate changes in the Length, Shaft Flex, Swingweight and Total Weight/Shaft Weight are going to be noticed more by the better player much sooner than the other specifications which have an effect on **Feel**.

The net result is that many times when the better player might be looking for more **Distance**, better **Accuracy** or a change in **Trajectory** and **Backspin**, the change that occurs in the **Feel** of the club, which happens as an offshoot of trying to change the other shotmaking factors, becomes more important to the player in the long run.

The Shaft Rules ALL (at least they think so)

Ask most good players which part of the golf club is the most important and they'll probably say the shaft. Part of the reason for this perception is the fact that good players, because of their increased sense of **Feel**, tend to notice differences (or think they do based on certain preconceived notions about a brand, or a stated design of a shaft) from one shaft to another sooner than average players. Because of this, the better player is going to place more shotmaking importance on the shaft than most other types of golfers. As a result, **the clubmaker has to take a little longer time to fit the shaft to the better player, using the techniques outlined in Chapter 7. A significant portion of that time must be used to communicate to the golfer what each aspect of the shaft is intended to address in the low handicapper's game, especially with regard to Feel.**

Swingweight/Golf Club Balance Point is Key

Fitting a high handicap golfer with the wrong swingweight/golf club balance point is just as important as pinpointing the same specification for the low handicapper. However, because the higher handicap player makes many more swing errors, as well as a greater variety of swing errors, many bad shots will still occur even with the correct swingweight/golf club balance point in the higher handicapper's golf clubs. On the other hand, because the better player does not make as many swing errors or possess as many different swing problems, **finding the right swingweight/golf club balance point in the better player's clubs is very critical to swing consistency, especially with regard to the tempo and rhythm of the swing.** What this means is that the clubmaker can expect to experiment with different swingweights for the clubs and waiting for feed back from the player based on hitting shots before arriving on the final decision.

Time Soon Tells the Answer – Patience is a Virtue

Better players are much more fickle than higher handicappers. The low handicapper is so much more aware of the **Feel** of the golf club that what feels good one day might not the next, depending on how well the player happens to swing at the ball one day versus another. Because of this, the better player will be much more likely to return to the clubmaker's shop for changes to be made in the clubs after the set is built than will the higher handicap player. As a result, **the clubmaker who is called upon to make a** new set for the better player would be well advised to build a test 5-iron and/or driver and work with the player to fine tune these initial clubs before even beginning to assemble the full set. Doing so can save the clubmaker a lot of frustration and go a long way toward winning the respect of the lower handicap player.

Appearance vs Performance

Every player, regardless of handicap, has to like the appearance of the clubs he/she is going to use. However, there is no doubt the vast majority of lower handicap golfers are going to be much more demanding about the look of the club when it is placed behind the ball in the address position than will the average to less skilled player. In general, the lower the handicap, the less the player will be concerned about color and finish and the more he/she will be attuned to the shape of the head and its 'look' behind the ball. As a result, **when building clubs for the better player, be sure to take plenty of time to let the player see the actual clubheads before a final selection is made**. Remember, better players either tend to like more traditional shape clubheads (slightly smaller clubheads, less hosel offset), or they tend to follow the crowd and like what the tournament professionals are using.

Macho is a Disease to be Carefully Treated

Perhaps because it takes a lot of time to become a good player, or because there are so few good players as opposed to higher handicap players, there is no doubt the better player has a much more elevated sense of self image as a golfer than does the average player. This can often translate into the better player wanting to play with stiffer shafts, clubheads with fewer game improvement features, or in general, clubs which might not necessarily be well suited to his/her game, especially as the better player advances in age. Perhaps the most common scenario of this type is the better player who insists on using S or X flex shafts when the clubhead speed and downswing acceleration indicate otherwise. While communication is always the best tool for handling the better player who wants to tell the clubmaker what he/she needs, rather than fight the customer, the clubmaker should always remember two things; 1) Building a test 5-iron or driver is always a better procedure when fitting the good player than jumping headlong into the full set, and 2) Shaft flex letter codes are virtually meaningless because of differences in design philosophy from one shaft company to the next. Using the RSSR method of shaft fitting (See Chapter 7), it is always possible for the clubmaker to find an S or even an X-flex marked shaft which can match well to the swing speed and downswing acceleration of the player. This way the player sees what he/she wants on the shaft and the clubmaker has fit the golfer into the stiffness level best for his/her game.

Listen to the Player but Educate in Return (Trends & Fads)

The better the player, the more the golfer *thinks* he/she knows about golf clubs and fitting. Perhaps such a statement is a bit harsh and stereotypical, but many times, if the customer's handicap is lower than the clubmaker's, the customer will profess to know more about golf equipment than the clubmaker. An interesting offshoot of this observation is the fact that almost above all other segments of golfers the better player is more susceptible to following equipment fads and trends of the day than is the average to less able player. The reason is because while the higher handicap player knows he/she cannot play with the same equipment being used by the tournament professionals in competition, the better player does not. As a result, it is very common to encounter a good player who is so enamored by a particular clubhead or shaft or clubmaking trend of the time that he/she may insist on using that piece of equipment even though the characteristics of his/her game may indicate the selection would not enhance his/her playing ability.

This is one area of fitting which requires a great deal of patience, diplomacy and technical clubmaking knowledge on behalf of the clubmaker. If the clubmaker is sure the better player's insistence of using a particular clubhead or shaft, or a certain loft, length or swingweight specification would not be beneficial, it is the duty of the clubmaker to state this belief and be able to back up the opinion with an understandable technical explanation. **If the golfer still wishes to pursue a particular trend or fad, the clubmaker would be well advised to build a single test club with the demanded specification so the golfer is able to determine whether the desired feature is beneficial or not**. Again, just as with the advice given above, it is never wise to fight with a customer, only to educate and let the golfer experience for themselves what the equipment change will do without having the experience cost the golfer too much money. In short, whenever possible, build a single test club from which the final decision for the full set can be made.

IV. FITTING PHYSICALLY CHALLENGED GOLFERS

The Key Specifications for Fitting Physically Challenged Golfers

In no area of clubfitting will the clubmaker ever be called upon to use his/her creativity and imagination as when called upon to fit golf clubs for people who are physically challenged. Because there are many different physical challenges which can affect the way a person tries to play golf, there is only one set rule of fitting when it comes to actually making the golf clubs... comfort and ease for the physically challenged person. In other words, regardless of the disadvantage facing the golfer, the clubmaker has to approach the task with the goal of doing everything possible to make the golfer more comfortable as he/she swings the golf club at the ball.

When fitting physically challenged golfers, many of the 'rules of clubfitting' have to be tossed out the window, so to speak. In my career, I have had an opportunity to develop golf clubs for golfers with an assortment of physical challenges which ranged from paralysis to severe restriction of body or hand movement due to severe arthritis. Each situation can pose a different challenge, but **keeping the goal of offering swing comfort and ease to the golfer above all else, the clubmaker can possibly enjoy the most satisfying experience of all in clubfitting – helping a golfer play the game who might not otherwise have been able to do so**.

Pain in the shoulders, arms, wrists and hands, when severe enough, can create so much discomfort the golfer might be forced to stop playing. There is no doubt that severe arthritis, tendonitis or related discomfort can only be helped to a minor extent, because no matter what, the sheer requirement of hitting a hard golf ball with a clubhead made from a hard material will generate a feeling of impact which can aggravate the painful condition. In addition, the nature of the golf swing itself, in which the club completely changes direction at the top of the backswing, is such that a reverse in the direction of the force applied to the club can aggravate the discomfort felt in the hands, wrists, elbows and/or shoulders.

However, there are a few alterations which can be done to the golf clubs that allow some golfers to play the game with a reduction in discomfort when traditionally assembled equipment does not fit the need. When the back, shoulders, elbows, wrists and hands are creating pain during the swing, any change in the golf equipment which will make the golf club much lighter can help reduce the amount of discomfort during the swing.

Lighter Weight Golf Clubs

* **When the goal is a lighter weight golf club to help the player with joint and/or tendon discomfort, the primary focus should be made to decrease the total weight long before the swingweight is ever decreased**. Remember the specifications which have a Major effect on the Total Weight of the golf club without robbing the club of the proper feeling of head weight necessary to generate better swing tempo and rhythm – shaft weight and grip weight.

Shafts which weigh less than 70g and grips which weigh less than 40g will create golf clubs with the lightest possible total weights, thus allowing the golfer to expend less energy of motion when swinging the golf club. Swing effort creates the possibility of more pain, so any golf club which requires less force to swing will help this type of physically challenged player.

* The other way the golf club can be made to reduce the effort required to execute the swing is to reduce the swingweight. While a club which is 'head light' can definitely be easier to swing than one which is 'head heavy', **clubmakers must look at reducing swingweight as a last resort for the player with joint or tendon pain. The lighter the head weight, the more the head could transmit vibration to the golfer, especially when the shot is hit off-center**. This is why the only type of physically

challenged golfer who should be considered a candidate for a much lighter swingweight is the player who swings extremely slow at the ball because of the particular joint or tendon problem.

Absorbing the Shock of Impact with the Ball

* Even though the trends of the 1990s have brought about an increase in equipment components which claim to reduce the amount of impact vibration transmitted up the shaft to the golfer's hands, arms, upper body joints and tendons, there is no vibration reduction product which can totally eliminate the feeling of the clubhead hitting the ball. **In other words, the clubmaker can use vibration dampening devices to slightly reduce the severity of discomfort produced by impact with the ball, but it cannot be eliminated**.

* The first equipment change to employ in an effort to try to reduce the vibration of impact with the ball is to use a much larger diameter grip, which should also be very soft and cushioned in its composition and **Feel**. Traditional grip sizing techniques are not to be followed for fitting the diameter of the grip to the arthritic player. **The more the discomfort, i.e. the less the golfer can close his/her hands around the grip due to arthritis, the larger and softer the grip will have to be**. For example, it is not uncommon for clubmakers to increase the diameter of a grip such as the Avon Chamois or Golf Pride Air Cushion/Tour Velvet with 12, 15 or even 20 layers of masking tape to make the grip large enough so the golfer does not experience as much pain before the shot is hit.

Do not worry about re-swingweighting the clubs when jumbo oversizing is called for to alleviate hand or joint pain. To simply allow the golfer to close the hands around the grip with less discomfort will be a huge success. Adding weight back to the head could put more stress back on the hands during the swing, negating the original goal of improving comfort. However, if the huge oversizing of a grip for such a player causes the player to complain of swing tempo and timing problems, some weight may have to be added back to the clubhead on a trial and error basis to find the right combination of grip size to head weight **Feel**.

Remember, imagination is the key to success in fitting the golfer with special needs. Perhaps the golfer has much more trouble with pain in one hand compared to the other. In this case the clubmaker might greatly increase the diameter of the grip for the more affected hand. For example, I recall creating a very special custom made grip for a right-handed ex-pilot who had minor arthritis in the right hand, but had such a severe problem in the left hand that he had an extremely limited ability to close the hand around a normal shaped round grip.

After determining how much the golfer could close his hands and assume a grip before encountering pain, I created a grip for each club which was made up of the lower 6" of a normal grip, installed with 12 layers of masking tape for the right hand section of the grip. Butted up against that half grip for the golfer's lower hand, I then cut and used the top 4" of a training grip mounted on the end of the shaft with 20 layers of build-up tape for the upper hand. While the grips looked extremely strange, this golfer was able to resume playing for the first time in years because he could hold on to the club without having to close the fingers of his left hand more than 1/2". Remember, imagination and comfort are the keys.

* **The next alternatives to use to help reduce painful vibrations from the impact are the Sensi-Core insert found in selected True Temper shaft designs or the Sims Shock Relief Insert from PowerBilt**, both distributed by Golfsmith. Both devices are intended to decrease the vibration of the golf shaft as a way to reduce pain in the hands and elbows from minor arthritis or tendonitis. While both products do an excellent job of reducing the vibration of the shaft, if the player has moderate to severe pain, the experience of hitting shots with either device will still produce enough discomfort to prevent the player from enjoying the game.

Shock or vibration dampening devices are helpful in reducing the pain experienced by people with minor or very slight arthritic or tendonitis problems but will not bring about significant relief for people with much more severe discomfort problems. However, when it comes to trying to get the player back on the course when the physical problem is threatening to put a stop to his/her golfing life, everything that can possibly be done must be tried to see if the level of pain can be reduced to the threshold of being bearable.

The primary use of the vibration dampening devices should be for players who are just in the beginning stages of tendonitis or hand, wrist or shoulder discomfort. Because golfers who only have a slight amount of discomfort are less likely to mention the problem, it is very important for the clubmaker to probe this area during the Player Interview.

* The material of the shaft is another way the clubmaker can offer a minor amount of relief to the golfer suffering from hand, wrist, elbow or shoulder pain during the swing. Much has been written about the shock absorbing/vibration dampening benefits of graphite shafts. While there is no doubt graphite (and titanium as well) does transmit less impact vibration up the shaft to the golfer, when it comes to real pain, the dampening effect of graphite or titanium is slight at best, especially if the golfer is accustomed to taking a divot at impact. Once again, when it comes to trying to create golf clubs which will prolong the time the golfer can spend on the golf course, the clubmaker must use everything at his/her disposal.

For that reason, **graphite, aluminum and titanium shafts must be considered over steel for the golfer with joint or tendonitis pain**. Of the choices, even though studies have shown titanium is as good as to slightly better than graphite in reducing vibration, recommending graphite shafts (in particular, ultra lightweight graphite) would be better because of its lighter weight advantage over titanium and aluminum shafts.

* The material and weight distribution of the clubhead can also have a slight benefit when it comes to absorbing the shock of impact and bring-

ing about a reduction of joint/tendonitis discomfort. **Just like the shaft material, clubheads made from graphite, aluminum or titanium can absorb the shock of off-center impact and transmit less vibration up the shaft to the golfer**. Keep in mind, if any type of clubhead is hit on-center, the vibration felt by the golfer will be minimal. The fact is, golfers do not hit the ball on-center as much as they would like, so the clubhead material must be chosen on the basis of how well it will dampen vibration when impact takes place off the center of the clubface.

Also relating to the matter of off-center impact and how well the vibration is dampened is the weight distribution of the clubhead. Obviously, **perimeter weighted designs which are also made from materials which have the ability to dampen vibration would be the best choice for any golfer with any type of hand, wrist, elbow or shoulder discomfort**. This means aluminum or graphite wood heads over titanium or steel and deep cavity backed over muscleback or shallow cavity backed irons.

Reduced Mobility in the Swing

As virtually all golfers advance in age, body flexibility will decrease. In addition, injuries or chronic maladies can occur which may also limit or severely restrict the mobility of the golfer. Body flexibility is very important in playing golf because good shotmaking and, especially hitting the ball to a satisfying **Distance,** requires the golfer to be able to make an adequate shoulder and hip turn during the swing. Because mobility debilitating conditions are common, virtually every clubmaker will encounter golfers who have lost the ability to complete a full shoulder or hip turn or who are not able to adequately transfer weight from the back to the front foot during the downswing. In these cases, **the key golf club specifications on which to focus to make up for the loss of flexibility will be the length, total weight and swing weight, the shaft flex and loft of the clubheads**.

* Longer woods can be much more difficult to accomplish a **Distance** increase with than longer irons. Remember the cardinal rule of clubmaking – The longer the club, the stronger the loft, the heavier the club and the stiffer the shaft, the harder the club will be to hit. **One of the worst mistakes a clubmaker can make for a below average to poor physically coordinated golfer who has lost body mobility and wants to restore lost Distance is to increase the length of the woods and long irons**. So many people who have lost **Distance** have also lost strength. This is another factor which makes it much more difficult to rhythmically swing a very long golf club, and yet another reason to be very careful when attempting to restore **Distance** with a substantial length increase.

Numerous studies with actual golfers have proven that the ability of the golfer to gain **Distance** from an increase in club length is directly proportional to the natural rhythm, tempo and swing timing of the golfer. The better the swing timing, rhythm and tempo of the golfer to begin with, the more chance there will be for success in achieving an increase in **Distance** from an increase in the length of the woods. However, because there are so few changes which can be made to actually restore lost

Distance, if the clubmaker decides to try a length increase to help the golfer with limited flexibility, the total weight of the club must be as light as possible, which means the shaft and the grip must be as light as possible as well.

In addition, should the clubmaker wish to make the length of the woods more than 2" longer than the old traditional standards for length (43" men's driver/37.5 men's #5-iron), the clubheads should be lighter than normal component levels (<202g driver/<257g #5-iron) to help the task by preventing the longer finished clubs from feeling too head heavy.

On the other side of the set of clubs, longer middle and short irons are not normally as hard for the golfer to use as are longer woods. This is because the irons are naturally shorter and have much more loft than the woods to begin with. **Therefore, if it is not possible to use a length increase with the woods to restore lost Distance, the clubmaker still can increase the length of the middle and short irons so the goal of more Distance can at least be partially achieved.**

Golfers with a decrease in body mobility and flexibility who cannot come close to demonstrating a full turn or who cannot execute an average weight shift during the swing are perfect candidates for either increasing the length of the middle and short irons (#5 or 6 through the wedges), or for decreasing the incremental length change between the irons. By changing the separation in length from iron to iron from the normal 1/2" to 3/8" or even 1/4", the shorter the iron, the more potential for increasing shot **Distance** can result. Remember, if it is not possible to increase driver **Distance,** the golfer can still pick up enough yardage to make the game a little more enjoyable through the irons. Still, **such changes in length in the irons should also be accompanied by a decrease in shaft and grip weight to help make the longer clubs as easy as possible to swing**.

* **One of the most important changes to make in the set for the golfer who has lost body mobility is to decrease the total weight of the clubs**. As mentioned many times, the shaft and grip weight control the total weight of the club, so the clubmaker's recommendation should be to combine a very light shaft with a very light grip to make the club not only easier to swing, but to help squeeze a little more clubhead speed out of the golfer's swing.

Because ultralight weight graphite shafts are among the more expensive of all composite shafts, it is important to remind clubmakers that golfers with decreased flexibility do not necessarily have to be penalized in the pocketbook just because of their loss of mobility. When it comes to recommending a much lighter total weight for this type of golfer, what is important is the amount of total weight change being made.

If the golfer previously owned a set of steel shafted clubs, a change to graphite shafts which weigh 70-75g and grips which weight less than 40g will represent a huge change in total weight, likely enough to make the clubs both easier to swing and able to gain back some **Distance**. Shafts which weigh 70-75g are not nearly as expensive as those which weigh less than 60g. While it is always nice for the clubmaker to make the clubs as light as possible for this type of player, to drop the total weight by 2oz will be a very effective change, which is the difference between a steel shafted set and clubs made with 75g graphite shafts and 40g grips.

In addition, steel shafts which weigh in the range of 90g are also available as a lower-priced alternative to graphite. While not as light as the conventional and ultralight graphite shafts, when cost is a factor, even a change from the normal 120g steel shaft and 52g rubber grip to a 90g steel shaft and sub 40g grip will help the golfer a lot.

If the golfer with the lack of mobility has already been using graphite shafts, obviously, not as much can be done in the area of lowering the total weight of the clubs. Still, because virtually all of the sets built with graphite shafts up to 1995 were assembled with 80-90g shafts and 50-55g grips, the possible combination of a sub 60g shafts with sub 40g grips will bring about a change which can be very helpful.

When talking about greatly decreasing the total weight for the golfer who does not possess a normal range of body flexibility/mobility, the swing-weight must also be carefully considered as well. If the golfer still exhibits a reasonably high level of strength even with the lack of mobility, the swingweight of the light total weight clubs should be kept slightly to moderately higher than normal, in the range of D3-D6, based on a 44" driver or a 38" #5-iron length. However, because many people with decreased flexibility may also be lacking in overall strength, for most of these golfers the swingweight may need to be normal to slightly lower than normal. Only with extreme cases of lack of mobility should the swingweight be allowed to fall below the C7 range for men, based on modern lengths. (By comparison, ladies' swingweights would be two or three swingweight points lower for each 1/2" the clubs are made shorter than the men's).

* While the Practical Fitting Program does not award a **MAJOR** role to shaft flex, **when it comes to fitting the golfer with a lack of physical flexibility or body mobility, the flex of the shaft can become a little more important**. Tests performed by Grafalloy Shaft Corporation in the mid-1990s demonstrated that clubhead speed could be increased by as much as 10 percent with a significant decrease in shaft flex.

While such information may give the impression the Practical Fitting Program has made a mistake in ranking flex as only a **MEDIUM** factor of **Distance**, the point is that the test results Grafalloy obtained were based on decreases to levels of greater shaft flexibility which would not be acceptable to most golfers from a **Feel** and possibly, an **Accuracy** and **Trajectory** standpoint. In short, a golfer who swings a shaft with a base frequency of 200cpm after hitting a club with a 300cpm shaft could experience a 10mph swing speed increase, but would or could the golfer play with that 200cpm shaft? What if that golfer's swing speed was 100mph? Would the 200cpm shaft be well fit into the hands of a golfer with a 100mph swing speed? Not very likely (although anything is possible in fitting!).

What the Grafalloy test information can tell the clubmaker is that in extreme cases, shaft flex can contribute significantly to **Distance**. Since a severe lack of body mobility can certainly qualify as an extreme case, **clubmakers should consider fitting the golfer with very limited body mobility with a much more flexible shaft in an effort to make up for some of the clubhead speed lost due to the lack of flexibility or mobility**. Look at it this way – when the ability to execute a full turn is severely restricted or reduced, **Distance** will go away much faster than **Accuracy** or **Trajectory**. Most golfers faced with this delimma will be glad to adjust to whatever **Trajectory** or **Feel** differences come about from a switch to a very flexible shaft in an effort to gain back some of the lost yardage. As a result, this is what shafts like the Fiberspeed FS Series are for, which are far more flexible than normal shaft design parameters.

Do remember that the effect of the various inter-relationships between golf club specifications outlined extensively in Chapter 2 must be kept in mind when fitting the physically challenged golfer as well. For example, if the golfer with limited mobility or flexibility has an accomplished enough tempo and sense of rhythm to be able to use a very long golf club, the effect of that length on the shaft flex must be taken into account.

For example, the famous golfing trick shot artist Dennis Walters, who was paralyzed below the waist in a tragic accident after becoming a tournament professional, uses an average R-flex shaft (@ 250cpm if tested at 43.5"/D1) but at the 49" driver length he desires and has the ability to play, that R flex is bending as much as a 200cpm shaft will at 43" in the hands of a non-professional golfer. With his skill, Dennis knows he needs to draw upon every possible source for increasing clubhead speed for the days he plays a 'regular' round of golf instead of entertaining people with his amazing array of trick shots.

With absolutely no movement of his hips or legs, strapped to a chair mounted on a golf cart and only able to generate 40° of shoulder rotation as opposed to the desired 90°, with the extreme length and flexibility of the shaft, combined with a 195g head weight, Dennis is able to fly the ball over 225 yards with his driver! While regularly able to break 80 and often still shoot par, Dennis is an exceptional example of the golfer with limited mobility and flexibility because he has the swing timing of a professional golfer. But the point still remains – of course it is Dennis' incredible sense of timing and rhythm that makes the difference in his being able to hit a 49" long driver and 41" #5-iron, but the increased flex is a large part of the **Distance** he is able to generate.

* In most cases, the more the golfer lacks mobility and flexibility, the more loft will be required on the clubheads to generate the desired **Trajectory** for maximum carry **Distance**. This is because the more the golfer lacks mobility and flexibility, the lower the clubhead speed will be and with it, the lower the launch angle will be, and the less **Backspin** will be imparted on the ball.

Unless they already hit the ball high because of ball position or a swing movement, players who no longer hit the driver 200 yards should not be using a driver with less than 15° loft or a 5-iron with less than 28° loft.

* Other tips for helping the golfer with limited flexibility or a lack of body mobility are to select or make the irons with a much more radiused sole from front to back. As the ability to generate a full turn on the ball is decreased greatly, so to is the ability of the player to hit down and through the ball. Often, the percentage of 'fat' shots increases as well from the restricted shoulder turn or weight transfer. Players with decreased mobility are much better off learning how to sweep the ball off the ground. Irons with much greater front to back radius are more beneficial in helping the golfer achieve that goal.

A golf swing which is made with far less than a full turn or executed with a poor weight transfer will always put more stress on the hands and arms. Because they are able to help relax the muscles of the forearms and afford comfort at the same time, greatly oversized grips are a very helpful addition to the set being made for the golfer with limited flexibility.

Whether for challenged or non-physically challenged golfers, the set makeup is still one of the most important of all fitting factors. Many times, the golfer who encounters a decrease in flexibility or mobility will not have had the problem his/her entire golfing life. As such, it is likely the old set will be of a traditional #1, 3, 5 woods with 3-PW, SW set makeup. The rule of thumb for selecting the set makeup for the golfer with limited mobility or flexibility is the same for all golfers - replace the hard to hit clubs with clubs which are easier to hit which will achieve the desired shotmaking results.

For the golfer with limited mobility or flexibility, this means a higher lofted driver (or no driver at all), high lofted fairway woods, no iron longer than a 5- or 6-iron and extra wedges or a chipper to help enhance the ability to score.

Appendix I

The cardinal rules of clubfitting

1. The longer the shaft, the stronger the loft, the heavier the total weight, the stiffer the shaft, the harder the club will be to hit for any golfer.

2. The higher the handicap and the less the frequency of play, the more Rule #1 applies to the fitting process.

3. Unless they have a definite, substantiated reason to request otherwise, fit all golfers into the lightest, most flexible shaft which they can control.

4. The higher the handicap and the less the frequency of play, the more Rule #3 applies to the fitting process.

5. A change in the face angle of the woods is by far the best fitting prescription to improve the Accuracy of the golfer.

6. A light total weight combined with a higher than normal swingweight (> D2) is a good combination for a very wide range of players.

7. The stronger the upper body, the arms, the hands, the higher the swingweight will need to be. Add fast tempo to that mix and the total weight may have to be increased as well.

8. Slow swing speeds need substantially more loft on the driver, long and possibly middle irons. Driver swing speed 80mph or less = Driver loft no less than 15°, unless the player already possesses a high Trajectory to begin with.

9. Golfers with slow swing speeds can decrease loft on the #4 and higher number fairway woods and shorter irons (#6 - wedges) to increase Distance.

10. Ball position, alignment to the target and the hand position at address for chip shots are three areas of swing teaching that all clubmakers should check and correct for the golfer during the fitting session. Leave all others to a qualified teacher of the swing.

11. It is far easier to increase Trajectory for any golfer than to decrease Trajectory.

12. Make it a practice to build far more sets of irons without the #3 iron than with it.

13. More iron sole radius from front to back is better than less for all golfers.

14. Less vertical roll radius on the woods is better for all golfers.

15. With 99 percent of your golfers, always err on the side of more flexibility when fitting the shaft.

16. Never use the flex letter code as a method of determining the stiffness of a shaft. Swing speed ratings or actual frequency measurement

comparisons are much more accurate.

17. Unless the low torque shaft is also made with very low frequency like the Grafalloy Nitro Flex, try to fit less than 1 percent of your golfers with a shaft which has a torque measurement of less than 3°.

18. In a world of super jumbo drivers, be careful to avoid a tall face height on the matching fairway woods. For 99 percent of all golfers, 40mm (1.5") is too deep for a fairway wood.

19. When in doubt, build the club two swingweight points higher.

20. Hosel Offset is to be chosen for appearance long before performance.

21. Shaft Bend Point is to be chosen for Feel long before performance.

22. The greater the number of test clubs in a fitting session, the greater the amount of confusion.

23. Increasing club length can do more to harm Accuracy than help increase Distance.

24. Lead tape is for changing swingweight, not for changing center of gravity or weight distribution.

25. A medium change in ball flight requires a major change in the specifications.

26. No matter what, the golf swing always has the ability to overcome, negate or offset any changes the clubmaker can make in the golf clubs.

27. A positive change in the Feel of the golf club is just as much of a success in fitting as a positive change in Distance, Accuracy, Trajectory or Backspin.

28. To ignore fitting the wedges and putter is to lose one of the two most significant opportunities to help the golfer actually score better.

29. When it comes to the shaft, a little too flexible is a lot better than a little too stiff.

30. Downswing acceleration should be used to modify and fine tune the selection of stiffness made from clubhead speed. Downswing acceleration should not be used as the only determinant of shaft flex or the golfer can be robbed of the benefits of proper Feel.

APPENDIX 2

THE COMPLETE CONDENSED PROCEDURES OF THE GOLFSMITH PRACTICAL FITTING PROGRAM

STEP 1

Ask the golfer to fill out the Practical Fitting Program Player Interview Form. Tell him/her to be as complete and honest as he/she can be in making his/her responses. If the player has no idea of the answer to a particular question, he/she should leave that question blank. If the player is not familiar with the equipment information being indicated by any particular question but is curious about that aspect of the clubs, he/she may place a (?) question mark beside that point.

The player does not have to answer every question. However, do urge the golfer to list as much information about his/her ball striking tendencies, playing goals and equipment preferences as he/she can. The more information provided on the Player Interview Form, the more accurate will be the fitting.

STEP 2

While the golfer is filling out the Player Interview Form, the clubmaker should perform the Equipment Evaluation by measuring only the specifications which are outlined on the form. Remember to find out if the fitting session is for a full set of new clubs, a driver only, a full set of woods only, a set of irons only or fitting only for the wedges or putter. This will save time by performing only the equipment specification measurements which are pertinent to the fitting.

Remember to note the information provided in Chapters 4 and 6 which outlines which measurements are necessary to make and which are not to complete the Equipment Evaluation.

STEP 3

After the golfer completes the Player Interview Form, perform the Final Fitting Procedure tests of Dynamic Lie fitting, Wrist to Floor measurement, Grip Size determination and Driver and 5-iron Swing Speed measurement. After the swing tests, note the Equipment Preferences from the Player Interview and either with a catalog or with real clubhead samples, ask the player to choose two or three different clubhead designs which would be cosmetically pleasing in appearance.

This will complete your data gathering from the player. The player can leave, after which you can go over all the data from the Player Interview, the Equipment Evaluation and the Final Fitting Procedures to compile the Preliminary Fitting recommendation.

STEP 4

Look at the Preliminary Fitting Recommendation and determine if the required specifications for the clubhead can be achieved on one of the clubhead models chosen by the player. For example, not every clubhead the player might choose from a shape and style standpoint will be available with all of the specifications that are called for in the Fitting Recommendation. In these cases, the clubmaker must decide which of the specifications could be modified or compromised to let the golfer use one of the head designs he/she chose. If it is not possible to give the golfer the shape and style features with the required custom specifications, the golfer will have to be called back, the situation explained, and a new clubhead selection made with the clubmaker offering the reasons why.

STEP 5

The clubmaker should order a driver and a 5 or 7-iron (5-iron for the better player, 7-iron for the average to higher handicapper) of the selected clubhead and build those two clubs to the complete specifications dictated by the Preliminary Fitting Recommendation for the golfer to try before finishing out the full set. Ideally, the clubmaker should leave these two starting clubs with the golfer for two weeks. This would give the golfer enough time to try the new fitting specifications and report back to the clubmaker. If the specifications of the clubs need modification or changing in any way, the clubmaker can make the changes on the sample clubs before the rest of the set is built. Once the golfer is pleased with the initial clubs, the rest of the set should then be ordered and built.

CONCLUSION

The Practical Fitting Program identifies the path to game improvement through a new set of clubs by limiting the variables to **Distance, Accuracy, Trajectory, Backspin** or **Feel**, and by then identifying which specifications will have a **MAJOR** or **MEDIUM** effect on each game improvement factor. The Program then identifies the changes in those specifications which are capable of making the desired game improvement changes. The Program thus shortens the fitting session, avoids the extensive use of test clubs, does not exhaust the golfer with endless ball striking tests, and, best of all, results in a more accurate fitting.

If the Practical Fitting Program is confusing in any way to this point, it is strongly suggested the clubmaker go back through chapters 1, 2, 3, 4, 6 and 7 and read the bold type entries to get the highlights of the program. Remember, the purpose of any book is to explain the subject in its fullest extent. Each chapter contains the most complete explanation of every single point in the Practical Fitting Program so there can be no doubt why a particular decision or conclusion is made. But the book is also designed to explain the same points in a shorter format through the use of the bold type sections as well as the **FAST FACT** segments.

When all else fails, always remember the simplicity of the Practical Fitting Program is in the fact that the clubmaker need only find out how the golfer wants to improve his/her **Distance, Accuracy, Trajectory, Backspin** or **Feel** and then proceed to change only the specifications which have a **MAJOR** or **MEDIUM** effect on the game improvement factors the golfer wishes to change.

APPENDIX 3

EVERYTHING YOU WANTED TO KNOW ABOUT SHAFT FITTING AND ANALYSIS

PROCEDURES FOR SHAFT FITTING

STEP 1

Record the separate swing speeds of the golfer with a driver and a 5-iron after the golfer has warmed up sufficiently. Have the golfer hit five or six shots each with the driver and the 5-iron. Note and retain the swing speed as the most frequently seen swing speeds obtained with each club (plastic practice balls may be used with a swing speed recording device).

Shaft fitting example:
Swing speed with driver = 85mph
Swing speed with 5-iron = 65mph

STEP 2

Choose the shaft weight range from which the shaft is to be selected. The shaft weight range is selected based on the golfer's requirement for total weight, which will be based upon the golfer's need for **Distance, Accuracy** and **Feel**.

The following chart lists the shaft weight ranges along with the approximate driver and 5-iron total weights each shaft weight will create.

Shaft Weight Classification	Shaft Weight Range	Driver Tot. Wt.	5-Iron Tot. Wt.
Heavy Weight	110g +	>12.7oz	>14.7oz
Medium Weight	96-110g	12.2 - 12.7oz	14.2 - 14.7oz
Light Weight	81-95g	11.7 - 12.2oz	13.7 - 14.2oz
Very Light Weight	66-80g	11.2 - 11.7oz	13.2 - 13.7oz
Ultra Light Weight	50-65g	10.7 - 11.2oz	12.7 - 13.2oz

NOTE: Based on 50g grip weight. If using 38g lightweight grips, subtract 0.4oz from the total weight in the range for each classification of shaft weight.

Shaft fitting example (Continued):

From STEP 1 –
Swing speed measurement with driver = 85mph
Swing speed measurement with 5-iron = 65mph

From STEP 2 –
Recommended shaft weight range from preliminary fitting
Recommendation (Chapter 6) = 66g to 80g for wood shafts;
110 + g for Iron shafts

STEP 3

Use the Data Chart "RSSR x Shaft Weight Range," found in the supplement to this book, to find the group of eligible shafts which conform to the swing speed requirement and the desired shaft weight range for both the woods and the irons. Following is a section from the chart to help explain the fitting of the example golfer with an 85mph driver swing speed, a 65mph 5-iron swing speed, who needs a 66-80g graphite shaft in the woods and a 96-110g steel shaft in the irons.

<u>Shaft Fitting Example (Continued):</u>

From STEP 1 -
Swing speed measurement with driver = 85mph
Swing speed measurement with 5-iron = 65mph

From STEP 2 -
Recommended shaft weight range from preliminary fitting
Recommendation (Chapter 6) = 66g to 80g for wood shafts;
110 + g for iron shafts

From STEP 3 -
All wood shafts rated at 85mph with a 66g-80g shaft weight

80-90mph/66-80g
(L/M) Golfsmith Carbon Stick Ultralite • R-flex
(M) Aldila SpeedFit-80
(H) True Temper Dynamic Lite graphite • R-flex
(L)Aldila Low Torque 5.0 • Firm flex
(M) True Temper Lite graphite • R-flex

All iron shafts rated at 65mph with a 96-110g shaft weight

60-70mph/96-110g
(L) Ti-Tour Titanium 140
(M) True Temper Stratus • A-flex
(H) True Temper Dynamic graphite • R-flex
(M) True Temper TT Lite taper tip • L-flex

STEP 4

Eliminate any possible shafts from the initial list of eligible shafts which do not conform to how much the golfer wants to pay for the set of clubs. How the golfer's cost requirements is handled is a matter between the clubmaker and the golfer, based largely upon how much the clubmaker is going to charge for clubs which are made with shafts of different costs.

The example fitting will not use a cost restriction so the clubmaker can see the full scope of the shafts which may be selected without a cost consideration.

STEP 5

Determine the golfer's downswing acceleration capability using either simple judgment or by using one of the various test devices which have been created to make such an assessment. Adjust the golfer's RSSR requirement based on the measurement or judgment of their downswing acceleration force. (See Chapter 7 for instructions for using the True Temper Determinator as a method of judging the downswing acceleration)

Shaft Fitting Example (Continued):

From STEP 1 –
Swing speed measurement with driver = 85mph
Swing speed measurement with 5-iron = 65mph

From STEP 2 –
Recommended shaft weight range from preliminary fitting
Recommendation (Chapter 6) = 66g to 80g for wood shafts;
110 + g for iron shafts

From STEP 3 –
All wood shafts rated at 85mph with a 66g-80g shaft weight

80-90mph/66-80g
(L/M) Golfsmith Carbon Stick Ultralite • R-flex
(M) Aldila SpeedFit-80
(H) True Temper Dynamic Lite graphite • R-flex
(L)Aldila Low Torque 5.0 • Firm flex
(M) True Temper Lite graphite • R-flex

All iron shafts rated at 65mph with a 96-110g shaft weight

60-70mph/96-110g
(L) Ti-Tour Titanium 140
(M) True Temper Stratus • A-flex
(H) True Temper Dynamic graphite • R-flex
(M) True Temper TT Lite taper tip • L-flex

From STEP 5 –

Downswing acceleration judgment/measurement –

Average tempo, but a Determinator reading of 8 = Move the RSSR shaft selection range down by 5mph.

Wood shafts at 85mph/66g-80g shaft weight/-5mph on RSSR (The clubmaker is now looking for an 80mph wood shaft on an 85 mph driver swing speed golfer because of a low downswing acceleration measurement.)

75-85mph/66-80g

(L) Aldila Low Torque 5.0 • Strong flex
(M) Grafalloy Classic • A-flex
(L) G. Loomis Sport • S-flex
(M) Fenwick Scoreline • S-flex
(M) Swix Performa 80 • A-flex

Iron shafts at 65mph/110g+ shaft weight/-5mph on RSSR (The clubmaker is now looking for a 60mph iron shaft on a 65mph 5-iron swing speed golfer because of the low downswing acceleration measurement.)

55-65mph/96-110g

(L) True Temper Release • Men's flexible
(M) True Temper Gold Plus • L300 flex

STEP 6

In the Player Interview, if questions like "I want to **Feel** the clubhead more", "I want to **Feel** more kick in the shaft", or "I want to hit the ball more solid" are marked by the player, among the shafts now left through the process of elimination, choose the one(s) which are known to have a Low Bend Point. For the average to high handicap players, or players in search of a more solid **Feel** choose the shaft(s) among the remaining options which have a low bend point.

Only if the player has the very solid swing fundamentals of a full shoulder turn, a late release of the club into the ball, a driving movement through impact with the lower body, or if the player specifically requests, should the clubmaker search for a shaft with a High or Mid Bend Point among those shafts which are left from the process of elimination. If ever in doubt as to whether to select a Low or Mid/High Bend Point for the player, always select the Low Bend Point.

APPENDIX 4

THE GOLFSMITH PRACTICAL FITTING PROGRAM CLUBFITTING FORMS

To use the Golfsmith Practical Fitting Program to perform accurate and efficient clubfitting sesssions, it is vital to use fitting forms which can reveal the information that is necessary to make the proper fitting decisions. Appendix 4 contains each of the three forms employed by the Practical Fitting Program to enable clubmakers to use the forms in an actual fitting session. While clubmakers are free to develop their own fitting forms, we do urge clubmakers to consider using these forms to maintain continuity with the Practical Fitting Program. For your continued use, each of the following forms, The Player Interview, The Equipment Evaluation and the Preliminary Fitting Recommendation are available in the Golfsmith Clubhead and Components Catalog.

In Addition, Appendix 4 also offers a number of the fitting aids which may be used in the Practical Fitting Program. For more information on these or future fitting devices, contact Golfsmith International, Inc. at 1-800-456-3344.

THE GOLFSMITH

Practical
CLUBFITTING
PROGRAM

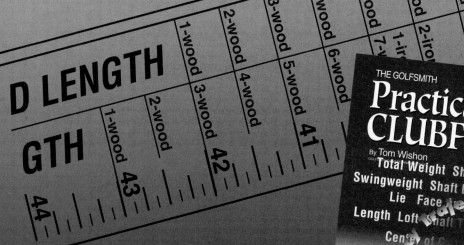

A player information survey
for custom fitting golf clubs
to be used in conjunction with the
Golfsmith Practical Golf Clubfitting Program.

Golfsmith®

PART 1

PLAYER INFORMATION

NAME_____ DATE_____

ADDRESS_____ CITY_____

STATE_____ ZIP_____ PHONE_____

HEIGHT	WEIGHT	AGE

YEARS PLAYING GOLF	HANDICAP	AVERAGE SCORE
		18 Holes

AVERAGE GREENS HIT	AVERAGE PUTTS	UP & DOWN IN TWO (%)	
18 Holes	18 Holes	CHIPS	SAND

ROUNDS PER WEEK	PRACTICES PER WEEK		PHYSICAL DISCOMFORT
	LONG GAME	SHORT GAME	

CURRENT SET MAKE-UP

CIRCLE ALL WOODS AND IRONS IN YOUR CURRENT SET; ENTER THE LOFT (IF KNOWN) OF ANY WEDGES IN YOUR SET; SPECIFY THE SOLE-WIDTH OF YOUR WEDGE.

WOODS	IRONS	PITCHING WEDGE (S)	
1 3 5 7 9 2 4 6 ___	1 3 5 7 9 2 4 6 8	LOFT °	WIDE SOLE___ MED. SOLE___ THIN SOLE___

SAND WEDGE (S)		OTHER WEDGE (S)		PUTTER	
LOFT °	WIDE SOLE___ MED. SOLE___ THIN SOLE___	LOFT °	WIDE SOLE___ MED. SOLE___ THIN SOLE___	TYPE	BLADE___ HEEL/TOE___ MALLET___

FAVORITE CLUBS	LEAST FAVORITE CLUBS	LONGEST CLUBS HIT WELL	
		WOOD	IRON

PART 2

BALL-STRIKING TENDENCIES

CHECK ANY SHOTMAKING TENDENCIES THAT APPLY TO EACH EQUIPMENT AREA IN YOUR GAME.
ESTIMATE CARRY DISTANCES AS CLOSELY AS POSSIBLE.

	TRAJECTORY			PREDOMINANT POINT OF IMPACT							SHOT PATTERN	EST. CARRY DISTANCE
	HIGH	MED	LOW	TOP	FAT	THIN	SKY	TOE	HEEL	CEN		
DRIVER											A B C D E F G H I	1w
F'WAY WDS.											A B C D E F G H I	5w
1,2,3 IRONS											A B C D E F G H I	3i
4,5,6 IRONS											A B C D E F G H I	5i
7,8,9 IRONS											A B C D E F G H I	7i
WEDGES											A B C D E F G H I	PW

Where do your shots go?

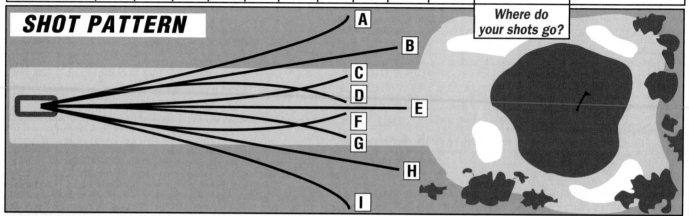

SHOT PATTERN

A
B
C
D
E
F
G
H
I

PART 3

PLAYING GOALS

CHECK THE BOX OF EACH GOAL YOU WOULD LIKE TO REACH AND CIRCLE IF FOR WOODS, IRONS OR BOTH.

1. I WANT TO HIT THE WOODS/IRONS HIGHER.	12. I WANT TO STOP HITTING THE WOODS/IRONS FAT.
2. I WANT TO HIT THE WOODS/IRONS LOWER.	13. I WANT TO HIT THE WOODS/IRONS MORE SOLIDLY.
3. I WANT TO HIT THE WOODS/IRONS FARTHER.	14. I WANT BETTER CLUBHEAD FEEL IN WOODS/IRONS.
4. I WANT TO HIT THE WOODS/IRONS STRAIGHTER.	15. I WANT TO FEEL MORE KICK IN THE WOOD/IRON SHAFT.
5. I WANT TO STOP SLICING THE WOODS/IRONS.	16. I WANT TO FEEL THE CLUBHEAD MORE AT THE TOP OF
6. I WANT TO STOP HOOKING THE WOODS/IRONS.	THE BACKSWING WITH THE WOODS/IRONS.
7. I WANT TO STOP PUSHING THE WOODS/IRONS.	17. I WANT TO HIT MY CHIPS LESS FAT.
8. I WANT TO STOP PULLING THE WOODS/IRONS.	18. I WANT TO HIT MY CHIPS LESS THIN.
9. I WANT TO STOP TOPPING THE WOODS/IRONS.	19. I WANT TO HIT MY SAND SHOTS LESS FAT.
10. I WANT TO STOP SKYING THE WOODS/IRONS.	20. I WANT TO HIT MY SAND SHOTS LESS THIN.
11. I WANT TO STOP HITTING THE WOODS/IRONS THIN.	21. I WANT A BETTER HOLD ON THE CLUB.

OVERALL GAME IMPROVEMENT DESIRES:

1. I WANT MORE DISTANCE. WOODS/IRONS	4. I WANT A LOWER TRAJECTORY. WOODS/IRONS
2. I WANT MORE ACCURACY. WOODS/IRONS	5. I WANT MORE BACKSPIN. IRONS/WEDGES
3. I WANT A HIGHER TRAJECTORY. WOODS IRONS	6. I WANT BETTER FEEL. WOODS/IRONS

PART 4

EQUIPMENT PREFERENCES

MARK ANY OF THE EQUIPMENT DESIGN FEATURES YOU PREFER. LEAVE BLANK IF YOU HAVE NO OPINION.

☐	1. I PREFER A PERSIMMON WOOD.
☐	2. I PREFER A LAMINATED MAPLE WOOD.
☐	3. I PREFER A METAL WOOD.
☐	4. I PREFER A GRAPHITE WOOD.
☐	5. I PREFER A TITANIUM WOOD.
☐	6. I PREFER AN INVESTMENT-CAST IRON HEAD.
☐	7. I PREFER A FORGED IRON HEAD.
☐	8. I PREFER A GRAPHITE IRON HEAD.
☐	9. I PREFER A STANDARD-WEIGHT SHAFT.
☐	10. I PREFER A LIGHTWEIGHT SHAFT.
☐	11. I PREFER A VERY LIGHTWEIGHT SHAFT.
☐	12. I PREFER A GRAPHITE SHAFT. WOODS/IRONS
☐	13. I PREFER A TITANIUM SHAFT. WOODS/IRONS
☐	14. I PREFER A STEEL SHAFT. WOODS/IRONS
☐	15. I PREFER A _____ SHAFT.

☐	16. I PREFER L A R S X SHAFT FLEX. (circle)
☐	17. NO PREFERRED SHAFT FLEX
☐	18. I PREFER A STANDARD GRIP.
☐	19. I PREFER A HALF-CORD GRIP.
☐	20. I PREFER A FULL-CORD GRIP.
☐	21. I PREFER A TACKY RUBBER GRIP.
☐	22. I PREFER A LEATHER GRIP.
☐	23. I PREFER A SOFT (CUSHION) GRIP.
☐	24. I PREFER A HARD (NON-CUSHION) GRIP.
☐	25. I PREFER A RIBBED GRIP.
☐	26. I PREFER A ROUND GRIP.
☐	27. I PREFER AN OVERSIZE GRIP.
☐	28. I PREFER AN UNDERSIZE GRIP.
☐	29. I PREFER A STANDARD-SIZE GRIP.
☐	

CIRCLE EQUIPMENT DESIGN FEATURES YOU LIKE OR DISLIKE FOR THE CHOICES OFFERED; LEAVE BLANK IF YOU HAVE NO OPINION.

1. I LIKE/DISLIKE AN OFFSET HOSEL ON THE IRONS.
2. I LIKE/DISLIKE AN OFFSET HOSEL ON THE WOODS.
3. I LIKE/DISLIKE AN OVERSIZE DRIVER.
4. I LIKE/DISLIKE OVERSIZE FAIRWAY WOODS
5. I LIKE/DISLIKE A MID SIZE DRIVER.
6. I LIKE/DISLIKE MID SIZE FAIRWAY WOODS.
7. I LIKE/DISLIKE A STANDARD SIZE DRIVER.
8. I LIKE/DISLIKE STANDARD SIZE FAIRWAY WOODS.
9. I LIKE/DISLIKE A HOOK FACED DRIVER OR WOODS.
10. I LIKE/DISLIKE AN OPEN FACED DRIVER OR WOODS.
11. I LIKE/DISLIKE A DEEP FACE DRIVER OR WOODS.
12. I LIKE/DISLIKE A STANDARD FACE HEIGHT DRIVER.
13. I LIKE/DISLIKE A SHALLOW FACE DRIVER.

14. I LIKE/DISLIKE A LONGER THAN NORMAL DRIVER.
15. I LIKE/DISLIKE COMPACT SIZE IRONHEADS.
16. I LIKE/DISLIKE STANDARD SIZE IRONHEADS.
17. I LIKE/DISLIKE OVERSIZE IRONHEADS.
18. I LIKE/DISLIKE A CAVITY BACK IRONHEAD DESIGN.
19. I LIKE/DISLIKE A MUSCLEBACK IRON DESIGN.
20. I LIKE/DISLIKE WIDE SOLE IRONS/WEDGES.
21. I LIKE/DISLIKE THIN SOLE IRONS/WEDGES.
22. I LIKE/DISLIKE A FERRULE ON MY WOODS.
23. I LIKE/DISLIKE A FERRULE ON MY IRONS.
24. I LIKE/DISLIKE COLORFUL GRAPHITE SHAFTS.
25. I LIKE/DISLIKE A SHINY CLUBHEAD SURFACE.
26. I LIKE/DISLIKE A SATIN CLUBHEAD SURFACE.

Golfsmith® PRACTICAL CLUBFITTING PROGRAM

THE GOLFSMITH
Practical CLUBFITTING PROGRAM

EQUIPMENT EVALUATION FORM

NAME _____   HANDICAP/AVG. SCORE _____   HEIGHT _____

ADDRESS _____   WRIST TO FLOOR LENGTH RECOMMENDATION 1w: _____ 5 i: _____

CITY _____ STATE _____ ZIP _____   SWING SPEED 1w (3w): _____ mph 5 i: _____ mph

PHONE Home: (__) _____ Work: (__) _____   DYNAMIC LIE FITTING   ☐ Center of Sole   ☐ _____ " Toward Heel
                                                   ☐ RH ☐ LH   ☐ _____ " Toward Toe

CURRENT WOODS

Brand/Model: _____   ☐ Traditional Size ☐ Offset ☐ Non-offset ☐ Oversize ☐ Mid-oversize ☐ Mid-size

SET MAKEUP	LOFT	FACE ANGLE	TOTAL WEIGHT	SWING WEIGHT	LENGTH	SHAFT MODEL /FLEX	BEND POINT	FREQ.	EST. TORQUE°	RSSR mph
☐ 1										
☐ 2										
☐ 3										
☐ 4										
☐ 5										
☐ 6										
☐ 7										
☐ 9										
☐ ___										
☐ ___										

SHAFT WEIGHT DRIVER
☐ Heavy 110g +
☐ Medium 96-110g
☐ Light 81-95g
☐ Very Light 66-80g
☐ Ultra Light 50-65g

WOODS GRIP SIZE
☐ Undersize ___ / ___ "
☐ Std. Men's/Ladies
☐ + 1/64
☐ + 1/32
☐ + 1/16
☐
Grip Type: _____

CURRENT IRONS

Brand/Model: _____   ☐ Offset ☐ Non-offset ☐ Prog.Offset ☐ Oversize ☐ Mid-size ☐ Compact ☐ Cavity Back ☐ Muscle

SET MAKEUP	LOFT	TOTAL WEIGHT	SWING WEIGHT	LENGTH	SHAFT MODEL /FLEX	BEND POINT	FREQ.	EST. TORQUE°	RSSR mph
☐ 1									
☐ 2									
☐ 3									
☐ 4									
☐ 5									
☐ 6									
☐ 7									
☐ 8									
☐ 9									
☐ PW ☐ (10)									
☐ SW									
___ ☐									
PT ☐									

SHAFT WEIGHT 5-IRON
☐ Heavy 110g +
☐ Medium 96-110g
☐ Light 81-95g
☐ Very Light 66-80g
☐ Ultra Light 50-65g

IRONS GRIP SIZE
☐ Undersize ___ / ___ "
☐ Std. Men's/Ladies
☐ + 1/64
☐ + 1/32
☐ + 1/16
☐
Grip Type: _____

SOLE ANGLE
___° ☐ Sq. ☐ Bounce
___° ☐ Sq. ☐ Bounce
___° ☐ Sq. ☐ Bounce

THE GOLFSMITH
Practical CLUBFITTING PROGRAM

PRELIMINARY FITTING RECOMMENDATION

NAME _____

ADDRESS _____

PHONE Home: (____) _____ Work: (____) _____

CITY _____ STATE _____ ZIP _____

SET MAKEUP   *Circle & write in recommended set makeup*

WOODS   1 **2** 3 4 **5** 7 9 ____ ____ ____ ____

IRONS   1 **2** 3 **4** **5** 6 7 8 **9** ____ ____ ____

WEDGES   ☐ PW   ☐ SW   _____ Other wedges

LOFT ANGLES   *Enter recommended loft angles for each*

WOODS   #1 _____°   #3 _____°   #5 _____°   #__ _____°

IRONS   #3 _____°   #5 _____°   #7 _____°   #9 _____°

WEDGES   PW _____°   SW _____°   _____ _____°

CLUBHEAD DESIGN   *Check all recommended features*

WOODS   ☐ Jumbo   ☐ Oversize   ☐ Mid-size   ☐ Traditional

☐ Steel   ☐ Aluminum   ☐ Titanium   ☐ Graphite   ☐ Other _____

☐ Deep Face   ☐ Standard Face   ☐ Shallow Face   ☐ Offset ☐ Non-offset   ☐ Low CG   ☐ Mid-high CG

IRONS   ☐ Cavity Back ☐ Muscle Back   ☐ Compact ☐ Std ☐ Oversize

☐ Offset ☐ Non-offset   ☐ Wide Sole ☐ Std ☐ Thin Sole

WEDGES   PW – ☐ Wide Sole ☐ Medium ☐ Thin Sole   ____ – ☐ Wide Sole ☐ Medium ☐ Thin Sole (for 3rd or 4th wedge)

SW – ☐ Wide Sole ☐ Medium ☐ Thin Sole

LENGTH   *List each length; indicate incremental change in length between irons*

WOODS   1w ____"   3w ____"   5w ____"   #___w ____" (for 7w, 9w or other)

IRONS   5i ____"   Incremental Change _____"   WEDGES PW ____" SW ____" Other ____ ____"

SWINGWEIGHT   *List swing weight for woods & irons*

WOODS _____   IRONS _____   WEDGES PW _____ SW _____ Other ____ ____

TOTAL WEIGHT   *Check driver range; Indicate Fairway woods to match or other by listing shaft weight*

WOODS   1w – ☐ < 11.25 oz.   ☐ 11.25 - 11.75 oz.   ☐ 11.75 - 12.25 oz.   ☐ 12.25 - 12.75 oz.   ☐ > 12.75 oz.

Fairway Woods – ☐ To match to 1w   Other _____

IRONS   ☐ Match Wood Range   Other _____

FACE ANGLE   *Check angle*

WOODS   1w – _____°   ☐ Hook ☐ Square ☐ Open   Fairway Woods – _____°   ☐ Hook ☐ Square ☐ Open

---

BULGE/ROLL

WOODS   1w – Bulge _____"   Roll _____"   ☐ Std   Fairway Woods – Bulge _____"   Roll _____"   ☐ Std

---

GRIP SIZE   *Check size or indicate other size for woods/irons*

WOODS   ☐ Jumbo   ☐ + 1/16"   ☐ + 1/32"   ☐ + 1/64"   ☐ Std.   ☐ – 1/64"   ☐ Other _____

IRONS   ☐ Jumbo   ☐ + 1/16"   ☐ + 1/32"   ☐ + 1/64"   ☐ Std.   ☐ – 1/64"   ☐ Other _____

GRIP TYPE/WEIGHT   *Write in grip name and check weight range*

WOODS   Type – _____   Weight – ☐ < 40g   ☐ 40-50g   ☐ >50g

IRONS   Type – _____   Weight – ☐ < 40g   ☐ 40-50g   ☐ >50g

SHAFT WEIGHT   *Check shaft weight range and material for each*

WOODS   1w – ☐ < 65g   ☐ 66 - 80g   ☐ 81 - 95g   ☐ 96 - 110g   ☐ > 110g   ☐ Graphite ☐ Steel ☐ Other

Fairway Woods – ☐ < 65g   ☐ 66 - 80g   ☐ 81 - 95g   ☐ 96 - 110g   ☐ > 110g   ☐ Graphite ☐ Steel ☐ Other

IRONS   5i – ☐ < 65g   ☐ 66 - 80g   ☐ 81 - 95g   ☐ 96 - 110g   ☐ > 110g   ☐ Graphite ☐ Steel ☐ Other

---

SHAFT FLEX (RSSR) & BEND POINT   *Enter swing speeds - check downswing acceleration; indicate mph range for shaft*

WOODS   1w – Swing Speed – _____ mph   Downswing – ☐ Fast ☐ Avg ☐ Slow   RSSR – _____ – _____ mph

IRONS   5i – Swing Speed – _____ mph   Downswing – ☐ Fast ☐ Avg ☐ Slow   RSSR – _____ – _____ mph

WOOD BEND POINT   ☐ Low ☐ Mid/High   IRON BEND POINT   ☐ Low ☐ Mid/High

GOLFSMITH CLUBFITTING TOOLS AND SUPPLIES

BELTRONICS SWINGMATE

The SwingMate is reliable, accurate, and extremely easy to use: enter your club selection, swing, and read the swing speed plus estimated distance. Memory function stores the data from 10 swings and then calculates the average. Auto-shutoff feature; one-year manufacturer's warranty. *Takes one 9v battery, not included.*

Stock No. 4960R

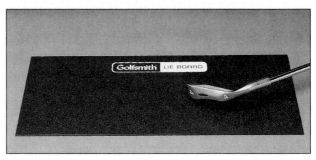

GOLFSMITH LIE BOARD

Special hitting surface material leaves a small, temporary mark on the sole of the clubhead indicating lie angle at impact. For best results, have the golfer stand level with the board, which is ⅛" thick including the special impact surface top. Durable size is 8" x 15½"

Stock No. 4990

48" COMINATION RULER

A durable 48" ruler that measures true, accurate playing length of golf clubs. Use it to measure and mark the accurate length of complete clubs by placing the ruler along the back of the shaft with the club at address; then read the length directly at the butt of the grip. Handy charts with Golfsmith's recommended men's and ladies' standard club lengths are printed on the ruler for easy reference.

Stock No. 460

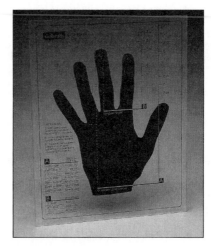

GRIP SIZER

Sturdy plastic chart incorporates finger and palm size separately for maximum accuracy in grip fitting. Lends reliability, standardization and professionalism to the process. Works on right or left hand.

Stock No. 937

FREQUENCY ANALYZER

Golfsmith's Shaft Frequency Analyzer is the first of its kind not to rely on an optical sensor near the tip of the shaft to obtain its frequency readings. The machine employs dual strain gauges and a microprocessor mounted under the clamp to obtain fail-safe frequency readings. Useful in calculating shaft fitting recommedations based on swing speed, analyzing proprietary or unmarked shafts, and verifying the accuracy of shaft fitting and installation.

Stock No. 8720

PUTTER LIE/LENGTH CALCULATOR

Fits the putter to the individual rather than forcing the player to adjust his or her stance to accomodate a new putter. Shaft adjusts to any golfer's preferred length (40" to 30") and putting stance, and provides accurate length and lie measurements.

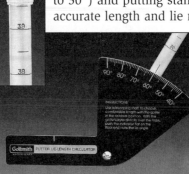

Features telescoping shaft with an easy-to-use precision twist-lock mechanism. Fits both left and right hand golfers.

Stock No. 467

INDEX

H

I

J

K

L

Q

R

S

T

U

V

W